Bridges Not Walls

A Book About Interpersonal Communication

NINTH EDITION

John Stewart
University of Dubuque

Boston   Burr Ridge, IL   Dubuque, IA   Madison, WI   New York
San Francisco   St. Louis   Bangkok   Bogotá   Caracas   Kuala Lumpur
Lisbon   London   Madrid   Mexico City   Milan   Montreal   New Delhi
Santiago   Seoul   Singapore   Sydney   Taipei   Toronto

Higher Education

BRIDGES NOT WALLS: A BOOK ABOUT INTERPERSONAL COMMUNICATION

Published by McGraw-Hill, a business unit of The McGraw-Hill Companies, Inc., 1221 Avenue of the Americas, New York, NY, 10020. Copyright © 2006, 2002, 1999, 1995, 1990, 1986, 1982, 1977, 1973, by The McGraw-Hill Companies, Inc. All rights reserved. No part of this publication may be reproduced or distributed in any form or by any means, or stored in a database or retrieval system, without the prior written consent of The McGraw-Hill Companies, Inc., including, but not limited to, in any network or other electronic storage or transmission, or broadcast for distance learning.
Some ancillaries, including electronic and print components, may not be available to customers outside the United States.

This book is printed on acid-free paper.

2 3 4 5 6 7 8 9 0 DOC/DOC 0 9 8 7 6

ISBN-13: 978-0-07-286286-7
ISBN-10: 0-07-286286-6

Editor in Chief: *Emily Barrosse*
Publisher: *Phillip A. Butcher*
Executive Editor: *Nanette Giles*
Senior Marketing Manager: *Leslie Oberhuber*
Associate Developmental Editor: *Joshua F. Hawkins*
Managing Editor: *Jean Dal Porto*
Production Service: *Marilyn Rothenberger*
Art Director: *Jeanne Schreiber*
Lead Designer: *Gino Cieslik*
Text Designer: *Cher Marie Ruden*
Cover Designer: *Gino Cieslik*
Art Manager: *Robin Mouat*
Photo Research Coordinator: *Nora Agbayani*
Cover Credit: *@ Getty Images*
Production Supervisor: *Jason Huls*
Media Producer: *Nancy Garcia*
Permissions Editor: *Karyn Morrison*
Composition: *Carlisle Communications, Ltd.*
Printing: *45# New Era Matte, R.R. Donnelley and Sons, Inc/Crawfordsville, IN*

Credits: The credits section for this book begins on page C–1 and is considered an extension of the copyright page.

Library of Congress Control Number: 2005927927

The Internet addresses listed in the text were accurate at the time of publication. The inclusion of a Web site does not indicate an endorsement by the authors of McGraw-Hill, and McGraw-Hill does not guarantee the accuracy of the information presented at these sites.

www.mhhe.com

About the Author

JOHN STEWART taught interpersonal communication at the University of Washington from 1969 to 2001. He attended Centralia Community College and Pacific Lutheran University, then got his M.A. at Northwestern University and completed his Ph.D. at the University of Southern California in 1970. In 2001 John moved to the University of Dubuque in northeast Iowa, where he is Vice President for Academic Affairs and Dean of the Graduate School. He continues to teach interpersonal communication at UD. He has two children and two grandchildren, is married to Kris Stewart, and they have a son, Lincoln, who was twelve years old in 2005.

Books and People

Imagine yourself in a situation where you are alone, wholly alone on earth, and you are offered one of the two, books or [people]. I often hear [speakers] prizing their solitude, but that is only because there are still [people] somewhere on earth, even though in the far distance. I knew nothing of books when I came forth from the womb of my mother, and I shall die without books, with another human hand in my own. I do, indeed, close my door at times and surrender myself to a book, but only because I can open the door again and see a human being looking at me.

—Martin Buber

Contents

Part IV
BRIDGES NOT WALLS

Part V
APPROACHES TO INTERPERSONAL COMMUNICATION

Preface

This edition of *Bridges Not Walls* maintains the approach and basic format of the previous eight editions. This time around, I have kept the chapter sequence, maintained the four approaches in Part V, and updated several chapters to reflect current communication concerns and directions of current research and teaching. For example, an excerpt from Susan Scott's best-selling book *Fierce Conversations* has been added to Chapter 2; in Chapter 3, Richard Rodriguez speaks about identity from his book, *Brown;* Mark Knapp and Judith A. Hall's treatment of nonverbal communicating updates Chapter 4; three new authors, including the highly respected John Gottman, write about listening in Chapter 5; long-distance relationships and romance in cyberspace are the topics of two new essays in Chapter 8; and there is an updated and simplified discussion of conflict transformation in Chapter 10. I have also made additional efforts to clarify that interpersonal communication involves much more than just friendly agreement by adding essays about verbal abuse and exploitative power.

Bridges Not Walls is still designed primarily for college students enrolled in interpersonal communication classes. But the materials discuss topics also included in social work, humanities, counseling, and sociology courses. Chapters treat the standard topics covered in most interpersonal communication courses, and a majority of the readings are authored by communication scholars and teachers. But there are also materials from authors in a range of disciplines, including education, organizational development, clinical and social psychology, cultural and media studies, and philosophy.

Since the first edition of *Bridges* was published in 1973, the approach to communication that has guided this collection of readings has been a relational one that focuses on the kind or quality of contact that people create *together*. In other words, as the first two chapters explain, "communication" is understood basically as the term humans use for our collaborative processes of meaning-making. To say that humans are "social animals" is to say that we make sense of things *with others*, and "communication" is the general label for these processes.

When I call these processes "collaborative," I obviously do not mean that humans always agree as we make meanings together, but only that we "co-labor," or work out meanings in response to one another. All this implies that communication is not simply an activity that one person performs or does "to" another, but is a process that happens *between* people. For those with theoretical interests, these basic ideas can be found in primary works by Mikhail Bakhtin, Martin Buber, Martin Heidegger, Alfred Schutz, Hans-Georg Gadamer, and theorists labeled "social constructionist."

Interpersonal communication is a subset of this process, a type or kind of contact that happens when the people involved talk and listen in ways that maximize the presence of the personal. This approach to interpersonal communication emphasizes the prominence of culture and highlights the ways communication affects social and personal identities. In other words, although communication can clearly be expressive and instrumental, this approach emphasizes that it is also person-building, which is to say that *who humans are* gets worked out in our verbal/nonverbal contact. Virtually all of the authors represented here acknowledge these features of communication, and many comment directly on them.

This is a book for people who want practical suggestions and skills that will help them communicate more effectively with their friends, partners, spouses, family, and co-workers. But unlike much of the self-help literature, *Bridges* resists the tendency to gloss over conceptual issues and to reduce interpersonal effectiveness to techniques or formulas. The authors of these readings recognize that there is much more to effective communication than simply "being open and honest." For example, there are thought-provoking discussions of the nature of interpersonal contact, the inseparability of verbal and nonverbal cues, identity management and social intelligence, listening, deception and betrayal, interpersonal ethics, family intimacy, verbal abuse, transformational conflict management, cultural diversity, and dialogue, and there are four philosophies of communication outlined at the end of the book in Chapters 13 to 16. *Bridges* also includes systematic treatments of self-awareness, functions of nonverbal behavior, social perception, listening, disclosure, gender patterns, hurtful messages, and power. But no reading claims to offer the definitive "six steps" or "twelve easy techniques" for guaranteed success. The authors emphasize that unique situations, the constancy of change, and especially the element of human choice all make it impossible to design and execute a purely technical approach to *human* relationships.

This point is rooted in the book's definition of its subject matter, which I've already sketched. *Bridges* does not define interpersonal communication as something that only happens in face-to-face settings, during discussions of weighty topics, or in long-term intimate relationships. Instead, the term "interpersonal" designates a kind or quality of contact that emerges between people whenever they are willing and able to highlight in their speaking and listening aspects of what makes them human. The editor's introduction in Chapter 1 and the first essay in Chapter 2 explain this definition, and subsequent readings extend and develop it. Throughout the book, the point is also made that different kinds or qualities of contact are appropriate in different situations. "More" interpersonal communicating is *not* always better. There is much more to it than that, as the readings in Chapters 9, 10, and 11 especially demonstrate. At the same time, materials in the first two chapters and the four approaches at the end of the book clarify how most people's personal, educational, and work lives could profit from increased interpersonal contact.

Readings in Chapters 1, 2, 3, 5, 7, 8, 11, 12, 14, 15, and 16 also emphasize the point made earlier that communication is more than just a way to get things done, because it affects who we are, our identities. I introduce this idea at the beginning of the book. Stuart Sigman, Daniel Goleman, Harold Barrett, Kathleen Galvin, Carma L. Bylund, Bernard J. Brommel, Ken Cissna, Evelyn Sieburg, Karen Zediker, Saskia Witteborn, and I develop and extend the early discussions, and the person-building dimension of communication is a profound part of Martin Buber's essay in Chapter 16.

These theoretical and conceptual commitments are complemented by my desire to make the book as readable as possible. This is the main reason why few research articles from scholarly journals are included. As in all earlier editions, I have tried to select substantive materials that speak directly to the student reader. I continue to search for authors who "write with their ears," or talk with their readers. Selections from past editions by Gerald and Marianne Corey, Virginia Satir, Carl Rogers, Julia Wood, Hugh and Gayle Prather, C. Roland Christensen, and Parker Palmer continue in this edition partly because they do this so well. I have also found this accessibility in some new authors, especially Susan Scott, Richard Rodriguez, Karen Kissel Wegela, and Pui Yee Beryl Tsang.

New Features

As I noted, the new features in this edition include additional coverage of the most challenging elements of interpersonal communicating, including verbal abuse, long-distance relating, power, and conflict. Beverly Engel's "Confronting Abusive Relationships" (Chapter 6) and Patricia Evans's "Children and Verbal Abuse" (Chapter 9) are both new. Joyce A. Arditti and Melissa Kauffman contribute "Staying Close When Apart: Intimacy and Meaning in Long-Distance Dating Relationships" to Chapter 8. There are two new treatments of power in Chapter 9, and, as noted, new materials on conflict in Chapter 10.

The treatment of several other topics has also been updated. The models of communicating and interpersonal communicating in Chapters 1 and 2 have been simplified and revised to reflect current research. Two of the five discussions of identity management in Chapter 3 are new. Four of the six discussions of listening in Chapter 4 are new. Two of the five essays about communication with intimate partners are new. There are also two new essays in the dialogue chapter (12), one about relational responsibility and the other about a near cousin of dialogue, "skillful discussion."

This edition keeps the simplified organization introduced in 2002, especially because people who use the book responded favorably to it. I've maintained the sequence of topics in Part I, the Inhaling/Exhaling metaphor that organizes Part II, and the central themes of Parts III, IV, and V. Continued work with dialogue theory and practice justifies the inclusion of an updated chapter on that topic.

As before, I have also tried to include diverse voices. Thirty-two of the 71 authors are women; Richard Rodriguez essays Hispanic identity; Pui Yee Beryl Tsang writes of her interracial marriage, and Marsha Houston explains why dialogues between black and white women are difficult. There are discussions of nontraditional families and gay, lesbian, and bisexual friends; an explanation of gendered standpoints on personal relationships; and two approaches written in Quaker and Jewish voices. I hope these materials will help readers feel more at home in contexts in which they are a minority and empower them to treat "different" others with respect and appreciation.

Other Features

As in earlier editions, my introduction shows how *Bridges Not Walls* is different from the standard, faceless, "objective" college textbook. I want readers to consider the potential for, and the limits of, interpersonal communicating between writer and reader. I also want them to remember that a book or essay is always somebody's point of view. I'd like readers to respond to what's here not as "true because it's printed in black and white" but as the thoughtful speech of a person addressing them. In the Introduction, I tell readers a little about myself, give a rationale for the way the book is put together, and argue for the link between quality of communication and quality of life.

Each time *Bridges* is reviewed, I get some complaints that the final reading by Martin Buber is "too dense," "too hard to read," and "too heavy," to say nothing of the sometimes archaic and sexist language. Happily, I also hear and see what happens when students in my classes—and in classes I observe being taught by graduate teaching assistants—actually begin to connect with Buber and his ideas. When teacher and student are patient and diligent, they often find that Buber can significantly deepen their understanding of interpersonal communicating. This experience frequently motivates them to apply these ideas, even in the face of hardships and challenges. All this continues to make teaching Buber rewarding for me and for many of the people I work with.

Two sets of questions follow each reading. The first, "Review Questions," are designed to prompt the reader's recall of key ideas. If the student can respond to these, there is some clear indication that he or she understands what's in the reading. Then "Probes" ask the reader to take some additional steps by extending, criticizing, or applying the author's ideas. Some "Probes" also explore links between readings in various chapters.

Many of the readings include extensive bibliographies or references. There are lengthy lists of additional sources, for example, accompanying the readings that discuss the book's approach, verbal and nonverbal dimensions of talk, nonverbal messages, person perception, listening, family communication, hurtful messages, identity management, and gender stereotyping. A detailed index also locates and provides cross-references to authors and key ideas.

As before, I want to remind readers that this book *about* interpersonal communicating cannot substitute for direct contact between persons in the concrete, everyday world. This is why I've once again begun the book with Buber's comment about "Books and People" and ended with Hugh Prather's reflections on the world of ideas and the world of "messy mortals."

Acknowledgments

This book would not be possible without the cooperation of the authors and publishers of the material reprinted here. Thanks to all of them for their permission.

I am also grateful to reviewers of the earlier edition. The following people offered insightful comments that guided the revision process this time: Ken Cissna, University of South Florida; Timothy R. Cline, College of Notre Dame of Maryland; Paul Duax, American River College; Carole Kenner, Vanderbilt University; Betty Jane Lawrence, Bradley University; Frank Mueller, Oakland City University; Christopher N. Poulos, University of North Carolina, Greensboro; Ronald K. Pyle, Whitworth College; Patricia J. Sotirin, Michigan Technological University; Jianglong Wang, Western Washington University.

Many people I am fortunate enough to contact regularly have also contributed in direct and indirect ways to what's here. I appreciate many current and past interpersonal communication teachers in the program at the University of Washington, including Milt Thomas, Lyall Crawford, Kathy Hendrix, Jeff Kerssen-Griep, Lisa Coutu, Roberta Gray, Laura Manning, Tasha Souza, Amanda Graham, Laura Black, Jody Koenig Kellas, Andi Hamilton Zamora, and Aimee Carillo Rowe. I also deeply appreciate past contacts with colleagues who have supported and challenged my ideas, including Gerry Philipsen, Barbara Warnick, Valerie Manusov, Jody Nyquist, Ken Cissna, John Shotter, and, since 2001, new colleagues at the University of Dubuque, including Paula Carlson, Bob Reid, John Hatch, Peter Smith, David Moessner, Brad Longfield, and Tammy Walsh. I continue to notice how both the greatest tests and the most solid confirmations of what's in this book emerge in my most important living relationships with Kris, Lincoln, Marcia, Lisa, Jamie, Josh, Barbara, Helene, and other family members.

Two things that still have not changed through all nine editions of *Bridges Not Walls* are my awareness of the difficulty and the necessity of interpersonal communicating and my excitement about the challenge of working toward achieving it. I hope that some of this excitement will rub off on you.

John Stewart

PART ONE

Entering the Interpersonal Arena

CHAPTER 1

Introduction to the Editor and to This Book

Writing about interpersonal communication, especially in a book that's used mainly as a text, is difficult because it's almost impossible to practice what you preach. Like many other text authors and editors, I could think of you as just "reader" or "student" and of myself as just "editor" or "teacher" and proceed to tell you what I want you to know. But if I did, we'd have something a lot closer to *impersonal* rather than *interpersonal* communication.

Why? Because, if I write simply as "teacher," and address you simply as "student," or "reader," and if you respond the same way, we will be relating to each other only in terms of our social roles, not in terms of who we are *as persons*. If I use the vocabulary introduced in the next chapter, this kind of contact would connect us as interchangeable parts.

But there's more to it than that. Both you and I are *non*interchangeable, multidimensional persons with distinctive ideas, convictions, wants, and needs. For my part, my name is John Stewart, I've been teaching college for almost 40 years, I am now serving as a college administrator, and I like almost everything about my job. For the past 12 years I've been in the exciting, demanding, and very rewarding position of being a 50-plus-year-old parent. This is my second time around as a dad. My daughters, who were born shortly after I finished high school, are in their early 40s, the grandkids are 18 and 16, and our son Lincoln is 12. So Lincoln is an uncle to a niece and nephew older than he, and is also one of the younger members of a large extended family of aunts, uncles, and cousins.

I'm a native of the northwest corner of the United States and have recently moved to northeast Iowa. I love the smell of saltwater and the fizz it makes behind a quiet boat; the exhilaration of biking and downhill skiing; the dazzling brightness of a winter sun on Midwest snow; the babble of a crowded family gathering; and the opportunity to leave home each day to respond to a calling, rather than just to do a job. I dislike phony smiles, grandiose flattery or apologies, pretentious academicians, rules that are vaguely stated but rigidly enforced, oysters, and machinery that runs roughly. I also get impatient with people who have trouble saying what they mean and meaning what they say. I was raised in a small town in Washington State and now live on the Mississippi, right at the point where Iowa, Illinois, and Wisconsin meet. I like the challenges of helping people in my classes learn new and old ideas, mentoring young faculty, and helping our small college live according to its mission. I feel very fortunate to have my occupation, family, and health.

The longer I study and teach interpersonal communication, the more I'm struck by how much the person I am today has been molded by the relationships I've experienced. Some of the most important people in my life are no longer alive: for example, my dad and mom; my father-in-law; my first real "boss," Marc Burdick; college teachers Peter Ristuben and "Prof" Karl; and Allen Clark, the friend who introduced me to Martin Buber's writings. Some others I've almost completely lost contact with, like high school and college teachers, co-workers in the pea cannery, and graduate school classmates. But many other relationships continue to teach and mold me, including those I have with Lincoln and my wife Kris, Kris's mother, my sister Barbara, cousins Jim and Carol, and close friends Karen Zediker, Tim Milander, David Moessner, Paula Carlson, Father Ralph Carskadden, Dennis and Julie Shaw, Cheryl Pope, and Jeff Bullock. I've also been affected by relationships with many authors who have made themselves available in their writing, especially Martin Buber, Hans-Georg Gadamer, Mikhail Bakhtin, John Shotter, Eric Voegelin, Martin Heidegger, Parker Palmer, and Carl Rogers. Contacts with all these persons have helped shape me. At the same time, I sense the presence of a continuous "me" who's never static but who's firmly anchored in values, understandings, weaknesses, and strengths that make me who I am.

If I stuck to being just "writer" or "teacher," I could also skip the fact that I am almost as grateful and excited about doing this ninth edition of *Bridges Not Walls* as I was about the first edition, and that I continue to be a little amazed that this book speaks to so many different people. Each mention of the book by a student who has read it or a teacher who has used it is a delight, and I especially like hearing from the communication graduate students and teachers who tell me that this was their introduction to the field. It's a gift to be able to share some ideas and feelings about interpersonal communication in this way, and I'm pleased that readers continue to allow me to talk relatively personally rather than just in the safe, sterile, and distant style of some "educational materials."

The impersonal approach I mentioned would also get in the way of the contact between you and me, because *you* are not simply "reader" or "student." Where were you born and raised, and how has that affected you? Are you reading this book because you want to or because somebody required it? If you're reading it as part of a college course, how do you expect the course to turn out? Challenging? Boring? Threatening? Useful? Inhibiting? Exciting? How do you generally feel about required texts? About going to school? What groups have you been in or are you a part of? A sports team? Neighborhood gang? A band? Campfire or Scouts? Natural Helpers? A church group? A sorority or fraternity? Alateen? What important choices have you made recently? To end a relationship? Move? Change majors? Quit work? Make a new commitment?

I'm not saying that you have to pry into the intimate details of somebody's life before you can communicate with him or her, but I am saying that interpersonal communication happens between *persons*, not between roles, masks, or stereotypes. Interpersonal communication can happen between you and me only to the degree that each of us makes available some of what makes us a person *and* at the same time is aware of some of what makes the other a person, too.

One way to conceptualize what I'm saying is to think about what could be called your Contact Quotient, or CQ. Your CQ is a measure of how you connect with another person. It's the quotient that expresses the ratio between the quality of contact you experience and the quality of contact that's possible. In other words,

$$\frac{\text{Richness or quality of contact achieved}}{\text{Richness or quality of contact possible}}$$

A husband and wife who have been married for 40 years have a huge CQ de-nominator (the figure below the line)—let's say 10,000. When one is giving the other the silent treatment, their numerator (the figure above the line) is painfully small—maybe 15. So their CQ in this instance would be 15/10,000—pretty low. But when they spend an afternoon and evening together in conversation, mutu-ally enjoyed activities, and lovemaking, their numerator is very high—perhaps 9,500—and their CQ approaches 10,000/10,000. You and I, on the other hand, have a pretty small denominator. This means that the absolute quality of contact we can achieve by way of this book is relatively low. But we can still work toward a CQ of unity—maybe 100/100—and this is one of my goals in this in-troduction and the other materials I've written for this book.

It's going to be difficult, though, to maximize the CQ between you and me. I can continue to tell you some of who I am, but I don't know whether what I write is what you need in order to know me as me. In addition, I know almost nothing about what makes you a person—nothing about your choices, feelings, hopes, fears, insights, blind spots—your individuality. This is why *writing* about interpersonal communication can sometimes be frustrating. Interpersonal com-munication can be discussed in print, but not much of it can happen here.

More can happen, though, than usually does with a textbook. Our relation-ship can be at least a little closer to interpersonal than it often is. I will work to-ward this end by continuing to share some of what I'm thinking and feeling in my introductions to the readings, in the Review Questions and Probes at the end of each selection, and in the six essays I've authored or co-authored. I hope you'll be willing to make yourself available by becoming involved enough in this book to recognize clearly which ideas and skills are worthwhile for you and which are not. I also hope you'll be willing and able to make yourself available to other persons reading this book, so they can benefit from your insights and you can benefit from theirs.

WHY APPROACH INTERPERSONAL COMMUNICATION THIS WAY?

Before we begin breaking human communication down into manageable parts, I want to talk about a couple of beliefs that guide my selection and organization of the materials in this book. I believe that when you know something about this book's rationale, it'll be easier for you to understand what's being said about each topic, and you'll be in a better position to accept what works for you, while leaving aside the rest.

Quality of Communication and Quality of Life

One of my basic assumptions is that *there's a direct link between the quality of your communication and the quality of your life.* I can best explain this idea with a little bit more of my history.

After high school, I attended a community college for two years and then transferred to a four-year college to finish my degree. I took a basic speech communication course at both schools, and noticed that in each, something was missing. The teachers emphasized how to inform others and persuade them to do what you want. They showed our classes how to research and outline ideas, how to move and gesture effectively, and how to use vocal variety to keep our listeners' attention. Students were required to write papers and give speeches to demonstrate that they'd mastered these skills. But the courses seemed to overlook something important. Neither the textbooks nor the instructors said anything about the connection between the quality of your communication and the quality of your life.

Other texts and teachers did. In my literature and anthropology classes, I read that "no human is an island," and that "the human is a social animal." Psychology books reported studies of infants who suffered profoundly when they were deprived of touch, talk, or other kinds of contact. A philosophy text made the same point in these words: "communication means life or death to persons. . . . Both the individual and society derive their basic meaning from the relations that exist between [persons]. It is through dialogue that [humans] accomplish the miracle of personhood and community."[1]

The speech texts and teachers promised that they could help students learn to make ideas clear, be entertaining, and persuade others to agree with them. But they seemed to miss the communication impact of the point being made in literature, anthropology, psychology, and philosophy. If humans really are social beings, then *communication is where humanness happens.* In other words, although communication is definitely a way to express ideas, get things done, and entertain, convince, and persuade others, it's also more than that. It's the process that defines who we are. As a result, *if we experience mainly distant, objective, impersonal communicating, we're liable to grow up pretty one-sided, but if we experience our share of close, supportive, interpersonal communicating, we're likely to develop more of our human potential.* This is how the quality of your communication affects the quality of your life.

One reason I started teaching interpersonal communication is that I figured out the truth of this idea, and this same point has motivated me to edit this book. I've also been impressed with some research that supports this reason for studying interpersonal communication.

Medical doctors have done some of the most impressive studies. James J. Lynch was co-director of the Psychophysiological Clinic and Laboratories at the University of Maryland School of Medicine when he introduced one of his books with these words:

> As we shall see, study after study reveals that human dialogue not only affects our hearts significantly but can even alter the biochemistry of individual tissues at the farthest extremities of the body. Since blood flows through every human tissue, the entire body is influenced by dialogue.[2]

In other words, Lynch is saying that the quality of your communication affects the *physical* quality of your life. One of his important discoveries is that blood pressure changes much more rapidly and frequently than people used to believe, and that some of the most significant blood pressure changes occur when people speak and are spoken to. Computerized instruments permit Lynch and other researchers to monitor blood pressure constantly and to map the effects of a person's entering the room, engaging in nonverbal contact, reading aloud, and conversing. Speech appears to directly affect blood pressure; in one study the mean arterial pressure of healthy nurses went from 92 when they were quiet to 100 when they "talked calmly."[3] Listening has the opposite effect. Rather than just returning to baseline when a person stops speaking, blood pressure actually drops below baseline when one concentrates on the other person.[4] And this happens only when we talk with people; "conversation" with pets does not produce the same result.[5]

In an earlier book, Lynch discusses some of the more global effects of essentially the same phenomenon. There he reports the results of hundreds of medical studies that correlate loneliness and poor health. For example, people with few interpersonal relationships tend to die before their counterparts who enjoy a network of family and friends.[6] In fact, a study of identical twins found that smoking habits, obesity, and cholesterol levels of the twins who had heart attacks were not significantly different from the twins with healthier hearts. But there were some other important differences, one of which was what the doctors called "poor childhood and adult interpersonal relationships."[7]

What conclusions can be drawn from evidence like this? Lynch puts it this way:

> Human companionship does affect our heart, and . . . there is reflected in our hearts a biological basis for our need for loving human relationships, which we fail to fulfill at our peril. . . . The ultimate decision is simple: we must either learn to live together or increase our chances of prematurely dying alone.[8]

In other words, if you view quality of life physically, it becomes apparent that there's more to it than ample food, warm clothing, shelter, education, and modern conveniences. The quality of your existence is linked directly to the quality of your communication.

If you go beyond physical quality of life, the same point can be made even more strongly. In fact, nonmedical people have been talking about the link between the quality of your communication and the quality of your life for many years. For example, the philosopher Martin Buber wrote:

> The unique thing about the human world is that something is continually happening between one person and another, something that never happens in the animal or plant world. . . . *Humans are made human by that happening.* . . . This special event begins by one human turning to another, seeing him or her as this particular other being, and offering to communicate with the other in a mutual way, building from the individual world each person experiences to a world they share together.[9]

Jesuit psychologist John Powell put the same idea in simpler terms: "What I am, at any given moment in the process of my becoming a person, will be determined by my relationships with those who love me or refuse to love me, with those I love or refuse to love."[10]

"Okay," you might be saying, "I don't disagree with the lofty ideals expressed by all these people, and I can see how quality of life and quality of communication are related, but let's be a little practical. It's not always *possible* to treat everybody as a personal friend, and more important, it's not always *wise*. So you can't realistically expect your communication always to be friendly and supportive. Impersonal communication happens all the time, and often it's exactly the right kind of communication to have."

I agree. And this is an important point. Many factors make interpersonal communication difficult or even impossible. Role definitions, status relationships, cultural differences, physical surroundings, and even the amount of time available can all be obstacles to interpersonal contact. Lack of awareness and lack of skills can also affect your CQ. One person may want to connect interpersonally with someone else, but may simply not know how to do it.

In other situations it may be possible but, as you point out, it may not be wise. The power relationships or amount of hostility may make it too risky. Everyday communication also includes a great deal of deception. One study concluded that 62 percent of statements made in conversations could be classified as deceptive, and in two other large surveys, more than one-third of the respondents admitted to lying to close friends about important topics.[11] I know a man who used to teach interpersonal communication as part of a Living Skills program in a prison work-release facility. Eric also worked there as a guard. His power as a guard—he had the authority to send people back to the county jail—drastically affected what he could accomplish as an interpersonal communication teacher. Some people in his classes responded openly to his efforts to connect with them. Others were so hardened by their years in various prisons that they could think only about maintaining their own power in the convict hierarchy and getting out as soon as possible—legally or otherwise. It simply didn't make good sense for Eric to try to communicate with all the persons in his class in consistently interpersonal ways. The bottom line is that all of our contacts certainly cannot be interpersonal, but in most cases, more of them could be. And if they were, the quality of our lives would be enhanced.

Human Being Results from Human Contact

The second, closely related basic assumption behind the materials in this book is that *there is a basic movement in the human world, and it is toward relation, not division*. This might sound a little vague, but I think it'll get clearer if you bear with me for a couple of paragraphs. First, I believe that human life is a process and that the general kind of process we humans are engaged in is growing into fully developed persons. So far, no big deal, right?

Second, humans are relational, not solitary, beings. We fundamentally or existentially need contact with other persons. If you could combine a human egg and sperm in a completely impersonal environment, what you'd end up with would not be a person. This is different from cloning. I'm thinking about an artificial womb, machine-assisted birth, mechanical feeding and changing, and so on. Why wouldn't the being that was created this way be a person? Because in order to become a person, the human needs to experience relationships with other persons. This point can't be proved experimentally, of course, because it would be unethical to treat any human organism that way. But some empirical evidence supports this claim; I'm thinking of studies of "feral," or "wild," children—children discovered after they'd been raised for a time by wolves or other animals. One book tells about the Wild Boy of Aveyron, a "remarkable creature" who came out of the woods near a small village in southern France on January 9, 1800, and was captured while digging for vegetables in a village garden. According to the people who knew him, the creature

> was human in bodily form and walked erect. Everything else about him suggested an animal. He was naked except for the tatters of a shirt and showed no modesty, no awareness of himself as a human person related in any way to the people who had captured him. He could not speak and made only weird, meaningless cries. Though very short, he appeared to be a boy of about eleven or twelve.[12]

The creature was taken to a distinguished physician named Dr. Pinel, one of the founders of psychiatry. The doctor was unable to help, partly because "the boy had no human sense of being in the world. He had no sense of himself as a person related to other persons."[13] The "savage of Aveyron" made progress toward becoming human only after he was taken on as a project by another medical doctor named Jean-Marc Gaspard Itard. Itard's first move was to give the boy a foster family and to put him in the care of a mature, loving mother, Mme. Guerin. In this household the boy was able to learn to "use his own chamber pot," dress himself, come when he was called, and even associate some letters of the alphabet with some pictures.

Itard's first report about his year of efforts to socialize the wild boy emphasizes the importance of human contact in becoming a person. Itard describes in detail events that demonstrate the significance of "the feeling of friendship" between him and the boy and especially between the boy and Mme. Guerin: "Perhaps I shall be understood if people remember the major influence on a child of those endless cooings and caresses, those kindly nothings which come naturally from a mother's heart and which bring forth the first smiles and joys in a human life."[14] Without this contact, the young human organism was a creature, a savage. With contact, he began to develop into a person.

Accounts like this one help make the point that *human being results from human contact.* Our genes give us the potential to develop into humans, but without contact, this potential cannot be realized. People definitely are affected by solitude, meditation, and quiet reflection, but mostly because those individualized activities happen in the context of ongoing relationships. As many writers have pointed out, we are molded by our contacts with nature, our contacts with other humans, and our contacts with whatever supreme being, higher power, or god we believe in. This book focuses on the second kind—our contacts with people.

This is *why* there is a direct connection between the quality of your communication and the quality of your life. This is also why I encourage you to think about your communicating in terms of its Contact Quotient. You certainly cannot have the same quality of contact with everybody you meet, in every situation. But you can recognize the quality of contact that's possible between you and the other person(s) and work toward a CQ of 1/1.

Again, I'm not saying that if everybody just holds hands, smiles, and stares at the sunset, all conflict will disappear and the world will be a happy place. I'm not that naïve. But the kind of communicating discussed in this book is not just a trendy, pop-psychology, Western, white, middle-class exercise in narcissism or New Age good-feeling. It's grounded in some basic beliefs about who human beings are and what communication means in human life—regardless of ethnicity, gender, class, or age. In the first reading of Chapter 2, I say more about this point. When you read those pages, you might want to refer to the two assumptions I just described.

PREVIEW OF THE BOOK

So far I've tried to say that for me, interpersonal communication differs from impersonal communication in that it consists of *contact between (inter) persons*. This means that for interpersonal communication to happen, each participant has to be willing and able to talk and listen in ways that maximize the presence of the personal. This willingness and ability will happen only when the people involved (1) are familiar with the basic ingredients of the human communication process, (2) are willing and able to accurately perceive and listen to themselves and others, and to make themselves and their ideas available to others, (3) recognize how the basic communication processes work in various relationships, (4) have some resources to deal with communication difficulties, and (5) can put the whole complex of attitudes and skills together in a human synthesis that works for them.

This is why I've organized *Bridges Not Walls* into five sections, or parts; the readings in each part are designed to do what I've just outlined. So the next three chapters, which complete Part One, explore the rest of the basic ingredients—your overall view of the communication process (Chapter 2), the communicative or social nature of who we are (Chapter 3), and the verbal and nonverbal parts of the process (Chapter 4). Part Two is organized around the metaphors "inhaling-exhaling." I explain the reasons for this metaphor in the introduction to Chapter 5. Basically, I use the term *inhaling* to highlight the perception and listening parts of the communication process and *exhaling* to focus attention on the messages that are expressed. The allusion to breathing emphasizes the impossibility, in actual practice, of separating these two processes.

Chapter 5 treats various parts of inhaling, including person perception and listening. Chapter 6 is made up of articles discussing self-expression, self-disclosure, and confronting abuse. Together, Parts One and Two lay out the general communication process and specific information about each of its main subparts.

The last three sections of this book focus solidly on application. The two chapters of Part Three discuss applications to relationships. First there are readings about family and friend relationships (Chapter 7) and five treatments of communication between intimate partners in Chapter 8. Next are the four chapters that make up Part Four, "Bridges Not Walls," where 30 different authors grapple with some of the most difficult situations where communication knowledge and skills are applied. Chapter 9 focuses on some of the kinds of communication that generate walls: hurtful messages, deception, betrayal, aggression, disconfirmation, power, and verbal abuse. Then in Chapter 10, nine authors offer suggestions about how to manage conflict by turning walls like these into bridges. This is followed by a chapter that focuses on the special difficulties that often emerge in contacts between members of different cultures—ethnic groups, genders, ages, and so on. The final chapter in Part Four describes dialogue, a kind of communicating that, at the beginning of the 21st century, many people are offering as the best way to build bridges not walls.

The final part of the book consists of four overall approaches to interpersonal communicating described by a teacher, a counselor, a spiritual guide, and a philosopher. These readings illustrate how the individual insights, attitudes, and skills talked about in all the other chapters can be condensed and synthesized. They also suggest some additional ways to take this content out of the classroom and into your life.

Before each reading there are some introductory comments that pinpoint what I think are the key ideas that appear there. At the end of each reading I've also included two kinds of questions. Review Questions prompt your recall of key ideas. Probes are questions intended to provoke your thinking and discussion, especially about how the ideas in the reading relate (1) to your own life experience and (2) to ideas in other readings.

One final note: A few of the essays that I have reprinted here were written before people learned about the destructive potential of the historical male bias in the English language. As a result, when these authors mean "humanity," "humans," or "humankind," they write *man* or *mankind*. And when they are using a pronoun to refer to a person in the abstract, it's always *he* rather than *she* or *he and she*. In some cases, I've tried to delete offensive uses or to substitute terms in brackets. In other cases, that kind of editing would make the essay very awkward and difficult to read. This is especially a problem in the reading by Martin Buber (Chapter 16). I hope in this case that you'll be able to read beyond the sexist language for the important ideas.

I also hope that you can have some fun with at least parts of what's ahead. Sometimes the topics are serious, and occasionally the concepts are complex. But this book is about familiar activities that all of us engage in just about all the time. By the time you're finished with it, you should be an even more effective communicator than you already are. This kind of learning can be exciting!

NOTES

1. Reuel Howe, *The Miracle of Dialogue* (New York: Seabury, 1963), cited in *The Human Dialogue,* ed. F. W. Matson and A. Montagu (New York: Free Press, 1968), pp. 148–49.
2. James J. Lynch, *The Language of the Heart: The Body's Response to Human Dialogue* (New York: Basic Books, 1985), p. 3.
3. Lynch, pp. 123–24.
4. Lynch, pp. 160ff.
5. Lynch, pp. 150–55.
6. James J. Lynch, *The Broken Heart: The Medical Consequences of Loneliness* (New York: Basic Books, 1977), pp. 42–51.
7. E. A. Liljefors and R. H. Rahe, "Psychosocial Characteristics of Subjects with Myocardial Infarction in Stockholm," in *Life Stress Illness,* ed. E. K. Gunderson and R. H. Rahe (Springfield, IL: Charles C. Thomas, 1974), pp. 90–104.
8. Lynch, *The Broken Heart,* p. 14.
9. Paraphrased from Martin Buber, *Between Man and Man* (New York: Macmillan, 1965), p. 203.
10. John Powell, *Why Am I Afraid to Tell You Who I Am?* (Chicago: Argus Communications, 1969), p. 43.
11. H. Dan O'Hair and Michael J. Cody, "Deception," in *The Dark Side of Interpersonal Communication,* ed. Wm. R. Cupach and B. H. Spitzberg (Hillsdale, NJ: Lawrence Erlbaum, 1994), pp. 183–84.
12. Roger Shattuck, *The Forbidden Experiment: The Story of the Wild Boy of Aveyron* (New York: Farrar Straus Giroux, 1980), p. 5.
13. Shattuck, p. 37.
14. Shattuck, p. 119.

CHAPTER 2

Defining Communication and Interpersonal Communication

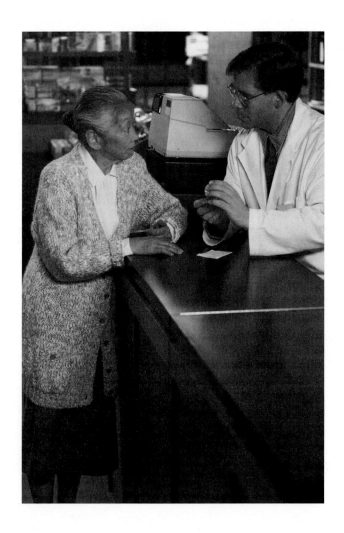

One of the best courses I took during my first year of college was Introduction to Philosophy. Part of the appeal was the teacher. He knew his stuff, and he loved to teach it. But as I discovered a few years later, I also enjoyed the course because I liked the kind of thinking that was going on in the materials we read and the discussions we had. As I continued through college, I supplemented my communication courses with other work in philosophy. The topics I talk about in this essay reflect this dual interest.

One definition of philosophy is "the systematic critique of presuppositions." This means that philosophers are interested first in principles, basic understandings, and underlying assumptions. If you've read much philosophy, you may have the impression that it can be stuffy or even nitpicky to the point of irrelevance. But it can also be exciting and important, because the philosopher says something like, "Hold it! Before you go off to spin a complicated web of explanations about something important—like how people should treat each other, principles of economics and business, or how people communicate—try to get clear about some *basic* things. When you're talking about human communication, for example, what are you assuming about what actually gets passed between people as they communicate? Ideas? Meanings? Or just light and sound waves?" The philosopher might say, "Since meanings are internal, and all that gets exchanged are light and sound, one person can communicate only with *his or her perceptions of* another person. This means I can *never* communicate directly with you. All I can do, when it comes right down to it, is communicate with myself!"

Basic issues like these intrigue me, mainly because they have so many practical effects. Our assumptions about things "leak" out in everything we do. For example, do you know somebody who fundamentally believes that it's a dog-eat-dog world? Watch him or her walk. Listen to the way that person answers the phone. Look at his or her typical facial expression. People's everyday choices about both big and small beliefs and actions grow out of their assumptions—about what's right, what's important, what's honorable, what will provide the best income, or whatever.

So it's important to think about these assumptions and change them when they aren't working well. I know that many potentially exciting conversations have been squelched by someone's dogmatic insistence that all participants "define their terms." But I also know that a great deal of fuzziness can be cleared up and many unhealthy choices can be revised when a conversation starts with some shared understandings about the assumptions behind and definitions of what's being discussed.

In the following essay, I describe my definition of the topic of this book—interpersonal communication. I begin with a six-part description of communication in general that includes a practical implication of each of the six parts. Then I discuss interpersonal communication as a subset of the more general term.

As you'll notice, the views of communication and interpersonal communication that I develop here extend the point I make in Chapter 1 about quality of communication and quality of life. One of the most important things I want to emphasize throughout this book is that communication functions partly to negotiate identities, or selves. In other words, who I am emerges in my listening and talking. This is why the reading begins with an extended explanation of how human worlds or realities are collaboratively constructed (built, modified, torn down, rebuilt) in communication. And the definition of interpersonal communication grows out of this point. In brief, interpersonal communication, as I put it, happens when the people involved talk and listen in ways that maximize the presence of the personal.

The reading is a little long, and I apologize for that. But I'm using it to frame just about everything that follows in this book.

Communicating and Interpersonal Communicating

John Stewart

Communication is an intriguing topic to study because, on the one hand, you and I have been doing it since at least the day we were born, so we have some claim to being "experts," and on the other hand, many of the difficulties that people experience are communication difficulties, which suggests that we all have a lot to learn. If your communication life is trouble-free, this book and the course it is probably a part of might not be for you. But if your experience is anything like mine, you might be interested in some help. After almost 40 years of communication study and teaching, I still experience plenty of misunderstandings, but I've found that some basic insights about what communication is and how it works can smooth many of the rough spots. That's why this introduction describes the general subject matter of communication and this book's specific focus, interpersonal communication. I don't want to make too much out of "defining our terms," but as I think you'll discover, there are some common ways of thinking about these topics that can actually make things harder rather than easier. And there are some important features of communication and interpersonal communication that significantly affect how they work.

COMMUNICATING[1]

In the most general sense, the terms "communication" and "communicating" label *the continuous, complex, collaborative process of verbal and nonverbal meaning-making.* When somebody says, "She's a good communicator" or "We communicate well," it basically means that contacts with these persons tend to go smoothly and that there aren't many confusions or misunderstandings, which is to say that the meanings the people build together generally work okay. By the same token, people talk about "poor communication" when they experience confusing, ambiguous, frustrating, disrespectful, or incomplete meanings.

The word "continuous" in the definition reminds us that communication was going on when we were born and it will continue well after we're dead. "Complex" means that there are many elements or dimensions of every communicative event, including facial expression, tone of voice, choice of words, past history, social roles, and dozens of other factors. The words "verbal and nonverbal" highlight the two basic codes that humans work with. And the term "collaborative" just means that we co-labor, or work together on the meanings we make. Even when two parties are in the midst of a violent disagreement, they are still co-constructing their meanings of anger, hostility, fairness, and respect. So whether you're talking about written or spoken communication, face-to-face or computer-mediated, conflict or cooperation, the process basically involves humans making meaning together.

Meaning is what makes the human world different from the spaces inhabited by other living beings—worms, dogs and cats, and even, so far as we now know, chimpanzees, whales, and dolphins. Since humans live in worlds of meaning—rather than worlds made up of only objects or things—communication is a major part of human living.

To clarify this idea that humans live in worlds of meaning, consider the part of your world that's your "home." If someone asked you to describe your home, you probably wouldn't just talk about how many square feet it has, how tall it is, the distance from your home to some prominent landmark, or the color of the bedroom walls (objective features). Instead, you'd talk about what it *means* to live in a place this small or this big, what you think and feel about the wall color, and what it *means* to live where your home is located. Similarly, the transportation part of your world is significant not simply because you travel by bike or on a bus, in your own old or new sedan or convertible, on foot or on a motorcycle, but because of what it *means* in your family, group of friends, and culture to get around this way. And the meanings of all these parts of our worlds get built up (constructed) and changed in communication—the written and oral, verbal and nonverbal contact people have with each other.

When each of us was born, this process of meaning-making was going on all around us, and we entered it kind of like a chunk of potato when it's plopped into a pot of simmering soup. The soup was there before we were born, it will be simmering all the time we're alive, and these communication processes will continue after we die. As individuals and groups, we certainly affect our worlds a whole lot more than a chunk of potato affects a pot of soup. But each of us is also a participant in an ongoing process that we do not completely control, a process as old and as large as the history of humanity. All the time, everywhere, in all the contacts that make us social animals, humans are constructing meaning together, and "communication" is the name of this ongoing process.

Interpersonal communication is a subset of this general process, a particular kind or type of communication. I'll describe what it is later. But first I want to explain six important features of all kinds of communication, the first of which I've already introduced, and an important implication or practical application of each of the six:

1. **Meaning** Humans live in worlds of meaning, and communication is the process of collaboratively making these meanings.
   Implication #1: No one person can completely control a communication event, and no single person or action causes—or can be blamed for—a communication outcome.
2. **Choice** All communication involves choices, some of which we actively consider and others that follow cultural norms and seem almost automatic.
   Implication #2: The choices communicators make reveal their ethical standards and commitments.
3. **Culture** Culture and communication are intertwined. Ethnicity, gender, age, social class, sexual orientation, and other cultural features always affect communication and are affected by it.
   Implication #3: Your cultures, and mine, affect what I say about communication in this book and how you respond to it.
4. **Identities** Some of the most important meanings people collaboratively construct are identities. All communicating involves negotiating identities or selves.
   Implication #4: Identity messages are always in play.
5. **Conversation** The most influential communication events are conversations.
   Implication #5: The most ordinary communication events are generally the most significant.
6. **Nexting** The most important single communication skill is "nexting."
   Implication #6: Whenever you face a communication challenge or problem, the most useful question you can ask yourself is, "What can I help to happen next?"

1. Humans live in worlds of meaning, and communication is the process of collaboratively making these meanings.

When I introduced this idea, you might have thought it was kind of strange. Most people don't give much thought to their definition of *communication,* and if pressed, a person who's new to this subject matter might just say that communication basically means "getting your ideas across," or "sending and receiving messages." In fact, there's a widespread belief in many cultures that communication

- begins when a sender gets an idea he or she wants to communicate,
- works by having the sender translate the idea into words or some other kind of message,
- requires the receiver to perceive the message and retranslate it into an idea,

- can be evaluated in terms of the match, fit, or, fidelity between message sent and message received, and
- can be analyzed by figuring out who *caused* its successes or failures (who's responsible, who gets the credit, who's at fault or to blame).

According to this definition, the general process of communication can be diagrammed this way:

$$\text{Idea}_1 \rightarrow \text{Message Sent} \rightarrow \text{Message Received} \rightarrow \text{Idea}_2$$

When idea$_2$ is the same as idea$_1$, then communication is successful. When the two ideas don't match, there's a misunderstanding that's somebody's "fault."

This might sound like a fairly reasonable, even accurate, understanding of communication. **But all these common beliefs about communication are misleading, and if you act on them, you're likely to have problems.**

Let's consider each briefly.

Communication Consists Mainly of "Getting Your Ideas Across"   This belief focuses attention on the topic or content of the communicating—the ideas people talk about. And it's reasonable to believe that idea transmission or information sharing is the most important function of communication. But to test this belief, look for a minute at an excerpt from an actual conversation:

1. JOHN: So what do you THINK about the bicycles on campus?
2. JUDY: I think they're terrible.
3. JOHN: Sure is about a MILLION of 'em.
4. JUDY: Eh, heh.
5. JOHN: (Overlapping Judy) Duzit SEEM to you . . . there's a lot more people this year?
6. JUDY: The re-yeah, for sure.
7. JOHN: (Overlapping) Go-GOD, there seems to be a mILLion people.
8. JUDY: Yeah. (brief pause) YEah, there's way too many. I can't . . . at TIMES the bicycles get so bad I just get off mine and . . . hhh . . . give up.
9. JOHN: (Overlapping) Oh, really . . .
10. JOHN: I dunno, when I DODGE one then I have to DODGE another one, 'n it's an endless cycle.
11. JUDY: Yeah (brief pause), oh they're TERrible.
12. JOHN: 'S so many people.
13. JUDY: Um hmm.[2]

The content of this conversation—bicycles on campus—is only a small part of what's going on here. John and Judy are college students who have just met, and they are using the topic of bicycles in part to figure out who they are to and for each other. In fact, the most important parts of this conversation are probably not John's and Judy's ideas about bicycles, but the commonality that their similar opinions creates, combined with the subtle power relationship that's constructed when John defines the topic and overlaps Judy's talk, and

Judy is willing to go along with this slightly one-up/one-down relationship. In other words, especially if you remember that John and Judy don't know each other well, you'd probably agree that the most important features of this conversation are what communication researchers call the *identity messages* or *relationship messages*. These are the verbal and nonverbal indicators of how John defines himself, how he views Judy, and what he thinks Judy thinks of him, along with Judy's verbal and nonverbal ways of defining herself, what she thinks of John, and what she thinks John thinks of her. These messages about the identities, or selves, of the persons involved and their relationships with each other are at least as important as the idea content, and often more so. So the first part of the common definition of communication is misleading because human communication always involves more than simply getting ideas across.

Communication Works by Having the Sender Translate the Idea into Words or Some Other Kind of Message   This belief assumes that speech happens when a speaker changes a mental idea into spoken words. But this conversation didn't just "start" when John got a nonverbal idea about bicycles in his head. He's encountering Judy in a particular context—in this case, they're both volunteer subjects in a communication experiment. Their social, political, and religious cultures help define how similar-age men and women strangers relate to one another, and they're probably each looking for ways to make the encounter as comfortable as possible. So the topic of bicycles emerges out of a context much broader than John's mind. In addition, before John spoke, there was probably no clearly identifiable, singular piece of mental content (an idea) located somewhere in his brain. The phenomena called "ideas" are complex and always changing; they're made up not simply of synapse patterns or cognitions but of words, intonation, stress, pauses, and facial expression; and they change as they are being uttered. This means that there is no unitary, identifiable thing inside a person's head (an idea) that gets translated or encoded into spoken words.

Communication Requires the Receiver to Perceive the Message and Retranslate It into an Idea   This belief suggests that listeners are doing the same things that speakers are, only in reverse. But again, human communication is not this simple. First, notice that neither John nor Judy is simply "sender" or "receiver" at any point in this exchange; in fact, they're both sending and receiving at every moment. *As she speaks,* Judy is noticing John's response (she is receiving) and is modifying what she says and how she says it. John is doing the same thing. *As he listens,* he's "saying" things to Judy with his face and body. And this goes on all the time. Human communicators are always sending and receiving simultaneously. As a result, each communicator has the opportunity to change how things are going at any time in the process. When this excerpt of the conversation ends, John and Judy are at a point of potential change, and the next utterance may move them closer together or farther apart. John could pick up on Judy's disclosure that she is a cyclist, for example, or Judy could introduce a new topic that's more important to her than this one. The point is, much more is going on here than back-and-forth translation and retranslation of individual ideas.

Communication Can Be Evaluated in Terms of the Match, Fit, or Fidelity between Message Sent and Message Received   This belief suggests that you could isolate and define John's and Judy's mental contents (ideas) so you could figure out how well they match or fit. But since ideas are so fluid and dynamic, and since communication happens as much in talk as in people's heads, the fidelity model doesn't fit living conversation very well. In order to apply this notion of matching or fitting, you'd have to slow down and distort the exchange to the point where it wouldn't be anything like what actually happened. Communication success has more to do with the people's ability to continue relating smoothly with each other than with matching mental contents.

Communication Problems Can Be Analyzed by Identifying Fault and Blame
To say that a problem is somebody's "fault" is to say that she or he *caused* it, like a temperature below 0°C causes water to freeze, or pushing down on one end of a lever causes the other end to rise. In other words, this belief assumes that human communication is governed by laws of cause and effect. But is it? If Judy noticed the one-up/one-down power relationship with John, she might believe that it's John's fault because he asserted power by taking on the roles of topic definer and overlapping speaker.[3] John, on the other hand, might think that any power imbalance between them is due to Judy's initial silence, or her willingness to go along with his topic choice. Who's right? Whose fault is it really? Who's really to blame?

One problem with questions like these is that they require somebody to identify where the exchange *started,* so they can determine what's "cause" and what's "effect." But as I've already noted, some of what's going on in a conversation is as old as the participants themselves, or older. And this is literally always true. Every single thing the participants say and do may be understood as a *response* to what preceded it in their lives. No living human is the original Adam or Eve, the first one to disturb the cosmic silence of the universe. An enormous amount of communication precedes everything all of us communicate.[4] Even the first "hi" in a relationship can be understood as a response to a smile, the situation, or a lesson your parents taught you about being polite. In John and Judy's conversation, some of what's said can be traced back to the gender definitions that each of them developed when they were growing up. And these influences could be traced back to John's and Judy's parents' definitions of themselves, which came in part from *their* parents, and so on. This is the kind of complex mess a search for original causes can suck you into. And for the sake of

argument, let's assume that John and Judy finally agree on just where the exchange started and whose fault some part of it was. What then? Will the resulting guilt feelings or an apology from the accused party fix the problem? Not
usually. Even when people agree on fault and blame, that agreement doesn't
usually improve things much. The reason is that human communication is
much too complex to be profitably analyzed into simple cause-effect, fault-
blame sequences.

In short, two things can be learned from this brief example:

- Some of the most common understandings or definitions of human communication are plausible but misleading.
- Since the way you think about or define something determines what you
  experience, and what you experience determines the responses you make
  (in other words assumptions, as I said before, "leak" out in all our beliefs
  and behaviors), it's important to have a workable definition of human
  communication so you can respond in ways that help you communicate
  effectively.

The main reason that this common definition of communication is misleading is that it's oversimplified.

**Communication Is the Continuous, Complex, Collaborative Process of Verbal
and Nonverbal Meaning-Making**   As I mentioned before, it's *continuous* because humans are always making meaning—figuring out, making sense of, or
interpreting what's happening. It's *complex* because it involves not just words
and ideas but also intonation, facial expression, eye contact, touch, and several
other nonverbal elements, and it always includes identity and relationship
messages, culture and gender cues, more or less hidden agendas, unspoken expectations, and literally dozens of other features that usually become apparent
only when they create problems. It's *collaborative,* because we do it with other
people; we don't communicate alone.[5] "Co-labor-ating" just means working together, and collaboration can be as anonymous as obeying traffic laws and
speaking the local language, or as intimate as attending to your partner's lovemaking preferences.

**Implication #1: No one person can completely control a communication
event, and no single person or action causes—or can be blamed for—a communication outcome.**   Many people come to communication classes or
workshops wanting to learn how to "do it right." They want to know how to
solve the communication problems they experience—to get their parents off
their backs; eliminate misunderstandings with roommates, co-workers, or
dating partners; deal with a critical and complaining boss; end a painful relationship; become a masterful salesperson. Some of these people want to learn
the surefire techniques that will give them control over their communication

lives. These people are disappointed, and some are even angry, when they learn that it isn't that simple. They are even more uncomfortable when they learn that it's an illusion to believe that surefire techniques of human communication even exist! As philosopher William Barrett put it over 30 years ago in his book *The Illusion of Technique,* "Technical thinking cannot deal with our human problems."[6]

I don't mean that technical thinking is hopeless or that there's nothing to be gained from scientific and social experiments. But one direct implication of the recognition that communication is a *collaborative* process is that no one person can completely control any communication event, and that no technique or set of communication moves can definitely determine its outcome.

Regardless of how clearly I write or speak, you may still interpret me in a variety of different ways. Regardless of how carefully I plan a meeting, one or more people are likely to have agendas very different from mine. Even a successful dictator whose orders are consistently followed can't control how people understand or feel about his or her demands. And as I mentioned, even though I've been working on my communication for years, I still experience difficulties that I cannot completely predict or control in relationships with family members, friends, co-workers, and acquaintances.

I believe that your skill as a communicator will be enhanced if you try to manage your expectations about control and perfection. The more you understand how communication works and the more communication skills you develop, the more effective and competent you will be. It is possible to learn how to give and get criticism gracefully, to manage conflict effectively, and to develop relationships smoothly. But not 100 percent of the time.

Cause-effect, fault-blame thinking is one of the oversimplifications people often fall into. I won't repeat what I said in the discussion of John and Judy's communication, but I do want to reemphasize it in this context. Problems obviously happen in communication, and the choices of the people involved help create, maintain, worsen, and solve these problems. But when you understand that communication is *continuous, complex,* and *collaborative,* you cannot coherently blame one person or one set of actions for whatever you might see as problematic. For one thing, fault and blame ignore the continuousness of communication. In order to say someone is at fault, you need to assume that whatever happened *began with the guilty person's action.* But all the people involved have been engaged in communication literally since they were born and have developed and reinforced each other's ways of speaking, listening, and interpreting since at least the time they met. So the person who you say is at fault because he didn't call you back to confirm the meeting may be remembering your complaints about "getting all those annoying calls" and your insistence that it's only necessary to call if meeting plans change.

Fault and blame also ignore the fact that communication is collaborative. When directions are unclear, for example, it's due to both the direction-giver and the direction-receiver. Did the receiver ask about what confused her? Did the giver check the receiver's understanding? It may have seemed perfectly legitimate to one person to assume that everybody understood that the meeting was at 8:00 P.M. and not 8:00 A.M., for example, or that the family would gather for the holiday dinner just like they had in the past. But others might have radically different assumptions that lead to significantly different interpretations.

Does this mean that when there are problems, nobody's responsible? Does this idea eliminate any possibility of accountability? No, not at all. Individual responses still make a difference, and some are definitely more ethical, appropriate, or humane than others. But I'm trying to replace the oversimplified and distorted notions of fault and blame with a broader focus on both or all "sides" of the communication process. I do not mean to replace, "It's his fault" with "It's her fault," "It's both of their faults," or "It's nobody's fault." Instead, I encourage you to give up the notion of fault altogether, at least when you're thinking or talking about human communication.

Another way to put this point is to say that this view of communication redefines what responsibility means. Traditionally, being responsible means that you *caused* something to happen, that it was your fault. But from the perspective I'm developing here, responsibility means *ability to respond,* not fault, blame, or credit. It means *"response-able."* You are response-able when you have the willingness and the ability to contribute in some way to how things are unfolding, rather than ignoring what's going on or dropping out of the event. "Irresponsible" people are not responsive; they act without taking into account what else is going on or how their actions may influence others. Responsible (response-able) actions consider the larger wholes that they help make up. This idea is related to the basic skill of "nexting" that's discussed in feature 6.

2. Choice. All communication involves choices, some of which people actively consider, and others that follow cultural norms and seem almost automatic.

Human meanings are inherently ethical because they involve choices. Individually and collectively, humans create and abide by guidelines for evaluating actions as right or wrong, good or bad, and appropriate or inappropriate. These ethical standards influence people's actions but do not always determine them. Interpersonal communication, as I'll explain, involves reflective and responsive choices.

Some of the choices people make don't feel much like choices. For example, shaking hands and bowing are two culturally influenced actions that one may choose to engage in when meeting another person for a business lunch. Although decisions about how long and how firmly to shake a hand or how deep to bow may be something you actively consider, the initial behavior of shaking or bowing may not be. You may not actively choose the tone of voice you use with your sibling in the same way you may consider how to talk with your best friend, because the norms for interaction in your family culture may be taken for granted, but not in your friendship.

Implication #2: The choices communicators make reveal their ethical standards and commitments.   Consider the issue of shoplifting food from a grocery store, for example. Many people admit to stealing a candy bar as a kid, a choice made for the thrill, as a response to peer pressure, or just because they wanted one and didn't have the money at the time. They might have had an ethical standard that stealing was wrong and another competing standard that said that the adrenaline rush, fitting in with friends, or immediate gratification was good. They had to choose between competing standards, and in this case, the stealing-is-wrong ethic carried less weight. Other people cannot understand how anyone could ever decide to steal. For these people, the stealing-is-wrong ethical standard is more heavily weighted, perhaps in response to explicit lessons from family, teachers, or a religious community. But whether you would or would not steal something from a grocery store, how would you evaluate an individual who had been involuntarily unemployed for months, exhausted by limited resources of the local food bank, and decided that the only way members of her family would eat today would be if she took a loaf of bread and a jar of peanut butter without paying for them? In this case, is the stealing right or wrong? A good or bad choice? An appropriate or inappropriate action?

The point is that there are always competing forces in human lives, and that part of what it means to be human is to make meaningful choices between them. If communication is a collaboratively constructed process, no one individual has complete control over its outcome. All of our choices are made within the context of our personal experience and are evaluated in relation to cultural norms and expectations. Standards for evaluation can differ from person to person, family to family, and culture to culture over time.

3. Culture. Culture and communication are intertwined. Ethnicity, gender, age, social class, sexual orientation, and other cultural features always affect communication and are affected by it.

When many people think about culture, they envision a group's customs, cooking, and clothing, but there's much more to it than that. In a very general sense, culture provides you with ways to make meaning. One way to talk about culture is to say that *culture means shared norms, values, and beliefs related to how people live and how people communicate.* These shared values, norms, and beliefs influence every part of people's lives.

Dating, for example, is one context in which the interaction of culture and communication can be observed. In some cultures, dating is a means to an end—a way to select a life partner, and whom you date is your business. In other cultures, it would be inappropriate to bring someone home to meet the folks, because "the folks" (parents, community members, or tribal leaders) will already have made arrangements for marriage.

When you think about culture this way, you'll realize that it involves much more than just national identity. People who share ways of living and speaking—belong to "the same culture"—can be members of different ethnic groups. Even two members of the same family (a heterosexual brother and his lesbian sister) inhabit different cultures.

Especially today, with the increasing globalization of sports, music, media, business, education, and religion; with the explosion of international communication via the Internet and the World Wide Web; and with the growing recognition in education and business that diversity in organizations is a strength rather than a threat, culture is on almost everybody's minds. This is partly why I say that culture figures prominently in communication.

But there is a more basic reason: Culture becomes concrete in communication. What it *means* to belong to a culture is to communicate in certain ways—to use certain expressions that members of other cultures don't use, to prefer certain kinds of meetings, to honor certain styles of speaking, to maintain certain distances, to touch in certain ways, and so on. This means that your culture is present in your communicating and other people's cultures are present in their communicating, too.

Implication #3: Your cultures—and mine—affect what I say about communication in this book and how you respond to it.   Importantly for each author in this book—and for you as reader—*our* cultures are present in our communicating, too. I consider myself to be culturally Western, Anglo, middle-class, late middle-aged, heterosexual, gendered, a parent, and a teacher–scholar. This means that my communication content and style in this book will embody these cultural features (and probably others I am not aware of). You'll get cultural information about some of the other authors in this book, and none about other authors. If you do *not* identify yourself culturally with an author, you may legitimately ask, "How are this person's ideas relevant to me? If culture and communication are so intertwined, what can I—an African-American, perhaps, or Latino, 20-year old, gay or lesbian, engineering or chemistry student—learn from writings by this person?"

Enough, I hope, to keep you reading. This book offers some knowledge and skills about communication that are supported by evidence from a variety of cultures, and its authors speak from positions in cultures with fairly large memberships and fairly wide ranges of influence. If you are not a member of one or more of the cultures an author belongs to, this material can still be useful to you in at least two ways: (1) You can test generalizations against your experience in your own cultures to determine which apply and which don't, and (2) when an author's ideas don't apply in one or more of your cultures, you can use them to enhance your ability to communicate with people in the cultures the author inhabits.

For example, my first three claims about human communication are that humans live in worlds of meaning that are constructed in communicating, that choices embody ethical standards, and that culture figures prominently in all communication. I believe that there is ample evidence to demonstrate that these points are true about all people in all cultures, *not* just Western, Anglo, middle-class, late middle-aged, heterosexual, gendered, parent, and teacher–scholar cultures. Do you? I encourage you to test these generalizations against your own experience and to discuss the results with your instructor and classmates. On the other hand, as just one example, this book's readings about nonverbal communication may contain some generalizations about space or eye contact that don't ring true for one or more of your cultures. If so, you can combine your understanding of your own culture with what the author says about hers or his, and use this knowledge about space or eye contact in the author's culture to enhance your ability to communicate outside your own culture, with people in the culture the author inhabits.

And notice that you can do this without being co-opted. If you feel culturally different from some of the writers in this book, you don't have to give up your distinctiveness to profit from what's here. You can operate like a global businessperson. People who have to serve customers or work with producers outside their own cultures routinely learn how to adapt to these other cultures, but from their own position of strength—as a representative of their business. These people want to do business in another culture, so their adaptation is based on that foundation; it doesn't mean that their values or morals are co-opted. Regardless of the culture you enter or the adaptations you may choose to make, you can do so from a comparable position of strength.

4. Some of the most important meanings people collaboratively create are identities; all communicating involves negotiating identities, or selves.

Communication theorist and teacher John Shotter emphasizes this point when he says that our "ways of being, our 'selves,' are produced in our . . . ways of interrelating ourselves to each other—these are the terms in which we are socially accountable in our society—and these 'traditional' or 'basic' (dominant) ways of talking are productive of our 'traditional' or 'basic' psychological and social [identities]."[7] In other words, who we are—our identities—is built in our communicating. People come to each encounter with an identifiable "self," built through past interactions, and *as we talk,* we adapt ourselves to fit the topic we're discussing and the people we're talking with, and we are changed by what happens to us as we communicate.

The way communication and identity are closely related became especially apparent in a conversation I had with a friend who was going through a painful divorce. "Mary Kay is not the person she used to be," Dale said. "Sometimes I hardly know her. I wish we could communicate and enjoy each other like we did when we were first married."

The times Dale was remembering were before Mary Kay was a mother, before she completed medical school, before she suffered through her residency in an urban hospital 2,000 miles from home, before she joined a prestigious medical clinic, and before she became a full-fledged practicing physician. They were also before Dale was a dad, before he started his import-export business, before he became active in his state professional association, and before he began attending church regularly. Dale was forgetting that Mary Kay could not possibly still be "the person she used to be." Neither could he. Both of them had experienced many relationships that changed them decisively. Mary Kay had been treated like a medical student—required to cram scientific information into her head and spout it on command—and like a first-year resident—forced to go without sleep, stand up to authoritarian doctors, and cope with hospital administrators. Now nurses obey her, many patients highly respect her for her skills, and prestigious doctors treat her like an equal. And she's treated as a mom by her son. Dale has also experienced many different relationships, and he's changed, too. He's treated as a boss by his employees and as "a respected American businessman" by his Japanese customers. Because of the contacts both have experienced, each is a different person. And the process continues as both Mary Kay and Dale continue to be changed by their communication.

Obviously these identity changes are limited. Most people don't change their gender, ethnicity, or family of origin. But some changes are inevitable over time, and others can happen in the short term. For example, a woman can communicate in ways that say she is more feminine—or more masculine—than her conversation partner, and as a person with greater or less authority or power than her conversation partner has. The other person's responses will contribute to the identity as it's negotiated verbally and nonverbally.

Consider the difference, for example, between "Shut the door, stupid!" and "Please close the door." The command projects the identity of a superior speaking to a subordinate. On the other hand, the request identifies the speaker as an equal to the person being addressed. The person who's told to "Shut the door, stupid!" may silently comply, in which case he or she is reinforcing part of the identities of superior and subordinate. Or the person may respond, "Shut it yourself!" which is a negotiation move that says, in effect, "You're not my superior; we're equals."

Implication #4: Identity issues are always in play.   The point is that *identity negotiation, or the collaborative construction of selves, is going on whenever people communicate.* It definitely is not the *only* thing that's happening, but it's one of the very important processes, and it often gets overlooked. When it does, troubles usually result. By contrast, people who are aware of identity negotiation processes can communicate more effectively and successfully in many different situations. So whenever you communicate—on the telephone, via e-mail, face-to-face, in meetings, even in front of the television—part of what is happening is identity negotiation.

Communication content is important too, and sometimes problems can be solved only when the parties involved have more or better information. Policies may be out of date, data may be incomplete, and people may have misread or misheard key instructions. In these cases, the people involved may need to complete, refine, or recalibrate the information they're working with.

But as I noted, effective communicators understand and manage what they're verbally and nonverbally "saying" about *who they are* to the people they're communicating with. Identities are communicated in many different ways. Topic choice and vocabulary are important. Grooming and dress also contribute to this process, as people offer definitions of themselves using nose rings and other body piercing, tatoos, starched white shirts or blouses, and conservative business suits. Tone of voice is similarly identity-defining. Some people foster misunderstanding by unknowingly sounding like they're skeptical, hostile, or bored, and other tones of voice help their listeners feel genuinely appreciated and supported. Facial expressions also help define a person as attentive, careful, positive, or their opposites.

Especially when you're troubleshooting—or just trying to live through—a disagreement or conflict, it usually works best to start by understanding the identities that are in play. Who might be getting defined as inattentive, insensitive, or incompetent? What communication moves make one person appear more important, trustworthy, moral, or thorough than the other? Does everybody involved feel able to influence the ways they're viewed by the others? Or are identities being treated as unchangable? By the time you've worked through this book, you should have a wealth of ideas and practical skills for constructively managing how you define yourself and how others define you.

5. The most influential communication events are conversations.

If you had to identify one event that humans all over the world engage in characteristically—because they're humans—routinely, naturally, and almost constantly, what would it be? We all breathe, but so do other animals. We eat and drink, but not constantly, and again, other animals do too. The one activity that marks us as human and that occupies a large part of our personal and occupational lives is conversation, verbal and nonverbal exchange in real time, either face-to-face or mediated by some electronic medium (e.g., the computer).

For a long time, people who studied communication and language tended to overlook this point. Language scholars focused on rules of grammar and syntax, dictionary definitions, and other features of writing, and speech research and teaching paid primary attention to public speaking and deliberation in law courts and legislatures. But in the last third of the 20th century, an increasing number of scholars and teachers have shown how written and formal kinds of communicating are derived from the most basic human activity, informal conversation. Recently, for example, two well-known psychologists from Stanford

University began a report of their National Science Foundation–supported research with these words:

> Conversation is the fundamental site of language use. For many people, even for whole societies, it is the only site, and it is the primary one for children acquiring language. From this perspective other arenas of language use—novels, newspapers, lectures, street signs, rituals—are derivative or secondary.[8]

Another respected scholar puts it more simply. "Conversation," he writes, "is sociological bedrock,"[9] the absolute foundation or base for everything humans do as social beings. This explains the sense of the title of one of communication theorist John Shotter's recent books, *Conversational Realities: Constructing Life through Language*.[10] Shotter's book explains in detail how human realities get constructed in communication—our point 1—and emphasizes that the most characteristic form of this communication is *conversation*.

Implication #5: The most ordinary communication events are the most significant.   The reason I highlight this idea as one of the five main points about human communication is that it justifies paying close attention to something common and ordinary. The fact that humans engage in conversation so constantly, and so often almost without thinking, is part of what makes the process so important. As organizational theorist and trainer Peter Senge puts it, effective conversation is "the single greatest learning tool in your organization—more important than computers or sophisticated research."[11] Whether in a living group, a family-run shop, a small work team, or a multinational corporation, the real organizational structure and rules—as contrasted with what's on the organizational chart—get defined in the subtleties of verbal and nonverbal conversation. (Susan Scott makes this point later in this chapter.) Superior and subordinate status get negotiated in face-to-face contacts. Key decisions are heavily influenced by brief informal contacts in the bathrooms and halls as much as they are by formal presentations in meetings. And when the organization needs to change and there are feelings about rights or two worthwhile principles in conflict, the only realistic options are some form of authoritarianism or some form of problem-solving conversation. Similarly, conversation is the primary way families have of making decisions and negotiating differences. And children become effective participants in play groups, classrooms, sports teams, and their own families by learning how to converse well.

This means that one very important way to improve your communication competence is to pay close attention to the most common and everyday kind of communicating—conversation. When you do, you'll discover that you already have a great deal of experience with many of the concepts and skills this book discusses. This means that you have a solid foundation to build on. Even if you don't believe you're very good at conversation, you've done it often and well enough, and it's going on around you so much, that you can build on the experiences you have. One way is with point 6.

6. The most useful single communication skill is "nexting."

Nexting is a strange term, I admit. But it's the best one I've come up with for this skill. If, as you read this section, you come up with a better one, please let me know.

By "nexting" I mean doing something helpful next, responding fruitfully to what's just happened, taking an additional step in the communication process. If you've grasped how I've described communication so far, this is the most important single skill you can build on this understanding. Here's why:

Since you realize that communication is complex, continuous, and collaborative, you'll always recognize that, no matter what's happened before and no matter how bad things currently look, you always have the option to try a *next* step. No matter how many times the same insult has been repeated, the next response can be creative rather than retaliatory. No matter how long the parties have not been speaking to each other, the next time they meet, one of them could speak. No matter how ingrained and toxic the pattern is that two groups are caught in, the next move one side makes could be positive. No matter how much you feel "thrown" by what the other person just said and did, if you give yourself a little time to regroup, you can make a next move that could help get the relationship back on track. No matter how little power the system gives you, your next communication choice can maximize the power you have. Even when it is very difficult not to strike back, your next comment could conceivably be helpful rather than abusive.

When you understand that communication is continuous and collaborative, you'll recognize the potential value of what you do next. Why? Because since no one person determines all the outcomes of a communication event, you can help determine some outcomes, even if you feel almost powerless. Since no one person is 100 percent to blame or at fault, and all parties share response-ability, your next contribution can affect what's happening. Since all communication is collaborative—remember, even prizefighters are co-labor-ating—your next communication move can make a change in the situation, or at least keep the conversation going.

Implication #6: Whenever you face a communication challenge or problem, the most useful question you can ask yourself is, "What can I help to happen next?"   You can apply the skill of nexting by remembering that no human system is ever completely determined or cast in stone. Regardless of how well or badly things are going between you and someone else, remember that what you do next will help maintain or destroy this quality. It almost goes without saying that in some cases you may not *want* to try to improve a bad situation or to maintain a good one. You may have tried to make positive contributions and have been continually rebuffed, and you may be out of patience, resources, or caring. You may in this particular case decide not to make a positive, supportive, or conciliatory move. You may also decide to let silence remain, to keep your distance, or to let the hostility fester. But if you understand the world-constructing nature of human communication, you can understand these options for what they are—*responses,* choices, decisions about what you are going to do *next.* They have their benefits and their consequences, just as other responses would.

To put it simply, people who understand communication to be the kind of process I've outlined so far are not generally thrown off balance by communication difficulties. They understand that the most important thing to consider is what they are going to do *next.*

INTERPERSONAL COMMUNICATING

As I said at the start of this chapter, interpersonal communication is a subset of communication in general. This means that collaboration, choices, culture, identities, conversation, and nexting are all parts of interpersonal communicating, too. The kind of communication I'm calling "interpersonal" doesn't happen all the time, but it can take place in families, between friends, during an argument, in business situations, and in the classroom. It can also happen on the telephone, online, among jurors, at a party, across a bargaining table, and even during public speeches or presentations. The main characteristic of interpersonal communication is that the people involved are contacting each other *as persons.* This might sound pretty simple, but again, there's a little more to it than you might think.

For one thing, as you and I move through our daily family, work, social, and school lives, we tend to relate with others in two different ways. Sometimes we treat others and are treated by them *impersonally* as role-fillers (bank teller, receptionist, employer, bus driver, etc.). And sometimes we connect with others *personally,* as a unique individual (not just role-filler or cultural representative). I don't mean that there are sharp divisions; sometimes we move back and forth between impersonal and interpersonal contact. But these two terms can anchor a sliding scale or continuum that models the qualities or kinds of communication that people experience.

QUALITIES OF COMMUNICATION	
Impersonal ———————————————————	Interpersonal

The left side of the continuum, the impersonal side, is characterized by communication that is based on social roles and exchanges that minimize the presence of the communicators' personal identities. Impersonal communication is the label I use to describe your typical experiences at the bank, convenience store, fast-food restaurant, and in front of the television. In these situations, people usually connect in ways that emphasize their social roles—teller/customer; buyer/seller; server/diner, and so on. Even though human beings are obviously involved, they all function pretty much like interchangeable parts of an automobile or computer. So long as the teller, buyer, or server knows his or her job (social role), and so long as the customer, seller, or diner remains in his or her role, it doesn't matter much who they are as individuals. I call this quality of communication *impersonal* because it's the most generic kind of human contact. There is human association but little or no close human contact.

Often, of course, this is exactly the best kind of communicating to have. For one thing, it's efficient. Nobody wants to wait in line while the Burger King cashier has a personal chat with each customer. It's also often the most appropriate kind of communicating. We don't ordinarily approach bank tellers, ticket sellers, or driver's license clerks expecting or wanting to have a deep conversation.

However, not all impersonal communicating takes place with people we hardly know. It is not unusual to engage in efficient, issue-centered communication with people we know well and care about. We also engage in generic greeting rituals with our best friends and family members as well as strangers. It's not uncommon to hear parents involve role-based communication patterns with their children (e.g., "Because I'm the mom, that's why!"). The important point is that impersonal communicating is a common, normal, useful, and often very appropriate way of relating.

But some of almost every day's communicating also fits near the right-hand end of the scale. During a committee meeting or team activity you may contact another person as a unique individual, and you may get treated that way by him or her. The same kind of communicating can happen in your conversations with a dating partner, a parent, a sibling, your roommate, co-workers, or close friends.

No one's communication life can be packaged into neat boxes; that's why the model is a sliding scale. At one moment you may be contacting someone impersonally and at the next moment your communication may become interpersonal. But what I've said so far clarifies what I mean when I define interpersonal communication, the main topic of this book, as *the type or kind of communication that happens when the people involved talk and listen in ways that maximize the presence of the personal.*

Notice that this definition is not based on the number of people involved or whether they are in the same place. I believe that it is possible to communicate interpersonally in groups and even through phone lines or e-mail. When communication emphasizes the persons involved rather than just their roles or stereotypical characteristics, interpersonal communication is happening.

Features of the Personal

So what do I mean by "the personal"? Many philosophers, anthropologists, and communication scholars have defined what it means to be a person and how persons differ from other kinds of animals. One widely recognized description was created by a philosopher of communication named Martin Buber. (Buber was born in 1878, lived in Austria, Germany, and Israel, visited the United States a couple of times, and died in 1965.) He suggested that there are five qualities, or characteristics, that distinguish persons across many—though perhaps not all—cultures: uniqueness, measurability, responsiveness, reflectiveness, and addressability.[12] These five define what I mean by "the personal," and I will use the five and their opposites to distinguish *impersonal* from *interpersonal* communicating.

Unique   Uniqueness means noninterchangeability. We, as persons, can be treated as if we were interchangeable parts, but each of us can also be thought of as unique in a couple of ways, genetically and experientially. The main reason that genetic cloning experiments are controversial is that they threaten this quality. Unless they are cloned or are identical twins, the probability that two persons would have the same genetic materials is 1 in 10 to the ten-thousandth power. That's less than one chance in a billion trillion!

But cloning wouldn't really threaten uniqueness, because even when persons have the same biological raw material, each experiences the world differently. For example, recall identical twins you've known. Both twins might see the same film in the same theater on the same night at the same time, sitting next to each other. Both might leave the theater at the same time and say exactly the same words about it: "I liked that film." At a superficial level, someone might suggest that the experiences of the two are, in this situation, interchangeable. But additional talk will show that they aren't. Did both twins like the film for the same reasons? Did they recall the same experiences as they interpreted the film? Will the film have the same effect on both of them? Will both remember the same things about it? If you asked the twins these questions, you'd get different answers, and you'd discover what you probably knew before you began the process: Each human is unique.

When people are communicating with each other impersonally, they're overlooking most of this uniqueness and focusing on the similarities among all those who play a given social role. All of us naturally and constantly fill many different roles—student, daughter or son, sibling, employee, and so on. And role relationships are an inescapable part of communicating. But the sliding scale emphasizes that people can move from impersonal communication to interpersonal contact.

So the first feature that distinguishes *persons* is experiential and, in most cases, genetic uniqueness. Some cultures downplay this feature, but most Western cultures emphasize it. The more present this feature is in your communicating, the farther your communication is toward the right-hand side of the impersonal–interpersonal continuum.

Unmeasurable   Objects are measurable; they fit within boundaries. An event is of a certain duration; it lasts a measurable amount of time. Even extremely complex objects, such as sophisticated supercomputers, 70-story buildings, and space vehicles, can be completely described in space-and-time terms. This is what blueprints do. They record all the measurements necessary to recreate the object—length, height, width, mass, specific gravity, amperage, voltage, velocity, circumference, hardness, ductility, malleability, conductivity, and so on. Although it's difficult to measure some things directly—the temperature of a kiss, the velocity of a photon, the duration of an explosion—no object or event has any parts that are unmeasurable, in theory at least.

It's different with persons. Even if your physician accurately identifies your height, weight, temperature, blood pressure, serum cholesterol level, hemoglobin count, and all your other data right down to the electric potential in your seventh cranial nerve, the doctor still will not have exhaustively accounted for the person you are, because there are parts of you that can't be measured. Many scientists, social scientists, philosophers, and theologians have made this point. Some cognitive scientists, for example, include in their model of the person components they call "schematas," or "cognitive patterns" that don't have any space-and-time (measurable) existence, but that can be inferred from observations of behavior. Others call the unmeasurable elements of a person the "human spirit," "psyche," or "soul." But whatever you call it, it's there.

Emotions or feelings are the clearest observable evidence of this unmeasurable part. Although instruments can measure things related to feelings—brain waves, sweaty palms, heart rate, paper-and-pencil responses—what the measurements record is a long way from the feelings themselves. "Pulse 110, respiration 72, Likert rating 5.39, palmar conductivity 0.036 ohms" may be accurate, but it doesn't quite capture what's going on inside when you encounter somebody you can't stand or greet somebody you love.

One other thing: These emotions or feelings are *always* a part of what we are experiencing. Psychologists and educators agree that it's unrealistic to try to separate the intellectual or objective aspect of a person or a subject matter from the affective or emotional parts. This is because humans are always thinking *and* feeling. As one writer puts it, "It should be apparent that there is no intellectual learning without some sort of feeling and there are no feelings without the mind's somehow being involved."[13]

Even though feelings are always present, some communication acknowledges them and some communication doesn't. The cashier who's dedicated to her social role will greet people with a smile and wish them a "nice day" even if she feels lousy. Servers in a restaurant are taught not to bring their feelings to work. Two persons who are in a minority may share similar feelings of isolation or exclusion, but they may or may not talk about them. On the other hand, when people are communicating interpersonally, some of their feelings are in play. This does not mean that you have to wear your heart on your sleeve to communicate interpersonally. It just means that when people are making interpersonal contact, some feelings are appropriately acknowledged and shared.

Responsive   Humans are thoroughly and uniquely responsive beings. Objects can only react; they cannot respond. They cannot choose what to do next.

Automatic pilots, photoelectric switches, personal and industrial robots, thermostats, and computers can sometimes seem to operate on their own or turn themselves off and on, but they too are dependent on actions initiated outside them. The computers and robots have to be programmed, the thermostat reacts to temperature, which reacts to the sun's rays, which are affected by the earth's rotation, and so on. Similarly, a ball can go only where it's kicked, and if you were good enough at physics calculations, you could figure out how far and where it would go, on the basis of weight, velocity, aerodynamics, the shape of your shoe, atmospheric conditions, and so on.

But what if you were to kick a person? It's an entirely different kind of activity, and you cannot accurately predict what will happen. The reason you can't is that when persons are involved, the outcome depends on *response*, not simply *reaction*. If you tap my knee, you may cause a reflex jerk, but the feelings that occur are not completely predictable, and the behavior or actions that accompany my reflex may be anything from giggles to a slap in the face.

The range of responses is limited, of course. We can't instantly change sex, become three years younger, or memorize the contents of the Library of Congress. But we can decide whether to use a conventional word or an obscene one, we can choose how to prioritize our time commitments, and, as will be discussed in later chapters, choice is even a part of the feelings we experience.

In fact, the more you realize your freedom and power to respond rather than simply react, the more of a person you can be. Sometimes it's easy to get out of touch with this freedom and power. You feel like saying, "I *had* to shout back; he was making me look silly!" or "I just *couldn't* say anything!" These statements make it sound like you don't have any choice, like what you do is completely *caused* by what another person does. But as the discussion of fault and blame noted, even when circumstances are exerting pressure, persons still have some freedom and power to choose how to respond. It may mean resisting a culturally rooted preference or breaking some well-established habit patterns, and it may take lots of practice, but it's possible to become aware of your responses and, when you want to, to change them. The reason it's important to learn this skill is that when you believe you're just reacting, you've lost touch with part of what it means to be a person. So, all communication involves choices because persons are responsive, and the more you remember and act on this feature, the more interpersonal your communicating can become.

Reflective   A fourth distinguishing characteristic is that persons are reflective. Being reflective means not only that we are aware of what's around us, but also that we can be aware of our awareness. As one author puts it, "No matter how much of yourself you are able to objectify and examine, the quintessential, living part of yourself will always elude you, i.e., the part of you that is conducting the examination,"[14] the reflective part. Wrenches, rocks, and rowboats aren't aware at all. Dogs, cats, armadillos, and giraffes are all aware of their environments, but we don't have any evidence that they are aware of their awareness.

So far as we know, only humans compose and save histories of their lives, elaborately bury their dead, explore their extrasensory powers, question the meaning of life, and speculate about the past and future. And only humans are aware that we do all these things.

Reflection is not a process that affects only philosophers and people who know that they don't have long to live. Healthy, "ordinary" people reflect, too. I wonder from time to time whether I'm spending my work time wisely and whether I'm making the right parenting decisions. Sometimes you probably wonder what you'll be doing five years from now. Before you make an important decision, you ask questions of yourself and others about priorities and probable consequences. On clear days you may notice the beauty of the landscape around you and reflect on how fortunate you are to live where you do. Like all persons, you ask questions and reflect.

When people ignore the fact that persons are reflective, their communication usually shows it. For example, you may stick with superficial topics—the weather, recent news items, gossip. On the other hand, when you're aware of your own and others' reflectiveness, you can respond to more of what's going on as you communicate. Questions can be a clear indicator that a person is reflecting. Often people who express their opinions with absolute certainty have forgotten to reflect, to ask what they might be unsure of and what they might not have thought about. But the reflective person will often explicitly express appropriate reservations and qualifications— "I think this is the right thing to do, but I'm not absolutely sure." Or "I know I don't want to lie to him, but I'm not sure how or when to tell him."

Addressable   Beings who are addressable can recognize when they are addressed, that is, when they are called or spoken to in language, and can also respond in language. Addressability is what makes the difference between talking *to* and talking *with*. Neither baseball bats nor dogs and cats are addressable, because you can talk to them, but not with them. You can call them, curse them, scold them, and praise them, but you cannot carry on a mutual conversation, even with an "almost human" pet.

One student described what addressability meant to her by recounting her experience as a child with her imaginary playmate, Sharla. Mary said that Sharla went everywhere with her and was always dressed appropriately. Sharla was also (in Mary's mind) always sympathetic to what Mary was doing and feeling. Mary would talk *to* Sharla constantly, telling her how she felt, complaining about her parents and older sister, and sometimes making elaborate plans. Occasionally Mary would talk *about* Sharla to her friends or her mother. But of course Sharla never responded out loud. She never talked back. Mary could talk *to* and *about* Sharla, but not *with* her. Sharla was not addressable; she wasn't a person.

Communication theorist John Shotter talks about this feature of human communication under the heading of "addressivity," which he defines as "the quality of being directed toward someone."[15] "Addressed" speech is directed or "aimed" speech, and one characteristic of persons is that they can recognize address and respond in kind. So, for example, as you sit in an audience of several hundred, the speaker can single you out for immediate contact: "Holly Tartar? Are you here? Your question is about job programs, and I want to try to answer it now." Or even more commonly and more directly, you may sit across from a friend and know from the friend's eyes, the touch of his hand, and his voice that he means *you*; he's *present* with you, you are being addressed.

Definition of Interpersonal Communication

Remember that communicators are always both talking and listening, sending and receiving, giving off cues and taking them in—Part Two of this book calls it "exhaling" and "inhaling." These five features—unique, unmeasurable, responsive, reflective, and addressable—can be used to describe how communicators engage in these exhaling and inhaling processes. That is, these five can describe what people are giving out (exhaling) and what they are taking in (inhaling). And, as I noted a few paragraphs earlier, **the term *interpersonal* labels the kind of communication that happens when the people involved talk and listen in ways that maximize the presence of the personal.** When communicators give and receive or talk and listen in ways that emphasize their uniqueness, unmeasureability, responsiveness, reflectiveness, and addressability, then the communication between them is interpersonal. When they listen and talk in ways that highlight the opposites of these five features—interchangeability, measurable aspects, reactivity, unreflectiveness, and imperviousness, their communicating fits on the impersonal end of the sliding scale.

Interpersonal communication is easiest when there are only two of you and you already know and trust each other. But it can also occur early in a relationship—even at first meeting—and, as I've already mentioned, it can occur over the telephone, during an argument, on the job, in group meetings, and even in public speaking or presentation situations. The important thing is not how many people there are or where they're located, but the peoples' willingness and ability to choose personal over impersonal communication attitudes and behaviors.

Importantly, the terms *impersonal* and *interpersonal* are *descriptive*, not *prescriptive*. Interpersonal communication can be appropriate, effective, or "good" in some situations, and "bad" in others, and the same goes for impersonal contact. The point of this simple model is to give you some control over where your communication is on the impersonal–interpersonal scale.

So the basic definition of interpersonal communication is pretty simple. It's the counterpart of impersonal communication. But as you'll see, I base this book's entire approach on this simple definition. As I've already explained in Chapter 1, each major division of the book, each chapter, and each reading extend a part of the approach to communication, and to interpersonal communication, that I've outlined here. So although this book contains writings by 75 different people, we all view interpersonal communication in similar ways. As a result, by the time you're finished with the book, you ought to have developed not only a deeper understanding of interpersonal communication but also a more powerful and effective sense of how to help make it happen when you want to.

REVIEW QUESTIONS

1. According to this reading, what is the main distinction between the world inhabited by a dog, cat, chimpanzee, or dolphin and the world inhabited by a human?
2. Why is it misleading to think about human communication in terms of senders and receivers?
3. Complete the sentence: Communication is the c _____ , c _____ , c _____ process of verbal and _____ meaning-making.
4. According to this reading, what's the difference between responsibility and response-ability?
5. List three qualities in addition to ethnicity that make up a person's culture.
6. True or False: Identity negotiation is the only process that's occurring when humans communicate. Explain.
7. Define *nexting* and give an example of it from your own communication experience.
8. What is the clearest example of the unmeasurable part of persons?
9. What's the difference between a reaction and a response?
10. The presence of questions in one's communicating is a clear example of which of the following: uniqueness, unmeasurability, responsiveness, reflectiveness, or addressability?
11. Complete the following: This reading defines *interpersonal communication* as the kind of _____ that happens when the people involved _____ and _____ in ways that _____ the presence of the _____.

PROBES

1. At the start of this reading, I outline five common but misleading ideas about communication: that it happens between sender and receiver, that it starts when an idea is translated into a message, that it continues when a message is retranslated into another idea, that it can be evaluated in terms of fidelity, and that it can be understood in terms of cause and effect. Which of these five are part(s) of your understanding of communication? Which are you least willing to give up or change?
2. How often does your communication focus on issues of fault and blame? How productive are these discussions? What alternative do you hear me proposing here?
3. Paraphrase the point I make when I say that collaboration doesn't necessarily mean agreement.

4. Implication 1 says, "No one person can completely control a communication event, and no single person or action causes—or can be blamed for—a communication outcome." How do you respond to this claim?
5. How would you describe the greatest cultural distance between you and the author of this reading? Where are you and this author culturally closest?
6. Describe the identity that you understand me (the author of this reading and the editor of this book) to be trying to develop so far in this book.
7. Without reading ahead to Chapter 3, which do you believe are more important in the identity-negotiation process, verbal or nonverbal cues?
8. Which of the five features of the personal—uniqueness, unmeasurability, responsiveness, reflectiveness, or addressability—do you believe is most important in interpersonal communicating?

NOTES

1. "Communica*tion*" or "communica*ting*?" I started with the "-ion" form because it's a little more familiar. But many "-ion" words, like *education, expression, persuasion,* and *sensation,* call to mind the finished product rather than the ongoing process. Education, for example, is something I get at school and expression is something that comes from my voice or body. "Educa*ting*," on the other hand, calls to mind events, occurrences, and processes, just like such terms as *singing, laughing, arguing,* and *making love.* It's helpful to remember that the topics of this reading are processes. This is why the reading title and main headings use the "-ing" forms.
2. Adapted from an example in Douglas W. Maynard, "Perspective-Display Sequences in Conversation," *Western Journal of Speech Communication* 53 (1989), p. 107.
3. Interruptions, or overlapping speech, can manifest a variety of power relationships between conversation partners. Sometimes overlaps can be supportive, and at other times they are denigrating. See, for example, Deborah Tannen, *Talking from 9 to 5* (New York: Wm. Morrow, 1994), pp. 232–34.
4. Russian communication theorist Mikhail Bakhtin put it this way: "Any concrete utterance is a link in the chain of speech communication of a particular sphere. . . . Each utterance is filled with echoes and reverberation of other utterances to which it is related by the communality of the sphere of speech communication. . . . The speaker is not Adam, and therefore the subject of his speech itself inevitably becomes the arena where his opinions meet those of his partners." *Speech Genres and Other Essays,* trans. Vern W. McGee, ed. Caryl Emerson and Michael Holquist (Austin: Univ. of Texas Press, 1986), pp. 91, 94.

5. Some people call talking to yourself or thinking out loud "intrapersonal communication," or communication "within" one person. I prefer to reserve the term *communication* for what happens between two or more people. The main reason is that *common* or *commune* is the root of *communication*, and you can't make something common that's not divided or separated. While any one person obviously has various "parts" or "sides," I think it's most useful to understand the human as a whole, a unity captured by such terms as *I, me,* or *the person*. Talking to yourself and thinking out loud are important processes, but they are fundamentally different from connecting with an *other*, someone who is not you. In addition, I want to emphasize that humans are first and foremost "social animals," relational beings. Humans become who we are in our contacts with others, not mainly as a result of thinking and talking to ourselves.

6. William Barrett, *The Illusion of Technique: A Search for Meaning in a Technological Civilization* (Garden City, NY: Anchor Doubleday), 1978, p. xx.

7. John Shotter, "Epilogue," *Conversational Realities: Constructing Life through Language* (London: Sage, 1993), p. 180.

8. Herbert H. Clark and Deanna Wilkes-Gibbs, "Referring as a Collaborative Process," *Cognition* 22 (1986), p. 1.

9. Emanuel A. Schegloff, "Discourse as an Interactional Achievement III: The Omnirelevance of Action," *Research on Language and Social Interaction* 28 (1995), pp. 186–87.

10. Shotter, 1993.

11. Peter M. Senge, Art Kleiner, Charlotte Roberts, Richard B. Ross, and Bryan J. Smith, *The Fifth Discipline Fieldbook: Strategies and Tools for Building a Learning Organization* (New York: Doubleday, 1994), p. 14.

12. Buber was an international citizen whose major book has been translated into over 20 languages. So he believed that his definition of the person applied across cultures. Many people agree, but others argue that his view of the person is in some ways more Western than Eastern. Some people in cultures that emphasize group identity (Japan, for example) believe that Buber's emphasis on the individual was misleading. But most people in Western cultures think that his description fits their experience pretty well. What do you think? See Martin Buber, *I and Thou*, trans. Walter Kaufmann (New York: Scribner's, 1970).

13. For a discussion of this point, see George Isaac Brown, *Human Teaching for Human Learning: An Introduction to Confluent Education* (New York: Viking Press, 1971).

14. Fredrick Buechner, *Wishful Thinking: A Theological ABC* (New York: Harper Collins, 1973), p. 64.

15. John Shotter, *Cultural Politics of Everyday Life: Social Constructionism, Rhetoric and Knowing of the Third Kind* (Toronto: Univ. of Toronto Press, 1993), p. 176.

D avid Bohm was, until his death in 1992, a world-renowned British physicist. He became interested in communication because of his commitment to improve life on this planet, and his ideas about communication emerged from his studies of the natural world. His basic insight was about the pervasiveness of interconnection—that humans and nature are interconnected, cultures are interconnected, and even the things we call "thoughts" are generated and sustained collectively.

In this short overview Bohm applies this insight about interconnection to our basic understanding of the processes we call "communication" or "communicating." He starts by noting how aggression and violence happen when people forget how interconnected we actually are. This often happens, he says, because we get stuck in a "crude and insensitive" way of thinking and talking about communication. We tend to believe, implicitly or explicitly, that communication "makes common" ideas or information that are already known to at least one of the people communicating. But if we examine communicating carefully, we can see that what is often actually happening is that the people are negotiating a variety of *differences* in order to generate something new that they then hold "in common." So the first view treats differences as problems to be eliminated, and the second view treats differences as contributions to the collaborative mix. To put it another way, we could say that the distorted view treats communication as a process whereby one person injects her ideas into another person's head, so they both supposedly end up with the same idea, and the better view understands communication as a process whereby two or more people co-construct a meaning that neither had before they communicated.

Importantly, this doesn't mean that communicators always agree. Opposing political candidates and spouses in a divorce build meanings together just as lovers do.

Bohm argues that even relationships with inanimate objects and with nature are collaborative or mutual. For example, in science there is a back-and-forth movement between observation and testing that generates new ideas, which are eventually extended into practical applications.

In art, science, and human relationships, the key to this kind of collaborative creativity is effective *listening*. As Bohm sees it, the general human tendency is to believe that we are already listening to the other person in the proper way, even though we may be what Bohm calls "blocked" about certain questions. This condition generates defensiveness—the tendency to protect one's own meanings rather than opening them to collaborative revision. But if we can learn to notice how we are blocking collaborative meaning-making in this way, "then we may be able to create something new between us, something of very great significance for bringing to an end the at present insoluble problems of the individual and of society."

On Communication

David Bohm

During the past few decades, modern technology, with radio, television, air travel, and satellites, has woven a network of communications which puts each part of the world into almost instant contact with all the other parts. Yet, in spite of this world-wide system of linkages, there is, at this very moment, a general feeling that communication is breaking down everywhere, on an unparalleled scale. People living in different nations, with different economic and political systems, are hardly able to talk to each other without fighting. And within any single nation, different social classes and economic and political groups are caught in a similar pattern of inability to understand each other. Indeed, even within each limited group, people are talking of a "generation gap," which is such that older and younger members do not communicate, except perhaps in a superficial way. Moreover, in schools and universities, students tend to feel that their teachers are overwhelming them with a flood of information which they suspect is irrelevant to actual life. And what appears on the radio and television, as well as in the newspapers and magazines, is generally at best a collection of trivial and almost unrelated fragments, while at worst, it can often be a really harmful source of confusion and misinformation.

Because of widespread dissatisfaction with the state of affairs described above, there has been a growing feeling of concern to solve what is now commonly called "the problem of communication." But if one observes efforts to solve this problem, he [or she] will notice that different groups who are trying to do this are not actually able to listen to each other. As a result, the very attempt to improve communication leads frequently to yet more confusion, and the consequent sense of frustration inclines people ever further toward aggression and violence, rather than toward mutual understanding and trust.

If one considers the fact that communication is breaking down and that in the present context efforts to prevent this from happening generally tend to accelerate the breakdown, [one] may perhaps pause in his [or her] thinking, to give opportunity to ask whether the difficulty does not originate in some more subtle way that has escaped our mode of formulating what is going wrong. Is it not possible that our crude and insensitive manner of thinking about communication and talking about it is a major factor behind our inability to see what would be an intelligent action that would end the present difficulties?

It may be useful to begin to discuss this question by considering the meaning of the word "communication." This is based on the Latin *commun* and the suffix "ie" which is similar to "fie," in that it means "to make or to do." So one meaning of "to communicate" is "to make something common," i.e., to convey information or knowledge from one person to another in as accurate a way as possible. This meaning is appropriate in a wide range of contexts. Thus, one person may communicate

From *On Dialogue* by David Bohm, 1996. Reprinted by permission of Routledge.

to another a set of directions as to how to carry out a certain operation. Clearly, a great deal of our industry and technology depends on this kind of communication.

Nevertheless, this meaning does not cover all that is signified by communication. For example, consider a dialogue. In such a dialogue, when one person says something, the other person does not in general respond with exactly the same meaning as that seen by the first person. Rather, the meanings are only *similar* and not identical. Thus, when the second person replies, the first person sees a *difference* between what she meant to say and what the other person understood. On considering this difference, she may then be able to see something new, which is relevant both to her own views and to those of the other person. And so it can go back and forth, with the continual emergence of a new content that is common to both participants. Thus, in a dialogue, each person does not attempt to *make common* certain ideas or items of information that are already known. Rather, it may be said that the two people are making something *in common*, i.e., creating something new together.

But of course such communication can lead to the creation of something new only if people are able freely to listen to each other, without prejudice, and without trying to influence each other. Each has to be interested primarily in truth and coherence, so that he is ready to drop his old ideas and intentions, and be ready to go on to something different, when this is called for. If, however, two people merely want to convey certain ideas or points of view to each other, as if these were items of information, then they must inevitably fail to meet. For each will hear the other through the screen of his own thoughts, which he tends to maintain and defend, regardless of whether or not they are true or coherent. The result will of course be just the sort of confusion that leads to the insoluble "problem of communication" which has been pointed out and discussed earlier.

Evidently, communication in the sense described above is necessary in all aspects of life. Thus, if people are to cooperate (i.e., literally to "work together") they have to be able to create something in common, something that takes shape in their mutual discussions and actions, rather than something that is conveyed from one person who acts as an authority to the others, who act as passive instruments of this authority.

Even in relationships with inanimate objects and with nature in general, something very like communication is involved. Consider, for example, the work of an artist. Can it properly be said that the artist is *expressing himself*, i.e., literally "pushing outward" something that is already formed inside of him? Such a description is not in fact generally accurate or adequate. Rather, what usually happens is that the first thing the artist does is only *similar* in certain ways to what he may have in mind. As in a conversation between two people, he sees the similarity and the difference, and from this perception something further emerges in his next action. Thus, something new is continually created that is common to the artist and the material on which he is working.

The scientist is engaged in a similar "dialogue" with nature (as well as with her fellow human beings). Thus, when a scientist has an idea, this is tested by observation. When it is found (as generally happens) that what is observed is only similar to what she had in mind and not identical, then from a consideration of the similarities and the differences she gets a new idea which is in turn tested. And so it goes, with the continual emergence of something new that is common to the thought of scientists and what is observed in nature. This extends onward into practical activities, which lead to the creation of new structures that are common to humans and to the overall environment in which we live.

It is clear that if we are to live in harmony with ourselves and with nature, we need to be able to communicate freely in a creative movement in which no one permanently holds to or otherwise defends his [or her] own ideas. Why then is it so difficult actually to bring about such communication?

This is a very complex and subtle question. But it may perhaps be said that when one comes to do something (and not merely to talk about it or think about it), one tends to believe that one *already is* listening to the other person in a proper way. It seems then that the main trouble is that the other person is the one who is prejudiced and not listening. After all, it is easy for each one of us to see that other people are "blocked" about certain questions, so that without being aware of it, they are avoiding the confrontation of contradictions in certain ideas that may be extremely dear to them.

The very nature of such a "block" is, however, that it is a kind of insensitivity or "anesthesia" about one's own contradictions. Evidently then, what is crucial is to be aware of the nature of one's own "blocks." If one is alert and attentive, one can see for example that whenever certain questions arise, there are fleeting sensations of fear, which push the person away from consideration of these questions, and of pleasure, which attract his thoughts and cause them to be occupied with other questions. So one is able to keep away from whatever it is that he thinks may disturb him. And as a result, he can be subtly defending his own ideas, when he supposes that he is really listening to what other people have to say.

When we come together to talk, or otherwise to act in common, can each one of us be aware of the subtle fear and pleasure sensations that "block" our ability to listen freely? Without this awareness, the injunction to listen to the whole of what is said will have little meaning. But if each one of us can give full attention to what is actually "blocking" communication while also attending properly to the content of what is communicated, then we may be able to create something new between us, something of very great significance for bringing to an end the at present insoluble problems of the individual and of society.

REVIEW QUESTIONS

1. Bohm starts by saying that modern technology has woven a vast network of communication, but that this has also created a basic problem. What is the problem?
2. According to Bohm, what is the major benefit of becoming aware of a *difference* between your idea and somebody else's?

3. Bohm briefly extends his treatment of communication to include not only contacts between persons but also what other type of contacts?

4. What does Bohm mean by "a kind of insensitivity or 'anesthesia' about one's own contradictions"?

PROBES

1. Paraphrase the distinction Bohm makes between treating communication as an "attempt to *make common*" and as "making something *in common.*" How might this difference affect the way you communicate with a friend or co-worker?

2. When you're talking with a close friend about a topic that's important to you, is the main point of your talk to *eliminate* differences or to *integrate* them into your mutual understanding?

3. Compare Bohm's understanding of collaboration with the understanding developed in the first reading in this chapter.

4. Talk with an artist you know (painter, sculptor, poet, etc.) about the idea Bohm introduces in the eighth paragraph of this essay. Is it most accurate to see art as an "expression" of the artist or as a negotiated, collaborative, creative engagement?

5. How often do you believe—without thinking about it—that you are "already listening to the other person in a proper way"? How might your communicating become "unblocked" if you were to reconsider this assumption about your own listening?

————————

This brief reading responds to the question, "Why should I study communication?"

Some people believe that, since we've all been communicating since at least the day we were born, we don't need to study it. Others claim that if you study something as normal and everyday as communication, you turn it into something mechanical and artificial. Still others argue that human communication is so complex and changeable that it is impossible to generalize about it without distorting what actually occurs.

Stuart Sigman argues here that we should study communication because it "matters." It matters because it affects the kinds of lives people lead. And importantly, this impact is more due to the *ways* people communicate than to *what* they say. Process is more important than content.

You will hear this idea developed in several of the following chapters. By the time you're finished with the readings in this book, you should be able to talk in some detail about how and why communication *matters.*

Toward Study of the Consequentiality (Not Consequences) of Communication

Stuart J. Sigman

State University of New York, Albany

Communication matters. It matters whether a word is spoken with a certain inflection, a gesture is displayed at a particular body height and with a particular intensity, an article of clothing is donned, or a bodily incision is endured at just some moment in an activity sequence. *What* persons do when constructing messages with others has an impact on the kinds of lives they lead, the kinds of institutions and organizations they find themselves inhabiting, and the kinds of connections with other persons they make—separated across space, time, and rank.

Thus, this book is concerned with the idea that the communication process is consequential in and to people's lives. This consequentiality cannot be explained by primary recourse to cultural, psychological, or sociological variables and theorizing, however. It is the ebb and flow of the communication process itself that must be studied, and a theory of communication consequentiality apart from anthropological, psychological, or sociological theory that must be developed.

As detailed later, *consequentiality of communication* means that *what* transpires during, within, and as part of persons' interactive dealings with each other has consequences for those persons. Those consequences come from the communication process, not the structure of language or the mediation of particular personality characteristics or social structures. Communication is consequential both in the sense that it is the primary process engendering and constituting sociocultural reality, and in the sense that, as it transpires, constraints on and affordances to people's behavior momentarily emerge. In this view, communication is not a neutral vehicle by which an external reality is communicated about, and by which factors of psychology, social structure, cultural norms, and the like are transmitted or are influential. The communication process: (a) exerts a role in the personal identities and self-concepts experienced by persons; (b) shapes the range of permissible and impermissible relationships between persons, and so produces a social structure; and (c) represents the process through which cultural values, beliefs, goals, and the like are formulated and lived.

Thus, to study the consequentiality of communication is to envision a world composed of a continuous process of meaning production, rather than conditions antecedent and subsequent to this production. To study the consequentiality of communication is to take seriously—for purposes of description and analysis—a world sustained by persons behaving, engaged in the negotiation and renegotiation of messages, not a world of a priori (or a posteriori) cognitive states, cultural rules, social roles, or the like.

REVIEW QUESTIONS

1. When Sigman says communication "matters," what does he mean?
2. Explain what it means to say that the process of communication often has more impact than the content.

PROBES

1. What is the relationship between this short reading and my essay that begins this chapter?
2. Assume that you are a communication major and that you've decided to focus your undergraduate studies on communication. At a family gathering, an aunt or uncle asks you what you're studying and why. Using the readings in this chapter, respond to your aunt or uncle.

Susan Scott is an executive educator who has helped clients around the world transform the cultures of their organizations. In this excerpt from her best-selling book, she explains how, as I noted earlier in the chapter, conversations are the most important communication events people experience. As she puts it, "our work, our relationships, and, in fact, our very lives succeed or fail gradually, then suddenly, *one conversation at a time.*"

Although Scott's primary audience is businesspeople rather than college students, her main points apply to everyone. Regardless of your station in life, when you face an important challenge, your first step should be to resist what she calls the "accountability shuffle" of blaming others and the second should be to "identify the conversations out there with your name on them and resolve to have them with all the courage, grace, and vulnerability they require." If life is good, you can also realize that you got here "gradually, then suddenly, one *successful* conversation at a time." And her advice applies as much to experiences at home as it does to experiences at work.

Scott reinforces what other authors in this chapter have also said: Relationships exist in the conversations that make them up. Whether you're thinking about a dating relationship, a marriage relationship, a work relationship, or a family relationship, "the conversation is the relationship." Relationship problems begin in specific conversations, negative spirals can be tracked through conversations, and improvement can occur when conversations change.

By "fierce conversation," Scott explains that she means intense, strong, powerful, passionate, eager, and robust conversation. "Fierce" does not mean angry or hostile; it emphasizes the importance of being genuinely present and authentic in as many as possible of the conversations you experience. Scott urges her readers to embrace the possibility that fierce conversations are opportunities to be known, seen, and changed.

Near the end of this reading, Scott tells her story of discovering the importance of conversation while working with business leaders on issues that undercut their effectiveness. As she explains, her brief and superficial explanation of what she did for a living was "I ran think tanks for corporate leaders and worked with them one-to-one." But "what I really did was extend an intimate invitation to my clients, that of conversation." And most clients experienced significant improvement in their effectiveness and their job satisfaction.

This reading ends with a challenge for you to begin working to make more of your conversations genuinely authentic or "fierce." The rest of Scott's 290-page book effectively details how to do this. But as a contribution to the second chapter of this book, I hope her words emphasize how crucially important it is for you to pay attention to the communication events that most define your reality and determine your success and happiness: conversations.

Fierce Conversations

Susan Scott

... Over ten thousand hours of one-to-one conversations with industry leaders, as well as workshops with men and women from all walks of life confronting issues of relationship and life direction, have convinced me that our work, our relationships, and, in fact, our very lives succeed or fail gradually, then suddenly, *one conversation at a time.*

Equally provocative has been my realization that while no single conversation is guaranteed to change the trajectory of a business, a career, a marriage, or a life, any single conversation *can*. . . .

Whether you intend to maintain positive results in your life or turn things around, considering all of the conversations you need to have could feel a bit discouraging, so let's take the curse off the somewhat daunting field of "communications." I'd like you to simply take it *one conversation at a time*, beginning with the person who next stands in front of you. Perhaps there are very few conversations in between you and what you desire.

. . . Once you get the hang of it, once you master the courage and the skills and, more important, enjoy the benefits of fierce conversations, there will be no going back. It could change the world. It will certainly change *your* world.

When *Here* Is Troubling

Be patient with yourself. You got here—wherever "here" is—one conversation at a time. Allow the changes needed at home or at work to reveal themselves one conversation at a time.

Sometimes *here* just happens. Following the high-tech carnage, crashing economies, corporate layoffs, and terrorist attacks of 2001, which altered our individual and collective realities in a heartbeat, it would be easy to conclude that life has grown too unpredictable, that there's nothing to do but hang on and muddle through as best you can.

Perhaps you received a major wake-up call. You lost your biggest customer—the one that counted for 40 percent of your net profit. Or you lost your most valued employee. Or you lost your job, and it wasn't due to a layoff. You lost the loyalty of your team. You lost your eighteen-year marriage, or the cohesiveness of your family.

Perhaps your company is experiencing turnover, turf wars, rumors, departments not cooperating with one another, long overdue reports and projects, strategic plans that still aren't off the ground, and lots of very good reasons and excuses why things can't be any different or better.

To experience what happens for many individuals and organizations facing challenges, put your right arm out and point your finger, then visualize pointing it at someone who is the bane of your professional or personal life right now. That's called the *accountability shuffle*. He did it, she did it, they did it to me.

Blame isn't the answer, nor is cocooning in the perceived safety of your home. Once you reflect on the path that led you to a disappointing or difficult point and place in time, you may remember, often in vivid detail, the conversation that set things in motion, ensuring that you would end up exactly where you find yourself today. It is very likely that you arrived at this destination one *failed* conversation at a time.

Ask yourself, "How did I get *here?* How is it that I find myself in a company, a role, a relationship, or a life from which I've absented my spirit? How did I lose my way?"

So many times I've heard people say, "We never addressed the real issue, never came to terms with reality." Or, "We never stated our needs. We never told each other what we were really thinking and feeling. In the end, there were so many things we needed to talk about, the wheels came off the cart."

In February 2002, Robert Kaiser and David Ottaway wrote an article for the *Washington Post* about the fragility of U.S.-Saudi ties. Brent Scowcroft, national security adviser to the first President Bush, is quoted as saying, "Have we [the United States and Saudi Arabia] understood each other particularly well? . . . Probably not. And I think, in a sense, we probably avoid talking about the things that are the real problems between us because it's a very polite relationship. We don't get all that much below the surface."

Take your finger and touch your nose. This is where the resolution begins. This is the accountable position. If you want to make progress toward a better "here" in your professional or personal life, identify the conversations out there with your name on them and resolve to have them with all the courage, grace, and vulnerability they require.

When *Here* Is Wonderful

And on the positive side, you finally landed that huge customer, the one your competition would kill for. Or you successfully recruited a valuable new employee. Or you discovered that your team is committed to you at the deepest level. Or you just received a promotion. Or you enjoy a deeply fulfilling relationship. You are clear and passionate about your life.

You got to this good place in your life, this satisfying career path, this terrific relationship, gradually, then suddenly, one *successful* conversation at a time. Perhaps one marvelously *fierce* conversation at a time. And now you are determined to ensure the quality of your ongoing conversations with the people central to your success and happiness.

If you want better results at home or at work, you've come to the right place. After reading this, gathering your courage, and working with the tools we'll explore together, you will return to your colleagues at work, to your partner at home, and, most important, to your *self*, prepared to engage in ongoing, groundbreaking conversations that will profoundly transform your life.

While it was tempting to give in to suggestions that I write two books— *Fierce Conversations in the Workplace* and *Fierce Conversations at Home*—breaking this material into two books would have been a mistake. Perhaps you've bought into the premise that we respond differently depending on whom we are with, that our work and home personas are really quite different. Perhaps you pay fierce attention to conversations at work but slip into a conversational coma at home, convinced there's nothing new, interesting, or energizing to discuss, preferring the company of the remote control. Perhaps you leave your warmth, playfulness, and authenticity at home and prop up an automaton at your desk at work, afraid to let your authentic self show up lest you be judged as poor fodder for the corporate feast. Perhaps you've told yourself that conversations at work are unavoidably and substantially different from conversations at home. That that's just the way it has to be. This is not true.

Each of us must discard the notion that we respond differently depending on whom we're with and that our work and home conversations are really quite different.

When you squeeze an orange, what comes out of it? Orange juice. Why? Because that's what's inside it. The orange doesn't care whether it's on a boardroom table or beside the kitchen sink. It doesn't leak orange juice at home and tomato juice at work.

When we get squeezed—*when things aren't going well for us*—what comes out of us? Whatever's inside us. To pretend that what's going on in our personal lives can be boxed, taped shut, and left in the garage while we are at work is hogwash. It seeps in everywhere. Who we are is who we are, all over the place. So if your conversations at work are yielding disappointing results, I'd be willing to bet you're getting similar results at home. The principles and skills needed to engage in conversations that produce mind-blowing, world-class results in the workplace are exactly the same principles and skills that produce mind-blowing, world-class results at home.

The Conversation Is the Relationship

Going hand in hand with the discovery that our lives succeed or fail one conversation at a time is a second insight, courtesy of poet and author David Whyte. During a keynote speech at TEC International's annual conference several years ago, David suggested that in the typical marriage, the young man, newly married, is often frustrated that this person with whom he intends to enjoy the rest of his life seemingly needs to talk, yet again, about the same thing they talked about last weekend. And it often has something to do with their relationship. He wonders, Why are we talking about this again? I thought we settled this. Couldn't we just have one huge conversation about our relationship and then coast for a year or two?

Apparently not, because here she is again. Eventually, if he is paying attention, it occurs to him, Whyte suggests, that "this ongoing, robust conversation he has been having with his wife is not about the relationship. The conversation *is* the relationship."

The conversation is the relationship. If the conversation stops, all of the possibilities for the relationship become smaller and all of the possibilities for the individuals in the relationship become smaller, until one day we overhear ourselves in midsentence, making *ourselves* smaller in every encounter, behaving as if we are just the space around our shoes, engaged in yet another three-minute conversation so empty of meaning it crackles.

Incremental degradation—if we compromise at work or at home; if we lower the standards about how often we talk, what we talk about, and, most important, what degree of authenticity we bring to our conversations—it's a slow and deadly slide. One company president has been known to stop candid input in its tracks with the pronouncement "Howard, I do not consider that a career-enhancing response."

Fortunately, few leaders exhibit such exaggerated violations of the general rules of communication. However, many work teams as well as couples have a list of undiscussables, issues they avoid broaching at all costs in order to preserve a modicum of peace, to preserve the relationship. In reality, the relationship steadily deteriorates for lack of the very conversations they so carefully avoid. It's difficult to raise the level if the slide has lasted over a period of years, and that's what keeps many of us stuck.

In our significant relationships, in the workplace, and in our conversations with ourselves, we'd like to tell the truth. We'd like to be able to successfully tackle the topic that's keeping us stuck or apart, but the task is too hard, we don't know how to avoid the all-too-familiar outcome of talks gone south, and besides, we've learned to live with it. Why wreck another meeting with our colleagues, another weekend with our life partner, trying to resolve the tough issues or answer the big questions? We're tired and we just want peace in the land.

The problem is, whether you are running an organization or your life, you are required to be responsive to your world. And that response often requires change. We effect change by engaging in robust conversations with ourselves and others.

Each conversation we have with our coworkers, customers, significant others, and children either enhances those relationships, flatlines them, or takes them down. Given this, what words and what level of attention do you wish to bring to your conversations with the people most important to you? Throughout the book we will explore principles and practices that will help you engage in conversations that enrich relationships, no matter how sensitive or challenging the topic.

What Is a "Fierce" Conversation?

But a "fierce" conversation? Doesn't "fierce" suggest menacing, cruel, barbarous, threatening? Sounds like raised voices, frowns, blood on the floor, no fun at all. In *Roget's Thesaurus*, however, the word *fierce* has the following synonyms: robust, intense, strong, powerful, passionate, eager, unbridled, uncurbed, untamed. In its simplest form, *a fierce conversation is one in which we come out from behind ourselves into the conversation and make it real.*

While many are afraid of "real," it is the unreal conversation that should scare us to death. Whoever said talk is cheap was mistaken. Unreal conversations are incredibly expensive for organizations and for individuals. Every organization wants to feel it's having a real conversation with its employees, its customers, its territory, and with the unknown future that is emerging around it. Each individual wants to have conversations that are somehow building his or her world of meaning.

If you are a leader, your job is to accomplish the goals of the organization. How will you do that in today's workplace? In large part, by making every conversation you have as real as possible. Today's employees consider themselves owners and investors. They own their time, their energy, and their expertise. They are willing to invest these things in support of the individuals, ideals, and goals in which they believe. Give them something real in which to believe.

What I've witnessed over and over is that when the conversation is real, the change occurs before the conversation has even ended.

Being real is not the risk. The real risk is that:

> *I will be known.*
>
> *I will be seen.*
>
> *I will be changed.*

Think about it. What are the conversations you've been unable or unwilling to have—with your boss, colleague, employee, customer; with your husband, wife, parent, child; or with *yourself*—that, if you *were* able to have, might change everything?

My Own Journey

For thirteen years, I worked with corporate leaders through the auspices of TEC International, an organization dedicated to increasing the effectiveness and enhancing the lives of CEOs. Thousands of CEOs in eighteen countries meet for monthly one-to-one conversations with someone like myself to focus on their businesses and lives—from budgets, strategies, acquisitions, personnel, and profitability (or the lack thereof) to faltering marriages, health issues, or kids who are upside down.

Twelve conversations over the course of a year with each CEO. Since time is a CEO's most precious commodity, it seemed essential that our time together be qualitatively different from time spent with others. Each conversation needed to accomplish something useful. My success, and that of my peers, depended on our ability to engage leaders in conversations that provoked significant change.

In the beginning, a fair number of my conversations were less than fierce. They were somewhat useful, but we remained in relatively familiar, safe territory. Some, I confess, were pathetic. No guts, no glory. I wimped out. Either I didn't have it in me that day, or I looked at the expression on my TEC member's face and took pity. I don't remember those conversations. They had no lasting impact. And I am certain my TEC members would say the same.

The fierce conversations I remember. The topics, the emotions, the expressions on our faces. It was as if, together, we created a force field by asking the questions, by saying the words out loud. Things happened as a result of those conversations.

When people asked me what I did, I told them that I ran think tanks for corporate leaders and worked with them one-to-one. That was the elevator speech. What I really did was extend an intimate invitation to my clients, that of conversation. And my job was to make each conversation as real as possible.

As my practice of robust conversations became increasingly compelling to me, I imagined that I was turning into a conversational cartographer, mapping a way toward deepening authenticity for myself and for those who wanted to join me. The CEOs with whom I worked became increasingly candid, and with that candor came a growing sense of personal freedom, vitality, and effectiveness. The most successful leaders invariably determined to engage in an ongoing, robust conversation with themselves, paying fierce attention to their work and lives, resulting in a high level of personal authenticity, ferocious integrity, emotional honesty, and a greater capacity to hold true to their vision and enroll others in it.

My colleagues worldwide asked me to conduct workshops on what I was doing, to pass along the skills needed for these conversations about which I had become so passionate. This required me to articulate for myself the approach I was developing. I led my first workshop in 1990.

In January 1999, I ran a redesigned, incredibly "fierce" workshop attended by sixteen extraordinary individuals from seven countries. In my workshops there is no role-play. No one pretends to be someone else. No one works on imaginary issues. It's all *real* play. All the participants engage in conversations as themselves, using real, current, significant issues as the focus for our practice sessions. Following one of the exercises, a colleague from Newcastle on Tyne, England, had tears in his eyes.

"I've longed for conversations like this all my life," he said, "but I didn't know they were possible. I don't think I can settle for anything less going forward."

Attendees e-mailed others about the impact of the workshop, about how they were applying the principles and using the tools they had learned, and about the results they were enjoying with their colleagues and family members. Word spread and the demand grew. Each subsequent workshop had a waiting list and each workshop went deeper. Corporate clients invited me to work with their key executives to foster courageous dialogue within their companies.

In November 2001, I recognized that my travel schedule had gotten out of hand when I sat down in my seat at the Sydney Opera House and reached for my seat belt. But my work with clients has been worth it. Over time I recognized that we were exploring core principles, which, when embraced, dramatically changed lives . . . one conversation at a time. Fierce conversations are about moral courage, clear requests, and taking action. *Fierce* is an attitude. A way of conducting business. A way of leading. A way of life.

Many times I hear words to this effect: "Your work has profoundly improved our leadership team's ability to tackle and resolve tough challenges. The practical tools allow leaders to become fierce agents for positive change." Or this: "You've helped me engage my workforce in moving the company to a position of competitive superiority!" Or this: "A fierce conversation is like the first parachute jump from an airplane. In anticipation, you perspire and your mouth goes dry. Once you've left the plane, it's an adrenaline rush that is indescribable." Or this: "This weekend my wife and I had the best conversation we've had in ten years. It feels like falling in love all over again." . . .

Getting Started

Here is what I'd like you to do. Begin listening to yourself as you've never listened before.

Begin to overhear yourself avoiding the topic, changing the subject, holding back, telling little lies (and big ones), being imprecise in your language, being uninteresting even to yourself. And at least once *today*, when something inside you says, "This is an opportunity to be fierce," stop for a moment, take a deep breath, then come out from behind yourself into the conversation and make it real. Say something that is true for you. For example, my friend Ed Brown sometimes stops in midsentence and says, "What I just said isn't quite right. Let me see if I can get closer to what I really want to say." I listen intently to the next words he speaks.

When you come out from behind yourself into the conversation and make it real, whatever happens from there will happen. It could go well or it could be a little bumpy, but at least you will have taken the plunge. You will have said at least one real thing today, one thing that was real for you. And something will have been set in motion, and you will have grown from that moment. . . .

REVIEW QUESTIONS

1. What is the "accountability shuffle"? Why is it ineffective?
2. What does it mean to say, "the conversation is the relationship"?
3. Explain Scott's notion of "fierce" conversation.
4. According to Scott, what does it take to make a conversation "real"?

PROBES

1. Scott argues that similar successes and problems occur in conversations at work and conversations at home. Do you agree? If you do, what are some implications of this fact for your communicating?
2. What does Scott say about the risks of being known, being seen, and being changed? How do you respond to what she says?
3. How can the job of "mak[ing] each conversation as real as possible" actually be meaningful and productive?

I n this reading, Neil Postman presents an "opposing" viewpoint. Postman offers a sensible and compelling argument *against* the notion that all we have to do to solve our problems is to communicate more effectively. Better communication, he says, is *not* a panacea, especially if by better communication we mean self-disclosing, that is, "saying what's on your mind," and "expressing your feelings honestly."

Postman reminds us, as do some communication researchers, that one of the important functions of speech communication is concealment. Civility is a necessary part of society, he argues, and civility sometimes requires that we keep our feelings to ourselves. It's pretty hard to ignore the way he makes his point; as he puts it in one place, "There is no dishonesty in a baboon cage, and yet, for all that, it holds only baboons."

Postman maintains that when people disagree fundamentally—for example, about racial issues—honest openness may not help at all. He writes, "There is no good reason . . . for parents always to be honest with their children."

You may find it tempting to dismiss Postman as some kind of fascist and to reject his remarks as inflammatory hate-mongering. Try not to take that easy way out. His main point is, as he puts it, "that 'authentic communication' is a two-edged sword," and I think that's an idea that's well worth thinking about and discussing.

I feel frustrated and disappointed when my students—or readers of this book—conclude that the main message in all of this is just that we need to "be open and honest." That's a vast oversimplification, and it's also a dangerous one. One of Postman's most important points is that in any given situation we do not have *an* "honest feeling" but a complex of often conflicting "authentic" feelings. So the expression of one feeling may be no more or less "honest" or "dishonest" than the expression of another.

I hope this essay will prompt the kind of reflection and discussion that can move well beyond a simplistic belief in the universal value of "being open and honest."

The Communication Panacea

Neil Postman

In the search for the Holy Grail of complete harmony, liberation, and integrity, which it is the duty of all true Americans to conduct, adventurers have stumbled upon a road sign which appears promising. It says in bold letters, **"All problems arise through lack of communication."** Under it, in smaller print, it says: "Say

what is on your mind. Express your feelings honestly. This way lies the answer."
A dangerous road, it seems to me. It is just as true to say. This way lies disaster.

I would not go so far as Oliver Goldsmith, who observed that the principal function of language is to *conceal* our thoughts. But I do think that concealment is one of the important functions of language, and on no account should it be dismissed categorically. As I have tried to make clear earlier, semantic environments have legitimate and necessary purposes of their own which do not always coincide with the particular and pressing needs of every individual within them. One of the main purposes of many of our semantic environments, for example, is to help us maintain a minimum level of civility in conducting our affairs. Civility requires not that we deny our feelings, only that we keep them to ourselves when they are not relevant to the situation at hand. Contrary to what many people believe, Freud does not teach us that we are "better off" when we express our deepest feelings. He teaches exactly the opposite: that civilization is impossible without inhibition. Silence, reticence, restraint, and, yes, even dishonesty can be great virtues, in certain circumstances. They are, for example, frequently necessary in order for people to work together harmoniously. To learn how to say no is important in achieving personal goals, but to learn how to say yes when you want to say no is at the core of civilized behavior. There is no dishonesty in a baboon cage, and yet, for all that, it holds only baboons.

Now there are, to be sure, many situations in which trouble develops because some people are unaware of what other people are thinking and feeling. "If I'd only *known* that!" the refrain goes, when it is too late. But there are just as many situations which would get worse, not better, if everyone knew exactly what everyone else was thinking. I have in mind, for example, a conflict over school busing that occurred some time ago in New York City but has been replicated many times in different places. Whites against blacks. The whites maintained that they did not want their children to go to other neighborhoods. They wanted them close at hand, so that the children could walk home for lunch and enjoy all the benefits of a "neighborhood school." The blacks maintained that the schools their children attended were run-down and had inadequate facilities. They wanted their children to have the benefits of a good educational plant. It was most fortunate, I think, that these two groups were not reduced to "sharing with each other" their real feelings about the matter. For the whites' part, much of it amounted to, "I don't want to live, eat, or do anything else with niggers. Period." For the blacks' part, some of it, at least, included, "You honky bastards have had your own way at my expense for so long that I couldn't care less what happens to you or your children." Had these people communicated such feelings to each other, it is more than likely that there could have been no resolution to this problem. (This seems to have been the case in Boston.) As it was, the issue could be dealt with *as if* such hatred did not exist, and therefore, a reasonable political compromise was reached.

It is true enough, incidentally, that in this dispute and others like it, the charge of racism was made. But the word *racism,* for all its ominous overtones, is a euphemism. It conceals more than it reveals. What Americans call a *racist* public remark is something like "The Jews own the banks" or "The blacks are lazy." Such remarks are bad enough. But they are honorifics when compared to the "true" feelings that underlie them.

I must stress that the "school problem" did not arise in the first place through lack of communication. It arose because of certain historical, sociological, economic, and political facts which could not be made to disappear through the "miracle of communication." Sometimes, the less people know about other people, the better off everyone is. In fact, political language at its best can be viewed as an attempt to find solutions to problems by circumventing the authentic hostile feelings of concerned parties.

In our personal lives, surely each of us must have ample evidence by now that the capacity of words to exacerbate, wound, and destroy is at least as great as their capacity to clarify, heal, and organize. There is no good reason, for example, for parents always to be honest with their children (or their children always to be honest with them). The goal of parenthood is not to be honest, but to raise children to be loving, generous, confident, and competent human beings. Where full and open revelation helps to further that end, it is "good." Where it would defeat it, it is stupid talk. Similarly, there is no good reason why your boss always needs to know what you are thinking. It might, in the first place, scare him out of his wits and you out of a job. Then, too, many of the problems you and he have do not arise from lack of communication, but from the nature of the employer-employee relationship, which sometimes means that the less money you make, the more he does. This is a "problem" for a labor organizer, not a communication specialist.

Some large American corporations have, of late, taken the line that "improved communication" between employees and management will solve important problems. But very often this amounts to a kind of pacification program, designed to direct attention away from fundamental economic relationships. It is also worth noting that a number of such corporations have ceased to hold "communication seminars" in which executives were encouraged to express their "true" feelings. What happened, apparently, is that some of them decided they hated their jobs (or each other) and quit. Whether this is "good" or not depends on your point of view. The corporations don't think it's so good, and probably the families of the men don't either.

The main point I want to make is that "authentic communication" is a two-edged sword. In some circumstances, it helps. In others, it defeats. This is a simple enough idea, and sensible people have always understood it. I am stressing it here only because there has grown up in America something amounting to a holy crusade in the cause of Communication. One of the terms blazoned on its banners is the phrase *real* (or *authentic*) feelings. Another is the motto "Get in touch with your feelings!" From what I have been able to observe, this mostly means expressing anger and hostility. When is the last time someone said to you, "Let me be *lovingly* frank"? The expression of warmth and gentleness is usually considered to be a façade, masking what you are really thinking. To be certified as authentically in touch with your feelings, you more or less have to be nasty. Like all crusades, the Communication Crusade has the magical power to endow the most barbarous behavior with a purity of motive that excuses and obscures just about all its consequences. No human relationship is so tender, apparently, that it cannot be "purified" by sacrificing one or another of its participants on the altar of "Truth." Or, to paraphrase a widely known remark on another subject, "Brutality in the cause of honesty needs no defense." The point is that getting in touch with your feelings often amounts to losing touch with the feelings of others. Or at least losing touch with the purposes for which people have come together.

A final word on the matter of "honesty." As I have said before, human purposes are exceedingly complex—multileveled and multilayered. This means that, in any given situation, one does not have *an* "honest feeling," but a whole complex of different feelings. And, more often than not, some of these feelings are in conflict. If anger predominates at one instant, this does not mean it is more "authentic" than the love or sorrow or concern with which it is mingled. And the expression of the anger, alone, is no less "dishonest" than any other partial representation of what one is feeling. By *dishonesty*, then, I do not merely mean saying the opposite of what you believe to be true. Sometimes it is necessary to do even this in the interests of what you construe to be a worthwhile purpose. But more often, dishonesty takes the form of your simply not saying *all* that you are thinking about or feeling in a given situation. And, since our motives and feelings are never all that clear, to our own eyes in any case, most of us are "dishonest" in this sense most of the time. To be aware of this fact and to temper one's talk in the light of it is a sign of what we might call "intelligence." Other words for it are discretion and tact.

The relevant point is that communication is most sensibly viewed as a means through which desirable ends may be achieved. As an end in itself, it is disappointing, even meaningless. And it certainly does not make a very good deity.

REVIEW QUESTIONS

1. What does Postman mean by "civility"?
2. Some persons insist that *whenever* humans disagree, to *some* extent there's a communication problem. Postman clearly doesn't agree. What is his position on this issue?
3. True or false: Postman urges the reader *not* always to "be honest." Explain.
4. What does Postman mean by "the Communication Crusade"? Where have you experienced this "crusade"?

PROBES

1. In your experience, is what Postman calls "civility" more a function of keeping feelings to one's self or expressing them in "constructive" ways? How so?

2. Do you agree or disagree with Postman's characterization of the perceptions and feelings that are "really" behind racist remarks? Discuss.

3. What's an example from your own experience of the accuracy of Postman's claim that "sometimes, the less people know about other people, the better off everyone is"?

4. In what specific ways do you agree or disagree with what Postman says about parenting?

5. What does Postman mean when he says that authentic communication is a two-edged sword? What are the two "edges"? How can the sword "cut" two ways?

6. Discuss an example from your own experience where you felt a complex of inconsistent or perhaps contradictory "honest feelings." How did you handle them in that situation?

CHAPTER 3

Defining Ourselves as Communicators

Now that we've defined communication and interpersonal communication, the next step is to think about the people who engage in it. For most of the past 300 years, westerners have understood people to be individuals, separate, singular selves. But in the last half of the twentieth century, some European and American researchers rediscovered an idea that had been clear to our Greek forebears and to most members of Eastern cultures for a long time: Humans are more than singular individuals. We are relational beings, unique selves mixed from many ingredients. The readings in this chapter develop this understanding of humans *as communicators*.

I introduced this idea in the first reading of Chapter 2 when I said that communication always involves negotiating identities or selves. Every time you or I communicate with anybody, one thing we're doing is mutually working out who we are for and with each other. Identities are always in play.

One way to talk about this identity-negotiation or identity-management part of communication is to use the vocabulary of "co-constructing selves," which is what Karen Zediker, Saskia Witteborn, and I do in this reading. This essay comes from a basic interpersonal communication text that the three of us wrote together. We begin with some examples of how this co-construction process operates to demonstrate that it's going on all the time. We point out that, since it is a continuous process, nobody always does it perfectly or poorly. As we emphasize, there is no one best or worst way to participate in this process. There are just outcomes of how you do it, results that people may or may not want. We also make the point that this process goes on in every culture, wherever humans communicate. And the reason it's important to understand this process is that when you want to influence where your communicating is on the impersonal ⟷ interpersonal continuum explained in Chapter 2, you need to pay attention to how you're co-constructing selves.

We define identity or self as a constellation of features or labels that establish social expectations that we have of ourselves and others. Then we contrast old and new views of identities. We point out that the individualistic, Western view is very narrow, and that increasing numbers of researchers and teachers are recognizing that identities are relational and multidimensional. They get built in the contacts we experience with others, and they are made up of many different elements.

This multidimensionality is part of the first of the four characteristics of identities or selves that we discuss. The second is that selves are responders. No human starts behaving from ground zero, so that everything we do can be understood to be in reply or answer to something else (this idea surfaces again in Chapter 12). The third feature is that identities are developed in past and present relationships. The families we are raised in significantly affect who we are, and our identities are also shaped by friends, dating partners, and work relationships. The fourth characteristic is that identities can be both avowed and ascribed. This means that we can verbally and/or nonverbally "assert" an identity—avowal—and that others can ascribe identity features to us. This is one reason why it is important to be reflective about your communicating—because in every conversation you're not only expressing your ideas, you're also defining who you are.

The readings in Chapter 3 will flesh out this basic understanding of how selves—who people are—get co-constructed in people's communicating.

Constructing Identities
John Stewart, Karen E. Zediker, and Saskia Witteborn

WHAT IS IDENTITY OR SELF?

Notice what happens in the following conversation:

ALIA: Hi, just wanted to introduce myself. I'm Alia. I'm your new roommate. Just switched universities. Kind of sucks to move in your senior year, but well . . .

CHERYL: Cool. I'm Cheryl. Nice to meet you, finally. I just knew that a girl named Alia—how do you pronounce your name?—would be my new roommate, that's all. Anyways, good to meet you. Any preference in terms of where you wanna sleep?

ALIA: Not really.

CHERYL: I'm just asking because I just got back from Germany. Exchange student, you know? I was sleeping in a dorm there and was glad that my roommate let me sleep by the window. I'm kind of claustrophobic. Ha-ha. Don't worry; otherwise I'm pretty much together. Let me guess where you're from. Honestly, you don't quite look as if you were from around here.

ALIA: Well, whatdaya think?

CHERYL: Greece. Oh no, Italy.

ALIA: Naaa.

CHERYL: Spain or South America?

ALIA: Wrong again. Born in Chicago, my parents are from Iraq. Where are you from?

CHERYL: Born in Detroit and raised in Oregon.

J. Stewart, K. E. Zediker, and S. Witteborn, *Together: Communicating Interpersonally, a Social Construction Approach*, 6th ed. (Los Angeles: Roxbury, 2005.)

ALIA: So you are American, too?

CHERYL: Absolutely, although it's not that important to me, really. No kidding. Could have sworn you were from Greece. My best friend in Germany looks like you, and she's Greek. Well, I feel stupid to ask this, but . . . aren't you supposed to wear a scarf?

ALIA: Guess what? I am a Christian, Chaldean to be exact. Not all Arabs are Muslims, and not all Muslims are Arabs. Islam's the biggest religion in the Arab world, but there're also lots of Christians.

CHERYL: Wow. Let's talk more about that. That's exciting. I'm living with an Iraqi woman.

ALIA: Iraqi American is better. I was born here. Chicago, remember?

CHERYL: You're right, I'm sorry I went off on this cultural thing. I'm really, really glad to finally live with someone who is from another culture. I'm still in a kind of culture shock, coming back to the States from Germany. That's why I'm so glad about you.

ALIA: Sure, but first, if you don't mind, could you show me around here? I need to register before classes start.

CHERYL: Yep, no problem. I'm sorry if I talked too much. Let's start with the library.

Cheryl and Alia are constructing themselves together. At first, Cheryl gives Alia a national identity that Alia does not identify with. Cheryl does this mainly because of how Alia looks. For a minute Cheryl restricts Alia's self to her nationality and religion. Alia is the "Iraqi woman," even though she would probably have liked to be the *person* Alia first, or the senior who is new to the university. Cheryl, on the other hand, constructs herself as a curious and outspoken young woman, a student, and someone who has been exposed to different cultures.

This conversation shows how identities or selves are outcomes of conversations and something that we do, rather than are. Cheryl and Alia move from negotiating their student identities when they talk about being a senior and an exchange student, to negotiating their national and ethnic identities, and back to negotiating their student selves again. Alia does not want to be known only as an Iraqi and an Arab. She wants Cheryl to recognize her multiple identities as a woman, a student, a Chaldean Christian, and an Iraqi American. Cheryl also emphasizes that her national identity is not that important to her. At that moment, she wants to be perceived as a knowledgeable and open person and a possible friend, and not just as an American. As you can see, identities are fluid, not static. No one wants to be put in an ethnic, national, or gender box, especially at the beginning of a relationship.

Here is another example of how identities are constructed in verbal and nonverbal talk:

Conversation 2:

JAN: Hey, how's it goin'?

HEATHER: (Silence and a scowl)

JAN: What's the matter?

HEATHER: Nothing. Forget it.
JAN: What are you so pissed about?
HEATHER: Forget it! Just drop it.
JAN: Well, all right! Pout! I don't give a damn!

Here, even though Jan and Heather are not talking about any specific object, issue, or event, they are definitely constructing identities together. In this conversation Heather's definition of herself and of Jan goes something like this:

> Right now I identify myself as independent of you (Silence. "Nothing. Forget it."). You're butting into my space, and you probably think I'm antisocial. But I've got good reasons for my anger.

On the other hand, Jan's definition of herself and of Heather is something like this:

> Right now I identify myself as friendly and concerned ("Hey, how's it goin'?" "What's the matter?"). I'm willing to stick my neck out a little, but you're obviously not interested in being civil. So there's a limit to how long I'll *stay* friendly and concerned. ("Well, all right! Pout! I don't give a damn!").

We want to emphasize that nobody in these conversations is constructing identities perfectly or poorly, right or wrong. In one sense, there is no right or wrong way to participate in this process. There are just *outcomes* of how you do it, *results* that you may or may not want.

We also want to emphasize that none of the people in these conversations could avoid constructing selves. It's a process that happens whenever people communicate. Some of the most important meanings we collaboratively construct are our identities, and all communicating involves constructing identities or selves. No matter how brief or extended the contact, whether it's written or oral, mediated or face-to-face, impersonal or interpersonal, the people involved will be directly or indirectly constructing definitions of themselves and responding to the definitions offered by others. Radio talk show hosts and television newscasters are continually building identities. The person who writes a letter longhand on colorful stationery is defining him- or herself differently from the person who writes the same letter on a word processor. The person who answers the telephone, "Yeah?" is defining him- or herself differently from the one who answers, "Good morning. May I help you?"

Research on intercultural communication shows how identity construction occurs in different cultures. For instance, Bailey (2000) shows how young Dominican Americans negotiate their cultural identities by switching between Spanish and English. Speaking in Spanish indicates solidarity with their peers who are similar in cultural background. In another study, Hegde (1998) shows how immigrants from India navigate between their Indian identity and their new American identity. Saskia has also studied Arab identities and has found that people of Arab descent enact multiple national and religious identities and feel more or less strongly Arab at various times, but it really depends on the context. For instance, some people say that they call themselves Arab American mostly when they have to fill out official forms, and that they feel Arab rather than Arab American when they talk about families because family is so important in the Arab world. As Scotton (1983) summarizes, in various cultural contexts, speakers use language choices "imaginatively . . . a range of options is open to them within a normative framework, and . . . taking one option rather than another is the *negotiation of identities.*"

So two reasons why it's important to understand the process of identity construction are (1) that you're doing it whenever you communicate—and everybody else is, too—and (2) that the process affects who you are in relation to others. The third reason why it's important is that *your negotiation responses also affect where your communication is on the impersonal ⟷ interpersonal continuum.* As we'll explain in the final section of this chapter, some responses just about guarantee that your communication will be impersonal. Others lead to more interpersonal communicating. So if you want to help change the quality of your contacts with your dating partner, employer, roommate, sister, or parent in either direction on the continuum, you'll probably want to learn as much as you can about this process.

Definition of Identity

As identity or self is made up of interlocking features that mark how we behave and respond to others, identities are constellations of labels that establish social expectations that we have of ourselves and others. These social expectations can include roles that we want or have to play in specific situations and the languages or dialects we speak and expect others to speak. When you enter a classroom in the United States, you expect your instructor to talk and behave in certain ways. For instance, most North Americans expect that a person enacting the identity of an "instructor" should normally stand in front of the class, speak in a loud and intelligible voice, have control in the classroom, and, unless it's a foreign language class, express him- or herself in some form of English. And in order to enact the role of instructor, this person needs students who enact their role. Notice how we say "enact." This is another way of emphasizing that identities are something that we *do* rather than what we *are* (Collier and Thomas 1988; Hecht, Jackson, and Ribeau 2003). You are not born to be a student for all of your life, but you are socialized into this identity, and it becomes salient in different times and places.

Old versus Current Views of Identity

It may sound weird to you to say that identities or selves are co-constructed in verbal and nonverbal talk. You might think of your *self* as fairly stable, identifiable, and clearly bounded. If so, you're not alone. Most people in Western cultures have been taught to think of their selves as individual containers that enclose their unique essence. As one book puts it,

> There is an individualist mode of thought, distinctive of modern Western cultures, which, though we may criticize it in part or in whole, we cannot escape. . . . This inescapable cultural vise has given us—or, at least, the dominant social groups in the West—a sense of themselves as distinctive, independent agents who own themselves and have relatively clear boundaries to protect in order to ensure their integrity and permit them to function more effectively in the world. (Sampson 1993, 31)

Most members of dominant social groups in the Western world think of the boundary of the individual as the same as the boundary of the body, and that the body houses or contains the self. Common metaphors reflect this view, as when people say that a person is *"filled* with anger," "unable to *contain* her joy," *"brimming* with laughter," or "trying to get anger *out of our system"* (Lakoff 1987, 383). Some theories of psychology reinforce this view of identity or the self. Psychologists influenced by the famous therapist Sigmund Freud, for example, think of society as made up of individual selves who are each working out their inner tensions. One Freudian insisted that a student revolt against university administrators was caused by the students' unresolved conflicts with their fathers. In his view,

> protestors were taking out their inner conflicts with parental authority by acting against the authority represented by the University. It was as though there were no legitimate problems with the University; it only symbolized protestors' unresolved Oedipal conflicts with the real source of their troubles, their fathers. (Sampson 1993, 44)

For this psychologist, selves were individual and internal.

But in the last decades of the twentieth century, the development of space travel, satellite television, and the World Wide Web; the globalization of music and business; and the end of the Cold War have all helped Westerners understand that this view of the person as a bounded individual is, as one anthropologist puts it, rather "peculiar" (Geertz 1979, 229). For centuries, people in many cultures outside the West have not been thinking this way. For example, if a North American is asked to explain why someone financially cheated another person, the North American's tendency will be to locate the cause in "the kind of person she is." A Hindu, by contrast, is more likely to offer a social explanation—"The man is unemployed. He is not in a position to give that money" (Miller 1984, 968). This is because many members of the Hindu culture don't think of identity or the self as individual, but as social or communal. For them, identity is a function of cultural or group memberships. Or, to take another example, in a study of U.S. and Samoan child care workers, U.S. preschool teachers tended to help children socialize by developing their individuality, whereas Samoan caregivers' efforts "were directed towards helping the children learn how better to fit into their in-group" (Ochs 1988, 199). In their broader culture, Samoans in this study also recognized the central role of other people in events that were deemed worthy of praise or compliments. So one researcher reported that when a Samoan passenger complimented a driver with language that translates, "Well done the driving," the driver typically responded, "Well done the support." "In this Samoan view, if a performance went well, it is the supporters' merit as much as the performer's" (Ochs 1988, 200). Many Japanese understand the person in a similar way. In Japan, one author notes, "The concept of a self completely independent from the environment is very foreign" (Kojima 1984, 972). Rather, Japanese think of individuals in terms of the social context they fit into—their family, work group, and so on. The United States, Canada, Australia, Great Britain, and some other Western cultures have a strong belief in the individual self, but many European countries (e.g., Spain, Austria, and Finland) and most Asian and Latin American cultures understand identities or selves as social, relational, or group-oriented (Hofstede 1980).

It's easier to understand how identity construction works—and how to manage your own identity constructing—if you adopt what has historically been a more Eastern perspective. This doesn't mean that you have to change cultures or religions, or to pretend to be somebody you're not. In fact, this understanding is being accepted by communication scholars, psychologists, anthropologists, and other students of human behavior all over the world. Especially in the final decade of the twentieth century, many of these scholars and teachers recognized that selves or identities are relational from birth, or maybe even before. They began taking seriously what Lev Vygotsky and George Herbert Mead, two very influential human development researchers, said several decades ago: namely, that infants are first *social* beings and only later in life learn to see themselves as *individuals*. As psychologist Edward Sampson explains,

> Both Vygotsky and Mead clearly emphasize the necessary social bases of human thinking, cognition, and mindedness. Indeed, rather than viewing the individual's mind as setting forth the terms for the social order, the reverse describes the actual event: the social process—namely, dialogue and conversation—precedes, and is the foundation for, any subsequent psychological processes that emerge. (Sampson 1993, 103)

In short, the English terms, *self* and *identity* and their meanings are only about 300 years old. Studies of history and of other cultures illustrate that the Western definition developed over the last 275 of these 300 years is very narrow. Today, this idea that selves are individual containers is being revised as communication scholars and psychologists are recognizing how much our selves are developed in communication with others. Westerners increasingly recognize that identities or selves are multidimensional and that they change in response to the people and institutions we connect with. Each of our identities has athletic, artistic, ethnic, gendered, occupational, scientific, political, economic, and religious dimensions, and all of these shift in content and importance as we move from situation to situation.

FOUR CHARACTERISTICS OF IDENTITIES OR SELVES

This understanding of identities or selves can be summarized in four primary characteristics.

1. Identities Are Multidimensional and Changing

One feature of selves is that we're complex. On the one hand, each of us is characterized by some stabilities or patterns. A person's genetic makeup is stable, and your ethnic identity also probably hasn't changed and probably won't. Someone who's known you all your life can probably identify some features you had when you were 4 or 5 years old that you still have, and as you look at old photographs of yourself, you might recognize how the identity of the person in the picture is in some ways "the same" as who you are today.

On the other hand, you are different in at least as many ways as you are the same. Think, for example, of who you were at age 9 or 10 and who you were at age 14 or 15. Adolescence is a time of *significant* change in our selves. Or, if it fits you, think of yourself before you were married and after, or your identity before and after you had children.

Some researchers broadly classify identities or selves into personal, relational, and communal features (Hecht, Jackson, and Ribeau 2003). *Personal* identity is all the characteristics that you think make you a unique person, such as being friendly, helpful, disciplined, hard working, beautiful, and so forth. *Relational* identities are based on relationships you have with others, such as mother-daughter, teacher-student, or employer-employee. *Communal* identities are usually related to larger groups, such as ethnicities, race, religion, gender, or nationality.

2. Selves Are Responders

We've already introduced this second feature of selves in Chapter Three when we said that responsiveness is one of the five features that makes each of us a person. Our main point there was to contrast responding with simply reacting. Now we want to build the meaning of this idea by noting that responding implies both *choice* (not just reacting) and *connection* with what's already happened.

To say that selves are responders is to say that we grow out of and fit into a context of actions and events that we behave-in-relation-to. On the one hand, this is just another way of saying that selves are relational or social. Remember how Alia responded to Cheryl's question about where she is from and how they both constructed their student and ethnic/national identities? They responded to each other. In one instance, Cheryl might be regarded as just reacting when she asks about Alia's absent scarf. However, in most instances, both women are responding to each other, which includes reflecting about what the other person just said. Responding means that all human action is joint action. No human starts behaving from ground zero, so that everything we do, from the very beginning, is in reply or answer to something else.

Humans begin responding from the first moment we develop any aware-ness, which, as we noted earlier, probably happens before birth. Every baby is born into a world of verbal and nonverbal talk, family relationships, gender pat-terns, ongoing activities, and social and political events. This is the sense in which no person is, "after all, the first speaker, the one who disturbs the eternal silence of the universe." Since none of us is Adam or Eve, all of our actions more or less effectively connect with or fit into the activities and language systems that surround us (Bakhtin 1986, 69).

3. Identities Are Developed in Past and Present Relationships

The reason selves change over time is that we develop who we are in relation-ships with the people around us. Some of the most important parts of each per-son's identity are established in one's family of origin, the people with whom you spend the first five to seven years of your life. One of your parents may have consistently introduced you to new people from the time you were old enough to talk, and today you may still find it easy to make acquaintances. Or you may have moved around a lot when you were young, and today you feel secure only when you have your own "place" and you prefer to spend holidays close to home. You may treasure a wonderful relationship with your dad, or you may have had the opposite kind of experience. Your family is the role model for many types of relational, religious, or ethnic identities. For instance, you learn what it means to be a good friend or a good neighbor, a good brother or sister or mother or father, or perhaps not such a good one:

> My father is an alcoholic. He has never admitted to that fact. He and my mom used to get in lots of fights when I lived at home. The six of us kids were used as pawns in their war games. I always wondered whether or not I was respon-sible for his drinking. When the fights were going on, I always retreated to my room. There I felt secure. Now, I am 22, and have been married for two years. I have this affliction that, whenever the slightest thing happens, I always say I am so sorry. I am sorry when the milk is not cold, sorry that the wet towel was left in the gym bag. I just want to take the blame for everything, even things I have no control over. (Black 1982, 9)

Many current studies about dysfunctional families emphasize how people with addictions to alcohol, cocaine, prescription drugs, and other chemicals de-veloped the communication patterns that reinforce these addictions in their fam-ilies of origin (Fuller et al. 2003). Other research focuses on how addictions affect the children or other family members of addicted persons. One review of studies about adult children of alcoholics concludes that, regardless of gender, socioeco-nomic group, or ethnic identity, these people develop 13 common features. For ex-ample, many adult children of alcoholics "have difficulty following a project through from beginning to end," "lie when it would be just as easy to tell the truth," "judge themselves without mercy," "take themselves very seriously," "constantly seek approval and affirmation," and "are extremely loyal, even in the face of evidence that the loyalty is undeserved" (Beatty 1989). These books and articles illustrate how much our family of origin contributes to the response patterns that we follow in identity construction. We talk about one of these patterns, codependence, in detail in Chapter Ten. But our main point here is that past relationships contribute a great deal to the patterns that help make up our present selves.

Present relationships are also important. When you realize that a new friend really likes you, it can do great things for your self-definition. Getting a top grade from a teacher you respect can affect how you see yourself. At work, a positive performance evaluation from your supervisor or a raise can improve not only your mood and your bank account but also your perception of yourself. And again, the reverse can obviously also happen. The point is, genetic makeup does not determine your identity, and we call the communication process that produces these identities *identity construction*.

4. Identities Can Be Avowed and Ascribed

Finally, identities or selves can be ascribed and avowed. *Ascribed* means that others assign you an identity that you may or may not agree with; *avowed* means that you personally assign yourself an identity and act it out. People also try to negotiate this avowal and ascription process. Remember the conversation between Cheryl and Alia? Cheryl ascribed to Alia a somewhat stereotyped national and religious identity that Alia did not accept as her main identity in that particular situation. During the conversation they both put their student and cultural identities on the table (being from Detroit and growing up in Oregon can imply two different regional identities) and reached somewhat of an alignment on how they wanted to be perceived in this initial encounter. However, sometimes when people stereotype, they rigidly stick with their opinions about people and make them one dimensional. For instance, sometimes people talk slower when they realize that English is Saskia's second language or start immediately to talk about beer when they hear that Saskia is from Germany. It can be entertaining for a while, but then Saskia wants to be perceived as Saskia or a woman or an instructor and not only as German. Rigid ascription of identities can become a problem for the person who is ascribed the identity. This is also true for many African Americans, Latinas, or Asian Americans. People are often judged on their looks and language and not who else they are or want to be. The question of ascription and avowal will come up again when we talk about response options.

REVIEW QUESTIONS

1. Fill in the blank: "_____ appear and are constructed or worked out in verbal and nonverbal talk."
2. Identify three plausible features of the identity being offered by the person who answers the telephone with a loud, "Yeah?" What are three plausible features of the identity of the person who answers the telephone, "Good morning. May I help you?"

3. What is the difference between a reaction and a response?
4. Describe one feature of your *personal* identity. Label one feature of your *relational* identity. Describe one feature of your *communal* identity.

PROBES

1. The old view of selves is that individuality comes first, and then individuals interact to form social groups. The new view reverses this sequence. Explain how.
2. Since no person is Adam or Eve, and we are all responding to what happens around us, (a) what does this say about the claim, "He started it!" and (b) what's the most accurate way to define "creativity"?
3. What can a person do about the parts of his or her identity that were formed in past relationships? If you're the child of an alcoholic, for example, what can you do about the parts of your self that were formed by that set of experiences?
4. Does the ethnicity or culture that you primarily identify with generally view selves as individualistic or relational? How does this affect your own sense of self?
5. What past relationships most affected the development of your self? Which present relationships are having the most impact on the current development of your self?
6. If you are mainly a product of your relationships, what happens to your individual integrity?

REFERENCES

Bach, G. R., and Wyden, P. 1968. *The Intimate Enemy: How to Fight Fair in Love and Marriage.* New York: Avon Books.

Bailey, B. 2000. "Language and Negotiation of Ethnic/Racial Identity Among Dominican Americans." *Language in Society*, 29: 555–582.

Bakhtin, M. M. 1986. *Speech Genres and Other Late Essays.* (Translated by V. W. McGee). Austin: University of Texas Press. (Originally published 1953.)

Beatty, M. 1989. *Beyond Codependency.* New York: Harper/Hazelden.

Black, C. 1982. *'It Will Never Happen to Me!' Children of Alcoholics as Youngsters— Adolescents—Adults.* Denver: M.A.C.

Cissna, K. N. L., and Sieburg, E. 1981. "Patterns of Interactional Confirmation and Disconfirmation." In C. Wilder-Mott and J. H. Weakland (eds.), *Rigor and Imagination: Essays from the Legacy of Gregory Bateson.* New York: Praeger. Pages 230–239.

Collier, M. J., and Thomas, M. 1988. "Cultural Identity: An Interpretive Perspective." In Y. Y. Kim and W. B. Gudykunst (eds.), *Theories of Intercultural Communication.* Newbury Park, CA: Sage. Pages 99–120.

Fuller, B. E., Chermack, S. T., Cruise, K. A., Kirsch, E., Fitzgerald, H. E., and Zucker, R. A. 2003. "Predictors of Aggression across Three Generations among Sons of Alcoholics: Relationships Involving Grandparental and Parental Alcoholism, Child Aggression, Marital Aggression and Parenting Practices." *Journal of Studies on Alcohol*, 64: 472–484.

Geertz, C. 1979. "From the Native's Point of View: On the Nature of Anthropological Understanding." In P. Rabinow and W. M. Sullivan (eds.), *Interpretive Social Science*. Berkeley: University of California Press. Pages 225–246.

Hall, B. J. 2002. *Among Cultures: The Challenge of Communication*. New York: Harcourt College Publishers.

Hecht, M. L., Jackson II, R. L., and Ribeau, S. A. 2003. *African American Communication: Exploring Identity and Culture*. 2nd ed. Mahwah, NJ: Erlbaum.

Hegde, R. S. 1998. "A View From Elsewhere: Locating Difference and the Politics of Representation From a Transnational Feminist Perspective." *Communication Theory*, 8: 271–297.

Hofstede, G. 1980. *Culture's Consequences: International Differences in Work-Related Values*. Beverly Hills, CA: Sage.

Kojima, H. 1984. "A Significant Stride Toward the Comparative Study of Control." *American Psychologist*, 39: 972–973.

Laing, R. D. 1961. *The Self and Others*. New York: Pantheon.

———. 1969. *The Self and Others*. Baltimore: Penguin Books.

Lakoff, G. 1987. *Women, Fire, and Dangerous Things*. Chicago: University of Chicago Press.

Miller, J. G. 1984. *The Development of Women's Sense of Self*. Work in Progress, No. 12. Wellesley, MA: Stone Center Working Paper Series.

Ochs, E. 1988. *Culture and Language Development: Language Acquisition and Language Socialization in a Samoan Village*. Cambridge: Cambridge University Press.

Rogers, C. R. 1965. "Dialogue Between Martin Buber and Carl R. Rogers." In M. Friedman and R. G. Smith (eds.), *The Knowledge of Man*. London: Allen and Unwin.

Sampson, E. E. 1993. *Celebrating the Other: A Dialogic Account of Human Nature*. Boulder, CO: Westview.

Scotton, C. M. 1983. "The Negotiation of Identities in Conversation: A Theory of Markedness and Code Choice." *International Journal of Sociological Linguistics*, 44: 119–125.

This next reading helps show how human selves are fundamentally communicative by defining the counterpart of IQ (Intelligence Quotient), as EQ (Emotional Quotient), which is basically the willingness and ability to connect effectively with others. For a long time, at least in the Western world, people have trusted IQ tests as the best measure of a person's "smarts." For many decades, IQ tests have been given to school children, and IQ scores have been used to define people as "gifted," "special needs," or "genius." Daniel Goleman argues that these tests are fundamentally flawed because they measure only part of what it means to be intelligent. There is a very important, complementary set of human competencies that he calls "emotional intelligence," and these are embodied in our ways of relating with others.

In other words, emotional intelligence is basically interpersonal intelligence. It is made up of four main abilities: organizing groups, negotiating solutions, personal connecting, and social analysis. Each is significantly different from the kinds of intelligence that standard IQ tests measure.

The first involves "initiating and coordinating the efforts of a network of people." The second is the talent of a mediator—resolving conflicts. The third kind of emotional intelligence is the capacity for empathy—reading emotions and responding appropriately to them. And the fourth consists of being able to "detect and have insights about people's feelings, motives, and concerns."

Goleman briefly describes how these abilities are related to other kinds of emotional intelligence. For example, the person who is empathic is also able to notice his or her own emotions, to fine-tune them to fit the situation, and to adjust them flexibly. He also cites the same research about self-monitoring that is discussed in Chapter 5 by Trenholm and Jensen to make the point that it's important to have a balance of the emotional capabilities of empathy and the awareness of your *own* needs and feelings.

In a section of the reading called "The Making of a Social Incompetent," Goleman discusses some of the experiences that help shape individual emotional intelligence. He quotes a psychologist who emphasizes that children need to be taught "to speak directly to others when spoken to; to initiate social contact, not always wait for others; to carry on a conversation, not simply fall back on yes or no or other one-word replies; to express gratitude toward others, . . . to thank others, to say 'please,' to share," and so on. Young children learn these capabilities—or fail to learn them—in countless informal contacts with family members, schoolmates, and friends, and this fact underscores the significance, in the early years, of these everyday, mundane activities. Goleman notes that psychologists have coined the term *dyssemia* to label people who haven't learned to read the nonverbal messages that primarily communicate emotions. He also points out that this difficulty affects not only a child's interpersonal life but also his or her academic success.

One of the primary tests of a young child's emotional intelligence is being on the edge of a group that the child wants to join. Some research indicates that even popular second- and third-graders are rejected almost a quarter of the time they attempt to join in such groups. And as each of us can probably remember, young children can be brutally candid in this situation. Researchers observe these events in classrooms and on playgrounds in order to assess individual abilities and clarify the features of emotional intelligence.

The selection ends with a description of an event of "emotional brilliance" that a friend of Goleman's observed on a train outside Tokyo. This story, along with the rest of this reading, should enable you to evaluate your own emotional or interpersonal intelligence and to recognize how this kind of knowledge affects your perceptions of people, relationships, and social situations.

The Rudiments of Social Intelligence

Daniel Goleman

It's recess at a preschool, and a band of boys is running across the grass. Reggie trips, hurts his knee, and starts crying, but the other boys keep right on running— save for Roger, who stops. As Reggie's sobs subside Roger reaches down and rubs his own knee, calling out, "I hurt my knee, too!"

Roger is cited as having exemplary interpersonal intelligence by Thomas Hatch, a colleague of Howard Gardner at Spectrum, the school based on the concept of multiple intelligences.[1] Roger, it seems, is unusually adept at recognizing the feelings of his playmates and making rapid, smooth connections with them. It was only Roger who noticed Reggie's plight and pain, and only Roger who tried to provide some solace, even if all he could offer was rubbing his own knee. This small gesture bespeaks a talent for rapport, an emotional skill essential for the preservation of close relationships, whether in a marriage, a friendship, or a business partnership. Such skills in preschoolers are the buds of talents that ripen through life.

Roger's talent represents one of four separate abilities that Hatch and Gardner identify as components of interpersonal intelligence:

- *Organizing groups*—the essential skill of the leader, this involves initiating and coordinating the efforts of a network of people. This is the talent seen in theater directors or producers, in military officers, and in effective heads of organizations and units of all kinds. On the playground, this is the child who takes the lead in deciding what everyone will play, or becomes team captain.
- *Negotiating solutions*—the talent of the mediator, preventing conflicts or resolving those that flare up. People who have this ability excel in dealmaking, in arbitrating or mediating disputes; they might have a career in diplomacy, in arbitration or law, or as middlemen or managers of takeovers. These are the kids who settle arguments on the playing field.
- *Personal connection*—Roger's talent, that of empathy and connecting. This makes it easy to enter into an encounter or to recognize and respond

fittingly to people's feelings and concerns—the art of relationship. Such people make good "team players," dependable spouses, good friends or business partners; in the business world they do well as salespeople or managers, or can be excellent teachers. Children like Roger get along well with virtually everyone else, easily enter into playing with them, and are happy doing so. These children tend to be best at reading emotions from facial expressions and are most liked by their classmates.

- *Social analysis*—being able to detect and have insights about people's feelings, motives, and concerns. This knowledge of how others feel can lead to an easy intimacy or sense of rapport. At its best, this ability makes one a competent therapist or counselor—or, if combined with some literary talent, a gifted novelist or dramatist.

Taken together, these skills are the stuff of interpersonal polish, the necessary ingredients for charm, social success, even charisma. Those who are adept in social intelligence can connect with people quite smoothly, be astute in reading their reactions and feelings, lead and organize, and handle the disputes that are bound to flare up in any human activity. They are the natural leaders, the people who can express the unspoken collective sentiment and articulate it so as to guide a group toward its goals. They are the kind of people others like to be with because they are emotionally nourishing—they leave other people in a good mood, and evoke the comment, "What a pleasure to be around someone like that."

These interpersonal abilities build on other emotional intelligences. People who make an excellent social impression, for example, are adept at monitoring their own expression of emotion, are keenly attuned to the ways others are reacting, and so are able to continually fine-tune their social performance, adjusting it to make sure they are having the desired effect. In that sense, they are like skilled actors.

However, if these interpersonal abilities are not balanced by an astute sense of one's own needs and feelings and how to fulfill them, they can lead to a hollow social success—a popularity won at the cost of one's true satisfaction. Such is the argument of Mark Snyder, a University of Minnesota psychologist who has studied people whose social skills make them first-rate social chameleons, champions at making a good impression.[2] Their psychological credo might well be a remark by W. H. Auden, who said that his private image of himself "is very different from the image which I try to create in the minds of others in order that they may love me." That trade-off can be made if social skills outstrip the ability to know and honor one's own feelings: in order to be loved—or at least liked—the social chameleon will seem to be whatever those he [or she] is with seem to want. The sign that someone falls into this pattern, Snyder finds, is that they make an excellent impression, yet have few stable or satisfying intimate relationships. A more healthy pattern, of course, is to balance being true to oneself with social skills, using them with integrity.

Social chameleons, though, don't mind in the least saying one thing and doing another, if that will win them social approval. They simply live with the discrepancy between their public face and their private reality. Helena Deutsch, a psychoanalyst, called such people the "as-if personality," shifting personas with remarkable plasticity as they pick up signals from those around them. "For some people," Snyder told me, "the public and private person meshes well, while for others there seems to be only a kaleidoscope of changing appearances. They are like Woody Allen's character Zelig, madly trying to fit in with whomever they are with."

Such people try to scan someone for a hint as to what is wanted from them before they make a response, rather than simply saying what they truly feel. To get along and be liked, they are willing to make people they dislike think they are friendly with them. And they use their social abilities to mold their actions as disparate social situations demand, so that they may act like very different people depending on whom they are with, swinging from bubbly sociability, say, to reserved withdrawal. To be sure, to the extent that these traits lead to effective impression management, they are highly prized in certain professions, notably acting, trial law, sales, diplomacy, and politics.

Another, perhaps more crucial kind of self-monitoring seems to make the difference between those who end up as anchorless social chameleons, trying to impress everyone, and those who can use their social polish more in keeping with their true feelings. That is the capacity to be true, as the saying has it, "to thine own self," which allows acting in accord with one's deepest feelings and values no matter what the social consequences. Such emotional integrity could well lead to, say, deliberately provoking a confrontation in order to cut through duplicity or denial—a clearing of the air that a social chameleon would never attempt.

THE MAKING OF A SOCIAL INCOMPETENT

There was no doubt Cecil was bright; he was a college-trained expert in foreign languages, superb at translating. But there were crucial ways in which he was completely inept. Cecil seemed to lack the simplest social skills. He would muff a casual conversation over coffee, and fumble when having to pass the time of day; in short, he seemed incapable of the most routine social exchange. Because his lack of social grace was most profound when he was around women, Cecil came to therapy wondering if perhaps he had "homosexual tendencies of an underlying nature," as he put it, though he had no such fantasies.

The real problem, Cecil confided to his therapist, was that he feared that nothing he could say would be of any interest to anybody. This underlying fear only compounded a profound paucity of social graces. His nervousness during encounters led him to snicker and laugh at the most awkward moments, even though he failed to laugh when someone said something genuinely funny. Cecil's awkwardness, he confided to his therapist, went back to childhood; all his life he had felt socially at ease only when he was with his older brother, who somehow helped ease things for him. But once he left home, his ineptitude was overwhelming; he was socially paralyzed.

The tale is told by Lakin Phillips, a psychologist at George Washington University, who proposes that Cecil's plight stems from a failure to learn in childhood the most elementary lessons of social interaction:

> What could Cecil have been taught earlier? To speak directly to others when spoken to; to initiate social contact, not always wait for others; to carry on a conversation, not simply fall back on yes or no or other one-word replies; to express gratitude toward others, to let another person walk before one in passing through a door; to wait until one is served something . . . to thank others, to say "please," to share, and all the other elementary interactions we begin to teach children from age 2 onward.[3]

Whether Cecil's deficiency was due to another's failure to teach him such rudiments of social civility or to his own inability to learn is unclear. But whatever its roots, Cecil's story is instructive because it points up the crucial nature of the countless lessons children get in interaction synchrony and the unspoken rules of social harmony. The net effect of failing to follow these rules is to create waves, to make those around us uncomfortable. The function of these rules, of course, is to keep everyone involved in a social exchange at ease; awkwardness spawns anxiety. People who lack these skills are inept not just at social niceties, but at handling the emotions of those they encounter; they inevitably leave disturbance in their wake.

We all have known Cecils, people with an annoying lack of social graces—people who don't seem to know when to end a conversation or phone call and who keep on talking, oblivious to all cues and hints to say good-bye; people whose conversation centers on themselves all the time, without the least interest in anyone else, and who ignore tentative attempts to refocus on another topic; people who intrude or ask "nosy" questions. These derailments of a smooth social trajectory all bespeak a deficit in the rudimentary building blocks of interaction.

Psychologists have coined the term *dyssemia* (from the Greek *dys-* for "difficulty" and *semes* for "signal") for what amounts to a learning disability in the realm of nonverbal messages; about one in ten children has one or more problems in this realm.[4] The problem can be in a poor sense of personal space, so that a child stands too close while talking or spreads their belongings into other people's territory; in interpreting or using body language poorly; in misinterpreting or misusing facial expressions by, say, failing to make eye contact; or in a poor sense of prosody, the emotional quality of speech, so that they talk too shrilly or flatly.

Much research has focused on spotting children who show signs of social deficiency, children whose awkwardness makes them neglected or rejected by their playmates. Apart from children who are spurned because they are bullies, those whom other children avoid are invariably deficient in the rudiments of face-to-face interaction, particularly the unspoken rules that govern encounters. If children do poorly in language, people assume they are not very bright or poorly educated; but when they do poorly in the nonverbal rules of interaction, people—especially playmates—see them as "strange," and avoid them. These are the children who don't know how to join a game gracefully, who touch others in ways that make for discomfort rather than camaraderie—in short, who are "off." They are children who have failed to master the silent language of emotion, and who unwittingly send messages that create uneasiness.

As Stephen Nowicki, an Emory University psychologist who studies children's nonverbal abilities, put it, "Children who can't read or express emotions well constantly feel frustrated. In essence, they don't understand what's going on. This kind of communication is a constant subtext of everything you do; you can't stop showing your facial expression or posture, or hide your tone of voice. If you make mistakes in what emotional messages you send, you constantly experience that people react to you in funny ways—you get rebuffed and don't know why. If you're thinking you're acting happy but actually seem too hyper or angry, you find other kids getting angry at you in turn, and you don't realize why. Such kids end up feeling no sense of control over how other people treat them, that their actions have no impact on what happens to them. It leaves them feeling powerless, depressed, and apathetic."

Apart from becoming social isolates, such children also suffer academically. The classroom, of course, is as much a social situation as an academic one; the socially awkward child is as likely to misread and misrespond to a teacher as to another child. The resulting anxiety and bewilderment can themselves interfere with their ability to learn effectively. Indeed, as tests of children's nonverbal sensitivity have shown, those who misread emotional cues tend to do poorly in school compared to their academic potential as reflected in IQ tests.[5]

"WE HATE YOU": AT THE THRESHOLD

Social ineptitude is perhaps most painful and explicit when it comes to one of the more perilous moments in the life of a young child: being on the edge of a group at play you want to join. It is a moment of peril, one when being liked or hated, belonging or not, is made all too public. For that reason that crucial moment has been the subject of intense scrutiny by students of child development, revealing a stark contrast in approach strategies used by popular children and by social outcasts. The findings highlight just how crucial it is for social competence to notice, interpret, and respond to emotional and interpersonal cues. While it is poignant to see a child hover on the edge of others at play, wanting to join in but being left out, it is a universal predicament. Even the most popular children are sometimes rejected—a study of second and third graders found that 26 percent of the time the most well liked children were rebuffed when they tried to enter a group already at play.

Young children are brutally candid about the emotional judgment implicit in such rejections. Witness the following dialogue from four-year-olds in a preschool.[6] Linda wants to join Barbara, Nancy, and Bill, who are playing with toy animals and building blocks. She watches for a minute, then makes her approach, sitting next to Barbara and starting to play with the animals. Barbara turns to her and says, "You can't play!"

"Yes, I can," Linda counters. "I can have some animals, too."

"No, you can't," Barbara says bluntly. "We don't like you today."

When Bill protests on Linda's behalf, Nancy joins the attack: "We hate her today."

Because of the danger of being told, either explicitly or implicitly, "We hate you," all children are understandably cautious on the threshold of approaching a group. That anxiety, of course, is probably not much different from that felt by a grown-up at a cocktail party with strangers who hangs back from a happily chatting group who seem to be intimate friends. Because this moment at the threshold of a group is so momentous for a child, it is also, as one researcher put it, "highly diagnostic . . . quickly revealing differences in social skillfulness."[7]

Typically, newcomers simply watch for a time, then join in very tentatively at first, being more assertive only in very cautious steps. What matters most for whether a child is accepted or not is how well he or she is able to enter into the group's frame of reference, sensing what kind of play is in flow, what's out of place.

The two cardinal sins that almost always lead to rejection are trying to take the lead too soon and being out of synch with the frame of reference. But this is exactly what unpopular children tend to do: they push their way into a group, trying to change the subject too abruptly or too soon, or offering their own opinions, or simply disagreeing with the others right away—all apparent attempts to draw attention to themselves. Paradoxically, this results in their being ignored or rejected. By contrast, popular children spend time observing the group to understand what's going on before entering in, and then do something that shows they accept it; they wait to have their status in the group confirmed before taking initiative in suggesting what the group should do.

Let's return to Roger, the four-year-old whom Thomas Hatch spotted exhibiting a high level of interpersonal intelligence.[8] Roger's tactic for entering a group was first to observe, then to imitate what another child was doing, and finally to talk to the child and fully join the activity—a winning strategy. Roger's skill was shown, for instance, when he and Warren were playing at putting "bombs" (actually pebbles) in their socks. Warren asks Roger if he wants to be in a helicopter or an airplane. Roger asks, before committing himself, "Are you in a helicopter?"

This seemingly innocuous moment reveals sensitivity to others' concerns, and the ability to act on that knowledge in a way that maintains the connection. Hatch comments about Roger, "He 'checks in' with his playmate so that they and their play remain connected. I have watched many other children who simply get in their own helicopters or planes and, literally and figuratively, fly away from each other."

EMOTIONAL BRILLIANCE: A CASE REPORT

If the test of social skill is the ability to calm distressing emotions in others, then handling someone at the peak of rage is perhaps the ultimate measure of mastery. The data on self-regulation of anger and emotional contagion suggest that one effective strategy might be to distract the angry person, empathize with his feelings and perspective, and then draw him into an alternative focus, one that attunes him with a more positive range of feeling—a kind of emotional judo.

Such refined skill in the fine art of emotional influence is perhaps best exemplified by a story told by an old friend, the late Terry Dobson, who in the 1950s was one of the first Americans ever to study the martial art aikido in Japan. One afternoon he was riding home on a suburban Tokyo train when a huge, bellicose, and very drunk and begrimed laborer got on. The man, staggering, began terrorizing the passengers: screaming curses, he took a swing at a woman holding a baby, sending her sprawling in the laps of an elderly couple, who then jumped up and joined a stampede to the other end of the car. The drunk, taking a few other swings (and, in his rage, missing), grabbed the metal pole in the middle of the car with a roar and tried to tear it out of its socket.

At that point Terry, who was in peak physical condition from daily eight-hour aikido workouts, felt called upon to intervene, lest someone get seriously hurt. But he recalled the words of his teacher: "Aikido is the art of reconciliation. Whoever has the mind to fight has broken his connection with the universe. If you try to dominate people you are already defeated. We study how to resolve conflict, not how to start it."

Indeed, Terry had agreed upon beginning lessons with his teacher never to pick a fight, and to use his martial-arts skills only in defense. Now, at last, he saw his chance to test his aikido abilities in real life, in what was clearly a legitimate opportunity. So, as all the other passengers sat frozen in their seats, Terry stood up, slowly and with deliberation.

Seeing him, the drunk roared, "Aha! A foreigner! You need a lesson in Japanese manners!" and began gathering himself to take on Terry.

But just as the drunk was on the verge of making his move, someone gave an earsplitting, oddly joyous shout: "Hey!"

The shout had the cheery tone of someone who has suddenly come upon a fond friend. The drunk, surprised, spun around to see a tiny Japanese man, probably in his seventies, sitting there in a kimono. The old man beamed with delight at the drunk, and beckoned him over with a light wave of his hand and a lilting "C'mere."

The drunk strode over with a belligerent, "Why the hell should I talk to you?" Meanwhile, Terry was ready to fell the drunk in a moment if he made the least violent move.

"What'cha been drinking?" the old man asked, his eyes beaming at the drunken laborer.

"I been drinking sake, and it's none of your business," the drunk bellowed.

"Oh, that's wonderful, absolutely wonderful," the old man replied in a warm tone. "You see, I love sake, too. Every night, me and my wife (she's seventy-six, you know), we warm up a little bottle of sake and take it out into the garden, and we sit on an old wooden bench . . ." He continued on about the persimmon tree in his backyard, the fortunes of his garden, enjoying sake in the evening.

The drunk's face began to soften as he listened to the old man; his fists unclenched. "Yeah . . . I love persimmons, too . . . ," he said, his voice trailing off.

"Yes," the old man replied in a sprightly voice, "and I'm sure you have a won-derful wife."

"No," said the laborer. "My wife died. . . ." Sobbing, he launched into a sad tale of losing his wife, his home, his job, of being ashamed of himself.

Just then the train came to Terry's stop, and as he was getting off he turned to hear the old man invite the drunk to join him and tell him all about it, and to see the drunk sprawl along the seat, his head in the old man's lap.

That is emotional brilliance.

REVIEW QUESTIONS

1. What's the difference between ability 3, "personal connection," and ability 4, "social analysis"?
2. What does Goleman mean when he says that emotionally intelligent people are "nourishing" to others?
3. How is the discussion of self-monitoring in this reading similar to and different from the discussion of the same construct in chapter five's first reading, by Trenholm and Jensen?
4. What's *dyssemia*, and how does it fit into this reading?
5. Goleman says that "the two cardinal sins that almost always lead to rejec-tion" are (a) trying to _____ too soon and (b) being _____ the frame of reference."
6. How did the old man on the train outside Tokyo demonstrate a key princi-ple of aikido?

PROBES

1. Explain the balance that Goleman emphasizes is necessary between emo-tional intelligence and "an astute sense of one's own needs and feelings and how to fulfill them."
2. In this selection, Goleman does not describe in detail *how* emotional intelli-gence can result in using one's social polish in keeping with one's true feel-ings, rather than becoming an "anchorless social chameleon." What do you believe it takes to do this?
3. It's relatively easy to describe what Cecil in Goleman's example failed to learn—"to speak directly to others when spoken to; . . . to carry on a con-versation, not simply fall back on yes or no . . . replies," and so on. But it's more difficult to describe what parents (and other caregivers) need *to do* to be sure their children learn all these things. What do you believe are the most important ways to help young children learn emotional intelligence?
4. How does Goleman's focus on *nonverbal* communication support or chal-lenge what's said about nonverbal communication in the last two readings in Chapter 4?

5. Young children can be brutally candid in their rejection of would-be play-mates. Do adults communicate these same messages in other ways? Or is rejection less common among adults? Discuss.
6. Goleman discusses a child named Roger who shows his emotional intelligence by checking with his playmate before committing himself "to be in a helicopter or an airplane." Describe an adult version of this same communication move.

NOTES

1. Thomas Hatch, "Social Intelligence in Young Children," paper delivered at the annual meeting of the American Psychological Association (1990).
2. Social chameleons: Mark Snyder, "Impression Management: The Self in Social Interaction," in L. S. Wrightsman and K. Deaux, *Social Psychology in the '80s* (Monterey, CA: Brooks/Cole, 1981).
3. E. Lakin Phillips, *The Social Skills Basis of Psychopathology* (New York: Grune and Stratton, 1978), p. 140.
4. Nonverbal learning disorders: Stephen Nowicki and Marshall Duke, *Helping the Child Who Doesn't Fit In* (Atlanta: Peachtree Publishers, 1992). See also Byron Rourke, *Nonverbal Learning Disabilities* (New York: Guilford Press, 1989).
5. Nowicki and Duke, *Helping the Child Who Doesn't Fit In.*
6. This vignette, and the review of research on entering a group, is from Martha Putallaz and Aviva Wasserman, "Children's Entry Behavior," in Steven Asher and John Coie, eds., *Peer Rejection in Childhood* (New York: Cambridge University Press, 1990).
7. Putallaz and Wasserman, "Children's Entry Behavior."
8. Hatch, "Social Intelligence in Young Children."

This chapter's first two readings explain how our selves are relational or communicative and define interpersonal intelligence. This one is more personal. It comes from a book written to help college and university students of all ages who want to expand their self-awareness and explore the choices available to them in significant areas of their lives. It is a personal reading partly because it asks you to focus on yourself as you read it, and partly because its authors, Gerald Corey and Marianne Schneider-Corey, write about their personal experiences. This reading encourages you to look critically at the *why* of your existence and to clarify the sources of your values. The

authors emphasize the importance of listening to your own inner desires and feelings as you ask three key questions, "Who am I?" "Where
am I going?" and "Why?" But they also make the point that "meaning
in life is found through intense relationships with others, not through
an exclusive and narrow pursuit of self-realization."

The Coreys encourage you to reflect on your philosophy of life,
your response to religion, and your values. You might think a discussion of religion is out of place in a textbook, but, as they point out, religious faith can be a powerful source of meaning and purpose. Even
reflection that begins with the question "Is there a God?" is religious,
and as you extend your exploration of some of the related questions
they suggest, you can often learn a great deal about your self. When I
grew up, for example, church was just something the family automatically did on Sunday, and my responses were predictable. I didn't hate
it, but I also didn't get much out of it. For a time I didn't have much
connection with religion, but when I attended a church-sponsored college and developed some religious friends, I discovered some deep
resonances between my fundamental values and those I saw being
lived out by some of the religious people I knew. Since then I've prof-
ited a great deal from the academic writings of some theologians and
from friendships with people with a variety of religious commitments.
My spiritual life is important to me, and I define myself in part as a
"religious" person.

Your experience might be totally different. But the point these authors reinforce is that, as part of your study of interpersonal communication, it can be helpful to reflect on your own philosophy, values, and
religious beliefs. Why? Because (a) they have been developed in your
past communication experiences, (b) they will be changed by communication you experience in the future, and (c) your philosophy, values,
and religious beliefs affect how you communicate with others today.

Meaning and Values

Gerald Corey and Marianne Schneider-Corey

In this chapter we encourage you to look critically at the *why* of your existence,
to clarify the sources of your values, and to reflect on questions such as these: In
what direction am I moving in my life? What do I have to show for my years on
this earth so far? Where have I been, where am I now, and where do I want to
go? What steps can I take to make the changes I have decided on?

Many who are fortunate enough to achieve power, fame, success, and material comfort nevertheless experience a sense of emptiness. Although they may not be able to articulate what is lacking in their lives, they know that something is amiss. The astronomical number of pills and drugs consumed to allay the symptoms of this "existential vacuum"—depression and anxiety—is evidence of our failure to find values that allow us to make sense of our place in the world. In *Habits of the Heart*, Bellah and his colleagues (1985) found among the people they interviewed a growing interest in finding purpose in their lives. Although our achievements as a society are enormous, we seem to be hovering on the very brink of disaster, not only from internal conflict but also from societal incoherence. Bellah and his associates assert that the core problem with our society is that we have put our own good, as individuals and as groups, ahead of the common good.

The need for a sense of meaning is manifested by the increased interest in religion, especially among young people in college. A student told us recently that in her English class of twenty students, four of them had selected religion as a topic for a composition dealing with a conflict in their lives. Other signs of the search for meaning include the widespread interest in Eastern and other philosophies, the use of meditation, the number of self-help and inspirational books published each year, the experimentation with different lifestyles, and even the college courses in personal adjustment!

The paradox of our contemporary society is that although we have the benefits of technological progress, we are still not satisfied. We have become increasingly troubled about ourselves and our place in the world, we have less certainty about morality, and we are less sure that there is any meaning or purpose in the universe (Carr, 1988, p. 167). It seems fair to say that we are caught up in a crisis of meaning and values.

OUR SEARCH FOR IDENTITY

The discovery of meaning and values is essentially related to our achievement of identity as a person. The quest for identity involves a commitment to give birth to ourselves by exploring the meaning of our uniqueness and humanity. A major problem for many people is that they have lost a sense of self, because they have directed their search for identity outside themselves. In their attempt to be liked and accepted by everyone, they have become finely tuned to what *others* expect of them but alienated from their *own* inner desires and feelings. As Rollo May (1973) observes, they are able to *respond* but not to *choose*. Indeed, May sees inner emptiness as the chief problem in contemporary society; too many of us, he says, have become "hollow people" who have very little understanding of who we are and what we feel. He cites one person's succinct description: "I'm just a collection of mirrors, reflecting what everyone expects of me" (p. 15).

Moustakas (1975) describes the same alienation from self that May talks about. For Moustakas, alienation is "the developing of a life outlined and determined by others, rather than a life based on one's own inner experience" (p. 31). If we become alienated from ourselves, we don't trust our own feelings but respond automatically to others as we think they want us to respond. As a consequence, Moustakas writes, we live in a world devoid of excitement, risk, and meaning. . . .

Achieving identity doesn't necessarily mean stubbornly clinging to a certain way of thinking or behaving. Instead, it may involve trusting ourselves enough to become open to new possibilities. Nor is an identity something we achieve for all time; rather, we need to be continually willing to reexamine our patterns and our priorities, our habits and relationships. Above all, we need to develop the ability to listen to our inner selves and trust what we hear. To take just one example, some students for whom academic life has become stale and empty have chosen to leave it in response to their inner feelings. Some have opted to travel and live modestly for a time, taking in new cultures and even assimilating into them for a while. They may not be directly engaged in preparing for a career and, in that sense, "establishing" themselves, but they are achieving their own identities by being open to new experiences and ways of being. For some of them, it may take real courage to resist the pressure to settle down in a career or "complete" their education.

Our search for identity involves asking three key existential questions, none of which has easy or definite answers: Who am I? Where am I going? Why?

The question Who am I? is never settled once and for all, for it can be answered differently at different times in our life. We need to revise our life, especially when old identities no longer seem to supply a meaning or give us direction. As we have seen, we must decide whether to let others tell us who we are or to take a stand and define ourselves.

Where am I going? This issue relates to our plans for a lifetime and the means we expect to use in attaining our goals. Like the previous question, this one demands periodic review. Our life goals are not set once and for all. Again, do we show the courage it takes to decide for ourselves where we are going, or do we look for a guru to show us where to go?

Asking the question Why? and searching for reasons are characteristics of being human. We face a rapidly changing world in which old values give way to new ones or to none at all. Part of shaping an identity implies that we are actively searching for meaning, trying to make sense of the world in which we find ourselves. . . .

Finding Meaning by Transcending Personal Interests

Carr (1988) concludes that what most of us want is to make a difference in the world. The process of becoming self-actualizing begins as a personal search. Although self-acceptance is a prerequisite for meaningful interpersonal relationships, there is a quest to go beyond self-centered interests. Ultimately, we want to establish connections with others in society, and we want to make a contribution. Likewise, Bellah and his colleagues (1985) conclude that meaning in life is found through intense relationships with others, not through an exclusive and narrow pursuit of self-realization. In their interviews with many people they found a desire to move beyond the isolated self. Our common life requires more than an exclusive concern with material accumulation. These authors maintain that a reconstituting of the social world is required, involving a transformation of consciousness.

Developing a Philosophy of Life

A philosophy of life is made up of the fundamental beliefs, attitudes, and values that govern a person's behavior. Many students have said that they hadn't really thought much about their philosophy of life. However, the fact that we've never explicitly defined the components of our philosophy doesn't mean that we are completely without one. All of us do operate on the basis of general assumptions about ourselves, others, and the world. Thus, the first step in actively developing a philosophy of life is to formulate a clearer picture of our present attitudes and beliefs.

We have all been developing an implicit philosophy of life since we first began, as children, to wonder about life and death, love and hate, joy and fear, and the nature of the universe. We probably didn't need to be taught to be curious about such questions; raising them seems to be a natural part of human development. If we were fortunate, adults took the time to engage in dialogue with us, instead of discouraging us from asking questions and deadening some of our innate curiosity.

During the adolescent years the process of questioning usually assumes new dimensions. Adolescents who have been allowed to question and think for themselves as children begin to get involved in a more advanced set of issues. Many of the adolescents we've encountered in classes and workshops have at one time or another struggled with questions such as the following:

- Are the values that I've believed in for all these years the values I want to continue to live by?
- Where did I get my values? Are they still valid for me? Are there additional sources from which I can derive new values?
- Is there a God? What is the nature of the hereafter? What is my conception of a God? What does religion mean in my life? What kind of religion do I choose for myself? Does religion have any value for me?
- What do I base my ethical and moral decisions on? Peer-group standards? Parental standards? The normative values of my society?
- What explains the inhumanity I see in our world?
- What kind of future do I want? What can I do about actively creating this kind of future?

These are only a few of the questions that many adolescents think about and perhaps answer for themselves. However, a philosophy of life is not something we arrive at once and for all during our adolescent years. The development of a philosophy of life continues as long as we live. As long as we remain curious and open to new learning, we can revise and rebuild our conceptions of the world. Life may have a particular meaning for us during adolescence, a new meaning during adulthood, and still another meaning as we reach old age. Indeed, if we don't remain open to basic changes in our views of life, we may find it difficult to adjust to changed circumstances.

Keeping in mind that developing a philosophy of life is a continuing activity of examining and modifying the values we live by, you may find the following suggestions helpful as you go about formulating and reforming your own philosophy:

- Frequently create time to be alone in reflective thought.
- Consider what meaning the fact of your eventual death has for the present moment.
- Make use of significant contacts with others who are willing to challenge your beliefs and the degree to which you live by them.
- Adopt an accepting attitude toward those whose belief systems differ from yours, and develop a willingness to test your own beliefs. . . .

Religion and Meaning: A Personal View

Religious faith can be a powerful source of meaning and purpose. Religion helps many people make sense out of the universe and the mystery of our purpose in living. Like any other potential source of meaning, religious faith seems most authentic and valuable when it enables us to become as fully human as possible. This means that religion helps us get in touch with our own powers of thinking, feeling, deciding, willing, and acting. You might consider reflecting on the following questions about your religion to determine whether it is a constructive force in your life:

- Does my religion provide me with a set of values that is congruent with the way I live my life?
- Does my religion assist me in better understanding the meaning of life and death?
- Does my religion allow tolerance for others who see the world differently from me?
- Does my religion provide me with a sense of peace and serenity?
- Is my religious faith something that I actively choose or passively accept?
- Do my religious beliefs help me live life fully and treat others with respect and concern?
- Does my religion help me integrate my experience and make sense of the world?
- Does my religion encourage me to exercise my freedom and to assume the responsibility for the direction of my own life?
- Are my religious beliefs helping me become more of the person I'd like to become?
- Does my religion encourage me to question life and keep myself open to new learning?

As you take time for self-examination, how able are you to answer these questions in a way that is meaningful and satisfying to you? If you are honest with yourself, perhaps you will find that you have not really critically evaluated the sources of your spiritual and religious beliefs. Although you may hesitate to question your belief system out of a fear of weakening or undermining your faith, the opposite might well be true: demonstrating the courage to question your beliefs and values might strengthen them. As we have mentioned, increasing numbers of people seem to be deciding that a religious faith is necessary if they are to find an order and purpose in life. At the same time, many others insist that religion only impedes the quest for meaning or that it is incompatible with contemporary beliefs in other areas of life. What seems essential is that our acceptance or rejection of religious faith come authentically from within ourselves and that we remain open to new experience and learning, whatever points of view we decide on.

It is perhaps worth emphasizing that a "religion" may take the form of a system of beliefs and values concerning the ultimate questions in life rather than (or in addition to) membership in a church. People who belong to a church may not be "religious" in this sense, and others may consider themselves religious even though they are atheists or agnostics. Like almost anything else in human life, religion (or irreligion) can be bent to worthwhile or base purposes.

In my own experience, I (Jerry) have found religion most valuable when it is a challenge to broaden my choices and potential, rather than a restrictive influence. Until I was about 30, I tended to think of my religion as a package of ready-made answers for all the crises of life and was willing to let my church make many key decisions for me. I now think that I was experiencing too much anxiety in many areas of life to take full responsibility for my choices. My religious training had taught me that I should look to the authority of the church for ultimate answers in the areas of morality, value, and purpose. Like many other people I was encouraged to learn the "correct" answers and conform my thinking to them. Now, when I think of religion as a positive force, I think of it as being *freeing*, in the sense that it encourages me to trust myself, to discover the sources of strength and integrity within myself, and to assume responsibility for my own choices.

Although as an adult I've questioned and altered many of the religious teachings with which I was raised, I haven't discarded many of my past moral and religious values. Many of them served a purpose earlier in my life and, with modification, are still meaningful for me. However, whether or not I continue to hold the beliefs and values I've been taught, it seems crucial to me that I be willing to subject them to scrutiny. If they hold up under challenge, I can reincorporate them; by the same token, I can continue to examine the new beliefs and values I acquire.

My (Marianne's) religious faith has always been a positive force in my life. Sometimes people who are religious suffer from feelings of guilt and fears of damnation. This saddens me greatly, for if this is the case, religion ceases being a positive and powerful force in one's life. For me, religion helps me with an inner strength on which I can rely and that helps me to overcome difficulties that life presents. Although religion was encouraged in my childhood, it was never forced on me. It was a practice that I wanted to emulate because I saw the positive effects it had on the people in my life. Religion was practiced more than it was preached. The questions that we asked you to reflect on earlier are ones that I pose to myself as well. I want to be sure that I am aware of my beliefs and the necessity for making changes if I am not satisfied with my answers. . . .

Becoming Aware of How Your Values Operate

Your values influence what you do; your daily behavior is an expression of your basic values. We encourage you to make the time to continue examining the source of your values to determine if they are appropriate for you at this time in your life. Furthermore, it is essential that you be aware of the significant impact your value system has on your relationships with others. In our view, it is not appropriate for you to push your values on others, to assume a judgmental stance toward those who have a different world view, or to strive to convert others to adopt your perspective on life. Indeed, if you are secure in your values and basic beliefs, you will not be threatened by those who have a different set of beliefs and values.

In *God's Love Song,* Maier (1991) wonders how anyone can claim to have found the only way, not only for himself or herself but also for everyone else. We strongly agree with his view that there is a unique way for each person, however different that may be from the way of anyone else. As a minister, Sam Maier teaches that diversity shared not only is beautiful but also fosters understanding, caring, and the creation of community. He puts this message in a powerful and poetic way:

> It is heartening to find communities where the emphasis is placed upon each person having the opportunity to:
> * share what is vital and meaningful out of one's own experience;
> * listen to what is vital and meaningful to others;
> * not expect or demand that anyone else do it exactly the same way as oneself.
> (p. 3)

Reverend Maier's message is well worth contemplating. Although you might clarify a set of values that seem to work for you, we would hope that you respect the values of others that may be quite different from yours. It is not that one is right and the other is wrong. The diversity of cultures, religions, and world views implies a necessity not only to tolerate differences but also to embrace diverse paths toward meaning in life.

Whatever your own values are, they can be further clarified and strengthened if you entertain open discussion of various viewpoints and cultivate a nonjudgmental attitude toward diversity. You might raise questions such as:

* Where did I develop my values?
* Are my values open to modification?
* Have I challenged my values, and am I open to being challenged by others?

- Do I insist that the world remain the same now as it was earlier in my life?
- Do I feel so deeply committed to any of my values that I'm likely to push my friends and family members to accept them?
- How would I communicate my values to others without imposing those values?
- How do my own values and beliefs affect my behavior?
- Am I willing to accept people who hold different values?
- Do I avoid judging others if they think, feel, or act in different ways from myself? . . .

WHERE TO GO FROM HERE: CONTINUING YOUR PERSONAL GROWTH

. . . As you consider what experiences for continued personal growth you are likely to choose at this time, be aware that your meaning in life is not cast in concrete. As you change, you can expect that what brings meaning to your life will also change. The projects that you were deeply absorbed in as an adolescent may hold little meaning for you today. And where and how you discover meaning today may not be the pattern for some future period.

You can deliberately choose experiences that will help you actualize your potentials. Perhaps you remember reading a book or seeing a film that had a profound impact on you and really seemed to put things in perspective. Certainly, reading books that deal with significant issues in your life can be a growth experience in itself, as well as an encouragement to try new things.

Often, we make all sorts of resolutions about what we'd like to be doing in our life or about experiences we want to share with others, and then we fail to carry them out. Is this true of you? Are there activities you value yet rarely get around to doing? Perhaps you tell yourself that you prize making new friendships; yet you find that you do very little to actually initiate any contacts. Or perhaps you derive satisfaction from growing vegetables or puttering in your garden and yet find many reasons to neglect this activity. You might tell yourself that you'd love to take a day or two just to be alone and yet never get around to arranging it. When you stop to think about it, aren't there choices you could be making right now that would make your life a richer one? How would you really like to be spending your time? What changes are you willing to make today, this week, this month, this year?

In addition to activities that you enjoy but don't engage in as often as you'd like, there are undoubtedly many new things you might consider trying out as ways of adding meaning to your life and developing your potentials. You might consider making a contract with yourself to start now on a definite plan of action, instead of putting it off until next week or next year. Some of the ways in which many people choose to challenge themselves to grow include the following:

- finding hobbies that develop new sides of themselves
- going to plays, concerts, and museums

- taking courses in pottery making, wine tasting, guitar playing, and innumerable other special interests
- getting involved in exciting work projects or actively pursuing forms of work that will lead to the development of hidden talents
- spending time alone to reflect on the quality of their lives
- initiating contacts with others and perhaps developing an intimate relationship
- enrolling in continuing-education courses or earning a degree primarily for the satisfaction of learning
- doing volunteer work and helping to make others' lives better
- experiencing the mountains, the desert, and the ocean—by hiking, sailing, and so on
- becoming involved in religious activities or pursuing a spiritual path that is meaningful to them
- traveling to new places, especially to experience different cultures
- keeping a journal in which they record feelings and dreams
- sharing some of their dreams with a person they trust

Any list of ways of growing is only a sample, of course; the avenues to personal growth are as various as the people who choose them. Growth can occur in small ways, and there are many things that you can do on your own (or with friends or family) to continue your personal development. Perhaps the greatest hindrance to our growth as a person is our failure to allow ourselves to imagine all the possibilities that are open to us.

REVIEW QUESTIONS

1. What do these authors mean by "existential vacuum"?
2. What does it generally mean to "find meaning by transcending personal interests"?
3. According to these authors, how much of a person's philosophy of life is stable, and how much changes?
4. What rationale do the Coreys give for including the topic of religion in this chapter?
5. What's the difference between religious influences and values?
6. How do these authors view individual choice? How important is it?

PROBES

1. Do you agree that there is a widespread need for a sense of meaning among people you know, or do you think that these authors exaggerate the problem?
2. Before you read this essay, did you believe you had a "philosophy of life"? Do you now believe you do? What's it made up of?

3. What feelings are generated in you by this reading's discussion of religion? What experiences with others (family, friends, etc.) do those feelings grow out of?
4. How do you respond to Jerry's and Marianne's individual discussions of the roles of religion in their lives?
5. Do you agree that you can make conscious choices to change the directions of your personal growth? What examples from your own experience reinforce your view?

REFERENCES

1. Bellah, R. N., Madsen, R., Sullivan, W. M., Swidler, A., & Tipton, S. M. (1985). *Habits of the Heart: Individualism and Commitment in American Life.* New York: Harper & Row.
2. Carr, J. B. (1988). *Crisis In Intimacy: When Expectations Don't Meet Reality.* Pacific Grove, CA: Brooks/Cole.
3. Maier, S. (1991). *God's Love Song.* Corvallis, OR: Postal Instant Press.
4. May, R. (1973). *Man's Search for Himself.* New York: Dell.
5. Moustakas, C. (1975). *Finding Yourself, Finding Others.* Englewood Cliffs, NJ: Prentice-Hall.

––––––––

Harold Barrett is an award-winning professor of communication at California State University, Hayward. This reading is taken from his book, which approaches interpersonal communication from what he argues is the normal, natural, and pervasive human tendency to protect the self. As he puts it early in the reading, "our persistent and compelling need in communication is to give an account of ourselves." Barrett offers some specific ways to overcome the detrimental effects of defensiveness.

Barrett begins from the idea that, whenever we communicate, we want to influence our listeners—he calls them "audiences"—favorably about ourselves. Yet we can never be sure of their attitude toward us or of our capability to relate to their attitude. So we adopt a more or less rigid posture of defensiveness. Barrett anchors his analysis in the neo-Freudian explanation of the human self put forward by a psychologist named Heinz Kohut. Kohut argued that unless a person has had just about completely perfect parents and has been raised in a perfect network of relationships, he or she carries some "shame," some feelings of "emptiness, unfulfillment, and deficiency." So from this perspective shame is not necessarily bad; it's just part of what each human experiences. And this experience leads us "to invent modes of maintaining the self," some of which work positively and some of which work negatively.

One tension that arises in this situation is that "rewards of individualism increasingly come into conflict with rewards of community affiliation." That is, people can get caught between the "rock" of individual integrity and the "hard place" of getting along with others. Culture, especially ethnicity, helps determine how we cope with these tensions. But regardless of culture or ethnicity, Barrett writes, we're all struggling with similar issues. In short, regardless of who you are, says Barrett, "the great commandment is to maintain the self." And interpersonal contacts are the ones that both pose the greatest threats to the self and provide the most maintenance of it. This means that selves are "in play" in every interpersonal encounter—as Barrett puts it, in "every conversation, public speech, interview, and discussion." But there are also at least eight specific self-maintenance resources available to every communicator, and the last major section of this reading explains these eight resources—Barrett uses the term *topoi*—that people use to maintain their threatened selves.

Barrett begins by talking about how control can help maintain your sense of self. Then he discusses achievement, which can also help, so long as you avoid its extreme, which is perfectionism. The third resource, or *topos,* is opposition, which means "standing up for oneself." The fourth is attribution, or identifying responsibility. Anger, denial, withdrawal, and lying are the final four resources, or *topoi.* The last page of the reading encourages you to reflect on which resources you draw on in various situations.

I put this reading into this chapter in order to offer the opportunity to reflect on how the natural tendency to "protect your own ego" affects your interpersonal communicating. If Barrett and the scholars he cites are right, defensiveness is a normal and always-present human tendency. It can be helpful to think and talk about how this dynamic operates in our own communicating.

Maintaining the Self in Communication

Harold Barrett

LOOKING AFTER THE SELF

Interpersonal security is currently a common topic in the media. An example is a recent interview with Harvard political scientist Robert D. Putnam. Putnam believes that Americans have lost much of their willingness to trust. A generation

"Maintaining the Self in Communication" by Harold Barrett, from *Maintaining the Self in Communication.*

ago, when asked if they trusted other people, two-thirds said yes; now two-thirds say no. Americans are untrusting because they don't know each other, Putnam says. Today they are less connected to each other—and less happy.[1]

One result of this lack of connection and trust is a greater dedication to self-protection in communicating with others. Given a condition of insecurity, the solution is predictable: purposeful effort to look after and justify the self. Insecurity and protectiveness have always been a part of human interaction; the issue of the moment is about their increase. . . .

Self-maintenance behavior arises from some sense of uncertainty with others, from a perception of danger to the self—whether negligible or great, obscure or obvious. Thus we have defense mechanisms, as they are called. Theorist Karl E. Scheibe holds that *defense* mechanisms are so named in psychoanalytic theory because "the ego is considered to be under a more or less constant state of siege."[2] And, I would add, the communicator's response to the siege is *constant*.

It's easy to find testimony to the pervasiveness of insecurity and consequent safeguarding. Psychoanalytic theorist Marshall Edelson holds that defensiveness is "a ubiquitous aspect of human action." (Indeed, *any* use of language is defensive, he believes.)[3] Just yesterday I heard down at my little post office, "Why is everyone so damned defensive these days?"

A FUNCTION OF COMMUNICATION

Gregory Rochlin . . . offers this truth on the self (and self-esteem): "Its defense may bring the highest honors and justify the lowest violence."[4] Defending and thus maintaining the self, an ordinary function of communication, has both good and bad dimensions. Moreover, no mode of conduct is more fascinating in the drama of human interaction, as is apparent in the life stories of communicators, including those whose deeds we celebrate: Washington and Lincoln, Churchill and Roosevelt, Joan of Arc and Susan B. Anthony, Martin Luther and Martin Luther King, Jr.—as well as in those whose deeds we deplore: Joseph Stalin, Richard III, Adolf Hitler, and Joseph McCarthy. All of these notable figures were self-defenders in their communicating. Sigmund Freud said that defenses of the self direct the daily functioning of humankind. That's true, for better or worse.

There's high adventure and peril in communication, a fact that all of us seem to feel. Using athletic talk about teams playing defense ("D"), we can say that in the risky interactive game called communication, we play "D" at every moment. Knowing our ways, advisers urge, "Don't explain, don't complain!" ("Don't be defensive!") That's appealing advice, yet asking us not to look after ourselves is like asking us to give up being human.

Every Communicator's Story

Plots of every communicator's story are built around self-maintenance. Why so? Because self-worth is always at issue in communication; it hurts to be disrespected, dismissed, or disregarded. This may explain why **our persistent and compelling need in communication is to give an account of ourselves.** Intense or minimal, our motivation will never cease; protective messages will continue, whether as simple explanations, subtle excuses, hostile retorts, or anxious retreats. Such is our uneasiness about personal status and safety—apparent now more than ever before. A generation ago, Dean C. Barnlund saw signs of increasing interpersonal vulnerability—if not danger—and noted that a common use of communication is to act on our own behalf: "Communication arises out of the need to reduce uncertainty, to act effectively, to defend or strengthen the ego."[5] Thus, in studying the act of communication, we must include the fundamental needs of self as sources of motivation.

Now, before expanding the discussion, I want to present some concepts in communication that will be basic from this point on.

A Rhetorical Perspective

In this exploration of ordinary human interaction, I am guided by a rhetorical perspective on communication: that we *choose* ways to be with others, always with *purpose,* always seeking to be *effective* with them. That's what it means to be rhetorical in communication. Whether succeeding or failing, our aim is to use self-sustaining methods that will help us be effective. Psychologist Guy E. Swanson, in his scientific study of defenses, holds that defensive strategies of daily life, grounded in social interaction and interdependence, "are justifications tailored to social relations that are in danger and need of preservation." In other words, the goal is to adapt to others and maintain connections to them. In this, the choices are "likely to be determined by the nature of the social relationship concerned."[6] What's useful in maintaining one relationship may not be useful in another.

Characterized by strategic choice in the exchange of messages, the interactive function of communication is rhetorical. **To be rhetorical is to make choices for success.** Consequently, I will always use the word *communication* in a rhetorical sense, i.e., to refer to the symbolic interactions of people *exercising options* in saying things and pursuing their respective *purposes.* The rhetorical function is at the heart of communication, for participants put messages together to secure responses from each other . . .

In terms of rhetorical theory, those with whom we relate and communicate are our "audiences." Moreover, as audience-conscious communicators, we're never innocent in our efforts to get a response, for our intent is to "get something"; most fundamentally, it is to secure confirmation of the person we believe we are—or want to be. That's why mindfulness of *self*-status is foremost in communication—*always,* regardless of the occasion or apparent meaning of the message. **We can never be sure of ourselves, especially of the other's attitude toward us or of our capability to relate to that.** Possessed of a vulnerable self and being rhetorically aware, we involve ourselves inventively with relevant ideas and feelings, dealing with issues of the moment, seeking to be successful: we want to identify with audiences and be confirmed by them. . . .

The Rhetorical Imperative   Our strategies of interaction arise from a powerful rhetorical imperative: to affect audiences favorably about ourselves. Most of our self-sustaining measures work fairly well most of the time and with most audiences. Swanson found that defenses "enable us to go on acting in a coherent fashion," promising to "afford us whatever gratification seems possible. In that sense they are adequate—sometimes ingeniously so."[7] Stories of brilliant accomplishment can be traced to this very ingenuity: for example, the eloquence of Winston Churchill.[8] Yet, other stories tell of inadequate self-maintenance strategy: stories of personal failure, strained relations, and communicative disaster.

And remember our internal messages, those we send to ourselves. In an *intra*personal sense, excuses, denials, rationalizations, and other kinds of validating messages to ourselves about ourselves can help us to feel good with ourselves and to accept ourselves. Being comfortable with ourselves is basic to acting comfortably with others.

SHAME

For a psychological grounding on the nature of the social threat to the self, we can do no better than to consult Heinz Kohut, founder of the school of self psychology. Kohut's study of human behavior led to an important challenge to classical Freudian psychoanalytic thought. Departing from classical theory on the conflict of drives as fundamental to human behavior, Kohut centered instead on humankind's sense of self-defectiveness. In arguing his theory, he contrasted the family environment of Freud's time with that of subsequent generations, finding great differences in influences on child development. He contrasted the close household involvements and constant family stimulation of Freud's Victorian era with conditions of more recent decades. Families now have looser ties. There's much greater emotional distance among members, and one result is understimulation.

In Freudian theory, the *neurosis* is the common psychological complaint; it's tied to guilt and overstimulation from the persistent presence of family members, particularly parents. Guilt results from felt transgression, e.g., in violation of parental or social rule. But more recently, reflecting shame from felt neglect or deprivation, particularly parental, it is *narcissism* that is the common condition.

Shame results from a sense of felt defectiveness. In the absence of optimal parental or social constraint, the self is inadequately responded to, resulting in the narcissistic feelings of emptiness, unfulfillment, and deficiency. Thus, Kohut concluded, this is "the era of the endangered self."[9] The prime motivator of our time is shame. As we strive to protect ourselves against shame, our communicating is affected. . . .

To counter the shame of personal deficit (felt inadequacy), humans invent modes of maintaining the self: some facilitative, others maladaptive. Of course, shame has always been with us, and the response to it is not a new behavioral act. But now the incidence is much higher, leading to a higher incidence of corrective activity to protect and justify ourselves. Of course guilt continues, but given increased narcissistic injury, e.g., from neglect, shame has become the master emotion. We live in an age of diminished parental presence and authority and in a general culture marked by increased social disregard. Consequently, we are provided with less feedback on connectedness and worth—or less constructive feedback. We are more on our own and more likely to question our adequacy, experience social endangerment, and respond self-protectively. The results—good and bad, hardly noticeable or blatant—appear in all daily communication: at home, on the job, at school—everywhere. . . .

ON CULTURE AND SOCIALIZATION

Consider the following premise and implications for communication: **Rewards of individualism increasingly come into conflict with rewards of community affiliation.** "I want to be *me,* but I need *you*" expresses this personal-interpersonal conflict of our time: Or "It's great to be a person apart from others, but I need things from them." Issues of the conflict can be set out in various subjective terms:

- being gloriously alone and independent versus being safely associated and interdependent
- magnifying personal differences versus acknowledging kinship with others
- keeping distance versus seeking intimacy
- suffering the pain of separation versus enjoying the compensations of communication

The communicator's dilemma is about wanting to rely on self-confirmation versus needing the confirmation of others. It's a question of in*tra*personal (individual) versus in*ter*personal (social) satisfaction. It's an old story but with numerous postmodern twists and significant connections to other conditions of this age.[10] The dilemma is basic to the study of maintaining the self in communication.

East and West

At the outset, let's recognize the fact of cultural diversity in communication patterns. For example, in the United States, there is variance from culture to culture in strategies of self-maintenance—and from family to family, gender to gender, and from region to region. Communicators and students of communication should be aware that differences exist, and should be attentive to specific instances, some of which may influence the character of a moment of communication.

Thus we take the workings of socialization into account when studying variations in communication methods. And though anthropologists occasionally point to an isolated culture in which constraints on infant behavior appear to be minimal, apparently all cultures impose a socialization process on their children, one that moderates expression of their natural and normal narcissism. Certain differences in self-perception observed among Western and Eastern cultures can be traced to variations in the tightness of socialization processes that are imposed, primarily during the first two years or so of life. In some cultures, the social framing of the self is keen, and narcissism is actively suppressed, i.e., expressions of self and self-fulfillment are discouraged. The most familiar examples are collectivistic cultures like those of Asia. In others, such as the traditionally individualistic cultures of North America, greater encouragement is given to development of a self and related behaviors.

We know that in East Asian cultures, shame is a product of ardent socialization and group association. But in North American cultures . . . individuals value independence, and they feel shame when they sense personal inadequacy. Thus they seek some kind of exoneration or justification when they perceive themselves to be in violation of their self-concept. Pride, respect, trust, specific kinds of prowess, and other personal mandates are among the major issues. East Asians feel shame when they violate group norms, when their behavior hurts the group.

But note the common property. While forces of socialization differ in intensity, people of every culture and background possess a self that is subject to threat and injury. And all are influenced by a concept of self. For instance, the pain that East Asians feel in bringing discredit to the group comes from knowing that they have violated their concept on group allegiance. Defending against that shame—maintaining or saving face—is necessary because self-worth and continuation of benefits of membership are in the balance. . . .

When interpersonally uncertain or threatened, people on all continents respond protectively. Thus **the great commandment is to maintain the self. . . .**

Of the Highest Order

Self-maintenance activity is more than mere habit; it pursues a major goal and is carried on with structures that have become integral to one's total being. Looking after the self has a place of the highest order in everyone's life.

. . . First of all, each of us has a self-concept: a demanding and assertive personal view of who we are and how we want to be seen and taken, of the kind of person we feel ourselves to be or the kind of person we think we *ought* to be. Specific reflections of this insistent self-concept appear in our attitudes, values and ideals, ways of doing, and positions on just about anything that is important to us.

Second, each of us needs to be treated as a worthy person and cared about—at least, to be taken seriously and respected. We need others to support and confirm us in who we are. In a word, self-esteem is a critical personal factor in communicating; it has to do with how you pay attention to my *self* needs and I to yours. **Climates of mutual support—and nonsupport—are created by the two of us together, as we bring our needy and sensitive selves to each other.**

. . . Effort to uphold and justify the self arises from threat to individual well-being—and it appears most obviously in *interpersonal* communication, as we put ourselves in association with others. And the fear of being hurt, offended, disqualified, or diminished in some way can be very strong. . . .

The All-Powerful Self-Concept

What do the incidents below suggest about the self-concept and the need to be regarded well? Note the variety of motivating circumstances and how the individuals met ordinary human challenges. The circumstances are in italics.

Offended and wanting revenge, he vowed, "I'm gonna tell everyone what I know about her!"

Pleased with acknowledgment and praise, he modestly admitted, "Well, yes, I was the one who assisted him with CPR."

Unwilling to accept an almost unbearable feeling of defeat, she proclaimed, "I feel great! No problem! None whatever!"

Stinging from a felt attack on her religion, she never said another word during the entire evening.

Jolted by a sudden and loud command to leave the room, she cringed and murmured submissively, "Yes, ma'am."

Consumed with jealousy, he held her shoulders tightly and demanded, "Where in hell were you when I called seventeen times last night?"

Add to these instances all those messages communicated by persons who feel *slighted, put down, praised only faintly, unfairly compared, ridiculed,* or *passed over.* There's pain in *feeling unwanted and rejected, "out of one's element," unappreciated and misunderstood, incompetent*—and *believing oneself to be an imposter, a victim, weak link, traitor to the cause, ugly duckling,* or *an outsider.*

What about You?

Then there's you. Are you ever defensive or anxious to prove your worth? Say "Yes," because I know you are. Like the rest of us, you have a vulnerable self. It's disturbing to you to feel neglected or perceived as less than you think you ought to be. You have pride but also occasional feelings of inadequacy; you need recognition and approval. Feeling insecure at times about your place in life or your status at home, work, or school, you try harder—you're anxious to do better, to feel good about yourself or show that you're somebody. Much of such effort to achieve is beneficial, but it doesn't always come off smoothly. Sometimes there's distracting anger and hostility, criticism of self and others, backing off, and hiding out.

Try This   Recall a recent intense urge to protect yourself: when you felt that "call to action," to justify your background, explain your sexual orientation, stand behind your family, or vindicate your profession or political party or favorite music group. Or think back to how you felt down deep when you sensed that someone was trying to

- manipulate you or boss you around. What was your response to this felt abuse?
- lord it over you, acting in a superior manner. How did you handle that interpersonal wrong?
- impose on you a rigid and unacceptable point of view. What did you do about that?
- be noncommittal with you, remaining adamantly silent and evasive. How did you meet that?

On such occasions, how did you react? With a self-maintenance strategy? Quite likely. If so, what form did it take?

HOW PREVALENT IS THIS BEHAVIOR?

Self-maintenance strategies in communication appear in all relationships and interpersonal events: in friendships, romantic relationships, family systems, professional situations, church organizations, political entities, all school groups, and so forth. . . .

Who can begin to calculate the vast amount of communicative energy spent in ordinary self-maintenance by one ordinary person in one ordinary day? That's a good question, for it suggests a fact: **A degree of uncertainty about one's social safety or status operates in every message sent: in every conversation, public speech, interview, and discussion.** And it's a part of every display of "attitude," as we call some kinds of scornful behavior or insolence.

Human uncertainty is one of the staple elements of television situation comedies. It's prominent in the lives of characters in novels, stage plays, movies, and comic strips. One of the most lovable insecure comic strip people is Cathy; her self-maintenance strategies are quite true to life. Without conditions of self-doubt and unpredictability on personal status, communication in the Doonesbury and Dilbert strips would be literally unreal. The conditions of characters would be false and the stories unappealing. Can you identify any important character in any well-written piece of fiction who is fully secure? I can't. The characters of *good* fiction are *real* in their self-maintenance activity.

Now, when talking about proving the self, justifying, and so forth, we must acknowledge (and be grateful for) the good results that often occur. Worthy accomplishment, professional success, and good works all have beginnings related to self-maintenance needs, in that all are associated with requirements of security and support—and of choices made to meet those requirements. Thus there are two possible consequences: Our self-protective ways *do* find positive and useful expression, but sometimes they function negatively against our best interests: for example, when they take the shape of neglectfulness or some kind of abuse. It follows that communicative interaction, energized with goals of self-maintenance, ranges from stimulating and constructive dialogue and rewarding interpersonal communication to personal attack and counter-attack. Whether obvious or indistinct, strategies of self-care are ever-present in communication. . . .

SELF-MAINTENANCE IN COMMUNICATION: EIGHT *TOPOI*

Is there a useful way to categorize self-maintenance resources available for communication? Classically, we have the psychological nomenclature called "defense mechanisms." Remember those? They have names like rationalization, repression, regression, projection, introjection, sublimation, and so forth.

But rather than adopt a list of mental "mechanisms" and end up with nothing but an outline of abstractions, we must find categories that will reflect a sense of the behavioral dynamics of communicative *interaction.* Any practical study of self-maintenance strategies will take account of the potent energy involved, while emphasizing the interactive give-and-take and ever-present fact of personal purpose. Consequently, we need action terms to depict what goes on, to give meaning to the justifying, qualifying, rationalizing, asserting, confronting, bragging, avoiding, excusing, soft-pedaling, soothing, supporting, and so forth of ordinary communicating. To this end, I have identified eight strategic groupings. They are expressed as common purposes: to control, achieve, oppose, attribute, express anger, deny, withdraw, and prevaricate.[11] Each of the eight *topoi* is a package, a collection of related options. Incidentally, *topoi* is a Greek word for topics. Aristotle used it. I like the word because it conveys the idea of *purposeful action* and connotes *strategic choice in interaction* and *variety of choice and opportunity in interaction.* . . . As you look over the eight categories, note those that seem to have appeared in your recent communications with others. You hear and see them every day.

1. Control

Needs of security and certainty move communicators to regulate events, to find strategies for making things happen favorably. The need to control may be compelling or casual, and specific behaviors are numerous. Aims relate to ordinary communicative effectiveness, e.g., in being ready to handle unwelcome surprises or shocks as they might arise. But the goal may extend beyond seeking ordinary communicative control and effectiveness. For example, contrast the simple act of a person's choosing appropriate telephone language in placing a catalog order (necessarily exercising some control) to the extreme of a parent's determination to regulate an adult child's social activities. Likewise, at work, one employee may be rather easygoing, getting the routine communicative jobs done without excessive exertion (though there's always *some* management of events in communication), while another person will act to gain complete personal dominance of all functions related to on-the-job interactions. The latter mode might be considered "more defensive" than the former. Yet another example is the individualistic, iron-handed executive who seems unable to delegate authority to others or make use of cooperative problem-solving methods.

2. Achievement

Achievement needs frequently lie behind acts like self-justification. Related strategies often operate at a sensible and relaxed level: for example, that of doing a job adequately and feeling good about it. But contrast that with a level of functioning that is tremendously intense—when the communicator is determined to be absolutely right or brilliant or unchallengeable—anxious to stand out over others. Behavior of this extreme type is commonly called "perfectionism."

An example of the extreme is the vice president whose quarterly reports consistently and unnecessarily double the length of other vps' reports. This person's fervent drive to achieve—and get credit for it—requires great expenditure of time and energy.

3. Opposition

Protection of the self is a purpose of messages using the *topos* of *Opposition*. In this instance, a communicator assumes a contrary stance in communication with others, e.g., in "standing up for oneself." It may be expressed in some cases as disagreement or disapproval and in other cases as abject repugnance or contempt. *Opposition*, whether taken as ordinary dissent, rebuttal, stubbornness, resistance, challenge, nonconformity, derision, obstinacy, negativity, or scorn—whether seen as spirited support of one's position or as fierce denunciation or counteraction—is prevalent in all quarters of daily life.

4. Attribution

Attribution is common in communication to maintain the self. Communicators frequently face "How did this happen?" issues and matters of cause, responsibility, fault, or blame. In "getting to the bottom of things," one may name someone responsible—or oneself. Whether the communicator's spirit is constructive or malicious, the motivation is often one of self-protection, from a need to ascribe blame or accountability, and so forth. In this way the communicator attempts to maintain personal equilibrium and satisfactory communication.

Examples include the employee who realizes his computation error and consequently accepts responsibility; an older brother who blames his little sister when he trips on the stairs; the baseball batter whose habit is to scowl at the umpire when he takes a called third strike; the well-intentioned soul who needs to know whom to *absolve*, and the person who is motivated to solve "Who dunnit?" puzzles of relationships, whether concerned with a minor disagreement or a serious interpersonal conflict. . . .

5. Anger

If or when one is inclined toward sustaining the self through *Anger*, one will express strong displeasure or perhaps resort to violent verbal attacks. Like all *topoi*, *Anger* may be either beneficial or harmful. Others may view the behavior as useful passion, righteous indignation, bad temper, sullenness, belligerence, wrath, resentment, or great furor.

One example is two drivers' heated exchange after racing to occupy that empty space in the parking lot. What's at the root of such expression? Fairness is an issue, as is self-worth. Thus do self-maintenance needs of these communicators enter in: They feel a need to stand up for themselves and protect their "rights." That's one reason why some businesses install a "Take-a-Number" system to facilitate fair turn-taking at the counter. Customers who become preoccupied with protecting themselves may be less likely to return than customers who feel secure.

6. Denial

When choosing *Denial* as a method of self-care, one seeks to dodge an unpleasant or threatening reality, whether with a customary strategy or a spur-of-the-moment choice. Such communication involves inventing a method to protect against facing the "truth" or the "facts." In refusing to perceive something that's psychologically menacing, the communicator attempts to insulate the self from it by negating reality.

For example, a person may deny the fact of someone's death and thus provide cushioning against loss. Another example is the middle-aged woman who prefers teenage-style clothes, thereby revealing both her self-perception and her protective regression. Then there's the father who, unwilling to accept his son's rather ordinary athletic ability, criticizes the coach for not nominating his boy to the all-star team.

7. Withdrawal

If maintaining the self through *Withdrawal,* one will shun a certain event or individual, retreat from a threatening scene, maintain silence and mental distance, assume a passive posture, repress thoughts or feelings, resist disclosure of feelings, or in any number of other ways protect against the dangers and discomforts of social participation or judgment.

8. Prevarication

Prevarication is self-protection involving falsehood, excuse-making, justification of personal beliefs or actions, inhibition, deceptive statement, evasion, and so forth. As with all *topoi*, the strategic aim is to uphold the self: the self-concept, self-esteem, or sense of worth. Other modes of *Prevarication* are equivocation, euphemizing, use of passive voice, and "waffling."

An example of *Prevarication* is the socially useful "white lie." Another is shown in the case of the project coordinator who when asked for a progress report responded evasively, "Everybody's working real hard on this one, Chief—yes sir. I'll have more to tell you at mid-week." In this case, what needs of the self is the communicator seeking to care for?

Selecting Useful *Topoi*

In the process of communication, one isn't restricted to drawing from only one of the eight *topoi*.[12] Some of us find ourselves using them all at various times. Also interesting is the view that choice of *topos* may depend on personality type. For instance, extroverts may favor expressions of *Anger,* while introverts may favor *Withdrawal*.[13] But our social consciousness dictates that our choice of *topos* will be influenced by our perception of the situation and conditions. Audience characteristics are particularly significant in communication. That is, we fashion our messages in accord with the likely reactions of others. Why? Because we humans are *rhetorical* creatures: practical, purposeful, and adaptable. That's a point not to be forgotten by communicators! . . .

Try This   From the twenty-five OCCASIONS FOR SELF-MAINTENANCE COMMUNICATION listed below, select one that relates to an experience you've had. Recall the occasion, and do the following:

1. Tell how in an insecure moment you came to perceive an exigence (some condition that required a response).
2. From which of the eight *topoi* did you draw for a strategic response? Was it one of the eight that I have discussed above? If not, what's your name for it?
3. Briefly stated, what message did you want to send? To whom did you send the message? What kinds of inward—intrapersonal—messages were a part of the process? Distinguish between verbal and nonverbal elements of the message. What result and feedback (response) did you want?

Occasions for Self-Maintenance Communication

When you . . .

- respond to the charge of damaging another's property
- are embarrassed after making a social error
- try to handle the boss's dissatisfaction with a job you've done
- seek satisfaction after an acquaintance spreads a false story
- feel hurt in not being invited to the party
- sense public criticism of your behavior
- take a comment as threatening to your self-image
- feel shunned by a friend
- feel slighted in a group activity
- don't want to face the facts or your true feelings

- hear a comment that seems to be critical of your race, religion, sex, family, or school
- are jolted by a loud command of a coach, parent, or other
- feel down deep that you do not believe yourself to be qualified, e.g., to be in college or a given profession ("I'm just an imposter.")
- feel apprehensive about a surprising change in company policy or a relationship
- have a feeling of not belonging in a certain group
- are jealous
- are unsure of your personal status with someone or some group
- feel socially awkward in a specific situation
- fear speaking up in class
- are denied an expected honor or reward
- sense diminishment of your reputation in the family or other group
- feel wronged by a boyfriend or girlfriend
- feel that you deserve better treatment from someone on whom you depend for confirmation
- feel incompetent as a writer, athlete, cook, mother, etc.
- feel lacking in good looks

REVIEW QUESTIONS

1. According to Barrett, what is a defense mechanism?
2. Barrett says he is "guided by a rhetorical perspective on communication." What does this mean?
3. Define *shame* as Barrett discusses it.
4. Explain the individual versus social-cultural tension that Barrett describes.
5. What's the difference between an individualistic and a collectivistic culture?
6. What's narcissism?
7. What's the difference between the first two *topoi*, control and achievement?

PROBES

1. I can imagine people agreeing with Barrett about the significance of defensiveness and appreciating the increased self-awareness that comes from reading this selection. And I can also imagine some people rejecting Barrett's analysis as too obscurely Freudian, negative and pessimistic, and ultimately not very productive. If we imagine a sliding scale between these two positions, where on the scale would you put your response to this reading?
2. Barrett argues that every single time we communicate we are partly engaged in defending our selves. Do you agree or disagree? Explain.

3. Which type of culture that Barrett discusses do you identify with—individualistic or collectivistic? How does this affect your communicating?

4. "Are you ever defensive or anxious to prove your worth?" Barrett asks. "Say 'Yes,' because I know you are. Like the rest of us, you have a vulnerable self." How do you respond to that part of the reading?

5. Compare and contrast Barrett's discussion of attribution and my discussion of fault and blame in Chapter 2.

6. What did you learn from the list of "occasions for self-maintenance communication" at the end of this selection?

NOTES

1. "Social Insecurity," *America West Airlines Magazine*, April 1996: 74, 76–77, 79–80.

2. "Historical Perspectives on the Presented Self," *The Self and Social Life*, ed. Barry R. Schlenker (New York: McGraw-Hill, 1985), pp. 33–64.

3. "Two Questions about Psychoanalysis and Poetry," *The Literary Freud: Mechanisms of Defense and the Poetic Will*, ed. Joseph H. Smith (New Haven: Yale UP, 1980), pp. 113–18. To demonstrate the ubiquity or prevalence of the defensiveness that Edelson notes, I can't resist quoting a line from a recent film version of *Shadowlands* (a story about the relationship of C. S. Lewis and Joy Davidman): "People read to know they're not alone." The quotation suggests that to be alone is to be unprotected, an unacceptable condition, and to read is to guard against that.

4. *Man's Aggression: The Defense of the Self* (Boston: Gambit, 1973), p. 216.

5. "Toward a Meaning-Centered Philosophy of Communication," *Journal of Communication* 12 (1962): 197–211.

6. *Ego Defenses and the Legitimation of Behavior* (Cambridge: Cambridge UP, 1988), p. 2.

7. *Ego Defenses*, p. 24.

8. See Heinz Kohut, *The Analysis of the Self* (London: Hogarth Press, 1971), pp. 108–9 and Kohut, *Self Psychology and the Humanities: Reflections on a New Psychoanalytic Approach*, ed. Charles B. Strozier (New York: Norton, 1985), pp. 12–13, 110, 198–99.

9. *The Restoration of the Self* (New York: International Universities Press, 1977), p. 290. For an important comment on Kohut's belief on shame as the central affect in narcissism, see Andrew P. Morrison, "Shame and the Psychology of the Self," *Kohut's Legacy: Contributions to Self Psychology*, ed. Paul E. Stepansky and Arnold Goldberg (Hillsdale: The Analytic Press, 1984).

10. In this regard, I recommend David Zarefsky's thoughtful (and rhetorical) exploration of the problem relating to the current conflict in the United States on diversity and community interests: *The Roots of American Community* (Boston: Allyn and Bacon, 1996).

11. Besides relying on my catalogue of extensive observations of human interaction and responses of focus groups, I have found two books particularly useful as sources for developing the eight *topoi:* Merle A. Fossum and Marilyn J. Mason, *Facing Shame: Families in Recovery* (New York: Norton, 1986) and Gershen Kaufman, *Shame: The Power of Caring,* 2nd ed. rev. (Cambridge, MA: Schenkman, 1985).
12. On the topic of choice in selecting maintenance strategies, defenses in particular, turn to George Vaillant, *The Wisdom of the Ego* (Cambridge: Harvard UP, 1993).
13. See Gershen Kaufman, *Shame,* p. 71.

T he previous readings in this chapter talk about the significance of identity in communication, and how people define themselves and each other as we communicate. This reading is a poignant example of how this process works, from the inside.

Richard Rodriguez is a widely-known, influential speaker and writer whose parents moved from Mexico to California. Rodriguez refers to himself as Hispanic rather than Latino, and the book this reading came from is simply called *Brown.*

The best way to "get the point" of this reading is to let yourself be drawn into it. Rodriguez is writing about how he defines himself and how he and other people like him are defined by the people with whom they communicate.

I purchased the book entitled *Brown* after listening to Rodriguez speak at what he refers to as his "collapsible double-irony on tour to hotel ballroom conferences and C-SPAN-televised luncheons and 'Diversity Week' lectures at universities." I was in the hotel ballroom room when, "for a fee," Rodriguez rose up to say, "I am not Latin American, because I am Hispanic. I am Hispanic because I live in the United States. *Thank you.*" As he puts it, "(For a larger fee, I will add there is no such thing as a Hispanic. *Thank you.*)" The group sponsoring the "hotel ballroom conference" I attended must have paid the larger fee, because I heard him say that, too.

What does it mean to negotiate this identity in the twenty-first century United States of America? What is risked? What rewards can be realized? How have the categories devised in 1973 by President Nixon's administration helped shape the culture U.S. citizens inhabit?

When Stuart Sigman writes in Chapter 2 that communication "matters," he is talking about the issues that Richard Rodriguez raises in this reading. When I talk about the connection between quality of communication and quality of life, I'm talking about the topics Rodriguez addresses here.

If you belong to a family that prefers "Latino" or "Chicano" to Hispanic, you will have some responses to Rodriguez that other readers don't have. How do these definitions position you in relation to him?

But regardless of your own ethnicity or other cultural identity, don't miss the basic point: self-definitions are negotiated (worked out) in communicating. And they matter.

Hispanic

Richard Rodriguez

Hi.spa'.nick. 1. Spanish, *adjective.* 2. Latin American, *adjective.* 3. Hispano, *noun.* An American citizen or resident of Spanish descent. 4. Ducking under the cyclone fence, *noun.* 5. Seen running from the scene of the crime, *adjective.* Clinging to a raft off the Florida coast. Elected mayor in New Jersey. Elevated to bishop or traded to the San Diego Padres. Awarded the golden pomegranate by the U.S. Census Bureau: "most fertile." Soon, an oxymoron: America's largest minority. An utter absurdity: "destined to outnumber blacks." A synonym for the future (salsa having replaced catsup on most American kitchen tables). Madonna's daughter. Sammy Sosa's son. Little Elián and his Great Big Family. A jillarioso novel about ten sisters, their sorrows and joys and intrauterine devices. The new face of American Protestantism: Evangelical minister, tats on his arms; wouldn't buy a used car from. Highest high school dropout rate; magical realism.

The question remains: Do Hispanics exist?

I tell myself, on mornings like this—the fog has burned off early—that I am really going to give it up. Hispanicism cannot interest me anymore. My desk a jumble of newspaper clippings. Look at all this! Folders. It looks like a set for *The Makropolous Case.* I will turn instead to the death agony of a moth, the gigantic shuddering of lantern-paper wings. Or I will count the wrinkles on Walden Pond. I will write some of those constipated, low-paying, fin de siècle essays about the difficulty of *saying* anything in this, our age. *Visi d'arte*, from now on, as Susan Sontag sang so memorably from the chapel of Sant' Andrea della Valle.

For years now I have pursued Hispanicism, as a solitary, self-appointed inspector in an old Hitchcock will dog some great hoax; amassing data; abstractedly setting down his coffee cup at a precarious angle to its saucer, to the stack of papers and books and maps on which it rests, because he is drawn to some flash-lit, spyglassed item in the morning paper. I am catching them up, slowly, inexorably, confident of the day—soon—when I shall publish my findings.

Soon. I take my collapsible double-irony on tour to hotel ballroom conferences and C-SPAN-televised luncheons and "Diversity Week" lectures at universities. For a fee, I rise to say I am not Latin American, because I am Hispanic. I am Hispanic because I live in the United States. *Thank you.* (For a larger fee, I will add there is no such thing as a Hispanic. *Thank you.*)

But this morning I have decided, after all, to join the hoax.

Hispanic has had its way with me. I suspect also with you. The years have convinced me that Hispanic is a noun that can't lose. An adjective with legs. There is money in it.

Hispanic (the noun, the adjective) has encouraged the Americanization of millions of Hispanics. But at the same time, Hispanic—the ascending tally announced by the U.S. Census Bureau—has encouraged the Latinization of non-Hispanics.

As a Hispanic, as a middle-aged noun, like Oscar Wilde descending to gaol, I now take my place in the booth provided within that unglamorous American fair devised by the Richard Nixon administration in 1973 (O.M.B. Statistical Directive 15). Within the Nixonian fair are five exposition halls:

BLACK;

WHITE;

ASIAN/PACIFIC ISLANDER;

NATIVE AMERICAN/ESKIMO;

HISPANIC.

They aren't much, these drafty rooms—about what you'd expect of government issue. Nixon's fair attempted to describe the world that exists by portraying a world that doesn't. Statisticians in overalls moved India—*oufff*—that heavy, spooled and whirligigged piece of Victorian mahogany, over beneath the green silk tent of Asia. Mayan Indians from the Yucatán were directed to the Hispanic pavilion (Spanish colonial), which they must share with Argentine tangoistas, Colombian drug dealers, and Russian Jews who remember Cuba from the viewpoint of Miami. Of the five ports, Hispanic has the least reference to blood. There is no such thing as Hispanic blood. (*Do I not bleed?*) Though I meet young Hispanics who imagine they descend from it.

Nixon's fair does at least succeed in portraying the United States in relation to the world. One can infer a globe from a pentagram.

Over my head, as I write these words, a New World Indian is singing in the language of the conquistador. (A Korean contractor, hired by my landlord, has enlisted a tribe of blue-jumpered Mexican Indians to reroof the apartment building where I live.) In trustworthy falsetto, the young man lodges a complaint against an intangible mistress unfond, as high above him as the stars, and as cold. Yesterday, as he was about to hoist a roll of tar paper, this same young man told me the choir of roofers, excepting "*el patron*," originate from a single village in a far state of Mexico. And a few minutes ago, I overheard them all—the Mexicans and the Korean contractor—negotiating their business in pidgin (Spanish, curiously; I would have expected English). Then my ceiling shook with their footfalls. And with bolts of tar paper flung upon it. My library leapt in its shelves—those ladies and gentlemen, so unaccustomed.

Tomorrow, having secured my abstractions against the rainy season, the Mexican Indians will fly away to some other rooftop in the city, while I must remain at this desk.

Why must I? Because my literary agent has encouraged from me a book that answers a simple question: *What do Hispanics mean to the life of America?* He asked me that question several years ago in a French restaurant on East Fifty-seventh Street, as I watched a waiter approach our table holding before him a shimmering *îles flottantes*. . . .

Surviving Chicanos (one still meets them) scorn the term Hispanic, in part because it was Richard Nixon who drafted the noun and who made the adjective uniform. Chicanos resist the term, as well, because it reduces the many and complicated stories of the Mexican in America to a mere chapter of a much larger saga that now includes Hondurans and Peruvians and Cubans. Chicanos resent having to share mythic space with parvenus and numerically lesser immigrant Latin American populations. After all, Mexican Americans number more than seventy percent of the nation's total Hispanics. And, Chicanos say, borrowing a tabula rasa from American Indians, we are not just another "immigrant" population in the United States. We were here before the *Mayflower*. Which is true enough, though "we" and "here" are blurred by imprecision. California was once Mexico, as were other parts of the Southwestern United States. So we were here when here was there. In truth, however, the majority of Mexican Americans, or our ancestors, crossed a border.

One meets Hispanics who refuse Hispanic because of its colonial tooling. Hispanic, they say, places Latin America (once more) under the rubric of Spain. An alternate noun the disaffected prefer is "Latino," because they imagine the term locates them in the Americas, which the term now does in all revised American dictionaries, because Latinos insist that it does. (What is language other than an agreement, like Greenwich Mean Time?) In fact, Latino commits Latin America to Iberian memory as surely as does Hispanic. And Latino is a Spanish word, thus also paying linguistic obeisance to Spain. For what, after all, does "Latin" refer to, if not the imperial root system?

Hispanicus sui.

My private argument with Latino is no more complicated than my dislike for a dictation of terms. I am Latino against my will: I write for several newspapers—the *Los Angeles Times* most often—papers that have chosen to warrant "Latino" over "Hispanic" as correct usage. The newspaper's computer becomes sensitive, not to say jumpy, as regards correct political usage. Every Hispanic the computer busts is digitally repatriated to Latino. As I therefore also become.

In fact, I do have a preference for Hispanic over Latino. To call oneself Hispanic is to admit a relationship to Latin America in English. *Soy* Hispanic is a brown assertion.

Hispanic nativists who, of course, would never call themselves Hispanic, nonetheless have a telling name for their next-door neighbors who are not Hispanic. The word is "Anglo." Do Irish Americans become Anglos? And do you suppose a Chinese American or an African American is an Anglo? Does the term define a group of Americans by virtue of a linguistic tie to England or by the lack of a tie to Spain? (Come now, think. Did no one in your family take a Spanish course? In high school?) In which case, the more interesting question becomes whether Hispanics who call Anglos Anglo are themselves Anglo?

Nevertheless, in a Texas high school, according to the *Dallas Morning News*, a gang of "Anglos" and a gang of "Hispanics" shed real blood in a nonfictional cafeteria, in imitation of a sixteenth-century sea battle the students doubtlessly never heard of. Who could have guessed that a European rivalry would play itself out several hundred years after Philip's Armada was sunk by Elizabeth's navie? And here? No other country in the world has been so confident of its freedom from memory. Yet Americans comically (because unknowingly) assume proxy roles within a centuries-old quarrel of tongues.

REVIEW QUESTIONS

1. Explain the distinctions Rodriguez makes among Hispanic, Latino, and Chicano. Why does he prefer Hispanic?
2. What does the presence of the Nixon-era categories say about how ethnicity is defined and negotiated in the United States?

PROBES

1. Rodriguez pokes fun at the way he takes "a fee" to appear before various, mainly white, audiences to say, "I am Hispanic" and in some situations, "There is no such thing as a Hispanic." What do you believe is his point here, on the surface and below? Is he ridiculing the groups who pay him these fees? Is he sad at having to continue to say this? Is he resolute in his battle with "Chicanos" and "Latinos"?

CHAPTER 4

Making Contact Verbally and Nonverbally

Τhis next reading starts with its own introduction and is longer than most, so I'll make this short. These pages come from the 1998 edition of an interpersonal communication text that I coauthored with Carole Logan, a colleague who teaches communication at the University of San Diego. As you can tell from the title, the reading reverses the popular tendency to discuss verbal and nonverbal communicating in separate chapters. We explain why at the start.

This selection is broad enough in coverage to give you a fairly comprehensive introduction to both language and most nonverbal cues. We resist the "verbal/nonverbal" dichotomy by locating the main communication building blocks on a continuum or sliding scale that runs from primarily verbal (written words) to mixed (vocal pacing, pause, loudness, pitch, and silence) to primarily nonverbal (gestures, eye gaze, facial expression, touch, and space). Our goal is to encourage you to view these aspects of your communicating as holistically as you can and to notice the ways the various kinds of cues affect each other.

We briefly review the three main ways language has been discussed—as a system of symbols, an activity, and what we call a "soup." Then we discuss some features of mixed and primarily nonverbal cues. If you read both this introductory overview and the three other readings in this chapter, I think you'll have a pretty decent understanding of these parts of communication's basic ingredients.

Verbal and Nonverbal Dimensions of Talk

John Stewart and Carole Logan

Interpersonal communication texts typically devote one chapter to verbal codes and a separate one to nonverbal communication. This practice began in the late 1960s when communication researchers and teachers first discovered the importance of the nonverbal parts of communicating—eye contact, body movement, facial expression, tone of voice, touch, silence, and so on. For about 30 years, most textbooks treated each subject as significant and distinct.

But now research is focusing more and more closely on conversations as people actually experience them, and it has become obvious that you can't really separate the verbal and nonverbal parts. In the words of two researchers, "It is impossible to study either verbal or nonverbal communication as isolated structures. Rather, these systems should be regarded as a unified communication construct."[1] And as teacher and theorist Wendy Leeds-Hurwitz puts it, "In discussing communication as consisting of verbal and nonverbal modes . . . we leave ourselves open to the impression that the two are somehow distinct and

"Verbal and Nonverbal Dimensions of Talk" by John Stewart and Carole Logan. Reprinted by permission of the senior author.

should be studied separately. This is not at all the case, and there is now a current body of literature devoted to rejoining the two."[2]

Interestingly, almost this same point was made at the beginning of the twentieth century by Ferdinand de Saussure, one of the founders of linguistics. Saussure said that language is like a sheet of paper, where sound makes up one side of the page and the concepts or thoughts make up the other. You can't pick up one side of the paper without picking up the other, and you can't cut one side without cutting the other. So it's best to think of them together.[3] We think the same way about the verbal and the nonverbal parts of communication; they're like the two sides of one sheet of paper.

This is actually the way they occur in human experience. For example, consider this conversation:

SCOTT: *(Smiling and nodding)* Hi, John Paul. Howzit goin'?

JOHN PAUL: *(Excited look)* Scott! *(Shaking hands)* It's good to see you! I heard you'd moved. Where've you *been?*

SCOTT: *(Smiling knowingly)* Nowhere, really. I've just been working and going to school. But Heather and I have been hangin' around together quite a bit.

JOHN PAUL: *(Teasing)* Yeah, I heard that. What's the story with you two anyway?

SCOTT: *(Playful but cagey)* What do you mean "What's the story"? We just like each other, and we spend a lot of time together.

JOHN PAUL: *(Still teasing)* Yeah, like all weekend. And every night. And most of the rest of the time.

SCOTT: *(Turning the tables)* Well, what about you and Bill? I've heard you two are a duo . . . partners . . . an item.

JOHN PAUL: *(A little shy)* Where'd you hear that? Yeah, it's pretty true. *(Brighter)* And it's kind of neat, actually. It's the first time I've felt like part of *a couple.* We might even get an apartment together. But he's got to get a job that pays more. I can't support both of us.

SCOTT: *(Friendly)* Sounds like you've got the same questions Heather and I have. But her folks are also a problem.

JOHN PAUL: *(Serious)* My mom and dad are fine. But Bill's parents don't know anything about us, and I'm trying to get him to change that. In fact, I was thinking that I'd like to talk to you about that. I also wonder how you and Heather plan to actually set up living together. But I've got to get to work now. Give me your new number so I can give you a call, okay?

John Paul and Scott build this conversation together by using verbal and nonverbal aspects of language simultaneously. There is never a point in the talk where these two parts of communicating are separate. When Scott's intent is to be "playful," he communicates this verbally and nonverbally to John Paul. When the tone of the conversation turns "serious," John Paul communicates this through posture, facial expression, and tone of voice, as well as through the words he chooses.

This chapter emphasizes the fact that people engaged in conversation construct all verbal and nonverbal aspects of talk together. To put it in researchers' terms, utterance meaning and nonverbal meaning are not discrete and independent.[4] This is true even of words written on a page. What you might consider to be "purely verbal" written words appear in a designed typeface, on a certain weight and color of paper, and surrounded by more or less white space. All of these nonverbal elements affect how people interpret the written words of any language. Similarly, even purely nonverbal behaviors, such as gestures or eye behavior, occur in the context of some spoken or written words. One way to sort out the verbal and nonverbal aspects of language is to think in terms of a continuum or sliding scale like the following.

Primarily Verbal ——— Mixed ——————— Primarily Nonverbal
written words　　　　vocal pacing,　　　　gestures, eye gaze,
　　　　　　　　　　pause, loudness,　　　 facial expression,
　　　　　　　　　　pitch, silence　　　　 touch, space

Written words are classified as primarily verbal for the reasons we just gave. They appear in a nonverbal typeface surrounded by nonverbal space, but readers interpret or make meaning primarily on the basis of the words' verbal content. To the degree that you can isolate the words speakers use, they might be considered primarily verbal, too. But spoken words always come with vocal pacing, pause, loudness, pitch, and silence, and as a result these are labeled mixed. Gestures, facial expression, and so on are labeled primarily nonverbal because they can occur without words, but they are usually interpreted in the context of spoken words.

It would be possible to highlight some of the verbal parts of Scott and John Paul's conversation. Scott says, "Howzit going'?" rather than "How is it going?" or the even more formal "It's good to see you again." He uses the general phrase "spending a lot of time together" rather than a more specific description of his and Heather's activities. For John Paul, the word "couple" is significant. The two share an understanding of what it means, in this context, to say that parents are a "problem."

We could also pinpoint some nonverbal aspects of the conversation. For example, Scott's initial tone of voice is pretty low-key, but John Paul sounds excited to see him. They touch briefly as they shake hands. Their smiles "say" several different things—"It's good to see you." "I like you." "I'm teasing." "I'm teasing back." "We've got something in common." Since they're friends, they stand fairly close together.

In order to focus on the exclusively verbal or exclusively nonverbal parts, however, we'd have to distort what actually happens in Scott and John Paul's conversation. As we've said, the verbal and nonverbal aspects of the conversation are as inseparable as the two sides of a piece of paper. So in this reading:

We describe three approaches to *primarily verbal* cues ("language") that help clarify our reasons for combining verbal and nonverbal communication.

We discuss how several *mixed* cues affect meaning-making and how facial expression and gestures work together with words.

We describe the five most influential *primarily nonverbal* cues—facial expression, eye contact and gaze, space, touch, and body movement and gesture.

THREE APPROACHES TO STUDYING PRIMARILY VERBAL CUES (LANGUAGE)

1. Language Is a System of Symbols

Historically, this is the oldest point of view. From this perspective, language is a system made up of different kinds of words and the rules governing their combinations. Your grade-school teachers emphasized the systematic features of language when they helped you learn the differences among nouns, verbs, adjectives, and adverbs and the rules for making grammatical sentences. When you think of German, Mandarin Chinese, or Spanish as a "language," you're thinking of it as a language *system*. Dictionaries record a part of a language system and provide a record of, for example, word histories and new words like ROM, uplink, and downsize.

Those who study language as a system emphasize that it is a system of symbols. They develop a point made about 2,500 years ago when the Greek philosopher Aristotle began one of his major works on language this way: "Spoken words are the symbols of mental experience and written words are the symbols of spoken words."[5] As a contemporary linguist explains, "This criterion implies that for anything to be a language it must function so as to *symbolize* (represent for the organism) the not-necessarily-*here* and not-necessarily-*now*."[6] In brief, since a symbol is something that stands for something else, this approach emphasizes that units of language—words, usually—represent, or stand for, chunks or pieces of nonlinguistic reality. In the simplest terms, the word "cat" stands for the furry, purring, tail-twitching animal sitting in the corner.

One of the features of symbols that this approach also highlights is that they're *arbitrary*. This means that there is no necessary relationship between the word and the thing it symbolizes. Even though the word *five* is physically smaller than the word *three*, the quantity that *five* symbolizes is larger. So there's no necessary relationship between word (in this case, its size) and meaning. Or consider the words that people from different language communities use to symbolize a dwelling where someone lives: *casa* in Spanish, *maison* in French, and *Haus* in German. This couldn't happen unless the relationship between the word and its meaning were arbitrary.

A classic book, first published in 1923, elaborated just this point. Its authors, C. K. Ogden and I. A. Richards, diagrammed this insight with their famous "triangle of meaning" (see Figure 4–1).[7] Ogden and Richards' triangle is

FIGURE 4–1 Ogden and Richards' triangle of meaning.

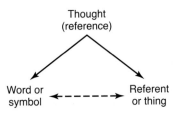

meant to illustrate how words are related to both thoughts and things. The word-thought relationship is direct—that's why the line is solid. For Aristotle, words stood for thoughts. The relationship between thought and thing was also more or less direct. But the word-thing relationship is arbitrary; there is no necessary relationship between the word and its referent. The dotted line across the bottom of the triangle emphasizes this point.

The main advantage of viewing language as a system of arbitrary symbols is that it alerts us to the dangers of abstractions and of the assumptions people make about what words mean by emphasizing that the *thought* or meaning associated with a word may or may not be directly related to the *thing* the word symbolizes. The clearest, most easily understood words are those that are easiest to connect with concrete reality: "this car," "my CD collection," "his blue hair." But from Ogden and Richards' point of view, people should be careful with abstract words like "safety," "style," "love," and "honesty," because the thoughts that they call up may or may not be linked to concrete realities that they symbolize. One person's writing or talk about safety may be connected with safety pins, bank vaults, or a seat belt, and because of the dotted-line relationship in the triangle, the individual to whom the person is writing or talking may not be able to tell the difference. We can also learn from this perspective that, since the relationship between words and meanings is arbitrary, we should never assume that another person means exactly what we do, even when he or she uses the same words. What does "early" mean, for example, when your mom or dad tells you to "get home early"? When your teacher says you should "get started early on your papers"? When the person you're dating feels it's too early in the relationship for sex? When you tell your roommate you want to get up early? Assumptions about identical word meaning often create communication problems.

This view of language is also drastically oversimplified, however. The triangle of meaning makes it appear that language is essentially made up of concrete nouns, labels for things in the world. It doesn't take much reflection to realize that language is much more complicated than that. Often the topic you're discussing and the ideas you want to express require abstract words, such as "love," "pride," and "homelessness." The advice to avoid these kinds of words because there are no "things" or "referents" to which they are even arbitrarily related is not very practical. And what about words like "and," "whether," "however," and "larger"? It can be really confusing to try to figure out what things these words symbolize. Even more important, we don't usually experience language as individual words, but as statements, utterances, messages, or parts of a conversation. So an approach that tries to explain living language by focusing on individual words has to be limited. All this is why it's partly true to say that language is a system of symbols, but there's much more to it than that.

2. Language Is an Activity

A second, more recent approach to the study of language views it as an activity. The most influential version of this approach began in the 1950s when several researchers showed how many utterances actually perform actions. They called these utterances "speech acts." For example, the words "I will" or "I do" in a marriage ceremony are not just symbolizing or referring to getting married. Rather, they are an important part of the activity of marrying itself. If they're not said at the right time by the right people, the marriage hasn't happened. Similarly, the words "I agree" or "Okay, it's a deal" can perform the activity of buying, selling, or contracting for work. And "Howzitgoin'?" is not about a greeting; it is the activity of greeting itself. A group of researchers called conversation analysts have shown how to extend and apply this insight about the action-performing function of language.

Conversation analysts, for instance, have identified the crucial features of many of the speech acts that people typically perform, such as promise, request, threat, offer, command, compliment, and greeting.[8] Each of these terms labels what certain utterances *do* rather than what they symbolize or say. And, these researchers point out, a given utterance won't perform this action unless it has certain features. For example, a *request* requires the speaker to ask for a preferred future behavior from the hearer, and the person who hasn't done this has not competently performed a request. A *promise* is also about a preferred future behavior, but it identifies what the speaker rather than the hearer will do.

If you understand the building blocks of each speech act, you can see why some *indirect* requests and promises will work and others won't. For example, "Are you taking your car to the game tonight?" could function as a *request* for a ride to the game, even though it does not actually identify a preferred future behavior. But it can only work as a request when the context allows both speaker and hearer to fill in the parts that the words themselves leave out. This explains how problems arise when one person fills in the blanks and another doesn't, or when one person means or hears a promise even though the crucial parts of the speech act are absent. For example, when Reggie and Kevin were discussing the game they both wanted to attend, Reggie heard Kevin's "Yeah, I'll be driving" as a *promise* to give him a ride. But Kevin meant it only as a response to Reggie's direct question. So he was surprised and a little angry when Reggie called to confirm the ride he'd "promised."

Conversation analysts have also studied several ways in which people collaborate to mutually construct some speech acts. For example, greetings, goodbyes, invitations, apologies, offers, and congratulations are all speech acts that almost always require two or more conversational moves rather than just one. If one conversation partner greets the other, the expectation is that the other will respond with another greeting. If this doesn't happen, the speech act of "greeting" has only partly occurred. The same thing happens with goodbyes; it takes both one person's "goodbye" *and* the other person's response. This requirement can create problems when one person means to be leaving and the other doesn't pick up on it. Similarly, an invitation is expected to be followed by an acceptance, questioning, or rejection of the invitation; an apology is expected to be followed by an acceptance or rejection, and so on. As one conversation analyst puts it:

> As we shall see, when one of these first actions has been produced, participants orient to the presence or absence of the relevant second action. There is an expectation by participants that the second action should be produced, and when it does not occur, participants behave as if it should have.[9]

Many insights into language use have been generated by people viewing it as an activity that people carry out by following certain sets of conversational rules. At the same time, the more researchers have studied communication as people actually experience it, the more they've recognized that although a great deal can be learned about the individual moves conversation partners make with their various speech acts, natural conversations almost always include unpredictable events or surprises. People improvise as much as they follow conversational rules. In other words, there is a structure to conversation, but it is less like the repetitive pattern followed by a supermarket checkout clerk and more like the loose and varied collaboration of five good musicians getting together to jam.

In summary, conversation analysts have demonstrated the value of studying language as an activity. They have shown that every time we say something, we're also doing something—that speech is a kind of action. They have catalogued many of the actions that people perform by talking and have also shown that some of these actions are produced collaboratively. But they have only been able to consider a few of the important nonverbal elements of conversation, and they have had to admit that there is almost as much improvisation as rule following. Every day people engage in greetings, goodbyes, promises, threats, compliments, offers, commands, requests, and dozens of other conversation acts. But we also improvise and modify expected patterns. Finally, conversation analysts have very little to say about the crucial identity-constructing function of communication. . . . We believe that the most helpful approach to language is the one that includes a focus on identities.

3. Language Is a Soup

This may sound a little weird, but stay with us for a few paragraphs. This approach does include identities.

Especially in the last 30 years, many scholars have recognized the limitations of both the system and action views of language. Both of these views treat language as a tool that humans manipulate, either to arbitrarily stand for some referent or to perform an action. As we have explained, there's some truth to these views, and they can teach us some important things about language. But language is more than a tool. If it were just a tool, we could lay it aside when we didn't need it and pick up some other tool, just as we can lay aside a screwdriver and pick up a hammer. But we can't do that. As humans, we're immersed in language, like a fish is immersed in water. And this quality is what the "soup" metaphor is meant to highlight. As one writer puts it:

> In all our knowledge of ourselves and in all knowledge of the world, we are always already encompassed by the language that is our own. We grow up, and we become acquainted with [people] and in the last analysis with ourselves when we learn to speak. Learning to speak does not mean learning to use a preexistent tool for designating a world already somehow familiar to us; it means acquiring a familiarity and acquaintance with the world itself and how it confronts us.[10]

This is what it means to say that language is a soup. We're immersed in it from birth to death, just as a fish is immersed in the water in which it lives.

In fact, language experience may begin even before birth. As soon as 20 weeks after conception, the human fetus has functioning ears and is beginning to respond to sounds.[11] Its mother's voice is clearly one sound the fetus learns to identify.[12] Some pregnant couples talk to and play music for their unborn child. When the infant is born, it typically enters an environment of exclamations and greetings. Then verbal and nonverbal communication experiences fill the infant's life. Touch, eye contact, smiles, and a great deal of talk are directed to him or her. As infants develop, parents and other caregivers invite them into conversations or exclude them from conversations by providing a context for talk, by encouraging them with positive attitudes toward talk or discouraging them with negative attitudes, and by interpreting, modeling, and extending talk.[13] This process continues right up to the last tearful goodbyes a person hears at death. In between, humans live more or less like nutritious morsels in a broth of language. This soup includes all the verbal and nonverbal parts of our communicative life. In fact, the theorists and researchers who treat language as a soup have begun to mean by "language" what used to be called "communication"—all the verbal and nonverbal, oral and nonoral, ways that humans make meaning together. As you might be assuming, this view of language fits most comfortably with the approach to communication outlined in Chapter 2.

Language and Perception   If this notion of language as a soup sounds a little abstract, consider one important practical implication of the fact that language is all-encompassing: Because we are immersed in language all our lives, language and perception are thoroughly interrelated. . . . When we perceive, we select, organize, and make meaning out of the things and events we see, hear, touch, taste, and smell. The point that language and perception are thoroughly interrelated means that everything we perceive, all the things that make up our world, is affected by the language in which we live. In the early 20th century, one version of this insight about language and perception was called the Sapir-Whorf hypothesis, for the two people who originally wrote about it, Edward Sapir and Benjamin Lee Whorf. It was summarized by Whorf in these words:

> The background linguistic system (in other words, the grammar) of each language is not merely a reproducing instrument for voicing ideas but rather is itself the shaper of ideas, the program and guide for the individual's mental

activity, for his [or her] analysis of impressions. . . . We dissect nature along lines
laid down by our native language.[14]

Thus, if you have spent enough time on boats and around the water to learn a
dozen different words for water conditions, you will perceive more differences
in the water than will the person who was born and raised in Cheyenne,
Oklahoma City, or Calgary. That person might distinguish between *waves* and
smooth water, but you will see and feel differences between *cats' paws*, *ripples*,
chop, and *swells* that he or she probably won't even notice.[15] Or if you have
learned important meanings for *latex*, *natural*, *lubricated*, and *spermicidal*, you can
make distinctions among condoms that were impossible for the high school
graduate of the 1970s or early 1980s.

A Chinese-American woman, Mandy Lam, made the point that she felt "sim-
ilar to the fish that lives in an area of water where the river mixes with the ocean.
I have only to travel a little further in either direction to experience the extremes."
Her grandparents speak only Chinese, and she relates to them, and often to her
parents and other elders, in Chinese ways. But all her premed classes are in
English, and she lives in an almost completely English world at school.

As the two of us try in this book to write about communication as a continuous, complex, collaborative meaning-making process, we especially notice two
particular ways in which our native language limits our perceptions. The first
has to do with the ways that the English language affects how people understand ongoing processes. Unlike some languages, English maintains clear
distinctions between noun subjects and verb predicates, causes and effects, beginnings and ends, and this affects how native English speakers perceive communication. A surprising number of other language systems do not do this.
According to one researcher, for example, Navajo speakers characteristically
talk in terms of processes—uncaused, ongoing, incomplete, dynamic happenings. The word that Navajos use for wagon, for example, translates roughly as
"wood rolls about hooplike."[16] The Navajo words that we would translate as
"He begins to carry a stone" mean not that the actor produces an action, but that
the person is simply linked with a given round object and with an already existing, continuous movement of all round objects in the universe. The English
language, by contrast, requires its users to talk in terms of present, past, future,
cause and effect, beginning and end. Problems arise when some things that
English speakers would like to discuss just can't be expressed in these terms. To
continue our example, we would like to be able to talk more clearly about the
emergent, ongoing nature of communication. . . . But, especially since communication doesn't always obey the rules of cause and effect, the noun-plus-verb-
plus-object structure of the English language makes it difficult to do this. For
this topic, Navajo would probably work better than English.

The second way in which we notice that the English language affects our
discussion of communication has to do with the ways English speakers perceive
gender differences. One accomplishment of research encouraged by the feminist
movement of the 1960s and 1970s is that people now recognize how the male

bias of standard American English has contributed to the ways in which English-speaking cultures perceive women and men. The fact that, until recently, there were no female firefighters was not caused simply by the existence of the word fire*man*. It's not that simple. But research indicates that gender-biased words affect perceptions in at least three ways. They shape people's attitudes about careers that are "appropriate" for one sex but not for the other, they lead some women to believe that certain jobs and roles aren't attainable, and they contribute to the belief that men deserve higher status in society than do women.[17] This is why changes in job titles have helped open several occupations to more equal male-female participation. Consider, for example, *parking checker* instead of *metermaid, chair* or *chairperson* instead of *chairman, salesperson* instead of *salesman,* and *server* instead of *waiter* or *waitress.* We have also just about stopped referring to female physicians as woman doctors and female attorneys as lady lawyers, and it is more than a coincidence that these changes have been accompanied by significant increases in the numbers of women in these two professions.

Since the mid-1990s, both scholarly and popular books have emphasized this point about gender, language, and perception by highlighting the differences between the language worlds into which men and women are socialized in North America. Sociolinguist Deborah Tannen's book *You Just Don't Understand: Women and Men in Communication*[18] was on the best-seller list for months, and John Gray has sold millions of copies of *Men Are from Mars, Women Are from Venus*[19] and *Mars and Venus in Love.*[20] All of these books describe the ways in which women's communication differs from men's and explain how many problems between genders are influenced by these differences. Some people complain that the books reinforce the very stereotypes they're trying to reduce by generalizing about "women's communication" and "men's communication." Despite the very real danger of this oversimplification, however, there is considerable research evidence to indicate that most North American, English-speaking women and most of their male counterparts do communicate differently. In other words, carefully controlled observations of how these men and women actually talk found that there are important gender-linked patterns.

The women observed in these studies generally use communication as a primary way to establish and maintain relationships with others, whereas the men generally talk to exert control, preserve independence, and enhance status. More specifically, most of these women's communicating is characterized by seven features that are not generally found in the men's talk: an emphasis on equality, support, attention to the relationship, inclusivity, concreteness, and tentativeness, and a preference for collaborative meaning-making. Men's communicating is described in this same research as functioning to exhibit knowledge or skill, accomplish goals, assert dominance, avoid tentativeness, stay abstract rather than concrete, and minimize relationship responsiveness.[21] . . .

To summarize, from the point of view of this soup or fish-in-water idea, language is more than a *system* we use or an *activity* we perform. It is larger than any of us; it happens to us and we are subject to it as much as we manipulate or use it. . . . When studied from this third perspective, language has both verbal and nonverbal aspects. Language researchers and teachers have become increasingly aware that languaging as people actually live it is less of a system or action and more of a mutual event or collaborative process. "Language" is the term these researchers and teachers use for the communicating that, as [was] said in Chapter 2, makes us who we are.

MIXED CUES: VOICE, SILENCE, FACE AND WORDS, GESTURES AND WORDS

The first section of this reading was about the primarily verbal parts of communication—the parts that are often called "language." By now, you know that language includes both verbal and nonverbal elements, but that it can still be distinguished from the "mixed" parts, which include the rate, pitch, volume, and quality of the voice; silence; facial expressions accompanying words; and gestures that accompany words. Let's consider next how these mixed cues operate.

Voice

Sometimes people overlook the fact that spoken language includes many different nonverbal vocal elements. The technical term for these cues is *paralinguistics*, and they include rate of speech, pitch variation, volume, and vocal quality. If you think about your perceptions of someone who speaks really rapidly or v-e-r-r-r-y s-l-o-o-o-w-l-y, you have a sense of how rate affects communicating. Listeners and conversation partners also make inferences about how monotone or melodic speech is, how softly or loudly someone speaks, and whether a speaker's vocal quality is resonant, squeaky, nasal, or breathy. Sometimes people manipulate these four dimensions of their voice to assist listeners in interpreting what they're saying, whether they're emphasizing various words or phrases, expressing feelings, or indicating when they're serious and when they're sarcastic or joking. In other cases, speakers don't mean to manipulate any of the four; they're "just talking normally" when people hear them as too fast, as too soft, as a monotone, or as too loud.

As these examples suggest, one of the ways people interpret others' vocal cues is to make stereotyped judgments about the speakers' personalities. It's not a good idea, but we do it nonetheless. For example, a male with a breathy voice is likely to be stereotyped as gay, or at least as young and artistic, whereas a female with the same vocal quality is usually thought of as "more feminine, prettier, more petite, more effervescent, more high-strung, and shallower."[22] Nasal voices are heard as undesirable for both males and females, and low, deep voices are perceived as being more sophisticated, more appealing, and sexier than are higher-pitched voices. People also use vocal cues to draw conclusions about the age, sex, and ethnicity of speakers they hear. What can you conclude from the fact that we use voices this way? According to Mark Knapp:

> You should be quick to challenge the cliché that vocal cues only concern how something is said—frequently they are what is said. What is said might be an attitude ("I like you" or "I'm superior to you"), it might be an emotion . . . or it might be the presentation of some aspect of your personality, background, or physical features. Vocal cues will, depending on the situation and the communicators, carry a great deal of information. . . .[23]

Silence

> With silence we express the most varied and conflicting states, sentiments, thoughts and desires. Silence is meaningful. There is the silence of fear and terror, of wonder and stupor, of pain and joy. . . . "Dumb silence" is a contradictory expression. Instead of describing the same thing the two terms exclude each other; silence is not dumb and whatever is dumb is not silent. Silence is a form of communication . . . dumbness, on the other hand, isolates and excludes us from all communication.[24]

The reason we classify silence as a mixed cue is that it most often becomes significant in the context of talk. As one author puts it, "A discourse without pauses [is] incomprehensible. Silence is not an interval . . . but the bridge that unites sounds."[25] In other words, silence is usually noticed because of the way it relates to speaking. Examples include the failure or refusal to respond to a question, and the pregnant pause. Even the silence of the forest, prairie, mountain, lake, or bayou is most meaningful because of the way it contrasts with the noises of city crowds.

Silence is one of the least understood nonverbal behaviors, partly because people use and interpret it in so many different ways. Silence can be interpreted to mean apathy, patience, boredom, fear, sadness, love, intimacy, anger, or intimidation. We have talked with married couples who use silence as a weapon. One husband, who knew his wife hated it when he didn't talk out a problem, sometimes would refuse to talk to her for two or three days. His wife said she found this "devastating." When there are prolonged silences in group meetings, people start shifting nervously and making inferences, such as "nobody is interested," "people don't like this group," and "nobody really cares what we're doing."

But silence also works in positive ways. Beginning teachers, for example, have to learn that the silence that sometimes comes after they ask their students a question can be very fruitful. A group's silence can mean that there's a lot of thinking going on. Two close friends may also say nothing to each other just so they can share the experience of the moment. Or in an interview, silence can be a welcome opportunity for the interviewee to elaborate, return to a topic discussed earlier, or simply reorganize her or his thoughts. A friend of ours reported that the long silences he and his mother shared during the last two days of her life were some of the richest times they had spent together. Love, warmth, and sympathy are sometimes best expressed through silent facial and body movements and touch.

Facial Expression and Words

[Later in] this reading, we'll discuss facial expression as a primarily nonverbal cue. But peoples' faces also connect with words when they help to regulate utterance "turns" in conversations, and when they do, they can be considered mixed cues. The next time you're in a conversation, notice how you know when it's your turn to talk. The other person's face and eyes will almost always "tell" you. People also use faces and eyes to tell someone who approaches them either that they are welcoming the person into conversation or that they would rather be left alone.

Eye behavior is an important part of facial expression, and people use specific forms of eye behavior to accomplish several general goals in most conversations. First, we look away when we're having difficulty putting our thoughts into words. The amount of information we seem to be getting from another's eyes can be intense enough to be distracting, so if we're having trouble saying what we want to say, we look away to reduce the amount of input.

We also use eye contact to monitor feedback, to check the other's responses to the conversation. If we notice that the person is looking at us, we infer that she or he is paying attention; if we see that the person is staring into space, or over our shoulder to something or someone behind us, we draw the opposite conclusion. This phenomenon often helps make "cocktail party" conversation uncomfortably superficial. Neither conversation partner wants to be left standing alone, so both are as concerned about the next conversation as they are about the current one. As a result, both divide their looking between eye contact with the other and the search for the next partner.

Visual contact is also a primary way to indicate whose turn it is to talk. When a person tries to "catch the eye" of a server in a restaurant, the point is to open the channel, to initiate talk. And the same thing happens in conversation; I can "tell" you that it's your turn to talk by making eye contact with you. One communication researcher summarizes the typical conversation pattern in this way: "As the speaker comes to the end of an utterance or thought unit, gazing at the listener will continue as the listener assumes the speaking role; the listener will maintain gaze until the speaking role is assumed when he or she will look away. When the speaker does not yield a speaking turn by glancing at the other, the listener will probably delay a response or fail to respond. . . ."[26] Of course, this description is accurate for some cultures and not for others. Like other nonverbal cues, the facial expressions that accompany words vary among ethnic groups, genders, social classes, and sexual preferences. Eye contact and facial expressions are so critical to regulating conversations that a speaker's elimination of either one will seriously affect the responses of the listener.

Gestures and Words

Researcher David McNeill emphasizes why gestures can be considered mixed cues by examining their connection to spoken words. In one of McNeill's articles, "So You Think Gestures Are Nonverbal?" he explains how they are not just nonverbal, because gestures and speech are part of the same language structure. As he puts it, certain "gestures are verbal. They are the overt products of the same internal processes that produce the other overt product, speech." He goes on to point out that this is another reason we have to change what we mean by "language." He writes, "We tend to consider linguistic what we can write down, and nonlinguistic, everything else...."[27] However, he says, we now know better. Language is made up of both verbal and nonverbal aspects. This is "contrary to the idea of body language, that is, a separate system of body movement and postural signals that is thought to obey its own laws and convey its own ... meanings."[28] It's misleading to talk of body language, McNeill argues, because posture and gesture are too intimately connected with the other part of language—words....

Communication researcher Janet Bavelas and her colleagues have extended McNeill's work by studying what they call interactive gestures. These are movements that are related not to the content of the conversation, but to the relationship between or among the people communicating. Interactive gestures include the listener and thus "act to maintain the conversation as a social system."[29] For example, Bavelas describes how one speaker was discussing the summer job options that would contribute the most to his career goal.

> The listener had suggested earlier that working for Canada Customs would be a good idea; the speaker, after listing several other possibilities, adds "and Customs is DEFINITELY career-oriented." As he said "Customs," the speaker moved his hand up and toward the other person (almost as if tossing something to him), with palm up, fingers slightly curled, and thumb pointing directly at the other at the peak of the movement. Our translation of this gesture is "which YOU suggested," that is, the speaker credits the other person with the idea.[30]

Other interactive gestures were translated as "Do you get what I mean?" "Would you give me the answer?" and "No, no, I'll get it myself." All of these gestures are connected not to the conversational topic, but to the other speaker. Thus, they add important social content to the conversation, content separate from what is contributed verbally. In this way, they take on part of the work of mutual meaning constructing that is normally thought to be done only by words. So these so-called nonverbal gestures are actually functioning exactly as words do to add substance to the conversation.

Bavelas and her colleagues explain the importance of this added substance when they write:

> An interesting, intrinsic problem in dialogue is that, while both partners must remain involved, only one person can talk at once. Whenever a speaker has the floor, there exists the possibility that the conversation could veer off into monologue. One solution to the problem ... is for the speaker to involve the listener regularly. To a certain extent, the speaker can do this by verbal statements, such as "You know," "As you said," "As you know," "I'm sure you agree," etc. However, the frequent use of verbal interjections and addenda would constantly disrupt the flow of content, so nonverbal means of seeking or maintaining involvement are well suited to this function....

> We propose that interactive gestures, for all their many specific forms and translations, form a class with the common function of including the listener and thereby counteracting the beginning of a drift toward monologue that is necessarily created every time one person has the floor.[31]

In summary, vocal rate, pitch, volume, and quality affect how people collaboratively construct meaning in communication; this is why they can be thought of as mixed cues. Silence is another influential mixed building block. In addition, many facial expressions, much eye behavior, and even many gestures work so intimately with spoken words that they should also be thought of as mixed.

PRIMARILY NONVERBAL CUES: FACE, EYE CONTACT AND GAZE, SPACE, TOUCH, MOVEMENT AND GESTURE

Although we're not going to present an exhaustive list of primarily nonverbal cues (for example, we omit appearance and dress, smells, time, and colors), we think that the following five categories will give you a broad sense of the most influential primarily nonverbal parts of your communicating.

Facial Expression

Your face is probably the most expressive part of your body and one of the most important focal points for nonverbal communicating. Most of the time, people are unaware of how much they rely on faces to give and get information. But a little reflection—or reading some of the research—can change your level of awareness. Consider, for example, how important the face is in expressing emotion. An extensive program of research has demonstrated that certain basic emotions are facially expressed in similar ways across cultures.[32] Every culture studied so far has been found to include some conventional facial expressions that people use to communicate joy or happiness, sadness, surprise, fear, anger, and disgust. There are some culture-specific rules for the display of these emotions, but they are expressed in very similar ways in most cultures.

Researchers have discovered these similarities by showing photographs of North American faces, for example, to Japanese or preliterate New Guinean observers, and then showing photographs of Japanese and New Guineans to North Americans. In most cases, members of one culture were able to identify accurately the emotions being expressed by the faces of persons from the other cultures.[33] They recognized, for example, that surprise is consistently communicated by a face with widened eyes, head tilted up, raised brow, and open mouth. Disgust is communicated with brows pulled down, wrinkled nose, and a mouth with raised upper lip and downturned corners.

Although the facial expression of emotions is similar across cultures, there are important differences in facial displays, for example, between Japanese and

North Americans. Historically, Japanese have been taught to mask negative facial expressions with smiles and laughter and to display less facial emotion overall.[34] There are a number of competing ideas about why these differences exist, but regardless of the origins, differences in expression have contributed to misunderstandings between Japanese and North American businesspeople. Many Japanese still appear to be some of the least facially expressive of all cultural groups, and persons from other cultures are learning to adapt to this difference.

Eye Contact and Gaze

Although eyes are obviously a part of facial expression, gaze and eye contact are important enough to discuss separately. Eye contact appears to be one of the first behaviors that infants develop. Within a few days of birth, infants seem to recognize and attend to the caregiver's eyes. In the weeks immediately after birth, researchers have observed that simply seeing the eyes of the caregiver is enough to produce a smiling reaction.[35] Eye contact also significantly affects development. Infants who lack mutual gaze do not appear to mature perceptually and socially as rapidly as those who experience regular eye contact.[36]

If you doubt the importance of eye contact, consider the inferences you make about someone who doesn't look you in the eye "enough." What "enough" means varies from person to person, and certainly from culture to culture, but most Caucasians in the U.S. infer that the person with too little eye contact is insincere, is disinterested, lacks confidence, is trying to avoid contact, or is lying. There aren't many other possibilities. And all these inferences are negative. Generally, there are *no* positive messages conveyed by too little eye contact in white U.S. cultures. . . .

One important function of eye gaze is to enhance the intimacy of the relationship. Especially when it is accompanied by forward lean, direct body orientation, and more gesturing, it can help promote closeness.[37] Some intimacy research has studied not sexual contact, but the kind of intimacy that increases the desire to help. Gaze has been found to increase the probability that a bystander will help a person with a medical problem or someone who has fallen.[38] But this phenomenon seems to characterize female-female contacts more than it does those involving males. As Judee Burgoon and her colleagues summarize, "Under some circumstances, prolonged gaze may serve as an affiliative cue in the form of a plea for help, while in other cases it may be seen as overly forward or aggressive behavior."[39]

Another primary function of eye behavior is to express emotions. Some of the same people who studied facial expressions have also researched how people use eyes and eyebrows to interpret the six common emotions. Generally eyes are used more than brows/forehead or lower face for the accurate perception of fear, but eyes help less for the accurate perception of anger and disgust.[40]

Feelings about others are also communicated visually. For example, if you perceive a person as being of significantly lower status than you are, the tendency will be for you to maintain considerable eye contact. On the other hand, communicators tend to look much less at high-status people. Generally, we also look more at people we like and at those who believe as we do. The obvious reason, as Albert Mehrabian explains, is that eye contact is a kind of approach behavior, and approach behaviors are connected with liking.[41] So one response to someone who is appealing is to approach by looking, and one way to avoid a person we dislike is to look away.

We also use gaze and eye behavior to make and influence credibility judgments. Several studies on persuasive effectiveness and willingness to hire a job applicant have underscored the importance of normal or nearly continuous gaze. It appears that gaze avoidance is interpreted negatively, as we mentioned above, and that it can significantly affect your chances of being perceived as credible.[42] This is why those who teach or coach people for public speaking or interview situations emphasize that speakers and interviewees should generally try to maintain eye contact 50 to 70 percent of the time. As we mentioned earlier, cultural identities affect this formula, but it is a reliable basic guideline for many North American communication situations.

The bottom line is that people give considerable weight to eye behavior and eye contact, because they apparently believe that the eyes are indeed the "windows of the soul." Especially in Western cultures, people are confident that they can spot even the most practiced liar if they can just "look the person in the eye"[43] (although detecting deception is more complicated than this, as we explain below). People are also generally impressed by the confidence and overall effectiveness of a speaker with good eye contact. But since different cultures have different estimates of what constitutes "good" eye contact, it's important not to oversimplify gaze and eye behavior and to remember that, especially because this category of nonverbal cues is given so much credence, it's important to become aware of and to learn to manage your own eye behavior.

Proximity or Space

You have probably noticed that you often feel possessive about some spaces—perhaps your room, yard, or car—and that you sometimes sit or stand very close to people with whom you're talking and at other times feel more comfortable several feet away. These feelings are related to what is known as *proxemics,* the study of the communicative effects of space or distance.

As [was] said in Chapter 2, space is one of the basic dimensions of every human's world, and the primary tension that describes this dimension is near-far. Because we all have basic human needs both for privacy (distance) and to be interdependent (nearness), one way we manage this tension is by defining and defending a *territory.* A territory is an identifiable geographic area that is occupied, controlled, and often defended by a person or group as an exclusive domain.[44] For example, for many North Americans, one's bedroom, or a particular space in a shared room, is yours whether you're in it or not, and one of the reasons you guard your right to keep it in your preferred state of neatness or disorder is to underscore the point that it's your territory. In a library, cafeteria, or other public space, people use overcoats, briefcases, newspapers, food trays, dishes, and utensils to establish a claim over "their" space, even though it's temporary.

A number of studies have identified differences between ways women and men use territory. For example, in most cultures, women are allowed less territory than are men. As Judy Pearson notes, "Few women have a particular and unviolated room in their homes while many men have dens, studies, or work areas which are off limits to others. Similarly, it appears that more men than women have particular chairs reserved for their use."[45]

Each of us also lives in our own personal space, a smaller, invisible, portable, and adjustable "bubble," which we maintain to protect ourselves from physical and emotional threats. The size of this bubble varies; how far away we sit or stand depends on our family and cultural memberships, the relationship we have with the other person, the situation or the context, and how we are feeling toward the other person at the time. Anthropologist Edward Hall says it this way:

> Some individuals never develop the public phase of their personalities and, therefore, cannot fill public spaces; they make very poor speakers or moderators. As many psychiatrists know, other people have trouble with the intimate and personal zones and cannot endure closeness to others.[46]

Within these limitations, Hall identifies four distances he observed among middle-class adults in the northeastern United States. Although the limits of each zone differ from culture to culture, something like these four types of space exist in many cultures.

Intimate Distance (Contact to 18 Inches)   This zone begins with skin contact and ranges to about a foot and a half. People usually reserve this distance for those to whom they feel emotionally close, and for comforting, protecting, caressing, or lovemaking. When forced into intimate distance with strangers— as on an elevator, for example—people tend to use other nonverbal cues to reestablish separateness. So we avoid eye contact, fold our arms, or perhaps hold a briefcase or purse in front of our body. Allowing someone to enter this zone is a sign of trust; it says we have willingly lowered our defenses. At this distance, not only touch, but also smells, body temperature, and the feel and smell of breath can be part of what we experience. Voices are usually kept at a low level to emphasize the "closed circle" established by intimates.

Personal Distance (1.5 to 4 Feet)   This is the distance preferred by most conversation partners in a public setting. Typically, subjects of personal interest and moderate involvement can be discussed at this distance. Touch is still possible, but it is limited to brief pats for emphasis and reassurance. Finer details of the other's skin, hair, eyes, and teeth are visible, but one can't discern body temperature or feel the breath.

The far range of this distance is just beyond where you can comfortably touch the other. Hall calls it the distance we can use to keep someone "at arm's length." John sometimes works as a communication consultant training people to do information-gathering interviews. In that context, he encourages the people he's training to try to work within this zone. It appears that three to four feet is far enough away not to threaten the other and yet close enough to encourage the kind of relatively candid responses that make the interviews most successful.

Social Distance (4 to 12 Feet)   More impersonal business generally is carried out at this distance. People who work together or who are attending a social gathering tend to use the closer ranges of social distance. Salespeople and customers typically are comfortable within the four- to seven-foot zone. Most people feel uncomfortable if a salesperson approaches within three feet, but five or six feet nonverbally "says," "I'm here to help but I don't want to be pushy."

At the farther ranges of this distance, eye contact becomes especially important. When a person is 10 or 11 feet away, it's easy to be uncertain about who the person is talking with until you can determine where the person is looking. This is also the distance we often use with people of significantly higher or lower status. Sitting at this distance from a superior will tend to create a much more formal conversation than might take place if one or both persons moved their chairs much closer. As a result, it can be more effective to reprimand using social distance and less effective to give praise in this zone.

Public Distance (12 to 25 Feet)   The closer range of this distance is the one commonly used by instructors and managers addressing work groups. The farthest end of this zone is usually reserved for public speeches. When communicating at this distance, voices need to be loud or electronically amplified. At the farther ranges of this distance, facial expression, movements, and gestures also need to be exaggerated in order to be meaningful.

Like many other general observations about human communication, these four distances need to be taken with a grain of salt. Several studies have shown, for example, that females sit and stand closer together than do males, and that mixed-sex pairs consistently adopt closer distances than do male-male pairs.[47] Interpersonal distance also generally increases with age from preschool and grade school through the teen years to adulthood, but this tendency is mitigated somewhat by the fact that people also tend to adopt closer distances with age peers than with those who are younger or older.[48] So people's interpretations of distance and closeness may depend not only on their cultural identity, but also on their gender and age and on the gender and age of the person with whom they're conversing.

Space is usually interpreted in the context of other nonverbal cues. For example, a Chinese-American student reported:

> [My grandfather] commands his presence with silence, limited facial expressions and lots of space between himself and others. I have never thought of jumping into his lap like Ol' St. Nick or even felt comfortable talking to him at any great length. When I do scrounge up the courage to speak to him, it is almost always to greet him or ask him to come to dinner. The speech used would have to be laden with respectful words.[49]

Touch

Touch is the most direct way that humans establish the contact that makes us who we are. "It is well documented that touch is essential to the physical, emotional, and psychological well-being of human infants and to their intellectual, social, and communication development."[50] Touch is equally important for adults, although taboos in many Western cultures make it much more difficult to accomplish. That's why some scholars believe that these cultures are "touch-starved."

Touch plays a part in just about every activity of our waking day—not just with other humans but also with objects. You may not be aware of the feel of your clothes; the chair, couch, or floor on which you're sitting, standing, or lying; or the feel of the book you're holding, the pencil or pen you're grasping, or the shoes you're wearing. But you couldn't write, walk, make a fist, smile, or comb your hair without the sense of touch. In addition, the ways in which we hold and handle such things as books, pencils, cups or glasses, and purses or briefcases can affect another person's responses to us.

Touch between persons is even more complex. Stan Jones and Elaine Yarbrough, two speech communication researchers, found that people touch to indicate positive feelings, to play, to control, as part of a greeting or departure ritual, to help accomplish a task, to combine greeting or departure with affection, and accidentally.[51] In their studies, control touches occurred most frequently, touches that were primarily interpreted to mean a request for compliance or attention getting. A spot touch with the hand to a nonvulnerable body part—hands, arms, shoulders, or upper back—frequently accompanies and emphasizes such statements as, "Move over," "Hurry up," "Stay here," "Be serious," and "Do it." A similar touch reinforces such messages as, "Listen to this," "Look at that," and "I want your attention." These touches are almost always accompanied by verbalization, and both sexes initiate these touches with almost equal frequency.

Positive affect touches were the second most frequent kind of touch Jones and Yarbrough observed. The highest number of these touches were expressions of affection. As you would expect, these occur predominantly in close relationships and include hugs, kisses, and often contacts with "vulnerable body parts"—head, neck, torso, lower back, buttocks, legs, or feet. But affection can also be communicated by touch in some business settings. Long-term work teams sometimes engage in spontaneous brief touches among team members that are interpreted as positive and supportive. On the other hand, . . . sexual harassment in the workplace often consists in part of inappropriate or manipulative positive affect touching.

Research such as that of Jones and Yarbrough is important because it helps us comprehend a poorly understood, and sometimes even feared, aspect of our communicating. As Mark Knapp says:

> Some people grow up learning "not to touch" a multitude of animate and inanimate objects; they are told not to touch their own body and later not to touch the body of their dating partner; care is taken so children do not see their parents

"touch" one another intimately; some parents demonstrate a noncontact norm through the use of twin beds; touching is associated with admonitions of "not nice" or "bad" and is punished accordingly—and frequent touching between father and son is thought to be something less than masculine.[52]

We know that touch is an enormously powerful kind of nonverbal communication; a very small amount of it can say a great deal. We can harness this power by becoming aware of how touch affects where our communication is on the social-cultural-interpersonal scale.

Body Movement and Gestures

The technical term for the study of movement and gesture is *kinesics*, from the Greek word for "motion." Some kinesic behaviors mean virtually the same thing whether they're performed by men or women, young or old people, and in the United States, Latin America, Europe, Australia, or Japan. For example, the head nod for agreement, shaking a fist in anger, clapping hands for approval, raising a hand for attention, yawning in boredom, rubbing hands to indicate coldness, and the thumbs-down gesture for disapproval are all interpreted similarly in at least several western hemisphere cultures.

Movements and gestures can also reflect the type of relationship that exists between partners or spouses. Communication researcher Mary Anne Fitzpatrick has distinguished among three general couple types who are identifiable in part by their patterns of movement and gesture. Traditionals accept conventional beliefs about relational roles, for example, about which are "the husband's" duties and which are "the wife's."[53] They value stability over spontaneity and affirm the traditional community customs that a woman should take her husband's last name when she marries, and the belief that infidelity is always inexcusable. Independent couples are at the opposite end of the ideological scale. They believe that one's relationship should not limit her or his individual freedom in any way. "The independent maintains a high level of companionship and sharing in marriage, but . . . [he or she] maintains separate physical spaces to control accessibility." Separates are conventional regarding marital and family issues but also support independent values. "They may espouse one set [of values] publicly while believing another privately. The separates have significantly less companionship and sharing in their marriage."[54] One of the ways to distinguish among the three couple types is to observe their movements and gestures when they are together.

Traditionals engage in a high number of meshed movements and actions. Each partner facilitates the other partner's actions. If the woman moves toward the door, for example, the man will typically move to open it for her. Separates, on the other hand, engage in very few meshed action sequences. They are disengaged from one another. However, even though their gestures and movements don't interconnect, they are often parallel. For example, one may move toward the door while the other moves to get his or her coat. Finally, the gestures and movements of independents clash more often than they are parallel. If one moves toward the door, the other may sit down or even try to keep the door closed.

People also communicate dominance and submission posturally. A male may hook his thumbs in his belt and both females and males may stand with hands on hips in the akimbo position. When a seated person leans back with hands clasped behind her or his head, this is typically another dominance posture. When a conversational group of three is approached by a fourth person, they typically rotate their bodies out to encourage the fourth to join them or in to discourage him or her.

Forward lean is commonly interpreted as more involved and usually more positive, while "seated male and female communicators both perceived a person leaning backward and away from them as having a more negative attitude than one who was leaning forward."[55] A direct vis-à-vis posture, movement toward the other, affirmative head nods, expressive hand gestures, and stretching are all rated as "warm" behaviors, while moving away, picking one's teeth, shaking the head, and playing with hair are rated as "cold."[56] All of these descriptions illustrate how body movement and gesture make up still another important category of nonverbal behaviors.

REVIEW QUESTIONS

1. To check your understanding of the relationship between verbal and nonverbal cues, itemize six nonverbal features of the words you find in this book.
2. Explain what it means to say that words are "arbitrary symbols."
3. What's the problem with an explanation of language based on an analysis of concrete nouns?
4. What's missing, according to Stewart and Logan, from the account of language as an activity?
5. Explain the Sapir-Whorf hypothesis in your own words.
6. Give an example from your own experience of gendered (masculine/feminine) language affecting your perception of someone or something.
7. What are paralinguistics?
8. Especially in conversation, silence, this reading argues, is much more than the absence of noise. Explain.
9. Why is facial expression discussed in two separate places in this reading?
10. What are interactive gestures?
11. What makes eye behavior so important in conversations?
12. Stewart and Logan make the point that a very small amount of touch can "say" a great deal. Which other mixed and primarily nonverbal cues are similarly high in potency—where a little can go a long way?

PROBES

1. Carole and I explain some disadvantages of separate discussions of verbal and nonverbal cues. What are some advantages?

2. When does it most seem as if language is a "system"? When does this label seem least appropriate?

3. One famous author expressed something very close to the "language is a soup" idea in these words: "The limits of my language are the limits of my world." With the "soup" metaphor in mind, explain what you believe that means.

4. Carole and I repeat the claims about the differences between masculine and feminine communication styles that have been popularized by Deborah Tannen and John Gray. The second reading in Chapter 8 challenges these claims. Flip forward in the book to Chapter 8 and make a note there to discuss whether you agree with this reading or that one.

5. In your experience, which kinds of mixed and primarily nonverbal cues vary the most between or among cultures? Which kinds of cues from other cultures are the most different from your preferred patterns?

6. Give an example from your own experience of gender differences in spatial nonverbal cues.

7. Summarize three pieces of advice about your own verbal and nonverbal communicating that you drew from this reading. If you are to take seriously what's here, what three changes might you make?

NOTES

1. D. J. Higginbotham and D. E. Yoder, "Communication within Natural Conversational Interaction: Implications for Severe Communicatively Impaired Persons." *Topics in Language Disorders* 2 (1982): 4.

2. Wendy Leeds-Hurwitz, *Communication in Everyday Life* (Norwood, NJ: Ablex, 1989), p. 102.

3. Ferdinand de Saussure, *Course in General Linguistics,* ed. Charles Bally and Albert Sechehaye, trans. Roy Harris (LaSalle, IL: Open Court, 1986), pp. 66–70. After making this point, de Saussure focused his attention on the *system* of language, in order to make linguistics a "science."

4. Robert E. Sanders, "The Interconnection of Utterances and Nonverbal Displays." *Research on Language and Social Interaction* 20 (1987): 141.

5. Aristotle, *De Interpretatione,* trans. E. M. Edgehill in *The Basic Works of Aristotle,* ed. Richard McKeon (New York: Random House, 1941), p. 20.

6. Charles E. Osgood, "What Is a Language?" in I. Rauch and G. F. Carr (eds.), *The Signifying Animal* (Bloomington, IN: Indiana University Press, 1980), p. 12.

7. C. K. Ogden and I. A. Richards, *The Meaning of Meaning,* 8th ed. (New York: Harcourt Brace, 1986), p. 11. If you're interested in reading more about this view of language and its problems, see John Stewart, *Language as Articulate Contact: Toward a Post-Semiotic Philosophy of Communication* (Albany, NY: State University of New York Press, 1995); and John Stewart (ed.), *Beyond the Symbol Model: Reflections on the Representational Nature of Language* (Albany, NY: State University of New York Press, 1996).

8. Robert E. Nofsinger, *Everyday Conversation* (Newbury Park, CA: Sage, 1991), pp. 19–26.

9. Nofsinger, p. 51.

10. Hans-Georg Gadamer, "Man and Language," in David E. Linge (ed.), *Philosophical Hermeneutics* (Berkeley, CA: University of California Press, 1976), pp. 62–63.

11. D. B. Chamberlain, "Consciousness at Birth: The Range of Empirical Evidence," in T. R. Verney (ed.), *Pre- and Perinatal Psychology: An Introduction* (New York: Human Sciences, 1987), pp. 70–86.

12. A. Tomatis, "Ontogenesis of the Faculty of Listening," in Verney (ed.), pp. 23–35.

13. Beth Haslett, "Acquiring Conversational Competence." *Western Journal of Speech Communication* 48 (1984): 120.

14. John B. Carroll (ed.), *Language; Thought and Reality: Selected Writings of Benjamin Lee Whorf* (New York: Wiley, 1956), pp. 212–213.

15. For over 50 years, linguistics, anthropology, and communication textbooks have used the example of Eskimo words for snow to illustrate how language and perception are interrelated. According to this account, the importance of snow in Eskimo culture is reflected in the many terms they have for "falling snow," "drifting snow," "snow on the ground," "slushy snow," and so on. Earlier editions of this text repeated this myth. But we now know it isn't true. The myth began in 1911 when an anthropologist working in Alaska compared the different Eskimo root words for "snow on the ground," "falling snow," "drifting snow," and "a snow drift" with different English root words for a variety of forms of water (liquid, lake, river, brook, rain, dew, wave, foam, and so on). The anthropologist's comment was popularized in a 1940 article and then found its way into literally hundreds of publications that confidently asserted that Eskimos had 9, 23, 50, and even 100 words for snow. But they don't. The best available source, *A Dictionary of the West Greenlandic Eskimo Language,* gives just two: *quanik,* meaning "snow in the air," and *aput,* meaning "snow on the ground." So if you hear or read of the Eskimo-words-for-snow example, feel free to correct it. Or at least don't repeat it. See Geoffrey Pullum, "The Great Eskimo Vocabulary Hoax." *Lingua Franca* 14 (June 1990): 28–29.

16. Harry Hoijer, "Cultural Implications of Some Navajo Linguistic Categories." *Language* 27 (1951): 117.

17. J. Birere and C. Lanktree, "Sex-Role Related Effects of Sex Bias in Language." *Sex Roles* 9 (1980): 625–632; D. K. Ivy, "Who's the Boss? He, He/She, or They?" Unpublished paper, 1986; cited in D. K. Ivy and Phil Backlund, *Exploring Gender Speak: Personal Effectiveness in Gender Communication* (New York: McGraw-Hill, 1994), p. 75.

18. Deborah Tannen, *You Just Don't Understand: Women and Men in Communication* (New York: Morrow, 1990).

19. John Gray, *Men Are from Mars, Women Are from Venus* (New York: HarperCollins, 1992).

20. John Gray, *Mars and Venus in Love* (New York: HarperCollins, 1996).

21. Julia T. Wood reviews this research in *Gendered Lives: Communication, Gender, and Culture* (Belmont, CA: Wadsworth, 1994), pp. 141–145.

22. D. W. Addington, "The Relationship of Selected Vocal Characteristics to Personality Perception." *Speech Monographs* 35 (1968): 492–503.
23. Mark L. Knapp, *Essentials of Nonverbal Communication* (New York: Holt, 1980), p. 361.
24. M. F. Sciacca, *Come Si Vinci a Waterloo* (Milan: Marzorati, 1963), p. 129; quoted in Gemma Corradi Fiumara, *The Other Side of Language: A Philosophy of Listening* (London: Routledge, 1990), p. 101.
25. Sciacca, p. 26, quoted in Corradi Fiumara, p. 102.
26. Knapp, p. 298.
27. D. McNeill, "So You Think Gestures Are Nonverbal." *Psychological Review* 92 (1985): 350–371.
28. McNeill, p. 350.
29. Janet Beavin Bavelas, Nicole Chovil, Douglas A. Lawrie, and Allan Wade, "Interactive Gestures." Paper presented at the International Communication Association, Chicago, 1991, p. 2.
30. Bavelas, Chovil, Lawrie, and Wade, p. 7.
31. Bavelas, Chovil, Lawrie, and Wade, pp. 10–11.
32. See, for example, Paul Ekman, "Universal and Cultural Differences in Facial Expressions of Emotions," in *Nebraska Symposium on Motivation*, Vol. 19, ed. J. K. Cole (Lincoln, NE: University of Nebraska Press, 1971), pp. 207–283; C. E. Izard, *Human Emotions* (New York: Plenum, 1977).
33. Paul Ekman, W. V. Friesen, and S. Ancoli, "Facial Signs of Emotional Experience." *Journal of Personality and Social Psychology* 39 (1980): 1125–1134; Paul Ekman and W.V. Friesen, *Unmasking the Face* (Englewood Cliffs, NJ: Prentice-Hall, 1975).
34. R. A. Miller, *Japan's Modern Myth: The Language and Beyond* (Tokyo: Weatherhill, 1982).
35. Michael Argyle and M. Cook, *Gaze and Mutual Gaze* (Cambridge, England: Cambridge University Press, 1976).
36. Janis Andersen, Peter Andersen, and J. Landgraf, "The Development of Nonverbal Communication Competence in Childhood." Paper presented at the annual meeting of the International Communication Association, Honolulu, May 1985.
37. Judee K. Burgoon, David B. Buller, and W. Gill Woodall, *Nonverbal Communication: The Unspoken Dialogue* (New York: Harper & Row, 1989), p. 438.
38. R. L. Shotland and M. P. Johnson, "Bystander Behavior and Kinesics: The Interaction between the Helper and Victim." *Environmental Psychology and Nonverbal Behavior* 2 (1978): 181–190.
39. Burgoon, Buller, and Goodall, p. 438.
40. Ekman and Friesen, *Unmasking the Face*, pp. 40–46.
41. Albert Mehrabian, *Silent Messages: Implicit Communication of Emotion and Attitudes*, 2nd ed. (New York: Random House, 1981), pp. 23–25.
42. See, for example, J. K. Burgoon, V. Manusov, P. Mineo, and J. L. Hale, "Effects of Eye Gaze on Hiring Credibility, Attraction, and Relational Message Interpretation." *Journal of Nonverbal Behavior* 9 (1985): 133–146.

43. We elaborate on the process of deception in Chapter 8. Closely related to the work on deception is research on equivocal communication. See, for example, Janet Beavin Bavelas, Alex Black, Nicole Chovil, and Jennifer Mullet, "Truths, Lies, and Equivocation," in *Equivocal Communication* (Newbury Park, CA: Sage, 1990), pp. 170–207.

44. Burgoon, Buller, and Woodall, p. 81.

45. Judy C. Pearson, *Communication in the Family* (New York: Harper & Row, 1989), p. 78.

46. Edward T. Hall, *The Hidden Dimension* (Garden City, NY: Doubleday, 1966), p. 115.

47. For example, N. M. Sussman and H. M. Rosenfeld, "Influence of Culture, Language, and Sex on Conversational Distance." *Journal of Personality and Social Psychology* 42 (1982): 66–74.

48. Burgoon, Buller, and Woodall, p. 110.

49. Mandy Lam, *Interpersonal Communication Journal*, October 19, 1996. Used with permission.

50. Burgoon, Buller, and Woodall, p. 75.

51. Unless otherwise noted, the material on touch is from Stanley E. Jones and A. Elaine Yarbrough, "A Naturalistic Study of the Meanings of Touch." *Communication Monographs* 52 (1985): 19–56.

52. Knapp, pp. 108–109.

53. Mary Anne Fitzpatrick, *Between Husbands and Wives* (Newbury Park, CA: Sage, 1988), p. 76.

54. Fitzpatrick, pp. 218–219.

55. Knapp, p. 224.

56. G. L. Clore, N. H. Wiggins, and S. Itkin, "Judging Attraction from Nonverbal Behavior: The Gain Phenomenon." *Journal of Consulting and Clinical Psychology* 43 (1975): 491–497.

———

Virginia Satir was a family counselor who spent over 40 years helping parents and children communicate. Her small book, *Making Contact*, is her response to the many persons who asked her to write down the ideas and suggestions that she shared in workshops and seminars. As she said in the introduction, "The framework of this book is the BARE BONES of the possible, which I believe applies to *all* human beings. You, the reader, can flesh out the framework to fit you."

I like the simple, straightforward, no-nonsense way she talks about words, and I think that she's pinpointed several insights that can help all of us communicate better. If we did, as she suggests, pay more attention to the ways we use the 10 key words she discusses, I'm convinced that we'd experience considerably less conflict, misunderstanding, and frustration. See if you agree.

Paying Attention to Words

Virginia Satir

Words are important tools for contact. They are used more consciously than any other form of contact. I think it is important to learn how to use words well in the service of our communication.

Words cannot be separated from sights, sounds, movements, and touch of the person using them. They are one package.

However, for the moment, let's consider only words. Using words is literally the outcome of a whole lot of processes that go on in the body. All the senses, the nervous system, brain, vocal chords, throat, lungs, and all parts of the mouth are involved. This means that physiologically, talking is a very complicated process. . . .

If you think of your brain as a computer, storing all your experiences on tapes, then the words you pick will have to come from those tapes. Those tapes represent all our past experiences, accumulated knowledge, rules, and guides. There is nothing else there until new tapes are added. I hope that what you are reading will help you to add new tapes out of getting new experiences.

The words we use have an effect on our health. They definitely influence emotional relationships between people and how people can work together.

WORDS HAVE POWER

Listen to what you say and see if you are really saying what you mean. Nine people out of ten can't remember what they said sixty seconds ago; others remember.

There are ten English words that it is well to pay close attention to, to use with caution and with loving care: *I, You, They, It, But, Yes, No, Always, Never, Should.*

If you were able to use these special words carefully it would already solve many contact problems created by misunderstanding.

I

Many people avoid the use of the word *I* because they feel they are trying to bring attention to themselves. They think they are being selfish. Shades of childhood, when you shouldn't show off, and who wants to be selfish? The most

From *Making Contact* by Virginia Satir, (Millbrae, CA: Celestial Arts, 1976). The excerpt covers twelve pages in the text of Satir's book. Courtesy of Celestial Arts Pub. Co., 231 Adrian Rd., Millbrae, CA 94030.

important thing is that using "I" clearly means that you are taking responsibility for what you say. Many people mix this up by starting off with saying "you." I have heard people say "You can't do that." This is often heard as a "put-down," whereas "I think you can't do that" makes a more equal relationship between the two. It gives the same information without the put-down.

"I" is the pronoun that clearly states "me" when I am talking so it is important to say it. If you want to be clear when you are talking, no matter what you say, it is important to state clearly your ownership of *your* statement.

> "I am saying that the moon is made of red cheese."
> (*This is clearly your picture*)

instead of saying . . .

> "The moon is made of red cheese."
> (*This is a new law*)

Being aware of your clear use of "I" is particularly crucial when people are already in crisis. It is more clear to say "It is my picture that . . ." (which is an ownership statement). Whoever has the presence of mind to do this can begin to alter an escalating situation. When "I" is not clear, it is easy for the hearer to get a "you" message, which very often is interpreted as a "put-down."

You

The use of the word *you* is also tricky. It can be felt as an accusation when only reporting or sharing is intended.

"You are making things worse" can sound quite different if the words "I think" are added. "I think you are making things worse. . . ."

When used in clear commands or directions, it is not so easily misunderstood. For example, "I want you to . . ." or "You are the one I wanted to speak to."

They

The use of *they* is often an indirect way of talking about "you." It is also often a loose way of spreading gossip.

> "They say . . ."

"They" can also be some kind of smorgasbord that refers to our negative fantasies. This is especially true in a situation where people are assessing blame. If we know who "they" are we can say so.

How many times do we hear "They won't let me." "They will be upset." "They don't like what I am doing." "They say . . ."

If someone else uses it, we can ask "Who is your *they?*"

The important part of this is to have clear who "they" are so that inaccurate information is not passed on and it is clear exactly who is being referred to.

Being clear in this way seems to add to everyone's security. Information becomes concrete, which one can get hold of, instead of being nebulous and perhaps posing some kind of threat.

It

It is a word that can easily be misunderstood because it often isn't clear what "it" refers to. "It" is a word that has to be used with care.

The more clear your "it" is, the less the hearer fills it in with his [or her] own meaning. Sometimes "it" is related to a hidden "I" message. One way to better understand your "it" is to substitute "I" and see what happens. "It isn't clear" changed to "I am not clear" could make things more accurate and therefore easier to respond to.

"It often happens to people" is a statement that when said straight could be a comfort message that says, "The thing you are talking about has happened to me. I know how feeling humiliated feels."

To be more sure that we are understood, it might be wiser to fill in the details.

But

Next is the word *but*.

"But" is often a way of saying "yes" and "no" in the same sentence.

"I love you *but* I wish you would change your underwear more often."

This kind of use can easily end up with the other person feeling very uncomfortable, uneasy, and frequently confused.

Try substituting the word "and" for "but," which will clarify the situation. Your body will even feel different.

By using "but" the speaker is often linking two different thoughts together, which is what causes the difficulty.

Thus "I love you, but I wish you would change your underwear more often" could be two expressions.

"I love you," and "I wish you would change your underwear more often."

It could also represent someone's best, although fearful, attempt to make an uncomfortable demand by couching the demand in a love context, hoping the other person would not feel hurt.

If this is the case, what would happen if the person were to say "I want to ask something of you that I feel very uncomfortable about. I would like you to change your underwear more often."

Yes, No

A clear "yes" and "no" are important. Too many people say "yes, but" or "yes, maybe" or "no" just to be on the safe side, especially if they are in a position of power.

When "yes" or "no" are said clearly, and they mean NOW and not forever, and it is further clear "yes" and "no" relate to an issue rather than a person's value, then "yes" and "no" are very helpful words in making contact.

People can get away with much misuse of words when trust and good feeling have been established and when the freedom to comment is around. However, so often people feel so unsure about themselves that the lack of clarity leaves a lot of room for misunderstanding and consequent bad feelings. It is easy to build up these bad feelings once they are started.

"No" is a word that we all need and need to be able to use when it fits. So often when people feel "no," they say "maybe" or "yes" to avoid meeting the issue. This is justified on the basis of sparing the other's feelings. It is a form of lying and usually invites distrust, which, of course, is death to making contact.

When the "no" isn't clear, the "yes" can also be mistrusted. Have you ever heard "He said yes, but he doesn't really mean it"?

Always, Never

Always is the positive form of a global word. *Never* is the negative form. For example:

Always clean up your plate.
Never leave anything on your plate.

The literal meaning of these words is seldom accurate and the directions seldom applicable to life situations. There are few cases in life where something is always *or* never. Therefore to try to follow these demands in all situations will surely end up in failure like the rules I described earlier.

Often the use of these words is a way to make emotional emphasis, like . . .

"You *always* make me mad."

meaning really . . .

"I am NOW very mad at you."

If the situation were as the speaker states, the adrenals would wear out.

Sometimes the words *always* and *never* hide ignorance. For example, someone has spent just five minutes with a person and announces,

"He is always bright."

In most cases the literal use of these two words could not be followed in all times, places and situations. Furthermore, they are frequently untrue. For the most part they become emotionally laden words that harm rather than nurture or enlighten the situation.

I find that these words are often used without any meaning in any literal sense. . . .

Should

"Ought" and "should" are other trap words from which it is easy to imply that there is something wrong with you—you have failed somehow to measure up.

Often the use of these words implies stupidity on someone's part . . .

"You should have known better."

This is frequently heard as an accusation. Sometimes it merely represents some friendly advice. When people use the words "ought" and "should," often they are trying to indicate a dilemma in which they have more than one direction to go at a time—one may be pulling harder than the rest although the others are equally important . . .

"I like this, but I should get that."

When your words are these, your body often feels tight. There are no easy answers to the pulls which "ought" and "should" represent. Biologically we really can go in only one direction at a time.

When your body feels tight your brain often freezes right along with your tight body, and so your thinking becomes limited as well.

Hearing yourself use the words "ought" and "should" can be a tip-off to you that you are engaged in a struggle. Perhaps instead of trying to deal with these opposing parts as one, you can separate them and make two parts.

"I like this . . ." (one part)
"But I should get that"

translated into . . .

"I also need that . . ." (a second part).

Such a separation may be helpful in considering each piece separately and then considering them together.

When you do this your body has a chance to become a little looser, thus freeing some energy to negotiate a bit better.

When I am in this spot, I can help myself by asking whether I will literally die in either situation. If the answer is no, then I have a different perspective, and I can more easily play around with alternatives, since I am now out of a win-loss feeling in myself. I won't die. I may be only a little deprived or inconvenienced at most.

Start paying attention to the words you use.

Who is your *they?*
What is your *it?*
What does your *no* mean?
What does your *yes* mean?
Is your *I* clear?

Are you saying *never* and *always* when you mean sometimes and when you want to make emotional emphasis?

How are you using *ought* and *should?*

REVIEW QUESTIONS

1. What reasons do people give for *not* using the word *I?*
2. What is similar about the problems Satir finds with the words *they* and *it?*
3. Does Satir suggest that we should not use the words *but, yes,* and *no?* What is she saying about these words?
4. How does a person's use of the words *ought* and *should* reflect that person's value system?

PROBES

1. When you're in a conversation, can you recall what you said 60 seconds earlier? Try it. What do you notice?
2. Notice how, as Virginia Satir says, *it* and *they* both often work to hide the fact that some *I* is actually talking. When do you hear yourself using *it* and *they* that way?
3. What happens when you substitute *and* for *but?*
4. Do you experience your body responding, as Satir describes, to the words *ought* and *should?*

K napp and Hall begin this next reading with a point made before: The line separating verbal from nonverbal communication is not distinct. Both are virtually always found together, and the main—perhaps the only—benefit of separating them is to make it a little easier to study them.

In this excerpt from their book, *Nonverbal Communication in Human Interaction,* Knapp and Hall divide nonverbal cues into three general categories, the communication environment, the communicators' physical characteristics, and body movement and position. Then they discuss some ways that nonverbal communication works in the overall communication process. When they turn to everyday life, their examples involve nonverbal elements of the criminal justice system, nonverbal cues in televised politics, nonverbal aspects of classroom behavior, and nonverbal courtship behavior.

Their comments about the physical environment should sensitize you to the ways that furniture, lighting conditions, colors, and music or environmental noise affect interpersonal communicating. They also sketch effects of *proxemics,* the study of the impact of space.

Their brief comments about communicators' physical characteristics are meant to remind their readers of the potential impact body shape, skin color, and body or breath odors can have on communication. Artifacts such as clothes, hairpieces, jewelry, and accessories such as purses or portable electronic devices—cell phones, PDAs, and so on—can also affect how people communicate.

The section on body movement and position is divided into six topics: gesture, posture, touch, facial expression, eye behavior, and vocal behavior. Knapp and Hall do not attempt to cover any of these topics thoroughly. They say just enough about each to remind readers of the potential impact of each category of cue. For example, forward-leaning posture, they note, has been associated with higher involvement, more liking, and lower status. Touching others is a highly ambiguous form of communicating that takes its meaning from the context, the nature of the relationship, and the way the touching is done, rather than the type of touch, per se. Eye behavior can significantly affect judgments of credibility and attraction. And such elements of vocal behavior as rate, loudness, precise versus slurred articulation, laughing, swallowing, and moaning can all be understood to be significant.

The second major section of the reading reasserts the point that since verbal and nonverbal signals are virtually always inseparable, it is difficult to distinguish between the primary functions of either. Nonetheless, some research has emphasized the importance of nonverbal cues in (a) expressing emotion, (b) conveying interpersonal like/dislike, dominance/submission, and so on, (c) presenting one's personality to others, and (d) accompanying speech for the purposes of managing turn taking, feedback, attention, and so on. Another researcher emphasized the importance of nonverbal cues in the communication of immediacy, status, and responsiveness.

The final part of the reading illustrates the pervasive importance of nonverbal communication in everyday life by highlighting some ways these cues function in four contexts. In the criminal justice system, some researchers have tried to associate facial features or styles of appearance and movement with "criminal type" people. These efforts have been debunked, but contemporary nonverbal studies do generate advice, for example, about how to walk on a crowded street in order to minimize your vulnerability. Courtroom studies also provide material for lawyers and their consultants to aid in the process of jury selection.

Everyone who's viewed political campaigning on television is aware of the importance of appearance, dress, and location or context in politics. Handlers or managers place their candidates in locations that emphasize aspects of their verbal messages—the factory gate to discuss labor-management legislation, the national park to discuss environmental politics, in front of Congress or the White House to emphasize national credibility. Studies of televised debates have attributed success and failure to facial expressions, eye gaze, and even to dress.

As you know first-hand, classroom communication also includes important nonverbal elements. Students learn where to sit to reinforce their self-definition as "involved" or "laid-back." They develop subtle and powerful rhythms of eye behavior to avoid being called on or to present themselves as interested and engaged. Professors announce that they make time for students and then contradict themselves by habitually glancing at their watches. And U-shaped or circular arrangement of chairs can facilitate interaction and make "hiding at the back of the room" more difficult. With respect to online learning, Knapp and Hall note that "the influence of nonverbal behavior that communicates warmth and closeness in conventional classrooms promises to be even more important to the success of distance education."

Their final topic is courtship behavior, and all of us have experienced the importance of nonverbal cues in this context. The authors note that research has not yet systematized or quantified the powerful elements that contribute toward attractiveness and signal availability or its opposite. They review results of some research on flirtation behavior between men and women in bars that you might usefully test against your own experience. Knapp and Hall also summarize some studies of the sequence of steps in courtship behavior, both generally—approach, turning toward the other, nonintimate touch, increasing eye gaze, and so on—and in specific nonverbal courtship behaviors—eye to body, eye to eye, hand to hand, and so on.

An entire course—or more—could be dedicated to the study of the nonverbal aspects of interpersonal communicating. This reading and the one that follows are designed to provide an overview of these processes and the ways they function. I hope that this reading will sensitize you to the many different ways you communicate nonverbally, and to the many nonverbal cues you interpret.

Nonverbal Communication: Basic Perspectives

Mark L. Knapp and Judith A. Hall

To most people, the phrase *nonverbal communication* refers to *communication effected by means other than words* (assuming words are the verbal element). Like most definitions, this one is generally useful, but it does not account adequately for the complexity of this phenomenon. As long as we understand and appreciate its limitations, this broad definition should serve us well.

[For example,] we need to understand that separating verbal and nonverbal behavior into two separate and distinct categories is virtually impossible. Consider, for example, the hand movements that make up American Sign Language (a language of the deaf). These gesticulations are mostly linguistic (verbal), yet hand gestures are often considered behavior that is "other than words." McNeill (1992) has demonstrated the linguistic qualities of some gestures by noting that different kinds of gestures disappear with different kinds of aphasia, namely, those gestures with linguistic functions similar to the specific verbal loss. Conversely, not all spoken words are clearly or singularly verbal—as, for example, onomatopoeic words such as *buzz* or *murmur* and nonpropositional speech used by auctioneers and some aphasics. . . .

Another way of defining nonverbal communication is to look at the things people study. The theory and research associated with nonverbal communication focus on three primary units: the environmental structures and conditions within which communication takes place, the physical characteristics of the communicators themselves, and the various behaviors manifested by the communicators. A detailed breakdown of these three features follows.

THE COMMUNICATION ENVIRONMENT

Physical Environment

Although most of the emphasis in nonverbal research is on the appearance and behavior of the persons communicating, increasing attention is being given to the influence of nonhuman factors on human transactions. People change environments to help them accomplish their communicative goals; conversely, environments can affect our moods, choices of words, and actions. Thus this category concerns those elements that impinge on the human relationship but are not directly a part of it. Environmental factors include the furniture, architectural style, interior decorating, lighting conditions, colors, temperature, additional noises or music, and the like, amid which the interaction occurs. Variations in arrangements, materials, shapes, or surfaces of objects in the interacting environment can be extremely influential on the outcome of an interpersonal relationship. This category also includes what might be called *traces of action*. For instance, as you observe cigarette butts, orange peels, and wastepaper left by the person you will soon interact with, you form an impression that will eventually influence your meeting. Perceptions of time and timing comprise another important part of the communicative environment. When something occurs, how frequently it occurs, and the tempo or rhythm of actions are clearly a part of the communicative world even though they are not a part of the physical environment per se.

Spatial Environment

Proxemics is the study of the use and perception of social and personal space. Under this heading is a body of work called *small group ecology*, which concerns itself with how people use and respond to spatial relationships in formal and informal group settings. Such studies deal with seating and spatial arrangements as related to leadership, communication flow, and the task at hand. On an even broader level, some attention has been given to spatial relationships in crowds and densely populated situations. Personal space orientation is sometimes studied in the context of conversation distance and how it varies according to sex, status, roles, cultural orientation, and so forth. The term *territoriality* is also used frequently in the study of proxemics to denote the human tendency to stake out personal territory (or untouchable space) much as wild animals and birds do.

THE COMMUNICATORS' PHYSICAL CHARACTERISTICS

This category covers things that remain relatively unchanged during the period of interaction. They are influential nonverbal cues that are not visibly movement bound. Included are physique or body shape, general attractiveness, height, weight, hair, skin color or tone, and so forth. Odors (body or breath) associated with the person are normally considered part of a person's physical appearance. Further, objects associated with the interactants also may affect their physical appearance. These are called *artifacts* and include things such as clothes, lipstick, eyeglasses, wigs and other hairpieces, false eyelashes, jewelry, and accessories such as attaché cases.

BODY MOVEMENT AND POSITION

Body movement and position typically includes gestures, movements of the body (limbs, hands, head, feet, and legs), facial expressions (smiles), eye behavior (blinking, direction and length of gaze, and pupil dilation), and posture. The furrow of the brow, the slump of a shoulder, and the tilt of a head are all considered body movements and positions. Specifically, the major areas are gestures, posture, touching behavior, facial expressions, and eye behavior.

Gestures

There are many different types of gestures (and variations of these types), but the most frequently studied are the following:

1. **Speech independent.** These gestures are not tied to speech, but they have a direct verbal translation or dictionary definition, usually consisting of a word or two or a phrase. There is high agreement among members of a culture or

subculture on the verbal "translation" of these signals. The gestures used to represent "A-OK" or "Peace" (also known as the "V-for-Victory" sign) are examples of speech-independent gestures for large segments of U.S. culture.

2. **Speech related.** These gestures are directly tied to, or accompany, speech—often serving to illustrate what is being said verbally. These movements may accent or emphasize a word or phrase, sketch a path of thought, point to present objects, depict a spatial relationship, depict the rhythm or pacing of an event, draw a picture of a referent, depict a bodily action, or serve as commentary on the regulation and organization of the interactive process.

Posture

Posture is normally studied in conjunction with other nonverbal signals to determine the degree of attention or involvement, the degree of status relative to the other interactive partner, or the degree of liking for the other interactant. A forward-leaning posture, for example, has been associated with higher involvement, more liking, and lower status in studies where the interactants did not know each other very well. Posture is also a key indicator of the intensity of some emotional states, for example, the dropping posture associated with sadness or the rigid, tense posture associated with anger. The extent to which the communicators mirror each other's posture may also reflect rapport or an attempt to build rapport.

Touching Behavior

Touching may be self-focused or other focused. Self-focused manipulations, not usually made for purposes of communicating, may reflect a person's particular state or a habit. Many are commonly called *nervous mannerisms*. Some of these actions are relics from an earlier time in life—times when we first learn how to manage our emotions, develop social contacts, or perform some instructional task. Sometimes we perform these manipulations as we adapt to such learning experiences, and they stay with us when we face similar situations later in life, often as only part of the original movement. Some refer to these types of self-focused manipulation as *adaptors*. These adaptors may involve various manipulations of one's own body such as licking, picking, holding, pinching, and scratching. Object adaptors are manipulations practiced in conjunction with an object, as when a reformed male cigarette smoker reaches toward his breast pocket for the nonexistent package of cigarettes. Of course, not all behaviors that reflect habitual actions or an anxious disposition can be traced to earlier adaptations, but they do represent a part of the overall pattern of bodily action.

One of the most potent forms of nonverbal communication occurs when two people touch. Touch can be virtually electric, but it also can irritate, condescend, or comfort.

Touch is a highly ambiguous form of behavior whose meaning often takes more from the context, the nature of the relationship, and the manner of execution than from the configuration of the touch per se. Some researchers are concerned with touching behavior as an important factor in the child's early development; some are concerned with adult touching behavior. Subcategories include stroking, hitting, greetings and farewells, holding, and guiding another's movements.

Facial Expressions

Most studies of the face are concerned with the configurations that display various emotional states. The six primary affects receiving the most study are anger, sadness, surprise, happiness, fear, and disgust. Facial expressions also can function as regulatory gestures, providing feedback and managing the flow of interaction. In fact, some researchers believe the primary function of the face is to communicate, not to express emotions.

Eye Behavior

Where we look, when we look, and how long we look during interaction are the primary foci for studies of gazing. *Gaze* refers to the eye movement we make in the general direction of another's face. *Mutual gaze* occurs when interactants look into each other's eyes. The dilation and constriction of our pupils also has interest to those who study nonverbal communication because it is sometimes an indicator of interest, attention, or involvement.

Vocal Behavior

Vocal behavior deals with *how* something is said, not what is said. It deals with the range of nonverbal vocal cues surrounding common speech behavior. Generally, a distinction is made between two types of sounds:

1. The sound variations made with the vocal cords during talk that are a function of changes in pitch, duration, loudness, and silence
2. Sounds that result primarily from physiological mechanisms other than the vocal cords, for example, the pharyngeal, oral, or nasal cavities

Most of the research on vocal behavior and its effects on human interaction has focused on pitch level and variability; the duration of sounds (clipped or drawn out); pauses within the speech stream and the latency of response during turn exchanges; loudness level and variability; resonance; precise or slurred articulation; rate; rhythm; and intruding sound during speech such as "uh" or "um." The study of vocal signals encompasses a broad range of interests, from questions focusing on stereotypes associated with certain voices to questions about the effects of vocal behavior on comprehension and persuasion. Thus even specialized sounds such as laughing, belching, yawning, swallowing, moaning, and the like, may be of interest to the extent that they may affect the outcome of interaction.

NONVERBAL COMMUNICATION IN THE TOTAL COMMUNICATION PROCESS

[A close examination of these varied cues reveals] the inseparable nature of verbal and nonverbal signals. Ray Birdwhistell, a pioneer in nonverbal research, reportedly said that studying only *nonverbal* communication is like studying *noncardiac* physiology. His point is well taken. It is not easy to dissect human interaction and make one diagnosis that concerns only verbal behavior and another that concerns only nonverbal behavior. The verbal dimension is so intimately woven and subtly represented in so much of what has been previously labeled *nonverbal* that the term does not always adequately describe the behavior under study. Some of the most noteworthy scholars associated with nonverbal study refuse to segregate words from gestures and hence work under the broader terms of *communication* or *face-to-face interaction* (McNeill, 2000). . . . Because verbal and nonverbal systems operate together as part of the larger communication process, efforts to distinguish clearly between the two have not been very successful. One common misconception, for example, assumes nonverbal behavior is used solely to communicate emotional messages, whereas verbal behavior is for conveying ideas. Words can carry much emotion—we can talk explicitly about emotions, and we also communicate emotion between the lines in verbal nuances. Conversely, nonverbal cues are often used for purposes other than showing emotion; as examples, people in conversation use eye movements to help tell each other when it is time to switch speaking turns, and people commonly use hand gestures while talking to help convey their ideas (McNeill, 2000).

Argyle (1988) has identified the following primary functions of nonverbal behavior in human communication as follows:

1. Expressing emotion
2. Conveying interpersonal attitudes (like/dislike, dominance/submission, etc.)
3. Presenting one's personality to others
4. Accompanying speech for the purposes of managing turn taking, feedback, attention, and so on.

Argyle also notes that nonverbal behaviors are important in many rituals, such as greeting. Notice that none of these functions of nonverbal behavior is limited to nonverbal behavior alone; that is, we can express emotions and attitudes, present ourselves in a particular light, and manage the interaction using verbal cues, too. This does not suggest, however, that in any given situation we might not rely more heavily on verbal behavior for some purposes and on nonverbal for others.

We also need to recognize that the ways we attribute meanings to verbal and nonverbal behavior are not all that different either. Nonverbal actions, like verbal ones, may communicate more than one message at a time—for example, the way you nonverbally make it clear to another person that you want to keep talking may simultaneously express your need for dominance over that person and, perhaps, your emotional state. When you grip a child's shoulder during a reprimand, you may increase comprehension and recall, but you may also elicit such a negative reaction that the child fails to obey. A smile can be a part of an emotional expression, an attitudinal message, part of a self-presentation, or a listener response to manage the interaction. And, like verbal behavior, the meanings attributed to nonverbal behavior may be stereotyped, idiomatic, or ambiguous. Furthermore, the same nonverbal behavior performed in different contexts may, like words, receive different attributions of meaning. For example, looking down at the floor may reflect sadness in one situation and submissiveness or lack of involvement in another. Finally, in an effort to identify the fundamental categories of meaning associated with nonverbal behavior, Mehrabian (1970, 1981) identified a threefold perspective resulting from his extensive testing:

1. **Immediacy.** Sometimes we react to things by evaluating them—positive or negative, good or bad, like or dislike.
2. **Status.** Sometimes we enact or perceive behaviors that indicate various aspects of status to us—strong or weak, superior or subordinate.
3. **Responsiveness.** This third category refers to our perceptions of activity— slow or fast, active or passive.

In various verbal and nonverbal studies over the past three decades, dimensions similar to Mehrabian's have been reported consistently by investigators from diverse fields studying diverse phenomena. It is reasonable to conclude, therefore, that these three dimensions are basic responses to our environment and are reflected in the way we assign meaning to both verbal and nonverbal behavior. Most of this work, however, depends on subjects translating their reactions to a nonverbal act into one identified by verbal descriptors. This issue has already been addressed in our discussion of the way the brain processes different pieces of information. In general, then, nonverbal signals, like words, can and do have multiple uses and meanings; like words, nonverbal signals have denotative and connotative meanings; and like words, nonverbal signals play an active role in communicating liking, power, and responsiveness. . . .

NONVERBAL COMMUNICATION IN EVERYDAY LIFE

Clearly nonverbal signals are a critical part of all our communicative endeavors. Sometimes nonverbal signals are the most important part of our message. Understanding and effectively using nonverbal behavior is crucial in virtually every sector of our society.

Consider the role of nonverbal signals in therapeutic situations. Therapists use nonverbal behavior to build rapport with clients (Tickle-Degnen & Rosenthal, 1994). Their ability to read nonverbal signals associated with client problems surely assists in diagnosis and treatment. A slight change in tone of voice or a glance away from the patient at the wrong time and a physician may communicate a message very different from intended (Buller & Street, 1992). In situations where verbal communication is often constrained, as in nurse-physician interaction during an operation, effective nonverbal communication is literally the difference between life and death. The significance of nonverbal cues in the arts—dance, theatrical performances, music, films, photography, and so on—is obvious. The nonverbal symbolism of various ceremonies and rituals (e.g., the trappings of the marriage ceremony, Christmas decorations, religious rituals, funerals, and so forth) creates important and necessary responses in the participants. Certainly, an understanding of nonverbal signals prepares us for communicating across cultures, classes, or age groups and with different ethnic groups within our culture (Lee, Matumoto, Kobayashi, Krupp, Maniatis, & Roberts, 1992). Nonverbal messages not only help determine how well you do in a job interview, but also play an integral part in your job performance—whether it involves public relations, customer service, marketing, advertising, supervision, or leadership (DePaulo, 1992; Hecker & Stewart, 1988). Diplomats often prefer implicit accommodation rather than explicit, thereby using and relying heavily on nonverbal signals.

A list of all the situations where nonverbal communication plays an important role would be interminable—especially if we included our everyday activities involving forming impressions of other people and building, maintaining, and ending relationships. Therefore, we limit our discussion in this chapter to four areas that touch all our lives: crime and punishment, televised politics, classroom behavior, and courtship behavior. . . .

Crime and Punishment

The desire to identify criminal types has been a subject of study for centuries. Because it is unlikely that a person will tell you that he or she is a criminal or potential criminal, nonverbal indicators become especially important. At one time, some people thought criminals could be identified by their facial features or the pattern of bumps on their head. In recent years, scientists have used a knowledge of nonverbal behavior to examine both criminal acts and the arena for assessing guilt or innocence, the courtroom.

One study analyzed the appearance and movements of people who walked through one of the highest assault areas in New York City (Grayson & Stein, 1981). Then, prisoners who had knowledge of such matters were asked to view the films of the potential victims and indicate the likelihood of assault. In addition to finding that older people are a prime target, the researchers also found that potential victims tended to move differently. They tended to take long or short strides (not medium); and their body parts did not seem to move in synchrony; that is, they seemed less graceful and fluid in their movement. Other studies have tried to identify nonverbal characteristics that rapists use to select their victims. Some rapists look for women who exhibit passivity, a lack of confidence, and vulnerability; others prefer the exact opposite, wishing to "put an uppity woman in her place." The conclusion seems to recommend a public nonverbal demeanor that is confident yet not aggressive (Myers, Templer, & Brown, 1984).

Another study that assessed potentially aggressive acts focused on mothers who abused their children (Givens, 1978). It was noted that even while playing with their children, these mothers communicated their dislike (turning away, not smiling, etc.) by their nonverbal behavior. Just as abusive and nonabusive mothers differ in their behavior, the children of abusive parents and nonabusive parents differ in their nonverbal behavior (Hecht, Foster, Dunn, Williams, Anderson, & Pulbratek, 1986). . . .

Because of the important implications of decisions made in courtrooms and the desire to maintain impartial communication, almost every facet of the courtroom process is being analyzed. Judges are cautioned to minimize possible signs of partiality in their voice and positioning. Research suggests that judges' attitudes and nonverbal cues may indeed influence the outcome of a trial (Blanck & Rosenthal, 1992). . . . In some cases, attorneys and witnesses have been videotaped in pretrial practice sessions to determine whether they are conveying nonverbally any messages they want to avoid. The study of nonverbal behavior is also important to the process of jury selection. Although this attention to nonverbal signals emanating from prospective jurors may indicate a degree of sensitivity that did not previously exist, we need not worry that attorneys or social scientists will become so skilled they can rig juries (Saks, 1976).

Televised Politics

Politicians have long recognized the important role of nonverbal behavior. . . . The tired, overweight, physically unappealing political bosses of yesteryear have been replaced by younger, good-looking, vigorous candidates who can capture the public's vote with an assist from their nonverbal attraction. The average American currently watches between 30 and 40 hours of television each week. Television has certainly helped to structure some of our nonverbal perceptions, and more and more political candidates recognize the tremendous influence these perceptions may have on the eventual election outcome. Television seems especially well suited to nonverbal signals that express positive relationship messages (e.g., facial expressions that communicate sincerity, body positions that suggest immediacy, or vocal tones that are perceived as caring). Television requires what Jamieson (1988) calls "a new eloquence—a softer, warmer style of communication." This in no way minimizes the necessity of a candidate also displaying nonverbal signals that would help to communicate assertiveness and energy. How have our presidential candidates fared? . . .

An analysis of the 1976 Carter-Ford presidential debates argues that Gerald Ford's "loss" was attributable to less eye gaze with the camera, grimmer facial expressions, and less favorable camera angles (Tiemens, 1978). Subsequently, Jimmy Carter's loss to Ronald Reagan in the 1980 debate was attributed to Carter's visible tension and his inability to "coordinate his nonverbal behavior with his verbal message" (Ritter & Henry, 1990). Effective leaders are often seen as people who confidently take stock of a situation, perform smoothly, and put those around them at ease. Many saw Reagan's nonverbal behavior this way. In 1984 Reagan's expressiveness and physical attractiveness were evident, whereas his opponent, Walter Mondale, was perceived as low in expressiveness and attractiveness (Patterson, Churchill, Burger, & Powell, 1992). Expressions of fear may be the biggest turnoff for voters. Looking down, hesitating, making rapid, jerky movements or seeming to freeze as Dan Quayle did when Lloyd Bentsen told him in the 1988 vice presidential debate, "You're no Jack Kennedy." Some even associated Walter Mondale's tense smile with a fear grimace (Masters, 1989; Sullivan et al., 1991).

Fortunately, media experts do not control all the variables—not the least of which is the public's increasing knowledge of how political images can be molded through television. One of Richard Nixon's image-makers in 1968, Roger Ailes, offered the following perspective 15 years later: "The TV public is very smart in the sense that somewhere, somehow, they make a judgment about the candidates they see. Anybody who claims he can figure out that process is full of it."

Classroom Behavior

Whether it takes place in the classroom itself or not, the teaching/learning process is a gold mine for discovering the richness and importance of nonverbal behavior (Andersen & Andersen, 1982; Babad, 1992; Philippot, Feldman, & McGee, 1992; Woolfolk & Brooks, 1983).

Acceptance and understanding of ideas and feelings by both teacher and student, encouraging and criticizing, silence, and questioning all involve nonverbal elements. Consider the following instances as representative of the variety of classroom nonverbal cues:

1. The frantic hand-waver who is sure he or she has the correct answer
2. The student who is sure she or he does not know the answer and tries to avoid eye contact with the teacher
3. The effects of student dress, hair length, and adornment on teacher-student interaction
4. The glowering facial expressions, threatening gestures, and critical tone of voice frequently used for discipline in elementary schools
5. Teachers who request student questioning and criticism, but whose nonverbal actions make it clear they will not be receptive
6. The way arrangement of seating and monitoring behavior during examinations reveal a teacher's degree of trust in students
7. Professors who announce they have plenty of time for student conferences, but whose fidgeting and glancing at a watch suggest otherwise
8. Teachers who try to assess visual feedback to determine student comprehension
9. The ways different classroom designs (wall colors, space between seats, windows) influence student participation and learning
10. The nonverbal cues that signal student-teacher closeness or distance

Subtle nonverbal influence in the classroom can sometimes have dramatic results, as Rosenthal and Jacobson (1968) found. Intelligence quotient (IQ) tests were given to elementary school pupils prior to their entering for the fall term. Randomly (that is, not according to scores), some students were labeled as high scorers on an "intellectual blooming test" indicating they would show unusual intellectual development in the following year. Teachers were given this information. These students showed a sharp rise on IQ tests given at the end of the year, which experimenters attributed to teacher expectations and to the way these students were treated.

> To summarize our speculations, we may say that by what she said, by how and when she said it, by her facial expressions, postures, and perhaps by her touch, the teacher may have communicated to the children of the experimental group that she expected improved intellectual performance. Such communications together with possible changes in teaching techniques may have helped the child learn by changing his self-concept, his expectations of his own behavior, and his motivation, as well as his cognitive style and skills. (p. 180) . . .

The influence of nonverbal behavior in the classroom can be a two-way street. Teachers who are perceived by their students as establishing physical and psychological closeness through nonverbal behavior produce positive learning outcomes. Furthermore, students whose nonverbal behavior are perceived by teachers as establishing this kind of immediacy seem more likely to elicit positive expressions from their teachers (Baringer & McCroskey, 2000). The influence of nonverbal behavior that communicates warmth and closeness in conventional classrooms promises to be even more important to the success of distance education (Guerrero & Miller, 1998; Mottet, 2000).

Courtship Behavior

One commentary on nonverbal courtship behavior is found in the following excerpts from the Beatles' song "Something":

Something in the way she moves
Attracts me like no other lover
Something in the way she woos me . . .
Something in her smile she knows
That I don't need no other lover
Something in her style that shows me . . .
You're asking me will my love grow . . .
You stick around, now
It may show . . .

As the song suggests, we know there is "something" highly influential in our nonverbal courtship behavior. We are, however, at a very early stage in quantifying these patterns of behavior. On a purely intuitive level, we know that some men and some women can exude such messages as "I'm available," "I'm knowledgeable," or "I want you" without saying a word. These messages can be expressed by the thrust of one's hips, touch gestures, extra long eye contact, carefully looking at the other's body, showing excitement and desire in fleeting facial expressions, and gaining close proximity. When subtle enough, these moves will allow both parties to deny that either had committed themselves to a courtship ritual.

Studies involving flirtation behavior between men and women in bars (singles bars, hotel cocktail lounges, bars within restaurants, etc.) provide some observational data on the role of nonverbal signals in the courtship process (McCormick & Jones, 1989; Moore, 1985; Perper & Weis, 1987). Most of the early signaling seemed to be performed by women. The most frequently observed behaviors included three types of eye gaze (a room-encompassing glance; a short, darting glance at a specific person; and a fixed gaze of at least 3 seconds at a specific other); smiling at a specific other person; laughing and giggling in response to another's comments; tossing one's head, a movement sometimes accompanied by stroking of the hair; grooming, primping, and adjustment of clothes; caressing objects such as keys or a glass; a solitary dance (keeping time to the music with visible movements); and a wide variety of seemingly "accidental" touching of a specific other. The researchers did not specifically examine the type of clothing, nor did they examine the tone of voice used—both of which are likely to be influential flirtation behaviors. In an effort to determine whether these behaviors were more likely to occur in a context where signaling interest in and attraction to others was expected, the researchers observed the behavior of women and men in snack bars, meetings, and libraries. None of these contexts revealed anything close to the number of flirting behaviors found in bars. . . .

Does the courtship process proceed according to a sequence of steps? Perper (1985) describes courtship's "core sequence" like this: The *approach* involves getting the two people in the same general proximity; *acknowledging and turning toward the other* is the invitation to begin talking; during *talk*, there will be an increasing amount of fleeting, *nonintimate touching and a gradually increasing intensity in eye gaze*; finally, Perper says the two will exhibit *more and more synchrony in their movements*. Obviously, either person can short-circuit the sequence at any point. . . .

Morris (1971) also believes that heterosexual couples in Western culture go through a sequence of steps, like courtship patterns of other animals, on the road to sexual intimacy. Notice the predominant nonverbal theme:

1. Eye to body
2. Eye to eye
3. Voice to voice
4. Hand to hand
5. Arm to shoulder
6. Arm to waist
7. Mouth to mouth

8. Hand to head
9. Hand to body
10. Mouth to breast
11. Hand to genitals
12. Genitals to genitals and/or mouth to genitals

Morris . . . believes these steps generally follow the same order, although he admits there are variations. Skipping steps or moving to a level of intimacy beyond what would be expected is found in socially formalized types of bodily contact, for example, a good-night kiss. It should be noted that any of the behaviors identified by . . . Morris can be performed in a more or less intimate way. Mouth-to-mouth kisses, for example, may be performed with little intimacy or with a great deal of it. . . .

Up to now, we have concentrated on the nonverbal courtship behavior of unmarried men and women. The use of specific types of gazing, touching, and other actions studied in heterosexual courtship patterns is also an important part of homosexual courtship (Delph, 1978).

SUMMARY

The term *nonverbal* is commonly used to describe all human communication events that transcend spoken or written words. At the same time, we should realize that these nonverbal events and behaviors can be interpreted through verbal symbols. We also found that any classification scheme that separates things into two discrete categories (e.g., verbal/nonverbal, left/right brain, vocal/nonvocal, etc.) will not be able to account for factors that do not seem to fit either category. We might more appropriately think of behaviors as existing on a continuum with some behaviors overlapping two continua. . . .

The theoretical writings and research on nonverbal communication can be broken down into the following three areas:

1. The communication environment (physical and spatial)
2. The communicator's physical characteristics
3. Body movement and position (gestures, posture, touching, facial expressions, eye behavior, and vocal behavior)

Nonverbal communication should not be studied as an isolated phenomenon but as an inseparable part of the total communication process. The interrelationships between verbal and nonverbal behavior were illustrated in our discussion of how nonverbal behavior functions in repeating, conflicting with, substituting for, complementing, accenting/moderating, and regulating verbal communication. Nonverbal communication is important because of its role in the total communication system, the tremendous quantity of informational cues it gives in any particular situation, and its use in fundamental areas of our daily life. . . .

REVIEW QUESTIONS

1. Define nonverbal communication in a way that does not depend on the "non" and that acknowledges the virtual impossibility of separating verbal and nonverbal cues.
2. What are "traces of action" and how have they affected your communicating?
3. Define: proxemics   territoriality   artifacts   adaptors   gaze.
4. Give an example of how nonverbal cues communicate immediacy. Do the same with status and responsiveness.
5. Describe three important nonverbal facets of a funeral and three different important nonverbal facets of a church service.
6. How is nonverbal communicating important in a job interview?
7. How do you think a judge's nonverbal behavior in the courtroom can affect the outcome of a trial?
8. Describe three obvious ways nonverbal communication functions in the interpersonal communication class that you are currently taking.

PROBES

1. What happens to your understanding when everyday human behavior is categorized into "spatial environment," "gestures," "eye behavior," "touching behavior" and the other categories used by nonverbal researchers?
2. Some research—and everyday experience—indicates that, when a person's verbal and nonverbal cues contradict each other, people tend to believe what's being communicated nonverbally. Do you agree or disagree? Explain why.
3. In your opinion, what is more important in dating contexts, eye gaze, vocal behavior, or touch? Explain.
4. From your dating experience, what are the two most important nonverbal elements of successful dating behavior?
5. Some people complain that an emphasis on nonverbal cues in the courts, politics, and the classroom focuses on what's trivial rather than on what's important. They argue that the main meanings should be in the words, the language that's used. What is your position on this issue?

REFERENCES

1. Andersen, P. A., & Andersen, J. (1982). Nonverbal immediacy in instruction. In L. L. Barker (Ed.), *Communication in the classroom.* Englewood Cliffs, NJ: Prentice-Hall.
2. Argyle, M. (1988). *Bodily communication* (2nd ed.). London: Methuen.
3. Babad, E. (1992). Teacher expectancies and nonverbal behavior. In R. S. Feldman (Ed.), *Applications of nonverbal behavioral theories and research.* Hillsdale, NJ: Erlbaum.

4. Baringer, D. K., and McCroskey, J. C. (2000). Immediacy in the classroom: Student immediacy. *Communication Education, 49,* 178–186.

5. Blanck, P. D., & Rosenthal, R. (1992). Nonverbal behavior in the courtroom. In R. S. Feldman (Ed.), *Applications of nonverbal behavioral theories and research.* Hillsdale, NJ: Erlbaum.

6. Buller, D. B., & Street, R. L., Jr. (1992). Physician-patient relationships. In R. S. Feldman (Ed.), *Applications of nonverbal behavioral theories and research.* Hillsdale, NJ: Erlbaum.

7. Delph, E. W. (1978). *The silent community: Public homosexual encounters.* Beverly Hills, CA: Sage.

8. DePaulo, P. J. (1992). Applications of nonverbal behavior research in marketing and management. In R. S. Feldman (Ed.), *Applications of nonverbal behavioral theories and research.* Hillsdale, NJ: Erlbaum.

9. Givens, D. B. (1978). Contrasting nonverbal styles in mother-child interaction: Examples from a study of child abuse. *Semiotica, 24,* 33–47.

10. Grayson, B., & Stein, M. I. (1981). Attracting assault: Victims' nonverbal cues. *Journal of Communication, 31,* 68–75.

11. Guerrero, L. K., & Miller, T. A. (1998). Associations between nonverbal behaviors and initial impressions of instructor competence and course content in videotaped distance education courses. *Communication Education, 47,* 30–42.

12. Hecht, M., Foster, S. H., Dunn, D. J., Williams, J. K., Anderson, D. R., & Pulbratek, D. (1986). Nonverbal behavior of young abused and neglected children. *Communication Education, 35,* 134–142.

13. Hecker, S., & Stewart, D. W. (Eds.). (1988). *Nonverbal communication in advertising.* Lexington, MA: Lexington.

14. Jamieson, K. H. (1988). *Eloquence in an electronic age.* New York: Oxford University Press.

15. Lee, M. E., Matsumoto, D., Kobayashi, M., Krupp, D., Maniatis, E. F., & Roberts, W. (1992). Cultural influences on nonverbal behavior in applied settings. In R. S. Feldman (Ed.), *Applications of nonverbal behavioral theories and research.* Hillsdale, NJ: Erlbaum.

16. Masters, R. D. (1989). *The nature of politics.* New Haven, CT: Yale University Press.

17. McCormick, N. B., & Jones, A. J. (1989). Gender differences in nonverbal flirtation. *Journal of Sex Education & Therapy, 15,* 271–282.

18. McNeill, D. (1992). *Hand and mind: What gestures reveal about thought.* Chicago: University of Chicago Press.

19. McNeill, D. (2000) (Ed.). *Language and gesture.* New York: Cambridge University Press.

20. Mehrabian, A. (1970). A semantic space for nonverbal behavior. *Journal of Consulting and Clinical Psychology, 35,* 248–257.

21. Mehrabian, A. (1981). *Silent messages* (2nd ed.). Belmont, CA: Wadsworth.

22. Moore, M. M. (1985). Nonverbal courtship patterns in women: Content and consequences. *Ethology and Sociobiology, 6,* 237–247.

23. Morris, D. (1971). *Intimate behavior.* New York: Random House.

24. Mottet, T. P. (2000). Interactive television instructors' perceptions of students' nonverbal responsiveness and their influence on distance teaching. *Communication Education, 49,* 146–164.

25. Patterson, M. L., Churchill, M. E., Burger, G. K., & Powell, J. L. (1992). Verbal and nonverbal modality effects on impressions of political candidates: Analysis from the 1984 presidential debates. *Communication Monographs, 59,* 231–242.

26. Perper, T. (1985). *Sex signals: The biology of love.* Philadelphia: ISI Press.

27. Perper, T., & Weis, D. L. (1987). Proceptive and rejective strategies of U.S. and Canadian college women. *Journal of Sex Research, 23,* 455–480.

28. Philippot, P., Feldman, R. S., & McGee, G. (1992). Nonverbal behavioral skills in an educational context: Typical and atypical populations. In R. S. Feldman (Ed.), *Applications of nonverbal behavioral theories and research.* Hillsdale, NJ: Erlbaum.

29. Ritter, K., & Henry, D. (1990). The 1980 Reagan-Carter presidential debate. In R. V. Friedenberg (Ed.), *Rhetorical studies of national political debates: 1960–1988.* New York: Praeger.

30. Rosenthal, R., & Jacobson, L. (1968). *Pygmalion in the classroom.* New York: Holt, Rinehart & Winston.

31. Saks, M. J. (1976). Social scientists can't rig juries. *Psychology Today, 9,* 48–50, 55–57.

32. Sullivan, D. G., Masters, R. D., Lanzetta, J. T., McHugo, G. J., Plate, E., & Englis, B. G. (1991). Facial displays and political leadership. In G. Schubert & R. Masters (Eds.), *Primate politics.* Carbondale: University of Southern Illinois Press.

33. Tickle-Degnen, L., Hall, J., & Rosenthal, R. (1994). Nonverbal behavior. In V. S. Ramachandran (Ed.), *Encyclopedia of human behavior* (Vol. 3). New York: Academic Press.

34. Tiemens, R. K. (1978). Television's portrayal of the 1976 presidential debates: An analysis of visual content. *Communication Monographs, 45,* 362–370.

35. Woolfolk, A. E., & Brooks, D. M. (1983). Nonverbal communication in teaching. In E. Gordon (Ed.), *Review of Research in Education, 10.* Washington, DC: American Educational Research Association.

The readings before this one describe what nonverbal communication "is" and this one describes some of what it "does." In this final reading in the chapter, three communication teacher-scholars identify some of the main *functions* of nonverbal cues.

Canary, Cody, and Manusov first point out that, most of the time, no single nonverbal cue operates by itself. This is why it's dangerous to interpret a cue like folded arms as always indicating "closure" or "rejection." Instead, for example, facial cues function along with eye be-havior, posture, and tone of voice to contribute to what's communicated.

One of the main functions of these nonverbal behaviors is to express emotions. The truth of this point is demonstrated every time someone says, "You say you love me, but I don't believe you," or screams "I'm not MAD!!" In each case the person interpreting the communication is read-ing emotions from the nonverbal cues, not the verbal ones. The words "I love you" express that complex emotion much less effectively than the amount of time one person spends with another, the quality of eye contact, and the amount and type of touch—all nonverbal cues. Similarly, the loud and harsh tone of voice accompanying the words "I'm not mad" reveals that the person's emotions are very different from what the words express.

The second function of nonverbal cues is to manage an individual's identity or the impression he or she leaves with others. The authors talk about the believability or "babyfaced" adults and the ways nonverbal attractiveness can lead to many other positive judgements. They note that people rely on nonverbal cues despite the potential errors in using them to assess others' identities. And they note how each of us wears certain "identity badges."

A third function is to manage conversation—to indicate whose turn it is to talk. Good conversations include the smooth exchange of speak-ing turns, and this is made possible mainly through nonverbal cues such as eye behavior, vocal pitch and tone, rate of speech, and gestures.

Relational messages are also sent nonverbally, and this is the fourth function discussed here. People indicate how close they feel toward oth-ers, whether power is balanced, and whether the relationship is formal or informal, for example. And they do these things, again, with eyes, voice, face, posture, gesture, and timing. People who want to change the definition of their relationship also often change nonverbal aspects of their communicating, for example, by standing closer or farther away, touching more or less, or changing the amount they smile and look the other person in the eye.

This reading and the previous one give you an overview of what nonverbal cues are and how they help people communicate.

Functions of Nonverbal Behavior

Daniel J. Canary, Michael J. Cody, and Valerie L. Manusov

[N]onverbal cues—whether unintended or intended, universal or culturally bound—play a significant role in our interactions with others. We might say that nonverbal cues perform a range of **communicative functions,** or tasks; they allow us to try to fulfill a number of our interpersonal goals. Such a functional approach to nonverbal behaviors makes two assumptions. First, it assumes that clusters of behaviors are used together to communicate a function; although a single behavior (e.g., gaze) may fulfill a function, it is more common for cues, including language, to work together. Second, the functional approach assumes that any one behavior can be used, alongside other cues, to communicate any of several functions. Proxemics, for example, may be a part of communicating a liking for another person or it may be an indication of the amount of power one person has over someone else.

Emotional Expression

For many people, the most obvious functions of nonverbal cues are to communicate how we feel and to reveal how others are feeling. In particular, the term "facial expression" shows the inherent connection often made between certain behaviors and their meanings. Although the previous discussion's warning against assuming an automatic, natural connection between behaviors and their meanings is important to keep in mind, nonverbal cues *are* a vital part of emotional expressions. When we are trying to understand what others are feeling, for example, we look at their face and their posture and listen to their vocal tone. When we want to communicate our feelings to others, we are inclined to do so nonverbally. But the relationship between nonverbal cues and emotional expression is complex, in large part because emotions themselves are complex.

Some researchers argue that **emotional expressions** reflect an area of universal communication that can be used and understood by all. To provide evidence for this, they point to studies that show that people from a range of cultures can recognize the emotions reflected in certain photographs (Ekman & Friesen, 1969). The similarity between the expressions used by humans and those used by other primates (e.g., showing aggression or sadness) also reflects that some expressions may have biological and evolutionary origins. However, most of the emotional expressions we actually use are modified through our culture's display rules. We learn, for example, *how* to show sadness, happiness, and anger in ways appropriate to our culture. In the United States, for example, we would likely show grief on our faces and in the quietness of our voices. We also have an idea of when our "grieving period" should be complete (i.e., a chronemic rule). In several African cultures, however, the way to show grief is through loud wailing for extended periods. The same emotion is reflected in different behaviors as dictated by the culture in which they occur.

Other work limits the extent to which emotional expressions form a simple, universal set of messages. Motley's (1993) studies revealed that most emotional expressions used in everyday conversations cannot be interpreted outside of the conversation in which they occur. Seldom do we use the kind of exaggerated expressions that led Ekman and Friesen (1969) to conclude that everyone can read emotional messages. Instead, most of the movements that our faces make in our

conversations with others act as "interjections" (e.g., communicating the equivalent of "gosh," "geez," "really," or "oh, please") and make sense only when we
have also heard the topic being discussed. Thus, although nonverbal behavior
is an important component of emotional expression, any particular cue (e.g., a
facial expression) is likely to need other behaviors (such as language or vocal
cues) to be interpreted accurately.

Impression Formation/Identity Management

Not only do we look toward another's expressions, we also make assessments
of his or her *expressiveness*, and this reflects our reliance on nonverbal cues for
assessing what another person is like. . . . In this section, the focus is on showing not only how nonverbal cues work as part of person perception **(impression
formation)**, but also the ways in which people work to get others to see them in
a certain way **(identity management)**.

Many of the examples given up to this point already highlight how important nonverbal cues are for judging others. In 1988, Berry and Zebrowitz-
McArthur showed not only the link between nonverbal cues and impressions,
but also the important *effects* that such impressions may have. These researchers
used a simulated courtroom trial to study the effects of physical attractiveness;
in particular, they looked at the importance of facial maturity on perceptions
and on trial outcomes. Berry and Zebrowitz-McArthur found that "babyfaced"
adults are thought to be more honest than adults with more mature facial features. Because of this, the babyfaced adults in the mock trial were seen to be less
likely to have intentionally committed a crime, and they subsequently received
shorter criminal sentences.

Berry and Zebrowitz-McArthur's study helps show the series of links that
people tend to make when judging others through nonverbal means. We see one
or more behaviors or cues (e.g., little gaze or physical attractiveness) and assume that the person has certain characteristics (e.g., shyness). We may then
treat that person in a particular way because we believe he or she has certain
characteristics; this treatment may actually help bring around those qualities,
creating a *self-fulfilling prophecy*. More likely . . . we tend to *notice* those behaviors
that are consistent with the beliefs we have about another and ignore those that
are inconsistent. Because of this process, we come to believe that we have made
the "right" judgment of another. Importantly, however, research has revealed
very few reliable personality characteristics that are revealed through nonverbal
means (Burgoon, Buller, & Woodall, 1989).

People still rely on nonverbal cues, despite the potential errors in using
them to assess others. For instance, besides helping us try to figure out what another person is like, we also reflect aspects of our *own* identity (or desired identity) through nonverbal means. Others are likely to know our sex or ethnicity by
observing our physical features. This ability to reflect certain aspects of ourselves to others is linked with others' ability to make judgments of us. Specifically, in her discussion of Tajfel's research, Burgoon (1994) says that,

Manifest indications of one's cultural, social, demographic, and personal characteristics serve as "identity badges," enabling individuals to project their own identification with various personal and social categories while simultaneously enabling observers to use the same cues as an instant means of classification. Thus, not only may individuals rely on their own nonverbal behavior as affirmation or self-verification of their identities . . . but others may also treat such information as outward reflections of the inner self. (p. 245)

Conversation Management

. . . The ways in which nonverbal cues allow for the structuring of conversation is known as **conversation management.**

Many examples show nonverbal cues' role in facilitating conversations (e.g., we gesture to make points and use high levels of gaze to show we are listening to another), but one of the most notable is how the behaviors help people take "turns" in their conversation (i.e., to know when it is our time to speak and to know when it is our conversational partner's time). According to Burgoon (1994), "[n]onverbal cues are the lubricant that keeps the conversation [turn-taking] machine well-oiled" (p. 268).

> Research has identified that speaker and listener behaviors determine whose turn it is to speak, auditor feedback cues that control speaker behavior, behaviors that mark changes in the tone and topic of interaction, the influence of interruptions and other dynamic cues on floor-holding and the flow of conversation, the role of distance and silence in maintaining engagement, and factors influencing the smoothness of interaction. (Burgoon, 1994, p. 268)

In most cases, "good" conversations include the smooth exchange of speaking turns; this is made possible largely through nonverbal cues such as eye behavior, vocal pitch and tone, rate of speech, and gestures. Cappella's work (reviewed in his 1994 chapter) refers to people's ability to *keep* the floor (i.e., to keep speaking when they want to, through both verbal and nonverbal means), and he has shown a strong link between holding the floor and others' assessments of the speaker's power and control. Those who are able to hold the floor the most tend to have more power than others have in a conversation. Not only are nonverbal cues important in how smoothly a conversation will flow, they are also vital in understanding the outcomes (e.g., perceived or actual power) of those conversations.

Relational Messages

Burgoon and Hale (1984, 1987) were some of the first researchers to discuss in depth the ways in which nonverbal cues both denote and change the relationship we have with others. For them, **relational messages** include the amount of intimacy two people share, whether the power balance is matched or not between interactants, and the degree to which one's relationship with another person is formal or informal. Overall, "relational communication addresses the processes and messages whereby people negotiate, express, and interpret their relationships with one another" (Burgoon et al., 1989, p. 289), and such messages are typically sent nonverbally.

One of the ways in which people may reflect both intimacy and equality with one another is through the degree of behavioral **synchrony** that exists. Synchrony can occur in many forms (i.e., mirroring, mimicry, or behavioral meshing), but overall it refers to the amount of coordination in peoples' behaviors (i.e., two people move in the same ways and/or their behaviors "fit" with the others). When two or more peoples' nonverbal cues are "in sync" with one another, the relational message sent is usually solidarity, agreement, support, and attraction.

Only behavior that appears to be *naturally* synchronous is likely to reflect positively on relationships. In one study, Manusov (1992) led some participants to believe that the person with whom they had interacted mirrored their behavior on purpose (the other person was actually a confederate in the study); she told others that the mirroring behavior was accidental, or she never discussed the behaviors (the control group). Those participants who were told that the behaviors were intentional judged the confederate to be less competent and attractive (and the behaviors as more disjointed and exaggerated) than he was judged when the participant was [sic] not led to think that the behaviors were purposeful, even though the confederate actually acted the same way each time. The negative evaluations were due in large part to participants' beliefs that they were being manipulated by the confederate, a common outcome of synchrony perceived to be "unnatural."

As noted, nonverbal cues can show the current state of a relationship *or* help interactants move to a different type of relationship. For example, Muehlenhard and his colleagues performed a series of studies relating specific behaviors with the intent to date (Muehlenhard, Koralewski, Andrews, & Burdick, 1986; Muehlenhard & McFall, 1981; Muehlenhard, Miller, & Burdick, 1983). Their participants watched videotapes of male-female interactions and rated the probability that the woman would accept if the man asked her for a date. Observers believed that the woman would be likely to accept a date if she maintained high levels of eye contact, smiled, leaned forward, leaned sideways, maintained a direct body orientation, moved closer to the man, touched him, and used animated speech, among other cues. Because these cues are often linked with desires to escalate a relationship, some subset of these cues is likely to help communicate that one person is ready for the relationship to change.

The process of moving from one level of relationship to another is often problematic, however, and this may be based in behavioral "mistakes" made in our quest to attain goals. Specifically, Abbey (1982) conducted a study in which male and female students engaged in a five-minute interaction while being observed from another room. After the conversation, both partners and the observers rated the extent to which the interactants were friendly, seductive, flirtatious, and promiscuous. Male and female observers saw the female interactants as friendly, but the male observers rated them as more seductive and flirtatious than did the female observers. Abbey concluded that males very often perceive a higher level of sexual intent than females do, and this could lead to different interpretations (i.e., "mistakes") for the same actions. Shotland and Craig (1988) contend, however, that there are objective distinctions between seductive behavior (e.g., long eye contact, softer speaking patterns, many short smiles, and comments that the other has been noticed before) and friendliness (e.g., more frequent brief eye contact, taking longer speaking turns, being distracted by other activities).

The idea of relational messages also connotes that nonverbal cues allow us *to relate* in a general sense to others. A recent book illustrates this idea. Cole (1998) conducted a series of interviews with people who could speak but could not rely on faces to communicate (some had Möbius syndrome, in which the face is immobile, and others were blind and therefore could not see *others'* faces). He was able to show that, unless people find another means of connecting with others (e.g., through vocal characteristics such as tone and volume), they often feel at odds with the social world. According to Cole, "without the feedback and reinforcement that facial gestures provide, there [is] little relatedness and engagement" (p. 10). This discussion shows just how profound social relationship to others is and highlights the importance of nonverbal cues in the process of engagement.

REVIEW QUESTIONS

1. Fill in the blank: "Although a single nonverbal behavior (e.g., gaze) may fulfill a function, it is more common for cues, including language, to_____."
2. How does culture affect the ways that nonverbal behaviors express emotions?
3. What is the difference between "impression formation" and "identity management"?
4. What is an "identity badge"?
5. Which nonverbal behaviors are used to manage turn-taking in conversation?

PROBES

1. Are nonverbal expressions of emotion (happiness, sadness, etc.) common across most situations, or is it likely that any particular cue will need language and vocal cues to be interpreted accurately? Explain.
2. What might you do nonverbally to communicate that you are "in sync" with your conversation partner? If you choose to do this, what danger do you need to avoid?
3. Give two examples of nonverbal cues you have used to help a relationship move from one level of relationship to another higher or lower level.

REFERENCES

1. Abbey, A. (1982). Sex differences in attributions for friendly behavior: Do males misperceive females' friendliness? *Journal of Personality and Social Psychology, 42*, pp. 830–88.
2. Berry, D. S., & Zebrowitz-McArthur, L. (1988). What's in a face? Facial maturity and the attribution of legal responsibility. *Personality and Social Psychology Bulletin, 14*, pp. 24–33.
3. Burgoon, J. K. (1994). Nonverbal signals. In M. L. Knapp and G. R. Miller (Eds.), *Handbook of interpersonal communication* (pp. 229–285). Beverly Hills, CA: Sage.
4. Burgoon, J. K. & Hale, J. L. (1984). The fundamental topic of relational communication. *Communication Monographs, 51*, pp. 193–214.
5. Burgoon, J. K. & Hale, J. L. (1987). Validation and measurement of fundamental themes of relational communication. *Communication Monographs, 54*, pp. 19–41.
6. Burgoon, J. K., Buller, D. B., & Woodall, W. G. *Nonverbal communication: The unspoken dialogue.* New York: HarperCollins, 1989.
7. Cappella, J. N. The management of conversational interaction in adults and infants. In *Handbook of Interpersonal Communication* (2nd ed.). D. M. L. Knapp and G. R. Miller, Thousand Oaks, CA: Sage, 1994.
8. Cole, J. *About face.* Cambridge, MA: Bradford/MIT Press, 1998.
9. Ekman, P. & Friesen, W. V. (1969). The repertoire of nonverbal behavior: Categories, origins, usage, and coding. *Semiotica, 1*, pp. 49–98.
10. Manusov, V. (1992). Mimicry or synchrony: The effects of intentionality attributions for nonverbal mirroring behavior. *Communication Quarterly, 40*, pp. 69–83.
11. Motley, M. T. (1993). Facial affect and verbal content in conversation. *Human communication research, 20*, pp. 3–40.
12. Muehlenhard, C. L. & McFall, R. M. (1981). Dating initiation from a woman's perspective. *Behavior Therapy, 12*, pp. 682–691.
13. Muehlenhard, C. L., Miller, C. L., & Burdick, C. A. (1983). Are high-frequency daters better cue readers? Men's interpretation of women's cues as a function of dating frequency and SHI scores. *Behavior Therapy, 14*, pp. 626–636.
14. Muehlenhard, C. L., Koralewski, M. A., Andrews, S. L., & Burdick, C. A. (1986). Verbal and nonverbal cues that convey interest in dating: Two studies. *Behavior Therapy, 17*, pp. 404–419.
15. Shotland, R. L. & Craig, J. M. (1988). Can men and women differentiate between friendly and sexually interested behavior? *Social Psychology Quarterly, 51*, pp. 66–73.

Making Meaning Together

"INHALING" AND "EXHALING"

A s I noted in the Preface, the next two chapters that make up Part Two are organized with the help of a breathing metaphor. At the most basic level, I use the terms *inhaling* and *exhaling* to begin to break down or organize the continuous, changing, multidimensional, often confusing processes called "communicating." One commonsense, close-to-experience way to organize this overall process is to divide it up into what people take in (inhaling) and what they give out (exhaling).

You can figure out my second and most important reason for choosing this metaphor if you try to inhale without exhaling, or vice versa. These labels allow me to separate communication into two of its important parts while still emphasizing that the parts happen together. As I noted in Chapter 2, communicators are always receiving and sending at the same time. *While we're talking,* we're noticing how people are responding, and *while we're listening,* we're giving off mixed and primarily nonverbal cues.

No metaphor is perfect, of course, and one problem with this one is that inhaling and exhaling happen *sequentially,* while perceiving and talking take place *simultaneously.* In this way, communication is even more dynamic than this metaphor suggests.

A third reason I'm using this metaphor is that it is organic. Breathing is a part of living for most of the organisms in the world. It's vital for humans and other animals, of course, but you can also think of the fish's intake and output of water and even the plant's intake of water and output of oxygen as forms of breathing.

The fourth reason is that this metaphor organizes breathing into a process that begins with input. If somebody asks, "What are the two parts of the breathing process?" the common answer is "inhaling and exhaling," not "exhaling and inhaling." So the metaphor allows me to focus *first* on perception and listening. This reverses the historical tendency to begin one's efforts to improve communication by focusing on what one *says.* I'm convinced that listening is the often neglected but crucially important half of the listening–speaking pair, and this metaphor makes it easier to redress some of this imbalance.

So Chapter 5 discusses how we "take in" information and impressions about others—how we perceive individuals, relationships, and social events, and how we listen. It begins with two readings about person perception, one that overviews the process and another that discusses stereotyping. This is followed by three readings that focus on listening. Then Chapter 6 covers what we "give out" or "exhale." Here, five different readings discuss being open, expressing thoughts and feelings, being assertive, nonverbal immediacy, and self-disclosure.

As you read these materials, remember that each of these chapters somewhat artificially emphasizes one part of a process that always happens as a whole—just like the inhaling and exhaling of normal breathing. It makes sense to break the process down into what's taken in and what's given out. But this isn't how we actually experience communication. As the title of Part II indicates, people make meaning *together,* and they do it by "inhaling" and "exhaling" *together.*

Understanding and Listening: Communication as Inhaling

Thus first reading surveys how people perceive persons, relationships, and social events. In the past couple of decades, research on
what's often called "social cognition" has exploded. Increasing
numbers of communication scholars have been figuring out how interpersonal communication is affected by such things as cognitive scripts,
episodes, prototypes, and self-monitoring. But the authors of this selection don't bore you with the details of all this research. Instead, Sarah
Trenholm and Arthur Jensen translate key findings into understandable
principles and tell you how they can be applied to your communication.

They summarize the information into four processes that people
engage in before, during, and after communicating: (1) identifying the
situation, (2) defining the other person, (3) defining yourself and your
relationship with the other, and (4) figuring out why things unfold the
way they do. This reading discusses each of the four.

First, they describe how we orient ourselves to the situations we're
in by defining what kind of *episode* it is. Definitions vary from culture to
culture, of course. Examples of Western middle-class episodes include
the big family dinner, the parent–teacher conference, TV viewing, and
such less enjoyable episodes as avoiding dad or mom when he or she is
drunk, and apologizing to the neighbor whose property you've damaged. Communication within various episodes often follows a script.
The major way we make overall sense of the situations we're in is to define the episode, figure out the script, and then identify the *consequences*
of being in the middle of this episode and following this script.

Second, we size up the people we're around. Again, we use several
strategies, including personal constructs, implicit personality theory,
self-fulfilling prophecies, and cognitive complexity. Trenholm and
Jensen explain each of these jargon terms and give examples of them, so
you can see how they operate in your own communication life. For example, they point out how people tend to group certain personality
traits together, so if we perceive someone as "friendly" and "quiet," we
may also believe them to be "intelligent," even though we have no evidence of how smart they are. This is how we apply an overall implicit
personality theory as we perceive others.

Third, we size up relationships. We begin with perceptions of
ourselves (as were discussed in the readings in Chapter 3), and then we
develop perceptions of who we are in relation to the person or people we're communicating with. In this section, Trenholm and Jensen
explain briefly the identity-negotiation process that is described much
more completely in the first reading in Chapter 3. They talk about how
we label relationships and manage our responses to fit the labels.

Finally, Trenholm and Jensen discuss under the heading *attribution theories* how we use communication to answer the questions
"Why did I do what I did?" and "Why did she or he do that?" These
theories explain how people attribute reasons or causes to the events

we experience. They distinguish between attributing events to surrounding situations (external) versus attributing them to somebody's personality traits (internal). They also describe some of the biases that affect people's attributions.

By the end of this reading you should have a pretty good overview of how perception processes affect your interpersonal communicating.

Interpretive Competence:

How We Perceive Individuals, Relationships, and Social Events

Sarah Trenholm and Arthur Jensen

To interact with others successfully requires a wealth of social knowledge. You must be able to perceive the information in your social environment accurately enough to know which of the hundreds of schemata in your memory bank are the best ones to pull out of the vault. This is, of course, a very complicated operation. Cognitive psychologists are just beginning to understand how we do it. We have tried to simplify the problem by highlighting four perceptual processes that people engage in before, during, and after social interaction. These include identifying (1) what the situation is, (2) who the other person is, (3) who you are and what kind of relationship between self and other is implied, and (4) why things unfold the way they do. Let's examine each of these processes more closely.

SIZING UP SITUATIONS

The more we know about the particular situations in which we interact with others, the more likely we are to produce effective messages. We propose three useful ways to manage situations: (1) identifying episodes, (2) knowing scripts, and (3) perceiving potential consequences of following scripts.

Orienting Ourselves: Episode Identification

At one time or another, we have all been in situations where we didn't know what was going on or what to do. Visiting a foreign culture or being initiated into a sorority or fraternity are examples of situations that are not very well defined for us. Knowing the situation can make interactions much easier. In its simplest form a situation is "a place plus a definition."[1] When we enter a place, our first task is to orient ourselves or get our bearings. One way to do this is to ask the simple question "Where am I?" We find ourselves in a variety of places every day: in the car, at home or work, in the shopping mall, at the zoo, church, or bus station, and so on. Where we are determines to a large extent what we can do socially. But identifying the place alone is not enough. For instance, a church building can serve as a place for worship, weddings, ice cream socials, even bingo. To communicate appropriately requires that we recognize the physical and social cues that define the episode or activity that is taking place. Each culture has an array of social episodes or activities for its members to follow. For the individual, **social episodes** are "internal cognitive representations about common, recurring interaction routines within a defined cultural milieu."[2] Some typical social episodes? Having a big family dinner, attending a parent-teacher conference, planning a party, gossiping. How do we know which episodes to enact? Often we have a particular episode in mind when we initiate a conversation with someone. Perhaps you know someone who likes to "pick fights" or tease a brother or sister in order to get him or her riled up. Often enacting an episode is a process of negotiation—one person suggests an activity, only to have the other counter with another option, as in this conversation:

LAURA: I noticed that Kmart is having a sale on lawn mowers.
BUD: This is the only evening I'm free all week. I don't want to spend it shopping for a lawn mower. Besides, the Battle of the Mack Trucks is going on at the fairgrounds tonight.

Social interaction is a continuous dance in which participants accept and decline each other's invitations to enact different episodes. For instance, when two old friends have a chance meeting on the street, the question "Can I buy you a drink?" is an invitation to engage in the episode of "talking over old times." Refusing the drink because you are not thirsty would be missing the point—it would reflect a failure to recognize the other's definition of the situation.

Using Scripts to Guide Interaction: Open, Closed, and Defined Episodes

When people play out an episode, they may also follow a script. As we have seen, a script is a highly predictable sequence of events. Some classroom learning episodes are highly scripted; others are not. For example, you may be able to predict (from experience) that every Wednesday morning your history professor will call the roll, hand out a quiz, collect the quizzes, lecture for 20 minutes, and end the class with a humorous anecdote. The more predictable the sequence of events, the more scripted the interaction is. Another class may be taught so differently that you never know for sure what will happen in a given class period. Both examples are classroom episodes, but only the first one follows a clearly identifiable script.

Scripts and episodes are useful guides to interaction. Identifying the episode narrows the range of possible actions and reactions. Knowing the script makes social life even more predictable. Michael Brenner has proposed that the vast majority of social episodes fall into one of three types: closed, open, and defined.[3]

Closed Episodes   When a situation is almost completely scripted, it is a **closed episode.** Rules for proper behavior are well known in advance and govern the flow of interaction. Rituals such as greetings and religious observances are closed episodes. Many business organizations tightly script interactions by training their personnel to follow carefully devised sets of procedures. If you've ever applied for a loan at a bank, you have probably participated in a closed episode. You have a standard set of questions you want answered (the loan rate, fixed or variable, length of repayment, and so on) and so does the loan officer (income, collateral, address, credit references, and so on). Other, less formal, interactions are also somewhat scripted. An episode of "small talk" has a limited range of topics, although the sequence in which these topics are discussed may vary.

Open Episodes   When participants enter a situation without any preconceived plan or with a very general one, they are involved in an **open episode.** In such situations there is greater freedom to create new forms of interaction and to change episodes midway through. Episodes such as "hanging out with friends" are sometimes scripted, but not always. When almost anything can be introduced as a topic of conversation or an activity to perform, the episode is an open one. An orchestra performing a John Philip Sousa march is clearly following a musical script, but a group of musicians having a "jam session" is not. The freedom to improvise or break the rules is typical of an open episode. Some open episodes may be unsettling, since there is no clear idea of what should be done next. Perhaps you have been in situations where nobody seemed to know what to do. We know of an instructor whose routine on the first day of class was to walk into the room, assume the lotus position on top of his desk, and say nothing for the first half of the class. His point was to show how communication is used to define ambiguous situations. Eventually, students would begin talking to one another, trying to figure out what he was doing. From the students' point of view, this was an open episode.

Defined Episodes   While closed episodes are known to be such in advance as a result of expectations, many situations are defined "in progress" as participants follow their own personal goals and plans to achieve a working consensus. Even so, the consensus is often temporary—definitions of the situation may fall apart as quickly as they develop. A **defined episode** is an open episode in which the participants are trying to negotiate some closure. The difference is that open episodes are experienced as creative and liberating; defined episodes are competitive attempts to control the activity. Brenner suggests that defined episodes are often ambiguous and unstructured interactions because each partner may be proposing alternative directions for the episode. For example, a not-very-good salesperson might initiate a "sales episode" but eventually succumb to a clever-but-unwilling-to-buy customer's definition of the situation as "shooting the breeze." A romantic evening can be spoiled quickly when a candlelight dinner becomes redefined as an episode of "stilted conversation" or "talking about the kids." In closed relationships people may spend a lot of time just deciding what episode to enact next. We know of four friends who, in the course of one evening, proposed over 20 different activities for that evening. Needless to say, they ended up doing nothing but talking about what they could be doing. Chances are none of the persons involved planned to spend the evening that way, but our observations lead us to believe that these two couples frequently end up playing this "what do you want to do tonight" episode.

Although we may think that closed episodes are too limiting and value open ones for the freedom they provide, stop and think how chaotic social life would be without any well-defined or scripted episodes. The important thing, of course, is that we recognize the types of episodes others propose so that we can accept the invitation or decline gracefully.

Identifying Consequences of Episodes and Scripts

Sometimes it is just as important to perceive the possible outcomes of a situation, like the chess player who sees several moves ahead, as it is to properly label that situation. We can avoid detrimental outcomes if we can see them coming. Salespeople often use the tried-and-true "yes technique" to set up unwitting customers. They ask questions that seem unrelated to selling their product, such as "Are those lovely photographs of *your* children?" or "I've had a hard time catching you at home. You must work awfully long hours." The customer's automatic "yes" in response to each question or comment establishes a habitual pattern that could cost a lot of money at the end of the episode.

Following a script can lead to positive or negative outcomes. Sometimes we know the script so well that we can tell our friends what they are going to say next. If we finish the sentence for them, they may be gratified that we understand them so well or offended that we cut them off. Another negative consequence is that scripted interactions can become boring or even damage a relationship if repeated too often. Researchers who study marital conflict patterns often comment that couples get caught up in "conflict scripts" that neither person intended to start but both felt compelled to see to the bitter end once the episode began. And as we have already seen, expecting the interaction to follow a script can prevent us from perceiving important messages the other may be sending our way. Following the script can also limit creativity, but only if we remain tied completely to the script. Minor alterations, improvisations, and other forms of playing with the script can add some spice to everyday interactions.

SIZING UP PEOPLE

As we interact, we come to an understanding of what other people are like. Knowing how to size up the individual is another way to reduce our uncertainty about communication. In studying the process of impression formation, researchers have discovered several factors that influence our judgment. We will discuss four of these factors: (1) the use of personal constructs, (2) implicit personality theory, (3) self-fulfilling prophecies, and (4) cognitive complexity.

The Use of Personal Constructs to Judge Others

. . . Personal constructs [are] mental yardsticks for evaluating objects, events, and people. . . . Since constructs are "personal," no two people will use them in exactly the same way. You and I may both observe Bill eating a sandwich in two bites, mustard dribbling down his chin. You may think he is "aggressive" while I argue that he is "messy" and "impolite." What we see in others is a combination of their actual behavior and our personal construct of their behavior. These constructs say as much about you and me as they do about Bill.

Even though we each use different constructs to judge others, we do use them in similar ways. Steven Duck has noted a typical pattern in the use of four different kinds of constructs.[4] The four types are:

- Physical constructs (tall-short, beautiful-ugly)
- Role constructs (buyer-seller, teacher-student)
- Interaction constructs (friendly-hostile, polite-rude)
- Psychological constructs (motivated-lazy, kind-cruel)

Our initial impressions are frequently based on physical attributes—we take stock of how people are dressed or how attractive they are. These are quickly followed by the formation of role constructs as we try to make sense out of each other's position in the social world. As we talk, we may focus attention on interaction constructs, or aspects of the other's style of communication. Finally, we use these observations to infer what makes the other tick (psychological constructs)—we begin to guess at motivations and build a personality for the other. When we reach this last stage, we have gone beyond simply interpreting what we see and hear; we've begun to assume that we know things about the person that we can't see.

Implicit Personality Theory: Organizing Trait Impressions

We don't simply form isolated opinions of other people; rather, we organize all of our individual perceptions into a more complete picture by filling in a lot of missing information. One of the ways we do this is through what is referred to as an **implicit personality theory.** This is the belief on our part that certain individual traits are related to other traits. If we observe a trait that we think is part of a cluster, we will assume that the person also has the rest of the traits in the cluster. Each of us has our own notions of what traits go together. For some, the traits (or constructs) "intelligent," "quiet," and "friendly" may cluster together.[5] If we observe behavior that we interpret as friendly and quiet, we may then attribute intelligence to that person without any firsthand evidence. . . .

Interpersonal Self-Fulfilling Prophecies

Another important perceptual tendency is the **self-fulfilling prophecy.** Unlike the more passive implicit personality theory (in which traits are associated in the mind), the self-fulfilling prophecy involves both perception *and* behavior.

It starts when one person—the observer—believing something to be true about another person—the target—begins acting toward the target as if the belief were fact. This action prompts the target to behave in line with the observer's expectations. If you believe your friend is "touchy," you are likely to avoid sensitive topics and be more hesitant in what you say. The effect of your behavior? Your friend becomes oversensitive because *you* are acting oversolicitous. Unaware that you helped create the prickly atmosphere, you say to yourself, "My God, it's true. You can't say anything to him."

Cognitive Complexity: Factors Affecting Impression Formation

Not everyone forms impressions in the same way. Observers differ in the number and quality of personal constructs they use to evaluate others. A **cognitively complex** person's system is greater in number of personal constructs (*differentiation*), includes more abstract psychological categories (*abstraction*), and has more elaborate ways of relating various constructs (*integration*).[6] A cognitively simple person has fewer, less abstract constructs about people and views those constructs as relatively isolated impressions. Let's look at an example comparing the two extremes.

Suppose Pat and Chris observe Marvin on several occasions. They are both present when Marvin (1) cheats on an English test, (2) takes charge and gets everyone out of a burning building, (3) refuses to help with a charity car wash, (4) helps a friend study for a difficult math test, (5) embarrasses another friend by pointing out her faults in front of a large group of people, and (6) always gives blood when there is an opportunity.

If you want to test yourself, you might write down your own impression of Marvin before reading on. Then come back and read the impressions that Chris and Pat formed.

To Pat, Marvin is "tall and handsome, but extremely selfish, difficult to get along with, and not trustworthy." When reminded of some of the positive things Marvin has done, Pat shrugs and says, "It's just a front. The real Marvin is a cheat."

To Chris, "Marvin seems selfish when he is unsure of himself, but quite selfless when he knows he can help out. Marvin is also very outspoken and direct—he says what is on his mind. If he believes in a cause, he'll support it. If he doesn't think it's important he won't give it the time of day." Chris sums up Marvin's behavior as being motivated by his insecurity: "If he didn't worry so much about being noticed, he wouldn't make himself look so bad. He has real potential."

Why are these two impressions so different? Pat uses fewer, more concrete constructs (for example, "tall and handsome") and ignores much of the information that doesn't fit with the emerging impression. If this impression is typical of her reactions, Pat's construct system is a relatively undeveloped one. Contrast that with Chris, who demonstrates a fairly high level of cognitive complexity. By integrating the apparent contradictions in Marvin's behavior, Chris has arrived at a more subtle understanding of Marvin, recognizing situational constraints as well as psychological motivations.

Research has shown cognitively complex persons to be more accurate in processing information about others, better at placing themselves in the role of the other person, and more patient in weighing most of the evidence before formulating a complete impression.[7] Less complex individuals tend to either stick with their original impression and ignore contradictory information or to change the impression to fit the most recent information they have.[8] They lack the ability to integrate the constructs they use into a more complete image of others.

Considering the differences between more complex and less complex persons, you might get the impression that the more complex, the better. Actually, it depends on the situation and the other person. Imagine Pat and Chris talking to each other. They would probably drive each other crazy. Pat would claim that Chris thinks too much and analyzes everybody. Chris would charge Pat with making snap judgments. In general, complex persons are more versatile in social situations and better at cross-cultural adaptation. . . . But a cognitively complex person is not necessarily a "better" person. Like any of us, such a person can abuse his or her abilities by being unethical, insensitive, and so on.

SIZING UP RELATIONSHIPS

As we read the situation and form impressions of the other, we also face the perceptual task of determining what relevant aspects of self fit the situation and how the emerging relationship between self and other should be interpreted.

Self-Monitoring: Deciding Who to Be

. . . Just as we form impressions of others, we form and present images of ourselves to others. The awareness of images of self and the ability to adapt these images to the situation at hand has been referred to as **self-monitoring.**[9] A high self-monitor tends to read the social situation first and then present an appropriate face, as opposed to simply presenting a consistent image of self in every situation.

Mark Snyder characterizes the difference between a high and low self-monitor in the form of the question each might ask in defining the situation.

> The high self-monitor asks, "Who does this situation want me to be and how can I be that person?" In so doing, the high self-monitoring individual reads the character of the situation to identify the type of person called for by that type of situation, constructs a mental image or representation of a person who best exemplifies that type of person, and uses the prototypic person's self-presentation and expressive behavior as a set of guidelines for monitoring his or her own verbal and nonverbal actions. [The low self-monitor asks] "Who am I and how can I be me in this situation?"[10]

Instead of calling on a prototype to guide his or her actions, the low self-monitor behaves in accordance with an image of his or her "real" self.

To test yourself, make a short list of five or six very different social situations you frequently take part in. Write down how you typically behave in each situation, or better yet, have someone observe you in each of those situations and write down what you do. Then compare your actual behavior to Snyder's - self-monitoring questions. Do you normally present a consistent self-image, or do you alter your self-presentation for each situation?

Our culture often sends us mixed messages. For instance, we are told to "be ourselves" and "remain true to self," messages that seem to endorse the low self-monitor's position. On the other hand, research demonstrates that being adaptable (being a high self-monitor) is one of the keys to social success. It is probably best to recognize that either extreme can be limiting. If we always try to maintain a consistent self-concept, we will be less versatile and probably less human because we won't experience the full range of human emotions and potentials. But if we are always changing to fit the situation or someone else's conception of us, we may compromise important standards and values. The best course is to ask ourselves which is more important in a given situation—being adaptable or being consistent. On one occasion it may be important for you to exert your individuality and violate the family rule that "everyone comes home for Christmas." The next year you might pass up a wonderful ski trip just to be home and fit in again.

Defining Relationships: Self in Relation to Others

When people interact, each presents an image of self to the other. These images are, however, usually quite fluid. We are responsive to the feedback of the other and begin quickly to negotiate a definition of the relationship between self and other. Thus, one important perceptual process is the identification of the type of relationship that applies in a given situation. Office workers at a company picnic may perceive that the superior-subordinate relationship with the boss no longer applies during a game of softball. As long as the boss sees things the same way, there is no problem. But what if the boss assumes he or she is still in charge and wants to pitch? The difference in perceptions may lead to negative feelings that were never intended.

A wide range of relationship labels are available to us. We can be casual or long-time acquaintances, friends, close friends, almost friends, just friends, co-workers, neighbors, bowling partners, platonic lovers, husbands and wives, ex-husbands and -wives, blood brothers or sisters, business associates, straight man and funnyman, roommates, counselor and advisee, master and slave, even student and teacher. The list could go on.

Once a relational label is firm in our mind, it tends to limit our perception of what we can do together. Most American couples who have just begun dating probably don't even think about drawing up and signing prenuptial agreements about finances, children, property, and so on. These actions are not perceived as having anything to do with "real" romantic relationships.

Several studies have demonstrated the existence of relational prototypes. In the same way that we have mental images of typical personalities, we also form cognitive models of the best example of a romantic relationship or a good friendship. Sally Planalp found that prototypes students held of the student-professor relationship seemed to be guided by their expectations about the respective rights and obligations that each party has in different situations. Planalp had students read three conversations between a professor and student: (1) a student asking to add the professor's class, (2) a student asking to make up an exam that had been missed, and (3) a student requesting a change of grade for the professor's class. Different students read different versions of the conversations, some in which the professor made dominant, neutral, or submissive statements and others in which the student's statements varied in terms of dominance or submissiveness. One week later, students were asked to identify whether the conversation they had read the week before contained the dominant, neutral, or submissive statements. As expected, students "remembered" (incorrectly) having read statements that were more in line with prototypical expectations than they were with the actual dialogues the students had read.[11]

Robert Carson has used the term **master contract** to refer to the worked-out definition of a relationship that guides the recurring interaction of any dyad.[12] This means that as relationships develop, perceptions that were originally guided by a prototype eventually give way to an understanding based on verbalized agreements or silent acceptance of established patterns of behavior. . . . It is important to recognize that identifying what type of relationship you're involved in may be just as crucial as knowing the situation or forming a useful impression of the other.

EXPLAINING BEHAVIOR: ATTRIBUTION THEORIES

When all is said and done, we are frequently left with the question "Why did he (or she) do that?" or "Why did I do that?" Most of the time we are quick to offer some type of explanation. If we think we understand what motivated our own or another's actions, we have reduced some uncertainty and made our world a little more predictable. Theories concerned with how the average person infers the cause(s) of social behavior have been called *attribution theories*. Before we examine some of these theories, let's look at a typical conversation and try to explain each person's behavior.

Imagine that you've been visiting your friends Angela and Howie for a few days. You are sitting at the kitchen table with Howie when Angela comes home from work. She looks very tired. The following conversation ensues:

HOWIE: (*looking up from the plastic model car kit he has been putting together*) Hi, honey. How was work?

ANGELA: (*after saying hello to you, she scans the room*) Howie! You haven't done the dishes yet? They're left over from last night. Can't you do anything you're asked to do?

HOWIE: It's been a busy morning. I just haven't had time.

ANGELA: No time! You don't have a job. You're not looking for work. And you can't find 15 minutes to do a dozen dishes?

HOWIE: I've been looking through the classifieds, for your information.
ANGELA: Did you send out any resumes?
HOWIE: No, not really . . .
ANGELA: Here we go again. Do I have to physically force you to sit down and
    write letters of application and send your resume out?
HOWIE: I'll do it. I'll do it.
ANGELA: You'll do what? The dishes or the resumes? . . .

How would you explain the communication behavior of your two friends? Is
Angela the kind of person who constantly nags and belittles others? Or did
Howie provoke this tirade? What other explanations could there be? . . .

Identifying Attributional Biases

If all the causes of behavior we attribute were clearly logical and made use of all
the relevant information, our social lives would be much easier to manage. Unfortunately, we humans are notoriously irrational at times. A number of perceptual biases affect how we arrive at causal attributions. We rely on some of
these biases when we have no prior knowledge of the persons being observed,
and at other times the biases just override whatever knowledge we do have.

Personality Bias Toward Others   The most common bias is to explain other people's behavior in terms of their personality dispositions.[13] We are especially prone
to this **personality bias** when we observe strangers. We just naturally assume that
a stranger who throws a shoe at the television screen lacks self-control or is mentally unstable. The bias is even stronger if the person's behavior is contrary to our
expectations.[14] Since we expect people in a restaurant to be eating or drinking, we
probably think that only a buffoon would start singing in that setting. Rarely do we
look for other explanations—such as the possibility that someone offered him $50
to do it or that the woman he was with accepted his proposal of marriage. Cognitively complex individuals may be less susceptible to this bias, perhaps because
of their tendency to engage in role-taking. When we try to see a situation from the
other person's point of view, we may see more situational or relational causes.

Situational Bias Toward Self   When we're asked to explain our own behavior,
the story is somewhat different—we're more likely to rely on **situational bias.**
If I throw a shoe at the television, I can explain that it was because of tension
built up at the office, a stupid call by the referee, or the loose morals of television producers. There are several reasons why we tend to attribute our own behavior to situational factors. In the case of negative behavior, blaming it on the
situation can serve as an excuse or justification for that behavior. Another reason is that we simply have more information about our own past and present
experience than an observer would. We know if we've had a bad day; an observer probably doesn't. Finally, our visual vantage point makes a difference.
When we behave, we don't see ourselves performing the action. What we do see

is other people and external circumstances. It's much more likely that we will reference the situation as the cause of our behavior.

Bias Toward Groups   In addition to these two biases, perceived group membership also produces a bias. We explain the behavior of members of highly stereotyped *out-groups* (groups we do not belong to) differently than the behavior of *in-group* members (such as our own friends, associates, or ethnic group). In general, researchers have found that we attribute positive behavior by in-group members to their personal dispositions, while negative behavior is explained in terms of situational factors. We explain the behavior of out-group members in exactly the opposite manner. Positive behavior is explained away as situationally produced, while negative behavior is seen as the product of personality or group culture.[15] For example, suppose you are watching a close friend play in a tennis tournament when she screams at the referee for calling her shot out of bounds. You turn to the person next to you and say, "She's been under a lot of pressure lately. I think she just needed to blow off some steam." Moments later, her opponent (from an arch-rival institution) heatedly disputes another out-of-bounds call. "Why do they let people without manners play this game?" you think to yourself.

Why are we so prone to discriminate in favor of friends and against members of other social groups? We usually think of friends as being similar to us in many ways, but apparently perceive them to be even more similar when compared to an outsider. This in-group/out-group comparison seems to set in motion a role-taking process in which we identify closely with the in-group member and view things from his or her perspective. As a result, we often seek a situational account for the behavior. In contrast, we tend to view the out-group member with very little empathy or understanding. This makes it easier to assume the person would behave negatively regardless of the situation.

Bias Toward Cultures   Culture also plays a significant role in producing attributional bias. Our culture is a very individualistic one. As a result, we have a greater tendency to believe that the individual person is responsible for his or her behavior. In collectivist cultures such as Japan or India, situational attributions are more common.[16] A *collectivist culture* is one in which group goals have a higher priority than individual goals; loyalty to the group is usually expressed by behaving according to the rules in different situations. Thus, in collectivist cultures people are more aware of situational constraints and less aware of individual differences.

How can knowledge of these casual schemata and attributional biases help improve interpersonal communication? The first step is to realize that our past interactions with a person influence how we decide to communicate in the present. To a large extent, what we remember about past interactions is stored in the form of attributions. If you have a tendency to explain interactions in terms of single causes (such as personal or stimulus attributions), your communication may frequently take the form of complaining about or blaming the other. You may even do this without realizing it. It may be beneficial to sit down occasionally and evaluate how you've been explaining the events that have happened in your important relationships. . . .

CONCLUSION

This [reading] has provided you with a lot of information about the perceptual process and some of the cognitive schemata that people use to make sense of their social world. We have tried to simplify what you need to know by structuring this information around four cognitive processes that influence interpersonal communication: how we size up situations, people, and relationships and how we explain the causes of social interaction. . . . Understanding social cognition processes is the first step to improving interpersonal communication because so much of the meaning we assign to messages depends on our *perceptions* of the social context and the persons involved.

REVIEW QUESTIONS

1. List the four perception processes this reading explains.
2. How are scripts related to episodes?
3. What's the difference between closed episodes and defined episodes?
4. What's the relationship between personal constructs and implicit personality theory?
5. What's an *interpersonal* self-fulfilling prophecy?
6. Explain the difference between a high self-monitor and a low self-monitor.
7. People use attribution theories to infer the _____ of other people's behavior.

PROBES

1. Trenholm and Jensen say at one point that "social interaction is a continuous dance in which participants accept and decline each other's invitations to enact different episodes." Extend their metaphor of "dance" to explain your own experience. In what ways are your conversations, say at work, like a dance?
2. What principle is exemplified by the salesperson's "yes technique"? What do you hear Trenholm and Jensen saying about this technique? Do they think it's a good tactic to use?
3. Do you agree or disagree with the claim that first impressions are formed solidly within the first four minutes of interaction with a stranger, and that we use these hastily formed impressions to decide whether to continue conversing or not? Explain.
4. Do you tend to be a high self-monitor or a low self-monitor? How does your tendency affect your communicating?
5. Give an example of a bias toward groups and a bias toward cultures that affects how you perceive some of the people you're communicating with.

NOTES

1. Stanley Deetz and Sheryl Stevenson, *Managing Interpersonal Communication* (New York: Harper & Row, 1986), p. 58.

2. Joseph Forgas, "Affective and Emotional Influences on Episode Representations," in *Social Cognition: Perspectives on Everyday Understanding,* ed. Joseph Forgas (London: Academic Press, 1981), pp. 165–80.

3. Michael Brenner, "Actors' Powers," in *The Analysis of Action: Recent Theoretical and Empirical Advances,* ed. M. von Cranach and Rom Harre (Cambridge: Cambridge University Press, 1982), pp. 213–30.

4. Steven Duck, "Interpersonal Communication in Developing Acquaintances," in *Explorations in Interpersonal Communication,* ed. Gerald R. Miller (Beverly Hills, Calif.: Sage, 1976), pp. 127–47.

5. Seymour Rosenberg and Andrea Sedlak, "Structural Representations of Implicit Personality Theory," in *Advances in Experimental Social Psychology* 6, ed. Leonard Berkowitz (New York: Academic Press, 1972).

6. Walter Crockett, "Cognitive Complexity and Impression Formation," in *Progress in Experimental Personality Research* 2, ed. B. A. Maher (New York: Academic Press, 1965). See also Jesse Delia, "Constructivism and the Study of Human Communication," *Quarterly Journal of Speech* 63 (1977): 68–83.

7. Jesse Delia, Ruth Ann Clark, and David Switzer, "Cognitive Complexity and Impression Formation in Informal Social Interaction," *Speech Monographs* 41 (1974): 299–308. See also Claudia Hale and Jesse Delia, "Cognitive Complexity and Social Perspective-Taking," *Communication Monographs* 43 (1976): 195–203.

8. Crockett, "Cognitive Complexity."

9. Mark L. Snyder, "The Self-Monitoring of Expressive Behavior," *Journal of Personality and Social Psychology* 30 (1974): 526–37.

10. Mark L. Snyder, "Self-Monitoring Processes," in *Advances in Experimental Social Psychology* 12, ed. Leonard Berkowitz (New York: Academic Press, 1979), pp. 86–131.

11. Sally Planalp, "Relational Schemata: A Test of Alternative Forms of Relational Knowledge as Guides to Communication," *Human Communication Research* 12 (1985): 3–29.

12. Robert Carson, *Interaction Concepts of Personality* (Chicago: Aldine, 1969).

13. For a review, see Lee Ross, "The Intuitive Psychologist and His Shortcomings: Distortions in the Attribution Process," in *Advances in Experimental Social Psychology* 10, ed. Leonard Berkowitz (New York: Academic Press, 1977).

14. E. E. Jones and D. McGillis, "Correspondent Inferences and the Attribution Cube: A Comparative Reappraisal," in *New Directions in Attribution Research* 1, ed. J. H. Harvey, W. J. Ickes, and R. F. Kidd (Hillsdale, N.J.: Lawrence Erlbaum, 1976).

15. J. Jaspars and M. Hewstone, "Cross-Cultural Interaction, Social Attribution, and Intergroup Relations," in *Cultures in Contact,* ed. S. Bochner (Elmsford,

N.Y.: Pergamon Press, 1982); B. Park and M. Rothbart, "Perceptions of Outgroup Homogeneity and Levels of Social Categorization: Memory for the Subordinate Attributes of In-Group and Out-Group Members," *Journal of Personality and Social Psychology* 42 (1982): 1051–68.
16. J. Miller, "Culture and the Development of Everyday Social Explanations," *Journal of Personality and Social Psychology* 46 (1984): 961–78.

Julia Wood teaches in the department of communication studies at the University of North Carolina at Chapel Hill, does research on gender and communication, and has published several interpersonal communication texts. This chapter comes from a recent book that she dedicates to enhancing its reader's understanding of "different meanings that people may attribute to what they say and do." In her book, Wood emphasizes how diversity can contribute to misunderstanding and how awareness and acceptance of diversity can help improve understanding.

As the subtitle of this selection says, this is a discussion of stereotyping, one of the most familiar and unfortunate features of the way we perceive people. As the subtitle also suggests, the key concept in this chapter is "totalizing." Wood explains that this word describes "communication that emphasizes one aspect of a person above all others." Totalizing means thinking and acting as if a single aspect of a person is the totality of that person. So calling Spike Lee a "black filmmaker" spotlights his race in a way that makes it the dominant feature that's being noticed. The same thing happens when people talk of "that short guy you dated," "a Japanese friend of mine," and "his deaf sister."

Wood makes the obvious—though important—point that totalizing has negative effects on the people who are its target. But she also describes some of the effects of totalizing on the people who do it. Basically, when we engage in totalizing, we cripple our perceiving by forcing ourselves to look through blinders. As Wood puts it, "we tend to perceive others through the labels we use to describe them."

One reason people stereotype or totalize is that it's easier to deal with a one-dimensional person than someone with many different important qualities. Another reason is that several automatic human brain processes produce classifications and generalizations. It would be impossible for us constantly to notice every detail of everything available to our senses, so our brain automatically classifies what we perceive to help keep us from going nuts.

But when we perceive people, this natural process can lead us to operate on the basis of what are called "implicit personality theories" (this same idea was discussed by Trenholm and Jensen in the previous reading). As both readings note, these are generalizations about groups of qualities that seem "obviously" to go together—like being overweight, happy, lazy, and undisciplined. Problems arise when we perceive one of these features—that a person is overweight, for example—and our implicit theory about the rest of the personality fills in other features that may or may not be parts of who the person is.

Wood discusses some of Dawn Braithwaite's research about how totalizing applies to people with disabilities. Even that term—*disabled*—is often hurtful because it makes it easier for others to reduce the amputee or the deaf or partly sighted person to the negative status of being incomplete or flawed in some vital way.

Near the end of this short reading, Wood includes 10 examples of statements that often come from well-meaning people, but that are usually heard by the people they're directed to as totalizing or stereotyping. (Compare these with the three statements Marsha Houston criticizes at the end of Chapter 11.) This list and the other ideas in this selection should help sensitize you to whatever tendencies you have to rely on stereotypes in your communication.

It's Only Skin Deep

Stereotyping and Totalizing Others

Julia T. Wood

I want to be known as a talented young filmmaker. That should be first. But the reality today is that no matter how successful you are, you're black first. (p. 92)

Those are Spike Lee's words. In an interview with Diane McDowell, reporter for *Time* magazine, the gifted filmmaker lamented the reality that most people see and respond to his blackness more than his other qualities and achievements. Sometimes, awareness of Lee's blackness overrides all other perceptions of him.

Distinguished historian John Hope Franklin made the same point in an interview with Mark McGurl, reporter for the *New York Times*. According to Franklin, many people assume that because he is an African American historian, he must study African Americans. He is often introduced as the author of 12 books on black history. In reality, Franklin points out, he is *not* a historian only of African Americans. His specialty is the history of the South and, as he notes, that history includes both whites and blacks. In fact, several of his books have focused primarily on whites in the South. Franklin has been elected president of the American Historical Association, the Organization of American Historians, and the Southern Historical Association—none of which is specifically an African American organization. Still, many people perceive his skin color above all else and they assume his ethnicity defines his work.

The misunderstanding of identity and achievement that Spike Lee and John Hope Franklin confront is not unique to people of minority races. Women report that they are often asked to serve on committees. Many times the person asking says, "We need a woman on the committee" or "We think you can provide the woman's perspective on the issues." Like Lee and Franklin, professional women may feel that all their accomplishments and abilities are erased by those who ask them to be "the woman on the committee." The language in the request communicates that all that is noticed is biological sex: She can fill the "woman slot" on the committee.

In this [reading], we focus on communication that highlights one aspect of a person—usually race, sex, sexual orientation, disability, or economic status. We discuss common instances of such communication and explore how it fosters misunderstandings and often offense.

UNDERSTANDING THE MISUNDERSTANDING

Scholars use the term *totalize* to describe communication that emphasizes one aspect of a person above all others. When someone totalizes, he or she acts as if a single facet of an individual is the totality of that person or as if that single aspect is all that's important about the person. For example, describing Spike Lee as a *black* filmmaker spotlights his race as what is worthy of attention. Calling John Hope Franklin a *black* historian emphasizes his race and obscures his professional expertise and accomplishments. Asking a professional to provide the *woman's* perspective highlights sex as the criterion for serving on committees. Referring to a person as *gay* stresses sexual orientation and obscures all the person's other qualities. Describing people as *blue collar* or *white collar* makes their class visible and everything else about them invisible.

Totalizing affects both those who do it and those who are its targets. When we feel that someone totalizes us, we are likely to be offended and resentful. We may also be hurt that we have been reduced to a single part of our identity—perhaps not the part most important to us in a particular context. These feelings create barriers to open, healthy communication and comfortable relationships.

Less obvious but no less important is the impact of totalizing on people who engage in it. Language shapes our perceptions by calling certain things to our attention. When we use language that focuses our attention on race, class, sex, or any [other] single aspect of another person, we limit our perception of that person. In other words, we tend to perceive others through the labels we use to describe them.

Kenneth Burke, a distinguished critic of language and literature, observes that language simultaneously reflects, selects, and deflects. In his book *Language as Symbolic Action*, Burke writes: "Any given terminology is a *reflection* of reality, by its very nature as a terminology it must be a *selection* of reality; and to this extent it must function also as a *deflection* of reality" (p. 45). Burke means that the words we use to reflect our perceptions select certain aspects of what we are describing while simultaneously deflecting, or neglecting, other aspects of what we are describing. When we select *woman, black, gay,* and so forth to describe people, other aspects of those people are deflected (neglected or added as an afterthought). Consequently, we may not see in others whatever our labels deflect. Thus, we are unlikely to interact with those others in their wholeness.

Most of us wouldn't intentionally reduce another person to one aspect of who he or she is, but it happens. One motive for totalizing is the desire for reducing uncertainty. We tend to be uncomfortable when we are unsure about others and situations. To ease discomfort, we often attempt to reduce our uncertainty about others and circumstances. One way to do this is to define others as belonging to a group about which we have definite ideas (although the ideas may not be accurate). It is easier to think of Spike Lee as black than to try to perceive him as a unique individual who is—among other things—male, young, a filmmaker, educated, and African American.

In the classic book *The Nature of Prejudice,* psychologist Gordon Allport observed that stereotyping and prejudice grow out of normal—not deviant or unusual—cognitive activities. Specifically, Allport identified classification and generalization as commonplace mental activities that can foster stereotypes and prejudice. One reason we use stereotypes, then, is that they reduce our uncertainty by grouping people into broad classes that obscure individual characteristics.

A second reason we stereotype is that we rely on what psychologists call implicit personality theory. Most of us have certain unspoken and perhaps unrecognized assumptions about qualities that go together in personalities. Many people assume that attractive individuals are more extroverted, intelligent, and socially skilled than less attractive individuals. Another common implicit personality theory (one that research does not support) is that people who are overweight are also lazy, undisciplined, and happy. In both examples, we attribute to others a constellation of qualities that we associate with a particular quality we have noticed.

If we meet an individual who is overweight (in our judgment), we may assume that the person meets our implicit personality theory of overweight people and is happy, lazy, and undisciplined. Our implicit personality theories may also lead us to think that a nice-looking person must be intelligent, outgoing, and socially skilled. When we rely on our implicit personality theories, we latch onto one quality of another person—often a characteristic we can see, such as race, sex, or weight—and attribute to the person other qualities that we perceive as consistent with the quality we have identified. . . .

One form of totalizing . . . involves defining individuals by their membership in a specific group. Years ago sociologist Louis Wirth conducted classic studies of racial prejudice. One of his more important conclusions was that when we perceive people primarily in terms of their membership in a particular racial or ethnic group, we tend to think about them and interact with them in terms of our stereotypes of race, regardless of their unique qualities, talents, and so forth. In other words, their individuality is lost, submerged in our preconceptions of the group to which we assign them.

A second form of totalizing reduces individuals to one quality or aspect of their identities. This type of totalizing is evident in some of the language used to describe persons who have disabilities. How we perceive and label people with disabilities is the research focus of Dawn Braithwaite, a communication scholar at Arizona State University West. From interviews with persons who have disabilities, Braithwaite learned that the term *disabled person* is likely to offend. The reason is that the term suggests that their personhood is disabled—that they are somehow inadequate or diminished as persons simply because they have disabilities. One of the people Braithwaite interviewed asserted, "I am a person like anyone else" (1994, p. 151). Another interviewee said, "If anyone refers to me as an amputee, that is guaranteed to get me madder than hell! I don't deny the leg amputation, but I am me. I am a whole person" (1994, p. 151).

Individuals who have disabilities have been vocal in resisting efforts to label them *disabled*. They point out that calling them disabled emphasizes their disabilities above all else. "We're people who have disabilities. People first," a deaf student explained to me. When someone with a disability is described as disabled, we highlight what they cannot do rather than all they can do. . . .

When we think stereotypically, we expect people to conform to our perceptions of the group to which we assign them. Sometimes, however, we meet someone who doesn't fit our stereotypes of the group to which we think he or she belongs. Have you ever said or heard the phrases "woman doctor," "male nurse," or "woman lawyer"? Notice how they call attention to the sex of the doctor, nurse, or lawyer. Have you ever heard or used the phrases "man doctor," "woman nurse," or "man lawyer"? Probably not—because it is considered normal for men to be doctors and lawyers and women to be nurses. Many people perceive it as unusual for women to practice law or medicine or men to be nurses. "Woman doctor," "male nurse," and "woman lawyer" spotlight the sex of individuals as the element worthy of notice. The phrases also reflect stereotyped views of the professional groups.

When we mark an individual as an exception to his or her group, we unknowingly reveal our own stereotypes. In fact, we may reinforce them because marking an individual who doesn't conform to the stereotype as unusual leaves our perceptions of the group unchanged. All we do is remove the "exceptional individual" from the group. Consider these statements:

White manager to black manager:	"You really are exceptional at your job."
	[*Translation:* Black women aren't usually successful.]

Male professional to female professional:	"You don't think like a woman." [*Translation:* Most women don't think like professionals.]
Able-bodied individual to person in wheelchair:	"I'm amazed at how well you get around." [*Translation:* I assume that people who use wheelchairs don't get out much.]
Upper-class person to working-class person:	"It's remarkable that you take college classes." [*Translation:* Most working-class people aren't interested in higher education.]
White person to African American:	"I can't believe you don't like to dance." [*Translation:* I think that all blacks dance, have rhythm.]
Heterosexual to lesbian:	"I think it's great that you have some male friends." [*Translation:* Most lesbians hate men.]
Homeowner to maid:	"You speak so articulately." [*Translation:* I assume most domestic workers don't speak well and/or aren't educated.]
White man to black man:	"I never think of you as black." [*Translation:* You don't fit my views of blacks; you're an exception to my (negative) stereotype of blacks.]
Christian to Jew:	"I'm surprised at how generous you are." [*Translation:* Most Jews are tight with money.]
African American to white person:	"You're not as stuffy as most of your people." [*Translation:* Most whites are stuffy, or up-tight, but you're not.]

Would any of the above statements be made to a member of the speaker's group? Would a heterosexual say to a heterosexual woman, "It's great that you have some male friends"? Would a white man say to another white man, "I never think of you as white"? Would a maid say to his or her employer, "You speak so articulately"? Would a white person say to another white person, "I can't believe you don't like to dance"? In each case, it's unlikely. By changing the speakers in the statements, we see how clearly the statements reflect stereotypes of groups.

Communicating that you perceive an individual as an exception to his or her group invites two dilemmas. First, it expresses your perception that the person belongs to a group about which you have preconceptions. Understandably, this may alienate the other person or make her or him defensive. The person may feel compelled to defend or redefine the group from which you have removed that individual. An African American might, for instance, say "Lots of blacks don't enjoy dancing." A working-class person might inform an upper-class person that "education has always been a priority in my family."

A second possible response to communication that marks an individual as an exception to her or his group is the effort to deny identification with the group. A professional woman may strive not to appear feminine to avoid being judged by her colleagues' negative perceptions of women. A white person may try to "talk black" or play music by black artists to prove he or she isn't like most whites. The group stereotypes—no matter how inaccurate—are left unchallenged.

Whether individuals defend or redefine their groups or separate themselves from the groups, one result is the same: The possibilities for open communication and honest relationships are compromised.

REVIEW QUESTIONS

1. Define *totalizing* in your own words, and give an example from your own experience of how totalizing can affect communication.
2. Specifically how does totalizing affect the person who *does* it?
3. Define and give an example of *implicit personality theory.*
4. My wife, Kris, is an attorney. Use Wood's article to explain why she does not like to be called a "woman lawyer."
5. Explain the point Wood is making when she asks, "Would a white man say to another white man, 'I never think of you as white'?"

PROBES

1. On the first day of class, the instructor says in a genuinely pleased way, "It's great to have so many persons of color in the class." Explain how this can be heard as a totalizing statement.
2. Wood quotes Gordon Allport to make the point that stereotyping is a normal, natural activity. But if it's normal and natural, then how much sense does it make to encourage people not to do it?
3. Privately, if you prefer, or with a classmate, if you're willing, explore some of your own implicit personality theories. For example, if you're not thinking carefully about it, what qualities do you presume a person has who is (a) a teenage African-American male, (b) a female athlete, (c) a 20-something gay male, (d) a middle-aged female nurse?
4. If it's obviously true that a person does not have normal sight, hearing, intelligence, or mobility, what is the problem with referring to that person as "disabled"?

5. What's the connection between the main point made in this reading and the social–cultural–interpersonal continuum discussed in Chapter 2?

REFERENCES

1. Allport, G. (1979). *The nature of prejudice.* Reading, MA: Addison-Wesley.
2. Braithwaite, D. (1994). Viewing persons with disabilities as a culture. In L. Samovar & R. Porter (Eds.), *Intercultural communication: A reader* (7th ed., pp. 148–154). Belmont, CA: Wadsworth.
3. Burke, K. (1966). *Language as symbolic action.* Berkeley, CA: University of California Press.
4. McDowell, D. (1989, July 17). He's got to have his way. *Time,* pp. 92–94.
5. McGurl, M. (1990, June 3). That's history, not black history. *The New York Times Book Review,* 13.
6. Wirth, L. (1945). The problem of minority groups. In R. Linton (Ed.), *The science of man* (pp. 347–372). New York: Columbia.

The first two readings in this chapter examine perception processes generally and the specific problems created by perception that stereotypes and totalizes others. Now we move beyond the psychological element of "inhaling" to the communication elements that surface in listening.

This part of the chapter starts with an excerpt from a book called *Practicing the Sacred Art of Listening.* I was originally attracted to the book by its emphasis on the idea that listening is a sacred art. To say that listening is "sacred" is to indicate that it is not just an everyday, run-of-the-mill part of communicating. Sacred things are regarded with reverence; they should be immune from violence. Communication is often thought of as mainly the process of "getting your ideas across," and this view overlooks the importance of listening. So this reading is meant to counter that imbalance. The treatment of listening starts here with the idea that listening is special—"sacred"—and that it is an art, something that cannot be reduced just to mechanical behaviors or skills.

Kay Lindahl argues that "deep listening is a forgotten art," because most of us spend the nonspeaking parts of our conversation time planning what to say next. We learn this approach to communication in our family of origin and from the poor examples of listening that bombard us in the media. She offers three alternative ways to think about listening, presenting each as "a way to think about listening [rather] than the 'right' answer" to the question, "What is listening?"

The first is that listening is a choice. Often our choice not to listen is made below the level of our conscious awareness. It is important to recognize that listening is not a passive activity but a very active one. Anyone who listens for a living—therapist, pastor, group facilitator—can tell you how exhausting it can be to listen well for several hours.

Lindahl's second way to define listening is that it is a gift, in fact, as she puts it, "one of the greatest gifts we can give another is to listen to her or him with total attention." Each of us can test this claim against our own experience. Remember how supportive, confirming, and gratifying it is to really be listened to.

Third, listening is an art. This definition emphasizes that genuine listening is more than just technique. It includes "something special that elevates the experience or act to an art." Lindahl discusses that something special as a deep presence to each other and to something beyond the individuals involved.

Lindahl also makes the point that listening nourishes both the person being listened to and the listener. "Not only is there the connection, but there also is a sense of opening to something new." There are no quick and easy ways to move into this kind of listening zone, but it can help to engage three foundational qualities of listening: silence, reflection, and presence. Lindahl does not develop these qualities here, but other readings in this chapter do discuss them. I hope that you gain from this reading the basic understanding that listening is crucial to interpersonal communicating and it is also special.

What Is Listening?

Kay Lindahl

Are you listening, are you really listening? The answer to this question is usually yes—since asking the question automatically causes us to pay attention, to listen up. In thinking about it, though, we might also respond by saying it all depends what you mean by listening. Am I hearing the words? Am I understanding what I hear? Am I relating to what I hear? There are any number of ways to regard listening. It's a skill that we take for granted. Of course we all listen to each other, but what do we mean when we say that? Many times we think that if we are not speaking we must be listening. It becomes part of our vocabulary of opposites: hot/cold, wet/dry, light/dark, listening/speaking.

Think of the difference it would make if each of us really felt listened to when we spoke. Imagine the time it would save to be heard the first time around, instead of having to repeat ourselves over and over again. Envision a conversation in which each person is listened to with respect, even those whose views are different from ours. This is all possible in conversations of the heart, when we practice the sacred art of listening. It takes intention and commitment. We need to slow down to expand our awareness of the possibilities of deep listening. The simple act of listening to each other can transform all of our relationships. Indeed, it can transform the world, as we practice being the change we wish to see in the world.

"When people talk, listen completely. . . . Most people never listen."[1] There are some interesting statistics that validate this claim by Ernest Hemingway. Most of us spend about 45 percent of our waking hours listening, yet we are distracted, preoccupied, or forgetful about 75 percent of that time. Marketing studies indicate that the average attention span for adults is 22 seconds. (Think about television commercials, which usually last 15 to 30 seconds.) When someone has finished speaking, we remember about half of what we heard. Within a few hours we can recall only about 20 percent. The number of adults who have had any training in listening skills is less than 5 percent of our population. It hasn't been part of the curriculum in most schools.

After hearing these statistics, a business executive reflected: "This is very interesting. I just realized that I spend a great deal of time preparing myself to speak. I don't think I have ever prepared myself to listen." Deep listening is a forgotten art.

Our families provide us with our first experiences in listening. Each of us has a certain style of listening based on our childhood environment. As we grew older and entered school, we discovered more sophisticated ways to communicate and developed additional styles of listening. Relationships with our peers added new habits and patterns. Unless we are part of the 5 percent who have had formal training in listening, we continue to pick up our skills from our surroundings, which may or may not be conducive to effective listening.

We are inundated with examples of poor listening in movies and on television. People are constantly interrupting each other. Shouting is used as a way to make a point or to convince someone to do something. Often the one who is supposedly listening to another person is actually working on the computer, writing a report, or engaged in some other activity. Resolving differences frequently involves physical or verbal violence. There are very few examples of peacemaking solutions. The use of sarcasm, humiliation, and put-downs is rampant. We are being educated in our communication skills by mass media. Learning how to listen well is left to us to discover on our own.

Another factor that adds to the importance of listening is that we live in a country with enormous cultural and religious diversity. Diversity provides us with one of the major challenges and opportunities of our time. We've become a laboratory for the world. If we can learn to live together in harmony in this country, it can be done anywhere. This calls for a way of listening that transcends words and belief systems. Learning to truly listen to one another is the beginning of new understanding and compassion, which deepens and broadens our sense of community. Listening is the first step in making people feel valued.

What is listening? There are many definitions—and we each have our own based on our personalities, backgrounds, and training. Here I consider three ways to define listening, and each one is more of a way to think about listening than the "right" answer.

The first assertion about listening is that it's choice. Choosing to listen to someone else is a decision. Most of the time we are completely unaware that we are making a choice. Have you ever had the experience of listening to someone and all of a sudden you realize that you haven't heard a word for the past minute or so? Your attention is no longer with the other person. You have unconsciously chosen not to listen.

It's easier to notice conscious choices. If we don't want to hear what someone is saying, we can tune him or her out in an instant. Sometimes it's because we are uncomfortable with the topic, or we are simply not interested in it. Sometimes we know that we should listen but we worry that if we really listen we might just have to change something about the way we think or the way we lead our lives. Or we may hear a person's words, but we're not really there—something in our own minds has become more important.

Most likely, we've all been on the other side of this, too, when we are speaking and other people tune us out. They are still physically present and may even look as if they are listening. We just sense that they have left us and are no longer paying attention to what we are saying. We keep talking and are relieved when they tune in again.

Listening is not a passive activity. It's not about being quiet or even hearing the words. It is an action, and it takes energy to listen. The first time I became aware of the energy factor was at an international gathering, where I was part of a small group of eight people. We were from four different continents, spoke four different languages, and worshiped in four different faith traditions. Our task was to make recommendations for one part of a document we were creating as a large body. For two days, I went to bed exhausted. I couldn't imagine why I was so tired because I was getting enough sleep and had not been physically active. All we had been doing was sitting around talking and listening. Then it occurred to me that it took a lot of energy to listen with such intention. I was acutely aware of each person as he or she spoke and was committed to understanding each contribution. It was quite a workout!

Once we become aware of listening as a choice, we will notice that we have many opportunities to practice choosing to listen in our daily lives. It is a profound awakening.

The second way to define listening is that it is a gift—in fact, one of the greatest gifts we can give another is to listen to her or him with total attention. Think about a time when someone was truly listening to you—not figuring out what to say next, wishing you would hurry up so she or he could speak, or mentally reviewing a to-do list. The person was simply there, listening to you. You felt understood, refreshed, whole, connected, healed. It's what we are looking for when we express our desire to be listened to. What a rare occurrence in this fast-paced, information-based culture of the twenty-first century!

You might also have had the experience of people thanking you for all the help you gave them at a particular point in their lives—and you're wondering what they're talking about because you can't remember doing anything. You had simply given them the gift of listening. Thinking about listening as a gift that you either give or receive places a new emphasis on the value of listening. It makes it easier to slow down and savor the conversation, either by opening up to receive the gift or by extending the hospitality of giving the gift.

A few years ago, a member of my family was going through a difficult time. My response was to check in once a week with a phone call. After I said hello, I spent the rest of the time listening. This went on for about six months. I didn't give it any further thought. Just recently this family member brought it up by telling me how much it meant that I had called every week, and how helpful it had been. I hadn't given advice, lectured, or offered resources. I just listened. Journalist and author Paul Hawken adds this wisdom: "When we listen to people our own language softens. Listening may be the cardinal act of giving. . . . I think it is the source of peace."[2]

Third, listening is an art. When we think of describing something as an art we may think of music, painting, dance, drama, poetry, drawing, photography, or architecture, to name a few. We also describe some experiences or actions as art, such as the art of teaching, the art of medicine, the art of counseling, the art of preaching, the art of coaching. What do we mean when we say that? I don't think we are referring to the technique involved. We are talking about that extra something, something special that elevates the experience or act to an art. It happens with listening, too.

There are many wonderful tools and techniques for more effective listening, such as active listening, empathic listening, relational listening, and body language. The premise of my work is that listening is more than technique. When two people are deeply listening to one another, we sense that not only are they present to each other, but they also are present to something beyond their individual selves—some call it spiritual, holy, or sacred. Musicians refer to it as aesthetic rapture, mystics describe it as ecstasy, athletes call it being in the zone, and jazz artists say they are in the groove. All of them speak about it as a moment when time stands still. They are simply being in the experience. It is the same with listening.

Being truly listened to is one of those experiences that we cannot observe in the moment. We can only describe it afterward. When we are in it, that's all there is. A friend told me about his encounter with a storeowner as he was shopping for a wedding gift. The elderly gentleman began to tell my friend a story about the time he was in a concentration camp during World War II. My friend listened, first in polite interest, then in fascination and appreciation until he got caught up in the moment. He described it as being taken to another world. Nothing else mattered. Other people in the store, whatever was going on outside—he was no longer aware of them. There was a tremendous connection between the two men, and my friend left feeling he had been blessed by the listening. He said it had been an honor to listen.

For years, as I was raising my family, it seemed as though I was the one doing all the listening. After my children grew up and left home, I found myself lonely. I can still remember the first time someone really listened to me. I felt as though that person was there just for me. I could share from my soul. I didn't have to censor what I said. It was healing and nurturing. There was a great sense of connection. The fountain of my being had been replenished. It brought me peace beyond understanding.

The listener is also nourished by these exchanges. Not only is there the connection, but there also is a sense of opening to something new. As the other person is sharing herself, speaking about the most important things in her life, the listener is also transformed. Once we begin to think about listening as a gift that we give to someone else, we often find that we open up the space for even more listening within ourselves. Our capacity to listen expands.

With the awareness of this possibility, the next question is, How do we get there? How do we access being in the zone? There are no quick and easy answers but, as with all arts, we can focus on some practices that prepare us for this experience by engaging three foundational qualities of listening: silence, reflection, and presence.

Anyone who wants to be good at something practices. Musicians, dancers, and athletes are always practicing, continuing to fine-tune their talent. Many musicians and dancers practice at least four to six hours or more each day. Those who excel in sports also spend hours every day working out. It's the practice that creates the miracles on the stage or the field or the court. It's the same with listening. We need to exercise our listening muscles, and we do that by practicing. We want to create the equivalent of muscle memory, a state when our response is automatic and we no longer have to think about it because we have practiced regularly. As we practice we begin to notice how these concepts relate to all areas of our lives. They are about being, not doing. We become a listening presence.

Each of us has our own unique perspective of the world, our own worldview. We listen from that view, mostly without recognizing that we are doing so. Once we acknowledge that the way we hear something may not be what was actually said, we are on the journey to sacred listening.

As with any new skill, learning to listen takes effort, attention, and practice. The motivation to learn to listen can come in many forms. It may be in the field of relationships—at home, at school, or on the job. Perhaps you would like to have more harmony, respect, and understanding in your relationships. Or you would like more closeness with others. Perhaps you'd like to have a conversation that opens up your heart; you'd like to talk about things that are meaningful to you but you don't know how to go about it. Maybe you'd like to slow down your fast pace so you can actually be aware of life in the moment. You may be looking for a better way to manage conflicts when they occur. Or you may be interested in exploring your spiritual journey in more depth.

Once you are committed to learning more about the art of listening, you are ready to start practicing. Each conversation becomes an opportunity for practice.

REVIEW QUESTIONS

1. Most of us spend about what percent of our waking hours listening?
   a. 25%
   b. 45%
   c. 95%
2. What percentage of our listening time are we distracted?
   a. 25%
   b. 45%
   c. 75%
3. Everyone who has attended school has taken composition or writing classes. A high percentage have taken coursework in speaking. About what percent have had formal training in listening?
4. Review Lindahl's three ways of defining listening: as a _____, _____, and _____.
5. How do you describe the "something special" that makes listening an art?

PROBES

1. Notice the sequence of chapters in Part II of *Bridges Not Walls*. Chapter 5 is about "Communication as Inhaling" and Chapter 6 is about "Communication as Exhaling." I could have reversed the order of these two chapters. But what point—that Lindahl also makes—is made by this sequence?
2. How consciously do you choose to listen or not to listen? How might you make this crucial communication choice more consciously?
3. Have you ever thanked someone for listening to you? Exactly what are you thanking them for?
4. Explain the two-sided, reciprocal benefits of good listening.
5. Philosopher of communication Martin Buber was described as a person who had the ability to be "present to the presentness of the other and able to call the other into presence with him." This is how I would define the "something special" that makes listening an art. What do you think?

NOTES

1. Ernest Hemingway, "Monologue to the Maestro: A High Seas Letter." *Esquire*, October, 1935. Reprinted in *By-Line: Ernest Hemingway*, Ed. Wm. White (NY: Bantom Books, 1967), p. 190.
2. Paul Hawken, "Listening Could Relieve Strife That Leads to War," *Philadelphia Inquirer*, August 22, 2002.

The previous reading emphasized the importance of thinking of listening as "sacred," and loosely and usefully defined it. This reading walks you through a number of very practical listening skills, illustrating each with examples from real conversations. I think you will find Karen Wegela's essay simple, clear, and helpful.

One of the main points Wegela makes—indirectly—is that good listening requires skillful talk. Listening involves more than just attentive silence. Effective listeners provide paraphrases of what they've heard, probe incomplete statements, offer supportive examples, and, as the last section of the reading emphasizes, they ask helpful questions. Learning to be a good listener means partly learning what to ask and say.

The first skill Wegela reviews is "paying attention." Direct eye contact (in many cultures), nodding, interjecting brief comments, and allowing silence are all part of this skill. The second skill is paraphrasing. The reading provides examples of effective and ineffective paraphrasing that make some important distinctions. Paraphrasing helps with what Wegela calls the third skill, listening for feelings.

As she points out, listening for feelings involves more than just trying to "get it right," to fully understand the other. This kind of listening can also function to help the other person clarify confusing, contradictory, or vague feelings. As Wegela writes, "As a listener we can also help others to focus." As she discusses this skill, Wegela makes a point that you also read in Chapter 4—when verbal and nonverbal messages contradict each other, listeners tend to believe the nonverbal one.

The section titled, "Dealing with Our Own Reactions" emphasizes that nobody can listen as a completely blank slate. We all bring our history, preferences, and biases to the listening process. But Wegela notes that the more fully we understand our own intentions, "the less likely we are mindlessly to impose our own needs on others." Her example of listening to a woman friend agonizing about whether to have an abortion or to go ahead with an unplanned pregnancy is striking.

The final section of the reading, as I mentioned, discusses the kinds of questions that can help or hinder good listening. Wegela gives many examples of both. One principle is to ask questions based on the present situation not on how things got to be this way. These questions tend to begin with what and how rather than why. Why questions usually are not helpful because, even if you don't mean to be attacking, they tend to promote defensiveness. Wegela provides a number of apt examples to reinforce this point. She also provides examples of how questions that begin with how or what can "open things up" and "help us to focus on what is happening right now."

Open, rather than closed questions are also important, as Wegela's examples demonstrate. At the end of the reading she emphasizes that, before a listener asks probing what and how questions, she needs to be sure that her conversation partner is inviting this kind of interaction. Sensitive listeners do not assume that others always want to be deeply heard.

As I said, I think you will find this reading simple, clear, and helpful.

Being a Good Listener

Karen Kissel Wegela

One of the ways we show people that we are present with them is by how we listen. Being a good listener seems to come naturally for some people, but most of us benefit from learning some basic listening skills. These are the same techniques taught to students training to be counselors and psychotherapists, and they can be useful to all kinds of helpers.

We often find that instead of listening, we are just waiting to speak. We might be busy planning what we are going to say next. We might even interrupt and jump in with our own ideas. The person who is speaking will quickly understand that we're not really paying attention. Sometimes people shut down when this happens. They stop talking about what matters to them. They stop telling us, and often they stop letting themselves know too. We are sending the message that their experience is not interesting or worthy of attention. Children especially take to heart these unspoken messages.

BASIC LISTENING SKILLS

The first basic listening skill to practice is really paying attention. From our meditation practice we know that our minds tend to jump around. First we're present and then we're not. The same thing happens when we are with others. We might begin by listening carefully; then suddenly we're lost in our own thoughts about something else. When we notice this, we can gently bring ourselves back. If we've been absent so long that we've lost track of what is being said, we can say so. This lets others know that we really do want to know what they're saying.

We can show that we are following, listening, by nodding and looking at the person who is talking. We can interject brief comments like, "I see," or "Umm hmmm." I have been told that in some cultures the expectation is that when one person talks the other people present listen. In those cultures one is not expected to show that one is listening. It is taken for granted. But most of us in the West don't feel heard unless listeners show us, by their body language or their words, that they are really attending.

Along with paying attention, we can work with allowing silence. We don't have to respond immediately. We can take our time and see what our reaction is and formulate what we want to say. This also helps us drop the pressure to come up with a reply before the other person is done speaking. Some people are not comfortable with silence and tend to fill it up right away. We can feel our way with this. For many, allowing there to be some silence provides an opportunity to slow down a bit. That can be quite a relief in itself. So the first skill of listening is learning to come back, to drop our own distractions, and to allow some space into the conversation.

The second skill is paraphrasing. We let the other person know that we are hearing them by letting them know what we have heard. We put what we have heard into our own words rather than simply repeating the same words as though we were parrots. Obviously, we can't say everything we've heard, but we make a statement that shows that we've heard what's been said.

When I work with couples in counseling, we often spend a lot of time practicing just this skill. We call it stop, say, go. After one partner speaks, the other one says, "This is what I heard you say. Is that right?" If the first speaker agrees that the paraphrase is correct, then the other partner speaks. The first speaker then does the same paraphrasing exercise. Obviously, the conversation gets very slowed down, but each person begins to feel heard. After all, most couples come for help when communication has become problematic, so learning to listen is extremely important.

I remember one couple I worked with: I'll call them Gina and Frank. Gina said something like, "I would like to have some time to do some of the things I used to do before we got married. I would like time to paint and take walks alone."

Frank's first paraphrase was, "You don't want to be with me."

"No, I want some time to do some things alone."

He tried again. "You want to be alone. You're tired of me."

Clearly, Frank was hearing more than Gina was saying. With another try, he got much closer. "You haven't been doing the things you used to do before we got together. You'd like to have some time alone to do things like paint and go for walks." Gina agreed that this was what she had meant. Next it was Frank's turn to speak.

"When you talk about wanting to be alone, I get afraid that you want to leave me and end the marriage."

Gina's first attempts at feeding back what she heard from Frank were not any more accurate than his had been.

"You want me to always be right there where you can see me. You don't trust me at all."

You can imagine the kinds of communication that were going on with both partners mind reading the way they were! Neither one felt heard, and both were quite fed up. Beginning to listen—or even trying to listen—was a powerful message of caring for these two people.

As helpers, we don't usually need to slow things down this much, but the skill involved is the same. We simply let the other person know that we have heard the substance of what they have said.

The next skill builds on this one. This one is listening for the feelings. Instead of just feeding back the content of what is said, in this skill we let the person know what feeling we are hearing in the words. The person may have referred to feelings directly or not.

For example, when Janie was complaining about her landlord and the burdens of looking for a new place to live, Carol could have paraphrased by saying, "Sounds like your landlord is causing you a lot of problems and you'll have a lot to do if you move." A response based on listening for the feelings might go deeper: "It sounds like you're pretty angry at your landlord and scared about finding another place to live."

This kind of listening is more active and invites the speaker to look more closely at what they are experiencing on the spot. Notice that when we reply with either a paraphrase or from listening for the feelings, we do not add anything of our own. All we are doing with these skills is helping others become more clear and present with their full experience.

As a listener we can also help others to focus. A skill we might use here is summarizing what we've heard. We've been listening to Glenn. "You've been talking about the problems you've been having with your boss and also about what's going on with your girlfriend. Now you're starting to talk about your plans for next summer. Would it be helpful to focus on one of those or is talking about a number of different things helpful right now?" Once again, we're not adding our own opinion about what Glenn should choose—or even that he should focus only on one thing. By summarizing we show him what we've heard and give him a chance to decide what he wants to do next.

A very simple technique that we teach to counselors in training is to repeat a word or phrase to show that we are listening. For example, let's look one more time at Gina's first statement about wanting time for herself. "I would like to have some time to do some of the things I used to do before we got married. I would like time to paint and take walks alone."

If I were responding by using this repeating skill, I might say, "Alone?" That seems like the most potent word in what she said. Someone else might pick a different word or phrase to repeat. For example, "Used to do?" or "Paint and take walks?" Each of these would invite a somewhat different response from Gina.

With all of these skills it is important to be really interested, not just to go through the motions that show we are interested and listening. I hear many jokes and see cartoons that make fun of therapists who might, for example, be shown listening to a suicidal client and then saying, "Oh, you're depressed and now you're planning to commit suicide."

Whenever we present the simple repeating skill to counseling students we are likely to get teased by them. I might ask, "Are there any questions?" And students will reply, "Questions?" or "Any?" or even "Are there?"

In my own training, I used to worry about when I should say, "um hmm" and when I should be quiet—as though my timing were so crucial! The most important thing is to really be there with the intention to hear what we are being told. We can trust our basic sanity to decide when to speak up and when to be quiet, when to merely listen and when to get more actively involved. First, though, we need to be able to hear.

Hearing includes not just what we're told in words. We also need to pay attention to tone of voice, body language, and all the clues that are part of communication. I once heard a speaker demonstrate the difference between listening only to the words and listening to the whole message. "I love you!" she shouted in an angry voice. "What would you believe?" she asked us, "My tone or my words?" Most of us believe the nonverbal message first and the words only if they match. When parents' nonverbal and verbal messages are in conflict too often, children grow up very confused and, some people say, are likely to become psychologically disturbed.

DEALING WITH OUR OWN REACTIONS

I've said that when we are listening we don't add anything of our own. Strictly speaking that's not really true. Whenever we listen we pick up on some things and don't pick up on others. This will affect what we respond to, which, in turn, may direct the conversation in one direction and not in another. I don't think we are ever completely neutral, but we can do our best to try to stay with the concerns and priorities of the person we are listening to and not to interject our own agendas. Again, the more we know about our own intentions, the less likely we are mindlessly to impose our own needs on others.

Sometimes we need to let other people know if we cannot put aside our own concerns. If I am trying to help a friend who is agonizing about whether to have an abortion or whether to go ahead with an unplanned pregnancy, it is probably important for me to let her know if I have a strong opinion of my own. If I do, I may or may not be able to listen and help her clarify her own mind. If because of my own mindfulness practice I am aware of the solidity of my views, I need to let her know that I might not be the right person to help with this problem right now and why.

On the other hand, if I tell her where I stand and she still wants to talk with me about her dilemma, maybe that's a clue for her about her own preferences. I find that often people choose to discuss things with someone who will reflect back to them what they really want to hear. That's fine. It's their intelligence at work, and we can make the process more visible by commenting on it.

For example, once a new student came to talk to me about a drug problem with which she was working. She had just stopped smoking marijuana for the first time in a number of years. By telling me—the head of her training program—she was making sure that she could not mindlessly go back to her old habits. She was blowing her cover. If I knew her to be indulging her old habit again, I would not be able to ignore it; it would most likely mean that she would be asked to leave the program. We were able to talk about how risky and intelligent it was for her to choose to discuss her situation with me.

I am often impressed by how important these simple listening skills are. Many times just being heard is comforting in itself. Sometimes all that people need to become more clear about what to do is to have the chance to air their thoughts and contact their feelings. These basic skills can provide the space and support that help people to see for themselves what to do next.

GOOD QUESTIONS

We probably all know what it is like to be asked questions that are not helpful. It can be irritating, confusing, and distracting when our well-intentioned friends and family rally around and bombard us with a thousand questions or suggestions just when we are trying to sort things out for ourselves.

"Well, why did you invest in that company anyway?" "Who is she going out with now? What did you do to drive her away?" "Isn't this exactly the same thing your father used to do?"

These questions tend to take the person away from their experience in the present moment. They may imply a sense of blame. Or they suggest that the answer is already known before the question is asked.

Probably the worst kind of question is like the old joke: "Answer yes or no, did you stop beating your wife?" Of course, if you never beat your wife, you can't answer with either yes or no. This is an example of asking the wrong question altogether.

How can we ask good and useful questions that lead others to become more clear about how they are feeling, what their concerns are, and what actions they want to take? How can we do this in a way that supports both their intelligence and the development of maitri?

There are some basic skills that we can learn and practice. The first steps in asking good questions are what we have already looked at: being present and listening. The more open we are to really hearing how things are for the other person, the less likely we are to impose our own biases on the situation. So the first step, as always, is to show up with an open mind and heart.

We can then ask questions that are based on the present situation. In general, it is rarely useful to get caught up in how things came to be this way. That might be an interesting pursuit some other time, but when people are in pain and need assistance, tracking history is not usually a helpful approach. It tends to take people away from their present experience, and it gives them the message that we are not as interested in helping as we are in trying to satisfy our own curiosity.

Questions that help people focus on the present moment tend to begin with what and how, and not with why. Let's look first at why questions.

Why did you do that?" "Why do you want to hurt me like this?" "Why aren't you more like your brother?"

Why questions invite people to explain and defend themselves. Usually this leads to their feeling attacked or blamed. It may not be our intention to attack or blame, yet it is the response most people feel. When they feel this way, they also feel pushed away by us. They tend to pull back and feel more guarded and wary. This may be just the opposite of what we intended when we asked our question. Another unwanted result of our asking why questions can be that the others receive the message that we think they are stupid or incompetent. "Why did you do that?" is easily heard as, "You nitwit! Why would anybody in their right mind do that?"

Another problem with why questions, but not limited to them, is that they often veil our own agendas. When we ask, "Why?" we may really be saying, "I think. . ." It looks as if we're asking, but we're really telling. For example, "Why did you accept that position?" may sound like "I never would have taken that position." "Begging the question" means to assume we know the answer and then to ask a question that nearly forces the other person to frame the situation as we have done.

"How come you came to dinner tonight dressed so inappropriately?" Notice that the options available to a teenager addressed in this way are pretty limited. He can defend his choice of attire; he can deny its inappropriateness; he can storm out of the room. What he probably hears is, "You've dressed inappropriately for dinner, and I think you are a bad person." Notice too that how come is just another way of saying why.

Finally, why questions invite others into the past; they don't help them become more present now. "Why" suggests that we look at what has already happened—that is not necessarily a bad idea for another occasion. But when help is needed, it is only by coming into the present moment that we can discover where we are and what needs to happen next.

We can try to explore for ourselves by noticing how we feel when others ask us questions that begin with why. Notice the difference in how you respond as you imagine someone asking you, "Why do you feel that?" and "What do you feel?"

Instead of asking why, we can ask how or what. "How does that make you feel?" "How does losing your job affect your plans?" "What do you think about that?" "What options are you considering?"

Questions that begin with how or what tend to open things up. They invite exploration and curiosity. When we feel distressed we are likely to close down. We may feel as if the world is quite small and options are very limited. We may feel trapped and hopeless. It is as if we are walking around in a dense fog. Things suddenly loom up out of the murkiness, but we can't get a sense of how things go together or what else is there, just out of sight. Our emotions may be in a swirl: we don't know how we feel. Or we feel numb. Anything that helps us to open up a bit, that disperses the fog, can be quite valuable.

Questions that begin with how or what can be good ways to help us focus on what is happening right now. Questions that invite us to be more present with our bodily experiences, with our emotions, and with our thoughts can be very useful.

Another dimension we can pay attention to when we ask questions is whether our questions are open-ended or closed-ended. We'll call these open or closed questions.

Closed questions call for a one-word or very brief answer. They are often questions that ask for yes or no as the answer. These questions can be helpful when someone is feeling very confused. They can be used to help the person focus and become more grounded in body and environment.

"Can you see me sitting here?" "Do you know where you are?" "How many fingers am I holding up?" Closed questions can also be used to gather factual information. "Was there anybody else in the car with you when you went into the ditch?" "What's your name?"

The drawback to closed questions is that they may keep the focus narrow when it is more helpful to open things up more.

On the other hand, open questions are good for helping us to explore things and to open up our minds. They are a way of inviting others to relax and let go of any fixed views that may be getting in their way.

"What would happen if you didn't go back to school?" "When you see your girlfriend talking to another guy, what do you imagine is going on?" Compare this question to a why question like, "Why do you get so jealous when you see your girlfriend talking to another guy?" The second one seems more blaming and also assumes that jealousy is the person's response.

Open questions invite the person to tap into their creativity and can also suggest that there is more than one way to look at things. Sometimes this provides welcome relief.

A mistake helpers often make is to ask more than one question at a time. "What are you feeling right now? Do you want to stop talking? Is it okay if I ask you about your mother?" Most people will find a series of questions confusing. More often than not, people answer only the last question asked.

One last thing to keep in mind when we begin to ask questions is whether we have been invited to do so. Any time we present ourselves as helpers it is good to be sensitive when we begin to go deeper. Whenever we ask questions, we are going more deeply into the other person's feelings and thoughts. When people are distressed it is harder for them to tell us that they wish we would go away. It is up to us to try to be sensitive to what is wanted and needed.

I have a friend who is also a therapist. Often our conversations are chatty and humorous. Sometimes one of us will want some help. We have developed a kind of password with each other. "Do you want to really talk about this?" one of us will ask the other. This is a way of asking permission before going further. There are no sure ways to know when we are being a help instead of a nuisance, but when we are in doubt we can check it out by asking what kind of help would be useful.

Soon after I began dating my husband Fred, I received some unwelcome news from a doctor. When Fred heard the news from me by phone, he asked if it would be helpful to me if he came over. He didn't assume that he knew what I needed. I felt respected and cared for by his thoughtfulness.

Here are some other possible questions. "Would it help if I asked you some questions?" "Is it okay to ask you more about that now?" "Would you rather be alone now?" "Do you know what you'd like me to do?"

If we're told that someone would rather be left alone, we should respect that. We can let the person know how to reach us, or we can stay nearby—for example, in another room—if that seems appropriate. This can be a very important message: we are saying that we respect the person; that we will not aggressively intrude; and that we are really listening.

REVIEW QUESTIONS

1. The first listening skill—paying attention—is the most nonverbal one Wegela discusses, and it also includes certain kinds of talk. What kinds?
2. The final reading in this chapter will also discuss paraphrasing, and it will identify the four parts of a paraphrase. From Wegela's discussion of this skill, can you figure out what the four parts are?
3. List three important features of "good questions" that listeners can ask.
4. Give two examples of questions you could ask that are based on the present situation and two examples of questions that focus a conversation on how things came to be this way.
5. Give an example of each of the following:
   - A closed question
   - An open question
   - More than one question at a time

PROBES

1. This reading makes the point that good listening can help the listener understand *and* it can help the speaker focus and clarify what he or she is thinking and feeling. How can you be sure, as a listener, that the person you're listening to *wants* this kind of focused attention? In other words, how can you keep from *imposing* good listening?
2. Wegela's comments about when to say "um hmmm" and when to be quiet make a point about the relationship between the technology of listening and the art of listening. What is her point?
3. For most people, conversations about abortion and drug use are rare. What are two examples from your communication experience where it was important to "let other people know if we cannot put aside our own concerns"?
4. *Why* is it helpful to avoid questions that begin with "Why"?
5. Wegela emphasizes the importance of focusing your listening efforts on the present rather than the past. What is her rationale for this emphasis?

———

The author of this reading is a renowned psychologist and best-selling author who has been studying couples' communication for many years. One of his best-sellers is *The Seven Principles for Making Marriage Work,* and this excerpt comes from his 2001 book, *The Relationship Cure.* John Gottman emphasizes from the beginning that, as I've put it before, people don't talk their way into good, close relationships, we listen our way into them.

Gottman offers some practical suggestions for listening in family, friend, and dating situations. For example, he encourages you to focus on being interested, not on being interesting. The point is not to perform but to understand where the other person is coming from. He explains the importance of asking questions, especially questions about people's goals and visions of the future.

Like the other readings on listening, Gottman emphasizes the importance of searching for commonalities and focusing or tuning in "with all your attention." It doesn't work to fake attention or to try to listen when you're really distracted. After outlining some additional practical suggestions, Gottman concludes this brief excerpt with, "Turn off the television."

As you review these paragraphs, you might be struck with just how commonsensical Gottman's advice sounds. And it is good, common sense. But the reason why his reading is here, and why millions of people buy and read Gottman's books, is that all of us violate these commonsense principles every day. In other words, even though these suggestions make good sense, we need to be reminded to practice them.

Above All, Just Listen

John M. Gottman

While understanding metaphors and all the various forms of nonverbal communication can boost your ability to connect with others, you won't get far without a strong foundation of good, basic listening skills. Your knack for drawing others out and expressing genuine curiosity about their lives can be a real boon to bidding for connection and establishing satisfying relationships. Good listening skills can help you to feel easy in all sorts of social situations, and to build the kind of rapport that leads to solid emotional bonds.

Focus on being interested, not interesting.   That's the counsel Dale Carnegie offered in his 1937 classic, *How to Win Friends and Influence People*, which is still a top seller more than six decades later. And after my three decades of observational research. I have to say that it's still some of the best advice available. Carnegie was right when he wrote. "You can make more friends in two months by becoming genuinely interested in other people than you can in two years by trying to get other people interested in you."

Although Carnegie's advice centered on friendship and salesmanship, my research shows that you can apply the same principle to building better relationships with your spouse, your siblings, your children, your boss—with anybody who plays a significant role in your life. That's because everybody wants to feel valued and appreciated. And nothing fosters such goodwill as your ability to pay sincere attention to the details of another person's life.

Start by asking questions.   Don't ask the kind that can be answered with simple one-word responses. Instead, ask questions that allow people to explain their points of view and elaborate. Questions that begin with the words "Why do you suppose . . ." and "How do you think . . ." are good for this. Avoid questions that are too open-ended—questions like "What's new?" or "How's it going?" Too often, people give pat responses to such queries, perhaps because they're not sure you really want to know. But if you can ask the same type of question in a more tailored way, you're sure to get meatier answers. Examples: "So what's your latest project [at school, in your department, around the house, etc.]?" "How's your summer going? Got any vacation plans?"

It's good to ask specific questions, but it's usually not good for a relationship to pry, or to manipulate people into telling more about themselves than they're comfortable revealing. To find the right balance of disclosure, let the other person take the lead as you ask open-ended questions related to information that person has already revealed.

Say, for example, that a new acquaintance has alluded to using drugs while in college. If you wanted to pursue that line of conversation, you could say, "Was there a lot of drug use where you went to school?" Then, depending on his level of comfort, he could choose to speak from personal experience or to talk more generally. This would probably work better than a pointed probe, such as, "Did you ever feel addicted to smoking pot?" which might get to a point of interest more quickly, but you'd risk losing the connection.

Ask questions about people's goals and visions of the future.   Such queries can be a great way to connect. I'm reminded of the way some couples in our apartment lab use the view outside the window as a way to launch conversations about one another's shared dreams and fantasies of the future. "Look at that boat," one husband said. "If you could sail away to anywhere in the world, where would you go?" Another asked, "If you had that kind of money, what would you spend it on? A boat, a cabin in the mountains, or what?"

Look for commonalities.   People are attracted to those with whom they have things in common, so make it a point to let others know when you share similar views or backgrounds. At the same time, don't try to make yourself the focus of conversation. Say enough to establish common ground and empathize, but always remember to share the floor.

When you want people to disclose information about themselves, it can help to reveal details about your own life first. Be sure to aim for balance, however. Sharing too much personal information too early can be harmful to relationships. Your conversation partner may feel overwhelmed by the intensity of what you're sharing, or feel pressured to become too close too soon.

Be sparing, also, when sharing past experiences with teenagers or children. Young people often have a hard time imagining that their elders were ever as young as they are. And it's especially hard for them to imagine that older people ever encountered challenges similar to the ones they're facing. Such lack of imagination is not their fault; it's just a normal part of being young. You can still let youngsters know that you understand what they're going through, how-ever. The best way is to engage them in friendly conversations about their own experiences. Ask pertinent questions, reflect back what you're hearing, and empathize.

Say, for example, that you're visiting your twelve-year-old niece, who has just gotten braces.

You could say, "I had braces when I was your age."

To which she might reply, "Oh."

Then you might say, "We didn't have those fancy colored braces back then."

To which she might reply, "Oh."

Or you could ask her questions about her own unique, current experience. Resulting in a much more direct emotional connection. That conversation might sound like this:

"How do your braces feel?"

"They're okay now. But the first night was really painful."

"I'll bet. Did you take something for it?"

"Yeah, some ibuprofen."

"And how did it feel to wear them to school for the first time?"

"I felt so weird!"

"I think I know what you mean—like self-conscious?"

"Yeah."

"Did any of your friends tease you?"

"My friends didn't, but there's this guy in my math class and he was like, 'Hey, Metal Mouth.' And I was like, 'Oh, my God!'"

"So you felt kind of embarrassed?"

"Yeah."

"But you're smiling when you tell me about it. Did you feel kind of glad that he noticed?"

"Yeah. I guess so. Because he's real funny and smart. And I didn't even think he knew my name."

"But now he can call you 'Metal Mouth.'"

"Yeah, cool, huh?"

The difference in the two conversations is focus. The adult lets the preteen know that she's understood without taking the spotlight off the girl's present situation. As a result, the girl feels that she has an engaged, sympathetic listener, so she continues revealing more about her life.

Tune in with all your attention.   Once you've encouraged somebody to talk, the next step is to listen—*really* listen. This probably sounds simpler than it is. Many people have an unfortunate habit in conversation of planning the next thing they're going to say rather than tuning in to what the other person is say-ing. It may help to think of your conversation as a tour of some aspect of this person's life. Be willing to go along for the ride, asking questions in ways that show your sincere interest and natural curiosity.

Listen in a way that feels natural, not forced. Your expressed interest ought to be genuine and consistent with your own personality.

Respond with an occasional brief nod or sound.   This indicates that you're paying attention. Research shows that candidates who nod during interviews get the job more often than those who don't. Verbal cues such as "mm-hmm," "yeah," or even a grunt serve a similar purpose.

From time to time, paraphrase what the speaker says.   Doing so tells the speaker that you're still interested, especially when you can restate the important parts. This also serves to ensure that you understand what's been said. A good time to paraphrase is when you introduce a question. For example: "You say you'd really love to go to Africa. Why do you think it would be a great place to visit?" Or, "It sounds like school has been really frustrating for you this spring. How is it harder for you now than last semester?"

Maintain the right amount of eye contact.   Allow the speaker to catch your eye. Studies show that we tend to look more while listening, less while talking. We look away when we first start talking during a conversation. We look back when handing the conversation back to a partner. Avoid staring, which can be interpreted as a sign of hostility or intrusiveness. But don't be afraid to look at the speaker. Avoiding eye contact altogether gives the impression of disinterest, nervousness, or lack of confidence. Be aware also that holding eye contact with a warm smile for several seconds may be interpreted as flirtatious or seductive.

Let go of your own agenda.   It's hard to be a good listener when you're struggling to direct the outcome of a conversation. Listening—especially when a friend or loved one is trying to work though a difficult emotional experience—requires instead that you let go of your desire to control the situation. In such instances it may be best to follow the maxim, "Don't just do something, stand there." Such passive, openhearted listening is rarely easy. More often, when loved ones are upset, people get the notion that they should "fix" what's wrong and "make it all better." There are many drawbacks to this approach. First, it falsely presupposes that people can know and determine how others should live. Second, it can be overwhelming to believe that you have to come up with all the solutions to another person's pain. Faced with such a burden, many people simply avoid the person who's having difficulties, or try to minimize or deny the negative feelings the other person expresses. And, finally, the optimum solutions to an individual's emotional problems rarely come from the outside; the best answers are usually the ones individuals discover for themselves. Although we can't eliminate all the pain life presents our friends and loved ones, we can offer one another immeasurable support in difficult times simply by listening in authentic, empathetic ways. Often it comes down to developing the kind of mindful presence I mentioned in chapter 3. The key is to look for those "emotional moments"—those unpredictable but golden opportunities we have to simply stop and say to another, "I understand how you're feeling right now."

Turn off the television. TV often interferes with people's ability to listen to one another. We haven't done an official study of the frequency with which people choose the television over social interaction, but time and again in our marriage lab, we have observed one partner make a bid for connection only to have the other partner "turn away" because he or she was more interested in the action on the television screen.

TV interferes with children's ability to connect, as well. A 1999 Kaiser Family Foundation study showed that American kids watch an average of two hours and forty-five minutes of TV a day. Some 17 percent watch over five hours daily. Compare this with other studies that show that kids spend just forty-five minutes a week talking to their parents.

More than two-thirds of kids over age eight in the Kaiser study said their families kept the TV on during meals, the times when you'd most expect kids and parents to be talking to each other. But with the families' eyes glued to the set, the quality of interaction can only deteriorate. Indeed, indicators of discontent—such as not getting along with parents, being unhappy at school, and getting into trouble a lot—are strongly associated with high media use, the study's authors say.

So, for the sake of your family relationships, limit TV watching. Be aware of occasions when TV gets in the way of your ability to respond lovingly to one another's bids for connection. And when you do watch television, try to choose programs you can enjoy watching together. Then talk about the TV programs afterward. Ask one another open-ended questions about what family members liked best and liked least about the program. How did the show make you feel? Did it remind you of any similar situations in your own life? If so, how? In other words, use the TV as a way to connect with one another, rather than as a means of isolation.

REVIEW QUESTIONS

1. Gottman emphasizes the importance of asking questions and also warns against asking some kinds of questions. Which questions don't work well?
2. How often in your last three conversations were you doing what Gottman calls "really listening," and how often were you planning what to say next?
3. Gottman's suggestion, "Turn off the television" can be taken literally or figuratively. At times when there is no actual television going, what can you do to follow this suggestion?

PROBES

1. "Focus on being interested, not interesting" is a deceptively simple suggestion. What is the normal or common focus of most people, most of the time? What does it require to focus this way? What do you have to give up? Why is it difficult to do this?
2. Think of a person you feel is very different from you. If you follow Gottman's advice to "look for commonalities," what can you find?

3. It is probably impossible to be completely free of any "agenda," so Gottman's advice to "Let go of your own agenda" can be difficult. What "agenda" could you focus on that would have the desired effect of his advice?

<hr>

This reading offers a fairly extended treatment of two kinds of helpful listening. Empathic listening enables you to understand the *other* person, thoroughly and fully. This is the kind of listening that is discussed by some of the other readings in this chapter. Dialogic listening takes the process one step farther. Rather than focusing mainly on what the other person is thinking and feeling, dialogic listening helps the two of you—or all the people in the conversation—build meaning together. So when dialogic listening works well, everybody understands each other *and* the people involved co-create new understandings that go beyond the individuals.

Karen, Saskia, and I break emphatic listening down into three main skill sets: focusing, encouraging, and reflecting. The focusing section develops what John Gottman wrote about—"really listening"—earlier in this chapter. We outline four specific ways to focus on the person you're listening to.

Encouraging skills are communication moves that "pull" more talk from the other person. They are designed to help your conversation partner(s) get more of what they're thinking and feeling on the table between you. Some encouraging skills are nonverbal, and some are verbal. We offer five ways to encourage people, and we also suggest two kinds of questions that are good to avoid.

Reflecting skills enable your conversation partner(s) to understand what you have heard and understood. This enables them to clarify their meanings, where necessary, and to correct any misunderstandings. The main reflecting skill is paraphrasing, and you've already read about it in other readings that make up this chapter. The reason it's repeated is that it is so important.

As we note, there are no "six easy steps" or "five sure-fire techniques" for dialogic listening. It takes a different level of understanding and practice. If you have trouble with this section of the reading, you might look over the materials in Chapter 12, "Promoting Dialogue." They reinforce what's discussed here and give some additional examples.

The primary ingredient for dialogic listening is *your willingness and ability to collaboratively co-construct meaning with your conversation partner(s)*. You can't listen dialogically until you move beyond your desire to "make sure she understands you" and "get your point across." Dialogic listening begins with the understanding that "the point" needs to be what's shared among those in the conversation, not just your ideas.

The primary metaphor for dialogic listening is "sculpting mutual meanings." We refer to the situation of two people seated on either side of a potter's wheel, with their four wet hands shaping the clay on the wheel. Taken figuratively, this is what it means to "sculpt mutual meaning."

But we don't just leave you with abstractions. We describe four specific communication moves that can help you listen dialogically: focus on "ours", paraphrase-plus, ask for a paraphrase, and run with the metaphor. We also offer an extended example conversation that illustrates these communication moves. Our goal, here and in Chapter 12, is to encourage you and empower you to work toward creating dialogic moments in more of your communicating.

Empathic and Dialogic Listening

John Stewart, Karen E. Zediker, and Saskia Witteborn

EMPATHIC LISTENING

When a person is listening empathically, he or she is receptive or sensitive to the full range of characteristics shared by the other person, but responds only with his or her own impersonal characteristics. Carl Rogers, a famous counselor who pioneered the technique of empathic listening, describes it as "entering the private perceptual world of the other and becoming thoroughly at home in it." He continued:

> It involves being sensitive, moment by moment, to the changing felt meanings which flow in this other person. . . . To be with another in this way means that for the time being, you lay aside your own views and values in order to enter another's world without prejudice. In some sense it means that you lay aside yourself. (Rogers 1980, 142–143)

This kind of listening is important, for example, when you are aware that your friend needs to vent and you are willing to listen without adding anything beyond your friend's point of view. In fact, if you respond in these situations by saying, "Well, if I were you . . ." your friend may insist, "I don't need your advice. I want you to just *listen* to me." It can also be important to listen empathically if you've been asked to mediate a dispute. You can't function very well as a mediator until you fully understand each person's point of view, and empathic listening can help you build this understanding.

Empathic listening is also an important skill for parents, teachers, and managers. Family communication research indicates, for example, that toddlers, children, and adolescents often feel that their parents listen only from their own point of view, rather than taking the time and effort to fully understand the young person's thinking and feeling. Books such as *How to Talk so Kids Will*

From J. Stewart, K. E. Zediker, and S. Witteborn, *Together: Communicating Interpersonally, A Social Construction Approach*, 6th ed. (Los Angeles: Roxbury, 2005.)

Listen and Listen so Kids Will Talk (Faber and Mazlish 1982) also emphasize how pity and advice can leave one feeling worse than before.

> But let someone really listen [empathically], let someone acknowledge my inner pain and give me a chance to talk more about what's troubling me and I begin to feel less upset, less confused, more able to cope with my feelings and my problem. (Faber and Mazlish 1982, 9)

Managers and teachers often need to listen empathically in order to understand how to help their subordinates or students, and counselors and doctors also routinely respond this way to their clients.

In order to listen empathically, it's important to develop three sets of competencies: focusing, encouraging, and reflecting skills (Bolton 1990). As with any complex process, it works best to select from among the various ways to focus, encourage, and reflect. Think of the specific skills like a salad bar—put on your plate the ones that you're comfortable with and that fit the situation you're in.

Focusing Skills

As with analytic listening, the first step is to orient your attention to the person you're listening to. This begins with an internal decision about how you are going to invest your time and energy. Here it helps to recall the distinction between *spending* time and *investing* it and to realize that empathic listening can often pay the dividends of any good investment. Then you remember that listening takes effort, and you put aside the other things you're doing to concentrate on the other person. At this point, focusing surfaces in four skills.

The first is *aiming your posture*. Turn your body so that you're facing or nearly facing the person you're listening to, and if you're seated, lean toward your conversation partner. This is a simple thing to do, and yet a variety of studies have underscored its importance. One textbook for counselors puts it this way: "Usually, the interested helper leans toward the helpee in a relaxed manner. Relaxation is important because tenseness tends to shift the focus from the helpee to the helper. . . ." (Brammer 1979, 70). It's been demonstrated that when listeners focus their bodies this way, the people they're talking with perceive them as more "warm" and accessible and consequently they find it's easier to volunteer more information (Reece and Whiteman 1962).

A second part of focusing is making *natural and appropriate eye contact.*In Western cultures, when you look the other person in the eye, you are not only acutely aware of him or her, but you are also directly available to that person. Studies of nonverbal listening behavior in these cultures typically identify eye contact and forward body lean or movement toward the other as two of the most important indicators of attraction and contact (Clore, Wiggins, and Itkin, 1975). So, if you cannot easily make eye contact with the other person, move to a position where you can. If you're talking with children, get down on the same level by kneeling or sitting, so that they can see you looking at them.

As we've already noted, the amount and kind of eye contact that are "appropriate" depend partly on the cultural identities of the people involved. If you're talking with a person from a culture that proscribes eye contact except between intimates or from a superior to an inferior, it's important to try to honor these guidelines. If you're from one of these cultures, and your conversation partner is not, it can help to alter your own behavior in the direction of the other person's expectations as far as you comfortably can. But so long as you are operating in a generally Western communication context, it's important to work toward making eye contact 50 percent to 70 percent of the time.

In cultures that value direct eye contact, breaking it while listening can create real problems. As one of our students put it, "Based on my own experience, and that of a few others I've talked with, when a listening partner suddenly breaks eye contact to focus on something else (say a friend who's walking by and waving), it can have an almost disconfirming effect on those of us who want to express ourselves" (Adams 1996).

The third and fourth ways to focus are to *move responsively* and to *make responsive sounds.* We've known people who believed they were listening intently when they sat staring at the other person, completely immobile, and with unchanging, deadpan expressions on their faces. There are two problems with this habit. The most obvious one is that, even though you may think you're listening well, it doesn't look like you are. Unless I see some response in your body and on your face, I'm not convinced that you're really being affected by what I'm saying. The second problem is more subtle: Actually you are not fully involved in what you're hearing until your body begins to register your involvement. So even though you might think you're focused when you're immobile and silent, you are not as focused as you will be when you start moving responsively and making responsive sounds. Since everybody's mind and body are intimately connected, the kinesthetic sensations of your body's responsiveness will actually help your mind stay focused.

By moving responsively, we mean smiling, nodding or shaking your head, moving your eyebrows, shrugging your shoulders, frowning, and so on. These actions should be prompted by, in response to, and linked up with what the other person says and does. So an effective listener isn't nodding or smiling all the time; she nods or smiles when that is responsive to what the other person is saying, and she frowns or shakes her head when that's responsive.

Responsive sounds include the "Mnnhuh," "Oh?" "Yeah . . ." "Ahh?" "Sure!" "Really?" "Awww" utterances that audibly tell the other person you're tuned in to what he or she is saying. If you doubt the importance of responsive sounds, try being completely silent the next time you're listening over the phone. After a very short time the other person will ask something like "Are you still there?" We need sounds like these to reassure us that our hearer is actually listening.

These four skills may seem overly obvious or simplistic, but it is quite clear from a number of communication studies that people differ greatly in their ability to apply these behaviors.

Encouraging Skills

The second set of empathic listening skills is designed to "pull" more talk from the other person. More talk is obviously not always a good thing. But when you want to understand as completely as possible where another person is coming from, you need to have enough verbal and nonverbal talk to make the picture clear. As a result, we want to make six specific suggestions about how to encourage.

The first is the most direct one: As a listener, respond when appropriate with "Say more," "Keep talking," "Could you elaborate on that?" or "For example?" One situation where this response can help is when someone makes a comment that sounds fuzzy or incomplete. Frequently the listener's inclination is to try to paraphrase what's been said or to act on the information even though it's uncertain whether he or she has the materials to do so. Of course, it would be pretty ridiculous to respond to "I wonder what time it is" with "Could you say more about that?" But each time you hear a new idea, a new topic, or an important point being made, we suggest you begin your empathic listening effort at that moment not by guessing what the other person means but by asking her or him to tell you. "Say more," "Keep talking," or some similar encouragement can help.

A second encouraging skill is called *mirroring*. Mirroring means repeating a key word or phrase of the other person's with a question on your face and in your voice. "Repeating?" Yes, you just pick up on one term, for example, and feed it back with a questioning inflection and raised eyebrows, and the other person will elaborate on what he has just said. "Elaborate?" Yeah—you know, he will give an example, or restate what he said in other terms, or make some such effort to clarify the point he is making. Just as we have been doing here.

A third encouraging response is the *clarifying question*. Often this takes the form "Do you mean. . . ?" or "When you say _____, do you mean _____?" You might ask the person to explain how he or she is defining a word or phrase, or you might ask for the implications of what is being said. In a job interview, for example, the interviewer might comment, "Our company is interested only in assertive people. . . ." and the candidate could ask, "When you say 'assertive,' what do you mean?" Tone of voice is an important part of clarifying questions. Remember, your questions are motivated by a need to understand more clearly; they are not meant to force the other person into a corner with a demand to "define your terms!"

Open questions are a fourth way to encourage. *Closed* questions call for a yes or no, single-word, or simple-sentence answer. *Open* questions just identify a topic area and encourage the other person to talk about it. So, "Who was that person I saw you with last night?" is a closed question, and "How's your love life going?" is a more open one. Open questions often begin with "What do you think about . . .?" or "How do you feel about . . .?" while a closed version of a similar question might begin "Do you think . . .?" "Do you like this chapter?" is a closed question; "Which parts of this chapter do you like best?" is more open.

Both types of questions can be useful, but when you want to encourage, use open ones.

A fifth way to encourage is by using *attentive silence.* As we've said before, the point of empathic listening is to develop and understand the perspective of the speaker. So, stay focused and give the other person plenty of room to talk. This is frequently all a person needs to be encouraged to contribute more.

Our two final suggestions about encouraging highlight what *not* to do. Encouraging obviously involves asking questions, but not just any question. We have already explained why using open questions is generally more effective than using closed questions. But there are also two types of questions that it helps to avoid. The first are what we call *pseudoquestions. Pseudo* means pretended, unreal, or fake, and a pseudoquestion is a judgment or opinion pretending to be a question. "Where do you think you're going?" is not really a question, it's a pseudoquestion. In other words, if you think about how this question functions in actual conversation, you can hear how it's almost always a complaint or a judgment one person is making about the other. "Where do you think you're going?" usually says something like "Get back here!" or "I don't want you to leave." "Is it safe to drive this fast?" is another pseudoquestion; here, the hidden statement is something like "I'm scared by your driving," or "I wish you'd slow down." At times, we may use pseudoquestions to soften a more directly negative evaluation of the other person (Goodman and Esterly 1990, 760). But often such softening attempts are confusing and add more frustration than they're worth. Our point here is that if you use them in your efforts to encourage, they can backfire. Instead of pseudoquestions, try to ask only real ones, genuine requests for information or elaboration.

A second kind of question to avoid is the one that begins with the word "Why," because these questions tend to promote defensiveness. When people hear "Why?" questions, they often believe the questioner is asking them for a rationale or an excuse. "Why did you decide to bring him to this meeting?" "Why are you turning that in now?" "Why didn't you call me?" "Why did you decide to do it that way?" Do you hear the implicit demand in these questions? The problem is that "Why?" questions often put the questioned person on the spot. They seem to call for a moral or value justification. As a result, they don't work as encouragers. In their place, try asking exactly the same question but begin it with different words. For example, try "How did you decide to . . . ?" or "What are your reasons for . . . ?" We believe that you will find it works better.

Reflecting Skills

This third set of skills will help you directly reflect the other person's perspective in the communication process. This is the central goal of empathic listening. There are three skills in this final set. The first is called *paraphrasing. A paraphrase is a restatement of the other's meaning in your own words, followed by a verification check.* This means there are four important parts to a paraphrase: (1) It's a restatement, not a question. A paraphrase doesn't start out by asking; it starts out by telling the other what you have heard. The first words of a paraphrase might be "So you believe that . . ." or "In other words, you're saying that . . ."(2) It's a restatement of the other's *meaning*, not a repeat of the other's words. Meanings include both ideas and feelings, and the fullest paraphrase captures some of both. Sometimes the feeling content is very important, and sometimes it is less so. But your paraphrase ought at least to suggest the emotion that's included in what the other person said. "So you're worried that . . ." or "It sounds like you are really upset because you believe that . . ." are two examples of restating feelings—"worry" and "upset." (3) A paraphrase has to be in your own words. We have already mentioned why when we talked about restatement in the section on analytic listening. Translating the other's meaning into your words demonstrates that you've thought about it, that it's gone through your brain cells. (4) After the restatement, you finish a paraphrase with an opportunity for the other person to verify your understanding. You can do this very simply—just by pausing and raising your eyebrows, or asking "Right?" or "Is that it?" Paraphrasing is such a powerful communication move that, if you follow these four steps periodically in your conversations, your empathic listening effectiveness will improve significantly.

The second reflective skill is *adding an example.* You can contribute to the listening process by asking the other person to respond to an example from your own experience that you believe illustrates his or her point. Remember that this is an effort to listen empathically, not to turn the conversation away from the other person's concerns and toward yours. So the example needs clearly to be one that makes his or her main point. Here is part of a conversation that illustrates what we mean.

LAURA: I've had my share of problems with this TA position, but in some ways this job is actually rewarding.

(clarifying question) HABIB: Since it's payday, are you talking about your check?

LAURA: No, one of my students just wrote this note on her copy of the exam we were going over in class: "I liked the way you were willing to listen to our side and to consider giving back some points. I think it takes real confidence as a teacher to do that."

(adds example) HABIB: That's really great. But I got a comment like that from a student once, and it turned out that he was being sarcastic. He was really ticked off about the way I graded his exam, and he even complained to the department chair. Do you think she could be setting you up?

(clarifies) LAURA: I never thought about that. No, I don't think so. This is a returning student, and I think she appreciates it when she feels she's being treated as an adult.

Remember that understanding is very different from agreement, and that neither the paraphrase nor adding an example requires you to agree with the other person. These listening responses are designed to promote the empathic listening process, to simply help you understand the other person's perspective.

The third and final reflecting skill also takes some finesse. The skill consists of *gently pursuing verbal and nonverbal inconsistencies.* The first step is to identify when you think they've occurred. You have to be sensitive enough to recognize when the words a person is speaking don't match the way she or he is saying them. As we noted earlier, a shouted, scowling "I'm not mad!!" is an obvious example of an inconsistency between verbal and nonverbal cues. Most of the time, though, it's much more subtle. John had a friend who declared she was not going to waste any more time being angry at her boss, and then spent the next half hour complaining about the boss's most recent actions. In other situations, facial expression and tone of voice accompanying a person's "Sure," "I don't care," "Go ahead with it," or "It doesn't make any difference to me" can reveal that the words are thin masks for disappointment, concern, or hurt feelings.

As a listener you can help move beyond surface-level meanings by gently pursuing the verbal/nonverbal inconsistencies you notice. We stress the word *gently.* When you notice an inconsistency, remember that it's your interpretation of what's going on; be willing to own it as your own. Remember, too, that if the other person also sees an inconsistency, there's a reason for its being there. He or she may not be ready or willing to admit the difference between cues at one level and cues at another. So don't use this skill as a license to clobber someone with a club made out of sidewalk psychoanalysis. Instead, just describe the inconsistency you think is there and open the door for the other person to talk about it.

For example, one group of professionals John worked with were experiencing some conflict over a proposal made by their new manager. The manager decided that the group needed to be more cohesive, so she proposed that each Friday afternoon the office close down an hour early so the workers could spend some time together informally chatting over wine and cheese. Most of the people welcomed the idea, but two resisted it. They didn't like what they saw as "forced socializing," and they resented the fact that only alcoholic drinks were being served. They didn't think it was appropriate to "drink on the job." John asked the group to discuss this issue as part of their listening training. Ann, the manager, turned to Gene, one of the two persons resisting the plan, and asked what he thought about these Friday afternoon get-togethers. Gene turned slightly away in his chair, folded his arms in front of him, looked down at the floor, and said, "Well . . . it's a pretty . . . good idea . . ." Ann smiled and softly said, "Gene, your words tell me one thing and your body says something else." Then she was silent. After a couple of seconds, Gene relaxed his body posture, smiled, and admitted that he actually didn't like the plan very much. This began a conversation that ended up redesigning the get-togethers to respond to Gene's concerns.

The primary reason this listening response works is that nonverbal cues can "leak" implicit or hidden messages. Thus, a person's tone of voice, posture, eye behavior, and even facial expression often reveal levels of meaning that are obscured by his or her choice of words. Sensitive listeners try to respond to such inconsistencies and, as we suggest, gently pursue them.

DIALOGIC LISTENING

There is no simple recipe for dialogic listening—no "six easy steps" or "five surefire techniques." This is something that anybody who wants to can definitely do, but it requires an overall approach to communicating that's different from the stance most people ordinarily take when they listen or talk. You also need to maintain a sometimes-difficult tension or balance (remember the idea of tension in Chapter Two) between holding your own ground and being open to the person(s) you're communicating with. The best way to get a sense of this approach and this tension is to understand a little bit about the idea of *dialogue.*

Ordinarily, dialogue means just conversation between two or more people, or between the characters in a novel or play. But in two periods of recent history, the term has taken on some special meanings. First, between about 1925 and the early 1960s, the philosopher and teacher Martin Buber and some other writers used the term to talk about a special kind of communication. In his famous book *I and Thou* and in many other books and articles, Buber tried to point toward a way of communicating that he had noticed in some factories, family homes, schools, political organizations, churches, and even buses and planes, a way of communicating that accomplished genuine inter*personal* contact. Buber readily admitted that people can't and don't communicate dialogically all the time, but he maintained that we could do more of it, and if we did, we'd be better off.

For Buber, dialogue basically meant communication characterized by what we call open sensitivity. As we've noted, this definitely doesn't require agreement, but it does require alignment. It can and does sometimes happen in committee meetings, family discussions, telephone calls between friends, doctor-patient exchanges, lovers' quarrels, and even occasionally between labor-management negotiators and political enemies.

Buber's view of dialogue lost credibility in the United States when it became associated with the hippie movement of the 1960s and 1970s. But since the early 1990s, the term and the ideas surrounding it have become prominent again. Today, though, the main writer everybody's quoting is another early-twentieth-century author with the initials MB, the Russian theorist Mikhail Bakhtin (Holquist 1981).

If you're going into business, it is very likely that you will run across Bakhtin's name in discussions about the importance of dialogue in what are called "learning organizations" (Senge 1990). Management theorists from the

Sloane School at M.I.T., Harvard, and other prominent business schools argue that in this age of globalization and constant rapid change, the only way a company can keep up is to be constantly learning from its successes and mistakes. And the only way to become a learning organization is to replace traditional hierarchical communication with dialogue. Beginning in the late 1990s, large organizations like Ford Motor Company and Boeing started investing thousands of hours and dollars in training designed to help their employees learn to open spaces in their organizations for dialogue.

Dialogue is also being promoted as the best way to improve the quality of public discourse in the United States (Roth, Chasin, Chason, Becker, and Herzig 1992) and Great Britain (in 1995 and 1996, British Telecommunications was engaged in a nationwide project to enhance the quality of interpersonal communication; several U.S. interpersonal communication scholars contributed to this effort). And some psychologists are arguing that the focus of the entire discipline of psychology needs to shift from the individual psyche to the dialogic person-in-relation (Sampson 1993). The concept is also being used more and more by communication researchers and teachers (Baxter and Montgomery 1996) and Chapter 12 of this book focuses on this concept. In short, increasing numbers of influential people are recognizing that dialogue is a seriously beneficial phenomenon. The three of us believe that dialogic listening is the most direct way to promote dialogue. By "promote" we mean that dialogue can't be guaranteed, but it can be encouraged. And dialogic listening will help open up a space for the kind of person-to-person contact that Buber, Bakhtin, and all these other theorists and teachers call dialogue.

Dia-logos as Meaning-Through

One good way to open up this space is to focus on the term *dialogue* itself. This term consists of two Greek words, *dia* and *logos*. The *logos* in dia-logos is the Greek word for *meaning or understanding*. (The Greek term logos has other meanings, too. Sometimes it is translated as "logic," and at other times it comes into English as "language." But its most fundamental meaning is "meaning.") The *dia* in dia-logos means not "two" but *"through"* (Bohm 1990). So dialogue is not restricted to two-person communicating, and it is an event where meaning emerges *through* all the participants. This is another way of saying that, in dialogue, meaning or understanding is *collaboratively co-constructed*. The important implication of this idea for each participant is that, when you're listening and talking dialogically, *you are not in control of what comes out of the communicating*. This point is stated clearly by Abraham Kaplan:

> When people are in [dialogue] . . . the content of what is being communicated does not exist prior to and independently of that particular context. There is no message, except in a post-hoc reconstruction, which is fixed and complete beforehand. If I am really talking with you, I have nothing to say; what I say arises as you and I genuinely relate to one another. I do not know beforehand who I will

be, because I am open to you just as you are open to me. (quoted in Anderson, Cissna, and Arnett 1994)

As communication teacher Bruce Hyde points out, the main obstacle to dialogic listening is the kind of self or identity that replaces this openness to collaboration with the conviction that the ideas I utter are tightly connected with who I am. There's a big difference, Bruce notes, "between being right about something and being committed to something. Being right makes somebody else wrong; being committed has room to engage productively with other points of view." In other words, if you're committed, you might even welcome the chance to talk with someone who believes differently from the way you believe, but if you're committed to being right, there's not much room for people who don't share your position to be anything but wrong. The key difference has to do with identity. The person who's caught up in being right identifies him- or herself first an advocate for a certain position. The person who's committed, on the other hand, identifies him- or herself first as a listener who's collaborating on, but not in control of, what comes out of the conversation. If you're going to listen dialogically, you have to be more interested in building-meaning-through than in being right. And this, Bruce writes, "in my experience is the hardest single thing you can ask of anyone." (We got this from an e-mail contribution by Hyde on August 29, 1996, to Redwood Forest Dialogue. Kimberly Pearce was crucial in sharpening what Bruce wrote.)

Communication theorist and teacher Barnett Pearce expresses basically this same idea but with a cultural slant, when he contrasts an *ethnocentric* with a *cosmopolitan* approach to communication. Recall that the term *ethnocentric* means viewing other cultures from the perspective of one's own. When I communicate from an ethnocentric attitude, I begin with the assumption that my culture's way is "normal," "natural," "preferred," and, in these important senses, "right." Barnett argues that "ethnocentric communication is the norm in contemporary American society. It is, of course, the stuff of racism, sexism, and the like. It also structures domestic political discourse" (Pearce 1989, 120). Another feature of ethnocentric communication is that it privileges *coherence*—the kind of sense that emerges when other ideas fit into a comfortable whole, in part by matching or echoing what's already there and hence what is "normal and natural." So a person who approaches communication with an ethnocentric attitude assumes that his or her ways of thinking and doing are normal and natural and that conversations ought to make the kind of sense that you get when feelings and ideas fit together into familiar patterns.

A cosmopolitan attitude, on the other hand, is one that embraces all the "politics" in the "cosmos." It is inclusive rather than exclusive. A person with a cosmopolitan attitude may be *committed* to an idea or position, but he or she does not assume that it is absolutely "right." As a result, cosmopolitan communication privileges *coordination* rather than *coherence*. There's no assumption that the only way to put ideas or people together is the "logical" way, or the way based on "what we've always believed and done." People with a cosmopolitan attitude are open to all kinds of creative syntheses of ideas, procedures, and past experiences. The main goal is to work toward alignment, even when there is little or no agreement. As psychologist Gordon Allport is reported to have said, this kind of communicator is "half-sure yet wholehearted." *Dialogic listening begins with a cosmopolitan rather than an ethnocentric attitude.* The first step toward dialogic listening is to recognize that each communication event is a ride on a tandem bicycle, and you may or may not be in the front seat.

Sculpting Mutual Meanings

To shift from the bicycle metaphor, we've found that it helps to think and talk about the nuts and bolts of dialogic listening with the help of the image of a potter's wheel (Stewart and Thomas 1990). The sculpting mutual meanings metaphor was created by communication teacher Milt Thomas, and he uses it to suggest a concrete, graphic image of what it means to listen dialogically.

Picture yourself sitting on one side of a potter's wheel with your conversation partner across from you. As you participate (talk) together, each of you adds clay to the form on the wheel, and each uses wet fingers, thumbs, and palms to shape the finished product. Like clay, verbal and nonverbal talk is tangible and malleable; they're out there between people to hear, to record, and to shape. If I am unclear or uncertain about what I am thinking about or what I want to say, I can put something out there and you can modify its shape, ask me to add more clay, or add some of your own. Your specific shaping, which you could only have done in response to the shape I formed, may move in a direction that I would never have envisioned. The clay you add may be an idea I've thought about before—although not here or in this form—or it may be completely new to me. Sometimes these "co-sculpting" sessions will be mostly playful, with general notions tossed on the wheel and the result looking like a vaguely shaped mass. At other times, the basic shape is well defined and conversation partners spend their time on detail and refinement. Peoples' efforts, though, always produce some kind of result, and frequently it can be very gratifying. Sometimes I feel that our talk helps me understand myself better than I could have alone. At other times, we produce something that transcends anything either of us could have conceived of separately. This is because the figure we sculpt is not mine or yours but *ours,* the outcome of both of our active shapings.

So in order to enter into the sculpting process effectively, you need to remember, as we have said many times before, that the meanings that count between people are not just the ones inside somebody's head but also the ones that are constructed in conversations. With this understanding you will be willing to sit down at the potter's wheel, throw your clay on the wheel, and encourage the other person to add clay, too. Then you need to be willing to get your hands dirty, to participate in the collaborative process of molding meanings together.

As you might have guessed, in order to put this basic attitude into action, you need to practice some special kinds of focusing and encouraging.

Focus on 'Ours'   We mentioned before that dialogic listening involves a crucial change from a focus on *me* or the *other* to a focus on *ours*, on what's *between* speaker(s) and listener(s). Contrast this with empathic listening, which requires you to try to experience what is "behind" another's outward communication. When you focus on ours, you don't look behind the verbal and nonverbal cues. You don't try to deduce or guess what internal state the other is experiencing. Instead, you concentrate on the meanings you and the other person are mutually creating between yourselves. Empathic listening can be helpful, as we said, but dialogic listening requires a move beyond empathy to a focus on ours.

It can make a big difference whether you are trying to identify what's going on inside the other person or whether you're focusing on building-meaning-between. When your focus is on the other's thoughts and feelings "behind" their words, you spend your time and mental energy searching for possible links between what you're seeing and hearing and what the other "must be" meaning. "Look at those crossed arms. She must be feeling angry and defensive." Or, "He said he'd 'never' pay all the money back. That means it's hopeless to try to change his mind." When you think this way, your attention is moving back and forth between what's outside, in the verbal and nonverbal talk, and what's inside the person's head. From this position, it's easy to believe that what's inside is more reliable, more important, more true, and hence more interesting than the talk on the surface.

But when you're focusing on ours, you concentrate on what's outside, not what's supposedly inside. We don't mean that you should be insensitive to the other person's feelings. In fact, you will be even more sensitive when you are focused on what's between you here and now. You concentrate on the verbal and nonverbal talk that the two (or more) of you are building together. In a sense, you take the conversation at face value; you never stop attending to *it* instead of focusing mainly on something you infer is behind it. This doesn't mean you uncritically accept everything that's said as "the whole truth and nothing but the truth." But you do realize that meaning is not just what's inside one person's head. Focusing on ours prepares you to respond and inquire in ways that make it clear that "getting to the meaning" is a mutual process.

Encouraging as Nexting   Dialogic listening also requires a special form of encouraging. Basically, instead of encouraging the other person(s) to "say more," you're encouraging him or her to respond to something you've just put on the potter's wheel in response to something he or she has just said. So your encouraging is a "nexting" move; it actively and relevantly keeps the collaborative co-construction process going.

One specific way to do this is with a *paraphrase-plus*. We've already said that a paraphrase consists of (1) a restatement, (2) of the other's meaning, (3) in your own verbal and nonverbal talk, (4) concluded with an opportunity for the other person to verify your understanding. The paraphrase-plus includes all of these elements *plus* a small but important addition.

The plus is your own response to the question "What's next?" or "Now what?" You start by remembering that the meanings you are developing are created between the two of you, and individual perspectives are only a part of that. If you stopped with just the paraphrase, you would be focusing on the *other* person exclusively instead of keeping the focus on what is happening *between* you. So, you follow your verifying or perception-checking paraphrase with whatever your good judgment tells you is your response to what the person said, and you conclude your paraphrase-plus with an invitation for the person to respond to your synthesis of his or her meaning and yours. The spirit of the paraphrase-plus is that each individual perspective is a building block for the team effort. For example, notice the three possible responses to Rita's comments.

RITA: I like having an "exclusive" relationship, and I want you to be committed to me. But I still sometimes want to go out with other people.

1. MUNEO: So even though part of you agrees with me about our plan not to date others, you're still a little uncertain about it. Right? (Paraphrase)

2. TIM: Oh, so you want me to hang around like an idiot while you go out and play social butterfly! Talk about a double standard! (Attack)

3. SCOTT: It sounds like you think there are some pluses and minuses in the kind of relationship we have now. I like it the way it is, but I don't like knowing that you aren't sure. I guess I want you to tell me some more about why you're questioning it. (Paraphrase-plus)

Muneo responds to Rita's comment with a paraphrase. This tells us that Muneo listened to Rita, but not much more. Tim makes a caricature of Rita's comment; his interpretation reflects his own uncertainty, anger, and fear. His comment is more a condemnation than a paraphrase. Scott offers a paraphrase-plus. He explains his interpretation of what Rita was saying, then he says briefly how he *responds* to her point, and then he moves the focus back between the two of them, to the middle, where both persons are present in the conversation and can work on the problem together. He does this by putting some of his own clay onto the potter's wheel. He paraphrases, but he also addresses the "What's next?" question as he interprets and responds to her comments. Then he concludes the paraphrase-plus with encouraging rather than simply verifying the accuracy of his paraphrase. When all this happens, both the paraphrase and the plus keep understanding growing between the individuals.

Another way to think about the paraphrase-plus is that you're broadening your goal beyond listening for "fidelity" or "correspondence." If you're paraphrasing for fidelity or correspondence, you're satisfied and "finished" with the task as soon as you've successfully *reproduced* "what she means." Your paraphrase is a success if it corresponds accurately to the other person's intent. We're suggesting that you go beyond correspondence to creativity, beyond reproducing to producing, to mutually constructing meanings or understandings between you.

Because paraphrasing is so potentially helpful, another sculpting skill is to *ask for a paraphrase*. Whenever you're uncertain about the extent of the other person's involvement or whether the two of you share an understanding, you can ask the person for his or her version of the point you're making. It is difficult to do this well. Often a request for a paraphrase sounds like an accusation: "Okay, stupid, why don't you try telling me what I just said." This is obviously is not going to contribute much to the co-sculpting process. The idea is to ask for a paraphrase without demanding a response and without setting up the person so you can play "Gotcha!" if she or he doesn't get it right. You can try putting it this way: "Just to make sure we're going in the same direction, could you tell me what you think we've agreed to so far?" Or you might say, "I'm not sure I've been clear—what do you hear me saying?" The point is, if it's done with an eye toward nexting, a paraphrase can promote collaborating whether it comes from your side or the other's. You can sometimes help that happen by asking for one.

Another skill you can use in the sculpting process is to *run with the metaphor.* You can build meaning into the conversation by extending whatever metaphors the other person has used to express her or his ideas, developing your own metaphors, and encouraging the other person to extend yours. As you probably know, metaphors are figures of speech that link two dissimilar objects or ideas in order to make a point. Besides "Communication is made up of inhaling and exhaling," "Conversation is a ride on a tandem bicycle," and "Dialogic listening is sculpting mutual meanings," "This place is a zoo," "My vacation was a circus," and "She's as nervous as a flea on a griddle" all contain metaphors. As these examples illustrate, metaphors don't appear only in poetry or other literature; they are a major part of most everyday conversation. In fact, it's becoming increasingly clear that virtually all language is metaphoric (Lakoff and Johnson 1980; Ricoeur 1978). In our label for this skill, "run with the metaphor," for example, the term *run* itself is metaphoric.

This skill consists of listening for both subtle and obvious metaphors and then weaving them into your responses. We have found that when other people hear their metaphor coming back to them, they can get a very quick and clear sense of how they're being heard, and they typically can develop the thought along the lines sketched by the metaphor. For example, in a workshop he was leading, John was listening to an engineer describe part of his job, which involved going before regulatory boards and municipal committees to answer questions and make arguments for various construction projects. Part of what Phil said about his job was that it was a "game." John tried to run with the metaphor by asking, "What's the name of the game?" "Winning," Phil responded. John recognized that his question had been ambiguous, so he continued: "Okay, but what kind of game is it—is it baseball, football, soccer, chess, or what?" "It's football," Phil replied. "What position do you play?" "Fullback." "And who's the offensive line?" "All the people in the office who give me the information I take to the meetings." "Who's the coach?" "We don't have one. That's the major problem." This was a telling response. In fact, from that point on, the workshop was focused on one of the major management problems that engineering firm was having.

Here's another example of how running with the metaphor can work in conversation:

TANYA: You look a lot less happy than when I saw you this morning. What's happening?

ANN: I just got out of my second two-hour class today, and I can't believe how much I have to do. I'm really feeling squashed.

TANYA: *Squashed* like you can't come up for air, or *squashed* as in you have to do what everybody else wants and you can't pursue your own ideas?

ANN: More like I can't come up for air. Every professor seems to think his or her class is the only one I'm taking.

Again, the purpose of running with the metaphor is to build the conversation between the two of you in order to produce as full as possible a response to the issues you're talking about. In addition, the metaphors themselves reframe or give a new perspective on the topic of your conversation. A project manager who sees her- or himself as a "fullback" is going to think and behave differently from one who thinks in other metaphorical terms, like "general," "Joan of Arc," "guide," or "mother hen." And the work stress that "squashes" you is different from the pressure that "keeps you jumping like a flea on a griddle." Listen for metaphors and take advantage of their power to shape and extend ideas.

Remember our point that all these specific listening skills are like dishes in a salad bar: You don't eat everything, and at different times you select different dishes. Let's look at an extended example of a conversation that illustrates some of the listening attitudes and skills we've discussed. Sally and Julio start out at opposite sides in their opinions about the class. But first Julio, and then both he and Sally dialogically listen to each other. As a result, their interpretations of the class and the teacher change; they build a meaning that neither of them had at the beginning of the conversation. At the left margins, we've labeled some of the specific empathic and dialogic listening skills they're using.

SALLY: That class drives me up a wall.

(open question) JULIO: I thought it was going pretty well. What happened?

SALLY: She's so strict! We can't miss more than five hours of class, everything has to be submitted electronically, she won't take late papers. I'll bet she wouldn't even allow a makeup exam if I was in the hospital!

(say more)   JULIO: I didn't know she wouldn't take late papers. Where did you hear that?

SALLY: Alaysha told me that on Tuesday she tried to hand in the article analysis that was due Monday and Dr. Clinton wouldn't accept it.

(clarifying question)   JULIO: Was there anything else going on? Hilary and I both turned in our journals late and she took them. I also thought the five-hour restriction and the e-mail requirement were pretty standard at this school.

(say more)   SALLY: Do you have them in other classes?

JULIO: Yeah. My geology prof allows only two days' absence and won't accept hardly any excuses.

(say more)   SALLY: Are your other profs so stiff and formal in class?

JULIO: Some are and some aren't. Clinton is a lot looser in her office. Have you ever talked to her there?

SALLY: No, I don't like the way she treated Alaysha.

(paraphrase)   JULIO: So Alaysha did the assignment like she was supposed to and Clinton wouldn't take it even though it was only one day late?

SALLY: Well, it wasn't e-mailed, but I still think it's pretty unreasonable. I haven't started the paper that's due this Friday, and I'll bet there's no way she'd accept it Monday.

(paraphrase-plus)   JULIO: I know how that feels. But if you've got a good reason, I'll bet she would. She told me last term that most of her rules come from what other profs tell her are the standards here. This school is really into developing responsibility and treating everybody like an adult. That's why I thought they required attendance and e-mailed papers. But I think Clinton is willing to listen, and she's bent the rules for me a couple of times. You've been doing fine in class, and I'd really be surprised if she turned you down.

SALLY: I didn't know that about this school; this is my first term here.

JULIO: Well, I didn't know about Alaysha, but she probably should have printed it out.

SALLY: Yeah. Well, thanks for listening—and for the information.

Remember that we do not mean to present these skills as a guaranteed step-by-step way to instant success. They are suggestions, guidelines, examples of ways you can behaviorally work the focusing, encouraging, and sculpting processes of dialogic listening. They won't work if you apply them woodenly or mechanically; you have to use them with sensitivity to the relationship and the situation.

As you begin using these skills—and this also applies to all the skills we have discussed—you may feel awkward and even phony. This is natural. It is part of learning any new skill, whether it's skiing, tennis, aerobics, or listening. Remember that the better you get with practice, the less awkward you will feel. Try not to let any initial feelings of discomfort distract you from working on specific ways to improve.

REVIEW QUESTIONS

1. Describe the basic similarities and differences between empathic and dialogic listening
2. Focusing skills take time. How can the distinction between "spending" and "investing" time encourage you to take the time to focus?
3. What is it important *not* to do with your eye contact, movement, and sound if you want to focus effectively?
4. What's the difference between a clarifying question and an open question?
5. What's a "pseudoquestion"? Why is it dangerous?
6. What are the four parts of a paraphrase?
7. "Dia-logos" means "meaning-through." Explain.
8. Distinguish "ethnocentric" from "cosmopolitan" communicating.
9. How is "focus on ours" different from the "focusing" that is part of empathic listening?

PROBES

1. How can people cope with the natural tendency to feel that practicing new communication skills will make their communicating sound phony and artificial?
2. What are some real-world exceptions to the authors' advice about "Why?" questions?
3. What danger accompanies the "adding an example" skill? (Hint: Recall John Gottman's first piece of advice in his "Above All, Just *Listen*" reading.)
4. How can you "gently pursue verbal/nonverbal inconsistencies" without playing "Gotcha!"?
5. Google the word "dialogue" and identify examples of what we discuss about its importance in business and public communication.
6. Give an example from your own experience where you or your conversation partner "ran with a metaphor."

REFERENCES

1. Adams, J. 1996. *Journal entry in SpCmu 103, Autumn 2001.* University of Washington. Used by permission.
2. Anderson, R., Cissna, K. N., and Arnett, R. C. (eds.) 1994. *The Reach of Dialogue: Confirmation, Voice, and Community.* Cresskill, NJ: Hampton Press.
3. Baxter, L. A., and Montgomery, B. M. 1996. *Relating: Dialogue and Dialectics.* New York: Guilford.
4. Bohm, D. 1990. *On Dialogue.* Ojai, CA: David Bohm Seminars.
5. Bolton, R. 1990. "Listening Is More than Merely Hearing." In J. Stewart (ed.), *Bridges Not Walls.* 5th ed. New York: McGraw-Hill. Pages 175–191.
6. Brammer, L. M. 1979. *The Helping Relationship: Process and Skills.* 2nd ed. Englewood Cliffs, NJ: Prentice Hall.
7. Buber, Martin. 1970. *I and Thou.* Trans. W. Kaufmann. New York: Scribner.
8. Cirksena, K. and Cuklanz, L. 1992. "Male Is to Female as——is to——: A Guided Tour of Five Feminist Frameworks for Communication Studies." In L. F. Rakow (ed.), *Women Making Meaning.* New York: Routledge. Page 370.
9. Clore, G. L., Wiggins, N. H., and Itkin, S. 1975. "Judging Attraction from Nonverbal Behavior: The Gait Phenomenon." *Journal of Counseling and Clinical Psychology,* 43: 491–497.
10. Faber, A., and Mazlish, E. 1982. *How to Talk so Kids Will Listen and Listen so Kids Will Talk.* New York: Avon.
11. Goodman, G., and Esterly, G. 1990. "Questions—The Most Popular Piece of Language." In J. Stewart (ed.), *Bridges Not Walls.* 5th ed. New York: McGraw-Hill, Page 760.
12. Gray, J. 1992. *Men Are from Mars, Women Are from Venus.* New York: HarperCollins.
13. Harding, S. 1991. *Whose Science? Whose Knowledge: Thinking from Women's Lives.* Ithaca, NY: Cornell University Press.
14. Holquist, M. (ed.) 1981. *Mikhail M. Bakhtin. The Dialogic Imagination.* Translated by C. Emerson and M. Holquist. Austin: University of Texas Press.
15. Lakoff, G. and Johnson, M. 1980. *Metaphors We Live By.* Chicago: University of Chicago Press.
16. Nichols, M. 1995. *The Lost Art of Listening.* New York: Guilford.
17. Pearce, B. 1989. *Communication and the Human Condition.* Carbondale: Southern Illinois University Press.
18. Rakow, L. F. 1992. *Women Making Meaning.* New York: Routledge.
19. Reece, M., and Whiteman, R. 1962. "Expressive Movements, Warmth and Nonverbal Reinforcement." *Journal of Abnormal and Social Psychology,* 64: 234–236.
20. Ricoeur, P. 1978. *The Rule of Metaphor.* Translated by R. Czerny, K. McLaughlin, and J. Costello. London: Routledge & Kegan Paul.
21. Rogers, C. R. 1980. *A Way of Being.* Boston: Houghton Mifflin.
22. Roth, S., Chasin, L., Chason, R., Becker, C., and Herzig, M. 1992. "From Debate to Dialogue: A Facilitating Role for Family Therapists in the Public Forum." *Dulwich Centre Newsletter,* 2: 41–48.

23. Sampson, E. E. 1993. *Celebrating the Other: A Dialogic Account of Human Nature.* Boulder, CO: Westview.
24. Senge, P. 1990. *The Fifth Discipline: The Art and Practice of the Learning Organization.* New York: Doubleday.
25. Shotter, J. 1993. *Conversational Realities: Constructing Life Through Language.* London: Sage.
26. Stewart, J., and Thomas, M. 1990. "Dialogic Listening: Sculpting Mutual Meanings." In J. Stewart (ed.), *Bridges Not Walls.* 6th ed. New York: McGraw-Hill. Pages 184–202.
27. Tannen, D. 1995. *Talking from 9 to 5.* New York: William Morrow.
28. Weaver, R. L. II 1987. *Understanding Interpersonal Communication.* 4th ed. New York: Scott-Foresman.

CHAPTER 6

Engaging Others:
Communication as Exhaling

T he first half of "making meaning together" (the title of Part II of *Bridges Not Walls*) is "inhaling," and the second half of this process involves what I'm calling "exhaling." As the metaphor indicates, this is the "output" or "sending" part of communication. The five readings in this chapter explain interpersonal openness, self-expression, assertiveness, nonverbal immediacy, and choosing what to disclose.

This first reading is from the 2000 edition of a book called *Reaching Out: Interpersonal Effectiveness and Self-Actualization,* by David Johnson, a teacher at the University of Minnesota. He begins with the notion that all of our relationships can be classified on a continuum from open to closed. Of course, an "open" work or school relationship is different from an "open" family or intimate relationship, but in all cases, Johnson claims, openness means both being open *with* other people (disclosing yourself to them) and openness *to* others (listening to them in an accepting way). Relationships of all sorts develop as both kinds of openness increase.

With a considerable amount of social scientific research in the background, Johnson defines self-disclosure and identifies four of its important characteristics. He notes that effective disclosure focuses on the present rather than the past, includes feelings as well as facts, has both breadth and depth, and, especially in the early stages of a relationship, needs to be reciprocal. Then Johnson outlines the impact self-disclosure has on relationships and describes some of its benefits. He argues that "if you cannot reveal yourself, you cannot become close to others, and you cannot be valued by others for who you are." Clearly there are various ways to self-disclose and various kinds of information to share. But this author makes a strong connection between disclosure and effective interpersonal communicating.

One benefit of disclosure is that it can begin and deepen your relationships, whether at work, home, or school. It can also increase your self-awareness and your understanding of yourself. Self-disclosure can provide, as Johnson puts it, "a freeing experience," and can also help you control challenging social situations. Another benefit of self-disclosure is that it can help you manage stress and adversity.

Johnson also lists eight ways to keep self-disclosures appropriate. I think each of the eight is useful. As he notes, disclosures need to be part of an ongoing relationship, not "off the wall" or "out of nowhere." They need to be focused on the people present and sensitive to others' possible distress. Disclosure ought to be intended to improve the relationship and should move to deeper levels only gradually. Johnson also usefully notes that "there are times when you will want to hide your reactions," and he explains when and why.

In the final section of this reading Johnson talks about the connection between self-disclosure and self-presentation. He discusses how all of us help manage others' impressions of who we are, in part with our self-disclosures. He compares and contrasts the motives of "strategic self-presentation," which means efforts to shape others' impression of us, and "self-verification," which is the desire to have others perceive us as we genuinely perceive ourselves. As he notes, "self-presentation and impression management are part of everyone's life," which is why Johnson believes that the more you know about self-disclosure, the more effective you can be at this part of your communicating.

Being Open with and to Other People

David W. Johnson

Relationships may be classified on a continuum from open to closed. **Openness** in a relationship refers to participants' willingness to share their ideas, feelings, and reactions to the current situation. On a professional basis, relationships among collaborators who are working to achieve mutual goals tend to be quite open, while relationships among competitors who are seeking advantages over each other tend to be quite closed. On a personal level, some relationships (such as friendships) are very open, while other relationships (such as casual acquaintances) are relatively closed. The more open participants in a relationship are with each other, the more positive, constructive, and effective the relationship tends to be.

Openness has two sides. To build good relationships you must be both open *with* other people (disclosing yourself to them) and open *to* others (listening to their disclosures in an accepting way). Usually, the more that people know about you, the more likely they are to like you. Yet self-disclosure does carry a degree of risk. For just as knowing you better is likely to result in a closer relationship, sometimes it could result in people liking you less. "Familiarity breeds contempt" means that some people may learn something about you that detracts from the relationship. Because disclosing is risky, some people prefer to hide themselves from others in the belief that no reaction is better than a possible negative reaction. "Nothing ventured, nothing gained," however, means that some risk is vital to achieving any worthwhile goal. To build a meaningful relationship you have to disclose yourself to the other person and take the risk that the other person may reject rather than like you.

The other side of the coin is responding to the other person's self-disclosures. Being open to another person means showing that you are interested in how he or she feels and thinks. This does not mean prying into the intimate areas of his or her life. It means being willing to listen in an accepting way to his or her reactions to the present situation and to what you are doing and saying. Even when a person's behavior offends you, you may wish to express acceptance of the person and disagreement with the way he or she behaves.

In order for the relationship to build and develop, both individuals have to disclose and be open to other people's disclosures. Openness depends on three factors: self-awareness, self-acceptance, and trust. . . .

OPENNESS WITH OTHER INDIVIDUALS

You are *open with* other persons when you disclose yourself to them, sharing your ideas, feelings, and reactions to the present situation, and letting other people know who you are as a person. To be open with another person you must (a) be aware of who you are, (b) accept yourself, and (c) take the risk of trusting the other person to be accepting of you. Openness thus can be described as being dependent on self-awareness (S), self-acceptance (A), and trust (T) (O = S A T). Commonly, openness is known as self-disclosure.

What Is Self-Disclosure?

Self-disclosure is revealing to another person how you perceive and are reacting to the present situation and giving any information about yourself and your past that is relevant to an understanding of your perceptions and reactions to the present. Effective self-disclosure has a number of characteristics:

1. **Self-disclosure focuses on the present, not the past.** Self-disclosure does not mean revealing intimate details of your past life. Making highly personal confessions about your past may lead to a temporary feeling of intimacy, but a relationship is built by disclosing your reactions to events you both are experiencing or to what the other person says or does. A person comes to know and understand you not through knowing your past history but through knowing how you react. Past history is helpful only if it clarifies why you are reacting in a certain way.
2. **Reactions to people and events include feelings as well as facts.** To be self-disclosing often means to share with another person how you feel about events that are occurring.
3. **Self-disclosures have two dimensions—breadth and depth.** As you get to know someone better and better, you cover more topics in your explanations (breadth) and make your explanations more personally revealing (depth).
4. **In the early stages of a relationship, self-disclosure needs to be reciprocal.** The amount of self-disclosure you engage in will influence the amount of self-disclosure the other person engages in and vice versa. The polite thing to do is to match the level of self-disclosure offered by new acquaintances, disclosing more if they do so and drawing back if their self-disclosure declines. Once a relationship is well established, strict reciprocity occurs much less frequently.

Impact of Self-Disclosure on Relationships

Healthy relationships are built on self-disclosure. A relationship grows and develops as two people become more open about themselves to each other. *If you cannot reveal yourself, you cannot become close to others, and you cannot be valued by others for who you are.* Two people who let each other know how they are reacting to situations and to each other are pulled together; two people who stay silent about their reactions and feelings stay strangers.

There are many ways in which self-disclosure initiates, builds, and maintains relationships. *First, self-disclosure enables you and other people to get to know each other.* Most relationships proceed from superficial exchanges to more intimate ones. At first, individuals disclose relatively little to another person and receive relatively little in return. When initial interactions are enjoyable or interesting, exchanges become (a) broader, involving more areas of your life and (b) deeper, involving more important and sensitive areas. In terms of breadth, from discussing the weather and sports, as the relationship develops you may discuss a wider range of topics (such as your family, your hopes and dreams, issues at work, and so forth) and share more diverse activities (such as going to movies or plays together, going bike riding or playing tennis together, and so forth). In terms of depth, you might willingly talk with a casual acquaintance about your preferences in food and music but reserve for close friends discussions of your anxieties and personal ambitions. The longer people interact, the more topics they tend to be willing to discuss and the more personally revealing they tend to become. This does not mean that getting to know another person is a simple process of being more and more open. You do not simply disclose more and more each day. Rather, there are cycles of seeking intimacy and avoiding it. Sometimes you are candid and confiding with a friend, and other times you are restrained and distant. The development of caring and commitment in a relationship, however, results from the cumulative history of self-disclosure in the relationship.

Second, self-disclosure allows you and other individuals to identify common goals and overlapping needs, interests, activities, and values. In order to know whether a relationship with another person is desirable, you have to know what the other person wants from the relationship, what the other person is interested in, what joint activities might be available, and what the other person values. Relationships are built on common goals, interests, activities, and values. If such information is not disclosed, the relationship may end before it has a chance to begin.

Third, once common goals have been identified, self-disclosure is necessary to work together to accomplish them. Working together requires constant self-disclosure to ensure effective communication, decision making, leadership, and resolution of conflict. Joint action to achieve mutual goals can not be effective unless collaborators are quite open in their interactions with each other.

Just as relationships are built through self-disclosure, *relationships can deteriorate for lack of self-disclosure.* Sometimes people hide their reactions from others through fear of rejection, fear of a potential or ongoing conflict, or feelings of shame and guilt. Whatever the reason, if you hide how you are reacting to the other person, your concealment can hurt the relationship, and the energy you pour into hiding is an additional stress on the relationship. Hiding your perceptions and feelings dulls your awareness of your own inner experience and decreases your ability to disclose your reactions even when it is perfectly safe and appropriate to do so. The result can be the end of the relationship. Being silent is not being strong—strength is the willingness to take a risk by disclosing yourself with the intention of building a better relationship.

Benefits of Self-Disclosure

We disclose information to another person for many reasons. *First, you begin and deepen a relationship by sharing reactions, feelings, personal information, and confidences.* This topic has already been discussed.

Second, self-disclosure improves the quality of relationships. We disclose to those we like. We like those who disclose to us. We like those to whom we have disclosed. Overall, it is through self-disclosure that caring is developed among individuals and commitment to each other is built.

Third, self-disclosure allows you to validate your perception of reality. Listeners provide useful information about social reality. The events taking place around us and the meaning of other people's behavior are often ambiguous, open to many different interpretations. By seeing how a listener reacts to your self-disclosures, you get information about the correctness and appropriateness of your views. Other people may reassure you that your reactions are "perfectly normal" or suggest that you are "blowing things out of proportion." If others have similar interpretations, we consider our perceptions to be valid. Comparing your perceptions and reactions with the reactions and perceptions of others is called **consensual validation.** Without self-disclosure, consensual validation could not take place.

Fourth, self-disclosure increases your self-awareness and clarifies your understanding of yourself. In explaining your feelings in watching a sunset or why you like a certain book, you clarify aspects of yourself to yourself. In sharing your feelings and experiences with others, you may gain greater self-understanding and self-awareness. Talking to a friend about a problem, for example, can help you clarify your thoughts about a situation. Sharing your reactions with others results in feedback from others, which contributes to a more objective perspective on your experiences.

Fifth, the expression of feelings and reactions is a freeing experience. Sometimes it helps to get emotions and reactions "off your chest." After a difficult day at work, it may release pent up feelings by telling a friend how angry you are at your boss or how unappreciated you feel. Even sharing long-term feelings of insecurity with a trusted friend may free you from such feelings. Simply being able to express your emotions is a reason for self-disclosure.

Sixth, you may disclose information about yourself or not as a means of social control. You may deliberately refrain from talking about yourself to end an interaction as quickly as possible or you may emphasize topics, beliefs, or ideas that you think will make a favorable impression on the other person.

Seventh, self-disclosing is an important part of managing stress and adversity. Communicating intimately with another person, especially in times of stress, seems to be a basic human need. By discussing your fear, you free yourself from it. By sharing your anxiety, you gain insight into ways to reduce it. By describing a problem, you see ways to solve it. The more you seek out a friend in times of adversity and discuss the situation openly, the more you will be able to deal with the stress and solve your problem.

Finally, self-disclosure fulfills a human need to be known intimately and accepted. Most people want someone to know them well and accept, appreciate, respect, and like them.

Keeping Your Self-Disclosures Appropriate

You only self-disclose when it is appropriate to do so. Just as you can disclose too little, you can also be too self-disclosing. Refusing to let anyone know anything about you keeps others away. Revealing too many of your reactions too fast may scare others away. Typically, a relationship is built gradually and develops in stages. Although you should sometimes take risks in sharing your reactions with others, you should ensure that the frequency and depth of your reactions are appropriate to the situation. When you are unsure about the appropriateness of your self-disclosures, you may wish to follow these guidelines:

1. I make sure my disclosures are not a random or isolated act but rather part of an ongoing relationship.
2. I focus my disclosures on what is going on within and between persons in the present.
3. I am sensitive to the effect a disclosure will have on the other person. Some disclosures may upset or cause considerable distress. What you want to say may seem inappropriate to the other person. Most people become uncomfortable when the level of self-disclosure exceeds their expectations.
4. I only disclose when it has a reasonable chance of improving the relationship.
5. I continue only if my disclosures are reciprocated. When you share your reactions, you should expect disclosure in return. When it is apparent that self-disclosures will not be reciprocated, you should limit the disclosures you make.
6. I increase my disclosures when a crisis develops in the relationship.
7. I gradually move my disclosures to a deeper level. Self-disclosures may begin with the information acquaintances commonly disclose (such as talking about hobbies, sports, school, and current events) and gradually move to more personal information. As a friendship develops, the depth of disclosure increases as well. Disclosures about deep feelings and concerns are most appropriate in close, well-established relationships.

8. I keep my reactions and feelings to myself when the other person is competitive or untrustworthy. While relationships are built through self-disclosure, there are times when you will want to hide your reactions. If a person has been untrustworthy and if you know from past experience that the other person will misinterpret or overreact to your self-disclosure, you may wish to keep silent. . . .

SELF-DISCLOSURE AND SELF-PRESENTATION

The image of myself which I try to create in my own mind that I may love myself is very different from the image which I try to create in the minds of others in order that they may love me.

—*W. H. Auden*

Self-disclosure is based on self-awareness, self-acceptance, and taking the risk of revealing yourself to others. Self-disclosure takes place in an ongoing social interaction in which you choose how you wish to present yourself to others. Most people are concerned about the images they present to others. The fashion industry, the cosmetic companies, diet centers, and the search for new drugs that grow hair, remove hair, whiten teeth, freshen breath, and smooth out wrinkles, all exploit our preoccupation with physical appearance. Manners, courtesy, and etiquette are all responses to concern about the impressions our behavior makes.

In *As You Like It*, William Shakespeare wrote, "All the world's a stage, and all the men and women merely players." Erving Goffman put Shakespeare's thought into social science by arguing that life can be viewed as a play in which each of us acts out certain scripted lines. Our scripts are a reflection of the social face or social identity that we want to present to others. **Self-presentation** is the process by which we try to shape what others think of us and what we think of ourselves. It is part of **impression management**—the general process by which you behave in particular ways to create a desired social image.

In presenting yourself to others, you have to recognize that there are many complex aspects of yourself. It is as if you have a number of selves that are tied to certain situations and certain groups of people with whom you interact. The self you present to your parents is usually different from the self you present to your peers. You present yourself differently to your boss, subordinates, colleagues, customers, neighbors, same-sex friends, opposite-sex friends, and strangers. When you are playing tennis, the aspect of yourself that loves physical exercise and competition may be most evident. When you attend a concert, the aspect of yourself that responds with deep emotion to classical music may be most evident. In church, your religious side may be most evident. In a singles bar, your interest in other people may be most evident. In different situations and with different people, different aspects of yourself will be relevant.

In presenting yourself to others, you have to vary your presentation to the audience. Societal norms virtually require that you present yourself in different ways to different audiences. You are expected to address someone considerably older than you differently from the way you address your peers. You are expected to address the president of the United States differently from how you address your next-door neighbor. In formal situations you are expected to act in ways different from how you would act in informal situations. Depending on the setting, the role relationship, and your previous experience with the person, you are expected to monitor your behavior and present yourself accordingly.

In presenting yourself to others, you basically have two motives: strategic self-presentation and self-verification. **Strategic self-presentation** consists of efforts to shape others' impressions in specific ways in order to gain influence, power, sympathy, or approval. Job interviews, personal ads, political campaign promises, and a defendant's appeal to a jury are examples. Your goal may be to be perceived as likable, competent, moral, dangerous, or even helpless, depending on the situation and the relationship. You communicate who you are and what you are like through your clothes, appearance, posture, eye contact, tone of voice, manners, and gestures. There are many people who believe that you will be perceived in quite different ways depending on your style of dress, manner, and cleanliness. Clothing, they believe, transmits messages about the wearer's personality, attitudes, social status, behavior, and group allegiances. People who wear clothes associated with high status tend to have more influence than those wearing low-status clothes. Somber hues (grays, dark blues, or browns) of clothing seem to communicate ambition, a taste for moderate risks and long-range planning, and a preference for tasks that have clear criteria for success and failure. Attention to clothes, posture, eye contact, tone of voice, manners, and gestures may be especially important for first impressions.

Related to strategic self-presentation are ingratiation and self-promotion. **Ingratiation** describes acts that are motivated by the desire to get along and be liked. When people want to be liked, they put their best foot forward, smile a lot, make eye contact, nod their heads, express agreement with what is said, and give compliments and favors. **Self-promotion** describes acts that are motivated by a desire to "get ahead" and be respected for one's competence. When people want to be respected for their competence, they try to impress others by talking about themselves and immodestly showing off their knowledge, status, and exploits.

The second self-presentation motive is **self-verification**—the desire to have others perceive us as we genuinely perceive ourselves. This is sometimes known as **open self-presentation,** which consists of efforts to let others see you as you believe yourself to be. People generally are quite motivated to verify their existing self-view in the eyes of others. People, for example, often selectively elicit, recall, and accept feedback that confirms their self-conceptions. This statement does not mean that they wish to fool others about who they are. People often work hard to correct others whose impressions of them are mistaken. They may want to make a good impression, but they also want others (especially their friends) to have an accurate impression, one that is consistent with their own self-concept.

Self-presentation and impression management are part of everyone's life. Some people do these things more consciously and successfully than others. People differ in their ability to present themselves appropriately and create the impression they want. The more self-monitoring you are, the more sensitive you tend to be to strategic self-presentation concerns, poised, ready, and able to modify your behavior as you move from one situation to another.

The self is an enduring aspect of human personality, an invisible "inner core" that is stable over time and slow to change. The struggle to "find yourself" or "be true to yourself" is based on this view. Yet at least part of the self is malleable, molded by life experiences and different from one situation to the next. In this sense, the self is multifaceted and has many different faces. Each of us has a private self consisting of our innermost thoughts and feelings, memories, and self-views. We also have an outer self, portrayed by the roles we play and the way we present ourselves in public. In fulfilling our social obligations and presenting ourselves to others, we base our presentations on the complexity of our personalities, the social norms specifying appropriate behavior, and the motives of revealing who we really are, verifying our views of ourselves, and creating strategic impressions.

REVIEW QUESTIONS

1. Explain the difference between being open *with* another person and being open *to* another person.
2. Explain O = S A T.
3. According to Johnson, what is the relationship between self-disclosure and liking?
4. List the eight possible benefits of self-disclosure.
5. Explain the relationship between self-disclosure and self-awareness.
6. Define "strategic self-presentation" and "self-verification."

PROBES

1. Johnson argues that "in order for the relationship to build and develop, both individuals have to disclose and be open to other people's disclosures." Do you agree? Is disclosure and openness to others necessary for the development of *all* relationships? Are there any exceptions?
2. Why does self-disclosure need to be reciprocal in the early stages of a relationship? Why can it be one-sided or non-reciprocal in some later stages of a relationship?
3. Johnson notes that "there are cycles of seeking intimacy and avoiding it." Explain what he means. Why is this important to understand and practice?
4. Give an example of how self-disclosure can function as a means of social control.

5. Is there a contradiction between Johnson's preference for "openness" and his argument that self-disclosure should be "appropriate"? Doesn't appropriateness require not always being open?
6. Johnson indicates that "you have a number of selves that are tied to certain situations and certain groups of people. . . ." Do you think he believes that people also have a "core" or stable, central self? Do you?

This reading, as the authors note in their introduction, "is about expressing yourself when it counts and to the people who matter to you. It tells you how to make clear and complete statements about your inner experience." In the previous reading, Johnson distinguished between facts and feelings, and McKay, Davis, and Fanning in this reading identify four kinds of expression: observations, thoughts, feelings, and needs. Even though in actual experience you can't separate the four, these distinctions can help you recognize whether you're trying to express something about what you've seen, heard, read, or experienced, something you've concluded or inferred, something you are feeling, or something you want.

There are various kinds of thoughts, including beliefs, opinions, and theories about what should, or will, happen. Expressions of thoughts are different from feeling statements, even though they sometimes sound similar. As the authors point out, "Sometimes I feel that you are very rigid" expresses an opinion or belief, *not* a feeling. Feeling statements label part of a person's visceral, affective experience—"I miss her," "I'm really excited," "I feel stunned and a little angry." Especially in close relationships it is important to learn to express needs rather than to expect the other person to read your mind. As the authors put it, "Trying to have a close relationship in which you don't express your needs is like driving a car without a steering wheel."

Whole messages, they note, include all four kinds of expression, and intimate relationships thrive on whole messages. Contaminated messages are mixed or mislabeled. As the authors' examples of contaminated messages illustrate, they create problems because they can be understood in more than one way and they don't tell the listener how to interpret them correctly.

The final section of this reading offers five rules for effective expression: Be direct, immediate, clear, straight, and supportive. Directness requires knowing when something needs to be said—rather than assumed or implied—and the willingness and ability to talk about it. Immediacy means not putting off discussions, either by avoiding them or by "gunnysacking." The authors identify two concrete benefits of immediacy.

They also provide six ways to enhance the clarity of your messages. The first is, "Don't ask questions when you need to make a statement." The second is to keep your messages congruent, which means to match, so far as you can, the external message and your internal experience. The third is to avoid double messages, and the fourth is to be as clear as you can about your wants and feelings. The final two suggestions for clarity are to distinguish between observations and feelings and to focus on one thing at a time.

The fourth rule for effective expression states that messages should be straight. Straight messages are those "in which the stated purpose is identical with the real purpose of the communication." In other words, the authors are suggesting that you avoid communication based on disguised intentions and hidden agendas. Examples of hidden agendas include "I'm helpless," "I'm fragile," "I'm tough," and "I know it all," any of which can be behind ambiguous talk. Being straight also means that you tell the truth. For example, "You don't say you're tired and want to go home if you're really angry and want more attention."

The final rule is that messages should be supportive, and the authors contrast supportive statements with six hurtful tactics. These include global labels, sarcasm, threats, and dragging up the past. The authors conclude by urging you to avoid communicating from a win/lose mind-set.

There are important cultural limitations of this reading. McKay, Davis, and Fanning do a very good job of articulating a Western, mainly white, middle-class perspective that helps define effective communicating in many U.S. and Canadian contexts, and in some contexts in Western Europe, Australia, and New Zealand—*but not all cultures in these countries.* And their perspective certainly does not apply in some other cultures. For example, the kind of directness they urge would be considered very inappropriate in Japan and in parts of Britain. People in some blue-collar cultures in the United States would also ridicule the advice to "be supportive." So this reading can definitely sharpen your communication skills in some cultural contexts, but I believe that it would be a mistake to apply all of these rules in every situation. Use the information presented to hone your knowledge about communication in the cultures that the authors belong to.

Expressing

Matthew McKay, Martha Davis, and Patrick Fanning

SAM: "Do we have to go down to the P.T.A. meeting tonight?"
JANE: "Why, does it bother you?"

From *Messages, The Communications Skills Book* by Matthew McKay, Ph.D., Martha Davis, Ph.D. and Patrick Fanning. Copied with permission from New Harbinger Publications, Oakland, CA.

SAM: "It's just the same old thing. I don't know."

JANE: "Did something happen last time?"

SAM: "It's nothing. Sometimes the speakers are interesting, but I don't know . . . and Mrs. Williams is running it now."

JANE: "You don't like how she's handling it?"

SAM: "She's all right. She's so . . . organized. Forget it, let's get a move on if we're going."

Sam is in for another deadly evening. Mrs. Williams will carry on like General Patton. A speaker will drone about "multicultural awareness." If Sam had been able to express himself, he might have persuaded Jane to skip a night, or to help him push for changes in the meeting format. As it is, Jane has no idea what's irking him and can't respond to his needs.

This [reading] is about expressing yourself when it counts and to the people who matter to you. It doesn't tell you how to assertively ask your butcher for a good cut of meat. But it does tell you how to make clear and complete statements about your inner experience.

THE FOUR KINDS OF EXPRESSION

Your communications to other people can be broken down into four categories: expressing your observations, thoughts, feelings, and needs. Each category requires a different style of expression, and often a very different vocabulary.

Observations

This is the language of the scientist, the detective, the TV repairman. It means reporting what your senses tell you. There are no speculations, inferences, or conclusions. Everything is simple fact. Here are some examples of observations:

1. "I read in the *Enquirer* that an ice age is due to start within five hundred years."
2. "My old address was 1996 Fell Street."
3. "She plans to wear a chiffon dress with white ruffled collar."
4. "I broke the toaster this morning."
5. "It was a very hot day when I left Kansas. A slight wind riffled the fields and a thunderhead was beginning to form up north."

All of these statements adhere strictly to what the person has heard, read, or personally experienced. If Sam had been able to talk about his observations at the P.T.A. meeting, he might have pointed out that the meetings invariably went overtime, that the speakers were selected by Mrs. Williams without consulting the group, and that certain parent-teacher problems were never discussed.

Thoughts

Your thoughts are conclusions, inferences drawn from what you have heard, read, and observed. They are attempts to synthesize your observations so you can see what's really going on and understand why and how events occur. They may also incorporate value judgments in which you decide that something is good or bad, wrong or right. Beliefs, opinions, and theories are all varieties of conclusions. Here are some examples:

1. "Unselfishness is essential for a successful marriage." *(belief)*
2. "I think the universe will keep exploding and collapsing, exploding and collapsing, forever." *(theory)*
3. "He must be afraid of his wife; he always seems nervous around her." *(theory)*
4. "Log Cabin is the only syrup worth buying." *(theory)*
5. "You were wrong to just stop seeing her." *(value judgment)*

If Sam had been able to express his thoughts about the P.T.A. meeting, he might have said that Mrs. Williams was dominating and grandiose. He might have suggested that she was deliberately squelching conflicts because she was friendly with the school administration.

Feelings

Probably the most difficult part of communication is expressing your feelings. Some people don't want to hear what you feel. They get bored or upset when feelings come up. Some people are selectively receptive. They can hear about your post-divorce melancholy, but not about your fear of death. Anger is the most discouraged feeling because it's threatening to the listener's self-esteem.

Since people are often threatened or frightened by emotion, you may have decided to keep many feelings to yourself. Yet how you feel is a large part of what makes you unique and special. Shared feelings are the building blocks of intimacy. When others are allowed to know what angers, frightens, and pleases you, two things happen: They have greater empathy and understanding and are better able to modify their behavior to meet your needs.

Examples of some feeling statements are:

1. "I missed Al and felt a real loss when he left for Europe."
2. "I feel like I let you down, and it really gnaws at me."
3. "I sit alone in the house, feel this tingling going up and down my spine, and get this wave of anxiety."
4. "I light up with joy when I see you. I feel this incredible rush of affection."
5. "I'm checking my reactions, and I feel stunned and a little angry."

Note that feeling statements are not observations, value judgments or opinions. For example, "Sometimes I feel that you are very rigid," has nothing to do with feelings. It's just a slightly buffered judgment.

If Sam had expressed his feelings to Jane, he might have told her that he felt bored at the meetings and that he was angry at Mrs. Williams. He also might have discussed his worries that the school has serious curriculum inadequacies and his frustration that nothing was being done about it.

Needs

No one knows what you want, except you. You are the expert, the highest authority on yourself. However, you may have a heavy injunction against expressing needs. You hope friends and family will be sensitive or clairvoyant enough to know what you want. "If you loved me, you'd know what's wrong" is a common assumption. Since you feel it's bad to ask for anything, your needs are often expressed with a head of anger or resentment. The anger says "I'm wrong to ask, and you're wrong to make me have to."

Trying to have a close relationship in which you don't express your needs is like driving a car without a steering wheel. You can go fast, but you can't change directions or steer around chuckholes. Relationships change, accommodate, and grow when both people can clearly and supportively express what they need. Some typical need statements are:

1. "Can you be home before seven? I'd love to go to a movie."
2. "I'm exhausted. Will you do the dishes and see that the kids are in bed?"
3. "I need a day to myself this weekend. Can we get together Sunday night?"
4. "I need to reserve time with you so we can sit down and work this out."
5. "Could you just hug me for a while?"

Needs are not pejorative or judgmental. They don't blame or assign fault. They are simple statements about what would help or please you. . . .

WHOLE MESSAGES

Whole messages include all four kinds of expressions: what you see, think, feel, and need. Intimate relationships thrive on whole messages. Your closest friends, your mate, and your family can't know the real you unless you share all of your experiences. That means not leaving things out, not covering up your anger, not squelching your wants. It means giving accurate feedback about what you observe, clearly stating your inferences and conclusions, saying how it all makes you feel, and if you need something or see possibilities for change, making straightforward requests or suggestions.

When you leave something out, it's called a *partial message*. Partial messages create confusion and distrust. People sense something is missing, but they don't know what. They're turned off when they hear judgments untempered by your feelings and hopes. They resist hearing anger that doesn't include the story of your frustration or hurt. They are suspicious of conclusions without supporting observations. They are uncomfortable with demands growing from unexpressed feelings and assumptions.

Not every relationship or situation requires whole messages. Effective communication with your garage mechanic probably won't involve a lot of deep feeling or discussion of your emotional needs. Even with intimates, the majority of messages are just informational. But partial messages, with something important left out or obscured, are always dangerous. They become relational boobytraps when used to express the complex issues that are an inevitable part of closeness.

You can test whether you are giving whole or partial messages by asking the following questions:

1. Have I expressed what I actually know to be fact? Is it based on what I've observed, read, or heard?
2. Have I expressed and clearly labeled my inferences and conclusions?
3. Have I expressed my feelings without blame or judgment?
4. Have I shared my needs without blame or judgment?

CONTAMINATED MESSAGES

Contamination takes place when your messages are mixed or mislabeled. For example, you might be contaminating feelings, thoughts, and observations if you said to your daughter, "I see you're wearing that old dress again." What you really needed to say were three very distinct things:

1. "That dress is a little frayed and still has the ink spot we were never able to get out." *(observation)*
2. "I don't think it's nice enough for a Sunday visit to Grandpa's." *(thought)*
3. "I feel anxious that your grandfather will think I'm not a very good parent if I let you wear a dress like that." *(feeling)*

Contaminated messages are at best confusing and at worst deeply alienating. The message "I see your wife gave you two juicy oranges for lunch" is confusing because the observation is contaminated by need. The need is only hinted at, and the listener has to decide if what he heard was really a covert appeal. The message "While you were feeding your dog, my dinner got cold" is alienating because what appears to be a simple observation contains undercurrents of anger and judgment ("You care more about your dog than me").

Contaminated messages differ from partial messages in that the problem is not merely one of omission. You haven't left the anger, the conclusion, or the need out of it. It's there all right, but in a disguised and covert form. The following are some examples of contaminated messages:

1. "Why don't you act a little human for a change?" In this message need is contaminated with a value judgment *(thought)*. A whole message might have been, "You say very little, and when you do it's in a soft, flat voice *(observation)*. It

makes me think that you don't care, that you have no emotions *(thought)*. I feel hurt *(emotion)*, but what I really want is for you to talk to me *(need)*."

2. "Every year you come home to visit with a different man. I don't know how you move from one to another like that." Said in an acid tone, this would be an observation contaminated with a value judgment *(thought)*. The whole message might be "Each year you come home with someone else *(observation)*. I wonder if it creates a sort of callousness, a shallow affection *(thought)*. I worry, and also feel disappointed when I start liking your friend and never see him again *(feeling)*. I hope you'll make a commitment to a life partner *(need)*."

3. "I know what your problem is, you like to get paid but you don't like to work." This is an example of feeling contaminated with a value judgment *(thought)*. The whole statement might be "You've been late six times in the last two weeks *(observation)*. It makes me think that you're trying to work as little as possible *(thought)*. The lateness irritates me *(feeling)* and I want you to be late no more than once a month *(need)*."

4. "I need to go home . . . another one of those headaches." Said in an angry voice at a party, this is an example of feelings contaminated with need. The person really wants to say "I've been standing by myself *(observation)*. You don't seem to care or draw me into conversation *(thought)*. I get to feeling hurt and angry *(feeling)*. I want you to involve me in things or I don't want to be here *(need)*."

5. "You eat your breakfast without a word, you get your hat, you leave, you get home, you mix a drink, you read the paper, you talk about golf and your secretary's legs at dinner, you fall asleep in front of the TV, and that's the way it is." In this case observation is contaminated with feelings. It seems like a straightforward recital of events, but the speaker really wants to say "I'm lonely and angry, please pay attention to me."

The easiest way to contaminate your messages is to make the content simple and straightforward, but say it in a tone of voice that betrays your feelings. "I want to stop interviewing people, we have enough already" can be said in a matter-of-fact or very annoyed voice. In one case it's a clear statement of need. In the other, need is contaminated with unacknowledged anger. The secret of avoiding contaminated messages is to separate out and express each part of the communication. . . .

RULES FOR EFFECTIVE EXPRESSION

Messages Should Be Direct

The first requirement for effective self-expression is knowing when something needs to be said. This means that you don't assume people know what you think or want.

Indirectness can be emotionally costly. Here are a few examples. One man whose wife divorced him after fifteen years complained that she had no right to call him undemonstrative. "She knew I loved her. I didn't have to say it in so many words. A thing like that is obvious." But it wasn't obvious. His wife withered emotionally without direct expression of his affection. A woman who had been distressed by her child's performance in school stopped nagging when his grades went up. She was surprised to learn that her son felt unappreciated and wanted some direct approval. A man who had developed a chronic back problem was afraid to ask for help with gardening and household maintenance. He suffered through these tasks in pain and experienced a growing irritation and resentment toward his family. A fifteen-year-old retreated to her room when her divorced mother became interested in a new man. She complained of headaches and excused herself whenever the boyfriend arrived. Her mother, who once told the children they would always come first, assumed that her daughter was just embarrassed and would soon get over it.

These are all examples of people who have something important to communicate. But they don't know it. They assume others realize how they feel. Communicating directly means you don't make any assumptions. In fact, you should assume that people are poor mind readers and haven't the faintest idea what goes on inside you.

Some people are aware of the times when they need to communicate, but are afraid to do so. Instead they try hinting, or telling third parties in hope that the target person will eventually hear. This indirectness is risky. Hints are often misinterpreted or ignored. One woman kept turning the sound down on the TV during commercials. She hoped her husband would take the hint and converse a little at the breaks. Instead he read the sports page until she finally blew up at him. Third-party communications are extremely dangerous because of the likelihood that your message will be distorted. Even if the message is accurately delivered, no one wants to hear about your anger, disappointment, or even your love secondhand.

Messages Should Be Immediate

If you're hurt or angry, or needing to change something, delaying communication will often exacerbate your feelings. Your anger may smoulder, your frustrated need become a chronic irritant. What you couldn't express at the moment will be communicated later in subtle or passive-aggressive ways. One woman was quite hurt at the thought of not being invited to Thanksgiving at her sister's house. She said nothing, but broke a date they had to go to the planetarium and "forgot" to send a Christmas card.

Sometimes unexpressed feeling is gunnysacked to the point where a small transgression triggers a major dumping of the accumulated rage and hurt. These dumping episodes alienate family and friends. A hospital ward secretary had a reputation with peers for being dangerous and volatile. For months she would be sweet, considerate, and accommodating. But sooner or later the explosion came. A slight criticism would be answered with megatons of gripes and resentments.

There are two main advantages to immediate communication: (1) Immediate feedback increases the likelihood that people will learn what you need and adjust their behavior accordingly. This is because a clear relationship is established between what they do (for example, driving too fast) and the consequences (your expressed anxiety). (2) Immediate communication increases intimacy because you share your responses now. You don't wait three weeks for things to get stale. Here-and-now communications are more exciting and serve to intensify your relationships.

Messages Should Be Clear

A clear message is a complete and accurate reflection of your thoughts, feelings, needs, and observations. You don't leave things out. You don't fudge by being vague or abstract. Some people are afraid to say what they really mean. They talk in muddy, theoretical jargon. Everything is explained by "vibes" or by psychological interpretations. One woman who was afraid to tell her boyfriend she was turned off by public petting said that she felt "a little strange" that day and thought that her parents' upcoming visit was "repressing her sexuality." This ambiguous message allowed her boyfriend to interpret her discomfort as a temporary condition. He never learned her true needs.

Keeping your messages clear depends on awareness. You have to know what you've observed, and then how you reacted to it. What you see and hear in the outside world is so easily confused with what you think and feel inside. Separating these elements will go a long way toward helping you express yourself clearly.

Here are some tips for staying clear:

1. **Don't ask questions when you need to make a statement.** Husband to wife: "Why do you have to go back to school? You have plenty of things to keep you busy." The statement hidden in the question is "I'm afraid if you go back to school I won't see you enough, I'll feel lonely. As you grow in independence I'll feel less control over the direction of our lives."

Wife to husband: "Do you think we need to make an appearance at your boss's barbeque today?" Imbedded in the question is the unexpressed need to relax and putter in the garden. By failing to plead her case clearly, her husband can either miss or safely ignore her needs.

Daughter to father: "Are we going to have a little three-foot tree this year?" What she thinks but doesn't say is that she likes the big trees seen at friends' houses—the ones full of lights and tinsel around which the family gathers. She wishes that her family did more things together, and thinks Christmas decorating would be a good place to start.

Father to son: "How much did that paint job cost?" He really wants to talk about the fact that his son lives above his means, and then borrows from Mom without any intention of paying back. He's worried about his son's relationship to money and angry because he feels circumvented.

2. **Keep your messages congruent.** The content, your tone of voice, and your body language should all fit together. If you congratulate someone on getting a fellowship, his response is congruent if the voice, facial gestures, and spoken messages all reflect pleasure. Incongruence is apparent if he thanks you with a frown, suggesting that he doesn't really want the compliment.

Incongruence confuses communication. Congruence promotes clarity and understanding. A man who spent the day in his delivery truck arrived home to a request that he make a run to the supermarket. His response was, "Sure, whatever you want." But his tone was sarcastic and his body slumped. His wife got the message and went herself. But she was irritated by the sarcastic tone and later started a fight about the dishes. A model asked soothingly to hear about her roommate's "boyfriend in trouble." But while the story unfolded, her eyes flitted always to the mirror and she sat on the edge of her chair. Her voice said, "I care," but her body said, "I'm bored, hurry up."

3. **Avoid double messages.** Double messages are like kicking a dog and petting it at the same time. They occur when you say two contradictory things at once. Husband to wife: "I want to take you, I do. I'll be lonely without you. But I don't think the convention will be much fun. Really, you'd be bored to death." This is a double message, because on the surface the husband seems to want his wife's company. But when you read between the lines, it's evident that he's trying to discourage her from coming.

Father to son: "Go ahead, have a good time. By the way, I noticed your report card has some real goof-off grades. What are you doing about them?" This is a rather obvious double message, but the effect is confusing. One message undercuts the other, and the son is left unclear about his father's real position. The most malignant double messages are the "come close, go away" and "I love you, I hate you" messages. These communications are found in parent-child and lover relationships, and inflict heavy psychological damage.

4. **Be clear about your wants and feelings.** Hinting around about your feelings and needs may seem safer than stating them clearly. But you end up confusing the listener. Friend to friend: "Why don't you quit volunteering at that crazy free clinic?" The clear message would be: "I'm afraid for you struggling in that conflict-ridden place. I think you are exhausting yourself, and I miss the days when we have time to spend an afternoon together. I want you to protect your health and have more time for me."

Husband to wife: "I see the professors and their wives at the faculty party, and I shudder at some of the grotesque relationships." The real message that couldn't be said was "When I see that terrible unhappiness, I realize what a fine life we have and how much I love you."

Mother to daughter: "I hope you visit Grandma this week." On the surface this seems straightforward, but underneath lurks the guilt and anxiety she feels about Grandma's loneliness. She worries about the old woman's health and, without explaining any of this, badgers her daughter to make frequent visits.

Two lovers: "I waited while you were on the phone and now our dinners are cold." The underlying statement is "I wonder how much you care about me when you take a phone call in the middle of dinner. I'm feeling hurt and angry."

5. **Distinguish between observations and thoughts.** You have to separate what you see and hear from your judgments, theories, beliefs, and opinions. "I see you've been fishing with Joe again" could be a straightforward observation. But in the context of a longstanding conflict about Joe, it becomes a barbed conclusion. Review the section on contaminated messages for more discussion of this issue.

6. **Focus on one thing at a time.** This means that you don't start complaining about your daughter's Spanish grades in the middle of a discussion about her boyfriend's marijuana habits. Stick with the topic at hand until both parties have made clear, whole messages. If you get unfocused, try using one of the following statements to clarify the message: "I'm feeling lost . . . what are we really talking about?" or "What do you hear me saying? I sense we've gotten off the track."

Messages Should Be Straight

A straight message is one in which the stated purpose is identical with the real purpose of the communication. Disguised intentions and hidden agendas destroy intimacy because they put you in a position of manipulating rather than relating to people. You can check if your messages are straight by asking these two questions: (1) Why am I saying this to this person? (2) Do I want him or her to hear it, or something else?

Hidden agendas . . . are usually necessitated by feelings of inadequacy and poor self-worth. You have to protect yourself, and that means creating a certain image. Some people take the *I'm good* position. Most of their communications are subtle opportunities to boast. Others play the *I'm good but you aren't* game. They are very busy putting everyone down and presenting themselves, by implication, as smarter, stronger, more successful. Agendas such as *I'm helpless, I'm fragile, I'm tough,* and *I know it all* are good defensive maneuvers to keep you from getting hurt. But the stated purpose of your communication is always different from your real purpose. While you are ostensibly discoursing on intricate Middle East politics, the real purpose is to show how knowledgeable you are. We all succumb to little vanities, but when your communications are dominated by one such agenda, you aren't being straight.

Being straight also means that you tell the truth. You state your real needs and feelings. You don't say you're tired and want to go home if you're really angry and want more attention. You don't angle for compliments or reassurance by putting yourself down. You don't say you're anxious about going to a couples therapist when actually you feel angry about being pushed to go. You don't describe your feelings as depression because your mate prefers that to irritation. You don't say you enjoy visiting your girlfriend's brother when the experience is one step below fingernails scraping on the chalkboard. Lies cut you off from others. Lies keep them from knowing what you need or feel. You lie to be nice, you lie to protect yourself, but you end up feeling alone with your closest friends.

Messages Should Be Supportive

Being supportive means you want the other person to be able to hear you without getting blown away. Ask yourself, "Do I want my message to be heard defensively or accurately? Is my purpose to hurt someone, to aggrandize myself, or to communicate?"

If you prefer to hurt your listener with your messages, use these six tactics:

1. **Global labels.** Stupid, ugly, selfish, evil, assinine, mean, disgusting, worthless, and lazy are a few of the huge list of hurtful words. . . . Making your point that way creates a total indictment of the person, instead of just a commentary on some specific behavior.
2. **Sarcasm.** This form of humor very clearly tells the listener that you have contempt for him. It's often a cover for feelings of anger and hurt. The effect on the listener is to push him away or make him angry.
3. **Dragging up the past.** This destroys any chance of clarifying how each of you feels about a present situation. You rake over old wounds and betrayals instead of examining your current dilemma.
4. **Negative comparisons.** "Why aren't you generous like your brother?" "Why don't you come home at six like other men?" "Sarah's getting A's and you can't even get a B in music appreciation." Comparisons are deadly because they not only contain "you're bad" messages, but they make people feel inferior to friends and family.
5. **Judgmental "you messages."** These are attacks that use an accusing form. "You don't love me anymore." "You're never here when I need you." "You never help around the house." "You turn me on about as much as a 1964 Plymouth."
6. **Threats.** If you want to bring meaningful communication to a halt, get out the big guns. Threaten to move out, threaten to quit, threaten violence. Threats are good topic changers, because instead of talking about uncomfortable issues, you can talk about the hostile things you plan to do.

Communicating supportively means that you avoid "win/lose" and "right/wrong" games. These are interactions in which the intention of one or both players is "winning" or proving the other person "wrong" rather than sharing and understanding. Your intention in communication will guide you toward a predictable result. Real communication produces understanding and closeness, while "win/lose" games produce warfare and distance. Ask yourself, "Do I want to win or do I want to communicate? Do I want to be right or do I want mutual understanding?" If you find yourself feeling defensive and wanting to criticize the other person, that's a clue that you're playing "win/lose."

Win/lose interactions can be avoided by sticking rigidly to the whole-message structure. You can also get around the win/lose pattern by making clear observations on your process. "I'm feeling pretty defensive and angry right now, and it looks like I've fallen into the old win/lose syndrome."

REVIEW QUESTIONS

1. What kinds of fear can make it difficult to express feelings?
2. How are feelings different from and similar to needs?
3. "Not every relationship or situation requires whole messages," the authors note. So why do they discuss them? When and where *are* they required?
4. How do contaminated messages differ from partial messages?
5. What do you believe might be some of the emotional cost of indirect messages?
6. What is "gunnysacking"? How can you avoid it?
7. What is a double message?
8. These authors encourage you to communicate "straight" messages. What is a "crooked" one?

PROBES

1. On the one hand, the distinction between observations and thoughts makes clear sense and is useful. But how much of your communicating actually consists of pure observations? How commonly are thoughts and feelings mixed into your messages?
2. One reason why it's difficult to express feelings is the feelings people experience *about* feelings. What is an example of this?
3. How effectively do you believe you express your needs? When is it easiest to do this? When is it most difficult?
4. What are some of the reasons why it is difficult to be direct? What gets in the way of directness?
5. You could argue that sometimes it's helpful to be indirect rather than direct, that questions can soften otherwise hard statements, and that it's not always wise to express your wants and needs. How do you believe McKay, Davis, and Fanning would respond to these reservations?
6. When, if any time, might you argue that messages should be, or could usefully be, nonsupportive?

In Chapter 5, prominent psychologist and researcher John Gottman emphasized the importance of listening. In this reading he explains and illustrates the value of putting feelings into words. One reason this skill is valuable is that feelings happen all the time, and they often create problems. Humans are inherently, constantly, and thoroughly "feeling creatures." Even the most objective and dispassionate person experiences feelings all the time. Unfortunately, when the feelings are negative, like fear, anger, or sadness,

A second reason it's useful to put feelings into words is that feelings are one of the most potent ways of making contact. As Gottman puts it, "naming your feelings and talking about them is essential for connecting with others."

Gottman offers some help for people who have trouble figuring out what they're feeling. He describes how to use a form of cognitive reflection to move from a vaguely uncomfortable feeling to a well-defined and clearly named condition—"I'm lonely and disappointed about not seeing my family and I'm also anxious about our investments."

This reading includes an exercise that is designed to help you put your emotions into words. There is also an emotional vocabulary list that can also help you name your feelings and talk about them.

Later in the reading, Gottman explains how metaphors can help you understand and express feelings. Consider how much emotional content there is when a person says, "Our marriage was a train wreck" or "My father likes to play God." Gottman points out that when conversation partners listen to each other's metaphors, they come to an improved understanding of their differences.

In many Western cultures, men are socialized out of discussing feelings. If you're one of those men, this reading might seem uncomfortable or even silly. Recognize Gottman's first point, though: feelings are part of every human being's experience. And you can significantly improve your communicating when you can learn to put your feelings into words.

Putting Feelings into Words

John M. Gottman

There are many good reasons to focus on your emotions, give them a name, and then talk about them.

First, naming your feelings engages the part of the brain that controls the functions of logic and language. So when you identify your feelings and put them into words, you get a better sense of control over them. This can help you to cope with negative emotions like fear, anger, or sadness.

Second, naming your feelings and talking about them is essential for connecting with others; people around you can't know for certain what you're feeling unless you tell them.

Relationships grow when one person helps the other to name his or her emotions. Here's a simple example: Your friend tells you that his favorite aunt just died. If you say, "That must be very sad for you," you show that you understand your friend's experience, which helps you to connect emotionally.

What's even more helpful, however, are those instances when a friend is not sure what he's feeling and you help him figure it out:

"Jenny left last night without even saying good-bye."

"That must have been upsetting."

"It was. I didn't know what to think."

"Were you angry?"

"Sort of. But it was more than that. We've always been so close."

"So it sounds like you're kind of disappointed and sad."

"Yes, I'm really sad. And kind of scared, too. I don't know what I'd do if she left for good."

The ability to identify feelings and express them in words comes easily for some. These people are often quite aware of what they're feeling moment by moment, and have a rich vocabulary with which to describe their emotions.

But other people struggle all their lives to understand their feelings, name them, and converse about them. They may know they're feeling *something*, but they're just not sure what the feeling is. For those who have this kind of challenge, it may be helpful to take an intellectually based, or "cognitive," approach to exploring emotion. This involves remembering recent experiences in your life and thinking about the way such experiences typically lead people to feel.

Here's an example: Carl comes home from work and finds a note from his wife. It says she's gone to a PTA meeting, his son has gone to a movie, and his daughter is off with her girlfriends. He rummages through the refrigerator, finds some leftover pizza, heats it in the microwave, and settles in front of the television to watch a news program, the topic of which is the unstable economy.

Later that night, as Carl is lying in bed, he's aware that he feels vaguely uncomfortable, but he's not sure why. In fact, he's not sure that he *wants* to know why. But he's tired of this undefined angst that seems to be haunting him, and he'd like to get to the bottom of it. So he begins to think about this negative energy he's experiencing.

At this point he can only describe his feelings as "unsettled." Then he starts to reflect back on the evening's events—how unpleasant it was to come home to a dark, empty house when he was expecting to see his wife, his kids, and dinner on the stove. There was definitely something missing for him in this situation. And he knows that when things are missing from people's lives, they often feel sad. So he concludes, "I wanted to be with my family and they weren't here. This made me feel lonely. Lonely and disappointed."

Still, Carl feels there's more to the evening's negative energy. He thinks about the TV program. The economy has been strong for quite a while, and he and his wife have enjoyed a nice sense of economic security. But the program talked about how volatile the markets have become—how investors could lose a great deal very quickly. The program made him realize that his investments might not be that secure after all. And he knows what happens when people question their safety. They begin to feel anxious and fearful. "So this energy I'm feeling is more than loneliness and disappointment about not seeing my family," he tells himself. "It's also anxiety. I'm anxious about our investments."

Now that his feelings of loneliness, disappointment, and anxiety are defined, Carl decides he can do something about the discomfort he's feeling. He can talk with his wife about how he missed seeing her and the kids that night; perhaps they can plan to do something enjoyable together in the next few days. He can talk to his financial adviser and his wife about their investments and make some adjustments if they decide that's a prudent course.

Exploring emotions in such an analytical way may seem strange to people who have a more intuitive sense of what they're feeling moment by moment. But this cognitive approach can be a real benefit to people like Carl, who lack easy access to words and concepts that can help them cope with their feelings. Rather than expressing a vague sense of irritation at his family over who-knows-what, Carl can now talk specifically about what he's feeling. This puts him in a better position to express his needs and to connect with others emotionally. Identifying his emotions in an analytical way gives him the structure he needs to take steps toward feeling more settled and peaceful.

EXERCISE: WHAT AM I FEELING?

This exercise is designed to help you to define what you're feeling and to put your emotions into words. It may also help you to be a better listener—somebody who helps others to name their feelings and talk about them.

To start, think about a recent experience that left you feeling uncomfortable or unsettled in a way that was hard for you to define. Write down a short description of the incident.

Then look at the following series of questions, which are intended to help you determine in a general way what you might have been feeling at the time. After you've answered these questions, scan the Emotional Vocabulary List on the following page to find more specific ways to describe your feelings.

Once you've identified the emotions you were feeling, do you feel as if you have a better idea of how to express those feelings to people that matter? Can you think of steps you can take to soothe uncomfortable feelings, or to solve problems that are causing the discomfort? Write about these insights in your Emotion Log as well.

First ask yourself if the emotion you're experiencing is pleasant (positive) or unpleasant (negative).

If the feeling is pleasant:

- Do you think you'd like to explore some topic or get to know some person better? If so, you're probably feeling *interested*.
- Did something good happen? If so, you're probably feeling *happy*.

If the feeling is unpleasant:

- Do you think that something is lost, absent, or missing from your life that ought to be there? If so, then you're probably feeling *sad*.
- Do you think there's an obstacle to what you're trying to accomplish? If your goal is blocked, then you're probably feeling *angry*.
- Are you thinking that things are unsafe in your world? If so, then you're probably feeling *fearful*.
- Are you thinking that someone or something should be judged as beneath you or against your values and morals? If so, then you're probably feeling *contemptuous*.
- Are you thinking that you just can't tolerate things as they are anymore, or that you just can't "swallow" a current situation? If so, then you're probably feeling *disgusted*.

EMOTIONAL VOCABULARY LIST

Describing your feelings can help you to connect emotionally. It can also help you to cope with difficult feelings. This list, divided into general categories of emotion, may help you to name your feelings and to talk about them.

Interested

Stimulated
Fascinated
Engrossed
Engaged
Involved
Attentive
Eager
Excited
Anticipatory
Looking forward to
In awe
Entertained
Amused

Happy

Pleasantly surprised
Pleased
Contented
Satisfied
Cheerful
Glad
Appreciative
Grateful
Feeling good
Gratified
Proud

Jovial
Delighted
Loving
Liking
Attached to
Affectionate toward
Adoring
Blissful
Joyful
Ecstatic
Elated
Euphoric
Jubilant

Sad

Unhappy
Sorry
Sorry for
Regretful
Depressed
Discouraged
Disappointed
Dejected
Glum
Despondent
Dismayed
Down in the dumps

Blue
Heartbroken
Heartsick
Miserable
Disheartened
Despairing
Grieving

Angry

Displeased
Dissatisfied
Envious
Jealous
Resentful
Offended
Frustrated
Annoyed
Irritated
Mad
Fuming
Irate
Heated
Cross
Crabby
Bitchy
Exasperated
Furious

Incensed

Livid

Enraged

Outraged

Fearful

Timid

Nervous

Uncomfortable

Scared

Afraid

Disturbed

Uneasy

Concerned

Apprehensive

Anxious

Worried

Dread

Petrified

Terrified

Horrified

Contemptuous

Offended

Appalled

Indignant

Judgmental

Disdaining

Disrespecting

Despising

Bitter

Disgusted

Dislike

Hate

Loathe

Repelled by

Repulsed by

Aversion to

Revulsion

Sickened

Aghast

Metaphorically Speaking

Just as the voice provides clues to what's happening in the hearts of people talking, so do the metaphors they choose.

Many of us learned about metaphors in a high school literature class, and often during a poetry lesson. Reading Alfred Noyes's words "The road was a ribbon of darkness over the purple moor," we understood that the road wasn't *really* a ribbon. It was made of soil and rocks, after all. But the metaphor helped us to *see* the road as a ribbon. And as we did, we could imagine the whole moonlit landscape just as the highwayman of the poem's title saw it. We could be there with him, hearing his horse's hoofbeats, feeling the night wind, experiencing his fateful ride.

The metaphors we use when we talk about our feelings do the same thing. We can use metaphors to convey our emotional perspectives more clearly. We can listen for metaphors when people talk about their feelings in order to experience matters from their points of view.

When people use metaphors as simple figures of speech, the imagery they choose can provide little windows into their emotional reality. And when people use metaphors to draw parallels between their current lives and what happened in the past, their metaphors can open entire doors into many kinds of emotional-heritage issues.

Either way, metaphors become one more tool as we bid and respond to others' bids for emotional connection.

Common Metaphorical Figures of Speech Can Be Revealing   Here are just a few examples of familiar metaphors you might hear in conversation, as well as the emotional meaning you can guess from their usage. Keep in mind that the meanings you draw from metaphors are just that—guesses. But they often provide a great springboard for conversation as you seek to learn more about another person's feelings. And once you understand that person's metaphors, you can then use them yourself in making bids for emotional connection. Here are some examples:

"Our marriage was a train wreck." The speaker feels that his marriage was broken and irreparable in a very chaotic and destructive way. It's likely that people got hurt. And because he characterizes it as an accident, he probably didn't expect this outcome. It wasn't supposed to happen this way.

"I want to stay afloat financially." The speaker believes that her finances could reach a crisis state where she'd be "over her head" in debt and "drowning." She fears that her financial survival may be in doubt.

"My father likes to play God." The speaker feels that her father is autocratic and controlling, like a benevolent dictator. She also feels that his attempts at benevolence lack integrity and commitment. He's not *being* God, he's only *playing* at it. Therefore, she not only resents his interference, she mistrusts it.

As the psychologist Richard Kopp writes in *Metaphor Therapy* (Brunner/Mazel, 1995), such figures of speech do more than provide us with colorful language; they help us create a framework upon which to consider significant matters. They influence how we perceive issues and think and feel about them, and what actions we take.

Kopp uses the example "Time is money." Once you accept this metaphor as true, you start acting it out. You become more conscious of how you "spend" your time. You stop "giving" your time to others without expecting something in return. Instead, you try to "save" time so that you can "invest" it in worthwhile activity.

Imagine how you might act differently, however, if you accepted the metaphor that "time is a river." It "flows" continually, so you don't have to worry about giving it away; there's always more time coming down the channel. Time "carries" you along whether you want to go or not, so you might as well relax and enjoy the ride.

Now imagine the conflicts that might arise in a partnership between two people, each of whom constructs his or her reality around these contradictory metaphors. Working together on a project, one person might constantly be struggling to "save time" as the other attempts to "let go" of time constraints. But by listening to each other's metaphors, the pair may be able to come to a better understanding of their differences.

Kopp speculates that one reason metaphors are so powerful is that they activate the same mechanisms in the brain that we used in infancy to think about the world. As babies, we could not think of abstract concepts such as "security," "nourishment," or "nurturing." But we did think about the concrete objects associated with such concepts. There was the blanket, the bottle of milk, the mother, and so on. Even though we didn't have words for these things, we had the images of how they looked in reality, and how they looked in our minds. The blanket *was* security. The milk *was* nourishment. The mother *was* nurturing.

Because concrete images were so important as our brains formed and our thinking processes developed, we continue throughout our lives to find such images useful for learning and communicating abstract concepts. Now, if we want to think about an abstract concept in a new way, comparing it to something tangible can help. (Time is a runaway train; there's no stopping it. Time is a furnace; it's burning our resources. Time is a carousel; we'll get another chance the next time around.) And from that new image we build a new conceptual framework, a new way to think about the concept, a new way to communicate with one another about it.

REVIEW QUESTIONS

1. Paraphrase Gottman's two main reasons for giving your emotions names and talking about them.
2. List the main steps in the cognitive approach to exploring emotion that Gottman outlines.
3. What do you believe the difference is between feeling contemptuous and feeling disgusted?
4. Explain the role metaphors play in learning how to put your feelings into words.

PROBES

1. Does Gottman's cognitive approach to exploring emotions seem helpful to you or strange? What do you think this says about you?
2. Which, if any, words in the Emotional Vocabulary List would you never use to describe how you are feeling? Why? What makes those words inappropriate for you?
3. Do you agree that the metaphors a person uses can say a great deal about what he or she means? Explain.

This reading about engaging others is a case study, rather than an analytical or theoretical discussion. The senior author, Lawrence Rosenfeld, is one of the field's foremost self-disclosure scholars, but this is not a report of his research. It's a story about how a new university student manages the challenges of what to disclose about herself, to whom, and when.

Katherine, the new student, misses an opportunity to talk with her dad about this important time in her life, encounters a new roommate, considers how to present herself to the rest of the people in the dorm, and meets some interesting guys. She also has to figure out how to respond to Russ, a guy she's interested in, when he puts down people with learning disabilities, especially because Katherine herself has attention deficit disorder. She gets some guidance from her mom and from a counselor at the learning disabilities center.

Katherine learns that when it comes to self-disclosure, every relationship is different, but some guidelines can help. The counselor at the center discusses them with Katherine and helps her decide what to tell her roommate and what to say to Russ. This story doesn't wrap up everything into a neat bundle, but it does show how one person you might be able to relate to copes with the practical applications of some of the principles and concepts that have been discussed in earlier readings in this chapter.

What to Tell

Deciding When, How, and What to Self-Disclose

Lawrence B. Rosenfeld and Jack M. Richman

The summer went by too quickly. All the plans for the trip to college had to fall into place *now*.

"Katy-Leigh, hurry up and get your bags down here so we can pack the car!" Katherine's mother shouts, even though the house is small enough that shouting isn't necessary.

Katherine's father comes into her room and helps move her bags out to the hallway. He stops by the door, turns, and tells Katherine, "I remember when I went off to college . . . the first day . . . getting ready. I was excited and scared, happy and downhearted. . . . Yes, I was a bit bewildered! So, I was wondering how you were feeling."

Katherine looks at her father, confused, thinking, *I thought Mom would be talking to me about this? What's Dad up to?* "Well, yeah," she tells him, "I'm feeling pretty okay about all this."

"Okay, let's get these bags into the car," Katherine's Dad tells her. "I guess we can talk later, if you want."

Three hours and a hundred and forty miles later, they arrive at Western State University. As Katherine looks at the long set of stairs leading up the hill to her dormitory, all she can think about is getting her stuff into her room, meeting her roommate, and getting started on her first year of college. She grabs the smallest, lightest bag and hustles up to her dorm room so she can get to see her roommate before her parents embarrass her!

"Hi, my name's Katherine."

"Great to meet you. I'm Kim. I guess we're going to be spending the year together."

"Yeah, I see you've got your stuff in the closets already. I guess you want that side of the room." Katherine thinks, *Maybe I wanted that side of the room,* but says, "No problem, I'll take this side. I need to warn you: my parents will be up here in a minute, and there's no telling what they'll ask you. Just nod a lot. My folks are really great . . . most of the time."

"No problem! My mom just left—and if you had been here she would have grilled you about anything and everything. She has to be sure her daughter isn't living with a lunatic!"

Katherine's parents enter loaded down with boxes and suitcases, and the process begins—of moving in, meeting Kim, and making jokes that cover the tension everyone feels. Within a few hours everything is put away, the beds are made, and Katherine and her parents, with Kim, go out for dinner.

Later, Katherine and Kim collapse on their beds and wonder what's next. The answer appears in the doorway in the shape of the Resident Advisor, "Sarah-the-RA" (which seems to be her full name), telling them about the dorm meeting scheduled for 8:00 P.M. Living in a co-ed dorm means meeting the other women and men.

"Kim?" Katherine asks without posing a question. "Do you realize that we have a rare opportunity here? I mean, in an hour we'll be meeting lots of people, but right now they don't know us. We can be whoever and whatever we want to be! I'm not sure whether I want to be 'Katherine' or 'Kathy,' or even 'Katy-Leigh,' my parents' nickname for me."

"I can be 'Kim' or 'Kimberly,' or even 'Kimmy,' but I never liked that nickname. My brother uses that when he wants to be really obnoxious."

"I'm not sure what kind of impression I should make. Should I be 'sophisticated Katherine'? Or should I be 'easy-to-get-to-know Kathy'? "

"I think we're going to be whoever we are, whatever we call ourselves. But I agree with you, we're probably all feeling a little insecure and flustered. When we get back here, you can let me know how I came across, and I'll let you know. But we have to be honest with each other!"

The meeting is in the lounge on the first floor, between the elevators and the Coke machines. A hundred people scatter on the chairs and floor, and lean against the walls. Sarah-the-RA calls the meeting to order, and what follows is a lengthy speech about rules and regulations, quiet hours, and planned social events. Ears perk up at the mention of social events. Then Sarah-the-RA offers soft drinks and cookies to encourage the residents to hang around.

"Kathy?" a voice calls out to her. "Kathy? It's me, Russ. I was a year ahead of you in high school—remember? We went out once. I've been here a year, but I still like living in the dorms."

"Oh, yeah, Russ . . . sure . . . high school. You were friends with those kids on the basketball team." Katherine thinks, *I really liked you . . . and wanted to get to know you better . . . I don't know why you never called me again after we went out.*

After a moment of awkward silence, Katherine asks, "How do you like Western? I'm registering for classes tomorrow. Any suggestions?"

They talk about Western, classes, the weather, majors, "do-ya-know-so-and-so" questions, and other topics that are safe and usual. They agree to meet the next day for lunch after registration. Kim walks up, nudges Katherine, and clears her throat loudly.

"Russ, this is Kim. She's my roommate. Kim, this is Russ . . . he's a sophomore here . . . and he went to my high school."

"Hi, Russ! Sorry to interrupt, but I just wanted to tell Katherine . . . or is it Kathy? . . . or is it Katy-Leigh—have you decided? Well, I just wanted to tell you that I'm meeting some friends from Smith Hall. There's a guy there I know from high school. See ya!" Without waiting for a response, Kim is gone.

"What's up with Kim? Doesn't she know your name?" Russ asks.

"Oh, it's nothing. She was just kidding."

Later that night, lying on her bed, Katherine stares at the ceiling and goes over the day in her head. *I never did get to have that conversation Dad wanted. . . . I can't believe I'm in college, in a dorm room, away from home! . . . What would I be doing at 10:00 P.M. at home on a Sunday night—probably not much less than this! . . . Am I boring? What is this place really, really like? I think Kim is already having a better social life than I am. . . . I wish she asked me to go with her! Why did she mention that "name thing" to Russ? How embarrassing!*

Katherine's thoughts come to an abrupt halt when she hears a key in the door. Kim comes in and says, "How was your night? Russ is cute!"

"Oh, we just talked for a few minutes. I'm meeting him tomorrow after registration. A lunch thing."

"Do you like him?"

Katherine hesitates. *I'd like to tell Kim that Russ and I went out once, and about my feelings for him, whatever they are. I want to talk to Kim and sort out my feelings—about Russ, being away for the first time,* college. *But . . . I'm not ready. I mean, should I trust her? What if I say something really stupid? What if she thinks I'm an immature jerk?* She says, "He's OK. What did you do?"

"It was weird! I went over to meet Mike, and the first thing I notice is he's cut all his hair off! I'm not sure I like that! I really liked him in high school, but I don't know if I want to jump into a relationship—not with all these other guys around! You see . . . I was in a relationship for two years, and while it was good in a lot of ways, it felt a little like prison . . . a nice prison, but a prison anyway. You know what I mean?"

"I've had some boyfriends, but nothing as serious as two years. What was it like?"

Katherine and Kim talk about high school and the pros and cons of dating someone for a long time, and Katherine wonders, *Maybe I can tell her how I felt being left at the meeting, and about her mentioning the Katherine-Kathy-Katy-Leigh thing to Russ. After all, she's told me so much about herself.* "When I was talking to Russ, and you left . . . and I came up here by myself. It was . . . well . . . a little scary. I mean, it dawned on me, I really am alone here."

"How terrible! I didn't mean to leave you! I know how that feels. You know? I've felt the same way. I grew up in a single-parent family, and had a lot of responsibility, and I used to think that I was alone, having to figure out every-thing for myself. I'm sorry."

Katherine thinks, *I'm lucky! Kim really seems to understand me . . . and she's a great listener!* "It's OK, I'm probably a little hyper today. First day. Our relation-ship isn't going to be a 'prison,' even if we're roomies for four years!"

Lunch the next day comes at the perfect moment: Katherine is closed out of several classes, registers for a class in Botany that meets a science requirement but isn't something she's particularly interested in taking, and finds herself with a schedule that requires being on campus from 8:00 A.M. until 5:00 P.M. five days a week. Frustrated, she meets Russ and plunks her books on the table. Russ tells her, "You look terrible!"

"Thanks. You would too if you had to work so hard to get the awful sched-ule I'm stuck with! I couldn't get Dr. Rawlings for English, like you told me to, so I had to sign up for Dr. Spencer. I hear she requires a lot of reading!"

"Well, welcome to college! Only the learning disabled *really* have trouble keeping up!"

Katherine is surprised: *He said "learning disabled" like it was a horrible disease, and he doesn't know that I "have it"! I wonder what he would think if he knew I was ADD? A lot of reading is a real challenge for me. I have to stick with it for a long time. I've worked so hard to overcome my disability . . . why does it have to be a problem?*

The rest of the conversation follows the first-lunch rules: Say nothing too deep, ask nothing too personal, and keep yourself looking good. And it ends with plans to meet again on the weekend. But later that day, Katherine recog-nizes old feelings: *How can I tell Russ about my ADD? I never even heard of atten-tion deficit disorder, much less "ADD," which is what everyone calls it, until I found out I had it. And why should I have to explain myself to him in the first place? What will he think about me? He seems to think that anyone with a learning disability is less than a real student? I like him, but can I have a relationship with him?*

Katherine needs some advice. She calls her mother and tells her about the problems with registration and with Russ. "What can I do?" she asks her mother.

"Look, Katy-Leigh, one reason we selected Western was because they're supposed to have a great Learning Disabilities Center. Remember, when we met Dr. O'Neill, he said to come by any time. So why not call him? I'm sure you're not alone in having to tell people about your ADD."

"I know I'm not alone, but I sure feel alone."

Following her mother's advice, Katherine calls the Learning Disabilities Center and makes an appointment for the next day with Dr. O'Neill.

"What's up, Katherine? I'm glad to see you choose Western. What can I do for you?"

"Well, for starters, you can give me a magic pill that'll get rid of my ADD!"

"You sound frustrated. How is your ADD a problem? Classes don't begin until next week."

Katherine recounts her conversation with Russ, and about needing some advice. "How can I tell him about my ADD, which I have to if I want any kind of relationship with him that's more than superficial? I'm afraid he'll not want any relationship at all if I tell him."

"OK, you're feeling conflict over being honest with him and with risking the potential for a close relationship."

"That's it! So what do I do?"

"First, you need to decide if being open with Russ is what you want to do. There are no hard-and-fast rules about when and what to tell someone about yourself. Don't panic; you're in control here. Now, is this about Russ thinking bad things about you, or is it about your own fears about college and how well you'll do?"

"It's not the ADD. I know my problem with organizing, about having to concentrate when I listen in class, about not getting distracted, about following through on assignments. I've learned ways to sustain my concentration and mental effort when I'm doing my school work. I know all that. I've been taught how to use structure in my life, use time-outs when I get really frustrated, and to keep a sense of humor about the whole thing."

"So what's the problem?"

"The problem is how do I tell Russ, and my roommate, Kim, and anybody else at Western—without feeling exposed, unprotected, and maybe unworthy of being here."

"OK, I get the point. You need some guidelines. Well, every relationship is different, and it's not safe to make generalizations, but that's never stopped me before! Really, here are some things to think about. First of all, you need to think about how important Russ or Kim or anyone else is to you. Is the person you want to tell a big risk or a small risk? I mean, how much can you trust the person to treat what you say confidentially and with respect? Holding back with people you don't feel comfortable with may not be a bad idea! Second, you have to think about whether what you want to say about yourself is an appropriate topic to talk about. Your ADD may be something important to tell your teachers, but not just any student in one of your classes. See what I mean?"

"I see. But it seems relevant to tell Russ because he obviously has negative feelings about people with a learning disability. And if we're going to have any friendship at all—of any kind—this has got to get cleared up. I guess I just decided it's worth the risk!"

"Seems like it! Also, think about *when* you're going to tell Russ. You need a space that's comfortable and that allows for privacy. You don't want Russ to feel as if he *has* to be polite and say the 'right thing.' And here's a last consideration. You need to think about the possible outcomes and be prepared for whatever might be said. Why don't we do a few role plays. I'll play you and you can be Russ, then you can be yourself and I'll play Russ. This way you're sure to be clear and understandable if you decide to be open with him."

Katherine and Dr. O'Neill practice what Katherine might say to Russ, and she leaves his office feeling more confident in her ability to interact with Russ successfully and deal with whatever his response might be. Walking up the stairs to her dorm room, she thinks: *If Kim asks me where I've been, I'll tell her about meeting Dr. O'Neill and see how she reacts. I think it's worth the risk with Kim. We're going to be living together, and she seems to be understanding.*

As if on cue, Kim asks her, "So what's going on?"

"I'm just getting back from the Learning Disabilities Center."

"Getting a tutoring job?"

"Not really—I may be one of those who needs tutoring!"

"I don't understand."

"I saw Dr. O'Neill, the Center's Director. I wanted to talk to him about how to tell people about my learning disability."

"Great, so tell me."

"I have ADD—that's Attention Deficit Disorder. And Russ made some insensitive put-down of people with learning disabilities. So Dr. O'Neill and I decided how best to deal with all this. Am I clear? I can hear myself sounding scattered—shifting topics. Welcome to my ADD! This is what happens when I get nervous."

"OK, so you have ADD. What's the problem? You must be doing something right if you got into Western."

"The problem is I need to work harder than most people just keeping myself on task, on organizing my work. And sometimes I think I don't belong here . . . and I'm afraid the other students are going to judge me. That's why I feel so alone sometimes!"

"I don't know much about ADD, but if it helps, it looks to me like you're pretty task oriented and you seem organized. Is there anything I can do?"

"No, just listening to me helps. It feels good just to have someone know and be supportive. It would be great if you could learn to sleep with the light on while I'm taking the extra time I need to study. Just kidding!"

"So what's the issue with Russ? He doesn't seem like a jerk, except maybe for his remark about learning disabilities."

"That's the point. I don't know."

"Well, if you talk to him, you can clarify how you feel and how he feels. I'm sure he'll tell you if you tell him! And then you'll get it off your chest. You know, he may even think you're brave to tell him. I think you're brave! It takes guts to be up front with someone. . . . Anyway, it'll give him a chance to understand how his remark hurt you and to apologize, or let you know he's not worth having a relationship with."

"That makes sense. But if he says more insensitive stuff, I'll probably be so frustrated and angry that I'll want to hit him!"

"Yeah, being rejected, even if it's by a jerk, still hurts. But, it's either tell him, or plan on nothing more than nodding hello when you pass him on campus."

"I'm meeting him this weekend. I'll take the risk."

That Saturday night, sitting across from each other at a local pizza parlor, Katherine looks Russ in the eyes and says, "You said something when we were having lunch a few days ago, and I need to talk to you about it."

REVIEW QUESTIONS

1. Is the relationship portrayed here between Katherine and her roommate Kim a realistic one? Explain.
2. Who do you think is more open in this story, Kim or Katherine?
3. Katherine believes that Russ's comment, "Only the learning disabled *really* have trouble keeping up," accurately reflects part of his view of people with ADD. Do you agree? Explain.

PROBES

1. Before they go to the dorm meeting, Katherine tells Kim, "We can be whoever and whatever we want to be" when they meet the other women and men. Do you agree? When you're new, do you have relatively complete freedom to present whatever self you want to others? Or are you strongly limited by your appearance, culture, and habits?
2. The readings in Chapter 2 emphasize that communication happens *between* people; it's not something one person does "to" another. In this story, Russ says, "Only the learning disabled *really* have trouble keeping up," and Katherine interprets this as a threat to her possible future with Russ. "The communication" emerges *between* them. Which parts of "the communication" are Russ's and which are Katherine's?
3. Write out the rest of the conversation between Katherine and Russ that Katherine begins at the end of the story.

REFERENCES

1. Cline, R. J. W. (1989). The politics of intimacy: Costs and benefits determining disclosure intimacy in male-female dyads. *Journal of Social and Personal Relationships, 6,* 5–20.
2. Derlega, V. J., Metts, S., Petronio, S., & Margulis, S. T. (1993). *Self-disclosure.* Newbury Park, CA: Sage.
3. Foubert, J. D., & Sholley, B. K. (1996). Effects of gender, gender role, and individualized trust on self-disclosure. *Journal of Social Behavior and Personality, 11*(5), 277–288.
4. Laurenceau, J. P., Barrett, L. F., & Pietromonaco, P. R. (1998). Intimacy as an interpersonal process: The importance of self-disclosure, partner disclosure, and perceived partner responsiveness in interpersonal exchanges. *Journal of Personality and Social Psychology, 74,* 1238–1251.
5. Petronio, S., Martin, J., & Littlefield, R. (1984). Prerequisite conditions for self-disclosing: A gender issue. *Communication Monographs, 51,* 268–273.

6. Rosenfeld, L. B. (2001). Overview of the ways privacy, secrecy, and disclosure are balanced in today's society. In S. Petronio (Ed.), *Balancing the secrets of private disclosures.* Mahwah, NJ: Lawrence Erlbaum.

7. Rosenfeld, L. B. (1979). Self-disclosure avoidance: Why I am afraid to tell you who I am. *Communication Monographs, 46,* 63–74.

8. Rosenfeld, L. B., & Kendrick, W. L. (1987). Choosing to be open:. Subjective reasons for self-disclosing. *Western Journal of Speech Communication, 48,* 326–343.

9. Toukmanian, S. G., & Brouwers, M. C. (1998). Cultural aspects of self-disclosure and psychotherapy. In S. S. Kazarian & D. R. Evans (Eds.), *Cultural clinical psychology: Theory, research, and practice* (pp. 106–124). New York: Oxford University Press.

10. Wintrob, H. L. (1987). Self-disclosure as a marketable commodity. *Journal of Social Behavior and Personality, 2,* 77–88.

———

This chapter on communication as exhaling ends with this reading that offers some guidelines about confronting emotional abuse. There is another reading about verbal abuse in the "Recognizing Communication Walls" chapter (Chapter 9), but this one emphasizes the "exhaling" parts of the process—the ways the abused person can stand up for him- or herself.

This reading begins with some examples that lead up to a definition of emotional abuse as any *nonphysical* behavior that is designed to control, intimidate, subjugate, demean, punish, or isolate another person through the use of degradation, humiliation, or fear. Clearly interpersonal communication cannot happen in situations marked by emotional abuse.

Emotional abuse, Engel explains, does its damage by attacking the abused person's self-esteem and confidence. People who are regularly abused often both blame themselves for the problems in the relationship and also believe that they are fundamentally unlovable.

When emotional abuse becomes mutual, each partner has to constantly fend off criticism and attacks, but, paradoxically, each also becomes increasingly dependent on the relationship. This destructive cycle seriously damages both of the partners and the relationship.

When one partner is doing the abusing, he or she will often refuse to get help. This means that the abused partner needs to act to diminish or stop the abuse. Engel argues that abused partners have more power than they realize, and she lays out some suggestions for confronting an abusive partner about his or her behavior.

In the book that this reading is taken from, Engel offers a number of suggestions for dealing with emotional abuse. This excerpt focuses only on how to confront emotional abuse. Engel notes that there are two kinds of confrontation, following through on a planned conversation or responding directly to the next instance of abuse. Important nonverbal parts of this kind of confrontation include confident posture, direct eye contact, beginning with a deep breath, and staying in the present. Engel suggests several steps for the "serious discussion" confrontation, including managing the context, a clear description of the abuse as you experience it, and the use, if the situation calls for it, of the statement, "You are being verbally abusive. Stop it right now."

Engel also offers four specific suggestions for the second option, confronting abuse at the time it happens. They include speaking up, standing your ground rather than arguing, being prepared for silence, and offering information if requested.

Obviously, this brief treatment of a communication problem as serious as verbal abuse will not answer all your questions, and, even if you follow Engel's advice, there is no guarantee that the problem will disappear. But there are some helpful basic suggestions here. With the help of a skilled counselor, a knowledgeable advisor, or a good friend, you can at least begin to confront whatever abuse you are experiencing.

Confronting Emotional Abuse

Beverly Engel

No matter what Tracey does, she just can't seem to please her boyfriend. He complains constantly—about the way she dresses, the way she talks, the amount of time she spends on the phone with her friends—and even though she's taken his concerns to heart and made changes in these areas, he always seems to find something else to complain about. "I love him and I want him to be happy, but I'm confused," Tracey explained to me. "Sometimes it seems like no matter what I do he never seems to be satisfied, and at other times I begin to think that maybe I do things deliberately just to upset him."

Robert's wife isn't speaking to him again. This time it's been two weeks. Although it's happened many times before, it still bothers him immensely. "I feel like a bad boy who is being punished by his mother. It's not just the silent treatment that bothers me, it's the dirty looks, as well."

Over the years, Robert has learned to stay away from his wife and give her time to cool down. "It doesn't do any good to try to apologize or explain my side of the story—she refuses to listen, and often it makes her more angry. When she's ready to start talking to me again, she will—until then, I just have to suffer in silence."

Jason's lover, Mark, is extremely possessive and jealous. "He has to know where I am twenty-four hours a day," Jason complained to me. "He calls me at work several times a day, and if I'm away from my desk, he gets really angry and wants to know where I was and what I was doing. There are several nice-looking men in my office, and Mark is convinced I'm going to have an affair with one of them. It does absolutely no good at all for me to try to reassure him. And he's constantly accusing me of flirting. The worst part about it is that I'm beginning to question myself. I don't think I flirt, but maybe I do without realizing it."

Although Tracey, Robert, and Jason don't realize it, they are all being emotionally abused. The same is true of thousands of other women and men like them. Slowly, systematically, their self-confidence is whittled away, their self-esteem is eroded, and their perception of themselves is distorted—and yet they don't even know it is happening.

An individual or a couple can remain locked in a prison of conflict, humiliation, fear, and anger for years without realizing that they are in an emotionally abusive relationship. They may assume that all couples fight as they do or that all women (or men) are treated as they are. Often, emotional abuse between couples is denied, made light of, or written off as simple conflicts or "love-spats" when in fact one or both partners are being severely damaged psychologically. Even those who realize they are being emotionally abused tend to blame themselves or make excuses for their partner's behavior. Little do they know that by allowing their partner to continue this kind of destructive behavior, they are actually participating in destroying their relationship. Emotional abuse is one of the prime factors in creating dysfunctional relationships and one of the major causes for separation or divorce.

WHAT IS EMOTIONAL ABUSE?

When most people think of emotional abuse, they usually think of one or both partners belittling or criticizing the other. But emotional abuse is much more than verbal abuse. Emotional abuse can be defined as any *nonphysical* behavior that is designed to control, intimidate, subjugate, demean, punish, or isolate another person through the use of degradation, humiliation, or fear.

Emotionally abusive behavior ranges from verbal abuse (belittling, berating, constant criticism) to more subtle tactics like intimidation, manipulation, and refusal to be pleased. We will take much more in-depth looks at the various types of emotional abuse in the next chapter, but for now, here are some examples of emotional abuse in intimate relationships:

- Humiliation and degradation
- Discounting and negating

- Domination and control
- Judging and criticizing
- Accusing and blaming
- Trivial and unreasonable demands or expectations
- Emotional distancing and the "silent treatment"
- Isolation

Emotional abuse can also include more subtle forms of behavior such as:

- Withholding of attention or affection
- Disapproving, dismissive, contemptuous, or condescending looks, comments, and behavior
- Sulking and pouting
- Projection and/or accusations
- Subtle threats of abandonment (either physical or emotional)

Emotional abuse is not only made up of negative behaviors but negative attitudes as well. Therefore, we need to include the word *attitude* in our definition of emotional abuse. A person who is emotionally abusive need not take any overt action whatsoever. All he or she needs to do is to exhibit an abusive attitude. Here are some examples:

- Believing that others should do as you say
- Not noticing how others feel
- Not caring how others feel
- Believing that everyone else is inferior to you
- Believing that you are always right

So emotional abuse is any nonphysical behavior or *attitude* that is designed to control, intimidate, subjugate, demean, punish, or isolate another person. But there are also some types of physical behavior that can be considered emotional abuse. These behaviors have a name: *symbolic violence*. This includes intimidating behavior such as slamming doors, kicking a wall, throwing dishes, furniture, or other objects, driving recklessly while the victim is in the car, and destroying or threatening to destroy objects the victim values. Even milder forms of violence such as shaking a fist or finger at the victim, making threatening gestures or faces, or acting like he or she wants to kill the victim carry symbolic threats of violence.

HOW EMOTIONAL ABUSE DOES DAMAGE

The primary effects of emotional abuse on the victim are depression, lack of motivation, confusion, difficulty concentrating or making decisions, low self-esteem, feelings of failure or worthlessness, feelings of hopelessness, self-blame, and self-destructiveness. Emotional abuse is like brainwashing in that it systematically wears away at the victim's self-confidence, sense of self-worth, trust in his or her perceptions, and self-concept. Whether it is by constant berating and belittling, by intimidation, or under the guise of "guidance" or teaching, the results are similar. Eventually, the recipient loses all sense of self and all remnants of personal value.

Abused partners tend either to take on the criticism and rejection of their partner or to be in constant turmoil, wondering things like: *Am I as bad as she makes me out to be, or is she just impossible to please? Should I stay in this relationship, or should I go? If I'm as incompetent as he says I am, maybe I can't make it on my own. Maybe no one will ever love me again.* Ultimately, given enough time, most victims of emotional abuse come not only to blame themselves for all the problems in the relationship but also to believe that they are inadequate, contemptuous, and even unlovable.

Emotional abuse is considered by many to be the most painful form of violence and the most detrimental to self-esteem. Emotional abuse cuts to the very core of a person, creating scars that may be longer lasting than physical ones. With emotional abuse, the insults, insinuations, criticism, and accusations slowly eat away at the victim's self-esteem until he or she is incapable of judging a situation realistically. She may begin to believe that there is something wrong with her or even fear that she is losing her mind. She has become so beaten down emotionally that she blames herself for the abuse.

Emotional abuse poisons a relationship and infuses it with hostility, contempt, and hatred. No matter how much a couple once loved each other, once emotional abuse becomes a consistent aspect of the relationship, that love is overshadowed by fear, anger, guilt, and shame. Whether it is one or both partners who are being emotionally abusive, the relationship becomes increasingly more toxic as time goes by. In this polluted environment it is difficult for love not only to grow but to survive.

At the very least, emotional abuse causes both the abuser and the victim to lose sight of any redeeming qualities his or her partner once had. The more a partner is allowed to degrade, criticize, or dominate her partner, the less she will respect her partner. And the more a partner is emotionally abused, the more he will slowly build up an intense hatred toward his abuser. The disrespect and hatred each partner begins to feel leads to more and more emotional abuse and to each partner justifying inappropriate, even destructive, behavior. Over time, anger can build up on the part of both abuser and victim, and emotional abuse can turn to physical violence.

When emotional abuse is mutual, it becomes a matter of survival, as each partner has to constantly fend off the criticism, verbal attacks, or rejection and shore up enough strength to go on with daily tasks. As the emotional abuse takes its toll and each partner becomes less and less self-assured, each clings to the relationship even more. A destructive cycle is created—even as the relationship becomes more and more abusive each person becomes more dependent on his or her partner. And as the relationship continues to deteriorate, each partner feels further justified in becoming even more abusive.

ACTION STEPS FOR THOSE BEING ABUSED

While the optimum situation would be for both you and your partner to commit to working on your relationship together, often abusive partners refuse to admit they are being abusive and are unwilling to seek help, even in the form of reading a book such as this one. This does not mean that there is no hope for your relationship, however. In many cases, the abused partner can be the one who stops the abuse. This is not to imply that you are to blame for the abuse or that you "cause it" or "ask for it" in any way. Nor does it mean that you can change the abuser. He or she is the only person who can do that. But it does mean that in some situations, changing your behavior may encourage the abuser to change his or her behavior, or at the very least modify it.

This may sound unbelievable to you. "What can *I* do to stop the abuse? I've tried everything and nothing works." Although I'm sure you've tried everything you could think of to make your partner stop abusing you, there are some specific things you may not have considered that may discourage your partner from continuing to treat you in an abusive way.

You have much more power than you realize. What may have been standing in the way of you getting in touch with this power is your personal history—a history that no doubt robbed you of your self-esteem and feelings of personal power.

Confront Your Partner on His or Her Abusive Behavior

It's very likely that you've already spent many hours trying to understand your partner's behavior, explaining to your partner why you are upset, or trying to figure out what went wrong in the relationship, only to discover that none of these methods were effective in stopping the abuse. Some of you have also discovered that the strategies of trying to reason with your partner or just complaining about his behavior have not been effective. You must begin to respond to his inappropriate or unacceptable behavior in a new way—a way that will make an impact on him. The following strategies will help you respond in such a way. I suggest you practice or role-play these strategies with a friend or counselor before you try them with your partner, especially if you tend to become overwhelmed, frightened, or tongue-tied when he or she is being abusive. If you don't have someone with whom to practice, you can put an empty chair in front of you and imagine that your partner is sitting in it. This will help you get over some of your fears about confronting him or her and will make you more confident about what you want to say. The following suggestions will further prepare you for your confrontations:

- Be sure to speak clearly and firmly. Hold your head up high and look directly into your partner's eyes.
- Make sure your feet are firmly planted on the ground, whether you are standing or sitting.

- Take a deep breath before beginning your confrontation and make sure your eyes are clear and that you are in the present. (Often emotional or verbal abuse can trigger childhood memories and catapult you into the past.)

There are two ways to confront. You can sit down with your partner and have a talk with him about the fact that he is being inappropriate or disrespectful toward you, or you can call him on his behavior or attitude the next time he is abusive. The way you choose to go about confronting your partner will have a lot to do with the status of your relationship. If you and your partner are still emotionally close a great deal of the time and are still able to communicate with one another over most issues, approach number one—a serious discussion—may be the best choice. This approach will be especially effective if you have not confronted him on his abusive behavior in the past. If, on the other hand, you have confronted him before and he has ignored you or insisted that you are making too much of it, then you may need to try the second approach and confront him whenever he commits the abusive behavior. This is also the best approach for couples who have grown distant and noncommunicative.

If you are in a relatively new relationship and have begun to see warning signs of emotional or verbal abuse, a serious discussion with your partner is probably the best approach. Many people are simply unaware that their behavior is abusive. If he is young or has little or no experience in a long-term relationship, he may simply be repeating one or both parents' behavior without being aware of how it affects his partner. Even if a person has been in previous relationships, their past partners may have put up with the abuse without saying anything or may have blamed themselves for their partner's behavior, never realizing that they were being abused.

Your decision whether to choose approach one or two may also have to do with whether your partner is a person who has abusive behavior or someone who is an abusive person by nature. If he or she simply has some bad behaviors, approach number one may work well to help him become more conscious of how his behavior affects you. But if he has an abusive personality, approach number two will work better since reasoning with him will not likely be effective.

Approach Number One—The Serious Discussion   Tell your partner that you have something important to talk to him or her about and that you'd like to set up a time to do so. Make sure you choose a time that is good for both of you and a time when you will not be distracted by the kids, the television, or the telephone. In fact, it is best to unplug the phone and turn off all distractions when you have your talk. If she becomes curious or anxious and wants to have the talk immediately, make sure you are in the right frame of mind before giving in to her request. If you are not prepared to have the talk, simply assure your partner that while the discussion is an important one, it can wait for a more appropriate time. If you feel you are unable to talk to her at all, write her a letter.

I suggest you begin by telling your partner that you have been unhappy with some of the ways she has been treating you or speaking to you. If this is the first time you've brought this up, let her know that you care about her but that the way she treats you is affecting the way you feel about her and that you are afraid it will ultimately destroy the relationship. If you have tried talking to her about this before, remind her of this. Let her know that you haven't noticed a change on her part and that this is unacceptable to you.

If she seems open to what you are saying, tell her you appreciate her willingness to work on the relationship, and ask her if she'd like some examples of the kinds of behavior you are talking about. At this point you do not need to define the behavior as emotionally or verbally abusive. It will be difficult enough for her to hear your examples without being accused of being abusive. Don't be surprised if she makes excuses or becomes defensive. This is understandable. But don't allow the discussion to turn into an argument. If she begins to accuse you of making things up, imagining things, or trying to create problems where none exist, say something like the following: "What you are doing right now is an example of the kind of behavior I have been talking about. You are negating my experience and making accusations. Please stop." If she gets angry and becomes verbally abusive, say, "You are being verbally abusive. Stop it right now."

Tell your partner that from now on you are going to let her know when her behavior has become offensive to you and that you hope she will cooperate by being open to these reminders so that she can begin to change her behavior.

Approach Number Two—Confronting at the Time   If you choose to tell your partner by confronting him the next time he is abusive, the following suggestions will help:

- *Speak up.* The very next time your partner says something that is abusive or treats you in an emotionally abusive way, immediately say to him, "I don't want you to talk to me that way (or treat me that way). It is abusive (or inconsiderate or disrespectful). I don't deserve to be treated that way."

    This will no doubt get his attention. He is likely to be startled by your response and may even be at a loss for words at first. But be prepared for an argument, excuses, and even anger. He may tell you that he didn't do any such thing, that you made him say what he said, or that he treated you as he did because of your behavior. This leads us to the next step.

- *Don't argue; just stand your ground.* If your partner defends himself by making excuses or blaming you, don't get caught up in the argument. Stand your ground by repeating the exact words you said before, "I don't want you to talk to me like that (or treat me like that). It is abusive and I don't deserve to be treated that way."

- *Be prepared for silence.* Instead of arguing, some partners will completely ignore you when you confront them about their behavior. This is itself disrespectful and abusive. In essence he is saying to you, "You're not even important enough for me to listen to or respond to." Don't let him get away with it. If he gives you the silent treatment, say, "Ignoring me and giving me the silent treatment is also emotionally abusive (or inappropriate, unacceptable, or disrespectful), and I don't appreciate it. I deserve to be heard and for my words to be honored."

- *Offer information if requested.* If your partner seems genuinely surprised by what you have said and sincerely asks you for more information about what you meant by it, by all means offer it to him. You can explain that you discovered through reading this book that you are being emotionally abused by his behavior. If he seems genuinely interested, give him the book to read, and/or suggest you seek counseling together.

Time will tell whether your confrontation has had an impact on your partner. Often such confrontations enable an abusive partner to recognize the inappropriateness of her behavior and to understand that her behavior is hurtful to her partner and is having a negative effect on her relationship. When these realizations are made, people do sometimes change. Even those who are aware that they are being abusive sometimes stop their abusive behavior when they discover that their partner realizes he is being abused, states he will no longer allow it, and means what he says.

It is also possible that your partner may have been testing you to see just how much she could get away with. As I've mentioned earlier, some partners lose respect for their mates when they allow abuse to occur. By speaking up and letting her know you will not tolerate such behavior, you may not only stop the abusive behavior but also gain back your partner's respect.

On the other hand, some people deliberately look for partners they can dominate and control or someone who will be a scapegoat for their anger. If your new partner is such a person, your confrontation will tip him off that you are not the kind of partner he is looking for, and he may choose to move on. If this is the case, you are better off without him.

Whether this confrontation and your continued attempts to confront your partner's abusive behavior are effective or not, your efforts will not be in vain. By continuing to confront your partner on his or her unacceptable behavior, you will affirm in your own mind that you do not deserve to be treated in these ways. This will, in turn, help raise your self-esteem and help you take one step closer to ending the relationship. In the future you will know that you can recognize emotional abuse when it occurs and that you can respond appropriately.

REVIEW QUESTIONS

1. List three of the ways that people in an emotionally abusive relationship convince themselves that it is not a problem.
2. Think about a dating relationship you are now in, or one that you have been in recently. Which, if any, of the abusive behaviors that Engel lists have you experienced? Which, if any, have you engaged in?
3. Explain how emotional abuse does damage.

4. Engel says to the abused person, "You have much more power than you realize." What power does an abused person have?
5. Which of the two ways of confronting an abusive partner sounds most effective to you—the serious discussion or confronting at the time? Explain.
6. Paraphrase the four principles involved in confronting emotional abuse as it happens.

PROBES

1. Chapter 10 points out that conflict is a part of all relationships; no relational partners can "be nice" to each other all the time. But emotional abuse is different from conflict. What makes it different?
2. Many people in relationships overlook the value of the planned discussion, whether it is to negotiate vacation plans or to confront something as serious as emotional abuse. Often this happens because these discussions cannot be completely spontaneous, and the partners value spontaneity over everything else. One of Engel's strategies is the planned "serious discussion." What can make this a good idea, even though it is not entirely spontaneous?
3. Which of the four principles for confronting emotional abuse as it happens sounds most difficult to you? Explain.

PART THREE

Changing Relationships

One of the ways to understand the organization of *Bridges Not Walls* is to think about Part III of the book as the place where we move from theory to practice. The three chapters in Part I defined communication and interpersonal communication, showed how selves get built and changed communicatively, and surveyed the two basic ways we make contact—verbally and nonverbally. Then the two chapters in Part II analyzed and illustrated how people make meaning together by taking in cues via perception and listening—"inhaling"—and giving off cues via self-expression, self-disclosure, assertiveness, and immediacy—"exhaling." Now we turn to the three main arenas or contexts where this communicating happens: family, friends, and intimate partners.

But if you've read the earlier chapters you know that this way of understanding them doesn't quite work, because they aren't all theory. Practice and theory have been woven together from the beginning, and this is an important part of studying interpersonal communication. The theories that scholars have developed are systematic descriptions of practice. In this field, there are no abstract theoretical generalizations that are totally disconnected from people's lived experiences. Every theoretical principle—for example, that culture is part of all communicating, that selves are built in verbal/nonverbal talk, and that all perception involves interpretation—grows out of and can significantly affect actual practice.

So the readings in Part III continue the marriage between theory and practice that characterizes all the materials in *Bridges Not Walls*.

CHAPTER 7

Communicating with Family and Friends

Stephanie Coontz, the author of this reading, teaches history and family studies at the Evergreen State College in Olympia, Washington, and is the Director of Research and Public Education for the Council on Contemporary Families. Her writings on families have been translated into French, Spanish, German, and Japanese. One of her primary goals is to remind her readers that American families are not what they used to be, and that inaccurate nostalgia about family life gets in the way of effective family functioning.

She begins this reading by reviewing the three general styles of parenting that have been identified by family researchers, authori*tarian*, permissive, and authori*tative*. She notes that antisocial behavior and poor school performance in young people are associated with both parental extremes (authoritarian and permissive). She also reviews various types or models of families, including the breadwinner-homemaker model, two-earner families, and single-parent, both heterosexual and gay or lesbian. She emphasizes that each model can function in either healthy or unhealthy ways. For example, she refers to research that demonstrates that "Children raised by gay and lesbian parents seem to be as well adjusted, on average, as children raised by heterosexual parents, with the same range of variation within each group." Coontz also debunks some other rumors about gay and lesbian families, including the notion that these parents "recruit" their children to their sexual preferences.

The reading discusses strengths and weaknesses of single-parent families in some detail. One research finding is that, "when combined with an extended network of concerned kin, the one parent family often can tender more emotional support and offer more options to family members than an isolated nuclear [two-parent] family." Single parents tend to spend less time supervising homework than adults in two-parent families, but they spend more time talking with their children than married parents do. Adolescents in single-parent families face fewer pressures to conform to traditional gender roles. Single-parenting is most difficult in cultures that most emphasize two-parent families and paternal authority, and it is most successful in cultural groups that have a history of tolerance and support for single mothers.

As in two-parent families, the maximum stress is placed on the single-family unit when its children are adolescents. For example, male children of single mothers often have more difficulty engaging in the normal adolescent separation behaviors than males in two-parent families, because they have been so close to their single mothers in the past. Just as in all families, one of the main challenges for parents involves setting clear limits and preserving generational boundaries. Coontz's main point in this section is that successful parenting can and does occur in both single- and two-parent families.

This reading makes some similarly useful points about the dangers of sweeping generalizations about remarriage and stepfamilies. One long-term study found that 80 percent of children in stepfamilies were doing well psychologically, a figure close to the 90 percent in intact biological families. But generalizations about these groups are problematic, partly because there are so many different variations. One research program identified nine "structurally distinct" types of remarried families, depending on the custody and visitation arrangements, the presence or absence of children, and whether the children are from one or both of the remarried parents' former families. Blended families are complex.

The two general pieces of advice Coontz offers parents considering remarriage are (a) don't marry just to find a mother or father for your child, and (b) don't be scared off, because many stepfamilies do well. Stepparents need to set aside traditional assumptions about how a family evolves and functions and be flexible about role relationships. Old-fashioned expectations about gender roles can create problems, and male children will have experiences different from their sisters and stepsisters. Relationships with extended kin also require attention. But when stepfamily members are willing and able to create their own "culture," they provide the same kinds of support, encouragement, resources, and love as traditional families.

This reading begins Chapter 7 because of its emphasis on "working with what we've got." Successful family communication in the twenty-first century must begin, I believe, with optimism about the possibilities for all sorts of families—one-parent, two-parent, nuclear, step, blended, extended, single-earner, two-earner, gay, and lesbian. Family members' experiences will not be determined by the structure of the family, but by the quality of its communication.

Working with What We've Got: The Strengths and Vulnerabilities of Today's Families

Stephanie Coontz

With 50 percent of American children living in something other than a married-couple family with both biological parents present, and with the tremendous variety of male and female responsibilities in today's different families, the time for abstract pronouncements about good or bad family structures and correct or incorrect parental roles is past. How a family functions is more important than its structure or its formal roles.

There are some principles of family functioning that, at a general level, seem to work well for every kind of family. Family researchers and psychologists, for example, distinguish three general styles of parenting, not all of which are equally effective.

Authoritarian parenting is restrictive, controlling, and more concerned with the adults' needs for order and obedience than with the children's developmental tasks. Lines of communication run from the top down, with little give-and-take in family discussions or decisions. Negotiation with children is seen as a violation of correct parent–child boundaries. Discipline often takes the form of punishment rather than figuring out ways to ensure that the child accepts the logical consequences of his or her acts. Parents hold the child to high standards, but they are not responsive to the child's needs and desires.

Permissive parents, by contrast, are responsive but undemanding, indulgent of their children's impulsive behaviors and almost always willing to negotiate or renegotiate a decision. They are often highly affectionate, but such parents are sometimes hard for a child to read because it's never clear when "no" really means no—or when a "yes" will be regretted.

Midway between these two extremes are authoritative parents, who are responsive and demanding at the same time. They set limits based on an understanding of what age-appropriate boundaries their child needs, but they also take their child's point of view into account when making decisions and are willing to negotiate new rules. Parents remain warm and emotionally supportive even when they are enforcing consequences. As their children age, they increasingly hold them accountable for their acts rather than restricting their behavior in advance. As one researcher describes such parents, they are accepting, democratic, but also firm.[1]

Antisocial behavior and poor school performance in young people is associated with both extremes. The permissive pattern of placing few demands on children does little to increase their self-confidence and competence, while inadequate monitoring is a problem for adolescents because it opens the door to involvement in undesirable activities. But coercive parenting can be even worse, as it may draw parent and child into a cycle of rebellion and hostility that culminates in the adolescent's premature break with the family or the parents' rejection of the child. The child's break only hardens his or her self-image as an alienated troublemaker, and parental rejection is "the most powerful predictor" of subsequent violence.[2]

Authoritative parenting, on the other hand, in every family structure and at all income levels, tends to produce close parent–child relations and self-confident, competent children. Of course, it's all very well to know that in the abstract, but it's harder in practice to be authoritative when many of us aren't sure what the "right" answers are in today's society, where the logical consequences of acts are different than they were a generation or two ago and where the line between monitoring, restricting, and overindulging seems very blurred.

I don't know many parents, in any kind of family, who are confident that they've got it right. General proclamations that "intact" families are most likely to function well, while one-parent families and stepfamilies are more likely to fail, are no more helpful to intact families trying to cope with their particular situations than they are to other kinds of families. What parents need today is more concrete research about how different families can create processes that work for their individual situations.

Knowing the form of a family tells us very little about the communication and problem solving that goes on within it, the child-rearing practices that hold sway, or most of the other important variables that determine effective child raising. Different family structures may produce different stress points or pose distinctive challenges, but ultimately every family form provides its members with some resources or strengths to build on and some vulnerabilities or danger points to avoid.

Take the breadwinner–homemaker model. In an economy where work, home, and school are in different locations, this family potentially provides kids with more maternal time, supervision, and homework help. The mother has more chances to meet with teachers, help out in school, and chauffeur children to extracurricular activities. The parents don't have to scramble to rearrange schedules when a child gets sick or needs extra attention.

Male breadwinner families seem to be especially beneficial to the health and happiness of men, so long as they can live up to their provider roles. Yet the pressures of being the sole provider may distance a father from his kids, while these families often isolate the mother and lower her self-esteem. Homemakers with young children, for example, tend to be more depressed than other groups of women. Furthermore, such families may have a tough time adjusting to rapid economic change. Parents with strong values about male breadwinning are *more* likely than other parents to experience conflict and severe distress if the father faces economic setbacks or the mother has to find a job.[3]

Two-earner families have less family time together, and they are more likely to quarrel over housework, sometimes to the point of rupture. Yet Arlie Hochschild found that "sharing the second shift improved a marriage *regardless* of what ideas either [spouse] had about men's and women's roles. Whether they were traditional or egalitarian, couples were happier when the men did more housework and childcare." Furthermore, families with a working mother are more likely to raise children who respect women—no small advantage in a world where women are rapidly becoming the majority of the workforce and old-fashioned notions about women are a potent cause of workplace hostilities.[4]

Neither of these family types seems to have a clear advantage over the other when it comes to raising children successfully, but different dynamics are at work in each. The best predictor of secure mother–child attachment in a dual-earner family is the mother's satisfaction with child care arrangements, while in a male breadwinner family it is the mother's personal coping skills.[5]

Both types of two-parent families have the advantage that more than one adult is available to the child. Parents can back each other up in discipline, compensate for each other's weaknesses, spell each other in tasks or time, and model healthy conflict resolution. On the other hand, many two-parent families have the illusion that a father's presence provides them with some magic psychological shield, which may lead the mother to avoid confronting damaging paternal behavior rather than risk a split. And as we've seen, a conflicted marriage can actually be worse for a child than a divorce.

Researchers from the Fatherhood Project at the Families and Work Institute in New York point out that "it is presence, not absence, that often lies at the heart of troubled families. It is common for family members to be in the same room and be oblivious to each other's thoughts and feelings." As Harvard psychologist Samuel Osherson puts it, "Sometimes a father or mother can be in the same room as a child, but emotionally already have walked out the door."[6]

Even harmonious couples and hands-on parents need to beware of certain pitfalls. Thinking their family self-sufficient, they may not expose their children to experiences and values that differ from their own. Such families occasionally foster an inward orientation that hinders a child from striking out in new directions or learning to appreciate difference in others. I was raised in neighborhoods where all adults felt free to act parentally toward children, and I have noticed that when I continue this tradition by commenting on something dangerous or hurtful that local children are doing, it is often youths from two-parent families who are the *most* hostile in their response: "You can't tell me that; you're not my mom."

Collaborative two-parent families certainly benefit children. But it *is* possible for single parents to find effective substitutes for the second parent. Occasionally, in fact, the need for more than one adult can be satisfied best by adding someone *other* than the father or a lover. In a random sample of Baltimore schoolchildren during their first two years of school, researchers found that family structure had no consistent effects on grades, with only one exception: "African American children in single-mother families where other adults are present got higher marks in reading at the beginning of first grade than did their counterparts in mother-only or mother–father families."[7]

It's worth noting that the two-parent advantage also applies to gay and lesbian couples, a point that gets lost in many debates over same-sex marriage, adoption, and custody issues. This is not a question that can be sidestepped by forbidding artificial insemination to unwed mothers or prohibiting homosexuals from adopting. Ninety-nine percent of children being raised in gay or lesbian families were born within marriage and live with a parent who came out after a divorce.[8]

Julie Schwartz Gottman, codirector of the Seattle Marital and Family Institute, compared three groups of adult women: one raised by divorced mothers who had stayed single, another by mothers who had divorced and remarried, and a third group raised by divorced mothers in lesbian couples. Using eighteen different scales of social adjustment, she found no significant differences among the groups, but there was a tendency for the daughters of heterosexual remarried women *and* of lesbian couples to exhibit more independence and leadership qualities than daughters of women who divorced and remained single.[9]

Gottman's finding of normal adjustment in children of gay and lesbian families, with a slight advantage for those whose parents had partners, has been confirmed by a considerable body of research. Children raised by gay and lesbian parents seem to be as well adjusted, on average, as children raised by heterosexual parents, with the same range of variation within each group. Dr. Charlotte Patterson found in her research with 4- to 9-year-old children that there were only two significant differences between children of lesbian and heterosexual parents: Children of lesbian mothers were more likely to report feelings of anger and fear than children of heterosexual mothers, but also more likely to report positive feelings such as contentment and a general sense of well-being. Researchers suspect this may be because they are more open than average about communicating feelings, good and bad.[10]

Children in gay and lesbian families face the disadvantage of negative feedback from outside the family, especially in early adolescence, but many such families have important countervailing strengths. Lesbian couples, for example, have greater parenting awareness skills, on average, than heterosexual parents. They are also more likely to share child care and housework equitably, a trait associated with higher parental satisfaction and child well-being in *all* types of families. Finally, and contrary to what stereotype might lead one to expect, lesbian mothers, in comparison to heterosexual single mothers, "have more congenial relations with ex-spouses and include men more regularly in their children's lives." When I talk with such mothers and the fathers of their children, they suggest that this is because sexual jealousy is not part of the ex-spouse dynamic. One man told me, "if she'd left me for another man, I'd have gone ballistic. But I can't compete with a woman and don't want to."[11]

Many people are concerned that lesbian or gay parents will "recruit" children to their sexual orientation. *Any* parent who proselytizes about sexuality has a problem—whether it's a father of a Spur Posse rapist bragging about the "virile specimens" he's sired or a homosexual parent urging a child to experiment with same-sex relations. But unlike the documented cases of fathers who encourage sons to "prove" their heterosexual masculinity, there is no evidence of gay and lesbian parents doing anything comparable with their children. The largest survey to date of adult sons of gay fathers found that more than 90 percent were heterosexual, no matter how long a time they had lived with their fathers. Similarly, comparisons of women raised by lesbian and heterosexual mothers show no differences in their gender identity or sexual orientation.[12]

What the research clearly reveals is that it is not helpful to children for gay or lesbian parents to hide their homosexuality. When children learn this information in adolescence or in custody disputes, it is harder for them to accept it than when they are given the information at a younger age and allowed to assimilate it gradually.[13]

The biggest problem for children of gay and lesbian parents is hostility or ridicule from the outside world. Yet youngsters whose parents are open and supportive seem to learn effective ways of coping—and it's worth remembering that in the long run it is not necessarily bad for adolescents to have something that sets them apart from peers. Being popular and successful in adolescence sometimes forestalls later growth, as youngsters peak too early and have difficulty moving on to new values and challenges. By contrast, painful adolescent experiences can contribute to a young person's future maturity and problem-solving abilities. This factor is also important to consider in evaluating how family changes such as divorce and remarriage affect children over the long haul.[14]

SINGLE-PARENT FAMILIES: STRENGTHS AND WEAKNESSES

Single-parent families have only one parent in the home to provide financial and emotional resources. When one adult is sad or angry, the whole house is upset. It also takes single-parent families longer than two-parent ones to recover from economic reverses. These are serious handicaps. Yet anthropologists point out that, "when combined with an extended network of concerned kin, the one-parent family often can tender more emotional support and offer more options to family members than an isolated nuclear family." In some situations, children of a single mother may get more attention and assistance from the mother's kin, for a greater total amount of support, than children whose mother moves away from her family to be with her husband.[15]

An African-American colleague of mine tells me that his single mother's lack of a stable marriage gave her the flexibility to link him up with a huge network of kin and close family friends. She sent him to live with whatever friends or relatives were employed or had contacts with successful men in the black community. He thus gained access to mentoring that his own irregularly employed (though never entirely absent) father could not provide. Today, my friend argues, the cutbacks in social programs, growth of unemployment, and increasing isolation of poor inner-city blacks from job networks make single motherhood much more problematic. Yet the community collapse that makes single motherhood harder also increases its likelihood, and heaping more blame on single mothers does not help.

As my friend's example suggests, single-parent families do not necessarily lack male role models. At lectures and workshops I've conducted, I have often been surprised by the vehemence with which many mothers in female-headed families deny that they are single parents. In many cases they appreciate the parenting that the nonresidential father contributes and want it to be recognized as a legitimate form of fathering. Research confirms their instincts. When nonresidential fathers behave as parents, rather than friends or entertainers, they can have a significant impact on children's development. "Fathers do not need to live with their child" to engage in monitoring, support, and other authoritative parenting practices, say researchers who have conducted an intensive study of rural Iowa families. It is also possible to involve never-married fathers with their children on a regular basis, and several innovative programs have had encouraging success in doing so.[16]

Still, there are certainly daily pressures on single parents that even the most supportive nonresidential parents cannot relieve. Adults in single-parent families, on average, spend less time supervising homework than adults in two-parent families, which can hold back a child's academic progress. Because they are often pressed for time, single parents are less likely than married ones to attend open-house nights at school, extracurricular activities, school programs, and parent–teacher association meetings. Yet such activities have been shown to be more effective than monitoring homework in promoting academic achievement. A teacher who has met a parent, for example, is more likely to work with the family in helping a child get past any temporary academic or behavior difficulties.[17]

Single parents spend more time talking with their children than married parents do, a behavior that can lead to accelerated academic and emotional maturity so long as the parent takes care not to confide too much anger or distress. (Ironically, children of mothers who have made a conscious choice for singlehood and do not go through the intense bitterness of a failed relationship have a potential advantage here. On the other hand, mothers in divorced families spend more time than either currently married or never-married women working on homework projects with their children.) Single parents are also more likely than two-parent families to praise good grades, which tends to produce higher academic performance. But single parents are more likely to get upset and angry when their children receive bad grades, a reaction that is associated with defiance and a further decline in grades.[18]

Adolescents in single-parent families face fewer pressures to conform to traditional gender roles. They tend to have greater maturity, autonomy, and self-confidence than teens in two-parent families. Depending on the dynamics of the family, this can lead either to more potentially dangerous risk taking *or* to more breadth and depth of thinking—or to both.

In some conditions, one researcher suggests, the lack of other domestic responsibilities and competing ties can make a single person a good candidate for a foster parent. Single adoptive or foster parents "may be particularly suitable for certain children who need more undivided attention."[19]

It's important to develop a balanced assessment of the strengths as well as the weaknesses in single-parent families because, despite periodic claims that our society glorifies single motherhood, one of the biggest problems for single-parent families is the persistent bias they face. In one study, teachers were shown a videotape of a child engaging in a variety of actions. The teachers consistently rated the child's actions much more negatively when they were told that he or she came from a single-parent family than when they believed the child came from an intact home. Children in one-parent families do just about as well as those in two-parent families on standardized tests, but they are rated much more negatively on subjective measures of achievement, such as teachers' evaluations or deportment ratings.[20]

The problems of single parenthood tend to be greatest among groups whose cultural values most emphasize two-parent families and paternal authority, and least among those who have a history of tolerance and support for single mothers. Sara McLanahan and Gary Sandefur found that family disruption is most likely to produce negative effects among Hispanics and least likely to do so among blacks, with whites falling in between. Living in a middle-income neighborhood has a strong positive effect for children from black single-parent homes, but children in white single-parent homes face a *greater* risk of rejection by peers when they live in middle-income neighborhoods than when they live in low-income neighborhoods.[21]

As these examples suggest, generalizations about family form and functioning are also complicated by many other factors. Variables such as the race, class, or ethnicity of the family have different impacts on children depending on their age, gender, individual temperament, and interaction with siblings. Higher proportions of boys than girls have trouble adjusting to divorce; higher proportions of girls have trouble adjusting to remarriage. In some cases, parenting styles that are destructive for white children are helpful to youths who must learn to deal with racial prejudice. Girls are disadvantaged by having many siblings, because they are often made to do too much caretaking. But they gain an advantage from having brothers because fathers are more likely to get involved with all their children when they have sons.[22]

The sex of the custodial parent has no clear relationship to the effectiveness of single-parent families. Some research in the early 1980s suggested that adolescents did better when living with the same-sex parent, but a 1992 study was unable to replicate this finding. There are, however, different dynamics in single-mother and single-father families. The greatest cause of stress for custodial single mothers is money. For custodial fathers, relations with the nonresidential mother are the biggest problem. Single fathers seem to monitor their children less effectively than single mothers. But when single mothers come into conflict with their boys, they tend to have longer, more drawn-out disputes, with increasing frustration on both sides.[23]

This problem is sometimes interpreted as a case of boys "needing a father's guidance," but the research doesn't bear this out. Stories I hear from single mothers and their children suggest that one of the reasons single mothers and adolescent boys often come into conflict is precisely because they have been so intimate in the past and are therefore more ambivalent about the normal process of adolescent disengagement. The boys seem threatened by the ties they still feel, and may find it necessary to assert their independence or supposed indifference all the more loudly. Mothers tell me that, in the absence of a partner, the child's normal adolescent withdrawal inspires a greater sense of loss, and that they must guard against a tendency to express their pain as anger and resentment.

In order to maintain communication, some mothers engage in a behavior that works very well with adult males, but has the effect of further frightening their sons: Mom redoubles her efforts to demonstrate, in words and body language, an intense interest in everything her child tells her. The mother feels as if she is demonstrating her attention and respect, which she knows from experience is very flattering to an adult male. The teenager, however, already acutely self-conscious about being the object of attention, feels as if he is being subjected to the third degree. Many single mothers tell me that they have had to adopt a masculine technique that used to annoy them when they were married: diffusing emotional intensity by conducting conversations while in the process of doing something else—playing cards or watching television, for example.

One of the difficulties for single parents of either sex is setting clear limits and preserving generational boundaries. In a two-parent family, the parent looks to the other parent for confirmation: "Johnny doesn't do very well when he stays up late, so let's make bedtime 9 P.M., okay?" In a single-parent family, the natural need for confirmation often comes out this way: "Johnny, you don't do very well when you stay up late, so let's make your bedtime 9 P.M., okay?" For years, Johnny will happily reply, "okay." But by the time he reaches early adolescence, he is likely to start saying no, leaving the parent in the awkward position of either backing down or having to rephrase as a command something that had been posed as a request. And adolescence is a little late to *start* issuing parental commands. . . .[24]

The maximum stress for single-parent families usually occurs in the early teen years, as youngsters begin to demand more freedom from parental control. It's easier to wear a parent down when she or he has no ally to reinforce resistance to a child's insistence that "everybody else's parents let them." Thus single parents are apt to relinquish parental decision-making rights too early, which encourages negative forms of behavior in their children. However, it is by no means inevitable that single parents will fall into this trap. Studies that control for family process have found that single parenthood is *not* related to early teen sexual behavior, but *rules* about dating are. It is sometimes harder to establish and enforce such rules when one is alone, though, which is why it is often helpful for single parents to have another adult join the household for a while or to become regularly involved in family routines.[25]

The stresses of single parenthood can be a challenge to effective child rearing. But as psychologist Bonnie R. Strickland puts it, "well-adjusted children of both sexes can be reared in families of varying configurations." The most critical ingredient in such families is how well the main caregiver functions. And those who care about the future of children ought to be supporting a wide range of social policies and programs to make sure that children's caregivers, whether they live singly or with a partner, have the resources they need to function well.[26]

REMARRIAGE AND STEPFAMILIES

The contradictory data on stepfamilies also illustrate the problem with sweeping generalizations about family structure. While remarriage tends to reduce stresses associated with economic insecurity, some studies suggest that children in stepfamilies, taken as a whole, have the same added risks for emotional problems as do children in one-parent families; they are actually *more* likely to repeat a grade than children whose mothers have never married. Yet most stepfamilies work quite well. In a recent long-term, ongoing government study, 80 percent of children in stepfamilies were judged to be doing well psychologically—not a whole lot worse than the 90 percent in intact biological families. The large majority of stepparents and children in one national survey rated their households as "relaxed" and "close," while less than one-third described their households as "tense" or "disorganized." Sibling conflict, found in all types of families, was only slightly more frequent in families with stepfathers.[27]

The trouble with generalizing about stepfamilies is that they are even more complicated and varied than other family types because there are so many possible routes to forming them. Kay Pasley and Marilyn Ihinger-Tallman have identified nine "structurally distinct" types of remarried families, depending on the custody and visitation arrangements of each partner, the presence of children from the new marriage, and whether there are children from one or both of the remarried parents' former families. The challenges of blending a new family mount with the complexity of the combinations that are being put together.[28]

There seem to be two pieces of advice we can confidently give to parents considering remarriage. The first is *not* to marry just to find a mother or father for your child. While remarriage may be helpful for single-parent families experiencing economic distress, those with adequate financial resources may find that their children's adjustment and academic performance are initially set back. Many children take longer to adjust to remarriage than to divorce, especially when they are teens.[29]

But the second piece of advice is not to be scared off. Most stepfamilies do well, and a good relationship with a stepparent does appear to strengthen a child's emotional life and academic achievement.[30]

Although stepfamilies create new stresses and adaptive challenges, write researchers Mavis Hetherington and James Bray, they "also offer opportunities for personal growth and more harmonious, fulfilling family and personal relationships." Children gain access to several different role models, get the chance to see their parents in a happier personal situation than in the past, and can benefit from the flexibility they learn in coping with new roles and relations.[31]

The most important thing to grasp about stepfamilies is that they require people to put aside traditional assumptions about how a family evolves and functions. Since the parent–child relationships predate the marriage, each parent and child brings a history of already formed family values, rules, rituals, and habits to the new household. This situation can lead to conflict and misunderstanding. Research does not support the stereotype that children in stepfamilies normally suffer from conflicting loyalties, but there is often considerable ambiguity about parenting roles and boundaries. For adolescents, the situation can be particularly tense. Their understandable resentment of the newcomer may cause their age-appropriate distancing from the biological parent to proceed too rapidly.[32]

Another major challenge to stepfamilies lies in the fact that traditional gender roles often conflict with the new family structure. As therapists Monica McGoldrick and Betty Carter put it, "if the old rules that called for women to rear children and men to earn and manage the financing are not working well in first-marriage families, which they are not, they have absolutely no chance at all in a system where some of the children are strangers to the wife, and where some of the finances include sources of income and expenditure that are not in the husband's power to control"—for example, alimony or child support.[33]

For stepfamilies to meet the needs of both adults and children, they have to create a new family "culture" that reworks older patterns into some kind of coherent whole, allowing members to mourn losses from the previous families without cutting off those relationships. The main barriers to doing this include leftover conflict from previous marriages, unrealistic expectations about instant bonding within the new family, and attempts to reproduce traditional nuclear family norms.[34]

As Lawrence Ganong and Marilyn Coleman point out, stepfamilies that try to function like a first-marriage nuclear family "must engage in massive denial and distortion of reality," pretending that former spouses, with their separate family histories, do not exist and cutting members off from important people or traditions in their life. This is not healthy. Nor is it realistic for the biological parent in the household to expect to have sole control over child-rearing decisions. Thus stepfamilies need to have "more permeable boundaries" than nuclear families usually maintain. And a stepparent–stepchild relationship probably *should* be less emotionally close than a parent–child relationship.[35]

Old-fashioned gender roles pose another problem for stepfamilies. *Stepmother* families have more conflicts, many specialists believe, because both women and men often expect the wife to shoulder responsibility for child care and for the general emotional well-being of the family. A stepmother may therefore try to solve problems between her husband and his children or the children and their biological mother, which sets the stepmother up to be the villain for both the children and the ex-wife. In stepfather families, a woman having trouble with her children may push her new husband to assume a disciplinary role far too early in the marriage, which tends to set back or even derail his developing relationship with the children.[36]

Therapists recommend that stepfamilies be encouraged to see the problems they face as a consequence of their structural complexities, not of ill will or personal inadequacy. Indeed, many of the difficulties may actually be a result of previous strengths in earlier family arrangements—the woman's desire to make relationships work, for example, or the children's strong commitments to older ties and habits. Hetherington found that sons "who were high in self-esteem, assertiveness, and social competence before the remarriage" were most likely to start out being "acrimonious and negative toward stepfathers." In the long run, though, these boys were especially likely to accept and benefit from a stepfather's addition to the household. Boys who were close to their mothers in the single-parent family tend to resent the establishment of a strong marital alliance in the new stepfamily. Girls are more likely to welcome a close marital relationship, possibly because it serves as a buffer "against the threat of inappropriate intimacy between stepfathers and stepdaughters."[37]

Experts agree that stepfamilies need to develop new norms permitting parental collaboration across household boundaries. They need to facilitate interactions between children and extended kin on the noncustodial parent's side of the family. They must let go of romantic fantasies about being able to start over. They also have to become much more flexible about gender roles. The biological parent, whether male or female, should be the primary parent, which means that women must control their tendency to fix everybody's emotional problems and men must control theirs to leave emotional intimacy to women. A new stepfather should resist his wife's desire to have him relieve her of disciplinary duties; similarly, a new wife should resist a husband's pressure to take on maternal roles such as managing schedules, supervising housework, or even making sure the kids remember their lunches on the way to school.[38]

What seems to work best is for a stepparent to initially play the role of camp counselor, uncle, aunt, or even sitter—someone who exercises more adult authority than a friend but is less responsible for direction and discipline than a parent. Behaving supportively toward stepchildren is more effective than trying to exercise control, although stepparents should back up their partners' disciplinary decisions in a matter-of-fact manner and help to keep track of children's whereabouts. Stepparents of adolescents have to recognize that even under the best circumstances, resistance to them is likely to continue for some time. If stepparents understand this reaction as normal, they can control their own natural impulse to feel rejected and to back away.[39]

Parenting in stepfamilies requires a thick skin, a sensitive ear, and a highly developed sense of balance. A successful stepfamily has to tolerate ambiguous, flexible, and often somewhat distant relationships, without allowing any member to disengage entirely. It has to accept a closer relationship between biological parent and child than between stepparent and child without letting that closeness evolve into a parent–child coalition that undermines the united front of the marriage partners. And effective communication skills are even more important in stepfamilies than they are in other kinds of families.[40]

These tasks are challenging, which may be why stepfamilies take longer to come together as a unified team, are more vulnerable to disruption, and often experience renewed turmoil during adolescence. But Jan Lawton, director of the Stepfamily Project in Queensland, Australia, points out that while the divorce rate among remarried families is high in the first two years, it then slows down. After five years, second marriages are more stable than first ones. And researchers have found that even modest, short-term training in communication and problem solving can dramatically increase the stability of stepfamilies.[41]

REVIEW QUESTIONS

1. The author of this reading teaches both history and family studies. Why is this particular combination of disciplines important?
2. Compare and contrast the three styles of parenting and explain why one is most effective.

3. List two disadvantages of the traditional two-parent, male-breadwinner family.
4. Summarize and comment on the results of the research by Julie Schwartz Gottman on adult women raised by divorced mothers who stayed single, divorced mothers who remarried, and divorced mothers in lesbian couples.
5. What is the main challenge for children in gay and lesbian families?
6. Summarize the strengths and weaknesses of single-parent families that Coontz discusses.
7. Single parenthood tends to be most disruptive in which ethnic/cultural group, and least disruptive in which ethnic/cultural group?
8. True or False: The sex of the custodial parent has no clear relationship to the effectiveness of single-parent families.
9. How can old-fashioned gender roles lead to the stepmother being viewed as a villain?
10. Fill in the blanks: "Parenting in stepfamilies requires a _____ _____, a sensitive ear, and a highly developed _____ _____ _____."

PROBES

1. "I don't know many parents, in any kind of family, who are confident that they've got it right," Coontz writes. Why is this important for parents and children to understand?
2. "... a conflicted marriage," Coontz writes, "can actually be worse for a child than a divorce." Explain.
3. How do you respond to Coontz's review of research that finds similar problems and similar success potential in families headed by heterosexual and gay or lesbian parents?
4. In some cases, single mothers learn that they can communicate best with their adolescent sons when they conduct conversations while playing cards or watching television. Explain why this works.
5. Explain what Coontz means when she writes, "the most important thing to grasp about stepfamilies is that they require people to put aside traditional assumptions about how a family evolves and functions."
6. Reflect on your own experience growing up. What kind(s) of family structure did you experience? Which of the family strengths and weaknesses that Coontz discusses did you experience? Where do your experiences confirm or reinforce what Coontz says? In what ways was your experience different?

NOTES

1. Laurence Steinberg, Nina Mounts, Susie Lamborn, and Sanford Dornbusch, "Authoritative Parenting across Varied Ecological Niches," *Journal of Research on Adolescence* 1 (1991), p. 19. The classic work on parenting styles was done by Diana Baumrind. See, for example, "Child

Care Practices Anteceding Three Patterns of Preschool Behavior," *Genetic Psychology Monographs* 75 (1967); "Current Patterns of Parental Authority," *Developmental Psychology Monographs* 4 (1971); "Parental Disciplinary Patterns and Social Competence in Children," *Youth and Society* 9 (1978).

2. Mary Elizabeth Curtner-Smith and Carol E. MacKinnon-Lewis, "Family Process Effects on Adolescent Males' Susceptibility to Antisocial Peer Pressure," *Family Relations* 43 (October 1994), pp. 462, 466; James Patrick Connell, Margaret Beale Spencer, and J. Lawrence Aber, "Educational Risk and Resilience in African-American Youth: Context, Self, Action, and Outcomes in School," *Child Development* 54 (1994), p. 504; Richard A. Mendel, *Prevention or Pork? A Hard-Headed Look at Youth-Oriented Anti-Crime Programs* (Washington, D.C.: American Youth Public Forum, 1995), pp. 4–5.

3. See Stephanie Coontz, *The Way We Never Were,* chapters 9 and 11. See also "Men Benefit More from Marriage," *Olympian,* October 12, 1993, p. D6; Betty Holcomb, "Why Is Everybody Picking on Working Moms?" *Working Mother,* January 1992, p. 49.

4. Arlie Hochschild with Anne Machung, *The Second Shift: Working Parents and the Revolution at Home* (New York: Viking, 1989), pp. 211–212; Anita Shreve, *Remaking Motherhood: How Working Mothers Are Shaping Our Children's Future* (New York: Viking, 1987); Harriet Mischel and Robert Fuhr, "Maternal Employment: Its Psychological Effects on Children and Their Families," in Sanford Dornbusch and Myra Strober, eds., *Feminism, Children, and the New Families* (New York: Guilford, 1988).

5. Martha Moorehouse, "Work and Family Dynamics," in Philip Cowan, Carolyn Pape Cowan, and Patricia Kerig, eds., *Family, Self, and Society: Toward a New Agenda for Family Research* (Hillsdale, N.J.: Lawrence Erlbaum, 1993), p. 271.

6. James A. Levine with Edward W. Pitt, *New Expectations: Community Strategies for Responsible Fatherhood* (New York: Families and Work Institute, 1995), p. 35.

7. Doris R. Entwisle and Karl L. Alexander, "Family Type and Children's Growth in Reading and Math Over the Primary Grades," *Journal of Marriage and the Family* 58 (May 1996), p. 341 (emphasis added).

8. David K. Flaks, Ilda Fischer, Frank Masterpasqua, and Gregory Joseph, "Lesbians Choosing Motherhood: A Comparative Study of Lesbian and Heterosexual Parents and Their Children," *Developmental Psychology* 31 (1995), p. 105.

9. Julie Schwartz Gottman, "Children of Gay and Lesbian Parents," in Frederick W. Bozett and Marvin B. Sussman, eds., *Homosexuality and Family Relations* (New York: The Haworth Press, 1990).

10. John Laird and Robert-Jay Green, eds., *Lesbians and Gays in Couples and Families: A Handbook for Therapists* (San Francisco: Jossey-Bass, 1996); Adele Eskeles Gottfried and Allen W. Gottfried, eds., *Redefining Families: Implications for Children's Development* (New York: Plenum, 1994), p. 225; Flaks et al., "Lesbians Choosing Motherhood," pp. 105–113; Daniel

Goleman, "Gay Parents Called No Disadvantage," *New York Times*, December 2, 1992, p. B7; Bianca Cody Murphy, "Difference and Diversity: Gay and Lesbian Couples" (New York: The Haworth Press, 1994); Charlotte Patterson, "Children of the Lesbian Baby Boom: Parents' Division of Labor and Children's Adjustment," *Developmental Psychology* 31 (1995).

11. Gottfried and Gottfried, eds., *Redefining Families*, p. 225; Flaks et al., "Lesbians Choosing Motherhood," p. 105; Esther Rothblum, ed., "Mental Health of Lesbians and Gay Men" (Special Issue), *Journal of Consulting and Clinical Psychology* 63 (1994); Patterson, "Children of the Lesbian Baby Boom," p. 115; Jan Hare and Leslie Richards, "Children Raised by Lesbian Couples: Does Context of Birth Affect Father and Partner Involvement?" *Family Relations* 42 (1993), p. 254.

12. J. Michael Bailey, David Bobrow, Marilyn Wolfe, and Sarah Mikach, "Sexual Orientation of Adult Sons of Gay Fathers," *Developmental Psychology* 31, no. 1 (1995), p. 124; Gottman, "Children of Gay and Lesbian Parents"; Laird and Green, *Lesbians and Gays in Couples and Families*. The Spur Posse father was quoted in the *New York Times*, March 29, 1993, p. A9.

13. Diana Baumrind, "Commentary on Sexual Orientation," *Developmental Psychology* 31 (1995), p. 125; Gottman, "Children of Gay and Lesbian Parents," p. 191; personal interview with Dr. Gottman.

14. Gottman, "Children of Gay and Lesbian Parents," p. 191; Gottfried and Gottfried, *Redefining Families*, p. 25; Arlene Skolnick, "The Family Revisited: Themes in Recent Social Science Research," *Journal of Interdisciplinary History* 4 (1975), p. 710; Jean MacFarlane, "Perspectives on Personality Consistency and Change from the Guidance Study," *Vita Humana* 7 (1964), p. 123.

15. Carol Stack, *All Our Kin: Strategies for Survival in a Black Community* (New York: Harper and Row, 1974); Barbara Bilge and Gladis Kaufman, "Children of Divorce and One-Parent Families: Cross-Cultural Perspectives," *Family Relations* 32 (January 1983), p. 69.

16. Ronald L. Simons and Associates, *Understanding Differences Between Divorced and Intact Families: Stress, Interaction, and Child Outcome* (Thousand Oaks, Calif.: Sage, 1996), p. 16; Theodora Lurie, "Fathers and Families: Forging Ties That Bind," *USA Today Magazine*, May 19, 1993; Sandra Danziger and Norma Radin, "Absent Does Not Equal Uninvolved: Predictors of Fathering in Teen Mother Families," *Journal of Marriage and the Family* 52 (1990); James Levine, Dennis Murphy, and Sherrill Wilson, *Getting Men Involved: Strategies for Early Childhood Programs* (New York: Scholastic, 1993).

17. Simons and Associates, *Understanding Differences Between Divorced and Intact Families*, p. 224; Mary Tabor, "Comprehensive Study Finds Parents and Peers Are Most Crucial Influences on Students," *New York Times*, August 7, 1996, p. A12.

18. Sara S. McLanahan, Nan Marie Astone, and Nadine F. Marks, "The Role of Mother-Only Families in Reproducing Poverty," in A. Huston, ed.,

Children and Poverty (New York: Cambridge University Press, 1991), p. 58;
Nan Marie Astone and Sara S. McLanahan, "Family Structure, Parental
Practice and High School Completion," *American Sociological Review* 56
(June 1991), p. 318; Alan Acock and David Demo, *Family Diversity and
Well-Being* (Thousand Oaks, Calif.: Sage, 1994), pp. 124–125; E. Mavis
Hetherington, "Coping with Family Transitions: Winners, Losers, and
Survivors," *Annual Progress in Child Psychiatry and Child Development* (New
York: Brunner/Mazel, 1990), p. 228; Leslie N. Richards and Cynthia J.
Schmlege, "Problems and Strengths of Single-Parent Families: Implications
for Practice and Policy," *Family Relations* 42 (1993), p. 278; Sanford
Dornbusch and Kathryn Gray, "Single-Parent Families," in Dornbusch and
Strober, *Feminism, Children, and the New Families* (New York: Guilford,
1988), pp. 286–287, 292; Nancy Morrison, "Successful Single-Parent
Families," *Journal of Divorce and Remarriage* 22 (1995).

19. Mukti Jan Campion, *Who's Fit to Be a Parent?* (New York: Routledge, 1995),
p. 216.

20. David Demo and Alan Acock, "The Impact of Divorce on Children," in
Alan Booth, ed., *Contemporary Families: Looking Forward, Looking Back*
(Minneapolis: National Council on Family Relations, 1991), p. 170; B. Berg
and R. Kelly, "The Measured Self-Esteem of Children from Broken, Rejected
and Accepted Families," *Journal of Divorce* 2 (1979); Barbara Cashion,
"Female-Headed Families: Effects on Children and Clinical Implications,"
Journal of Marital and Family Therapy 8, no. 2 (April 1982), p. 77; Lawrence H.
Ganong, Marilyn Coleman, and Dennis Mapes, "A Meta-analytic Review of
Family Structure Stereotypes," *Journal of Marriage and the Family* 52 (May
1990), p. 293; Blechman, "Children with One Parent," *Journal of Marriage
and the Family* 44 (1982), pp. 186, 189; Joseph Guttmann, Nehemia Geva,
and Sally Gefen, "Teachers' and School Children's Stereotypic Perception of
the Child of Divorce,'" *American Educational Research Journal* 25 (1988);
Sanford Dornbusch and Kathryn Gray, "Single-Parent Families," in
Dornbusch and Strober, *Feminism, Children, and the New Families*, pp. 286,
288; Krantz, "Children and Divorce," p. 255; Valerie Polakow, *Lives on the
Edge: Single Mothers and Their Children in the Other America* (Chicago:
University of Chicago Press, 1993); Doris R. Entwisle and Karl L.
Alexander, "A Parent's Economic Shadow: Family Structure Versus Family
Resources as Influences on Early School Achievement," *Journal of Marriage
and the Family* 57 (May 1995), p. 399. Stigmatization, or anxiety about it, can
also affect "objective" test scores. Dr. Claude Steele of Stanford University
found that when blacks and whites are given a test and told it is to measure
their abilities, most black students score below most whites. When a similar
mix of students is told it's just a lab test, with no practical purpose, the
difference between black and white scores is insignificant (Norman
Lockman, "Bell Curve Sure to Draw Fire," *Olympian*, November 24, 1994).

21. Bette J. Dickerson, *African American Single Mothers: Understanding Their
Lives and Families* (Thousand Oaks, Calif.: Sage, 1995); Sara McLanahan,

"The Consequences of Single Motherhood," *American Prospect,* Summer 1994, p. 49; Frank Furstenberg, Jr., and Andrew Cherlin, *Divided Families: What Happens to Children When Parents Part* (Cambridge, Mass.: Harvard University Press, 1991), pp. 99, 103, 105; Janis Kupersmidt, Pamela Griesler, Melissa DeRossier, Charlotte Patterson, and Paul Davis, "Childhood Aggression and Peer Relations in the Context of Family and Neighborhood Factors," *Child Development* 66 (1995), pp. 369–370.

22. Diana Baumrind, "An Exploratory Study of Socialization Effects on Black Children: Some Black–White Comparisons," *Child Development* 43 (1972); John Lewis McAdoo, "A Black Perspective on the Father's Role in Child Development," *Marriage and Family Review* 9 (1986); George Knight, Lynn Virdin, and Mark Roosa, "Socialization and Family Correlate of Mental Health Outcomes Among Hispanic and Anglo Children: Consideration of Cross-Ethnic Scalar Equivalence," *Child Development* 65 (1994), pp. 220–221; Carl Husemoller Nightingale, *On the Edge: A History of Poor Black Children and Their American Dreams* (New York: Basic Books, 1993); Judith Blake, "Number of Siblings and Personality," *Family Planning Perspectives* 23 (1991), p. 272; Judith Blake, *Family Size and Achievement* (Los Angeles: University of California, 1989); D. B. Downey, "When Bigger Is Not Better: Family Size, Parental Resources, and Children's Educational Performance," *American Sociological Review* 60 (1995); Kathleen Harris and S. Philip Morgan, "Fathers, Sons, and Daughters: Differential Paternal Involvement in Parenting," *Journal of Marriage and the Family* 53 (1991).

23. E. Mavis Hetherington and W. Glenn Clingempeel, *Coping with Marital Transitions: A Family Systems Perspective* (Chicago: Monographs of the Society for Research in Child Development, Serial No. 227, vol. 57, 1992), pp. 3–4; Gottfried and Gottfried, *Redefining Families,* p. 106; Barbara J. Risman and Kyung Park, "Just the Two of Us: Parent–Child Relationships in Single-Parent Homes," *Journal of Marriage and the Family* 50 (November 1988), p. 1059; Leslie N. Richards and Cynthia J. Schmlege, "Problems and Strengths of Single-Parent Families: Implications for Practice and Policy," *Family Relations* 42 (1993), p. 282; Mary Elizabeth Curtner-Smith and Carol E. MacKinnon-Lewis, "Family Process Effects on Adolescent Males' Susceptibility to Antisocial Peer Pressure," *Family Relations* 43 (October 1994), p. 466; Christy Buchanan, Eleanor Maccoby, and Sanford Dornbusch, "Adolescents and Their Families After Divorce: Three Residential Arrangements Compared," *Journal of Research on Adolescence* 2 (1992), pp. 285–286.

24. Robert E. Emery and Michele Tuer, "Parenting and the Marital Relationship," *Parenting: An Ecological Perspective* (Hillsdale, N.J.: Lawrence Erlbaum, 1993), p. 128; Cowan et al., "Transitions to Parenthood: His, Hers, and Theirs," *Journal of Family Issues* 6 (1986); Philip A. Cowan and Carolyn Pape Cowan, "Changes in Marriage During the Transition to Parenthood: Must We Blame the Baby?" in G. Y. Michaels and W. A. Goldberg, eds., *The Transition to Parenthood: Current Theory and Research*

(Cambridge: Cambridge University Press, 1988). Most of my evidence for the idea that financially secure single mothers may have an easier time in the first few months comes from stories I have been told at workshops around the country, and may therefore not be representative. Some written support for this impression is provided by Margaret Louise Fox, *Unmarried Adult Mothers: A Study of the Parenthood Transition from Late Pregnancy to Two Months Postpartum* (Boston University School of Education, Ann Arbor, Mich.: University Microfilms International, 1979).

25. Mel Hovell, Carol Sipan, Elaine Blumberg, Cathie Atkins, C. Richard Hofstetter, and Susan Kreitner, "Family Influences on Latino and Anglo Adolescents' Sexual Behavior," *Journal of Marriage and the Family* 56 (November 1994), p. 973.

26. Bonnie Strickland, "Research on Sexual Orientation and Human Development: A Commentary," *Developmental Psychology* 31 (1995), p. 139.

27. Barbara Dafoe Whitehead, "Dan Quayle Was Right," *Atlantic Monthly*, April 1993, p. 71; "School Dropout Rates for Families," *USA Today*, March 15, 1993; "Stepfamilies Aren't Bad for Most Kids," *USA Today*, August 17, 1992; Frank Mott, "The Impact of Father Absence from the Home on Subsequent Cognitive Development of Younger Children," Paper delivered at the American Sociological Association, August 1992; Furstenberg and Cherlin, *Divided Families*, p. 89; Andrew J. Cherlin and Frank F. Furstenberg, Jr., "Stepfamilies in the United States: A Reconsideration," *Annual Reviews in Sociology* 20 (1994), p. 372.

28. Kay Pasley and Marilyn Ihinger-Tallman, "Stress and the Remarried Family," *Family Perspectives* 12 (1982), p. 187.

29. James Bray and Sandra Berger, "Developmental Issues in Stepfamilies Research Project: Family Relationships and Parent–Child Interactions," *Journal of Family Psychology* 7, no. 1 (1993), p. 86; Hetherington and Clingempeel, *Coping with Marital Transitions*, pp. 205–206; William S. Aquilino, "The Life Course of Children Born to Unmarried Mothers: Childhood Living Arrangements and Young Adult Outcomes," *Journal of Marriage and the Family* 58 (May 1996), p. 307.

30. E. Mavis Hetherington, "An Overview of the Virginia Longitudinal Study of Divorce and Remarriage with a Focus on Early Adolescence," *Journal of Family Psychology* 7 (1993); Kay Pasley and Marilyn Ihinger-Tallman, *Remarriage and Stepparenting: Current Research and Theory* (New York: Guilford, 1987), pp. 105–109; Bray and Berger, "Development Issues in Stepfamilies Research Project," p. 89.

31. Alan Booth and Judy Dunn, eds., *Stepfamilies: Who Benefits? Who Does Not?* (Hillsdale, N.J.: Lawrence Erlbaum, 1994); Virginia Rutter, "Lessons from Stepfamilies," *Psychology Today* (May/June 1994), p. 32.

32. Lawrence H. Ganong and Marilyn Coleman, *Remarried Family Relationships* (Thousand Oaks, Calif.: Sage, 1994), p. 122; Pasley and Ihinger-Tallman, *Remarriage and Stepparenting*, p. 108; Hetherington and Clingempeel, *Coping with Marital Transitions*, pp. 200–205.

33. Monica McGoldrick and Betty Carter, "Forming a Remarried Family," in McGoldrick and Carter, eds., *The Changing Family Life Cycle: A Framework for Family Therapy*, 3rd ed. (Boston: Allyn and Bacon, in press).

34. John Visher and Emily Visher, *Therapy with Stepfamilies* (New York: Brunner/Mazel, 1996); McGoldrick and Carter, "Forming a Remarried Family."

35. Demo and Acock, "Impact of Divorce on Children," pp. 201–202; Ganong and Coleman, *Remarried Family Relationships*, pp. 123–137; James Bray and David Harvey, "Adolescents in Stepfamilies: Developmental Family Interventions," *Psychotherapy* 32 (1995), p. 125; Visher and Visher, *Therapy with Stepfamilies*; McGoldrick and Carter, "Forming a Remarried Family."

36. Lynn White, "Growing Up with Single Parents and Stepparents: Long-Term Effects on Family Solidarity," *Journal of Marriage and the Family* 56, no. 4 (November 1994); Rutter, "Lessons from Stepfamilies," p. 66; Furstenberg and Cherlin, *Divided Families*, p. 78; McGoldrick and Carter, "Forming a Remarried Family"; John Visher and Emily Visher, *Old Loyalties, New Ties: Therapeutic Strategies with Stepfamilies* (New York: Brunner/Mazel, 1988).

37. E. Mavis Hetherington, "Presidential Address: Families, Lies, and Videotapes," *Journal of Research on Adolescence* 1, no. 4 (1991), pp. 341, 344.

38. Ganong and Coleman, *Remarried Family Relationships*; James Bray and Sandra Berger, "Noncustodial Father and Paternal Grandparent Relationships in Stepfamilies," *Family Relations* 39 (1990).

39. Mark Fine and Lawrence Kurdek, "The Adjustment of Adolescents in Stepfather and Stepmother Families," *Journal of Marriage and the Family* 54 (1992); Bray and Harvey, "Adolescents in Stepfamilies"; Margaret Crosbie-Burnett and Jean Giles-Sims, "Adolescent Adjustment and Stepparenting Styles," *Family Relations* 43 (October 1994); Hetherington and Clingempeel, *Coping with Marital Transitions*, pp. 10, 200–205; Visher and Visher, *Old Loyalties, New Ties*.

40. McGoldrick and Carter, "Forming a Remarried Family"; Visher and Visher, *Therapy with Stepfamilies*; Nancy Burrell, "Community Patterns in Stepfamilies: Redefining Family Roles, Themes, and Conflict Styles," in Mary Anne Fitzpatrick and Anita Vangelisti, eds., *Explaining Family Interactions* (Thousand Oaks, Calif.: Sage, 1995); Carolyn Henry and Sandra Lovelace, "Family Resources and Adolescent Family Life Satisfaction in Remarried Family Households," *Journal of Family Issues* 16 (1995); Marilyn Coleman and Lawrence H. Ganong, "Family Reconfiguring Following Divorce," in Steve Duck and Julia Wood, eds., *Confronting Relationship Challenges*, vol. 5 (Thousand Oaks, Calif.: Sage, 1995).

41. Rutter, "Lessons from Stepfamilies," pp. 60–62; Phyllis Bronstein, Miriam Frankel Stoll, JoAnn Clauson, Craig L. Abrams, and Maria Briones, "Fathering After Separation or Divorce: Factors Predicting Children's Adjustment," *Family Relations* 43 (October 1994), p. 478.

There are overlaps between the next reading and some of the other materials in *Bridges Not Walls*. For example, these authors discuss confirmation, a topic that is covered extensively in the third reading of Chapter 9. Galvin, Bylund, and Brommel also review how self-disclosure operates, and that is also one of the topics in Chapter 6. But the focus of this reading is different from the other chapters. These three authors concentrate on how these kinds of communicating can contribute to and detract from family intimacy. Another distinctive feature of this reading is that it consists mainly of summaries of social scientific research on family intimacy. The conclusions that are reviewed here are anchored in careful, empirical studies.

The research that is reviewed examines six major factors that contribute to the development of intimacy: talk, confirmation, self-disclosure, sexual communication, commitment, and forgiveness. By "talk," the authors mean direct and indirect messages that create and reflect investment in a relationship. Confirmation is a label for verbal and nonverbal messages that communicate recognition and acceptance. The authors describe how confirmation is centrally important in families.

Self-disclosure is, as they put it, "an important, complex, and difficult type of communication." The authors identify several patterns from self-disclosure research, including the findings that disclosure tends to be reciprocal, that women tend to be higher disclosers than men, and that negative disclosure occurs more often in highly intimate settings than in less intimate ones. Then they explain how family background, along with spousal, partner, and parent-child relationships all affect how disclosure functions in families. The level and pace of activity does, too. The authors note that in many families, needed disclosures are limited by schedule pressures and family members' multiple commitments. They also note that disclosure can sometimes be used manipulatively, but that positive disclosure is generally experienced as a welcome event that enhances intimacy.

Sexuality and communication is Galvin, Bylund, and Brommel's fourth main topic. After decades of being a taboo topic, sexuality is now recognized as a centrally important part of every family's life. This topic includes not only sexual relations that are part of the intimacy between spouses, but also the ways families socialize their members into sex and gender roles, and how parents communicate about sex with children. As the authors summarize, "sexuality, including sexual attitudes and behavior, may be viewed as a topic of communication, a form of communication, and a contributing factor to overall relational intimacy and satisfaction."

Fundamental perceptions, opinions, and beliefs about sexuality are strongly influenced by one's family of origin—the family unit in which a child spends the first five to nine years of his or her life. Young girls and boys learn very early, for example, what it means to be feminine or masculine, and this learning happens below the level of awareness, just like most of the rest of acculturation. As one author summarizes, "When we do begin having sex in our society, our beliefs about woman/man strongly influence whom we have sex with, what sexual things we do, where and when we will have sex, the reasons we agree, and the feelings we have."

Some of this acculturation happens in the interactions about sex and sexuality that children have—or don't have—with their parents. Some differences exist between heterosexual families and gay and lesbian couples with children. But Galvin, Bylund, and Brommel report that few families have any kind of ongoing discussions about sex, and that a significant majority of both children and parents reports dissatisfaction with family discussions about sexual issues. So there is considerable room for improvement, and this reading includes some guidelines and suggestions for better parent-child communication about sex and sexuality. The authors argue that "pressing issues such as AIDS, sexually transmitted diseases, and a high percentage of unwanted pregnancies necessitate such discussions."

The next section surveys commitment in families. The authors distinguish among want-to, ought-to, and have-to kinds of commitment. They discuss how both talk and effort define, build, and can destroy commitment.

The reading concludes with a discussion of forgiveness, a topic relegated in the past to popular and religious writings on relationships. Researchers are attempting to define the topic and track its important impact on family intimacy. In families where members have difficulty forgiving others, there is more aggression and what the authors call "negative reciprocity patterns." Gender differences in forgiveness call for additional research.

The long reference list at the end of this reading demonstrates the solid research support for the points the authors make. I hope you will be able to use their discussion both to understand more clearly the family communication you experienced in your past and to improve the family communication in your future.

Intimacy and Closeness Within Families

Kathleen M. Galvin, Carma L. Bylund, and Bernard J. Brommel

COMMUNICATION AS A FOUNDATION OF INTIMACY

Countless studies of enduring and/or healthy marriages or families emphasize the importance of communication as a hallmark of successful family relationships (Stinnett & DeFrain, 1985; Pearson, 1992; Covey, 1997). The terminology

varies but similar factors emerge. Robinson and Blanton (1993) identify key characteristics of enduring marriages as intimacy balanced with autonomy, commitment, communication, congruence, and, in some cases, religious orientation.
Pearson's study of lasting happy marriages discussed the importance of positive
perceptions, commitment, understanding, and unconditional acceptance.

In this section we will examine six major factors that serve to undergird the
development of communicated-related intimacy. These are talk, confirmation,
self-disclosure, sexual communication, commitment, and forgiveness. We will
also briefly address effort and sacrifice. Their function varies with the unique
marital or family system, its ethnic heritage, and the maturity of its members.
Because closeness is co-constructed in the ongoing management of both interdependence and independence, differences and struggles are inevitable.

Talk

There are direct and indirect messages that create and reflect investment in a relationship. Direct relational talk occurs when partners share with each other their
feelings and desire to grow in the relationship: "I love you." "It's so great to have
a sister to go through life with. We are a pair, no matter what." According to Duck
and Pond (1989), not only do relationships "affect or influence talk, but also talk
defines the relationship" (p. 26). Both direct communication and intentional
metacommunication are essential to developing and maintaining intimacy
(Schnarch, 1991). Talk creates its own rewards. For example, trust is inspired
when both partners communicate that the relationship is a priority—something
they want to invest in for their own benefit as well as their partner's benefit
(Avery, 1989, p. 30). Talk serves as the underpinning for connection, as will be
evident as different types of connecting talk are explored.

Confirmation

Confirming messages communicate recognition and acceptance of another human being—a fundamental precondition to intimacy. Sieburg (1973) provides
four criteria for confirming messages. A confirming message (1) recognizes the
other person's existence, (2) acknowledges the other's communication by responding relevantly to it, (3) reflects and accepts the other's self-experience, and
(4) suggests a willingness to become involved with the other.

Confirming responses may be contrasted with two alternative responses: rejecting and disconfirming. Whereas *confirming responses* imply an acceptance of
the other person, *rejecting responses* imply the other is wrong or unacceptable.
Confirming messages do not necessarily imply one person agrees with the
other, but responses such as "I see" display one's regard without expressing
agreement (Canary, Cody, & Manusov, 2000). Rejecting messages might include
such statements as "That's really dumb" or "Don't act like a 2-year-old."
Disconfirming responses send the message "You don't exist"; they are a direct
invalidation of the person. Disconfirming responses occur when a person is

ignored, talked about as if he or she is invisible, excluded from a conversation, or excluded from physical contact (Stafford & Dainton, 1994). Confirming communication is characterized by recognition, dialogue, and acceptance, which indicate a willingness to be involved.

Recognition   Verbally, one may confirm another's existence by using the person's name, including him or her in conversation, or just acknowledging the individual's presence. Comments such as "I missed you" or "I'm glad to see you" serve to confirm another person's existence. Nonverbal confirmation is equally important in the recognition process. Touch, direct eye contact, and gestures also may serve to confirm another person within norms of ethnic culture.

Dialogue   Dialogue implies an interactive involvement between two people. Comments such as "Because I said so" and "You'll do it my way or not at all" do not reflect a dialogical attitude, whereas "What do you think?" or "I'm upset—can we talk about it?" open the door to dialogue and mutual exploration. Nonverbal dialogue occurs in families in which appropriate affectionate displays are mutually shared.

Acceptance   Acceptance gives a powerful sense of being all right. "When we feel acceptance, even though disagreed with, we do not feel tolerated; we feel loved" (Malone & Malone, 1987, p. 73). Acceptance avoids interpreting or judging one another. Rather, it lets one another be. This may involve allowing yourself to hear things you really do not want to hear or acknowledging that you understand another's perspective.

Confirming behavior often reflects cultural backgrounds and one's family-of-origin. Persons who grew up in a nonexpressive family may have trouble satisfying the reassurance and recognition needs of a spouse. Cultural differences in the use of eye contact or touch may create disconfirming feelings for one partner. Family intimacy develops from each member's sense of acceptance and care. If one "learns to love by being loved," then one learns to confirm by being confirmed.

Self-Disclosure

Self-disclosure is an important, complex, and difficult type of communication. In an original definition, *self-disclosure* is described as occurring when one person voluntarily tells another personal or private things about himself or herself that the other is unable to discern in a different manner (Pearce & Sharp, 1973). It involves risk on the part of the discloser and a willingness to accept such information or feelings on the part of the other. Historically, scholars assumed that the most powerful and profound awareness of oneself occurs with one's simultaneous opening up to another human (Malone & Malone, 1987). Such openness is experienced through sharing and receiving self-disclosure.

Trust, the essence of which is emotional safety, serves as the foundation for self-disclosure because "trust enables you to put your deepest feelings and fears in the palm of your partner's hand, knowing they will be handled with care" (Avery, 1989, p. 27). Self-disclosure, trust, and intimacy are frequently linked. High mutual self-disclosure is usually associated with voluntary relationships that have developed a strong relational culture and are characterized by trust, confirmation, and affection. Yet, high levels of negative self-disclosure may occur at points in such relationships, resulting in conflict and anger.

Traditionally, self-disclosure has been considered a skill for fostering intimate communication within families. Jourard (1971), an early researcher, describes the optimal marriage relationship as one "where each partner discloses himself without reserve" (p. 46). Many current marriage and family enrichment programs support self-disclosing behavior, as do popular texts on the subject of marital or parent-child interaction (Stafford & Dainton, 1994). Premarital counseling often focuses on revealing areas of feelings or information not yet shared by the couple.

Yet, some cautions about unrestrained self-disclosure need to be considered, since it can be destructive, manipulative, or at least a utopian premise (Wilder & Collins, 1994). Petronio (1991) suggests the process of boundary management is ongoing as partners decide which feelings and thoughts they are willing to share with each other, understanding the cost of greater sharing is personal vulnerability. Satisfaction and disclosure have a curvilinear relationship; that is, relational satisfaction is greatest at moderate levels of disclosure (Littlejohn, 1992, p. 273). Wood and Inman (1993) argue that verbal emotional disclosure is a more feminine style of relating, whereas the more masculine style may privilege sharing joint activities. Accordingly, women seem to receive more self-disclosures than do men (Pearson, West, & Turner, 1995). Therefore, selective, rather than total, self-disclosure contributes to intimacy development. Essentially, self-disclosure is coordinated through a boundary management process tied to partner or family rules (Petronio, 2000)....

Family Background   Family-of-origin, cultural heritage, and gender set expectations that influence self-disclosing behavior. Ethnic heritage may influence the amount and type of disclosure. For example, in many Asian families, the degree of intimacy is prescribed by position and status and relies heavily on nonverbal communication to share critical feelings and important messages (Chung, 1992). Whereas Jewish families exhibit verbal skill and a willingness to talk about trouble and feelings, Irish families may find themselves at a loss to describe inner feelings (Galvin, in press).

Spousal Relationships   Although the research on gender and disclosure is inconclusive, some studies find female pairs tend to be more disclosive than male pairs (Cline, 1989). Generally, women tend to be higher disclosers than men; they disclose more negative information, they provide less honest information, and they disclose more intimate information (Pearson, 1989). These differences may reflect socialization of females and males. Yet, some studies do not find that women self-disclose more than men (Dindia, Fitzpatrick, & Kenny, 1997).

Partner Relationships   Marital self-disclosure studies reveal consistent findings across groups. According to Fitzpatrick (1987), self-report studies show a positive correlation between the self-disclosures of husbands and wives and between self-disclosure and marital satisfaction. Yet, a high disclosure of negative feelings is negatively related to marital satisfaction. In addition, dual-career couples appear to be more able to disclose to one another. Married men are less likely to disclose to friends than married women, although of married men and women who reported high self-disclosure within the marriage, only the women reported moderate to high disclosure to a friend (Tschann, 1988). Couples who insist on no secrets frequently discover such openness obliterates any sense of individuality (Imber-Black, 1998).

Parent-Child Relationships   Parent-child disclosure has received some attention, revealing that self-disclosure does not involve all family members equally. Most mothers receive more self-disclosure than fathers (Waterman, 1979). Parents perceived as nurturing and supportive elicit more disclosure from children who find those encounters rewarding. College students are more likely to disclose more information more honestly to same-sex best friends than to either parent (Tardy, Hosman, & Bradac, 1981). In many families, parental primacy invasion occurs as parents and growing children struggle with autonomy and closeness–boundary conflicts (Petronio, 1994). Parental invasion may be met with secrecy or confrontation. Although one might imagine stepfamily members would report more secrets and single-parent family members would report fewer secrets, Caughlin and colleagues (2000) report the degree of openness, number of topics, and function of secrets was consistent across stepfamilies, single-parent families, and two-parent biological families.

Such a brief review only highlights certain issues but indicates the complexity of a subject that some popular writers tend to treat simplistically as they encourage unrestrained, open communication in family relationships....

The Practice of Self-Disclosure   If you think about family relationships in terms of these characteristics, you can see ways in which family systems tend to encourage or discourage self-disclosure. Considering the time it takes to do the functional things in families, you can understand that little time or energy may be available for self-disclosure. According to Montgomery (1994), "While self-disclosure may have significant impact in close relationships, it does not occur with great frequency even between the happiest of partners" (p. 78). Finding everyday time to talk sets a context for the occasional self-disclosure. Partners can lead parallel lives and may never get in the habit of sharing their lives with each other (Schwartz, 1994). Vangelisti and Banski (1993) report that if couples hold *debriefing conversations* and talk about how their days went, they are more likely to experience marital satisfaction, because such conversations set the groundwork for discussing riskier topics. Hence, risk-taking communication is not likely to occur frequently within family life, but certain developmental or unpredictable stresses may trigger extensive amounts of personal discussion.

The self-disclosure process has an overlooked nonverbal component. A sequence of appropriate nonverbal signals occurring in the context of verbal disclosure also contribute significantly to mutual understanding. For example, nonverbal signals may tell a husband that his wife is surprised that he is unaware of her feelings about a topic (Duck, Miell, & Miell, 1984, p. 305). Duck and colleagues propose the term *intimation sequences* for these signals in which both partners intimate new levels of evolving awareness within a discussion. Parents may become skilled at reading a child's face and recognizing a desire or need to talk. Thus, verbal self-disclosure and nonverbal intimation sequences are bound together in face-to face interaction.

If high levels of disclosure occur mainly in dyads, how often does a parent of four children get time alone with each one of them? When do a stepparent and stepchild make time alone for themselves? Many family members never spend one-on-one time with each other, yet such time is important for openness to develop in their relationships.

Families create unique opportunities for self-disclosure. Joint living provides the potential for such interaction. Yet, this can take place only where positive social relationships, including trust, exist. Parents may break a child's trust unwittingly because they discussed the child's concern with another adult, not respecting the child's privacy. Unless disclosers indicate how private certain information is to them, another person may accidentally reveal that information to others and . . . damage the relationship.

In some involuntary family relationships, especially those involving stepfamilies, the bases of trust and liking may be missing, thereby reducing the likelihood of openness developing within the first five years (Galvin & Cooper, 1990).

One is likely to repeat self-disclosing if it is rewarded or met with a positive response. In a family that indicates satisfaction at knowing what the members are thinking or feeling, even if the information itself is not necessarily pleasant, continued self-disclosure is likely. If self-disclosure is met with rejecting or disconfirming messages, the level of sharing will drop significantly. Families with strong secrets may discourage self-disclosure in order to protect highly bounded areas.

Some people are dishonest or inaccurate in their disclosures (Berger & Bradac, 1982, p. 87). Although self-disclosure enhances intimacy development, it can be used to manipulate or control another family member. Partial or dishonest disclosures can undermine trust in a relationship. Sometimes young persons or immature adults engage in pseudo self-disclosure to gain something else from the relationship. In this process, they take advantage of the other. Unauthentic disclosures may be difficult to detect, but once discovered, they may interfere with future believability and mutual self-disclosure. In marriage, partners may be caught between desires for openness and protectiveness. A husband may be dismayed by his wife's weight gain, but he knows that bringing up his feelings would feed her low self-esteem.

Self-disclosure bears a direct relationship to family levels of cohesion and adaptation. An extremely cohesive family may resist negative self-disclosure because it would threaten the connectedness, particularly if the family has a low capacity for adaptation. For example, a highly cohesive family with a theme of "We can depend only on each other" would resist negative disclosures that might threaten security and cause internal conflict. Such a theme might be accompanied by rigid boundaries that would limit self-disclosures to outsiders.

Families with very low cohesion may tolerate negative self-disclosure but have difficulty with positive self-disclosure, which might lead to greater cohesion. Families with moderate to high adaptation and cohesion capacities may cope relatively well with the effects of high levels of positive or negative self-disclosure. Self-disclosure is a complicated process that may result in increased intimacy. In short, self-disclosure, or "sharing what's inside—even if what's inside isn't pretty—is the supreme act of faith in another" (Avery, 1989, p. 31).

Sexuality and Communication

How would you describe sexuality? As a series of isolated physical encounters? As an integral part of a growing relationship? Do you see marital sexuality as restricted to "being good in bed"? For most partners, sexuality within a marital relationship involves far more than just physical performance; it involves the partners' sexual identities, their history of sexual issues, their mutual perceptions of each others' needs, and the messages contained within sexual expression.

The quality of the sexual relationship affects, and is affected by, the other characteristics of intimacy—the affectionate/loving relationship and a deep, detailed mutual knowledge of the two partners. In their study of over 6,000 couples, Blumstein and Schwartz (1983) conclude that a good sex life is central to a good relationship. Schwartz (1994) reports the importance of equitable sexuality in peer marriages.

How would you describe sexuality within the family relationship? According to Maddock (1989), healthy sexuality reflects the balanced expression of sexuality in family structures that enhance the personal identity and sexual health of members and the system as a whole.

At both the marital and family level, sexual issues are linked directly to communication. In fact, "communication plays an important role in the development of intimate sexuality" (Troth & Peterson, 2000, p. 195). Sex communication implies "people exchanging verbal and nonverbal messages in a mutual effort to co-create meaning about sexual beliefs, attitudes, values, and/or behavior" (Warren, 2003). Sexuality, including sexual attitudes and behavior, may be viewed as a topic of communication, a form of communication, and a contributing factor to overall relational intimacy and satisfaction. Sprecher and McKinney (1994) suggest, "Sex is not only an act of communication or self-disclosure. Verbal and nonverbal communication is essential for the accomplishment of rewarding sexual episodes" (p. 206). Sheehy (1997) argues that it is important for partners and family members to talk about sex because sexuality is part of the essence of who we are, and not to talk about it sends messages that there is something wrong with it.

Although sexuality and intimacy may be experienced as disconnected or unrelated in certain relationships, we believe sexuality is directly related to intimacy in partner and family ties. In the following pages, sexuality will be explored in terms of socialization, parent-child communication, partner communication, and communication breakdowns.

Socialization and Sexuality   The basis for a mutually intimate sexual relationship reflects each partner's orientation toward sexuality, particularly that which is learned in the family-of-origin. An individual's sexuality remains closely intertwined with his or her intrapersonal, interpersonal, and environmental systems—systems that interlock yet vary in importance according to an individual's age.

The sexual dimensions of family life are tied strongly to gender identities, boundaries, and developmental change. Much of your sexual conduct was originally learned, coded, and performed on the basis of biosocial beliefs regarding gender identity, learned in your family-of-origin. Parents possess a set of gender-specific ideas about males and females developed from their childhood experiences and from "typical" behaviors of girls or boys of similar ages to their children. In addition, strong ethnic influences convey expectations about what it means to be a man or woman. This identity is so strong that efforts to alter such socialization patterns must occur very early or they will have little impact. Your personal identities include sexual/gender identity as a core component, which influences later sexual experiences.

Parent-Child Communication   Many of today's adults grew up in a home atmosphere of sexual silence and now live in a world of open sexual discussion. Much of what you learned about sexuality took place within the rule-bound context of your family. In the earlier discussion of communication rules, you may recall that many sex-related rules are negative directives—"Do not ...." The extent to which a family encourages or discourages talk about issues such as pregnancy, birth control, masturbation, menstrual cycles, the initial sexual encounters of adolescents, and the sexual intimacy of the parents is related to communication and sexuality rules (Yerby, Buerkel-Rothfuss, & Bochner, 1990).

Sex communication within the family has become more open in the past decades due to greater societal openness, media references to sex, concerns about health issues, and greater parent comfort. Data are sometimes contradictory in this area, however. In 1986, Fisher found that college students and parents in high communication families have more similar sexual attitudes than those in low communicative families. Even in recent years, however, a low percentage of families (10 to 15 percent) still has any kind of ongoing discussions about sex (Warren, 1995).

Frequently, teenagers are more comfortable discussing sex than are their parents. A study of students' attitudes about parent-child discussions on sex-related topics reports that teenagers believe parents need to learn how to communicate supportively and empathically, even if there is disagreement (Bonnell & Caillovet, 1991). Often, family communication about sexual issues remains indirect, resulting in confusion, misinformation, or heightened curiosity, although close to 40 percent of parents say they are talking frequently with their children about sex (Family Chats, 1998). Many parents "recognize the importance of communication and want to communicate with their children but they lacked good sexual communication role models in their own lives and are unaware of how and when to initiate sexual conversations" (Hutchinson, 2002, p. 246).

The research of Warren and Neer relying heavily on their Family Sex Communication Quotient (FSCQ) instruments is summarized in the following points:

- *Satisfaction with family discussions about sex is dependent on the key factor of mutual dialogue.* Furthermore, children are most satisfied with patterns of family communication about sex when parents help them feel comfortable, or at least free, to initiate discussions. Thus, for best results, parents must move beyond the role of initiators and into the role of facilitators.
- *The ability to communicate supportively about sex revolves around an attitude of openness.* Teens want parents to talk with them, not at them, and to avoid preachy messages. Parents who want only to give their children instructions and commands are likely to have little success as communicators in this area.
- *For discussions to have the greatest impact, they should become part of the family patterns well before children reach age 16.* Many parents tend to put off talking about sex with their children; and the longer they wait, the harder it is to start. On the other hand, early initiation of discussion tends to facilitate more frequent discussion as well as children's perceptions that their parents are effective communicators.
- *Parent-child communication about sex that is frequent and that is regarded as effective tends to facilitate children's open discussion with dating partners.* The resonance effect is at work here, as children go on to model what they have encountered at home (Warren, 2003, p. 320; used with permission).

Families differ greatly in their approach to sexuality. Maddock (1989) has described communication behaviors of *sexually neglectful, sexually abusive,* and *sexually healthy families.* In some "sexually neglectful" families, sex is discussed little or not at all. If it must be addressed, sexual communication occurs on an abstract level so direct connection is not made between the topic and the personal experience of family members (p. 133). Messages like the previous example communicate an underlying attitude of anxiety or displeasure, but the direct issue remains hidden. Veiled messages often continue through adolescence and into adulthood. According to Satir (1988), many families use the rule:

> "Don't enjoy sex—yours or anyone else's—in any form." The common beginning for this rule is the denial of the genitals except as necessary nasty objects. "Keep them clean and out of sight and touch. Use them only when necessary and sparingly at that" (pp. 124–125).

In some families, the marital boundary remains so closed around the area of sexuality that children never see their parents as sexual beings—no playful jokes, hugging, or tickling occurs in view of the children. In such cases, children may not learn that sexual expression is central to marital intimacy or that men and women can express their sexuality in any direct affectionate way.

Yet, in other families, the marital boundary is so open that children encounter incestuous behaviors as they are co-opted into spousal roles. This "sexually abusive" family is typically a closed, rigid system with boundary confusion between individuals and generations. Communication reflects a perpetrator-victim interaction pattern, especially in cross-gender relationships, resulting in marital conflict and lack of emotional intimacy (Maddock, 1989, p. 134). Yet, in both the sexually neglectful and sexually abusive families, sexual attitudes and sexual behavior are seldom addressed directly.

According to Maddock (1989), sexually healthy families are characterized by (1) respect for both genders; (2) boundaries that are developmentally appropriate and support gender identities; (3) effective and flexible communication patterns that support intimacy, including appropriate erotic expression; and (4) a shared system of culturally relevant sexual values and meanings. Sheehy (1997) argues that children should see their parents teasing each other and enjoying each other because parents "can make jokes, they can communicate that sexuality is sacred, because actually sex is a lot of things. It's not just one thing. And I think kids need to know and see that."

Maddock (1989) suggests that sexually healthy families communicate effectively about sex "using language that can accurately cover sexual information, reflect feelings and attitudes of members, and facilitate decision making and problem solving regarding sexual issues" (p. 135). Sex education is accurate and set in a context of family values transmitted across generations. Talking about sexuality has been avoided by a great majority of parents (Roxema, 1986). After interviewing women in their thirties regarding their mother-daughter conversations about sex, Brock and Jennings (1993) report that memories were primarily of negative, nonverbal messages, and limited discussion focused on warnings and rules. The women wished for openness and discussions of feelings and choices. Interestingly, most of these women excused their mothers for their silence or discomfort, but indicated a desire to do better with their own children.

You may have noticed that we have been discussing partners throughout this section in recognition of the multiple types of adult and young adult sexual partnerships that exist. Most of the research on sexual communication has been based on married or romantic heterosexual pairs. Yet, there are variations based on partnership type that are worth noting. . . .

In their study of relationship quality for child-free lesbian couples and those with children, Koepke, Mare, and Moran (1992) found that both groups reported happy and solid relationships but that couples with children, who had been together longer, scored higher on relationship satisfaction and sexual relationship satisfaction. Lesbian couples are more likely to report fusion-related struggles as they attempt to develop high levels of cohesion (Laird, 1996). In some cases, fusion is blamed for diminishing sexual interest. In their classic study of American couples, Blumstein and Schwartz (1983) note that gay males have sex more often in the early years of their relationship, but after 10 years, they have sex far less frequently than do married couples. Lesbians have sex less frequently than other couple types, yet are likely to be sexually exclusive in their partnerships. In same-sex couples, it is the more emotionally expressive partner who initiates sex most frequently.

Discussing one's own homosexuality with a child raises particular issues. Father disclosure strategies may be direct, such as open discussion, or indirect, such as taking a child to gay social events (Bozett, 1987). Children who showed the greatest acceptance were gradually introduced to the subject of homosexuality through printed material, discussion, and meeting gay family friends before full parental disclosure. . . .

Today, direct parent-child communication about sexuality is not only important for healthy family functioning but for the long-term physical health of family members. Pressing issues such as AIDS, sexually transmitted diseases, and a high percentage of unwanted pregnancies necessitate such discussions. Parents need to be able to address issues of safe sex practices and ways of talking about sex with their children. . . .

Commitment

"If you have to work at a relationship, there's something wrong with it. A relationship is either good or it's not." These words capture a naive but common belief about marital and family relationships. How often have you heard people argue that relationships should not require attention or effort? Yet it is only through commitment that a loving relationship remains a vital part of one's life.

Commitment implies intense singular energy directed toward sustaining a relationship. As such, it emphasizes one relationship and may limit other possibilities. "Commitment represents extended time orientation, and highly committed individuals should accordingly behave in ways that are consistent with this perspective, acting to ensure that their relationships endure and are healthy" (Rusbult, Drigotas, & Verette, 1994, p. 123).

Knapp and Taylor (1994) describe relational commitments as (1) want-to, (2) ought-to, and (3) have-to. Want-to commitment is based on personal choice and desire, usually rooted in positive feelings. Ought-to commitment stems from a sense of obligation based on a promise, a sense of guilt, or a fear of hurting another. Have-to commitment is based on the perception that there is no good alternative to maintaining membership in this relationship. Similarly, Johnson, Caughlin, and Huston (1999) identify three distinct types of commitment as personal, or wanting to stay in the relationship; moral, or feeling morally obligated to stay; and structural, or feeling constrained to stay regardless of the level of personal or moral commitment.

Another view of commitment includes personal dedication and constraints (Stanley, 1998). *Personal dedication* involves one's internal devotion to the relationship, whereas *constraint commitment* refers to factors that keep people in relationships regardless of devotion. The latter include religious beliefs, promises, children, finances, or social pressure. Frequently, partnerships and families are held together by a combination of these types of commitments. At good times, members *want-to* be connected; during rough times, members stick it out because they *ought-to*. Under difficult conditions, they may *have-to* stay together. Schnarch (1991) suggests that adult mature commitment in intimate relationships goes deeper than an equity model of reciprocity. In such relationships "the bittersweet awareness of immutable separateness heightens the salience of intimacy" (p. 118) because of the depth of the commitment.

Commitment is associated with higher relationship satisfaction and stability and with behaviors that maintain and enhance the quality of relationships (Flanagan et al., 2002). Commitment may carry people through rocky feuds. In their study of marriage renewal rituals, Baxter and Braithwaite (2002) found that their couples viewed commitment as a "lifetime promise to stay in the marriage, not a fair-weather declaration to be abandoned when maintaining the relationship became effortful" (p. 103).

In her exploration of a marital life of commitment during a period of geographic separation, Diggs (2001) examines her own marriage to explore a 24-year African American marriage from inside the relationship. She captures the intensity of connection, the gender differences in emphasizing emotional versus physical presence, and concludes by suggesting that their commitment is characterized by "displays of love, and physical presence (emotional and instrumental), and dialoguing to find a connection (*I feel ya*; refocus on the person or values that keeps a couple together; and the awareness of levels or areas of unity)" (p. 25).

Intensity, repetition, explicitness, and codification support commitment talk (Knapp & Vangelisti, 2000). As described in the discussion of verbal relational currencies, certain phrases need to be repeated, and certain ideas need to be emphasized or reaffirmed. Explicitness reduces misunderstanding: "I will stand behind you even if I don't agree," "We are brothers and that means I will support you." Such comments make the commitment quite clear. Codifying communication may be reflected in anything from love letters to a written agreement of rules for fighting to a marital contract. Commitment is not always easy; words may be hard to find and say. According to Knapp and Vangelisti, "The way we enact our commitment talk is at least as important, if not more so, than the content itself" (p. 298).

Effort and Sacrifice Many factors compete for attention in your life. Meeting home, work, school, friendship, and community responsibilities take tremendous time and effort. The nurturing of marital or family relationships often gets the time and energy that is "left over," a minimal amount at best. In most cases, this limited attention spells relational disaster. Unless familial ties receive high priority, relationships will "go on automatic pilot" and eventually stagnate or deteriorate.

Because the family operates within larger systems including work and school, each system impacts the other. In describing the tensions between work and home obligations, Blumstein and Schwartz (1983) refer to the interaction between "where people put their emotional energy (home versus work) and their commitment to their relationship" (p. 173). In this era of dual-career couples and families, commuter marriages, and high technology and subsequent job loss or relocation, family intimacy can be lost in the shuffle.

Only a conscious and shared determination to focus on the relationship can keep marital and family ties high on one's list of priorities. Many couples and families seek out opportunities to enrich their lives, to reaffirm their connection to work on their relationships. . . .

Forgiveness

What is the relational impact of saying "I forgive you"? And what might that statement really mean? Until recently, the concept of forgiveness primarily appeared in popular and religious writings on relationships. Yet, current work on repairing relationship includes an emphasis on forgiveness. Defining *forgiveness* is difficult because of multiple meanings. It may be viewed as "a transformation in which motivation to seek revenge and to avoid contact with the transgressor is limited" (Fincham & Beach, 2002, p. 240) but this does not reflect a relational focus. Essentially, all this definition implies is avoiding retaliation. Other definitions emphasize acknowledging the wrong but also changing one's heart to engage in positive attitudes or behaviors such as compassion, affection, generosity, and love. Kelley (2003) captures this intent, saying, "Forgiveness, at its best, is 'abandoning' the negative and 'fostering the positive'" (p. 224). Frequently, forgiveness implies an explicit renegotiation of the relationship that usually involves metacommunication.

Forgiveness appears directly related to family interactions given the long-term nature of family ties and the intensity of connections. According to Fincham and Beach (2002), "Paradoxically, those we love are the ones we are most likely to hurt and may not always be the ones with whom we communicate most effectively" (p. 239). In his study of close relationships, Kelley (1998) found that over 70 percent of respondents' motivations for forgiveness included love, restoring the relationship, and well-being of the other. He also found family members reported being less motivated to offer forgiveness because of love, restoring the relationships, or the other's behavior toward making up. He suggests that the obligatory nature of family relationships may create a sense of stability and resiliency. It seems self-evident that motivation and ability to discuss forgiveness depends on the severity of the transgressions; family reasons for forgiveness could range from an affair or violent act to an insult or sharing of another's secrets.

Not surprisingly, forgiveness and marital satisfaction are related. Fincham (2000; Fincham & Beach, 2002) found that marital unforgiveness may be especially associated with patterns of negative reciprocity because partners often hurt each other and initiate negative reciprocity patterns that work against intimacy. The authors also found unforgiveness to be related to partner psychological aggression, and that, for husbands, readiness to forgive is a strong predictor of wives' constructive communication. The current research on forgiveness indicates gender differences that need greater exploration.

Essentially, forgoing retaliation is unlikely to increase relational intimacy; only a proactive attempt to engage a family member in reconciliation has much chance for positively increasing constructive communication and intimacy.

CONCLUSION

. . . Think about the kinds of interactions you see in the families around you. Is most of their communication strictly functional? Do you see attempts at intimacy through confirmation or self-disclosure? Are these people able to demonstrate an ability to touch each other comfortably?

All human beings long for intimacy, but it is a rare relationship in which the partners (spouses, parents and children, siblings) consciously strive for greater sharing over long periods of time. Such mutual commitment provides rewards known only to those in intimate relationships.

REVIEW QUESTIONS

1. What is confirmation? When family members ignore or disregard someone in the family, what is the label for this behavior? How does it function?
2. How can self-disclosure be manipulative?
3. Why do you believe negative disclosure occurs more frequently in highly intimate settings than in less intimate ones?
4. What does it mean to say that relational satisfaction and self-disclosure have a curvilinear relationship?
5. What are "intimation sequences"? Why are they called this?
6. Paraphrase this statement by Galvin, Bylund, and Brommel: "Families with moderate to high adaptation and cohesion capacities may cope relatively well with the effects of high levels of positive or negative self-disclosure."
7. What's the difference between sex and gender? Between sex and sexuality?
8. Identify—privately, to yourself—two features of your gender identity and two beliefs about sexuality that you learned in your family of origin.
9. What four features characterize sexually healthy families, according to Maddock?
10. Distinguish among want-to, ought-to, and have-to commitments.
11. Explain what the authors mean when they say that forgiveness "implies an explicit renegotiation of the relationship that usually involves metacommunication."

PROBES

1. What are the similarities and differences between Galvin, Bylund, and Brommel's discussion of self-disclosure in families and the general discussions of self-disclosure in Chapter 6?
2. Do you believe that, in a marriage, open self-disclosure is virtually always beneficial, or do you believe that spouses have the right to—and should— manage what they disclose to one another, both to protect their own privacy and to avoid being manipulative?
3. Identify, from your own family experience, some effects of ethnicity on disclosure behavior.
4. Did multiple commitments and a fast-paced lifestyle affect disclosure among the members of your family of origin? Explain.
5. In your experience, what are some of the special challenges to self-disclosure in stepfamily relationships?
6. Do you agree that "children are most satisfied with their family sex communication pattern when parents help them feel free to initiate discussions"?
7. These authors claim that effective sex communication in the family influences the child's attitudes toward birth control more than institutional sex education. Do you agree or disagree? Explain.
8. Explain what it means to say that talk can both enhance and embody commitment.
9. What experience have you had with forgiveness that reinforces or extends what these authors say about this kind of communication?

REFERENCES

1. Avery, C. (1989). How do you build intimacy in an age of divorce? *Psychology Today, 23*, 27–31.
2. Baxter, L. A., & Braithwaite, D. O. (2002). Performing marriage: Marriage renewal rituals as cultural performance. *Southern Communication Journal, 67*, 94–109.
3. Berger, C. R., & Bradac, J. J. (1982). *Language and social knowledge*. London: Edward Arnold.
4. Blumstein, P., & Schwartz, P. (1983). *American couples*. New York: William Morrow.
5. Bonnell, K. H., & Caillovet, L. M. (1991, April). *Partners and communication barriers between teenagers and parents about sex related topics: A survey of teenagers in sex education classes*. Paper presented at the meeting of the Central States Communication Association, Chicago.
6. Bozett, F. (Ed.). (1987). *Gay and lesbian parents*. New York: Praeger.
7. Brock, L., & Jennings, G. (1993). What daughters in their 30s wish their mothers had told them. *Family Relations, 42*, 61–65.

8. Canary, D. J., Cody, M. J., Manusov, V. L. (2000). *Interpersonal communication: A goals-based approach* (2nd ed.). Boston: Bedford/St. Martin's.

9. Caughlin, J. P., Golish, T. D., Olson, L. N., Sargent, J. E., Cook, J. S., & Petronio, S. (2000). Intrafamily secretes in various family configurations: A communication boundary management perspective. *Communication Studies, 51,* 116–134.

10. Chung, D. K. (1992). Asian cultural commonalities: A comparison with mainstream American culture. In S. M. Furuto, R. Biswas, K. Murase, & F. Ross-Sheriff (Eds.), *Social work practice with Asian Americans.* Newbury Park, CA: Sage.

11. Cline, K. (1989). The politics of intimacy: Costs and benefit determining disclosure intimacy in male-female dyads. *Journal of Social and Personal Relationships, 6,* 5–20.

12. Covey, S. R. (1977). *The 7 habits of highly effective families.* New York: Golden Books.

13. Diggs, R. C. (2001, November). *Searching for commitment with a radical(izing) method: The experiences of an African-American long-distance married couple.* Paper presented at National Communication Association Convention. Atlanta, GA.

14. Dindia, K., Fitzpatrick, M. A., & Kenny, D. A. (1997). Self-disclosure in spouse and stranger interaction: A social relations analysis. *Human Communication Research, 23,* 388–412.

15. Duck, S., Miell, D., & Miell, D. (1984). Relationship growth and decline. In H. Sypher & J. Applegate (Eds.), *Communication by children and adults* (pp. 292–312). Beverly Hills: Sage.

16. Duck, S., & Pond, K. (1989). Friends, Romans and countrymen, send me your retrospectives: Rhetoric and reality in personal relationships. In C. Hendrick (Ed.), *Close relationships* (pp. 17–38). Newbury Park, CA: Sage.

17. Fincham, F. D. (2000). The kiss of the porcupines: From attributing responsibility to forgiving. *Personal Relationships, 7,* 1–23.

18. Fincham, F. D., & Beach, S. R. (2002). Forgiveness in marriage: Implications for psychological aggression and constructive communication. *Personal Relationships, 9,* 239–251.

19. Fitzpatrick, M. A. (1987). Marital interaction. In C. Berger & S. Chaffee (Eds.), *Handbook of communication science* (pp. 564–618). Newbury Park, CA: Sage.

20. Flanagan, K. M., Clements, M. L., Whitton, S. W., Portney, M. J., Randall, D. W., & Markman, H. J. (2002). Retrospect and prospect in the psychological study of marital and couple relationships. In J. P. McHale & W. S. Grolnick (Eds.), *Retrospect and prospect in the psychological study of families* (pp. 99–128). Mahwah, NJ: Lawrence Erlbaum.

21. Galvin, K. M. (in press). It's not all blarney: Intergenerational transmission of communication patterns in Irish-American families. In P. Cooper & R. Hoel (Eds.), *Intercultural communication.* Boston: Allyn and Bacon.

22. Galvin, K. M., & Cooper, P. (1990). *Development of involuntary relationships: The stepparent/stepchild relationship.* Paper presented at the

meeting of the International Communication Association Conference, Dublin, Ireland.

23. Hutchinson, M. K. (2002). The influence of sexual risk communication between parents and daughters on sexual risk behaviors. *Family Relations, 51,* 238–247.

24. Johnson, M. P., Caughlin, J. P., & Huston, T. L. (1999)). The tripartite nature of marital commitment: Personal, moral, and structural reasons to stay married. *Journal of Marriage and the Family, 61,* 160–177.

25. Jourard, S. (1971). *The transparent self.* New York: Van Nostrand Reinhold.

26. Kelley, D. (1998). The communication of forgiveness. *Communication Studies, 49,* 255–271.

27. Knapp, M., & Taylor, E. (1994). Commitment and its communication in romantic relationships. In A. Weber & J. Harvey (Eds.), *Perspectives on close relationships* (pp. 153, 175). Boston: Allyn and Bacon.

28. Knapp, M. L., & Vangelisti, A. L. (2000). *Interpersonal communication and human relationships* (4th ed.). Boston: Allyn and Bacon.

29. Koepke, L., Mare, J., & Moran, P. (1992, April). Relationship quality in a sample of lesbian couples with children and child free. *Family Relations, 41,* 224–229.

30. Laird, J. (1996). Family-centered practice with lesbian and gay families. *Families in Society. The Journal of Contemporary Human Services,* 559–571.

31. Littlejohn, S. (1992). *Theories of human communication* (4th ed.). Belmont, CA: Wadsworth.

32. Maddock, J. (1989). Healthy family sexuality: Positive principles for educators and clinicians. *Family Relations, 38,* 130–136.

33. Malone, T., & Malone, P. (1987). *The art of intimacy.* New York: Prentice-Hall.

34. Montgomery, B. M. (1994). Communication in close relationships. In A. Weber & J. Harvey (Eds.), *Perspectives on close relationships* (pp. 67–87). Boston: Allyn and Bacon.

35. Pearce, W. B., & Sharp, S. M. (1973). Self-disclosing communication. *Journal of Communication, 23,* 409–425.

36. Pearson, J. (1992). *Lasting love.* Dubuque, IA: Wm. Brown.

37. Pearson, J. C., West, R., & Turner, L. H. (1995). *Gender and communication.* Madison, WI: Brown & Benchmark.

38. Petronio, S. (1991). Communication boundary management: A theoretical model of managing disclosure of private information between married couples. *Communication Theory, 1,* 311–335.

39. Petronio, S. (2000). The boundaries of privacy: Praxis of everyday life. In S. Petronio (Ed.), *Balancing the Secrets of Private Disclosures* (pp. 37–49). Mahwah, NJ: Lawrence Erlbaum.

40. Robinson, L., & Blanton, P. (1993). Marital strengths in enduring marriages. *Family Relations, 42,* 38–45.

41. Roxema, H. J. (1986). Defensive communication climate as a barrier to sex education in the home. *Family Relations, 35,* 531–537.

42. Rusbult, C. E., Drigotas, S. M., & Verette, J. (1994). An interdependence analysis of commitment processes and relationship maintenance phenomena. In D. J. Canary & L. Stafford (Eds.), *Communication and relational maintenance* (pp. 115–139). San Diego: Academic Press.
43. Satir, V. (1988). *The new peoplemaking.* Mountain View, CA: Science and Behavior Books.
44. Schwartz, P. (1994). *Peer marriage.* New York: Free Press.
45. Schnarch, C. M. (1991). *Constructing the sexual crucible: An integration of sexual and marital therapy.* New York: W. W. Norton.
46. Sheehy, M. (1997). *Interview in family communication.* Teleclass, available from PBS Adult Learning Satellite Service, 1320 Braddock, Pl., Alexandria, VA.
47. Sieburg, E. (1973). *Interpersonal confirmation: A paradigm for conceptualization and measurement.* Paper presented at the meeting of the International Communication Association, Montreal, Quebec. (ERIC document No. ED 098 634 1975.)
48. Sprecher, S., & McKinney, K. (1994). Sexuality in close relationships. In A. Weber & J. Harvey (Eds.), *Perspectives in close relationships* (pp. 193–216). Boston: Allyn and Bacon.
49. Stafford, L., & Dainton, M. (1994). The darkside of "normal" family interaction. In W. R. Cupach & B. H. Spitzberg (Eds.), *The darkside of interpersonal communication* (pp. 259–280). Mahwah, NJ: Lawrence Erlbaum.
50. Tardy, C., Hosman, L., & Bradac, J. (1981). Disclosing self to friends and family: A reexamining of initial questions. *Communication Quarterly, 29,* 263–268.
51. Troth, A., & Peterson, C. C. (2000). Factors predicting safe-sex talk and condom use in early sexual relationships. *Health Communication, 12,* 195–218.
52. Tschann, J. (1988). Self-disclosure in adult friendship: Gender and marital status differences. *Journal of Social and Personal Relationships, 5,* 65–81.
53. Vangelisti, A. L., & Banski, M. A. (1993). Couples debriefing conversations, the impact of gender, occupation and demographic characteristics. *Family Relations, 42,* 149–157.
54. Warren, C. (1995). Parent-child communication about sex. In T. J. Socha & G. H. Stamp (Eds.), *Parents, children and communication: Frontiers of theory and research* (pp. 173–201). Mahwah, NJ: Lawrence Erlbaum.
55. Warren, C. (2003). Communicating about sex with parents and partners. In K. M. Galvin & P. J. Cooper (Eds.), *Making connections: Readings in relational communication* (3rd ed., pp. 317–324). Los Angeles: Roxbury.
56. Waterman, J. (1979). Family patterns of self-disclosure. In G. Chelune & Associates (Eds.), *Self-disclosure* (pp. 225–242). San Francisco: Jossey-Bass.
57. Wilder, C., & Collins, S. (1994). Patterns of interactional paradoxes. In W. R. Cupach & B. H. Spitzberg (Eds.), *The darkside of interpersonal communication* (pp. 83–103). Mahwah, NJ: Lawrence Erlbaum.
58. Yerby, J., Buerkel-Rothfuss, N. L., & Bochner, A. (1990). *Understanding family communication.* Scottsdale, AZ: Gorsuch Scarisbrick.

Steve Duck, an interpersonal communication professor at the University of Iowa, has written a number of books about how to understand and improve personal relationships. He begins this reading by explaining how "relationshipping" is a skill that each of us is taught—more or less effectively—and that we can learn to do better. He doesn't believe that building friendships is *nothing but* a mechanical process of applying certain skills, but he is convinced that skills are part of this process, just like they're part of the process of painting the Mona Lisa. As he suggests, the main advantage of treating relationshipping this way is that it can give you confidence in your ability to improve the ways you make and keep friends.

Duck talks about the general features that people expect friends to have and the friendship rules that people generally expect to be observed. Then he dedicates the bulk of this reading to a discussion of what he calls the "provisions" of friendships, that is, what they "provide" or do for us. He explains six reasons why we need friends: belonging and sense of reliable alliance; emotional integration and stability; opportunities for communication about ourselves; assistance and physical support; reassurance of our worth and value and opportunity to help others; and personality support.

His discussion helps me understand important features of the friendships I enjoy. For example, a family friend sometimes picks Lincoln up from school—a clear example of her giving us "assistance and physical support." During the times Kris and I are around this friend, our friendship with her also gives both of us opportunities for communication about ourselves as we discuss how we share or differ with her priorities and values. Our friendship with her also provides us opportunities to help, which feel good because they provide reassurance of our worth and value. I can also sense some of what our friendship provides her, how we might change things to make our relationships even better. It's clear from just this brief example that the ideas in this reading can help you understand your friendships and even improve them.

Our Friends, Ourselves

Steve Duck

. . . "Relationshipping" is actually a very complicated and prolonged process with many pitfalls and challenges. Relationships do not just happen; they have to be made—made to start, made to work, made to develop, kept in good working order and preserved from going sour. To do all this we need to be active, thoughtful and skilled. To suggest that one simply starts a friendship, courtship, romantic partnership or marriage and "off it goes" is simple-minded. It is like believing that one can drive down the street merely by turning the ignition key, sitting back and letting the car take care of itself.

On the contrary, to develop a close personal relationship (with someone who was, after all, at first a stranger to us) careful adjustment and continuous monitoring are required, along with several very sophisticated skills. Some of these are: assessing the other person's needs accurately; adopting appropriate styles of communication; indicating liking and interest by means of minute bodily activities, like eye movements and postural shifts; finding out how to satisfy mutual personality needs; adjusting our behaviour to the relationship "tango" with the other person; selecting and revealing the right sorts of information or opinion in an inviting, encouraging way in the appropriate style and circumstances; building up trust, making suitable demands; and building up commitment. In short, one must perform many complex behaviours. These necessitate proficiency in presenting ourselves efficiently, attending to the right features of the other person at the right time, and pacing the friendship properly.

Rather as learning to drive a car does, learning to steer a relationship involves a range of different abilities and these must be coordinated. Just as when, even after we have learned to drive, we need to concentrate harder each time we get into a new model, drive in an unfamiliar country or travel through unknown streets, so when entering unfamiliar relationships we have to relearn, modify or re-concentrate on the things that we do. All of us have pet stories about the strain, embarrassment and awkwardness that occurred in a first meeting with a new neighbour or a "friend of a friend": some clumsy silence, an ill-judged phrase, a difficult situation. It is in such situations that the skills of friendship are bared and tested to the limits, and where intuition is so clearly not enough.

Because it is a skill, relationshipping—even in these novel situations—is something that can be improved, refined, polished (even coached and practised) like any other skill, trained like any other, and made more fluent. It can be taken right up to the level of expertise where it all flows so skillfully and automatically that we can metaphorically focus away from the position of the relational brakes or accelerator and devise ways to drive (the relationship) courteously, skillfully, carefully, or enjoyably, so that the others in it can have a smoother ride!

Since we are not usually disposed to think of friendship and close relationships in this new kind of way, people sometimes feel irrationally resistant to doing so. "How can you represent a close personal relationship as a simple mechanical skill?", they ask. "Isn't it more mystical, more magical, more moral, less manipulative than you make it sound?" Such people seem happy to see relationships merely as pleasant, passive states: relationships just happen to us and we don't have to do anything particular—let alone do anything properly.

My answer is clear: I am not saying that friendship is all mechanical, any more than making a beautiful piece of furniture or playing an enchanting piano rhapsody or winning a sports championship is simply a mechanical exercise. But each of these activities has some mechanical elements that must be mastered before the higher-level aspects of skill can be attempted. You can't paint the Mona Lisa until you know something about painting figures, using a canvas, holding a brush, mixing paints, and so on. Furthermore, research backs this up. Scholars now regard "relationship work" as a process that continues right through the life of the relationship, with a constant and perpetual need for the right actions and activities at the right time to keep it all alive (for example, Baxter and Dindia, 1990). . . .

There are many advantages to this way of looking at relationships. It leads to a direct and useful form of practical advice for people who are unhappy with one or more of their relationships, or who are lonely or frustrated. It focuses on the things that one can do to improve relationships. It also runs counter to the common, but rather simplistic, assumption that relationships are based only on the matching of two individuals' personalities. This pervasive myth says that there is a Mr. or a Ms. Right for everyone or that friends can be defined in advance. If this were true, then we could all list the characteristics of our perfect partner—looking for a partner or being attractive to one would be like shopping for or making a checklist of things we liked. By contrast, the new approach adopted here will focus on performance, on behaviour, on the simple mistakes that people make at the various stages of friendship development.

Is it such a strange and unacceptable idea that people can be trained to adopt more satisfactory styles in relationships? Not really. Therapists, social workers, doctors and dentists nowadays receive instruction on the ways to establish rapport with patients and how to develop a reassuring and constructive "bedside manner." We know also that insurance or car sales staff are trained in how to relate to possible customers, that airline cabin crew and the police alike receive instruction on relating to the public, and that managers are now encouraged to spend time building up good personal relationships with employees. Such emphasis on skills takes us beyond the trite commonsense advice for lonely persons to "go out and meet more people." It focuses us on the fact that relationship problems derive in part, if not on the whole, from people "doing relationships" wrongly rather than simply not getting enough opportunities to be in them.

The evidence suggests that all of us are probably missing out and not maximizing our potential for relationships. American research (Reisman, 1981) shows that people claim to have about fifteen "friends" on average, although the numbers change with age (17-year olds claim about nineteen, while 28-year olds have only twelve; 45-year olds have acquired sixteen, while people in their sixties enjoy an average of fifteen). When people are asked to focus only on the relationships that are most satisfying, intimate and close, however, the number drops dramatically to around six (5.6 to be precise). . . .

THE NATURE OF FRIENDSHIP

A friend of mine once defined a "friend" as someone who, seeing you drunk and about to stand up on a table and sing, would quietly take you aside to prevent you[r] doing it. This definition actually embodies quite a few of the important aspects of friendship: caring, support, loyalty and putting high priority on the other person's interests. We shall see later in the [reading] why these are important. However, when researchers have taken a more precise look at the meaning of friendship, they have focused on two specific things: the general *features* that humans expect friends to have and the *rules* of friendship that humans expect to be observed.

There are certain features that we find particularly desirable in friends and certain characteristics that everyone believes that being a friend demands. K. E. Davis and Todd (1985) found that we regularly expect a friend to be someone who is honest and open, shows affection, tells us his or her secrets and problems, gives us help when we need it, trusts us and is also trustworthy, shares time and activities with us, treats us with respect and obviously values us, and is prepared to work through disagreements. These are things that people *expect* a friend to do for them and expect to do for the friend in return. These features constitute a quite complex picture. However, when one looks at the *rules* of friendship that people actually adhere to, then the strongest ones are rather simple (Argyle & Henderson, 1985): hold conversations; do not disclose confidences to other people; refrain from public criticism; repay debts and favours. These researchers also demonstrate that emotional support, trust and confiding are among the rules that distinguish high-quality friendships from less close ones.

In ideal circumstances, then, a friend is an open, affectionate, trusting, helpful, reliable companion who respects our privacy, carries out interactions with all due respect to the norms of behaviour and ourselves, does not criticize us in public, and both does us favours and returns those that we do. In the real world, friendship is unlikely to live up to this ideal and we all have some range of tolerance. However, it is a *voluntary* bond between two people and the above ideals can be seen as part of an unwritten contract between them, whose violation can become the grounds for the dissolution of the relationship (Wiseman, 1986).

Another important view of friendship has been offered by Wright (1984). He too stresses the "voluntary interdependence" of friendship: it is important that people freely choose to be intertwined together in the relationship. He also places emphasis on the "person qua person" element, or the extent to which we enjoy the person for his or her own sake, rather than for the things that he or she does for us. More recent research on this idea (Lea, 1989) finds indeed that "self-referent rewards," or the way the other person makes us feel about ourselves, are just as important as these other things. The way in which the relationship helps us to feel about ourselves, and its voluntary nature, are crucial to the nature of friendship. There are good reasons why this is the case.

THE "PROVISIONS" OF FRIENDSHIP

There are several ways to start answering the large question: "Why do we need friends?" We could just decide that everyone needs intimacy, possibly as a result of dependency needs formed in childhood, just as the psychoanalysts tell us. There may be something to this, as we shall see, but there is more to the need for friendships than a need for intimacy—and there is more to the need for intimacy than we may suppose, anyway. For instance, we might want to ask how intimacy develops, how it is expressed, what else changes when it grows, and so on. We might also note the curious finding (Wheeler *et al.*, 1983; R. B. Hays, 1989) that both men and women prefer intimate partners who are women! Indeed, Arkin and Grove (1990) show that shy men prefer to talk to women even when they are not in an intimate encounter. Not only this, but those people who talk to more women during the day have better health than those who talk to fewer women (Reis, 1986). Clearly the nature of needs for intimacy and friendship is rather intriguing and may be mediated by gender and other social contexts. . . .

Belonging and a Sense of Reliable Alliance

In writing about loneliness and the "provisions" of relationships—what it is that they do for us—Weiss (1974) proposed that a major consequence of being in relationships is a sense of belonging and of "reliable alliance." He is touching on something very important about human experience. We all like to belong or to be accepted; even those who choose solitude want it to be the result of their own choice, not someone else's. No one wants to be an outcast, a pariah or a social reject. Indeed, the powerful effects of being made *not* to belong were long recognized as a severe punishment in Ancient Greece, where people could be ostracized and formally exiled or banished. The modern equivalent is found in the British trade union practice of "sending someone to Coventry" when they break the union rules: the person's workmates, colleagues, neighbours and associates are instructed to refuse to speak to the person about anything. . . .

By contrast, relationships give us a sense of inclusion, a sense of being a member of a group—and, as the advertisers keep emphasizing, membership has its privileges. One of these privileges is "reliable alliance"; that is to say, the existence of a bond that can be trusted to be there for you when you need it. To [quote] a phrase, "A friend in need is a friend indeed"—or in our terms, the existence of a friendship creates a reliable alliance: one of the signs that someone is a true friend is when they help you in times of trouble.

Emotional Integration and Stability

Importantly, communities of friends provide a lot more than just a sense of belonging and reliable alliance (Weiss, 1974). They also provide necessary anchor points for opinions, beliefs, and emotional responses. Friends are benchmarks that tell us how we should react appropriately, and they correct or guide our attitudes and beliefs in both obvious and subtle ways. As an example, consider how different cultures express grief differently. In some countries it is acceptable to fall to the ground, cover oneself with dust and wail loudly; in other cultures it is completely unacceptable to show such emotion, and the emphasis falls on dignified public composure. Imagine the reaction in Britain if the Queen were to roll on the ground as a way of demonstrating grief, or in the United States if the President and First Lady attended military funerals with their faces blacked and tearing their clothes. Humans have available many different ways of demonstrating grief but they typically cope with this strong emotion in a way particularly acceptable to their own culture.

Like cultures, friends and intimates develop their own sets of shared concerns, common interests and collective problems, as well as shared meanings, common responses to life and communal emotions. Friends are often appreciated exactly because they share private understandings, private jokes, or private language. Indeed, communication researchers (Hopper *et al.*, 1981; Bell *et al.*, 1987) have shown that friends and lovers develop their own "personal idioms" or ways of talking about such things as feelings, sex and bodily parts, so that they are obscure to third parties. By using a phrase with secret meaning, couples can communicate in public places about things that are private. Good examples are to be found in newspaper columns on St. Valentine's Day. What, for example, are we to make of a message I found in the local student newspaper: "Dinglet, All my dinkery forever, Love, Scrunnett"? Presumably it meant something both to the person who placed the advertisement and to the person who was the intended object of it. Be alert: the couple who announce that "We are going home to make some pancakes" may in fact be planning to have a night of passion!

Such language is just a localized version of the fact that different cultures use different dialects or languages. Equally, friends have routines of behaving or beliefs that are not shared by everyone in a particular country or culture, but for that reason they are more important in daily life. Loneliness is, and isolation can be, wretched precisely because it deprives people of such psychological benchmarks and anchor points. Lonely people lose the stability provided by the chance to compare their own reactions to life with the reactions of other people that they know, like and respect. . . .

So loneliness and isolation are disruptive because they deprive the person of the opportunity for comfortable comparison of opinions and attitudes with other people—of close friends. People who are parted from friends become anxious, disoriented, unhappy and even severely destabilized emotionally; they may become still more anxious just because they feel themselves behaving erratically, or they may experience unusual mood swings. They often report sudden changes of temper and loss of control, sometimes resulting in violent outbursts; but in any case their judgment becomes erratic and unreliable, and they may become unusually vigilant, suspicious or jumpy in the presence of other unfamiliar people.

Another function of friendship, then, a reason why we need friends, is to keep us emotionally stable and to help us see where we stand *vis-à-vis* other people and whether we are "doing OK." It is particularly noticeable in times of stress and crisis. I remember an occasion when all the lights [went out] in a student residence block where I was a [residence advisor]. The rational thing to do was to find a flashlight and await the restoration of power. What we all actually did was to stumble down to the common-room and chatter amongst ourselves: the need to compare our reactions to the emergency was so powerful and so universal that even the warden, a medical researcher who had doctoral degrees from both Oxford and Cambridge, did the same. Such behaviour often happens after any kind of stress or crisis, from the crowd of people who gather to swap stories after a fire or a car accident, to the nervous chatter that schoolchildren perform when the doctor comes to inject them against measles or TB. . . .

Opportunities for Communication about Ourselves

There is a third reason why we need friends (Weiss, 1974). A centrally important need is for communication. This particular wheel was strikingly reinvented by the Quaker prison reformers several generations ago, who attempted to cut down communication between criminals in prison in order to stop them educating one another about ways of committing crime. Accordingly, one of their proposals was that prisoners should be isolated from one another. What occurred was very instructive: the prisoners spent much of their time tapping out coded messages on walls and pipes, devising means of passing information to one another, and working out other clever ways of communicating. Evidently, people who are involuntarily isolated feel a need to communicate. One additional function that healthy friendships provide, then, is a place for such communication to occur—communication about anything, not just important events but also trivial stuff as well as personal, intimate details about oneself. In a study at the University of Iowa, I and my students (S. W. Duck, *et al.*, 1991) have found that most conversations with friends last very short periods of time (about three minutes on average) and deal with trivialities. They are nonetheless rated as extremely significant. They revitalize the relationship, reaffirm it and celebrate its existence, through the medium of conversation.

A mild form of this overwhelming need to communicate is to be found on railway trains, planes and long-distance buses. Here many lonely people strike up conversations—but usually monologues—which allow them to communicate to someone or to tell someone about themselves and their opinions. A striking thing about this is the intimacy of the stories that are often told. Perfect strangers can often be regaled with the life history, family details, and personal opinions of someone they have not seen before and will probably never see again. Indeed, that is probably a key part of it, for the listener who will not be seen again cannot divulge the "confession" to friends or colleagues and so damage the confessor's reputation. (In cases where it is known that the listener and confessor will meet again, as in the case of doctors and patients, priests and parishioners, counsellors and clients, or lawyers and consultants, the listeners are bound by strict professional ethical codes not to reveal what they have been told. On the train, the "ethics" are simply left to statistical chance, and the extreme improbability of the two strangers meeting one another's friends is a comfort in itself.) . . .

Provision of Assistance and Physical Support

Another "provision" of relationships is simply that they offer us support, whether physical, psychological or emotional (Hobfoll and Stokes, 1988). This section focuses on physical support and assistance, which are often as significant to us as is any other sort of support.

For example, when people lose a friend or a spouse through bereavement, they report a lack of support—they are cut off from someone who has helped them to cope with life and to adjust to its problems, tasks, and changing uncertainties. This can take one of two forms: physical support (such as help with day-to-day tasks) and psychological support (such as when someone shows that we are appreciated, or lets us know that our opinions are valued). Human beings need both of these types of support, but the types are significantly different.

This is very simply illustrated. When your friend gives you a birthday present you are supposed to accept it in a way that indicates your own unworthiness to receive it and also the kindness of the friend ("Oh you shouldn't have bothered. It really is very good of you"). In short, you repay your friend by accepting the gift as a token of friendship and by praising the friend. You "exchange" the gift for love and respect, as it were. Imagine what would happen if you repaid by giving the friend the exact value of the gift in money. The friend would certainly be insulted by the ineptness: you would have altered the nature of the social exchange and also, in so doing, the nature of the relationship, by focusing on money rather than the gift as a symbol for friendship. Indeed, Cheal (1986) has shown that gift-giving as a one-way donation is rare and gift *reciprocity* is the norm, indicating that it serves an important relational function. Gift exchange serves the symbolic function of cementing and celebrating the relationship.

There are other clear examples of this point—that the nature of the exchange or support helps to define the degree and type of relationship. For instance, many elderly people get resentful of the fact that they gradually become more and more physically dependent on other people for help in conducting the daily business of their lives. The elderly cannot reach things so easily, cannot look after themselves and are more dependent physically, while at the same time they are less able to repay their friends by doing services in return. This, then, is one reason why many people dislike or feel uneasy with old age: they resent the feeling of helpless dependency coupled with the feeling of perpetual indebtedness that can never be paid off. For many elderly people, then, the mending of a piece of furniture, the making of a fruit pie, or the knitting of a sweater can be traded off against dependency: elderly people *need to be allowed* to do things for other people as a way of demonstrating to themselves and to everyone else that they are valuable to others and can still make useful contributions to the world. . . .

Reassurance of Our Worth and Value, and Opportunity to Help Others

People who are lonely characteristically say that no one cares about them, that they are useless, uninteresting, of low value and good for nothing. Studies of the conversation of severely depressed people invariably reveal indications that they have lost their self-respect or self-esteem (Gotlib and Hooley, 1988). In other words, they have come to see themselves as valueless, worthless and insignificant, often because that is how they feel that everyone else sees them. Furthermore, analysis of suicide notes shows that many suicide attempts are carried out as a way of forcing some particular friend to re-evaluate the person, or to shock the friend into realizing just how much he or she really does esteem the person making the attempt. For this reason, Alfred Adler (1929) has claimed, with characteristic insight, that every suicide is always a reproach or a revenge.

One reason, then, that we appreciate friends is because of their contribution to our self-evaluation and self-esteem. Friends can do this both directly and indirectly: they may compliment us or tell us about other people's good opinions of us. Dale Carnegie's multimillion-seller book on *How to Win Friends and Influence People* stressed the positive consequences of doing this. Friends can also increase our self-esteem in other ways: by attending to what we do, listening, asking our advice, and generally acting in ways that indicate the value that they place on our opinions. However, there are less obvious and more indirect ways in which they can communicate this estimation of our value. For one thing, the fact that they choose to spend time with us rather than with someone else must show that they value our company more than the alternatives.

There is a subtler version of these points too. Just as we look to friends to provide us with all of these things, so we can get from friendship one other key benefit. Because friends trust us and depend on us, they give us the chance to help them. That gives us the opportunity to take responsibility for them, to see ourselves helping them with their lives, to give them our measured advice and consequently to feel good. Friends provide us with these possibilities of taking responsibility and nurturing other people.

Undoubtedly, these things are important in the conduct of relationships and in making them satisfactory for both partners, and it is critical that we learn to evince them effectively. However, one important point to note is that those people who are poor at doing this (e.g., people who are poor at indicating interest, or who seem to have little time for other people, or never let them help or let them give advice) will find that other people are unattracted to relationships with them. All people need indications of their estimability and need chances to nurture just as we do, and if we do not adequately provide such signs then these people will reject us—just as we would do in their position. . . .

Personality Support

Yet there is something even more fundamental to close relationships than this. Recent research indicates that each feature mentioned above—sense of community, emotional stability, communication, provision of help, maintenance of self-esteem—in its own way serves to support and integrate the person's personality (S. W. Duck and Lea, 1982). Each of us is characterized by many thoughts, doubts, beliefs, attitudes, questions, hopes, expectations and opinions about recurrent patterns in life. Our personalities are composed not only of our behavioural style (for example, our introversion or extraversion) but also of our thoughts, doubts and beliefs. It is a place full of symbols, a space where we are ourselves, a system of interlocking thoughts, experiences, interpretations, expectancies and personal meanings. Our personality would be useless to us if all of these opinions and meanings were not, by and large, supported. We would simply stop behaving if we had no trust in our thoughts or beliefs about why we should behave or how we should behave, just as we stop doing other things that we are convinced are wrong. Some schizophrenics and depressives actually do stop behaving when their thought-world falls apart: they just sit and stare.

Each of us needs to be assured regularly that our thought-worlds or symbolic spaces are sound and reliable. A friend can help us to see that we are wrong and how we can change, or that we are right about some part of our thinking. We may have vigorous discussions about different attitudes that we hold—but our friends are likely to be very similar to us in many of our attitudes and interests, so that these discussions are more probably supportive than destructive. However, we all know the anger and pain that follow a really serious disagreement with a close friend—much more unpleasant than a disagreement with an enemy. What we should deduce from all this is that we seek out as friends those people who help to support our thought-world-personality, and we feel chastened, sapped or undermined when they do not provide this support.

What sort of person best gives us the kind of personality support that I have described here? In the first instance, it is provided by people who share our way of thinking. The more of these "thought-ways" that we share with someone, the easier it is to communicate with that person: we can assume that our words and presumptions will be understood more easily by someone who is "our type" than by someone who is not—we shall not have the repetitive discomfort of perpetually explaining ourselves, our meanings and our jokes.

Yet there is much more to it than this, although it has taken researchers a long time to sort out the confusing detail of the picture. For one thing, the type of similarity that we need to share with someone in order to communicate effectively depends on the stage that the relationship has reached. At early stages it is quite enough that acquaintances are broadly similar, but at later stages the similarity must be more intricate, precise, refined, and detailed. One of the skills of friend-making is to know what sorts of similarity to look for at which times as the relationship proceeds. General similarity of attitudes is fine at the early to middle stages, but matters much less later if the partners do not work at discovering similarities at the deeper level of the ways in which they view other people and understand their characters. Very close friends must share the same specific sorts of framework for understanding the actions, dispositions and characters of other people in general, and in specific instances of mutual acquaintance. Such similarity is rare and prized. For that reason, if for no other, it is painful and extremely significant to lose the persons who offer it.

Loss or absence of particular intimates or friends deprives us of some measure of support for our personality, and it is essential to our psychological health that we have the skill to avoid this. Losing an intimate partner or friend not only makes us die a little, it leaves floating in the air those bits of our personality that the person used to support, and can make people fall apart psychologically. Of course, this will depend on how much our personality has been supported by that partner, which particular parts are involved, how readily these parts are supported by others, how much time we have had to anticipate and adjust to the loss, and so on. But essentially the loss or absence of friends and of close, satisfying relationships does not merely cause anxiety, grief or depression; it can cause other, more severe, forms of psychological disintegration or deterioration, often with the physical and mental side-effects noted earlier. Many of the well-known psychosomatic illnesses and hysterical states are actually caused by relationship problems, although this has not been realized by as many doctors as one might expect (see Lynch, 1977). For too long the accepted medical folklore has assumed that the person's inner mental state is a given, and that it causes psychosomatic effects when it gets out of balance. It is now quite clear that the surest way to upset people's mental balance is to disturb their close relationships (Gerstein and Tesser, 1987). We need friends to keep us healthy both physically and mentally: therefore it is doubly important that we perfect the ways of gaining and keeping friends. An important first step is to recognize the different needs that each relationship can fulfill for us, and the means by which this can be achieved.

REVIEW QUESTIONS

1. Define *relationshipping*.
2. How many "satisfying, intimate, and close" relationships does the research say that people of your age typically have?
3. Duck lists four main rules that characterize friendship, according to the research. What are they?
4. Fill in the blank, explain, and tell whether you agree or disagree and why: "Both men and women prefer intimate partners who are _____."
5. What does it mean to have "a sense of reliable alliance"?
6. Paraphrase and give an example from your own experience of the reality-checking function of friendships.
7. Explain what Duck means when he says that sometimes elderly people need to be allowed to do things for others.
8. According to Duck, what is the relationship between friendship networks and personal mental health? Do you agree or disagree with this claim?

PROBES

1. In what ways does Steve Duck's example of learning to drive a car fit your experience of learning how to "do" relationships? In what ways does it not fit?
2. Test Duck's claim about the average number of "friends" reported by people of your age and the average number of "satisfying, intimate, and close" relationships. Do you find any differences among the people you know?

3. What is the function in intimate relationships of private language and personal idioms? What does the presence of these private modes of expression suggest about the similarities between friendships and cultures?
4. What explanation does Duck give for the "stranger on the train (bus, plane)" phenomenon, where your seatmate, whom you don't know, tells you intimate details of his or her life? Why does this happen?
5. How do you respond to Duck's claim that, in some important ways, birthdays are times when many people give *gifts in exchange for* respect and love?
6. Paraphrase and respond to Duck's explanation of the role of similarities in friendship relationships.

REFERENCES

1. Adler, A. (1929). *What Your Life Should Mean to You.* New York: Bantam.
2. Argyle, M., & Henderson, M. (1985). *The Anatomy of Relationships.* London: Methuen.
3. Arkin, R., & Grove, T. (1990). Shyness, sociability and patterns of everyday affiliation. *Journal of Social and Personal Relationships* (7), 273–281.
4. Baxter, L. A., & Dindia, K. (1990). Marital partners' perceptions of marital maintenance strategies. *Journal of Social and Personal Relationships* (7), 187–208.
5. Bell, R. A., Buerkel-Rothfuss, N., & Gore, K. (1987). "Did you bring the yarmulke for the cabbage patch kid?": The idiomatic communication of young lovers. *Human Communication Research* (14), 47–67.
6. Cheal, D. J. (1986). The social dimensions of gift behaviour. *Journal of Social and Personal Relationships* (3), 423–39.
7. Davis, K. E., & Todd, M. (1985). Assessing friendship: Prototypes, paradigm cases, and relationship description, in S. W. Duck & D. Perlman (eds.), *Understanding Personal Relationships.* London: Sage.
8. Duck, W., & Lea, M. (1982). Breakdown of relationships as a threat to personal identity, in G. Breakwell (ed.), *Threatened Identities.* Chichester: Wiley.
9. Duck, S. W., Rutt, D. J., Hurst, M., & Strejc, H. (1991). Some evident truths about communication in everyday relationships: All communication is not created equal. *Human Communication Research* (18), 114–29.
10. Gerstein, I. H., & Tesser, A. (1987). Antecedents and responses associated with loneliness. *Journal of Social and Personal Relationships* (4), 329–63.
11. Gotlib, I. H., & Hooley, J. M. (1988). Depression and marital distress: Current and future directions, in S. W. Duck (ed.) with D. F. Hay, S. E. Hobfoll, W. Ickes, & B. Montgomery, *Handbook of Personal Relationships.* Chichester: Wiley.
12. Hays, R. B. (1989). The day-to-day functioning of close versus casual friendship. *Journal of Social and Personal Relationships* (1), 75–98.

13. Hobfoll, S. E., & Stokes, J. P. (1988). The process and mechanics of social support, in S. W. Duck (ed.) with D. F. Hay, S. E. Hobfoll, W. Ickes, & B. Montgomery, *Handbook of Personal Relationships* (Chichester, UK: Wiley).

14. Hopper, R., Knapp, M. L., & Scott, L. (1981). Couples' personal idioms: Exploring intimate talk. *Journal of Communication* (31), 23–33.

15. Lea, M. (1989). Factors underlying friendship: An analysis of responses on the acquaintance description form in relation to Wright's friendship model. *Journal of Social and Personal Relationships* (6), 275–92.

16. Lynch, J. J. (1977). *The Broken Heart: The Medical Consequences of Loneliness.* New York: Basic Books.

17. Reis, H. T. (1986). Gender effects in social participation: Intimacy, loneliness, and the conduct of social interaction, in R. Gilmour & S. W. Duck (eds.), *The Emerging Field of Personal Relationships.* Hillsdale, NJ: Lawrence Erlbaum.

18. Reisman, J. (1981). Adult friendships, in S. W. Duck & R. Gilmour (eds.), *Personal Relationships 2: Developing Personal Relationships.* London: Academic Press.

19. Weiss, R. S. (1974). The provisions of social relationships, in Z. Rubin (ed.), *Doing Unto Others.* Englewood Cliffs, NJ: Prentice-Hall.

20. Wheeler, L., Reis, H. T., & Nezelek, J. (1983). Loneliness, social interaction and sex roles. *Journal of Personality and Social Psychology* (35), 742–54.

21. Wiseman, J. P. (1986). Friendship: Bonds and binds in a voluntary relationship. *Journal of Social and Personal Relationships* (3), 191–211.

22. Wright, P. H. (1984). Self referent motivation and the intrinsic quality of friendship. *Journal of Social and Personal Relationships* (1), 114–30.

T he author of this essay has been a philosophy teacher at East Tennessee State University. The paper appeared in an unusual collection of readings that discusses several *philosophical* aspects of interpersonal relationships. As you'll see, John Hardwig's concern is that interpersonal contacts often raise important ethical issues, but that few people have thought or written about how ethics work in these situations. One of the reasons he offers for this neglect is that most philosophy has been written by men, and men typically favor impersonal topics over personal ones.

Whether or not you agree with this reason, notice how Hardwig outlines his ethics. He defines a *personal,* as contrasted with a quasi-personal or impersonal, relationship as one in which I want you as an end, not as a means to an end, as one in which I see "you and the realization of your goals as part of me and the realization of my goals."

A personal relationship also involves wanting to be in relation with precisely you, not just wanting something that could be provided by you or somebody else. He contrasts this kind of relationship with a *quasi-personal* one in which I want to have "the kind of friend" or "the kind of wife" or husband that you might be. These relationships may appear to be personal, but they're actually not, because I've chosen the person who fits into a *category* of desire, rather than choosing the person because of who he or she is as an individual. Hardwig also says that hatred can define a truly personal relationship when I hate you, not just some of the things you are, do, or stand for.

This analysis makes it easier to understand the kind of relationship where I want precisely *you*, but "you simply want to be loved and protected or to have a certain kind of marriage." As Hardwig points out, "relationships are often made or broken by the issue of whether I want you or 'someone who....'"

The main principle of Hardwig's ethics of personal relationships is that when attitudes or actions depersonalize personal relationships, they do violence to what these relationships are, and this kind of violence ought to be avoided. This principle heightens the importance of motives in personal relationships. Motives that are completely acceptable in some impersonal relationships—duty, obligation, and pity, for example—are often inappropriate in personal relationships. As he explains, "While it might be nice to feel yourself to be charitable, benevolent, or compassionate, who could endure being emotionally involved with someone who saw you essentially or even very often as an appropriate object of benevolence, charity, or pity?"

It follows that personal relationships between adults ought to be entered into and continued out of a shared sense of vitality and strength rather than weakness and need. I'm reminded of the person who said that, whenever I try to feed my friends from a cup that is anything other than overflowing, I feed them poison.

Another implication of Hardwig's central ethical principle is that people in personal relationships should act toward each other as purely as possible because they *want* to, not out of a sense of duty, obligation, or *quid pro quo* (you did it for me, so now I owe you). All this doesn't mean that motives such as duty, pity, and sympathy are *always* inappropriate in personal relationships, but only that they should be fallback positions, not the main focus of the relationship.

A third implication is that in personal relationships you can't really separate egoism and altruism—self-interest and interest in the other. This is because if the relationship is personal, "your ends are my ends too." So "the distinction between giving and receiving thus collapses." This is an important claim, and it's one I encourage you to try applying to your own personal relationships. It doesn't mean that there are *never* conflicts or that *all* interests are shared, but that mutuality is primary.

A fourth implication is that personal relationships can't and don't have to be justified by an appeal to some higher value such as love, pleasure, or social utility. They are ends in themselves, justified by their own existence. If you try to make them dependent on another value, you depersonalize them.

The final implication is that this ethics of personal relationships sees people not as individuals but as relational beings, intimately tied in with others. This doesn't make me *dependent* on your friendship or even your presence. But it does mean that if our relationship ends, I change— just as you do.

Hardwig concludes with an argument that when it's necessary to end a relationship, it is both possible and desirable to do so without depersonalizing it. Spouses and attorneys involved in divorces could usefully reflect on this claim.

I find this a thought-provoking essay, and I hope you do, too. It raises some important questions about friendships and other relationships that aren't often discussed, but that can provide helpful guidance when you are faced with a hard decision.

In Search of an Ethics of Personal Relationships

John Hardwig

Although it's been ten years, I can still see the student, hands on her hips, as she brought my beautiful lecture on Kant's ethics to a grinding halt: "Is Kant saying," she demanded, "that if I sleep with my boyfriend, I should sleep with him out of a sense of duty?" My response: "And when you're through, you should tell him that you would have done the same for anyone in his situation." What could I say?

We do not search for what we already have. Thus my title commits me to the thesis that we do not have an ethics of personal relationships. And that is in fact my view, a view grown out of incidents like this one.

More specifically, I believe that for at least the past 300 years or so, philosophers thinking about ethics have tacitly presupposed a very impersonal context. They have unconsciously assumed a context in which we mean little or nothing to each other and have then asked themselves what principles could be invoked to keep us from trampling each other in the pursuit of our separate and often conflicting interests. Consequently, I contend, what we now study and teach under the rubric of ethics is almost entirely the ethics of impersonal relationships.

Excerpted from "In Search of an Ethics of Personal Relationships," by John Hardwig, as appeared in *Person to Person,* ed. George Graham and Hugh Lafollette. Reprinted by permission of John Hardwig.

Various explanations might be offered as to why philosophers have thought in terms of impersonal relationships. Philosophers have historically been almost exclusively males, and males have generally believed that the public realm where impersonal relationships predominate is much more important and worthy of study than the private and personal dimensions of life. Or perhaps the assumption that we are talking about impersonal relationships reflects the growing impersonality of modern society or an awareness of the increasing ability given us by our technology to affect the lives of people quite remote from us.

However, even if philosophers were not thinking about personal relationships when developing their ethics, it might seem that an ethics adequate to impersonal relationships should work at least as well in personal contexts. For in personal relationships there would be less temptation to callously ignore or to ride roughshod over each other's interests, owing to the greater meaning each has for the other. Thus it seems reasonable to assume that the principles constituting the ethics of impersonal relationships will work satisfactorily in personal contexts as well.

But this assumption is false. An ethics of personal relationships must, I try to show, be quite different from the ethics of impersonal relationships. Traditional ethics is, at best, significantly incomplete, only a small part of the story of the ethics of personal relationships. Often it is much worse: basically misguided or wrong-headed and thus inapplicable in the context of personal relationships. In fact, much of traditional ethics urges us to act in ways that would be inappropriate in personal contexts; and thus traditional ethics would often be dangerous and destructive in those contexts.

We do not search for what we already have. I do not have an ethics of personal relationships, though I offer some suggestions about what such an ethics would and would *not* look like. Since my views about the ethics of personal relationships depend, naturally enough, on what I take a personal relationship to be, I begin with a brief discussion of the nature and structure of personal relationships.

But I'm going to cheat some: Throughout, I speak of personal relationships as if they were static. Although this is obviously a gross oversimplification, limitations of space and understanding preclude a discussion of the beginnings and endings and dynamics of personal relationships.

I

So what's a personal relationship? Personal relationships, as opposed to impersonal relationships, are of course relationships such as love, being lovers, friends, spouses, parents, and so on. But these sorts of relationships aren't always very *personal*, since there are all sorts of marriages of convenience, Aristotle's "friendships of utility," Hobbesian power alliances, and many varieties of quite impersonal sexual relationships. Consequently, we need to distinguish what are commonly *called* personal relationships (love, friendship, marriage) from personal relationships in a deeper sense. Even when they are not *personal* in the deeper sense, relationships like love, friendship, and marriage are not exactly impersonal relationships either. So I use the phrase "quasi-personal relationships" to cover such cases, reserving the term "personal relationships" for those relationships which are personal in the deeper sense I hope to explicate. I thus work with a threefold distinction between personal, quasi-personal, and impersonal relationships.

Let us begin with the distinction between personal and impersonal relationships. I want to say two things by way of characterizing personal relationships: (1) If I have a personal relationship with you, I want you. You (and your well-being) are then one of my *ends*. This would seem to be part of what it means to care for or care about another person. (2) If my relationship to you is to be personal, this end must be *you*—precisely you and not any other person. The persons in personal relationships are not substitutable. . . .

First, then, the idea of having you as one of my ends is to be contrasted with both sides of the Kantian dichotomy between respecting you as an end in yourself and treating you as a means to my ends. Kant would have me respect you as a person, just as I would respect any person, simply because you (all) are persons. To respect you as an end in yourself is to recognize that you have value apart from whatever use I might be able to make of you. It is, moreover, to recognize that your goals and purposes have validity independent of whatever goals and purposes I may have and to acknowledge in my action that your goals and purposes have an equal claim to realization. Although respect for you and your goals is a part of a personal relationship, it is not what makes a personal relationship *personal*, valuable, or even a relationship. Instead, having you as one of my ends is valuing you in *relation* to me; it is seeing you and the realization of your goals as part of me and the realization of my goals. This is not, of course, to reduce you to a means to my ends. On the contrary, I want you. You are one of my *ends*.

The second characteristic of a personal relationship—that I want precisely *you*—serves to highlight the difference between this kind of relationship and impersonal relationships, and also to further elucidate the difference between seeing you as one of my ends and seeing you either as an end in yourself or as a means to my ends. The characteristic intentions in personal relationships are different from those in impersonal relationships. It is the difference between:

wanting *to get* something T and wanting to get T *from you.*
wanting *to give* T and wanting to give T *to you.*
wanting *to do* T and wanting to do T *with you.*

The first set of intentions or desires structures impersonal relationships; the second, personal relationships. There is a big difference between wanting to be loved, for example, and wanting to be loved *by you*; a crucial difference between wanting to go to bed (with someone) and wanting to go to bed *with you*. This difference seems to retain its significance whether "T" ranges over relatively insignificant things like taking a walk, having your breakfast made, sharing a ride to a party, and going to a movie, or over crucially important things like baring your soul, receiving love and emotional support, sharing your living space, and having children.

If I want *something* (as opposed to wanting something *from you*), I depersonalize you, reducing you (in my eyes) to an *X* who is a possessor or producer of certain goods. For it's these good things I want, not you; anyone who could and would deliver these goods would do as well. The language captures the depersonalization nicely: I want "someone who. . . ." It is when I want *something* and you become for me a "someone who" is the possessor or producer of this good that I reduce you to a means to my ends. This kind of desire and the intentions it gives rise to structure an impersonal relationship, though many of what are usually called "personal relationships" are structured by precisely this sort of impersonal desire. . . .

Let us now turn to quasi-personal relationships. These are the relationships that are commonly *called* personal, but that are not personal relationships in the deeper sense I have discussed. Quasi-personal relationships can be analyzed along similar lines. Suppose that it's important to me to have *the kind of friend* or *the kind of wife* who will help me with my work. In such cases, my desire or our relationship is not simply impersonal, for it won't do for me just to get help with my work—I want help from a friend or from a wife. In this intermediate case, the kind of relationship you have to me (wife, lover, loved one, friend, child) is essential to the structure of my desire; a certain kind of relationship is one of my ends.

But our relationship is still abstract or impersonal in a sense. I want something from you *because you are my wife* (lover, friend, child). I'd want the same from *any* wife (lover, friend, kid). Thus *you* are not important to the structure of my desire, *you* are not one of my ends. In such cases, the relationship I want must be defined (by me) in terms of roles and rules for those roles. I call these relationships quasi-personal. They are important for an ethics of personal relationships, for we often get hurt in precisely these sorts of relationships, especially when we believe we are involved in a personal relationship.

Two additional points about personal relationships are important for the ethics of personal relationships. First, although I talk mainly about positive, healthy personal relationships, it is important to recognize that *hatred*, as well as love, can be a personal relationship. As can resentment, anger, contempt. Hatred is personal if I hate *you*, not just some of the things you are or do or stand for, not just "anyone who. . . ." In cases of personal hatred, I may well desire your overall ill-being. Hatred that is personal rather than impersonal is much more thoroughgoing and often more vicious. Good sense suggests that we should get out of or depersonalize relationships dominated by intractable hatred, anger, or resentment. Interestingly, however, haters often don't get out of personal relationships with those they hate. And this calls for explanation. Such explanation must acknowledge that if I continue to hate *you* and to have your ill-being as one of my ends, there must be some sort of bond between you and me. *You* are important to me or I wouldn't devote my life to making *you* miserable. The opposite of love is not hatred; the opposite of love is indifference.

A second point important for the ethics of personal relationships is the possibility of one-sided personal relationships. Suppose I want *you* and you simply want to be loved and protected or to have a certain kind of marriage. Do I then have a personal relationship with you while you have an impersonal or quasi-personal relationship with me? Perhaps. But this surely is not the kind of relationship I will normally want. Such relationships are ripe for exploitation and tragedy. They are, in any case, almost always deeply disappointing, for we usually want *mutually* personal relationships. This means that not only do I want *you* and not just some producer of certain goods and services, but I want you to want *me*, not "someone who. . . ."

Although the logical structure of personal, quasi-personal, and impersonal relationships seems quite distinct, there can be tremendous . . . difficulties facing those of us who would know what kinds of relationships we have. Do I want *you* or do I want *something* (from you)? Do I want a relationship *with you* or do I want a *kind* of relationship with "someone who . . ."? Even if I think I want you, is it because I'm picking up on something that is *you*, or is it because you happen to resemble my childhood sweetheart, perhaps, or because you are so successful? If I cannot fathom my desires and intentions enough to make these discriminations accurately, it would be possible for me not to know whether I have a personal relationship with you, much less whether you have a personal relationship with me. These . . . difficulties notwithstanding, it may be *critically* important—both ethically and psychologically—to know what kinds of relationships we actually do have. Relationships are often made or broken by the issue of whether I want you or "someone who. . . ."

. . . Obviously, these characterizations of personal and quasi-personal relationships are based on my own intuitions, with which others may not agree. Fortunately, my argument does not require that my characterizations be accepted as necessary conditions, much less as necessary and sufficient conditions, for a personal relationship. It is enough for my purposes if it is admitted that many very healthy and beautiful personal relationships have the structure I have ascribed to them and that the reasons we often have for wanting personal relationships are expressed in my formulations.

II

Now for the ethics of personal relationships. My main contention and basic principle is that ethics must not depersonalize personal relationships, for doing so does violence to what these relationships are; to what is characteristically and normatively going on in them; and to the intentions, desires, and hopes we have in becoming involved in them. Particular persons figure essentially in personal relationships. But most ways of thinking about ethics invite or require us to treat ourselves or our loved ones as a "someone who. . . ." And this leads to many difficulties, both on the level of metaethical theory and on the practical level of ethical or moral prescription. . . .

III

"I don't want you to take me out," my wife exploded. "I just want you to want to go out with me. If you don't want to go out, let's just forget it." Motives, intentions, and reasons for acting play a *much* larger role in the ethics of personal relationships than they do in the ethics of impersonal relationships. In fact, the motivation of those who are close to us is often more important than the things which result from it. And even when actions are important in personal relationships, it is often because they are seen as symbols or symptoms of underlying feelings, desires, or commitments. Thus actions often seem worthless or even perverse if the motivation behind them is inappropriate.

In impersonal situations and relationships, on the other hand, we are much more content to allow people to do the right thing for the wrong reason and we are often even willing to provide incentives (for example, legal and financial) to increase the chances that they will do the right thing and also that they will do it for the wrong reason. I wouldn't, for example, be very much concerned about the motives of my congressman if I could be sure that he would always vote right. I believe that he should be well paid to increase the chances that he will vote right. But I would be deeply upset to learn that my wife is staying with me primarily for financial reasons. And I might be even more upset if her actions all along had been scrupulously wifelike. An ethics of personal relationships must, then, place more emphasis on motives and intentions, less on actions and consequences than most ethical theories have.

However, the motives that ethicists have found praiseworthy in impersonal contexts are usually inappropriate and unacceptable in personal contexts. Actions motivated by duty, a sense of obligation, or even a sense of responsibility are often unacceptable in personal relationships. A healthy personal relationship cannot be based on this sort of motivation; indeed, it cannot even come into play very often. . . . [It would be] devastating . . . to learn that your spouse of thirty-seven years had stayed in your marriage purely or even primarily out of a sense of obligation stemming from the marriage contract.

For similar reasons, motives of benevolence, pity, or compassion are also not acceptable as the characteristic or dominant motives in personal relationships. Acts of charity, altruism, and mercy are also, in general, out. As are sacrifices of important interests or a sense of self-sacrifice. Paternalism and maternalism are also generally unacceptable among adults in personal relationships. While it might be nice to feel yourself to be charitable, benevolent, or compassionate, who could endure being emotionally involved with someone who saw you essentially or even very often as an appropriate object of benevolence, charity, or pity? Of course, there always will be some occasions when you *are* an appropriate object of these attitudes, and it's desirable that they then be forthcoming . . . so long as they are viewed as exceptions. And yet, even in cases of great misfortune—if I contracted a debilitating disease, for example—I don't think I'd want my wife or friends to stay with me if they were motivated predominantly by pity or benevolence.

If even this much is correct, I think we can draw several lessons that point toward a deeper understanding of ethics in personal relationships. First, personal relationships between adults (and perhaps also between adults and children) are to be entered into and continued out of a sense of strength, fullness, and vitality, both in yourself and in the other, not out of a sense of weakness, need, emptiness, or incapacity.

Anything other than a shared sense of vitality and strength would lead to the unacceptable motives already discussed. Moreover, if I see myself primarily as a being in need, I will be too focused on myself and my needs. I will then tend to depersonalize you into someone who can meet my needs. And I will also be generally unable to freely and joyously give: Since I see myself as not having enough as it is, my giving will seem to me a giving up. (Does this mean that those who most need a first-rate personal relationship will be unable to have one? I'm afraid that this might be true.)

The fact that giving characteristically must be free and joyous points to a second lesson about the ethics of personal relationships: Characteristically and normatively, the appropriate motive for action in personal relationships is simply that we want to do these things. Persons pursue whatever *ends* they have simply because they want to (that's what it means to say that something is an *end*, of course). And in a personal relationship, I and my well-being are ends of yours. From this vantage point it is easy to see why motives should play such a central role in personal relationships and also why *wanting* to do the things we do together is often the only acceptable motivation: That motivation is the touchstone of whether or not we have a personal relationship.

Of course, this is not to imply that personal relationships must rest simply on untutored feelings, taken as brute givens in the personalities of the participants. Indeed, it makes sense to talk about doing things, even for the wrong reasons, in order that doing those things will in time change you, your feelings, and your reasons. But it may be even more important to point out that continual attempts to create the right feelings in oneself are also not acceptable or satisfactory. If you must continually try to get yourself to want to do things with me, or for me, or for our relationship, we must at some point admit that I and my well-being are not among your ends and that we do not, therefore, have a personal relationship.

Nor am I claiming that actions motivated by a sense of duty or obligation, by altruism or self-sacrifice, by benevolence, pity, charity, sympathy, and so on *never* have a place in personal relationships. They may be appropriate in unusual circumstances. But such motives and actions are a fall-back mechanism which I compare to the safety net beneath a high wire act. We may be safer with a net, but the act is no good if the net actually comes into play very often. Similarly, the fall-back mechanisms may, in times of crisis, protect us and *some* of what we want, but they do not and cannot safeguard what is central to personal relationships. Thus when we find ourselves thinking characteristically or even very often in terms of the motives and concepts I have claimed are generally inappropriate in personal relationships, this is a symptom that our relationships are unsound, unhealthy, jeopardized, decayed, or that they never did become the personal relationships we wanted and hoped for. (Compare Hardwig, 1984.)

A third lesson about the ethics of personal relationships can be drawn from these reflections: The distinction between egoism and altruism is not characteristically applicable to personal relationships. Neither party magnanimously or ignominiously sacrifices personal interests, but the two interests are not independent, not really even two. For your ends are my ends too. The distinction between giving and receiving thus collapses. In impersonal contexts, if I respect your (independent) interests, that may be all you want of me. But in a personal context, you will want me to be interested in your interests. For if I am not interested in your interests, your well-being is not one of my ends.

This does not, of course, mean that all interests will be shared, but it means I am interested even in those of your interests I do not share. (I may have no appreciation of operas, but knowing how much they mean to you, it is important to me that your life include them. Operas for you are important to me in a way that operas for others who may love them just as much simply are not.) Nor, of course, am I claiming that there are *never* conflicts of interest in personal relationships. But such conflicts are set within the context of the meaning each has for the other and are therefore seen and handled differently. In personal relationships, conflicts of interest are conflicts within myself, a very different thing from a conflict of interest with someone separate from me.

A fourth lesson about ethics and personal relationships is this: Because personal relationships are ends—indeed, ultimate and incommensurable ends—they cannot and need not be justified by an appeal to some higher value such as love, pleasure, utility, or social utility. Any ethics that attempts to justify personal relationships in terms of more ultimate goods depersonalizes personal relationships. It construes us as wanting these higher goods, not each other.

Nor can the relative merits of personal relationships be adequately assessed in terms of abstract values. Each personal relationship is a good *sui generis*. Irreducibly involving the specific persons that they do, personal relationships cannot be reduced to common denominators that would permit comparison without depersonalizing them. Although persons caught in situations requiring choices between different personal relationships sometimes talk (and probably think) about comparing them in terms of abstract common denominators, evaluating relationships in this way Platonistically reduces our loved ones to mere instantiations of forms, thus depersonalizing them and our relationships to them.

A fifth and final lesson serves to summarize and conclude these reflections. The ethics of personal relationships must see persons in nonatomic terms; it must be based on a doctrine of internal relations. People see themselves in nonatomic terms if they see at least some other individuals not just as means to their well-being, but as part of their well-being. As I suggested earlier, there is no way to explain why I value a relationship with *you* (over and above the goods I desire from you and from this kind of relationship) except by saying that I feel a bond between us. I have come to see myself as a self that can only be fulfilled by a life that includes a relationship with you. Thus I see myself, in part, as part of a larger whole that is *us*. This does not mean that I see you as either a necessary or a sufficient condition for my well-being. If our relationship ends, my world will not fall apart and I may know that it won't. But if our relationship does end, I will have to alter my conception of myself and my well-being. . . .

Granted, we must remember that relationships can be viciously personal as well as gloriously personal. And it does seem plausible to maintain that we don't need an ethics for times when relationships are healthy and going smoothly. But again, I believe that the plausibility of this view reflects the limitations of the ways in which we have thought about ethics. I would contend, instead, that we *do* need an ethics for good times and for healthy, beautiful relationships—an ethics of *aspiration* that would serve to clarify what we aim for in personal relationships and to remind us of how they are best done.

Moreover, even when personal relationships become troubled, strained, or even vicious, it is not always possible or desirable to depersonalize the relationship. And an ethics must not tacitly urge or require us to depersonalize our relationships whenever serious conflicts arise. Within a personal relationship, the depersonalizing stance will often distort the issue beyond recognition. If we leave out my love for you, my turmoil over how often you drink yourself into oblivion vanishes, and with it, the issue that arises between us. For I can acknowledge with equanimity the drinking of others who are not personally related to me. My concern is simply not an impersonal concern that ranges indifferently over many possible objects of concern.

Depersonalizing (or ending) a relationship *may* be the appropriate final step in the face of intractable difficulties. But I would deny that depersonalizing is always the best course even here. For I think we should aspire to learn how to end relationships without depersonalizing them. If we can learn to continue to care and to care personally for our past loves, friends, and partners, we can be left happier, less bitter, wiser about the causes of the difficulties, and better able to go on to other relationships than if we end our relationships in hostility, anger, rejection, or even the kind of indifference characteristic of an impersonal stance.

What, then, is to be done? If we accept my position that we need an ethics of personal relationships and that such an ethics will have to be different from an ethics of impersonal relationships, the field of ethics opens up and ethical theory turns out to be a much less thoroughly explored domain than we might have thought. For my view implies that there are vast, largely uncharted regions beyond what we have come to know as ethics. I have tried to point to this region, but I have hardly begun to explore it.

1. We need to consider whether personal relationships are always better. If that view is correct, impersonal relationships would be only the result of the limitations of our sense of relatedness, and there would be a constant ethical

imperative to personalize social contexts whenever possible and to expand our sense of connectedness. I suspect, however, that some relationships are better left impersonal and also that, because enmity, resentment, disgust, and many forms of conflict are much more bitter and intractable when they are personal, there are situations where depersonalizing is a good strategy. We must also understand more clearly exactly what depersonalizing a relationship involves.

2. We need an ethics for quasi-personal relationships (love, marriage, friendship) when these relationships are not also *personal* (in the sense I have been trying to explicate). For it is perhaps in such contexts that people are most devastatingly used, abused, and mistreated. Still, quasi-personal relationships have important roles to play, both when they do and when they do not involve a personal relationship: Marriage is also a financial institution; our concept of a parent seeks to insure that children will be protected and raised, even if not loved; even living together is in part an arrangement for sharing the chores of daily life.

3. We need some way to deal with the conflicts and tensions arising in situations involving both personal and impersonal relationships. Is it moral, for example, for me to buy computer games and gold chains for my son while other children are starving, simply because he is *my son* and I have a personal relationship with him? The issues about the extent to which one can legitimately favor those to whom one is personally related are, for me, deeply troubling and almost impenetrable to my ethical insight. . . .

4. Then, when we have all this in view, we should perhaps reexamine our "stranger ethics" to see if we need to revise our ethics of impersonal relationships in light of the ethics of personal and quasi-personal relationships.

5. Finally, we undoubtedly need a more precise understanding of what makes relationships personal, a better grasp on the values of such relationships, and a much more rigorous and developed account of the ethics of personal relationships. For even if the present paper succeeds beyond my wildest dreams, it has only scratched the surface.

Until we have done all these things, it will be premature to make pronouncements about what constitutes "the moral point of view."

Note

Acknowledgments: This paper was begun in 1978 at a National Endowment for the Humanities Summer Seminar directed by Amelie Rorty. It has, in various versions, benefited from many helpful criticisms and suggestions from the members of that NEH seminar, from the Philosophy Departments at East Tennessee State University and Virginia Commonwealth University, from the members of Kathy Emmett's seminar on personal relationships, from the editors of the present volume, and especially from Amelie Rorty and Mary Read English. My many benefactors have left me with a whole sheaf of powerful and important ideas for revising, amending, and qualifying what I've said, but unfortunately too often without the wit and wisdom needed to incorporate their suggestions into this paper.

REVIEW QUESTIONS

1. Why does Hardwig believe that we don't yet have an ethics of personal relationships?
2. Paraphrase Hardwig's two main characteristics of personal relationships.
3. What does the "quasi" mean in quasi-personal relationships?
4. State and explain the basic principle of Hardwig's ethics of personal relationships.
5. Fill in the blanks and explain: "First, personal relationships between adults (and perhaps also between adults and children) are to be entered into and continued out of a sense of _____ , _____ and _____ , both in _____ and in the _____ . . . ."
6. Explain what Hardwig means by his fifth lesson about the ethics of personal relationships; namely, that it's necessary to "see persons in nonatomic terms." Since this is such an important point, give a couple of examples of what it means to see persons as nonatomic.

PROBES

1. Explain the difference between treating a person as a means to an end and treating the person as an end in him- or herself. Give an example to illustrate your explanation.
2. What is the link between Hardwig's second main characteristic of a personal relationship and my discussion of uniqueness, or noninterchangeability, in Chapter 2?
3. Why does Hardwig believe that a one-sided personal relationship is "ripe for exploitation and tragedy"?
4. Why do motives and intentions play so much larger of a role in personal relationships than in impersonal relationships?
5. Why does Hardwig discourage—but not completely reject—the motives of duty, altruism, pity, and sympathy in personal relationships?
6. Hardwig claims that the distinction between egoism and altruism is not normally applicable to personal relationships. Paraphrase the argument he makes to support this claim, and tell whether you agree or disagree.
7. Hardwig says that we should learn to end a relationship without depersonalizing it. Think back to the last time you ended a relationship. Did either of you depersonalize it? What effects did that have? How might you have kept it personal and yet ended it?

CHAPTER 8

Communicating with Intimate Partners

The changing relationships we have with intimates—romantic partners, spouses, and roommates or housemates—are some of the most challenging ones we face. Most people prefer to live with someone rather than living alone, and as the first reading in this chapter indicates, "marriage"—even if it's nontraditional—is still the dominant relationship in western culture. But, whether you're married or not, it isn't easy to live with someone over a long period of time. In other words, intimacy inevitably creates problems. The five readings in this chapter can help you cope with them.

First, two experienced counselors discuss how meaningful relationships work and review almost 20 qualities or characteristics of successful ones. Then two readings analyze gender and intimate communication. The first questions the widely held belief that, as one pop-psych book put it, "men are from Mars and women are from Venus." These authors argue that there are more similarities than differences in the ways men and women communicate. The next reading preserves what's sensible and accurate about differences between women and men. Then the last two readings in the chapter focus on challenges to intimate relationships. Two authors summarize what is known about long-distance relationships, and then the chapter ends with a discussion of romance in cyberspace. Each of these authors brings expertise to this topic, and each explains how you can practically apply their findings and advice.

This first excerpt comes from the fifth edition of an unusual book designed to help people of any age expand their self-awareness and explore the choices available to them. I've included it because it focuses on some of the most difficult and important topics to discuss—for example, what does it mean to be in an "intimate" relationship or to "love" someone—and it addresses these topics personally rather than impersonally. One author—Jerry—is a professor of human services and counseling, and the other—Marianne—is a marriage and family therapist.

One of the first important points they make is that "we have the power to bring about change [in our relationships] if we ourselves change and do not insist that the other person make quick and total changes." This means that the rule of quid pro quo (I only give something when I get something in return) should *not* be applied in personal relationships. The only part of the relationship that I have any control over is my own part. And, although changes by one person almost always precede changes in the other (just because a relationship is a system in which everything affects everything else), it doesn't work to focus your change efforts on anyone but yourself. With this in mind, the authors emphasize, "you can choose the kinds of relationships you want to experience."

This selection discusses 19 characteristics of a meaningful relationship. I won't repeat the whole list here, but I think several are worth paying close attention to. For example, the Coreys emphasize that intimacy doesn't mean losing your sense of self; people in healthy, close relationships maintain their own separate identities. This is often experienced and discussed as the difference between "wanting" the other person and "needing" him or her. Another is that, as Steve Duck emphasizes in Chapter 7, each person in a healthy relationship is willing to work at keeping the relationship alive. If the relationship includes a sexual component, this also means that each person also makes some attempt to keep the romance alive. Another feature is that each person finds meaning and nourishment outside the relationship, rather than being totally dependent on the other, and both avoid manipulating, exploiting, or using each other. Healthy relationships are also marked by the partners' abilities to deal with the anger that inevitably surfaces. And, perhaps most fundamentally, in a healthy intimate relationship, each person has a commitment to the other, an investment in their future together that can tide them over in times of conflict and crisis.

The second major section of the reading discusses how to deal with barriers to effective communication that inhibit the development and maintainence of intimate relationships. Poor listening is one of the major barriers, which means that the materials in Chapter 5 apply to this chapter, too. Awareness of different gender styles is also important. The Coreys acknowledge that there are important cultural differences in what makes personal communication "effective," and they list 11 characteristics of this kind of communication in Euro-American cultures.

The Coreys conclude by encouraging you to apply what they discuss to improve some of your most important relationships. As they put it, "it will be helpful to begin by working on one of these skills at a time."

Intimate Relationships

Gerald Corey and Marianne Schneider-Corey

INTRODUCTION

Although this [reading] focuses mainly on the role that relationships play in our lives, we deal with relationships from a broad perspective, and also with a range of lifestyles. The [reading] deals with friendships, marital relationships, intimacy between people who are not married, dating relationships, relationships between parents and children, same-gender relationships as well as opposite-gender relationships, alternative lifestyles, and other meaningful personal relationships.

Marriage is still the dominant relationship in our society, particularly if the term *marriage* is construed broadly to include the many couples who consider themselves committed to each other even though they are not legally married as well as those who are creating relationships that are different in many respects from the traditional marriage. Bellah and his colleagues (1985) found that in today's society most people still want to marry, even though many of them no longer see it as a life requirement. For increasing numbers of people it is not considered disgraceful to be unmarried, and more people are remaining single by choice. There is less pressure to have children, and starting a family tends to be more of a conscious decision than was true in the past. Most of those interviewed believe in love as a basis for an enduring relationship. Love and commitment appear to be highly valued, although maintaining these qualities is difficult. Most people value spontaneity and solidity, freedom and intimacy, and the sharing of thoughts, feelings, values, and life goals. They feel freer than in the past to leave a marriage that is not working, and divorce is seen as one (but not the only) solution to an unhappy marriage.

Whether you choose to marry or not, or whether your preference is a same-gender or an opposite-gender primary relationship, you probably have many different types of relationships. What is true for marriage is largely true for these other relationships as well. Allowing for the differences in relationships, the signs of growth and meaningfulness are much the same, and so are the problems. Consequently, whatever lifestyle you choose, you can use the ideas in this [reading] as a basis for thinking about the role relationships play in your life. [Our] aim is to stimulate your reflection on what you want from all of your special relationships, and also to invite you to take an honest look at the quality of these relationships.

TYPES OF INTIMACY

[Psychologist Erik] Erikson maintains that the challenge of forming intimate relationships is the major task of early adulthood. Intimacy implies that we are able to share significant aspects of ourselves with others. The issues we raise concerning barriers to intimacy and ways of enhancing intimacy can help you better understand the many different types of relationships in your life. The ideas in this [reading] are useful tools in rethinking what kind of relationships you want, as well as in clarifying some new choices that you may want to make. You can take a fresh look at these relationships, including both their frustrations and their delights, and you can think about initiating some changes.

Consider the case of Donald, who told us about how little closeness he had experienced with his father. He saw his father as uncaring, aloof, and preoccupied with his own concerns. Yet Donald deeply wished that he could be physically and emotionally closer to him, and he had no idea how to bring this about. He made the difficult decision to talk to his father and tell him how he felt and what he wanted. His father appeared to listen, and his eyes moistened, but then without saying much he quickly left the room. Donald reported how hurt and disappointed he was that his father had not been as responsive as he had hoped he would be. What Donald was missing were subtle, yet significant, signs that his father had been touched and was not as uncaring as he had imagined. That his father listened to him, that he responded with even a few clumsy words, that he touched Donald on the shoulder, and that he became emotional were all manifestations that Donald's overtures had been received. Donald needs to understand that his father is probably very uncomfortable in talking personally. His father may well be every bit as afraid of his son's rejection as Donald is of his father's rebuffs. Donald will need to show patience and continue "hanging in there" with his father if he is really interested in changing the ways they relate to each other.

The experience Donald had with his father could have occurred in any intimate relationship. We can experience feelings of awkwardness, unexpressed desires, and fears of rejection with our friends, lovers, spouses, parents, or children. A key point is that we have the power to bring about change if we ourselves change and do not insist that the other person make quick and total changes. It is up to us to teach others specific ways of becoming more personal. It does little good to invest our energy in lamenting all the ways in which the other person is not fulfilling our expectations, nor is it helpful to focus on remaking others. . . . When you take a passive stance and simply hope the other person will change in the ways that you would like, you are giving away a sense of your power.

The intimacy we share with another person can be emotional, intellectual, physical, spiritual, or any combination of these. It can be exclusive or nonexclusive, long-term or brief. . . .

When we avoid intimacy, we only rob ourselves. We may pass up the chance to really get to know neighbors and new acquaintances, because we fear that either we or our new friends will move and that the friendship will come to an end. Similarly, we may not want to open ourselves to intimacy with sick or dying persons, because we fear the pain of losing them. Although such fears may be natural ones, too often we allow them to cheat us of the uniquely rich experience of being truly close to another person. We can enhance our life greatly by daring to care about others and fully savoring the time we can share with them now.

The idea that we most want to stress is that you can choose the kinds of relationships you want to experience. Often, we fail to make our own choices and instead fall into a certain type of relationship because we think "This is the way it's *supposed* to be." For example, some people marry who in reality might prefer to remain single—particularly women who often feel the pressure to have a family because it's "natural" for them to do so. Sometimes people choose a heterosexual relationship because they think that it is what is expected of them, when they would really prefer a homosexual relationship. Instead of blindly accepting that relationships must be a certain way or that only one type of lifestyle is possible, you have the choice of giving real thought to the question of what types of intimacy have meaning for you.

MEANINGFUL RELATIONSHIPS: A PERSONAL VIEW

In this section we share some of our ideas about the characteristics of a mean-ingful relationship. Although these guidelines pertain to couples, they are also relevant to other personal relationships, such as those between parent and child and between friends of the same or opposite gender. Take, for example, the guideline "The persons involved are willing to work at keeping their relation-ship alive." Sometimes parents and children take each other for granted and rarely spend time talking about how they are getting along. Either parent or child may expect the other to assume the major responsibility for their relation-ship. The same principle applies to friends or to partners in a primary relation-ship. As you look over our list, adapt it to your own relationships, keeping in mind your particular cultural values. Since the values that are a part of your cultural background play an influential role in your relationships, you will need to adapt them in appropriate ways. As you review our list, ask yourself what qualities you think are most important in your relationships.

We see relationships as most meaningful when they are dynamic and evolv-ing rather than fixed or final. Thus, there may be periods of joy and excitement followed by times of struggle, pain, and distance. As long as the persons in a re-lationship are growing and changing, their relationship is bound to change as well. The following are some of the qualities of a relationship that seem most im-portant to us.

- *Each person in the relationship has a separate identity.* Kahlil Gibran (1923) ex-presses this thought in *The Prophet:* "But let there be spaces in your togeth-erness, and let the winds of the heavens dance between you" (p. 16). In *The Dance of Anger,* Harriet Goldhor Lerner (1985) says that making long-term relationships work is difficult because it is necessary to create and maintain a balance between separateness and togetherness. If there is not enough to-getherness in a relationship, people in it typically feel isolated and do not share feelings and experiences. If there is not enough separateness, they give up a sense of their own identity and control. They also devote much ef-fort to becoming what the other person expects.
- *Although each person desires the other, each can survive without the other.* This characteristic is an extension of the prior one, and it implies that people are in a relationship by choice. They are not so tightly bound together that if they are separated, one or the other becomes lost and empty. Thus, if a young man says "I simply can't live without my girlfriend," he is indeed in trouble. His dependency should not be interpreted as love but as the seek-ing of an object to make him feel complete.
- *Each is able to talk openly with the other about matters of significance to the rela-tionship.* The two persons can openly express grievances and let each other know the changes they desire. They can ask for what they want, rather than expecting the other to intuitively know what they want and give it to them. For example, assume that you are not satisfied with how you and your

mother spend time together. You can take the first step by letting her know, in a nonjudgmental way, that you would like to talk more personally. Rather than telling her how she is, you can focus more on telling her how you feel in your relationship with her.

- *Each person assumes responsibility for his or her own level of happiness and refrains from blaming the other if he or she is unhappy.* Of course, in a close relationship or friendship the unhappiness of the other person is bound to affect you, but you should not expect another person to *make* you happy, fulfilled, or excited. Although the way others feel will influence your life, they do not create or cause your feelings. Ultimately, you are responsible for defining your goals and your life, and you can take actions to change what *you* are doing if you are unhappy with a situation.

- *The persons involved are willing to work at keeping their relationship alive.* If we hope to keep a relationship vital, we must reevaluate and revise our way of being with each other from time to time. Consider how this guideline fits for your friendships. If you take a good friend for granted and show little interest in doing what is necessary to maintain your friendship, she may soon grow disenchanted and wonder what kind of friend you are.

- *The persons are able to have fun and to play together; they enjoy doing things with each other.* It is easy to become so serious that we forget to take the time to enjoy those we love. One way of changing drab relationships is to become aware of the infrequency of playful moments and then determine what things are getting in the way of enjoying life. Again, think of this guideline as it applies to your close friends.

- *Each person is growing, changing, and opening up to new experiences.* When you rely on others for your personal fulfillment and confirmation as a person, you are in trouble. The best way to build solid relationships with others is to work on developing your own personality. But do not be surprised if you encounter resistance to your growth and change. This resistance can come from within yourself as well as from others.

- *If the relationship contains a sexual component, each person makes some attempt to keep the romance alive.* The two persons may not always experience the intensity and novelty of the early period of their relationship, but they can devise ways of creating a climate of romance and closeness. They may go places they haven't been to before or otherwise vary their routine in some ways. They recognize when their life is getting dull and look for ways to eliminate its boring aspects. In their lovemaking they are sensitive to each other's needs and desires; at the same time, they are able to ask each other for what they want and need.

- *The two persons are equal in the relationship.* People who feel that they are typically the "givers" and that their partner is usually unavailable when they need him or her might question the balance in their relationship. In some relationships one person may feel compelled to assume a superior position relative to the other—for example, to be very willing to listen and give advice yet unwilling to go to the other person and show any vulnerability or need.

Lerner (1985) says that women often define their own wishes and preferences as being the same as those of their partner. In this case there surely is no equality in the relationship. Both parties need to be willing to look at aspects of inequality and demonstrate a willingness to negotiate changes.

- *Each person actively demonstrates concern for the other.* In a vital relationship the participants do more than just talk about how much they value each other. Their actions show their care and concern more eloquently than any words. Each person has a desire to give to the other. They have an interest in each other's welfare and a desire to see that the other person is fulfilled.

- *Each person finds meaning and sources of nourishment outside the relationship.* Sometimes people become very possessive in their friendships. A sign of a healthy relationship is that each avoids assuming an attitude of ownership toward the other. Although they may experience jealousy at times, they do not demand that the other person deaden his or her feelings for others. Their lives did not begin when they met each other, nor would their lives end if they should part.

- *Each avoids manipulating, exploiting, and using the other.* Each respects and cares for the other and is willing to see the world through the other's eyes. At times parent-child relationships are strained because either or both parties attempt to manipulate the other. Consider the father who brags about his son, Roger, to others and whose affection is based on Roger's being an outstanding athlete. Roger may feel used if his father is able to talk only of sports. What if he were to decide to quit playing sports? Would he still be earning his father's approval?

- *Each person is moving in a direction in life that is personally meaningful.* They are both excited about the quality of their lives and their projects. Applied to couples, this guideline implies that both individuals feel that their needs are being met within the relationship, but they also feel a sense of engagement in their work, play, and relationships with other friends and family members. Goldberg (1987) makes some excellent points pertaining to these issues:

> Probably the best or healthiest relationships begin without intensely romantic feelings, but where there is a genuine basis for being with each other on a friendship level and where there is enjoyment of each other's company without concern over commitment or future. Add to that a balanced flow of power, healthy conflict resolution free of blaming guilt, a sense of being known for who you are and knowing your partner, and a relaxed desire to be fully present with little need to escape or avoid through distraction, and you have a fine potential for growth in a good relationship. (p. 89) . . .

- *If they are in a committed relationship, they maintain this relationship by choice, not simply for the sake of any children involved, out of duty, or because of convenience.* They choose to keep their ties with each other even if things get rough or if they sometimes experience emptiness in their relationship. They share some common purposes and values, and therefore, they are willing to look at what is lacking in their relationship and to work on changing undesirable situations.

- *They are able to cope with anger in their relationship.* Couples often seek relationship counseling with the expectation that they will learn to stop fighting and that conflict will end. This is not a realistic goal. More important than the absence of fighting is learning how to fight cleanly and constructively, which entails an ongoing process of expressing anger and frustrations. It is the buildup of these emotions that creates trouble. If anger is not expressed and dealt with constructively, it will sour a relationship. Stored-up anger usually results in the target person's getting more than his or her share of deserved anger. At other times bottled-up anger is let out in indirect ways such as sarcasm and hostility. If the parties in a relationship are angry, they should try to express it in a direct way.

- *Each person recognizes the need for solitude and is willing to create the time in which to be alone.* Each allows the other a sense of privacy. Because they recognize each other's individual integrity, they avoid prying into every thought or manipulating the other to disclose what he or she wants to keep private. Sometimes parents are guilty of not respecting the privacy of their children. A father may be hurt if his daughter does not want to talk with him at any time that he feels like talking. He needs to realize that she is a separate person with her own needs and that she may need time alone at certain times when he wants to talk.

- *They do not expect the other to do for them what they are capable of doing for themselves.* They don't expect the other person to make them feel alive, take away their boredom, assume their risks, or make them feel valued and important. Each is working toward creating his or her own autonomous identity. Consequently, neither person depends on the other for confirmation of his or her personal worth; nor does one walk in the shadow of the other.

- *They encourage each other to become all that they are capable of becoming.* Unfortunately, people often have an investment in keeping those with whom they are intimately involved from changing. Their expectations and needs may lead them to resist changes in their partner and thus make it difficult for their partner to grow. If they recognize their fears, however, they can challenge their need to block their partner's progress.

- *Each has a commitment to the other.* Commitment is a vital part of an intimate relationship. It means that the people involved have an investment in their future together and that they are willing to stay with each other in times of crisis and conflict. Although many people express an aversion to any long-term commitment in a relationship, how deeply will they allow themselves to be loved if they believe that the relationship can be dissolved on a whim when things look bleak? Perhaps, for some people, a fear of intimacy gets in the way of developing a sense of commitment. Loving and being loved is both exciting and frightening, and we may have to struggle with the issue of how much anxiety we want to tolerate. Commitment to another person involves risks and carries a price, but it is an essential part of an intimate relationship.

DEALING WITH COMMUNICATION BLOCKS

A number of barriers to effective communication can inhibit the developing and maintaining of intimate relationships. Some of these barriers are failing to really listen to another person; selective listening—that is, hearing only what you want to hear; being overly concerned with getting your point across without considering the other's views; silently rehearsing what you will say next as you are "listening"; becoming defensive, with self-protection your primary concern; attempting to change others rather than first attempting to understand them; telling others how they are, rather than telling them how they affect you; bringing old patterns into the present and not allowing the other person to change; overreacting to a person; failing to state what your needs are and expecting others to know intuitively; making assumptions about another person without checking them out; using sarcasm and hostility instead of being direct; and speaking in vague terms such as "You manipulate me!"

In most of these cases you tend to be so concerned with getting your point across, defending your view of yourself, or changing another person that you cannot appreciate what the other person is thinking and feeling. These blocks make it very difficult to have what are called I-Thou encounters, in which two persons are open with themselves and each other, expressing what they think and feel and making genuine contact. Instead, the persons who are attempting to communicate typically feel distant from each other.

Deborah Tannen has written two best-selling books on the subject of communication between women and men. In *That's Not What I Meant* (1987), Tannen focuses on how conversational styles can make or break a relationship. She maintains that male-female communication can be considered cross-cultural. The language we use as we are growing up is influenced by our gender, ethnicity, class and cultural background, and location. Boys and girls grow up in different worlds, even if they are part of the same family. Furthermore, they carry many of the patterns they established in childhood into their transactions as adults. For Tannen, these cultural differences include different expectations about the role of communication in relationships. These factors make up our conversational style, and the subtle differences in this style can lead to overwhelming misunderstandings and disappointments. In her other book, *You Just Don't Understand* (1991), Tannen develops the idea that conversational style differences do not explain all the conflicts in relationships between women and men, but many problems result because partners are expressing their thoughts and feelings in different ways. She believes that if we can sort out these differences based on conversational style, then we are better able to confront real conflicts and find a form of communication that will allow for a negotiation of these differences.

[Carl R.] Rogers (1961) has written extensively on ways to improve personal relationships. For him, the main block to effective communication is our tendency to evaluate and judge the statements of others. He believes that what gets in the way of understanding another is the tendency to approve or disapprove, the unwillingness to put ourselves in the other's frame of reference, and the fear of being changed ourselves if we really listen to and understand a person with a viewpoint different from our own.

One of Roger's suggestions for testing the quality of our understanding of someone is as follows: The next time you get into an argument with your partner, your friend, or a small group of friends, just stop the discussion for a moment and, for an experiment, institute this rule: "Each person can speak up for himself only after he has restated the ideas and feelings of the previous speaker accurately, and to that speaker's satisfaction" (p. 332). Carrying out this experiment implies that you must strive to genuinely understand another person and achieve his or her perspective. Although this may sound simple, it can be extremely difficult to put into practice. It involves challenging yourself to go beyond what you find convenient to hear, examining your assumptions and prejudices, not attributing to statements meanings that were not intended, and not coming to quick conclusions based on superficial listening. If you are successful in challenging yourself in these ways, you can enter the subjective world of the significant person in your life; that is, you can acquire empathy, which is the necessary foundation for all intimate relationships. Rogers (1980) contends that the sensitive companionship offered by an empathic person is healing and that such a deep understanding is a precious gift to another.

Effective Personal Communication

Your culture influences both the content and the process of your communication. Some cultures prize direct communication, while other cultures see this behavior as rude and insensitive. In certain cultures direct eye contact is as insulting as the avoidance of eye contact is in other cultures. Harmony within the family is a cardinal value in certain cultures, and it may be inappropriate for adult children to confront their parents. As you read the following discussion, recognize that variations do exist among cultures. Our discussion has a Euro-American slant, which makes it essential that you adapt the principles we present to your own cultural framework. You need to examine the ways that your communication style has been influenced by your culture and then decide if you want to modify certain patterns that you have learned. For example, your culture might have taught you to control your feelings. You might decide to become more emotionally expressive if you discover that this pattern is restricting you in areas of your life where you would like to be freer.

From our perspective, when two persons are communicating meaningfully, they are involved in many of the following processes:

- They are facing each other and making eye contact, and one is listening while the other speaks.
- They do not rehearse their response while the other is speaking. The listener is able to summarize accurately what the speaker has said. ("So you're hurt when I don't call to tell you that I'll be late.")
- The language is specific and concrete. (A vague statement is "I feel manipulated." A concrete statement is "I don't like it when you bring me flowers

and then expect me to do something for you that I already told you I didn't want to do.")
- The speaker makes personal statements instead of bombarding the other with impersonal questions. (A questioning statement is "Where were you last night, and why did you come home so late?" A personal statement is "I was worried and scared because I didn't know where you were last night.")
- The listener takes a moment before responding to reflect on what was said and on how he or she is affected. There is a sincere effort to walk in the shoes of the other person. ("It must have been very hard for you when you didn't know where I was last night and thought I might have been in an accident.")
- Although each has reactions to what the other is saying, there is an absence of critical judgment. (A critical judgment is "You never think about anybody but yourself, and you're totally irresponsible." A more appropriate reaction would be "I appreciate it when you think to call me, knowing that I may be worried.")
- Each of the parties can be honest and direct without insensitively damaging the other's dignity. Each makes "I" statements, rather than second-guessing and speaking for the other. ("Sometimes I worry that you don't care about me, and I want to check that out with you, rather than assuming that it's true.")
- There is a respect for each other's differences and an avoidance of pressuring each other to accept a point of view. ("I look at this matter very differently than you do, but I understand that you have your own opinion.")
- There is a congruency (or a matching) between the verbal and nonverbal messages. (If she is expressing anger, she is not smiling.)
- Each person is open about how he or she is affected by the other. (An ineffective response is "You have no right to criticize me." An effective response is "I'm very disappointed that you don't like the work I've done.")
- Neither person is being mysterious, expecting the other to decode his or her messages.

These processes are essential for fostering any meaningful relationship. You might try observing yourself while you are communicating, and take note of the degree to which you practice these principles. Decide if the quality of your relationships is satisfying to you. If you determine that you want to improve certain relationships, it will be helpful to begin by working on one of these skills at a time.

REVIEW QUESTIONS

1. Give an example from your own experience of a relationship where the persons involved do not have very strong individual identities. Give an example of another relationship where they do.
2. What do the Coreys say about fault-finding and blaming in relationships?
3. Explain the conflict-management suggestion by Carl Rogers that the Coreys include in their discussion about communication blocks.
4. What do the Coreys mean when they say that effective communication involves "specific and concrete" language and "personal statements instead of impersonal questions"?

PROBES

1. How do you respond to these authors' comments about same-gender relationships? How might your response be reflected in your own communication with lesbian and homosexual individuals?
2. The Coreys say that in a meaningful relationship "each is able to talk openly with the other about matters of significance to the relationship." Are they suggesting that you need to be *completely* open and honest? What are some important limitations on this feature?
3. What might be the Coreys' rationale for beginning their discussion of "communication blocks" with a comment about *listening?* Why do they start at this end of the communication process?
4. Review the Coreys' 11 suggestions about effective communication from the perspective of a non-Euro-American culture. What differences do you believe characterize effective communication in another culture?

REFERENCES

1. Bellah, R. N., Madsen, R., Sullivan, W. M., Swidler, A., & Tipton, S. M. (1985). *Habits of the Heart: Individualism and Commitment in American Life.* New York: Harper & Row.
2. Gibran, K. (1923). *The Prophet.* New York: Knopf.
3. Goldberg, H. (1987). *The Inner Male: Overcoming Roadblocks to Intimacy.* New York: New American Library.
4. Lerner, H. G. (1985). *The Dance of Anger: A Woman's Guide to Changing the Patterns of Intimate Relationships.* New York: Harper & Row.
5. Rogers, C. R. (1961). *On Becoming a Person.* Boston: Houghton Mifflin.
6. Rogers, C. R. (1980). *A Way of Being.* Boston: Houghton Mifflin.
7. Tannen, D. (1987). *That's Not What I Meant: How Conversational Style Makes or Breaks Relationships.* New York: Ballantine.
8. Tannen, D. (1991). *You Just Don't Understand: Women and Men in Conversation.* New York: Ballantine.

One of the most dominant ideas in the late 1990s was that, as author John Gray put it, "men are from Mars and women are from Venus." According to a considerable amount of scholarly research and several popular accounts of this research in Gray's hugely successful book and several best-sellers by Deborah Tannen, men and women have significantly different communication styles. This literature argues that a great deal of the misunderstanding between men and women is due to these differences, and that it can help for both genders to learn to accept these differences, and even to communicate using the other gender's preferred style.

This excerpt from the 1997 book *Sex and Gender Differences in Personal Relationships* challenges almost every claim that Gray and Tannen make. Communication researcher and teacher Daniel Canary and his coauthors claim that most of the research on gender and communication, when it is examined carefully, "does *not* support the view that men and women come from separate cultures, let alone separate worlds." They argue that these "long-presumed differences in men's and women's interpersonal behavior simply do not reflect in the empirical research literature." In other words, this reading claims that, if you examine studies of what actually happens when men and women communicate, you will not find support for the "two cultures," "Mars and Venus" view.

Instead, there is evidence for much more similarity than difference. For example, a review of some 1,200 studies regarding sex differences in social behavior found that only about 1 percent of the variance in people's social behavior is attributable to sex or gender. "If men and women do originate from different cultures or worlds", these authors conclude, "they at least speak the same language about 99% of the time."

A major part of the problem, these authors argue, is that some of the people who contend that there are vast differences have stereotyped the women and men they have studied. Once these stereotypes are in the literature, they influence the studies that come after them. Canary, Emmers-Sommer, and Faulkner argue that, even though gender stereotypes offer simple answers to complex and troubling questions, there is in the end little to be gained by polarizing men and women in these ways. The serious problem, as these authors put it, is that "if one holds that men are from Mars and women are from Venus, then it follows that Earth provides no home for either sex."

This reading unpacks this problem, first, by defining *sex* and *gender* in order to clarify what's being studied in these articles and books. Then the authors analyze the presumption of differences between the genders. They acknowledge that there are obviously important distinctions in both sex and gender. But when one asks about whether there are consistent and important sex and gender differences in personal relationships, things are not so clear-cut.

One claim in the popular books is that women tend to be communal and men tend to be instrumental. But if one looks at much of the evidence, it is difficult to find these simple and clear differences. As this reading puts it, "expressive and instrumental characteristics are about equally prominent aspects of a strong friendship for both women and men." Another researcher concluded that "similarities between men and women [are] far greater than the differences, and that knowledge about a person's [sex] will give us little ability to accurately predict how a person will behave in many situations."

In place of the simplified stereotype, Canary and his colleagues propose what they call a "flowchart model" for predicting stereotypic interaction behavior. The model, which is presented in Figure 8–1 in this reading, indicates that sex-stereotyped behavior is liable to occur only when several of five conditions are present: (1) The people involved are focusing on gender, (2) their beliefs are consistent with stereotypes, (3) the context or situation is not one where men and women fill similar roles (e.g., managers or teachers), (4) the participants don't expect nonstereotyped behaviors, and (5) the partner's behavior promotes sexual stereotypes. When *these* conditions exist, then you're likely to observe "Mars vs. Venus" phenomena. But in the overwhelming percentage of the time when these conditions do not exist—for example, when the men and women are of similar role or status, when nobody is expecting sex-stereotyped behavior, and when sex or gender is irrelevant to the communicators—then there will be many more similarities than differences between women and men.

I chose this reading to challenge a currently popular set of beliefs about gender and communication, and to warn readers about the dangers of believing everything that's written in best-selling books. I hope these pages will encourage you to think again about the whole "Mars–Venus" hypothesis.

At the same time, I also hope you won't just accept *this* reading at face value. One of the reasons the "Mars–Venus" hypothesis is so popular is that *it resonates with many peoples' experiences.* Here, Canary and his colleagues argue that ordinary people have been misled, and that social science can free them from their confusion. Sometimes this is called the "cultural dopes" argument. It says that you can't trust laypeople to get it right, but that experts—usually some kind of scientists—can be trusted to have insight into the "truth". But does this idea make sense to you? Are laypeople this gullible? Or does the incredibly widespread acceptance of the "Mars–Venus" idea argue for its validity? I hope you'll think about these questions and discuss them in class.

Moving Beyond Sex and Gender Stereotypes

Daniel J. Canary and Tara M. Emmers-Sommer, with Sandra Faulkner

There are two types of people in this world—those who categorize people into one of two groups and those who do not.

—*Popular paradox*

How men and women communicate in their personal relationships has become a "hot" topic in both academic and popular discussions. A common assumption

"Moving Beyond Sex and Gender Stereotypes" by Daniel J. Canary, Michael J. Cody and Valerie L. Manusov from *Sex and Gender Differences in Personal Relationships,* pp. 1–23. Reprinted by permission of The Guilford Press.

stresses differences between men and women that might explain problems between the sexes, which is conveyed in generalizations that take the form "Women want this, whereas men want that." Such views also suggest that people have only one brand of each sex to choose from; that is, all men are alike and all women resemble each other. . . . We attempt to counter the prevailing notion that differences between the sexes are constant and reveal separate molds, and we present an alternative to categorical thinking about men and women in their personal relationships. . . .

One relevant influence [on us as authors] is the recent popular portrayal of men and women. In 1990, Deborah Tannen published her widely accepted quasi-academic book, *You Just Don't Understand,* wherein men and women were cast as though they come from different cultures. Academics and lay people alike read Tannen's accounts of various "composite" couples and appreciated the nuance that Tannen offered. In addition, the two-cultures approach offered an alternative, though not necessarily an opposite point of view, to the dominance perspective that was popular in the 1970s and 1980s. Then John Gray (1992) exaggerated sex differences even further with the analogy that men are from Mars and women are from Venus, a thought that was inspired by the film *E.T.* (Gleick, 1997). The "nonfiction" portrayals by Tannen and Gray of men's and women's communication remained best sellers for years.

[But] most of the research does *not* support the view that men and women come from separate cultures, let alone separate worlds. Long-presumed differences in men's and women's interpersonal behavior simply do not reflect in the empirical research literature. Sex differences do not emerge because many researchers (like lay individuals) rely on traditional sex stereotypes when constructing the difference argument (i.e., men are instrumental, assertive, insensitive, and dominant, whereas women are communal, passive, sensitive, and subordinate), and the research shows that sex stereotypes poorly predict interpersonal communication behaviors.

Indeed, research suggests far more similarity than differences in men's and women's communication. For example, Canary and Hause (1993) reviewed 15 meta-analyses (representing some 1,200 studies) regarding sex differences in social behavior and found that about only 1% of the variance in people's social behavior derives from sex differences. Likewise, in the area of organizational communication, Wilkins and Andersen's (1991) meta-analysis (which was missed by Canary & Hause) found only one-half of 1% variance in behavior that was due to sex differences. According to these objective summaries, men and women are much more similar than different. If men and women do originate from different cultures or worlds, they at least speak the same language about 99% of the time.

Yet no one can deny that men and women are different. The issue is to provide some account of sex or gender that provides more insights than stereotypes can offer. Recently, scholars in psychology, communication, sociology, and related fields have offered theoretical models regarding men's and women's interaction in general that do not rely on stereotypic beliefs (e.g., Deaux & Major, 1987). . . .

How scholars and lay people conceptualize sex and/or gender differences varies radically. Accordingly, we do not anticipate widespread agreement with the points we make. We do hope for continued discussion about how men and women do, in fact, communicate and create expectations.

Many people still rely on stereotypes for their judgments on the issue of sex differences. But such a reliance on stereotypes only serves to perpetuate them among students and lay persons. In our view, the perpetuation of stereotypes constitutes the most disheartening outcome of books that distort and emphasize sex differences. If people come to believe that they are from separate cultures or worlds and that their social behavior is cast from separate molds, then they may never accept the idea that they can create their own gendered identities. As a result, advances in social, political, and economic equity might be handicapped by outdated notions of what men and women are capable of doing. [Here, we attempt] to correct an antiquated, unfair portrayal of women and men. Many people still measure a man by his career advancement and intelligence and a woman by her looks and spending habits. In light of widespread acceptance of such notions, our goal is to examine men and women in close relationships without assuming one sex is attracted to the mall, and the other a "cave" (Gray, 1992).

DO MEN AND WOMEN INHABIT DIFFERENT WORLDS?

John Gray's *Men Are from Mars, Women Are from Venus* (1992) has sold over 6 million copies—more than any other nonfiction hardcover book (Gleick, 1997, p. 69). Gray argues that men and women are so entirely different that it appears they come from different planets. And these planets have alternative meanings for the same language. But somewhere along the way, we have forgotten that men and women originated in different worlds and that we need an interpreter (John Gray?) to help us understand each other. This analogy not only provides the foundation for Gray's portrayal of personal relationships between men and women, it also serves as the premise for the entire book (and several other books Gray has written). Gray's success in using this figurative analogy as a premise for understanding men and women cannot be denied in a social or monetary sense—Gray enjoys thousands of loyal followers and has earned approximately $18 million from book sales alone (i.e., not counting money he gets from seminars [$35,000 per engagement], Mars and Venus Counseling Centers, or multimedia [videos, CDs, etc.]; Gleick, 1997).

Of course, Gray's figurative analogy presents a polarized view of men and women communicating with each other. For example, consider the following passage about how one sex difference hurts relationships:

> Women generally do not understand how Martians [men] cope with stress. They expect men to open up and talk about all their problems the way Venusians [women] do. When a man is stuck in his cave, a woman resents his not being

more open. She feels hurt when he turns on the news or goes outside to play some basketball and ignores her.

To expect a man who is in his cave instantly to become open, responsive, and loving is as unrealistic as expecting a woman who is upset immediately to calm down and make complete sense. It is a mistake to expect a man to always be in touch with his loving feelings just as it is a mistake to expect a woman's feelings to always be rational and logical. (p. 33)

To the extent one accepts the premise that men and women are so different they seem to come from different social and psychological worlds, Gray's many prescriptions regarding communication make sense. However, to the extent one finds the premise grossly exaggerated (and it is), then such a polarizing and stereotypic presentation of men and women appears fictional and offensive (see Crawford, 1995, for other examples regarding Gray's extreme position).

Although polarized portrayals of men and women may be entertaining (see also Tannen, 1990), one must wonder at their effect on people's understanding of sex and gender roles and how men and women *should* act in their close relationships. Geis (1993), for example, has provided evidence that at a general social level stereotypes act as value-laden, self-fulfilling prophecies. In other words, stereotypes about men and women become standards for behavior. Moreover, people have a tendency to create bipolar constructs, and thereby they essentialize the "male" and "female" qualities (Thorne, 1990). The question then is whether such polarized views function for the social good, for scientific purposes, or whether they have little social or scientific payoff.

Putnam (1982) argued that nothing can be gained by polarizing men and women through reliance on stereotypes. More specifically, she pointed out that understanding sex/gender differences in social interaction behavior requires more than an affirmation of sex stereotypes that portray women as communal (i.e., primarily concerned with relational welfare) and men as instrumental (i.e., primarily concerned with task-related resources). She described the landscape of scientific theory on the issue as "barren," largely due to the polarizations of men and women that reside in traditional stereotypes.

Of course, many scholars have invested considerable effort in delineating the structure and content of sex stereotypes (e.g., Eagly & Steffen, 1984). Deaux and Lewis (1984) reported that the stereotypical man is instrumental, assertive, competitive, dynamic, and task-competent, whereas the stereotypical woman is kind, nurturing, sensitive, relationally oriented, and expressive. These authors found that their participants rely on such labels until they learn more specific information about one another, as partners do in close relationships.

Stereotypes can offer a means to explain sex and gender differences on at least two levels: (1) as a way to predict men's and women's behavioral differences; and (2) as a way that people establish baselines for expectations about other people's behavior. In the former case, researchers adopt sex role stereotypes to construct their own concepts and measures (e.g., Bem, 1974); in the latter case, researchers hold that participants rely on stereotypes to know how to behave or to judge behavior (e.g., Geis, 1993).

The problem does not reside in the theoretical construction and explanation of the understanding of the nature and function of stereotypes in interaction behavior; rather, the problem arises when researchers uncritically—and perhaps without realizing they do so—adopt stereotypes as a means for scientifically explaining and predicting sex and gender differences. Adopting stereotypic thinking represents a rather simple solution to the sex difference issues, although as a solution it is inadequate because people do not reliably conform in their interaction behavior to conventional sex stereotypes (Aries, 1996). Although we concur with Deaux (1984) and others who claim that sex stereotypes are pervasive, we also contend that they appear baldly essentializing in their portrayals of men's and women's behavior. In particular, we contend that stereotypes do not adequately or accurately represent men's and women's interactions in personal relationships.

We acknowledge that men and women sometimes differ in their interaction behavior and they sometimes rely on stereotypes as guidelines for interaction behavior (Deaux & Major, 1987). However, such stereotypes present an outdated view of men and women that distorts scientific understandings of male and female interaction, *especially in the context of personal relationships.* If one holds that men are from Mars and women are from Venus, then it follows that Earth provides no home for either sex.

INVESTIGATING SEX AND GENDER DIFFERENCES IN PERSONAL RELATIONSHIPS

Defining Sex and Gender

Defining terms is an important obligation because definitions establish the boundaries of a phenomenon and indicate one's understanding of it. We have considered several issues in the debate over the definition of the terms *sex* and *gender.* For instance, some scholars hold that gender is partially composed of one's biological sex, but that gender also entails "the psychological, social, and cultural features and characteristics strongly associated with the biological categories of male and female" (Gilbert, 1993, p. 11). Likewise, Moore (1994) has argued that the construct of sex entails both a reference to objective differences in the genetic/biological composition of men and women and to people's beliefs accompanying the term "sex"; gender refers to the cultural understandings and explanations that people have for sex. Accordingly, "sex" is partially socially constructed, is sometimes conflated with *sexuality,* and connotes sexual intercourse. In the scholarly debate about the term "gender," some argue that gender refers to cultural differences between men and women, whereas others argue that gender is a grammatical device (as in "masculine" nouns), and still others argue that gender refers exclusively to "women" and women's attitudes and behaviors (Scott, 1996).

Despite the definitional debates on the topic, which can appear quite nuanced, we opt for a clear distinction. More precisely, we adopt the advice set forth in the *Journal of Social and Personal Relationships (JSPR)* and define *sex* as the biological distinctions between men and women and *gender* as the social, psychological, and cultural differentiations between men and women (see also Deaux, 1985). This convention allows us to be clear about our terms, and this distinction appears to be gaining support among those who define *sex* versus *gender.* . . .

Assessing the Presumption of Differences

One does not need supporting research to claim that sex differences exist. Men and women obviously differ. Men's genetic code differs from women's, men have historically enjoyed greater sociopolitical power and status, and women have been conferred greater prestige in relationship matters. Yet precisely *how* men and women differ in their personal relationships remains quite a mystery, especially in comparison to sex differences on display in physical and sociopolitical realms of behavior. Sex and gender differences in personal relationships emerge in minute interaction behaviors, often in private contexts, and within different subcultures that defy sweeping, categorical generalizations about men's and women's behaviors in "society at large."

The issue of whether or not pervasive sex/gender differences exist in personal relationships is addressed variously and often inferred from research involving acquaintances or strangers. For example, Henley (1977) focused on how women suffer power deficits in the context of cross-sex interaction, arguing that men's greater occupational status affords them more power and freedom in several behavioral categories: space (e.g., women use less space in interactions with men), time (e.g., women wait on men), environment (e.g., women have less freedom to arrange their environment), language (e.g., men talk longer), demeanor (e.g., men act more relaxed), touch (men can, women cannot), eye contact (men stare, have higher visual dominance scores), and facial expression (e.g., women must offer a pleasant smile). Henley's review strongly supported the contention that men consistently dominate women through communication behavior.

More recently, scholars in the fields of communication, psychology, and family studies (among others) have begun to doubt findings regarding sex/gender differences that reflect the traditional women-as-communal and men-as-instrumental categories (e.g., various views by authors in Canary & Dindia, 1998). Ragan (1989) observed that the study of sex differences in communication presents no single consistent finding. In a noteworthy paper, Duck and Wright (1993) reversed their own earlier interpretations of two sets of data to conclude that, within the sexes, the friendships of men and women were more similar than different: "Within sexes, characteristics that are important in friendship do not fit readily into expressive vs. instrumental categories for either women or men. That is, according to our factor analyses, expressive and instrumental characteristics are about equally prominent aspects of a strong friendship for both women and men" (p. 724). Analyzing the research on group interaction using Interaction Process Analysis (IPA), Aries (1996) also reversed an earlier claim she made that supported the stereotype of men as instrumental and women as communal:

> . . . While the case has been made that men are instrumental and women expressive, a closer examination of these studies suggests that this stereotyped description of men and women is an exaggeration of the data, that the differences are small to moderate in magnitude, and that role differentiation along instrumental–expressive lines by males and females does not appear consistently in all group situations. (p. 27)

Aries (1996) proceeded to review, in detail, interaction differences between men and women in a variety of behavioral domains (i.e., self-disclosure, leadership behaviors, interruptions, conversational management, etc.), and she concluded, "I have gone back through the research literature to demonstrate that the data reveal similarities between men and women to be far greater than the differences, and that knowledge about a person's [sex] will give us little ability to accurately predict how a person will behave in many situations" (p. 189). . . .

A FLOWCHART MODEL PREDICTING STEREOTYPIC INTERACTION BEHAVIOR

We believe that sex differences exist, but the manner in which they emerge in interaction behavior between partners remains opaque. As indicated above, the primary culprit for the fuzzy picture appears to be researchers' reliance on and perpetuation of exaggerated, "main effect" polarization arising from stereotypes (see also Aries, 1996; Putnam, 1982; Ragan, 1989). If we consider various models for sex-linked behavior (i.e., that within-group differences exist for men and women), and if we allow for various countervailing influences on one's communication behavior, then we should find as invalid studies presuming that stereotypes are powerful influences. Figure 8–1 presents what researchers and readers need to address when presupposing stereotypic behavior.

The model we offer in Figure 8–1 indicates how sex-relevant beliefs affect interaction (see also Deaux & Major, 1987). The flowchart in Figure 8–1 offers five questions that people should consider regarding behavior between close relationship partners (e.g., self-disclosure, touch, conflict). Our objective in this exercise is to show some of the pitfalls contained in the presumption of stereotypic sex differences in personal relationships. We assume that the mediating factors listed in Figure 8–1 are most often significant in personal relationships. In addition, we assume that during interaction two people are communicating, although this model might apply to other contexts (e.g., small groups, organizations). Finally, we focus on the sex-relevant behaviors of one person at a time (i.e., the *actor*), which reflects other researchers' view of sex as an individual, structural variable. The same questions addressed at the dyadic level would double and become more difficult to answer. Nevertheless, the search for stereotypic sex differences progresses as one answers each of the questions [in Figure 8–1].

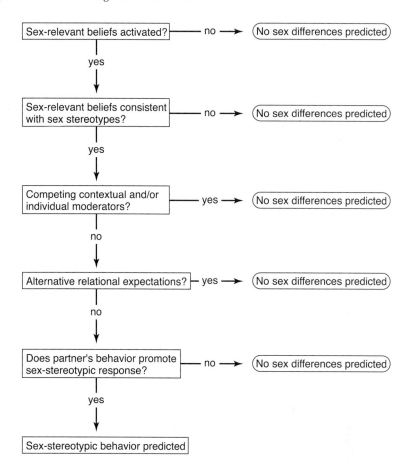

FIGURE 8–1 Model predicting sex-stereotypic interaction behaviors.

. . . Some authors argue that stereotypes are widely held and prompt people to conform to expectations implied by the stereotype in a self-fulfilling manner (Geis, 1993). At a social level, interactions exist wherein stereotypic responses may prevail and reinforce gender stereotypes (Deaux & Major, 1987). But the extent to which the self-fulfilling nature of stereotypes extends into personal relationships remains unclear, though we acknowledge that it happens. Geis (1993) noted that education about stereotypes and currently shifting occupational roles of men and women can counterbalance the self-fulfilling nature of stereotypes. One should be able to locate where the enactment and perception of stereotypic behavior occur in interaction that might prompt a stereotypic response. Whereas the data appear to support a few *general* trends among acquaintances regarding stereotyping and self-fulfilling behavior, the literature does not reveal specific stereotypic communication behaviors in close involvements. We question the assumption that stereotypic responses typify interaction in close, personal relationships (see also Duck & Wright, 1993).

CONCLUSION

Many social scientific researchers have examined sex and gender differences in interaction behavior for the past 50 years, though much of this research perpetuates stereotypic thinking of how men and women communicate in their personal relationships. Feminist reactions to sex differences have generally taken two routes, to deny difference or to celebrate women's differences. The meaning of difference has been problematic at best, restricting opportunities for both men and women and ignoring their experiences (Rhode, 1990).

Some people assume that differences between men and women reflect stable predispositions, leaving out potentially more important aspects of individuals and culture. In addition, as Deaux and Major (1990) stated, "Dualistic assumptions about gender may also preclude other relevant categories—race, class, age—from entering the analysis" (p. 89). We hope to locate places when difference should be questioned and when it should be celebrated. In our view, the quality of our close relationships depends on increased understanding of sex differences and similarities as well as the activities that reflect people's gender.

REVIEW QUESTIONS

1. The authors say that the "Mars–Venus" hypothesis is not supported by "the empirical research literature." What do they mean by "the empirical research literature"?
2. Explain the "Mars–Venus" hypothesis. According to this view, how do men generally communicate? How do women generally communicate?
3. Canary and his coauthors cite research that says that relational partners rely on stereotypes only until what happens?
4. Explain the difference between sex and gender.
5. What do you understand to be the basic message or insight of the flowchart model in Figure 8–1?
6. What do the authors mean in the conclusion when they agree with Deaux and Major, who wrote, "Dualistic assumptions about gender may also preclude other relevant categories—race, class, age—from entering the analysis"?

PROBES

1. You would certainly assume that authors like John Gray and Deborah Tannen, who support the "Mars–Venus" hypothesis do not *mean* to be reinforcing sex stereotypes. And yet Canary and his colleagues say that they are.

How does this literature end up doing what it doesn't appear to mean to be doing?

2. How do you respond to the quotation from Gray's "Mars–Venus" book [p. 366] that begins, "Women generally do not understand how Martians [men] cope with stress" and ends "just as it is a mistake to expect a woman's feelings to always be rational and logical"? Do you sense stereotyping in these two paragraphs?

3. Explain how the distinction between sex and gender can complicate the answer to the question, "How do men and women actually communicate in close, personal relationships?"

4. The flowchart model in Figure 8–1 says that sex-stereotyped communication behavior is likely to happen *only* when at least several of five conditions are present. The first is "sex-relevant beliefs activated." This means that in order to have "Mars–Venus" behavior, one thing the parties have to be doing is consciously thinking about some sex-relevant beliefs ("Is she likely to be feeling differently because she's a woman?" "Is this a guy thing?"). Explain the other four conditions.

REFERENCES

1. Aries, E. (1996). *Men and women in interaction: Reconsidering the differences.* New York: Oxford University Press.
2. Bem, S. L. (1974). The measurement of psychological androgyny. *Journal of Consulting and Clinical Psychology, 42,* 155–162.
3. Canary, D. J., & Dindia, K. (Eds.). (1998). *Sex differences and similarities in communication.* Mahwah, NJ: Erlbaum.
4. Canary, D. J., & Hause, I. S. (1993). Is there any reason to research sex differences in communication? *Communication Quarterly, 41,* 129–141.
5. Crawford, M. (1995). *Talking difference: On gender and language.* Thousand Oaks, CA: Sage.
6. Deaux, K. (1984). From individual differences to social categories: Analysis of a decade's research on gender. *American Psychologist, 39,* 105–116.
7. Deaux, K. (1985). Sex and gender. *Annual Review of Psychology, 36,* 49–81.
8. Deaux, K., & Lewis, L. L. (1984). The structure of gender stereotypes: Interrelationships among components and gender label. *Journal of Personality and Social Psychology, 46,* 991–1004.
9. Deaux, K., & Major, B. (1987). Putting gender into context: An interactive model of gender related behavior. *Psychological Review, 94,* 369–389.
10. Deaux, K., & Major. B. (1990). A social-psychological model of gender. In D. L. Rhode (Ed.), *Theoretical perspectives on sexual difference* (pp. 89–99). New Haven, CT: Yale University Press.
11. Duck, S., & Wright, P. (1993). Reexamining gender differences in same-gender friendships: A close look at two kinds of data. *Sex Roles, 28,* 709–727.

12. Eagly, A. H., & Steffen, V. (1984). Gender stereotypes stem from the distribution of women and men into social roles. *Journal of Personality and Social Psychology, 46*, 735–754.

13. Geis, F. L. (1993). Self-fulfilling prophecies: A social psychological view of gender. In A. E. Beall & R. U. Sternberg (Eds.), *The psychology of gender* (pp. 9–54). New York: Guilford Press.

14. Gilbert, L. A. (1993). *Two careers/one family: The promise of gender equality.* Newbury Park, CA: Sage.

15. Gleick, E. (1997). Tower of psychobabble. *Time, 149*, 69–70, 72.

16. Gray, J. (1992). *Men are from Mars, women are from Venus.* New York: Harper-Collins.

17. Henley, N. (1977). *Body politics: Power, sex, and non-verbal communication.* Englewood Cliffs, NJ: Prentice Hall.

18. Moore, H. L. (1994). Understanding sex and gender. In T. Ingold (Ed.), *Companion encyclopedia of anthropology* (pp. 813–830). New York: Routledge.

19. Putnam, L. L. (1982). In search of gender: A critique of communication and sex roles research. *Women's Studies in Communication, 5*, 1–9.

20. Ragan, S. L. (1989). Communication between the sexes: A consideration of differences in adult communication. In J. F. Nussbaum (Ed.), *Life-span communication: Normative processes* (pp. 179–193). Hillsdale, NJ: Erlbaum.

21. Rhode, D. L. (1990). Theoretical perspectives on sexual difference. In D. L. Rhode (Ed.), *Theoretical perspectives on sexual difference* (pp. 1–19). New Haven, CT: Yale University Press.

22. Scott, J. W. (1996). Gender: A useful category of historical analysis. In J. W. Scott (Ed.), *Feminism and history* (pp. 152–180). New York: Oxford University Press.

23. Tannen, D. (1990). *You just don't understand: Women and men in conversation.* New York: William Morrow.

24. Thorne, B. (1990). Children and gender: Construction of difference. In D. L. Rhode (Ed.), *Theoretical perspectives on sexual difference* (pp. 100–113). New Haven, CT: Yale University Press.

25. Wilkins, B. M., & Andersen, P. A. (1991). Gender differences and similarities in management communication: A meta-analysis. *Management Communication Quarterly, 5*, 6–35.

Without repeating the extreme generalizations of the "Mars/ Venus" popular books, communication teacher and scholar Julia Wood reviews some basic feminine and masculine standpoints on personal relationships. Wood acknowledges that "not all women operate from feminine standpoints and not all men act from masculine ones." But there are patterns and tendencies, she argues, and it is helpful to understand them.

These patterns arise mainly because of the different ways girls and boys are socialized. The speech communities we grow up in are gendered, Wood argues, and we learn how to be masculine or feminine there.

The two main principles that girls and women learn is that intimacy is a continuous process and that personal communication is the primary way to build relationships. So even when commitment is secure, women "tend to see partners and relationship as continuously evolving," which means that they continue to focus on and work with these relationships. Generally, the research indicates, women's communication is more emotionally expressive than men.

The two main principles that boys and men learn is that intimacy is "an event that is resolved at some point" and that relationships are built by activities more than by talk. As a result, many men feel that, after a commitment is made, no continuous work on the relationship is necessary. We also prefer to *do* things together to build a relationship, rather than *talking* about the relationship.

Differences between these standpoints suggest why misunderstandings between men and women often occur, and Wood briefly outlines how this can happen. She does not provide the magic remedy for all gender difficulties here, but she does offer some ways to understand the problems all of us have experienced with our cross-sex conversation partners. You can use this understanding to troubleshoot the difficulties you have.

Gendered Standpoints on Personal Relationships

Julia T. Wood

Writing in 1992, Sharon Brehm observed that "probably the most powerful individual difference that affects how we experience love is that of gender. . . . [M]ales and females construct their realities of love in very different terms" (p. 110). Research studies on topics ranging from emotional expressiveness (Christensen & Heavey, 1990), to love styles (Hendrick & Hendrick, 1988), to conflict styles (Gottman, 1994a; Jones & Gallois, 1989) report general differences between women and men. So significant are differences between the sexes' approaches to intimacy that a 1993 popular magazine (*Utne*, January) carried this cover headline: "Men and Women: Can We Get Along? Should We Even Try?" Although most of us seem to think it's worth the effort to get along, doing so is sometimes very frustrating and confusing. Much of the misunderstanding that plagues communication between women and men results from the fact that they are typically socialized in discrete speech communities. [According to] standpoint theory, social structures and processes in Western society foster gender-distinctive perspectives on relationships and equally distinctive communication and perceptions within relationships.

Gendered speech communities teach most men and women to understand, interpret, and communicate in ways consistent with society's views of femininity and masculinity. Through gender-differentiated contexts, activities, and instruction, a majority of boys and girls internalize views of relationships and how to interact that reflect their respective genders. Pragmatically, this implies that women and men, in general, may have somewhat different views of what closeness is and how to create, express, and sustain it (Inman, 1996; Wood & Inman, 1993). Numerous studies and reviews of research demonstrate that distinct gender cultures exist and that they differ systematically in some important respects (Aries, 1987; Beck, 1988; Coates & Cameron, 1989; Gottman & Carrère, 1994; Johnson, 1989; Kramarae, 1981; Maltz & Borker, 1982; Wood, 1993, 1994a, b, c, 1995, 1996, 1999). Although not all women operate from feminine standpoints and not all men act from masculine ones, research indicates that many women and men do adopt the standpoints of their respective speech communities.

FEMININE STANDPOINTS ON PERSONAL RELATIONSHIPS

Perhaps the two most basic principles of a feminine standpoint on relationships are that intimacy is understood as a continuous process and that personal communication is regarded as the primary dynamic that sustains connections with others (Riessman, 1990; Wood, 1986, 1993, 1996, 1999). Because women are generally taught to build and nurture relationships, they typically understand close connections as fluid processes. Thus, even when commitment is secure, women tend to see partners and relationships as continuously evolving in large and small ways (Gilligan, 1982; Schaef, 1981; Wood, 1986, 1993). From this standpoint, intimacy is never finished, never resolved in a final form. There is always more to be learned about each other, new layers of understanding and experience to be added to a relationship. Because women, more than men, are socialized to prioritize relationships, intimacy is a central and continuing focus of thought, interest, and investment (Acitelli, 1988, 1993; Gilligan, 1982; Wood, 1986, 1993b, 1999). A formal commitment such as marriage does not settle intimacy but is only one moment in an ongoing process.

Perhaps because feminine socialization emphasizes building and refining connections with others, women generally regard communication as a primary way to create, express, enlarge, and celebrate closeness with others. From her study of troubled marriages, Catherine Riessman (1990) concluded that women see talking deeply and closely as "the centerpiece of relationships" (p. 24). In general, women's communication is more emotionally expressive than men's (Christensen & Heavey, 1990; Roberts & Krokoff, 1990); it is also more verbally responsive to others than men's (Beck, 1988; Burleson, 1982; Miller, Berg, & Archer, 1983).

Expressive communication is especially prominent in some lesbian relationships. Lesbian partners, more than heterosexuals or gay men, rely on communication to provide emotional support and responsiveness (Eldridge & Gilbert, 1990; Kurdek & Schmitt, 1986; Wood, 1994b). Women are also more likely than men to find talking about a relationship rewarding, even when there are no major issues or problems (Acitelli, 1988; Wood, 1998b). Thus, spending an evening discussing a relationship may enrich a woman's sense of connection to a partner more than doing something together.

But what is meant by communicating? Substantial research indicates that women tend to place high priority on daily talk and the process of engaging others, whether or not the topics of discussion are important (Riessman, 1990; Wood, 1993, 1998b, 1999). Thus, most women find pleasure and significance in talking about unremarkable, daily issues with partners and see this as important to continually enriching personal relationships and keeping lives interwoven (Aries, 1987; Tannen, 1990). To capture how women typically create closeness, women's friendships are described as "an evolving dialogue" (Becker, 1987). Within a feminine perspective on relationships, talk is not just a means to other objectives such as resolving problems or coordinating activities. In addition, talk is a primary goal in its own right—the process of engaging is the *raison d'être* of communicating.

MASCULINE STANDPOINTS ON PERSONAL RELATIONSHIPS

Two linchpins of a masculine orientation toward close relationships are a view of intimacy as an event that is resolved at some point and a focus on activities as the heart of closeness. Unlike women in general, many men tend to see intimacy as something that is established at one time and then stays more or less in place (Rubin, 1985; Schaef, 1981). Thus, when a commitment is made, some men regard it as a given that does not need ongoing comment or attention. This diverges from a feminine view of relationships as ongoing processes that call for and are enriched by continuous attention and talk.

Because masculine socialization emphasizes accomplishments, an instrumental view of communication tends to be endorsed by most men (Block, 1973; Brehm, 1992). Thus, more than women, men tend to use communication as a way to achieve particular objectives—to settle a problem, express an idea, arrange a plan, and so forth. In other words, it should serve some purpose, should accomplish something (Maltz & Borker, 1982; Riessman, 1990; Wood, 1993c). From this perspective, small talk may seem pointless, and conversation about a relationship itself may seem unnecessary unless there are specific problems that need attention (Acitelli, 1988; Wood, 1993, 1998b). Masculine communication, both verbal and nonverbal, also tends to be relatively unexpressive verbally, because its focus is not feelings, but content, and because men, more than women, are socialized to control emotions (Christensen & Heavey, 1990;

Fletcher & Fitness, 1990; Roberts & Krokoff, 1990). Gay partners, both of whom usually are socialized in masculine speech communities, tend to be the least emotionally attentive and expressive of all types of couples (Blumstein & Schwartz, 1983; Eldridge & Gilbert, 1990; Kurdek & Schmit, 1986; Wood, 1994d).

In place of communication, activities tend to occupy center stage in how men generally create and express closeness. Dubbing this "closeness in the doing," Scott Swain (1989) found that men's friendships typically grow out of shared activities. Swain interpreted the focus on doing not as a substitute for intimacy but as an alternate path to closeness, as well as an alternative form. Research by other scholars (Paul & White, 1990; Sherrod, 1989; Tavris, 1992; Wood & Inman, 1993; Wright, 1988) supports Swain's findings and his interpretations that activities are a means to closeness, one that differs from but is just as legitimate as closeness through dialogue. Doing things with and for partners also seems to characterize many men's orientations toward heterosexual romantic relationships (Cancian, 1987, 1989; Inman, 1996; Riessman, 1990; Wood, 1993, 1998b). Thus, a man might wash his partner's car to express affection and might consider going out to a ball game a good way to celebrate an anniversary.

TENSIONS BETWEEN GENDERED VIEWS OF RELATIONSHIPS

Differences between masculine and feminine standpoints suggest why misunderstandings can—and often do—occur. For example, a woman may perceive a man's lack of interest in talking about a relationship as evidence he cares less about it than she does. Yet from his perspective, as long as the relationship is solid there's no need to focus on it. Similarly, men sometimes feel women's talk about small issues is trivial, and they regard women's interest in discussing a relationship that is in good shape as pointless. This interpretation, however, is based on only the content level of meaning, and it ignores the relationship level at which the point of talking is to connect with each other.

Another frequent frustration is what linguist Deborah Tannen (1990) calls "troubles talk." For example, a woman might tell her partner about a problem with a co-worker in the hope that he will sympathize with her and support her feelings. Instead, he may offer advice on how to solve the problem. To her, this may seem cold, because advice fails to acknowledge her feelings. Yet his intention was to support her by fixing the problem. He is communicating at the content level of meaning, she is communicating at the relationship level, and neither understands the other. Similarly, when men want to do things instead of talking, women sometimes feel the men are rejecting intimacy. Conversely, men generally experience closeness through activities, so they may not experience closeness in dialogue (Riessman, 1990; Wood & Inman, 1993). Problems arise not because either style of relating is bad but because partners don't understand each other's ways of expressing and creating closeness.

Lenny

> *Ever since I started having relationships with girls, it seems I've had problems. I did not understand why they obsessed on talking about a relationship when nothing was wrong, or why they would get bent out of shape if I suggested we watch a game or go to a movie instead of talking. Now I understand a lot more about what things mean to girls. Also, I'm now able to explain to my girlfriend what I mean. Like the last time I suggested we go out to a game, I explained to her that I felt close to her when we did things together. She mulled that one over a bit and agreed to go. We've been having some pretty interesting conversations about different ways we see things in our relationship.*

In sum, gendered standpoints are one of many influences on how partners view a relationship and how they interpret each other's actions. As we've seen, socialization is generally sex segregated to a large degree, so many women and men learn different ways of communicating and develop distinctive understandings of how intimacy operates. The differences themselves are not necessarily troublesome, but how we interpret or misinterpret each other can be toxic. Perhaps the soundest course of action is to avoid interpreting others through our own perspectives and to try, instead, to understand them on their own terms. Learning to do this requires partners to communicate openness to each other's ways of experiencing and expressing closeness.

REVIEW QUESTIONS

1. Explain what Wood means when she says that women and men are "typically socialized into discrete speech communities." What does "socialized" mean? What is a "speech community"?
2. Explain the two basic principles of a feminine standpoint on relationships and the two basic principles of a masculine standpoint on relationships.
3. Sometimes a woman will be frustrated by a man's unwillingness or disinterest in maintaining a relationship, especially if he doesn't want to *talk* about the relationship. From a masculine point of view, why does this unwillingness or disinterest make sense? From a woman's point of view, what's frustrating about it?
4. Small talk can seem pointless to men and important to women. Explain why.
5. Often when a woman tells a man about a problem, the man tries to fix or solve it. But in many situations, this is *not* what the woman wants. Why? What's happening here?

PROBES

1. Given the different ways they are socialized, how might women and men define communication differently? What could be the practical impact of this difference?

2. What do you believe is Wood's response to the argument made by Canary, Emmers-Sommer, and Faulkner in the previous reading?

3. Reflect on your own experience with communication and gender. Do you agree more with Wood or with Canary, Emmers-Sommer, and Faulkner? What do you find most insightful or helpful in the article you agree with *least?*

REFERENCES

1. Acitelli, L. (1988). When spouses talk to each other about their relationship. *Journal of Social and Personal Relationships, 5,* 185–199.

2. Acitelli, L. (1993). You, me, and us: Perspectives on relationship awareness. In S. W. Duck (Ed.), *Understanding relationship processes, 1: Individuals in relationships* (pp. 144–174). Newbury Park, CA: Sage.

3. Aries, E. (1987). Gender and communication. In P. Shaver (Ed.), *Sex and gender* (pp. 149–176). Newbury Park, CA: Sage.

4. Beck, A. (1988). *Love is never enough.* New York: Harper & Row.

5. Becker, C. S. (1987). Friendship between women: A phenomenological study of best friends. *Journal of Phenomenological Psychology, 18,* 59–72.

6. Block, J. H. (1973). Conceptions of sex role: Some cross-cultural and longitudinal perspectives. *American Psychologist, 28,* 512–526.

7. Blumenstein, P., & Schwartz, P. (1983). *American couples: Money, work, and sex.* New York: Morrow.

8. Brehm, S. (1992). *Intimate relationships.* New York: McGraw-Hill.

9. Burleson, B. R. (1982). The development of comforting communication skills in childhood and adolescence. *Child Development, 53,* 1578–1588.

10. Christensen, A., & Heavey, C. (1990). Gender and social structure in the demand/withdraw pattern in marital conflict. *Journal of Personality and Social Psychology, 59,* 73–81.

11. Coates, J., & Cameron, D. (Eds.). (1989). *Women and their speech communities.* New York: Longman.

12. Eldridge, N. S., & Gilbert, L. A. (1990). Correlates of relationship satisfaction in lesbian couples. *Psychology of Women Quarterly, 14,* 43–62.

13. Fletcher, G. J., & Fitness, J. (1990). Occurrent social cognition in close relationship interaction: The role of proximal and distal variables. *Journal of Personality and Social Psychology, 59,* 464–474.

14. Gilligan, C. (1982). *In a different voice: Psychological theory and women's development.* Cambridge, MA: Harvard University Press.

15. Gottman, J. (1994). *What predicts divorce? The relationship between marital processes and marital outcomes.* Hillsdale, NJ: Erlbaum.

16. Gottman, J., & Carrère, S. (1994). Why can't men and women get along? Developmental roots and marital inequities. In D. Canary & L. Stafford (Eds.), *Communication and relational maintenance* (pp. 203–229). New York: Academic Press.

17. Hendrick, C., & Hendrick, S. S. (1988). Lovers wear rose-colored glasses. *Journal of Social and Personal Relationships, 5,* 161–184.
18. Inman, C. C. (1996). Friendships among men: Closeness in the doing. In J. T. Wood (Ed.), *Gendered relationships* (pp. 95–110). Mountain View, CA: Mayfield.
19. Johnson, F. (1989). Women's culture and communication: An analytic perspective. In C. M. Lont & S. A. Friedley (Eds.), *Beyond boundaries: Sex and gender diversity in communication.* Fairfax, VA: George Mason University Press.
20. Jones, E., & Gallois, C. (1989). Spouses; impressions of rules for communication in public and private marital conflicts. *Journal of Marriage and the Family, 51,* 957–967.
21. Kramarae, C. (1981). *Women and men speaking: Frameworks for analysis.* Rowley, MA: Newbury House.
22. Kurdek, L. A., & Schmitt, J. P. (1986). Relationship quality of partners in heterosexual married, heterosexual cohabiting, and gay and lesbian relationships. *Journal of Personality and Social Psychology, 51,* 711–720.
23. Maltz, D. N., & Borker, R. (1982). A cultural approach to male-female miscommunication. In J. J. Gumpertz (Ed.), *Language and social identity* (pp. 196–216). Cambridge, England: Cambridge University Press.
24. Miller, L., Berg, J., & Archer, R. (1983). Openers: Individuals who elicit intimate self-disclosure. *Journal of Personality and Social Psychology, 44,* 1234–1244.
25. Paul, E., & White, K. (1990). The development of intimate relationships in late adolescence. *Adolescence, 25,* 375–400.
26. Riessman, C. (1990). *Divorce talk: Women and men make sense of personal relationships.* New Brunswick, NJ: Rutgers University Press.
27. Roberts, L. J., & Krokoff, L. L. (1990). A time-series analysis of withdrawal, hostility, and displeasure in satisfied and dissatisfied marriages. *Journal of Marriage and the Family, 52,* 95–105.
28. Rubin, L. (1985). *Just friends: The role of friendship in our lives.* New York: Harper & Row.
29. Schaef, A. W. (1981). *Women's reality.* St. Paul, MN: West.
30. Sherrod, D. (1989). The influence of gender on same-sex friendships. In C. Hendrick (Ed.), *Close relationships* (pp. 164–186). Newbury Park, CA: Sage.
31. Swain, S. (1989). Covert intimacy: Closeness in men's friendships. In B. J. Risman & P. Schwartz (Eds.), *Gender in intimate relationships* (pp. 71–86). Belmont, CA: Wadsworth.
32. Tannen, D. (1990). *You just don't understand: Women and men in conversation.* New York: Simon & Schuster.
33. Tavris, C. (1992). *The mismeasure of woman.* New York: Simon & Schuster.
34. Wood, J. T. (1986). Different voices in relationship crises: An extension of Gilligan's theory. *American Behavioral Scientist, 29,* 273–301.
35. Wood, J. T. (1993). Engendered relations: Interaction, caring, power, and responsibility in intimacy. In S. W. Duck (Ed.), *Understanding relationship*

processes, 3: Social context and relationships (pp. 26–54). Newbury Park,
CA: Sage.

36. Wood, J. T. (1994a). Engendered identities: Shaping voice and mind
    through gender. In D. Vocate (Ed.), *Interpersonal communication: Different
    voices, different minds* (pp. 145–167). Hillsdale, NJ: Erlbaum.

37. Wood, J. T. (1994b). Gender and relationship crises: Contrasting reasons,
    responses, and relational orientations. In J. Ringer (Ed.), *Queer words, queer
    images: The construction of homosexuality* (pp. 238–264). New York: New
    York University Press.

38. Wood, J. T. (1994c). Gender, communication, and culture. In L. Samovar &
    R. Porter (Eds.), *Intercultural communication: A reader* (7th ed.) (pp. 155–164).
    Belmont, CA: Wadsworth.

39. Wood, J. T. (1994d). *Who cares? Women, care and culture.* Carbondale:
    Southern Illinois University Press.

40. Wood, J. T. (1995). Feminist scholarship and research on personal
    relationships. *Journal of Social and Personal Relationships, 12,* 103–120.

41. Wood, J. T. (Ed.). (1996). *Gendered relationships.* Mountain View, CA:
    Mayfield.

42. Wood, J. T. (1999). *Gendered lives: Communication, gender, and culture* (3rd ed.).
    Belmont, CA: Wadsworth.

43. Wood, J. T. & Inman, C. C. (1993). In a different mode: Masculine styles of
    communicating closeness. *Journal of Applied Communication Research, 21,*
    279–295.

44. Wright, P. H. (1988). Interpreting research on gender differences in
    friendship: A case for moderation and a plea for caution. *Journal of Social
    and Personal Relationships, 5,* 367–373.

This reading is included in the Communicating with Intimate Partners chapter because students in my interpersonal communication classes often ask me about the topic it discusses—how to
cope with a long-distance relationship. When people who dated in high
school go to different colleges, when a parent's relocation forces a family move, when circumstances force a couple into a commuter marriage,
and when the increasingly common movement between jobs and
schools separates dating partners, the people involved have to face the
challenges of this kind of relationship.

This reading reports the results of interviews with 10 college students
who had dated their partners for at least six months in long-distance relationships. The researchers found, to nobody's surprise, that all the people
they interviewed relied primarily on the telephone to maintain contact.

Because they needed to take care of their individual commitments, couples also negotiated "rules" about the timing and duration of calls.

The activity of planning visits provided comfort during times of physical absence. Some partners also planned their academic schedules to facilitate meetings. Partners also reported that geographic distance was not related to how close partners felt.

Age, maturity, distaste for the "dating scene," and a desire to settle down and get married in the future were attributes that the students felt contributed to their commitments to their partners. Only one person interviewed believed he or she had the option of dating other people. The predominant view of the separation was that it was "an investment for the future." This belief did the most to enable the partners to cope with being apart. Many partners also felt that the separation made them stronger, as individuals and in the relationship. All the interviewees reported that they were sometimes lonely and sad because of the separation. But so long as they could view it as "necessary and temporary," they had the strength to cope.

I hope that this account will help you understand and cope with the long-distance relationships you may experience.

Staying Close When Apart: Intimacy and Meaning in Long-Distance Dating Relationships

Joyce A. Arditti and Melissa Kauffman

In recent years long-distance romantic relationships have become increasingly common. For example, about one-third of premarital relationships in university settings may be long-distance in nature. Job mobility as well as educational pursuits have created a need for many romantically involved couples to be geographically separated.

Long-distance relationships (LDRs) may suffer because they lack the support of shared social networks, and partners cannot easily communicate or be affectionate with each other. Physical separation also increases the potential for individuals to mislead each other. On the other hand, LDRs may provide a context whereby individuals are free to think about themselves, their partners, and their relationships in new and creative ways.

The purpose of this study was to explore long-distance dating relationships. Little information is available describing how couples maintain intimacy while geographically separated. What little we do know is based on research on commuter

"Staying Close When Apart" by Joyce Arditti and Melissa Kauffman from *Journal of Couple and Relationship Therapy*, Vol. 1, No. 1, 2004. Reprinted by permission of The Haworth Press and Joyce Arditti.

marriages that may not apply to single romantic partners. The main questions guiding the study were: How do long-distance couples stay close? What shared meanings do individuals have with their long-distance romantic partners? Why do individuals stay in long-distance relationships? Ten college students that had dated their partners for at least six months in long-distance relationships were interviewed.

How do LDRs stay emotionally connected? Every person we interviewed used the telephone to varying degrees, most used e-mail, and some planned regular visits with their distant partners to stay close. There was a wide range of tolerance for disconnection, and there were differences in how frequently they needed to contact their partners in order to feel close to them.

Every person relied on the telephone as the primary link with their partner, although individuals varied in the frequency of phone use. For some, the need to talk to their partner was more important than anything—finances, school, work, whatever. One woman said that she had to talk with her boyfriend every night and, if they missed a night, they talked even longer the next night. Sam, a teaching assistant, and his girlfriend called each other daily and talked as long as they wanted, ignoring expenses.

However, not everyone was interested in talking with their partners daily. For students who emphasized school, the LDRs met their relationship needs but they also gave each other enough "space" to do their work. For example, Kim and Amanda talked by phone with their partners about once a week, stating that they felt they needed to stay completely focused on academics. Kim explained that difficult engineering courses left her little time for leisure and therefore planned weekly phone conversations, supplementing them with short daily e-mails. She seemed satisfied with this mutually agreed-upon schedule. Amanda needed to spend hours on horticulture projects and said she lacked the free time to get distracted by calling her boyfriend. She was satisfied with having little contact with her boyfriend while she finished her degree:

> I almost don't want him up here. I would be too distracted, I wouldn't be able to concentrate as much on my school work. . . . Yeah, in a warped sort of way it is kind of good that he is not here. We stay close when we are apart by calling a lot, sending a lot of e-mails, just reinforcing that we are thinking about each other even though we are separated and things are a little bit different, but it is not really. You can still talk to each other and communicate about things when you need to.

Other couples had "rules" about limiting phone calls because of expenses. Most LDRs supplemented phone calls with e-mail to cut down on costs. Darren and his girlfriend creatively used a free internet program:

> We talk a lot on the phone, especially recently, because on the Internet you can make free phone calls, so we usually talk to each other at least every other day.

In addition, planning visits provided comfort during the physical absence. Of course, there were constraints concerning how often they were able to visit each other, such as money, academic schedules, proximity, and their willingness/ability to travel. Some participants were able to see each other every weekend, while others, separated by greater distances, had to wait until major school breaks.

Some students set up their academic schedules so that they could frequently visit their partners. For example, Marcus, who lived 300 miles from his partner, said:

> We have been seeing each other every 2 weeks . . . I set up my schedule so that I don't have anything on Friday at all. So I leave Thursday and I get back late Monday.

Sam and his girlfriend both loved road trips, so they viewed the five-hour drive separating them as an "inconvenience," but not a defining feature of the relationship:

> We have seen each other every single weekend. . . . It doesn't really feel like a long-distance relationship to me. It is a distance inconvenience, not a time inconvenience. We don't go long periods of time without seeing each other, because we are both willing to travel.

Both of these men demonstrated a willingness to travel frequently despite the distance. Having control over one's time and resources was connected with the ability to travel frequently. A positive view about the situation—minimizing the importance of geographic separation—also seemed to facilitate visiting and relationship satisfaction.

What shared meanings do individuals have with their long-distance romantic partners? Geographic distance was not related to how close partners felt. Instead, the meanings attached to their situation, regardless of how often they talked to or saw their partners, seemed to be most important. For example, meanings such as *not being distracted from academics* or the *importance of staying connected despite costs* made it easier for them to cope with separation.

Age, maturity, distaste for the "dating scene," and a desire to settle down and get married in the near future were attributes that the students felt contributed to their desires to be committed to their partners. These attributes also served to keep them out of new relationships that could threaten the LDRs. They took their relationships seriously and seemed to know what they were seeking in a lifetime partner. Sam emphasized his belief in committing to one person and his lack of interest in casual dating:

> I don't believe in dating other people. . . . If you date other people, you are obviously not in love and you are just kind of looking for . . . somebody to have sex with, somebody to hold your hand, or have some kind of affection.

Several others shared Sam's attitude about dating other people. They thought that it would have been acceptable at the beginning of their relationship to date other people because they had not explicitly committed themselves to their partners, but they felt a growing commitment over time. These individuals admitted that they neither had the time nor the desire to date others.

In fact, only one person still thought they had the option of dating other people.

> We talked about it a little bit and we just both decided that since we are both separated so much it would be better if we did date other people, if we wanted to. I haven't, and I didn't really ask him if he has. We did talk about it, but it is not something that we discuss all the time. . . . We date other people if either one of us wants to, but it is definitely more of a casual thing dating. It is not as if I think he would go out and find somebody that he would prefer over me. . . . We have known each other for so long . . . it is not something that is really a big deal.

Overall, these students were committed to their partners. They felt trust and exclusivity were central to their relationships. The issue of trust was particularly meaningful—several thought that without trust, LDRs would never work. For example, Lucy said: "I trust him. I mean that is the bottom line. I trust him, and I know he trusts me. I mean there is not even a question. We have established that." Despite this, she admitted that sometimes "her mind played tricks on her," and she felt insecure.

The predominant view of the separation was that it was an *investment for the future*. Most felt that changing academic plans in order to be geographically closer to their partners was not feasible. Academic and career plans were deemed essential to either their or their partners' professional growth. This was a critical part of the shared meaning system for some couples. Amanda's comments reflect her unwillingness to change her academic study for the relationship:

> I would not compromise my education, I wouldn't sacrifice anything . . . and he has such a good job . . . so I don't think he would move back up just until I finish school.

Most of them focused on the temporary nature of the separation. Having an end in sight made it easier for couples to deal with the long-distance status of their relationships. Jaime reflected this,

> We realized that it would be a temporary situation, and it is okay as long as I know we are going to be together after I do this. It is like a Christmas present, you know it is there, you are just waiting to open it.

Similarly, Darren, realizing that a two-year separation would create greater career potential:

> I look at it as a positive thing in the future, because we are both going to school for reasons, I guess to have better careers in the future, so in that way it would be better.

In addition to defining the separation as *necessary and temporary*, perceiving the separation as a factor that made them feel even closer to their partners made the experience more acceptable. Specifically, "not taking their partner for granted" and "developing a stronger connection through non-physical communication," were two issues that emerged from all of the interviews.

This suggests how important it was for them to think positively about the situation. Marcus explained that after coming to school he realized how "great his girlfriend was. It's just the more I was down here, the more I realized what I missed." Sam also mentioned that being away from his girlfriend had made him cherish her more:

> It has made us stronger. When you are constantly around somebody, you tend to take them for granted. I see a lot of that among my friends.

Not everyone felt that absence made their hearts grow fonder—for some the lack of physical intimacy was a negative part of the separation.

Why do individuals stay in long-distance relationships? Despite the sense of commitment to their partners, several people identified difficulties they had in maintaining the relationship. Among these were fear and uncertainty about being apart, the potential to "grow apart," and loneliness.

Lucy feared that the separation might affect the closeness she felt toward her partner if it was for a much longer period of time. She was unable to focus on the separation as temporary because she was not certain about when the separation would end, thus making her situation more ambiguous than the other respondents.

> As I start looking at this more closely, the longer we stay separated, that may cause a strain if we don't see one another. 'Cause there is a chance that we may grow apart.

Jaime admitted that the separation had negatively impacted both her and her boyfriend. "I am not as secure in our relationship because he is so far away, [and] I don't think either one of us are really as happy overall." Jaime was upset about the distance because she was unhappy about her boyfriend's decision to move away and get a job suggesting a lack of agreement about the need for the separation. Kim also clearly viewed the separation negatively. She initially stated that the distance did not really hurt that much, but deeper probing revealed that she believed the separation had kept the relationship from progressing. Kim admitted that she wished she had dated her boyfriend for longer before they were separated and was not convinced that she would be able to continue to connect as well with him from a distance. She explained:

> I don't think it is a good thing. . . . If we had started out earlier . . . before he left, it would have been better. I would know more about him, things like that, now he is far away, and it's kind of hard, you know.

It seemed that ambiguity regarding the length of the separation and the absence of an "end date" contributed to uncertainty about future plans and difficulty with the long-distance experience. Both Lucy and Kim were uncertain about how long they would be separated from their boyfriends. It is worth noting that Jaime was the only participant whose partner *left her* to go to a geographically distant location. The other nine participants were the ones who *left their partners*. The issue of who leaves and why has bearing on relationship satisfaction and on ways individuals handle the separation. If both members of a couple do not view the separation the same way, it seems more likely that the separation would contribute to either or both partners' unhappiness. The leaver may be less attached to the partner than the one who was left. It makes sense that the more attached an individual is to their romantic partner, the more distressed they will be when separated.

All of the respondents were occasionally lonely and sad over the lack of physical intimacy caused by separation. They discussed various ways that they dealt with these feelings, including thinking about the partner or by doing something to take their minds off their loneliness. Several of them coped by developing a "positive personal philosophy" about LDRs in general and about the specific effects of the separation on their relationships. Skip jokingly refuted the old adage, "Absence makes the heart grow fonder," by saying, "That is just a crock in my opinion!" His philosophy, *it's just one of those things,* made the separation into a "minor inconvenience." He felt that other problems in his relationship had been more difficult than the separation. "You know the distance is . . . nothing, a long-distance relationship is a cakewalk."

Personal philosophies about what constituted "good relationships" helped individuals cope by focusing on the positive aspects of their relationships. Lucy explained her philosophy: "I think when you both trust each other and you both love each other then you have a solid foundation. We have that foundation." Passionately explaining his philosophy on LDRs, Sam stated:

> If they fail, I think it is due to lack of effort, laziness, lack of character. If two people decide that they want something, then the only way it is not going to happen, is if they let it not happen. So if we broke up there is nobody to blame but ourselves. You can't blame the distance, you can't blame the time, you can't blame any of that, because if you truly love somebody, it is not an issue. . . .

Sam's personal philosophy emphasized working hard on the relationship and not giving up.

In summary, trust was cited as an essential aspect of satisfying LDRs. The mostly positive views about LDRs were helped by emphases on the temporary and necessary nature of the separations. Overall, respondents accepted their situations, although those who had been "left behind" or who were uncertain about when the geographic separation would end were less positive overall. Most believed that the distance did not affect how well they knew their partners. This may have been because they all considered their partners to be good friends, and they attributed the success of their relationships to this. Although admitting that LDRs could be difficult, they believed that their partner was "the one" for them—this belief helped support them being sexually faithful. Idealizing the partner may help the relationship continue by minimizing the possibility of meeting other potential mates and by justifying the separation as valid.

REVIEW QUESTIONS

1. Why did partners in long-distance relationships negotiate "rules" for their contact?
2. Why, according to this reading, was dating others not an option for most couples in this study?
3. What evidence is there in this study that "absence makes the heart grow fonder"?
4. When interviewees viewed the separation negatively, what were their reasons?

PROBES

1. Some people dislike "the dating scene," and some enjoy the variety and excitement that dating new people can generate. From what you've read here, do you think that people with the former attitude are the only ones who are likely to cope well with a long-distance relationship? Explain.
2. What can you learn from this study about your own experience with long-distance dating relationships? What will you try to do if you find yourself in this situation? Or, if you have been or are in this kind of relationship, what does this reading suggest you might have/could do differently?

When the Internet first created possibilities for people to meet and converse in cyberspace, the prevailing belief was that all online relationships would necessarily be superficial. Now we have had enough experience with chat rooms, listservs, distance education, and email to understand that the online environment affords opportunities for interpersonal communication that, for a long time, were considered to be highly unlikely, if not impossible. Students in online project teams develop strong working relationships, family members and dating partners maintain intimate connections, and strangers even develop unusually trusting, high-stakes commercial relationships via eBay. This reading explains some of what's been learned about romance in cyberspace.

The first sentence announces that the topic is "the healthy development of romantic relationships, which may indeed carry over into 'real life.'" The authors cite research that substantiates the notion that CMR (computer-mediated relating) can become as personal as FTF (face-to-face) relating. Some computer users even rated e-mail and computer conferencing as rich as FTF and telephone conversations, or richer.

One important and, many would say, desirable feature of CMR is that physical attractiveness does not influence relationship initiation as it does in FTF contexts. It is well-known that people overgeneralize from physical appearance when they meet someone face-to-face, whereas online, people meet many to whom they might not be attracted, were they face-to-face. As one researcher summarizes, in a FTF situation, we meet someone and then get to know him or her, and online, the processes are reversed. First we get to know someone and this may or may not lead to meeting him or her. If two people meet after having connected online, they may well have already developed some intimate bonds that serve as the context or frame for whatever impressions they may generate based on physical appearance.

Attraction is highest when the partner is perceived as being both physically attractive and attitudinally similar, and people who have difficulty connecting with others in FTF interactions have a better chance of meeting an attitudinally similar person online. Self-disclosure can also be facilitated in CMR because it is less risky than FTF disclosure. Each partner has more control over what is disclosed and how, and the resulting increase in confidence can be attractive to the relational partner. The more oral quality of online written messages maintains a quality of presence, even though each partner has time to reflect and compose, at least in asynchronous contexts.

Erotic connections can even be enhanced by the point already made—that emotional involvement rather than lustful attraction is the foundation of the relationship. As one scholar puts it, "Psychological intimacy . . . is an intangible, subtle, powerful motivator of our sexual expression." The interpersonal space that characterizes CMR can also minimize the impact of stereotyped gender roles on the development of intimacy. For example, women do not have to be primarily concerned about saying "no" online. Both men and women can experiment with their communication in ways that are impossible FTF.

This reading does not tell you how to develop a dating—or other kind of—relationship online, but it does provide a wealth of insights that can guide your own experiences with interpersonal communication in cyberspace.

Romance in Cyberspace: Understanding Online Attraction

Alvin Cooper and Leda Sportolari

This article presents and discusses ways in which the structure and process of online relating facilitates positive, warm interpersonal connections, including the healthy development of romantic relationships, which may indeed carry over into "real life." While recognizing that the Net can be used in sexually compulsive or deviant ways, we consider how sexual intensity may develop in positive ways within these relationships. By applying psychosocial theories of relationship formation as well as describing qualities of the interpersonal space that's created online, we account for the richness and depth relationships may take on via this seemingly impersonal medium.

A priori assumptions about Internet relating tend to be that it is less involving, less rich, and less personal than face-to-face (FTF) communication due to the lack of facial and body language cues, the lack of the "felt presence" of the other, the lack of a "shared social context" between the communicators, and the "lean" bandwidth of the medium (i.e., written text alone without visual, auditory, olfactory, and other nonverbal impressions of the other available) (Walther, 1994).

While some experimental research seemed to substantiate the notion that computer mediated communication (CMC) was less personally engaging and more task oriented than FTF communication, field research showed contrary results. CMC relationships were found to take longer to develop than FTF relationships because of the slowness of the communication exchange and the limited bandwidth (it takes longer to form impressions of the other), but over time they did become as personal as FTF relationships, along dimensions such as affection, immediacy, receptivity, trust, and depth (Walther and Burgoon, 1992). Asynchronous CMC was even found to allow for more personal relating than FTF when groups were involved in task completion, because the sender did not have to worry about slowing the whole group down by interjecting personal comments or asking personal questions, since receivers could individually read the comments addressed to the group at their own leisure (Walther and Burgoon, 1992). Indeed, some experienced computer users rated e-mail and computer conferencing as "rich" or "richer" than FTF and telephone conversations (Jaffe, Lee, Huang, and Oshagan, 1995).

ONLINE RELATIONSHIP DEVELOPMENT

To make sense of these research findings as well as the many popular press reports of online love affairs, both of which point to the personally involving, even captivating, nature of electronic relating—we turn to theories of interpersonal attraction and early relationship formation, which were conceptualized with FTF relating in mind, and apply them to this new high-tech forum. Many "real world" relationships begin with attraction based on external attributes, such as physical appearance. If the relationship progresses, the attraction then evolves into an attachment based on similarity of values and beliefs. The development of rapport, mutual self-disclosure, and the empathic understanding of the other (Brehm, 1992, p. 156) are involved in a deepening of the connection, which moves the relationship to a more intimate stage. The relationship may become sexualized at any point, either initially as a spark from physical attraction or later based on a sense of being intimately connected emotionally. Certainly, each relationship online as well as offline is unique and its evolution defies simple categorizing.

PHYSICAL ATTRACTIVENESS

Clearly, as the technology stands now, CMR [computer mediated relating] does not start off or develop due to attraction based on physical attributes. In a culture that emphasizes physical appearance, the Internet affords a different way of developing initial attraction. This may change if video cameras become standard equipment; for many people video imaging will likely be experienced as a loss of the freedom to not care about how they look when communicating. However, even with a videocam image, the physical press of the interaction will not be as powerful as it is in FTF interaction; it will be less salient, relegated to one aspect of the overall online presentation, rather than the overwhelmingly dominant one.

Initial impressions online are based on how someone describes and expresses him/herself. Online, one's physical presence—attractiveness, age, race, ethnicity, gender, and mannerisms—is not evident except through what is conveyed by a name unless users choose to describe these aspects of themselves. People can present themselves and be "seen" free from some of the conscious and unconscious stereotypic notions that affect FTF relating from the outset. Self-presentation is more under one's control online; people can make decisions about when and how to disclose negative information about themselves. Sometimes it is better (in terms of advancing the relationship) to reveal such information about oneself early on; under other conditions, it may be best to wait (Hendrick and Hendrick, 1983).

In FTF interaction, people make quick judgments based on physical attributes, and good-looking individuals have a distinct social advantage. People over-generalize from appearance, assuming that those who are attractive on the outside are also nicer on the inside and have better future prospects; this well known phenomenon has been termed the "what-is-beautiful-is-good stereotype" (Brehm, 1992, p. 65). People who may in FTF encounters unwittingly keep themselves from intimate relationships by being overly focused upon or critical of their or others' physical appearance are freed up online to develop connections. Electronic relating offers a different basis for interaction than that of the "meat market" of the singles scene: "Concepts of physical beauty on the Net don't apply. We are all just bits and bytes blowing in the phosphorous stream" (Deuel, 1996, p. 143).

On the Net, the vast array of people to whom we are not physically drawn, yet with whom we might connect quite well if given the opportunity, become available to us. As one online participant commented, "You meet everyone you pass on the street without speaking to . . . you learn to look at people differently" (Turkle, 1995, p. 224). The compelling but often risky appeal of chemistry or "love at first sight" is reduced. The experience of being swept away upon first contact often involves a combination of raw physical attraction and tangled up projections, and for many people would better serve as a red flag than a basis for jumping right in (Hendrix, 1988).

Rheingold reflects,

> The way you meet people in cyberspace puts a different spin on affiliation: In traditional kinds of communities, we are accustomed to meeting people, then getting to know them; in virtual communities we get to know someone and then choose to meet them. (Rheingold, 1993, pp. 26–27)

By the time people meet each other in person, an intimate bond can already be formed. The felt intensity and meaning of any unappealing physical traits are then more likely to be mitigated by the overall attraction that exists. Certainly, the subjective experience of knowing and liking someone can profoundly influence how attractive s/he *seems:* Perceived beauty correlates more strongly than objective beauty to interest in dating (Brehm, 1992).

Attraction is also known to be fostered through proximity and familiarity. There is some evidence that mere frequency of exposure can create a degree of attraction between people (Hendrick and Hendrick, 1983). Electronic communication

> creates a feeling of greater propinquity [spatial proximity] with others, regardless of their actual geographic dispersion. This 'electronic propinquity' might be expected to foster friendships, as actual propinquity is known to do. (Walther, 1992)

Rapport can develop easily and casually online. Frequent contact with others is possible with little inconvenience or cost, from the comfort and safety of one's own home or workplace. One can access synchronous groups anytime for immediate interaction and can e-mail others whenever desired without being concerned about intruding, since they can retrieve messages at their convenience.

SIMILARITY

Studies point to attraction being highest when the partner is perceived as being both physically attractive and attitudinally similar to oneself (Brehm, 1992). The Net increases one's chances of connecting with like-minded people due to the computer's ability to rapidly sort along many dimensions simultaneously.

People who have difficulty connecting with others in FTF interactions have a better chance of meeting a compatible person online. For instance, an obese woman who feels insecure approaching new people in FTF interactions because of her weight may interact online with a variety of people who share her interests. She may then

> put [her weight] out to 40 different potential partners and eventually one of them will say 'Your weight doesn't bother me.' Emotionally speaking, it's much harder to say that to 40 different people in person. But on the Internet, it feels a lot less painful. (Williams, 1996, p. 11)

SELF-DISCLOSURE

Mutual self-disclosure is a key ingredient in developing intimacy between two people. Partners who self-disclose more to each other report greater emotional involvement in dating relationships and greater satisfaction in marriage (Brehm, 1992). A person who discloses intimate information about him/herself is generally better liked than one who is superficial. New acquaintances tend to match each other's level of self-disclosure, each disclosing more if the other person does so and holding back if the other person withdraws (Hendrick and Hendrick, 1983).

CMR provides sufficient distance to make it safer for people who may be restrained in FTF encounters to reveal more than they normally would. A woman who married a man she met online states,

> Had we met each other in person, I think we would have talked, but I don't think we would have given each other the opportunity to know each other. . . . It's pretty easy to talk about feelings and hopes and hurts when you don't see the person and think you're never going to meet. (Puzzanghera, 1996, p. 1A)

People who are shy have an opportunity to relate online, developing social skills and increasing their confidence as they go. A shy so-called computer "nerd" may connect better online because he is more confident: ". . . being able to type fast and write well is equivalent to having great legs or a tight butt in the real world" (Branwyn, 1993, p. 784). He may be able to carry the confidence and the social skills acquired online with him into FTF encounters; if not, with the ease of meeting people online he may meet a compatible person who will accept him with all his social awkwardness off as well as online.

> Some people, many people, don't do well in spontaneous spoken interaction, but turn out to have valuable contributions to make in a conversation in which they might have time to think about what they say. These people, who might constitute a significant proportion of the population, can find written communication more authentic than the FTF kind. (Rheingold, 1993, p. 23)

For people who may normally stay clear of intimate relationships due to concerns about feeling trapped or burdened or losing themselves in some way, online relating makes it easier to feel in control and therefore to get involved. Net relating tends toward frequent small, casual interactions, as compared to a long talk that can induce a sense of pressure and so be avoided or put off. People are freer to engage and disengage when they want to, to modulate the intensity of their interactions.

> The computer is sort of practice to get into closer relationships with people in real life. If something is bothering me, you don't have to let the person know or you can let the person know (Turkle, 1995, p. 203)

or you can log off.

Because of its informality, online written text resembles oral communication more than most other forms of writing. At the same time, certain qualities distinctive to writing and unavailable in spoken interactions can heighten the experience of being intimately understood: Writing offers time for reflection and revision, so that what is communicated may be complete and intentional, with the author neither forgetting important points nor saying too much. Due to the diminished interpersonal press, the weakened link between sender and receiver in CMR, the receiver is able to offer focused attention while staying centered within him/herself. S/he can access the message when s/he has the time and in-clination to fully attend to it. Because words can be saved, they can be reread by the receiver, their importance not lost in a quickly spoken phrase, their meaning not denied in an anxious moment. There's quality of putting oneself on the line in writing, of being more vulnerable and exposed to the other, a confessional quality: "As high tech as it is, there's something very old-fashioned about it. The writing and the feelings . . . [sic]" (Puzzanghera, 1996).

EROTIC CONNECTION

All psychological intimacy has the potential to provoke an eroticization of the person with whom it is shared (Levine, 1992), a desire to physically express the intimate connection. Online relating has some features that may promote and heighten such an erotic connection in positive ways. By minimizing an initial at-traction based on physical attributes and facilitating intimate, less inhibited sharing, the Net allows erotic interests to develop out of emotional involvement rather than lustful attraction. "Psychological intimacy . . . is an intangible, sub-tle, powerful motivator of our sexual expression" (Levine, cited in Lobitz and Lobitz, 1996, p. 71). Desire is strongest and most enduring when both partners value sexuality as a means of expressing intimacy.

Communication is a key to maintaining robust erotic connections. Failing to communicate intimately can spill over and impair sexual relationships (Chesney, Blackeney, Cole, and Chen, 1981). Online, partners have to verbally communi-cate, they can't fall back on unstated romantic scripts and nonverbal cues: "It's not like you can go to the movie together and not say anything" (Anning, 1996, p. 1A). Turn taking is built in so both people need to put themselves forward and cannot interrupt each other or speak at the same time.

All too often, psychological intimacy and sexuality are disconnected rather than integrated, with gender strongly influencing how people hold these two dimensions of relating. The interpersonal space the Net provides, reducing the emotional and physical press of FTF dating, may facilitate men and women's freedom to deviate from constricting gender roles related to sexuality that are often automatically activated in FTF encounters.

Internet relating can be conducive to the way many females in our culture experience sexuality, linking sexual desire to the overall relationship context and the degree of emotional intimacy. Online relating also frees women from the concern that if they or their partner reveal too much too soon, the rela-tionship will get too intimate, too sexual too quickly: Women don't have to be primarily concerned about saying "no" online. In the anonymity and safety of Net-space, women may feel free to be more directly and explicitly sexual, to take charge of their desire, without fear of potential real life consequences (e.g., pregnancy, forced sex, or STD's) or the need to deal with the male's more powerful physical presence.

A woman who feels inhibited about presenting herself as sexual yet desires to be sexually attractive to men can experiment with being more flirtatious. She may find a way to describe herself online as attractive and sexually appealing, affording her the chance to incorporate this view into her self-image, off as well as online. Physical attractiveness is not merely a question of endowment; how one comes across has much to do with projecting confidence, knowing how to accent one's strengths and minimize one's flaws, appreciating and presenting oneself as uniquely beautiful even when one's looks don't fit society's standard images of attractiveness.

Conversely, men, who often feel pressure to move a developing relationship along by being appropriately assertive and "getting somewhere," may feel less responsible for setting the pace of the relationship, including pushing for its sexual development; men can relax and let relationships develop in a more organic way, with sexuality springing from an emotional connection rather than vice versa.

SUMMARY

While many people think that electronic relating promotes emotionally disconnected or superficially erotic contacts, the structure and process of online relating can facilitate positive interpersonal connections, including the healthy development of romantic relationships. Computer mediated relating (CMR) reduces the role that physical attributes play in the development of attraction, and enhances other factors such as propinquity, rapport, similarity, and mutual self-disclosure, thus promoting erotic connections that stem from emotional intimacy rather than lustful attraction. The Net is a model of intimate, yet separate, relating. It allows adult (and teen) men and women more freedom to deviate from typically constraining gender roles that are often automatically activated in face-to-face interactions.

REVIEW QUESTIONS

1. What makes online relating as rich or richer than face-to-face relating for some people?
2. Explain what these authors call the "what-is-beautiful-is-good stereotype."
3. Face-to-face, you meet someone and then, perhaps, get to know him or her. Online you first get to know someone and then, perhaps, meet him or her. Describe the benefits of each.
4. How does the relative distance of CMR make self-disclosure easier? Are there problems with this dynamic?

5. What are some of the benefits of the enhanced control that individuals have when they are relating online?

6. Explain two ways that women and men can escape gender stereotypes in their CMR experiences.

PROBES

1. Consider how your physical appearance affects how you develop relationships face-to-face. What would be some benefits, for you specifically, of developing a relationship online, where the other person would not be responding to your physical appearance?

2. When you're communicating online, you miss the immediate, real-time, subtle facial expressions and posture changes that tell you how your conversation partner is responding to what you're saying. Isn't this vitally important information? How can CMR be as fulfilling, honest, and trustworthy as FTF relating if all this presentness is missing?

3. Isn't the discussion of erotic connection in this reading a little far-fetched? Can you imagine—or have you experienced—examples of CMR that actually generate erotic connections between people? Explain.

REFERENCES

1. Anning, V. (1996). Doctors analyze effect of Internet on relationships. *Stanford Daily*, October 15.
2. Branwyn, G. (1993). Compu-sex: Erotica for cybernauts. *South Atlantic Quarterly, 92*(4), 779–791.
3. Brehm, S. (1992). *Intimate relationships*. New York: McGraw-Hill.
4. Chesney, A. P., Blackeney, P. E., Cole, C. M., and Chen, F. (1981). A comparison of couples who have sought sex therapy with couples who have not. *Journal of Sex and Marital Therapy, 7,* 131–140.
5. Deuel, N. (1996). Our passionate response to virtual reality. In S. Herring (Ed.), *Computer-mediated communication: Linguistic, social and cross-cultural perspectives*. Philadelphia: John Benjamin.
6. Hendrick, C., and Hendrick, S. (1983). *Liking, loving and relating*. Monterey: Brooks/Cole.
7. Hendrix, H. (1988). *Getting the love you want: A guide for couples*. New York: Henry Holt.
8. Jaffe, J. M., Lee, Y., Huang, L., and Oshagan, H. (1995). *Gender, pseudonyms and CMC: Masking identities and baring souls*. [Online]. Available: <http://www.iworld.net/~yesunny/gendereps.html>
9. Levine, S. B. (1992). *Sexual life: A clinician's guide*. New York: Plenum Press.
10. Lobitz, W. C., and Lobitz, G. K. (1996). Resolving the sexual intimacy paradoxes: A developmental model for the treatment of sexual desire disorder. *Journal of Sex and Marital Therapy, 22*(2), 71–84.

11. Puzzanghera, J. (1996). Double click on love. *San Jose Mercury News*, April 27, 1A.
12. Rheingold, H. (1993). *The virtual community: Homesteading on the electronic frontier.* Reading: Addison-Wesley.
13. Turkle, S. (1995). *Life on the screen.* New York: Simon and Schuster.
14. Walther, J. B. (1992). Interpersonal effects in computer-mediated interaction: A relational perspective. *Human Communication Research, 20*(4), 473–501.
15. ———. (1994). Anticipated ongoing interaction versus channel effects on relational communication in computer mediated interaction. *Human Communication Research, 20*(4), 473–501.
16. Walther, J. B., and Burgoon, J. K. (1992). Relational communication in computer mediated interaction. *Human Communication Research, 19,* 50–88.
17. Williams, M. (1996). Intimacy and the Internet. *Contemporary Sexuality, 30*(9), 1–11.

PART FOUR

Bridges Not Walls

CHAPTER 9

Recognizing Communication Walls

Part IV of this book focuses on ways to turn communication *walls* into *bridges*. This first chapter of Part IV describes a variety of painful kinds of communication walls—deception, betrayal, aggression, hurtful messages, disconfirmation, the manipulative use of power, and verbal abuse. The next chapter describes how to manage the general "wall" called conflict, Chapter 11 discusses how to bridge cultural differences, and Chapter 12 explains how dialogue can bring people together.

This first reading in the chapter about walls discusses three of the more difficult elements of interpersonal communicating: lying, betrayal, and aggression. The reading combines insights from recent research into these phenomena with some practical suggestions about how to cope with them.

Karen, Saskia, and I begin by reviewing some research and some suggestions about deception or lying. We make the point that, like all forms of communication, lying is a joint action. Some people make it relatively easy for others to lie to them, and others make it desirable. This is not to "blame the victim" of deception, but only to remind communicators that it takes more than one person to lie. It is also important to realize that lying can be both intentional and unintentional. Especially when people are paying attention to social expectations and rules—which is just about all the time—it can be almost impossible to "tell the whole truth and nothing but the truth."

We discuss six motives for lying that emerge from some recent research, three of which the researchers call "positive," and three "negative," because of their likely impact on receivers. We also describe some of the most common consequences of deception. We note that the collaborative nature of deception becomes clearest when the deceived person decides to expose his or her relational partner's lies, or to ignore or suppress them.

Then we summarize the viewpoint of another researcher who argues that there are no "positive" motives for lying. We ask you to consider which of these views makes most sense to you—that deception is inevitable and sometimes it is a good thing, or that lying always objectifies and dehumanizes the receiver, and that it should be avoided whenever possible.

The second major section of the reading focuses on betrayal, communication that violates trust and the expectations on which the relationship is based. We note that a very high percentage of relational and dating partners report that they have experienced betrayal, which is more common than you might think. We discuss five features of betrayal that may empower you to understand it more effectively the next time it happens to you, and that may also remind you how to reduce the number of times you betray others.

The final section discusses hurtful messages, aggression, and violence. The first part pulls highlights from the next reading in this chapter, the one by Anita Vangelisti. Dr. Vangelisti's research identified 10 types of hurtful messages that people experience in relationships with partners, friends, and family members. In the next reading in this chapter, she describes the outcomes of her research in more detail than we do here.

The section of the reading on verbal aggression defines the phenomenon and describes how it takes some of its various forms. We also offer some suggestions for dealing with the verbal aggression you experience.

The final section of this reading briefly treats psychological abuse and physical violence. These brief paragraphs certainly do not do justice to these important topics, but we hope enough is said here, and later in the chapter, to empower those who suffer abuse or violence to begin to understand and cope with it. I also hope that those who inflict psychological abuse or physical violence can see from what's here that these behaviors are more common than they might have realized, and that there are people who can understand them and can help.

Deception, Betrayal, and Aggression

John Stewart, Karen E. Zediker, and Saskia Witteborn

DECEPTION

I've been going out with my current boyfriend for several months now and we spend most of our time together. I went home for the weekend to visit my grandmother, and when I returned a friend of ours told me that Josh was out dancing with his ex-girlfriend while I was gone. Josh had told me that he didn't want to have anything to do with her anymore, so obviously I was hurt and confused. When I saw my boyfriend this morning I asked him about his weekend, and he didn't say anything about going out. I wonder if I should ask him if he was out with her, but I really don't want to hear it if he was. But I'm not sure I can trust him until I know the truth, and if it's truth I don't want to hear, I don't know how I can trust him any more in this relationship.

You've probably heard stories like this one. Perhaps you've even told a story like this, or had one told about you. The reality and even the perception of deception can profoundly affect interpersonal relationships. In the next several paragraphs, we explore the motives or reasons for deception in interpersonal communication and identify some of the potential consequences for the relationship.

From J. Stewart, K. E. Zediker, and S. Witteborn, *Together: Communicating Interpersonally A Social Construction Approach*, 6th ed. Los Angeles: Roxbury, 2005.

Motives for Deception   Deception can vary from blatant lies to indirect actions such as exaggerations and false implications (Hopper and Bell 1984).
Whereas most people believe that deception is intentional, it can also be unintentional, as when someone misremembers or mistakenly forgets or omits information. Like all other communication phenomena, deception is a joint action,
the outcome of a collaboration between or among communicators. Some people
make it relatively easy for others to lie to them when they make choices that are
either gullible or overly demanding. It can be easy to lie to the person who believes almost everything he hears, for example. Authoritarian people also help
create communication contexts in which lying is easier. If your parent is always
on your case, demanding to know what you are doing all the time, you may be
more inclined to lie in order to negotiate the tension between interdependence
and autonomy. Some people decide whether or not to deceive others based on
the threat of being caught. If the danger of being discovered is high, and discovery has undesirable consequences, then a person might choose not to lie.

In addition, sometimes you may know, or at least suspect, that you are not
being told the truth but decide not to confront others about their deception.
One of us has a friend who is a compulsive liar, and most people who know her
well understand that this is part of her way of being with others. We know the
verbal and nonverbal signs that accompany her deceptions, probably better
than she does herself, and we choose not to "call her" on every one of her lies.
Sometimes the choice to "let her lie" is made out of a desire to save time, because the issue of the lie is not central to the conversation or simply because
holding her accountable for her lies would require more of an emotional investment than we'd like to make at the time. Occasionally, couples even collaborate on lies, and this is called collusion (Andersen 1998). One partner may
routinely deceive the other about infidelities, for example, and although the
other suspects the truth, he or she agrees, for whatever reasons, to look the
other way. In short, like all other kinds of communication, deception is strongly
influenced by its context.

Communication researchers Dan O'Hair and Michael Cody (1994) identify
six motives or reasons people give for lying to their relational partners. Three of
the motives—*egoism, benevolence,* and *utility*—are labeled positive because they
generally have positive consequences for at least one individual and appear to
O'Hair and Cody to do no harm to the relationship. The other three—*exploitation,
malevolence,* and *regress*—are labeled negative because their consequences do include harm to at least one person in the relationship. Egoism and exploitation are
positive and negative forms of *self-related* motives, benevolence and malevolence
are related to the *other,* and utility and regress have to do with the *relationship.*

Self-related motives for deception highlight what an individual can gain or
retain through deception. Egoism helps to protect or promote the deceiver's self-
concept. Think about times when you have stretched the truth on a job application or told someone something about yourself that was not quite true in order
to be viewed in a positive light or to avoid embarrassment. Exploitation is lying
with a purely selfish motive. When you pretend to be interested in someone in

order to get information or to achieve some other personal goal, you have exploited the deceived. You may believe that your decision to exploit another is no different from beefing up your resumé, but arguably there is a difference in degree regarding both the effect on the relationship and the potential damage to the other person.

Benevolence and malevolence are deceptive practices that are other-focused. Benevolent lies are motivated by the desire to protect the self-esteem, safety, or general well-being of the other person. Lies told by people who were hiding Jews from the Nazis in World War II, by members of the Underground Railroad facilitating travel of runaway slaves in the U.S. Civil War era, or by networks designed to help protect wives or husbands in physically abusive relationships are all deceptions motivated by benevolence. Distorted truths or blatant lies that parents tell their children in order to protect the child's sense of worth or well-being are another kind of benevolent deception. Malevolence, on the other hand, is motivated by the desire to hurt others and may include deception designed to sabotage others or to get revenge or retaliation. The motive for benevolence may be viewed as pure even though the consequences of the deception may not be altogether productive, but malevolence has at its core negativity, and the results of malevolent deception are almost always negative for both the people involved and the relationship.

The two final motivations for deception focus on outcomes for the relationship itself. When someone employs utility as a motive for deception, the goal is to improve, enhance, escalate, or repair the relationship. In the example at the beginning of this chapter, Josh could have been trying to protect the relationship when he avoided telling his girlfriend about running into his ex while his girlfriend was out of town. Since his girlfriend was already worried about her grandmother's health, Josh may have believed that it wasn't useful to bring up a casual contact, especially when the fact that they were at the same club at the same time didn't mean much to him. Utility can also be a motivation to ignore a friend's compulsive lying. Ignoring another's deception is one way to keep the peace in a relationship, even when that stability is based on a lack of trust. Regress, on the other hand, means using a lie to damage or terminate a relationship. For instance, Jamal might tell his steady date Anna that they should go back to being "just friends" when the truth is that Jamal wants Anna to end the relationship. In this case, Jamal is manipulating Anna rather than being accountable for his own preference (O'Hair and Cody 1994, 196).

Consequences of Deception   Most acts of deception have unintended consequences. In fact, if people carefully considered the potential ramifications of deception, they would often find that, in the long run, it would be less trouble to tell the truth. One unintended consequence is that when deception is undetected, it becomes a burden for the deceiver. In some cases people who deceive others feel a sense of autonomy, privacy, or control, but often these feelings are compromised by feelings of shame or guilt for lying to others and perhaps even anger at or contempt for the person they are lying to. Frequently, in order to maintain a falsehood, additional lies must be told to additional people. Any deception requires the deceiver to remember the details of the lie for as long as it is maintained, coordinate subsequent supporting lies, and maintain a heightened awareness of both verbal and nonverbal cues. This increased attention to one's own communication usually generates stress, which is ironic, since stress avoidance may have been the reason for the deception in the first place.

Once a deception has been detected by or revealed to a relational partner, the consequences expand and are almost universally negative. Until people discover that someone has lied to them, they generally operate from a "truth bias," that is, a basic belief that the other communicator is telling the truth. This state quickly changes to a "lie bias" once deception is revealed (O'Hair and Cody 1994, 197). At this point, the deceived person is likely to assume that that communicator is always lying. This change in a relationship is one way that many people discover how trust is a precious commodity that, once lost, is difficult to fully regain.

The collaborative nature of deception becomes clearest when the deceived person decides to expose his or her relational partner's lies or to ignore or suppress them. Suppression may require increasingly monumental efforts, including lying to yourself about the fact that you are being lied to, accusing others of lying to you about a partner's indiscretions, and even lying to others about your relational partner's behaviors. Exposing the lie, however, means admitting to the deceiver and to others one's hurt, loss of esteem, anger, and increasing uncertainty about the future of the relationship. The deceiver who is caught and confronted by the deceived partner frequently also suffers embarrassment, guilt, and loss of credibility. Deception often increases tension, conflict, and even aggression in a relationship.

For these reasons and others, communication researcher and teacher Bill Wilmot argues that deception is *always* damaging to the other person and to the relationship. Wilmot contends that deception, by its very nature, is a self-centered act. Unlike O'Hair and Cody, Wilmot does not believe that any motives for deception are positive. Even when you convince yourself that your deception benefits the other or the relationship, Wilmot maintains that

> the recipient of the deception has no hand in deciding if it is "good" for the relationship or not—he or she is out of the loop. . . . Deception, even in its benign forms, is a form of information control that one exercises; you want to be the one determining the course of the relationship, so you withhold information from the partner. (Wilmot 1995, 107–108)

If indeed the lowest common denominator in a relationship is two, an individual's choice to deceive is also a choice to short circuit the relationship by leaving the other partner out.

Whether you view deception as self or other motivated, patterns of deception are established collaboratively in relationships, and you can choose to sustain them or alter them. You do not have ultimate control over the direction of your relationships' spirals, because it always takes at least two. But your choices do contribute to sustaining, revealing, and preventing deception in your inter-personal relationships. If you are aware of a pattern of deception in an intimate relationship, we think that it would be useful for you to consider the motives for deception and the consequences of it for yourself, your partner, and the relation-ship. It may be that deception is a way to meet your need for privacy, control, or belonging, but there are consequences for choosing deception as a way to achieve the balance you are seeking. Whether you are the one in the relationship doing more of the deceiving, or the person who has been or is being lied to, you can start to alter the communicative pattern you've helped establish by interjec-ting more honesty whenever possible. Sometimes revealing a lie and working through its aftermath can lead to relationship development and growth.

We hope it is obvious that we are not advising you to be brutally honest all of the time in all of your relationships. Telling your boss that you think she has a big nose, for example, is irrelevant to the working relationship and could be considered malevolent, to say nothing of how foolish it might be if you are up for review. But when a pattern of deception is present between you and the peo-ple closest to you, it is important to identify what is going on and to restore as much of the truth as the relationship can contain. We also hope that you will at least think carefully about our point that deception is a collaboratively created phenomenon. It takes two to develop and maintain patterns of deception, and if you want to change the patterns, you'll need to make a choice to change your role in sustaining them. If you decide not to change the patterns, then at least ac-knowledge personal accountability for your part in them.

BETRAYAL

Deception and betrayal are closely related; in fact, some researchers see them as almost synonymous. The difference is that betrayal violates the betrayed per-son's expectations and can do so even when the person doing the betraying tells the truth. Researchers Walter Jones and Marsha Parsons Burdette define betray-als as "violations of trust or expectations on which the relationship is based" (Jones and Burdette 1994, 244). Their research reveals five important features of betrayal.

First, betrayal appears to be common in interpersonal relationships. Over 90 percent of the participants in one study could easily provide stories of be-trayal episodes in which they either did the betraying or were betrayed. As people move from the impersonal end of the continuum toward the inter-personal end, they tend to develop a sense of trust and commitment that grows out of mutual expectations consistently being met, even when some of these expectations remain unstated. It is not surprising, then, that any violation of expectations can be viewed as a betrayal by at least one of the partners.

Many different types of betrayal have been reported, including extramarital and extrarelational affairs, lies, revealed confidences, drinking and drugging, lack of support from a partner, ignoring a friend or partner, criticism, and gossip. Some of the most extreme forms of betrayal reported, and also the most severe, include being abused or abandoned by a parent. Unfortunately, the most painful kinds of betrayal happen in the most important relationships, probably because the expectations about communication and behavior are the highest in relationships that are most important. In relatively impersonal relationships, expectations are more socially shaped, and when social expectations are unmet, the consequences are less profound.

A second feature of betrayal is that the consequences of a betrayal incident differ significantly, depending on whether one is the betrayer or the betrayed. It may seem obvious that those who are betrayed described the relationship as having worsened in the aftermath of the betrayal incident. But it is interesting to note that those who did the betraying generally reported that the relationship had stayed the same or even improved after their betrayal.

Despite this potential optimism, the third feature is that betrayal tends to be followed by relationship termination. This obviously happens in romantic relationships and friendships, which are often referred to as relationships of choice. But even involuntary relationships, such as those between family members and coworkers, suffer serious decline following incidents of betrayal. One major reason is that betrayal involves disconfirmation of expectations, norms of interaction, and, most important, disconfirmation of the other as significant in the relationship. As Jones and Burdette (1994) explain, "The treachery is not just in the actual harm done to another, but also in the fact that betrayals threaten a major source of one's feelings of identity and well-being" (245). That source is the relationship itself. Effects of betrayal can last for a long time, and mitigation often requires help from a counselor, pastor or priest, or a trusted friend.

A fourth finding from studies of betrayal is that gender differences are prominent. Women are more likely to betray and be betrayed by other women, usually when one woman reveals a confidence or secret. Men report betraying their romantic partners more than they betray partners in any other relationship, and most often the nature of their betrayal is sexual. However, men report that they are most often betrayed by coworkers with whom they compete. Men and women also classify incidents of betrayal in significantly different ways. Men are more likely to identify only overt acts or events as betrayals, whereas women are more likely to describe a general lack of emotional support as a betrayal.

Finally, Jones and Burdette conclude that some personality traits may correlate with betrayal behavior. People who are likely to betray others also appear to be generally more jealous, suspicious, envious, and resentful of others. In addition, they tend to have more personal problems, including alcoholism or other addictions, depression, and a self-reported inability to sustain intimate relationships. These characteristics distinguish between those who are more likely to betray others, and they also identify those who are most likely to be betrayed.

Like deception, betrayal involves actions that leave at least one person out of the decision-making loop as the person doing the betraying attempts to control the destiny of the relationship on his or her own. Also like deception, betrayal diminishes trust between relational partners and damages the relationship itself.

When you notice patterns of betrayal in your relationships, it can be helpful to reflect on your expectations of the other person(s) and of the relationship(s). If you can talk to your relational partner and make some of your expectations explicit, then it may be easier for him or her to meet them. You can also discuss what expectations are most important to each of you, because even when people share mutual expectations, the value each places on any expectation can vary dramatically. When you experience incidents of betrayal, you may find it useful to get some perspective on your communication patterns from a third party and to express your feelings about the choices you have made and those that have been made for you.

HURTFUL MESSAGES, AGGRESSION, AND VIOLENCE

Aggression and violence are two additional relational problems that are influenced by power dynamics. When one party asserts control and influence over the other, patterns of hurtful messages, aggression, and violence may occur. These patterns are not simply created by the person who strikes out in anger or frustration. Like all relational patterns, these are also coconstructed. We definitely do not condone the behaviors of friends, family members, and romantic partners who berate and abuse others. At the same time, we also do not encourage friends, family members, and romantic partners who choose to accept emotional abuse. We acknowledge that sometimes people with less power—children, the elderly, a person in an unfamiliar culture—may not have many choices available. But we urge victims of abuse not to believe that their only option is to accept or reinforce the pattern.

Hurtful Messages   Hurtful messages are one of the ways that people attempt to assert power. Communication teacher and researcher Anita Vangelisti (1994) identified 10 types of hurtful messages people experience in relationships with partners, friends, and family members. The people Anita questioned reported all of the following hurtful messages: *Accusations* about the other's negative behavior ("You are a liar"), *evaluations* of the other person's value as a human being ("You have got to be the most worthless son on the face of the planet"), *directives* or commands ("Just get out of my face"), *advice* ("You really ought to so something about your appearance"), *expressions of desire* ("I don't want to have anything to do with you"), *information disclosure* ("I'm really not attracted to you anymore"), *interrogating questions* ("Were you out with that no-good loser again?"), threats ("If you think you can leave me, you have another thing coming"), *jokes* that put down the other ("The way you do that, you'd think your hair was blonde!"), and *lies* ("No I didn't cheat on you with her last week"). Clearly there are many ways to hurt another person, and the extent of the pain associated with each type of hurtful message depends on the context and the nature of the relationship.

In fact, the experience of hurt is also a relational phenomenon. A message that may be viewed as innocuous from a friend can be very painful when uttered by a family member or romantic partner. Vangelisti (1994) identified three factors that seem to affect how hurtful messages are interpreted: (1) the intent of the person communicating the hurtful message; (2) whether the parties shared a family or nonfamily relationship; and (3) the level of intimacy. One's overall satisfaction with a relationship also influences the extent to which relational partners emphasize hurtful messages. If a relationship is not very satisfying, people come to expect hurtful messages and pay less attention to them. Of course, as hurtful messages increase, overall satisfaction with the relationship decreases, and patterns of put-downs tend to create and maintain degenerative spirals.

When you are angry with someone or frustrated by your circumstances, consider the effects your hurtful messages may have. Many hurtful messages are difficult to repair, and although Vangelisti notes that those in intimate or family relationships may be more forgiving of them, participants in her study reported that it was difficult to forget them. Often they remembered the specific words of a message even years after they were spoken. Hurtful statements have rarely led to positive change in relationships and are often a part of relationship termination.

Verbal Aggression   Two communication researchers who spearheaded the study of verbal aggression noted that when someone uses verbal aggression they attack the self-concepts of other people (Infante and Wigley 1986). Attacks on character, ridicule, rough teasing, and profanity are all forms of verbal aggression. In contrast to content or topic, verbally aggressive messages focus on the identity of the person being attacked. Karen recalls one verbally aggressive message that called into question her identity as a communication professional. An extended family member was frustrated when she felt out of the loop on the timing of a visit from Karen's dad, and rather than strike out at the members of the family with whom she lived, she chose to strike out at Karen by asking, "Don't you ever *use* that communication stuff you teach in your classes? What happened to all that stuff on family communication? Your family doesn't seem to be very good at it!"

As Wilmot and Hocker (2001) note, the forms that verbal aggression take can differ from relationship to relationship and culture to culture. They point out that in cultures that value individualism, verbally aggressive remarks are generally directed against a person (Carey and Mongeau 1996). Examples might include "You are so stupid!" "You're ugly," "I wish you had never been born!" and "You are such a slob." By contrast, verbal aggression in collectivist cultures generally takes the form of attacks against the group, village, tribe, or family the person being attacked identifies with (Vissing and Baily 1996). Examples of verbally aggressive statements toward the group may include "You Irishmen are just a bunch of drunken idiots" or "All Greeks are geeks."

In a study of verbal aggression among college-age couples, Sabourin (1995) found that aggressive partners would attack each other in escalating verbal exchanges in an attempt to gain control. Both would make escalating accusations and assertions in a pattern of domineering talk in which neither would accept the other's desire for control. As Sabourin notes, couples often found them-selves stuck in escalating spirals that seemed out of control. She writes,

> The boundaries between individuals and the potential for empathy are lost. The partner is no longer experienced as a distinct individual deserving of respect but instead, as an extension of [the aggressive person]. In the process of esca-lating aggression, paradoxically, the power of both partners is lost to the pattern between them. (Sabourin 1995, 281)

If you find that you are involved in battles of verbal aggression that seem to be spiraling out of control, what are some of your nexting choices? One effective way to shift away from verbal aggression is to focus on the content of the con-flict rather than the character of the other person(s). Remember, verbal aggres-sion is defined in part by the ways it attacks the character and self-concept of the other. Choosing to focus on the issue at hand rather than the identity of the other is one effective way to break degenerative spirals fueled by verbal aggression. If you and your partner do not curb your patterns of verbal aggression, you should be aware that sustained patterns of verbal aggression often lead to episodes of psychological abuse and even to patterns of violence. So, it is defi-nitely worth it to try to intervene.

Psychological Abuse   Psychological abuse, like verbal aggression, can take a variety of forms, and what feels abusive in one relationship may not be inter-preted the same way in another relationship. One researcher notes that instances of psychological abuse including the "creation of fear, isolation, economic abuse, monopolization, degradation, rigid sex-role expectations, withdrawal, [and] contingent expressions of love" are widespread enough to occur in some form in all intimate or close relationships (Marshall 1994, 294).

In many cases, psychological abuse, like other forms of aggression and vio-lence, is one way that relational partners assert dominance and control. The individual who chooses this form of verbal aggression is actively engaged in constructing an identity of the other that is subordinate and powerless. When, for whatever reason, their partner accepts this construction of identity, patterns of abuse are likely to continue. Students have reported that when they look back on relationships characterized by psychological abuse, they often wonder why they allowed their partner to define them as dependent when in most other con-texts and relationships they were independent or interdependent people. One of the ways to respond to psychological abuse and other forms of verbal ag-gression is to use perception checking. You may find it helpful to solicit the per-ceptions of a close friend, family member, religious leader, or counselor to check your own perceptions of yourself and those features of your identity that feel imposed on you by your abusive relational partner.

Physical Violence   You might wonder why anyone would stay in a relationship that is physically violent. Part of the reason may be that, like other forms of violence in relationships, physical violence is often part of a pattern that develops over time, sometimes without the participants being fully aware that they are cocreating it. Most often, however, incidents of relational violence can be predicted by the extent to which verbal aggression and psychological abuse are occurring. Rarely do episodes of physical abuse exist in isolation. Most of the reports of physical violence in intimate relationships indicate that women are more likely to be harmed than men, but both men and women use physical violence as a tactic. Adults are more likely to use physical violence with children as discipline and as a way to assert influence and control.

Unfortunately the occurrence of physical violence as a tactic for negotiating power in a relationship is more common than you might imagine. One report suggests that in dating couples, 30–40 percent report violent incidents, including "pushing, shoving, slapping, kicking, biting, hitting with fists, hitting or trying to hit with an object, beatings, and threats/use of a weapon" (Cate and Lloyd 1992, 97). Most of us have heard reports on the national news of children so determined to save themselves and their siblings from continued abuse by a parent that they feel their only recourse is to murder their mom or dad. Women who murder their abusive spouses have successfully used self-defense pleas to avoid life in prison for terminating abusive relationships by terminating their abusive partners.

Most people will not experience extreme forms of physical abuse in their relationships, but if you or someone you know is in an abusive or violent relationship, on either side of the situation, we hope that the information we have sketched here can help you gain a better understanding of what is happening and provide you with some choices about what to do next. Of course, the abuse will not magically disappear just because you—or others—understand that physical violence is related to verbal aggression or that physical abuse often follows a cyclical pattern of increasing tension, some precipitating event, and a physically violent act, followed by remorse and often some form of restitution. At the same time, you or the person you are trying to advise can make choices about the ways to negotiate power in your relationships so these relationships do not include violence. You may need to change the context in which the relationship is maintained, for example, by putting physical distance between you and your partner. It may also be necessary to seek outside counsel and support from a third party and to learn new patterns of communication using more productive strategies for negotiating power in the relationship. Our point is that one person can choose to alter his or her own behaviors that contribute to the patterns of communication enacted in a problematic relationship and can explore appropriate ways to use the power currencies he or she has in those relationships.

REVIEW QUESTIONS

1. Explain the difference between positive and negative motives for deception.
2. Define "truth bias" and "lie bias."
3. Describe what some research has suggested are the personality features of frequent betrayers.

4. How does betrayal fit into the common pattern of communication in the family of an addicted person?
5. Explain the three factors that affect how hurtful messages are interpreted.
6. Paraphrase: "In the process of escalating aggression, paradoxically, the power of both partners is lost to the pattern between them."

PROBES

1. O'Hair and Cody would probably view the lies told to Nazi soldiers to protect Jews in hiding as "benevolent" and therefore positive. But Wilmot does not believe that any motives for deception can be completely positive, and he briefly explains why. What do you believe? Explain.
2. What do you believe is the most negative motive for deception?
3. How do you respond to the claim that deception is collaborative?
4. The authors say that they are not advising you to be "brutally honest" in all your relationships. What are they advising?
5. What makes betrayal so interpersonally toxic?
6. What resources are available in your community for people who are experiencing physical violence in a close relationship?

REFERENCES

1. Andersen, P. (1998). *Nonverbal Communication: Forms and Functions*. New York: McGraw-Hill.
2. Carey, C., and Mongeau, P. (1996). "Communication and Violence in Courtship Relationships." In D. Cahn and S. Lloyd (eds.), *Family Violence from A Communication Perspective*. Hillsdale, NJ: Lawrence Erlbaum. Pages 127–150.
3. Cate, R. M., and Lloyd, S. A. (1992). *Courtship*. Thousand Oaks, CA: Sage.
4. Deutsch, M. (1973). "Conflicts: Productive and Destructive." In F. Jandt (ed.), *Conflict Resolution Through Communication*. New York: Harper and Row.
5. Emerson, R. (1962). "Power-Dependence Relations." *American Sociological Review*, 27: 31–41.
6. Hopper, R., and Bell, R. A. (1984). "Broadening the Deception Construct." *Quarterly Journal of Speech*, 70: 288–300.
7. Infante, D., and Wigley, C. (1986). "Verbal Aggressiveness: An Interpersonal Model and Measure." *Communication Monographs*, 53: 61–69.
8. Jones, W. H., and Burdette, M. P. (1994). "Betrayal in Relationships." In A. L. Weber and J. H. Harvey (eds.), *Perspectives On Close Relationships*. Boston: Allyn and Bacon. Pages 245–262.
9. Marshall, L. L. (1994). "Physical and Psychological Abuse." In W. Cupach and B. Spitzberg (eds.), *The Darkside of Interpersonal Communication*. Hillsdale, NJ: Lawrence Erlbaum. Pages 292–297.

10. McGraw, P. (2003). *Relationship Rescue: A Seven-Step Strategy for Reconnecting With Your Partner.* New York: Hyperion.
11. O'Hair, H. D., and Cody, M. J. (1994). "Deception." In W. Cupach and B. Spitzberg (eds.), *The Dark Side of Interpersonal Communication.* Hillsdale, NJ: Lawrence Erlbaum.
12. Sabourin, T. C. (1995). "The Role of Negative Reciprocity in Spouse Abuse: A Relational Control Analysis." *Journal of Applied Communication Research,* 23: 271–283.
13. Vangelisti, A. (1994). "Messages That Hurt." In W. Cupach and B. Spitzberg (eds.), *The Dark Side of Interpersonal Communication.* Hillsdale, NJ: Lawrence Erlbaum. Pages 61–79.
14. Vissing, Y., and Baily, W. (1996). "Parent-to-Child Verbal Aggression." In D. Cahn and S. Lloyd (eds.), *Family Violence From a Communication Perspective.* Hillsdale, NJ: Lawrence Erlbaum. Pages 85–107.
15. Wilmot, W. W. (1995). *Relational Communication.* New York: McGraw-Hill.
16. Wilmot, W., and Hocker, J. (2001). *Interpersonal Conflict.* Boston: McGraw-Hill.

I remember when Anita Vangelisti was an undergraduate student in my interpersonal communication class. Now she is a respected researcher and a professor in one of the best communication departments in the United States at the University of Texas. This reading, which I excerpted from a considerably longer chapter in a recent book, summarizes some of Anita's work on messages that hurt.

This selection reviews work done by others and reports on some studies Anita and her colleagues have done. As she reports, one of her early moves was to ask several hundred college students to recall a situation in which someone said something to them that hurt their feelings. From these data she was able to identify *categories* of hurtful messages. They are summarized in Table 9–1 and include accusations, evaluations, threats, lies, and six other types. She also identified nine *topics* of hurtful messages, including romantic relations, sexual behavior, physical appearance, personality traits, and so on. This early research gave Anita an overall view of the phenomenon she was studying.

One of her next moves was to explore why some messages hurt more than others. She found that informative messages hurt the worst, primarily because there seems to be little opportunity to defend oneself or repair the damage created by comments like, "You aren't a priority in my life," "I decided we can only be friends," or "I'm really attracted to Julie." As you might expect, messages centering on romantic relationships were also perceived as extremely hurtful. And again, their hurtfulness is partly a function of how much the recipient can do about the message. The most hurtful messages tend to be those that we can do the least to respond to. This is one of the reasons why recipients in at least one study responded to extremely hurtful messages by withdrawing—either by crying or by verbally complying.

Anita extends her discussion of these most hurtful messages by reviewing some attributions that people make to help them cope. (For a review of attributions, look back at the reading by Trenholm and Jensen in Chapter 5.) Sometimes people cope by providing a generous attribution about intent—"After all, she didn't *mean* to hurt my feelings." In other situations intent is clearer and the person receiving the message focuses on "How could anyone say something like that *on purpose?*"

The mental effort expended to make sense of hurtful messages varies, as you might expect, with the closeness of the relationship. Few people invest much effort in a hurtful message from a store clerk, but a comment from one's spouse might provoke considerable work. There are exceptions to this rule, however, including the son who excuses his father's put-downs with "I guess that's what fathers are supposed to do" and the abused wife who minimizes the negative messages received from her husband.

The final section of this reading focuses on how hurtful messages affect relationships. When the message is perceived to be unintentional, the impact on the relationship tends to be negligible. When the hurt is perceived to be intentional, there is a greater impact, but this tendency is balanced by the tendency to excuse intimates. In both family and dating relationships, hurtful messages are often forgiven.

Anita's research clearly demonstrates the inaccuracy of the old adage, "Sticks and stones can break my bones, but names can never hurt me." Hurt is a relational phenomenon that depends not only on what is said but when, by whom, to whom, and how seriously. But the potential of destructive words is clearly great. "Names" and other hurtful messages can cut deep.

Messages That Hurt

Anita L. Vangelisti

After my parents got divorced, my father sat down and had a long talk with me. He told me a lot of things that my mom did to hurt him and tried to explain his side of the story. I already knew most of what he said, but there was one thing that really surprised me. He said, "Your mother never really loved you as much as she did your brother or sister. . . . It was obvious from the start. You looked like me and she couldn't hide her feelings." He probably didn't mean this the way I took it, but it has bothered me ever since. I wish now he wouldn't have said it. I'm not sure why he did. I guess he was just expressing his anger.

Although most of us have used the old adage "sticks and stones may break my bones,"[1] few who study communication would argue that the impact of words on people and relationships is less than that of physical objects—whether those objects be sticks, stones, bats, or fists. Words not only "do" things when uttered (Austin, 1975), but they have the ability to hurt or harm in every bit as real a way as physical objects. A few ill-spoken words (e.g., "You're worthless," "You'll never amount to anything," "I don't love you anymore") can strongly affect individuals, interactions, and relationships.

Feeling hurt, by its nature, is a social phenomenon. Except in relatively rare circumstances, people feel hurt as a result of some interpersonal event—something they perceive was said or done by another individual. The hurtful utterance may be spoken with the best of intentions or it may be overtly aggressive. It may occur as a one-time event or it may be embedded in a long history of verbal abuse. It may be spoken by a complete stranger or by a life-long friend. Regardless of intentionality, context, or source, feelings of hurt are evoked by and expressed through communication. Although theorists of emotion and of communication have acknowledged the potential association between social interaction and the elicitation of emotions such as hurt, theoretical work has only recently begun to explain the processes that link communication and emotion (Averill, 1980; Bowers, Metts, & Duncanson, 1985; de Rivera & Grinkis, 1986; Shimanoff, 1985, 1987; Weiner, 1986).

Weiner (1986) suggested that emotions are determined, in part, by attributions. He and his colleagues have found, for example, that the attributions people make about interpersonal events distinguish whether individuals feel anger, guilt, or pity (Weiner, Graham, & Chandler, 1982). Given this, when people feel hurt, their attributions concerning the messages that initially evoked their feelings should distinguish those (hurt) feelings from other similarly "negative" emotions. Although researchers have begun to study the association between attribution and emotion, they have largely neglected the relationship between communication and attribution. Because attributions are based, in part, on individuals' observations of interpersonal events, the messages that people believe evoked their feelings of hurt are central to understanding how hurt is elicited.

The purpose of this reading is to begin to describe the social interactions that people define as hurtful. . . .

EXAMINING MESSAGES THAT HURT

To begin to describe hurtful messages, data collected from two groups of undergraduate students were examined. The first set of data was collected from students ($N = 179$) enrolled in a large, introductory communication course. The second data set was collected approximately 1 year later and consisted of responses from individuals (N = 183) enrolled in one of several introductory communication courses.

Respondents were instructed to recall a situation in which someone said something to them that hurt their feelings. Then they were asked to write a "script" of the interaction as they remembered it. They were told to include what was said before the hurtful comment was made, what the comment was, and how they reacted to the comment.[2] After completing their script, participants were asked to look back on the conversation they described and to rate how hurtful it was (a high score indicated that it was "Extremely Hurtful" and a low score that it was "Not At All Hurtful").[3]

Inductive analysis (Bulmer, 1979) was used to develop a category scheme to describe the acts of speech that characterize hurtful messages.[4] With the exception of the data from five respondents (who could not recall any particularly hurtful messages), over 96% of the messages were codable into the typology. Definitions and examples of the categories are provided in Table 9–1. . . . The most commonly perceived hurtful messages across both data sets were accusations, evaluations, and informative messages, whereas the least common were lies and threats.

TABLE 9–1 Typology of Hurtful Message Speech Acts

Definition	Examples
Accusation: A charge of fault or offense.	"You are a liar." "You're such a hypocrite."
Evaluation: A description of value, worth, or quality.	"Well, if I met him and liked him, I would have remembered him." "Going out with you was the biggest mistake of my life."
Directive: An order, set of directions, or a command.	"Just get off my back." "Just leave me alone, why don't you!"
Advice: A suggestion for a course of action.	"Break up with her so you can have some fun." "I think we should see other people."
Expression of Desire: A statement of preference.	"I don't want him to be like you." "I don't ever want to have anything to do with you."
Information: A disclosure of information.	"You aren't a priority in my life." "Well, I'm really attracted to Julie."
Question: An inquiry or interrogation.	"Why aren't you over this [a family death] yet?"
Threat: An expression of intention to inflict some sort of punishment under certain conditions.	"If I find out you are ever with that person, *never* come home again."
Joke: A witticism or prank.	"The statement was really an ethnic joke against my ethnicity."
Lie: An untrue, deceptive statement or question.	"The worst part was when he lied about something . . ."

TABLE 9–2 Example of Hurtful Topics

Topic	Example
Romantic Relations	"He never liked you anyway. He just used you to get back at me."
Nonromantic Relations	"You're trying too hard to be popular . . . you're ignoring your 'real' friends."
Sexual Behavior	"Why? Do you still want to sleep around?"
Physical Appearance	"God almighty you're fat!"
Abilities/Intelligence	"I guess it's hard for you teenage illiterates to write that stuff."
Personality Traits	"Well, I think you're selfish and spoiled!"
Self-Worth	"I don't need you anymore."
Time	"We don't do things together like we used to."
Ethnicity/Religion	"You're a stupid Jew!"

A brief perusal of these data suggested that the messages varied in terms of how hurtful they were to respondents. Interactions ranged from a former coach telling a respondent, "My, you seem to have put on a few pounds" to a physical education teacher exclaiming, "You are the worse [*sic*] player I've ever seen in my life!" In one case, a peer asked a respondent who was mourning her father's death, "When are you going to get over this?" In another, a respondent's step-mother told her, "You caused your grandmother's death. She died of a broken heart because you didn't show her how much you loved her." Although all of these examples were rated above the midpoint in terms of how hurtful they were to respondents, some were rated as more hurtful than others. . . .

The topics addressed by hurtful messages were coded using a procedure identical to the one outlined for the coding of message type. Initial categories were generated, the data were coded, the categories were refined, and the data were re-coded. Table 9–2 provides a list of topic categories as well as examples of each topic. Over 93% of the messages reported were codable into the typology. . . .

WHY SOME MESSAGES HURT MORE THAN OTHERS

Of the hurtful messages described, informative statements were the only speech acts that were rated extremely hurtful more often than they were rated low in hurtfulness. Informative statements, in short, were most typically seen as highly hurtful messages. Although potential explanations for this finding vary, the ability of recipients to "repair" or offer alternatives to the content of the message seems a particularly likely contributor. Whereas listeners are less likely than speakers to initiate repair (Schegloff, Jefferson, & Sacks, 1977), when accused or evaluated, recipients have the control to either overtly or covertly "defend" themselves against hurt. If the speaker does not initiate repair, the recipient may do so by offering alternatives to the accusation (e.g., accounts, excuses, justifi-cations) and even verifying those alternatives with examples from his or her own experiences.[5] On the other hand, when informed of something, there are few such arguments available. The opportunities for recipients to repair any damage to their own face are severely limited. If, for example, a person is accused of being selfish and inconsiderate, that person can point out instances in which that has not been the case. However, if the same person is informed by a lover that the lover is "seeing someone else," there is little the person can say to counter the statement.

Like informative statements, hurtful messages (in the second data set) centering on romantic relationships were, more often than not, perceived as extremely hurtful (although this difference was significant only for the second data set, messages in the first data set were similarly distributed). Given that over 54.5% of the informative messages concerned romantic relationships (i.e., "I don't love you anymore," "I've been sleeping with someone else," "I decided we can only be friends"), this finding is not surprising. It is interesting, however, that participants tended to rate these relational hurts as more hurtful, whereas they tended to rate some personal or individual hurts (i.e., statements regarding self-worth) as less hurtful. One explanation for this contrast involves the potential recency of the messages concerning romantic relationships. Because the sample for this study was college students, events centering on romantic relationships may have been more recent and therefore more salient in the minds of respondents. However, this was not the case ($F(1,283) = 1.76$, ns). Furthermore, participants' ratings of hurtfulness were positively correlated with the amount of time that had passed since the hurtful event. . . .

A second explanation is that hurtful messages focusing on relational issues, like those comprised of informative statements, may be more difficult for recipients to repair than messages that emphasize nonrelational issues. This explanation is supported by the finding (in the first data set) that hurtful messages concerning nonromantic relationships were seen as extremely hurtful more often than not. (In the second data set this difference was not significant, but the data were distributed in a similar pattern.) Because relationships involve two people, they are at once controllable and uncontrollable. Each individual has the power to influence, but neither has complete reign. In contrast, many nonrelational issues such as time management are more controllable. Recipients may repair by excusing, justifying, or apologizing for their behavior or choices (McLaughlin, 1984). Further, because recipients have access to a great deal of information concerning their own behavior (e.g., the situational parameters they face), they may be able to rationalize their limitations by adjusting their own criteria for evaluating the behavior. Other nonrelational issues such as physical appearance and intelligence are relatively uncontrollable. Recipients therefore need not take responsibility for evaluative remarks or questions from others.

In comparison to nonrelational issues, relational issues present both recipients and speakers with a unique situation. Neither has complete control or responsibility for relational outcomes. As a result, when one partner evaluates ("You aren't going to make a very good husband") or makes an accusation ("You don't care about our friendship at all") concerning the relationship, the other is faced with a dilemma. He or she must seek a repair strategy that addresses the (relational) issue at hand without threatening the face of either partner. In many cases, these two goals are incompatible. The difficulties of dealing with such incompatible goals are reflected by the findings of a pilot study that suggest that recipients tend to react to extremely hurtful messages by withdrawing—either by crying or verbally acquiescing to their conversational partner (Vangelisti, 1989).

In addition to presenting participants with potentially difficult behavioral choices, extremely hurtful messages may also create some difficult cognitive tasks. When a loved one says something that hurts, participants may make one of at least two attributional choices. First, they may reason that the person did not intend to hurt their feelings. If this choice is made, the message may evoke feelings of hurt, but might not have a major effect on the relationship ("After all, she didn't *mean* to hurt my feelings"). Second, participants may believe that the message was intentionally hurtful. If so, they will likely have more difficulty discounting the impact of the message on the relationship ("How could anyone say something like that *on purpose?*"). In some cases, people may examine the available data to determine whether or not a message was intended to hurt. In others, the need or desire to maintain a close relationship may encourage participants to make attributions that minimize the intentionality they attach to hurtful messages.

The cognitive "effort" that individuals expend to make sense of hurtful messages should depend, in part, on the individuals' relationship with the person who uttered the message. For example, if a clerk in a department store hurts a person's feelings, that person is probably less likely to spend time contemplating the clerk's motives than if the same person was treated badly by a friend, parent, or spouse. Why? In part because people expect to be treated by intimate relational partners in relatively positive ways.

Obviously, there are exceptions to this rule. For instance, when explaining why his father said something hurtful to him, one respondent noted, "I don't understand why he always puts me down. I guess that's what fathers are supposed to do." Clearly this respondent did not expect positive feedback from his father. The rather bewildered account of his father's behavior suggests that the hurtful message described by the respondent may have been one of many—that it was contextualized in an ongoing stream of verbal abuse (Leffler, 1988; Vissing, Straus, Gelles, & Harrop, 1991; Yelsma, 1992) and/or intentional verbal aggression (Infante, Riddle, Horvath, & Tumlin, 1992; Martin & Horvath, 1992). Another example would be a physically abused wife who comes to expect negative behavior from her spouse. Even in such extreme cases, however, researchers have found that both the abused and the abuser use cognitive strategies to minimize the control and intentionality associated with abusive acts (Andrews, 1992; Herbert, Silver, & Ellard, 1991; Holtzworth-Munroe, 1992). In the context of close relationships, acts of violence are often interpreted as representing "love" rather than more obvious emotions such as anger or rage (Cate, Henton, Koval, Christopher, & Lloyd, 1982; Henton, Cate, Koval, Lloyd, & Christopher, 1983; Roscoe & Kelsey, 1986). In short, relational intimacy, the type of relationship people have with those who utter hurtful messages, and the intentionality attributed to the message should affect the impact of hurtful messages on relationships. . . .

DISCUSSING THE IMPACT OF HURTFUL MESSAGES ON RELATIONSHIPS

Although the vast majority (64.8%) of hurtful messages were perceived to be unintentional, those that were seen as intentional had a significantly greater distancing effect on the relationship. Recipients' remarks regarding intentionality reflected their willingness to make allowances for a variety of speaker difficulties. When asked whether the speaker intended to hurt them, recipients often made comments such as "she was mad at someone else," "he just doesn't know how to fight," "he has a personal problem with alcohol," or "he said it because he loves me." If speakers seemed to regret the hurtful message (Knapp et al., 1986), or if the message was offered for the good of the recipient (Weber & Vangelisti, 1991), the message did not have as strong an effect on the relationship. In contrast, when recipients perceived that the message was intentionally hurtful, their remarks frequently focused on stable personality traits of the speaker: "She's just that sort of person," "he is very cruel and unforgiving," "he doesn't care about anyone except himself." . . .

The impact of hurtful messages on relational intimacy was also affected by ratings of relational closeness at the time the message was uttered. Ratings of relational closeness were negatively associated with the distancing effect of hurtful messages. Because there was not a similarly negative association between closeness and message hurtfulness, the apparent lack of distancing in more intimate relationships was not due to the fact that the messages hurt less. Instead, those who were involved in intimate relationships may be more willing to offer interpretations of the hurtful messages that are less harmful to the relationship. It is also possible that intimates have developed idiosyncratic patterns to deal with hurtful events (Montgomery, 1988), or that they have developed enough of a positive regard for one another that a single hurtful message does not affect relational intimacy (Knapp, 1984).

Similar explanations may be offered for the findings concerning family relationships. Although intimacy did not significantly differentiate between family and nonfamily relationships, results indicated that hurtful messages occurring in the context of the family had less of an effect on the relationship than did those occurring in nonfamily contexts. In contrast to intimate nonfamily relationships, family associations may encourage people to deal with hurtful messages by relying on the assumption that the relationships are involuntary and therefore virtually impossible to dissolve. One respondent noted in the margin of his questionnaire that "It seems if something happens with your family . . . [you are] a lot more apt to forgive them." Because family members are, for all practical purposes, irreplaceable, recipients of hurtful messages may feel more obligated to absorb the blow of a hurtful message without allowing it to impact the family relationship. In addition, the variety of circumstances family members have experienced together may create a sort of "immunity" to the impact of hurtful messages. Family members' experience with other negative interpersonal events may better prepare them for the feelings of hurt that can be elicited by other members. . . .

In sum, the findings of this research suggest that the old adage concerning "sticks and stones" requires, at the very least, a lengthy addendum. Hurt is a socially elicited emotion (de Rivera, 1977)—people feel hurt because of the interpersonal behavior of others. Because feelings of hurt are elicited through social interaction, words can "hurt"—both individuals and relationships.

REVIEW QUESTIONS

1. Paraphrase the relationship between attributions and hurtfulness that Anita outlines in the third paragraph of this reading.
2. What is the main characteristic of a hurtful message that informs?
3. Why does Anita believe that informative hurtful messages are so painful?
4. What is Anita's theoretical explanation for the finding that recipients tend to react to extremely hurtful messages by withdrawing?
5. How does the desire to maintain a close relationship sometimes affect attributions about a hurtful message?
6. What do you make out of the finding that almost 65 percent of hurtful messages were perceived to be unintentional?

PROBES

1. If you were a participant in Anita's first study, what two examples of hurtful messages would you first recall? Label them using the categories in Table 9–1. Then identify the topics of these messages, as in Table 9–2.
2. What is the frequency of hurtful messages in your life by topic type? Which topic in Table 9–2 do you hear the most hurtful messages about? What is ranked second and third?
3. "Time heals all wounds," the saying goes. Yet Anita found that "participants' ratings of hurtfulness were positively correlated with the amount of time that had passed since the hurtful event." Comment on this finding.
4. Explain how, in the context of close relationships, "acts of violence are often interpreted as representing 'love.'"
5. Anita found in her research that the distancing effects of hurtful messages in intimate relationships were less than she expected. How does she explain this finding?

NOTES

1. Steve Duck has informed me of a German proverb that provides a more accurate representation of the association between words and feelings of hurt: "Böse Disteln stechen sehr, böse Zungen stechen mehr." A colleague from Germany, Jurgen Streeck, confirmed the translation: "Nasty thistles hurt/stick a great deal, but nasty words hurt/stick more."

2. Respondents participating in the second data collection session were also asked to indicate how long ago the hurtful message occurred.

3. To reduce demand characteristics, participants were also informed that some people may not have experienced (or may not be able to remember) the type of conversations called for by the questionnaire and that part of the research project was to assess the percentage of people who could and could not do so. Subjects were further reminded that they would receive extra credit regardless of whether or not they completed the questionnaire (see Planalp & Honeycutt, 1985).

4. Because the data were collected approximately 1 year apart, the analyses were conducted separately (also approximately 1 year apart). The initial category scheme, therefore, was primarily developed using the first data set. The second set of data was collected, in part, to demonstrate the applicability of the category scheme and to replicate the frequencies found using the first data set.

5. Work on accounts, blaming, excuses, and attributions (e.g., Cody & McLaughlin, 1988; Fincham, Beach, & Nelson, 1987; Fincham & Jaspers, 1980; Harvey, Weber, & Orbuch, 1990; Hilton, 1990; McLaughlin, Cody, & French, 1990; Weber & Vangelisti, 1991; Weiner, Amirkhan, Folkes, & Verette, 1987) certainly supports the notion that people generate such alternatives to explain unexpected social circumstances, potentially negative behavior, or broken social contracts.

REFERENCES

1. Andrews, B. (1992). Attribution processes in victims of marital violence: Who do women blame and why? In J. H. Harvey, T. L. Orbuch, & A. L. Weber (Eds.), *Attributions, accounts, and close relationships* (pp. 176–193). New York: Springer-Verlag.

2. Austin, J. L. (1975). *How to do things with words* (2nd ed., J. O. Urmson & M. Sbisa, Eds.). Cambridge, MA: Harvard University Press.

3. Averill, J. R. (1980). A constructivist view of emotion. In R. Plutchik & K. Kellerman (Eds.), *Theories of emotion* (Vol. 1, pp. 305–339). New York: Academic Press.

4. Bowers, J. W., Metts, S. M., & Duncanson, W. T. (1985). Emotion and interpersonal communication. In M. L. Knapp & G. R. Miller (Eds.), *Handbook of interpersonal communication* (pp. 500–550). Beverly Hills, CA: Sage.

5. Bulmer, M. (1979). Concepts in the analysis of qualitative data. *Sociological Review, 27*, 651–677.
6. Cate, R. M., Henton, J. M., Koval, J., Christopher, F. S., & Lloyd, S. (1982). Premarital abuse: A social psychological perspective. *Journal of Family Issues, 3*, 79–90.
7. Cody, M. J., & McLaughlin, M. L. (1988). Accounts on trial: Oral arguments in traffic court. In C. Antake (Ed.), *Analyzing everyday explanation: A casebook of methods* (pp. 113–126). London: Sage.
8. de Rivera, J. (1977). *A structural theory of the emotions.* New York: International Universities Press.
9. de Rivera, J., & Grinkis, C. (1986). Emotions in social relationships. *Motivation and Emotion, 10*, 351–369.
10. Fincham, F. D., Beach, S., & Nelson, G. (1987). Attribution processes in distressed and nondistressed couples: III. Casual and responsibility attributions for spouse behavior. *Cognitive Therapy and Research, 11*, 77–86.
11. Fincham, F. D., & Jaspers, J. M. (1980). Attribution of responsibility: From man the scientist to man as lawyer. In L. Berkowitz (Ed.), *Advances in experimental social psychology* (Vol. 13, pp. 82–139). New York: Academic Press.
12. Harvery, J. H., Weber, A. L., & Orbuch, T. L. (1990). *Interpersonal accounts.* Oxford: Blackwell.
13. Henton, J. M., Cate, R. M., Koval, J., Lloyd, S., & Christopher, F. S. (1983). Romance and violence in dating relationships. *Journal of Family Issues, 4*, 467–482.
14. Herbert, T. B., Silver, R. C., & Ellard, J. H. (1991). Coping with an abusive relationship: I. How and why do women stay? *Journal of Marriage and the Family, 53*, 311–325.
15. Hilton, D. J. (1990). Conversational processes and causal explanation. *Psychological Bulletin, 107*, 65–81.
16. Holtzworth-Munroe, A. (1992). Attributions and maritally violent men: The role of cognitions in marital violence. In J. H. Harvery, T. L. Orbuch, & A. L. Weber (Eds.), *Attributions, accounts, and close relationships* (pp. 165–175). New York: Springer-Verlag.
17. Infante, D. A., Riddle, B. L., Horvath, C. L., & Tumlin, S. A. (1992). Verbal aggressiveness: Messages and reasons. *Communication Quarterly, 40*, 116–126.
18. Knapp, M. L. (1984). *Interpersonal communication and human relationships.* Boston: Allyn & Bacon.
19. Knapp, M. L., Stafford, L., & Daly, J. A. (1986). Regrettable messages: Things people wish they hadn't said. *Journal of Communication, 36*, 40–58.
20. Leffler, A. (1988). *Verbal abuse and psychological unavailability scales and relationship to self-esteem.* Paper presented at the annual meeting of the American Psychological Association, Atlanta, GA.

21. Martin, M. M., & Horvath, C. L. (1992, November). *Messages that hurt: What people think and feel about verbally aggressive messages.* Paper presented at the annual meeting of the Speech Communication Association, Chicago, IL.
22. McLaughlin, M. L. (1984). *Conversation: How talk is organized.* Beverly Hills, CA: Sage.
23. McLaughlin, M. L., Cody, M. J., & French, K. (1990). Account-giving and the attribution of responsibility: Impressions of traffic offenders. In M. J. Cody & M. L. McLaughlin (Eds.), *The psychology of tactical communication* (pp. 244–267). Clevedon, England: Multilingual Matters.
24. Montgomery, B. M. (1988). Quality communication in personal relationships. In S. W. Duck (Ed.), *Handbook of personal relationships* (pp. 343–359). New York: Wiley.
25. Planalp, S., & Honeycutt, J. M. (1985). Events that increase uncertainty in personal relationships. *Human Communication Research, 11,* 593–604.
26. Schegloff, E. A., Jefferson, G., & Sacks, H. (1977). The preference for self-correction in the organization of repair in conversation. *Language, 53,* 361–382.
27. Shimanoff, S. B. (1985). Rules governing the verbal expression of emotion between married couples. *Western Journal of Speech Communication, 49,* 147–165.
28. Shimanoff, S. B. (1987). Types of emotional disclosures and request compliance between spouses. *Communication Monographs, 54,* 85–100.
29. Vangelisti, A. L. (1989, November). *Messages that hurt: Perceptions of and reactions to hurtful messages in relationships.* Paper presented at the meeting of the Speech Communication Association, San Francisco, CA.
30. Vissing, Y. M., Straus, M. A., Gelles, R. J., & Harrop, J. W. (1991). Verbal aggression by parents and psychosocial problems of children. *Child Abuse and Neglect, 15,* 223–238.
31. Weber, D. J., & Vangelisti, A. L. (1991). "Because I love you": The use of tactical attributions in conversation. *Human Communication Research, 17,* 606–624.
32. Weiner, B. (1986). *An attributional theory of motivation and emotion.* New York: Springer-Verlag.
33. Weiner, B., Amirkhan, J., Folkes, V. S., & Verette, J. A. (1987). An attributional analysis of excuse giving: Studies of a naïve theory of emotion. *Journal of Personality and Social Psychology, 52,* 316–324.
34. Weiner, B., Graham, S., & Chandler, C. C. (1982). Pity, anger, and guilt: An attributional analysis. *Personality and Social Psychology Bulletin, 8,* 225–232.
35. Yelsma, P. (1992, July). *Affective orientations associated with couples' verbal abusiveness.* Paper presented at the bi-annual meeting of the International Society for the Study of Personal Relationships, Orono, ME.

This next reading describes and explains a communication wall that is often more subtle than hurtful messages, lying, betrayal, or aggression, but that can be equally damaging. It's disconfirmation, something that occurs when someone in a communication situation is cancelled out, ignored, or made invisible. Disconfirmation happens, for example, when a smile and a happy wave is met by a blank stare, or when a child's "Mommy! Look at this neat worm!" is met with "Go wash your hands!"

As you might guess, the opposite of disconfirmation is confirmation, and, as you learned in the second reading in Chapter 7, it means actively acknowledging a person as a person, recognizing him or her as a unique, unmeasurable, choosing, reflective, and addressable human. Martin Buber—who wrote the last essay in *Bridges Not Walls*—was the first to use these terms in this interpersonal sense, and he emphasized that confirmation or disconfirmation exists to some degree in *every* relationship. You can use the presence of these two qualities to distinguish the most positive relationships—they're the ones where there's lots of confirmation—from the most toxic ones—where disconfirmation rules.

Buber points out that confirmation is the quality that distinguishes the human world from the nonhuman. His point is that people discover their personhood or humanness as they make contact with others. In other words, I learn that I am a person when I experience confirmation from another person. This is what makes disconfirmation potentially so brutalizing. When it happens, it can threaten a person's fundamental sense of who he or she is.

Ken Cissna and Evelyn Sieburg are two communication teachers who studied confirmation and disconfirmation for several years. This essay is nicely organized into a section that defines and describes confirmation, a section that identifies its four main dimensions, and then a longer section that talks systematically about confirming and disconfirming behaviors.

The authors describe and illustrate how what they call indifferent responses, impervious responses, and disqualifying responses are all disconfirming. Indifference denies the other's existence, while imperviousness means responding only to my image of you, even if it contradicts your perception of yourself. People communicate indifference, for example, by avoiding eye contact or physical contact or by ignoring topics the other person brings up. Imperviousness can be communicated, for example, with "Don't be silly—of course you're not afraid," or, "Stop crying, there's nothing the matter with you!" Disqualification is the technique of denying without really saying "no," as people do when, for example, we utter the "sigh of martyrdom," respond tangentially to the other person, or say something like, "If I were going to criticize, I'd say your haircut looks awful, but I wouldn't say that."

Responses that confirm, the authors point out, are less clearly defined than disconfirming ones. However, they identify three clusters of confirmation: recognition, acknowledgment, and endorsement. They also emphasize that "confirming response is dialogic in structure; it is a reciprocal activity involving shared talk and sometimes shared silence."

Patterns of Interactional Confirmation and Disconfirmation

Kenneth N. Cissna and Evelyn Sieburg

The term "confirmation" was first used in an interpersonal sense by Martin Buber (1957), who attributed broad existential significance to confirmation, describing it as basic to humanness and as providing the test of the degree of humanity present in any society. Although Buber did not explicitly define confirmation, he consistently stressed its importance to human intercourse:

> The basis of man's life with man is twofold, and it is one—the wish of every man to be *confirmed* as what he is, even as what he can become, by men; and the innate capacity in man to confirm his fellow men in this way. . . . Actual humanity exists only where this capacity unfolds. [p. 102]

R. D. Laing (1961) quoted extensively from Buber in his description of confirmation and disconfirmation as communicated qualities which exist in the relationship between two or more persons. Confirmation is the process through which individuals are "endorsed" by others, which, as Laing described it, implies recognition and acknowledgment of them. Though Laing developed confirmation at a conceptual level more thoroughly than anyone prior to him, his focus remained psychiatric: he was concerned with the effects of pervasive disconfirmation within the families of patients who had come to be diagnosed as schizophrenic. In such families, Laing noted, one child is frequently singled out as the recipient of especially destructive communicative acts by the other members. As Laing explained it, the behavior of the family "does not so much involve a child who has been subjected to outright neglect or even to obvious trauma, but a child who has been subjected to subtle but persistent *disconfirmation*, usually unwittingly" (1961:83). Laing further equated confirmation with a special kind of love, which "lets the other be, but with affection and concern," as contrasted with disconfirmation (or violence), which "attempts to constrain the other's freedom, to force him to act in the way we desire, but with ultimate lack of concern, with indifference to the other's own existence or destiny" (1967:58). This theme of showing concern while relinquishing control is common in psychiatric writing and is an important element in confirmation as we understand it. Although Laing stressed the significance of confirmation, he made no attempt to define it in terms of specific behaviors, noting only its variety of modes:

> Modes of confirmation or disconfirmation vary. Confirmation could be through a responsive smile (visual), a handshake (tactile), an expression of sympathy (auditory). A confirmatory response is *relevant* to the evocative action, it accords recognition to the evocatory act, and accepts its significance for the other, if not for the respondent. A confirmatory reaction is a direct response, it is "to the point," "on the same wavelength," as the initiatory or evocatory action. [1961:82]

In 1967, Watzlawick, Beavin, and Jackson located confirmation within a more general framework of human communication and developed it as a necessary element of all human interaction, involving a subtle but powerful validation of the other's self-image. In addition to its content, they said each unit of interaction also contains relational information, offering first, a self-definition by a person (P) and then a response from the other (O) to that self-definition. According to Watzlawick *et al.*, this response may take any of three possible forms: it may confirm, it may reject, or it may disconfirm. The last, disconfirmation, implies the relational message, "You do not exist," and negates the other as a valid message source. Confirmation implies acceptance of the speaker's self-definition. "As far as we can see, this confirmation of *P*'s view of himself by O is probably the greatest single factor ensuring mental development and stability that has so far emerged from our study of communication" (p. 84). The descriptive material provided by Watzlawick *et al.* to illustrate disconfirmation includes instances of total unawareness of the person, lack of accurate perception of the other's point of view, and deliberate distortion or denial of the other's self-attributes.

Sieburg (1969) used the structure provided by Watzlawick as well as the concept of confirmation/disconfirmation to begin distinguishing between human communication which is growthful, productive, effective, functional, or "therapeutic," and communication which is not. She developed measurement systems for systematically observing confirming and disconfirming communication (1969, 1972); she devised the first scale which allowed for measurement of an individual's feeling of being confirmed by another person (1972). She has continued to refine the basic theory of confirmation (1975), and has recently used the concepts to describe both organizational (1976) and family communication systems. During this time, a growing body of theoretical development and empirical research has attempted to explore these important concerns (cf. Cissna, 1976a, 1976b). . . .

DIMENSIONS OF CONFIRMATION

In the few direct allusions in the literature to confirmation and disconfirmation, several different elements are suggested. Confirmation is, of course, tied by definition to self-experience; our first problem, therefore, was to identify the specific aspects of self-experience that could be influenced positively or negatively in interaction with others. Four such elements seemed significant for our purpose:

1. The element of existence (the individual sees self as existing)
2. The element of relating (the individual sees self as a being-in-relation with others)
3. The element of significance, or worth
4. The element of validity of experience

Thus, it was assumed that the behavior of one person toward another is confirming to the extent that it performs the following functions in regard to the other's self-experience:

1. It expresses recognition of the other's existence
2. It acknowledges a relationship of affiliation with the other
3. It expresses awareness of the significance or worth of the other
4. It accepts or "endorses" the other's self-experience (particularly emotional experience)

Each unit of response is assumed to evoke relational metamessages with regard to each of the above functions, which can identify it as either confirming or disconfirming:

Confirming	**Disconfirming**
"To me, you exist."	"To me, you do not exist."
"We are relating."	"We are not relating."
"To me, you are significant."	"To me, you are not significant."
"Your way of experiencing your world is valid."	"Your way of experiencing your world is invalid."

In attempting to find behavioral correlates of these functions, we acknowledge that it is not possible to point with certainty to particular behaviors that universally perform these confirming functions for all persons, since individuals differ in the way they interpret the same acts; that is, they interpret the stimuli and assign their own meaning to them. Despite this reservation about making firm causal connections between the behavior of one person and the internal experience of another, we have followed the symbolic interactionist view that certain symbolic cues do acquire consensual validation and therefore are consistently interpreted by most persons as reflecting certain attitudes toward them on the part of others. Such cues thus have message value and are capable of arousing in the receiver feelings of being recognized or ignored, accepted or rejected, understood or misunderstood, humanized or "thingified," valued or devalued. This assumption was borne out in a very general way by our research to date (Sieburg & Larson, 1971). . . .

SYSTEMATIZING DISCONFIRMING BEHAVIOR

A variety of specific acts and omissions have been noted by clinicians and theoreticians as being damaging to some aspect of the receiver's self-view. We have arranged these behaviors into three general groupings, or clusters, each representing a somewhat different style of response:

1. Indifferent response (denying existence or relation)
2. Impervious response (denying self-experience of the other)
3. Disqualifying response (denying the other's significance)

These clusters include verbal/nonverbal and vocal/nonvocal behaviors. Since they encompass both content and process features of interaction, scorers must be trained to evaluate each scoring unit in terms of its manifest content, its transactional features, and its underlying structure. In either case, no single utterance stands alone since it is always in response to some behavior or another, and is so experienced by the other as having implications about his or her self.

Disconfirmation by Indifference

To deny another's existence is to deny the most fundamental aspect of self-experience. Indifference may be total, as when presence is denied; it may imply rejection of relatedness with the other; or it may only deny the other's attempt to communicate.

Denial of Presence   The absence of even a minimal show of recognition has been associated with alienation, self-destructiveness, violence against others, and with psychosis. Laing used the case of "Peter," a psychotic patient of 25 to illustrate the possible long-term effects of chronic indifference toward a child who may, as a consequence, come to believe that he has no presence at all—or to feel guilty that he *does*, feeling that he has no right even to occupy space.

> Peter . . . was a young man who was preoccupied with guilt *because* he occupied a place in the world, even in a physical sense. He could not realize . . . that he had a right to have any presence for others . . . A peculiar aspect of his childhood was that his presence in the world was largely ignored. No weight was given to the fact that he was in the same room while his parents had intercourse. He had been physically cared for in that he had been well fed and kept warm, and underwent no physical separation from his parents during his earlier years. Yet he had been consistently treated as though he did not "really" exist. Perhaps worse than the experience of physical separation was to be in the same room as his parents and ignored, not malevolently, but through sheer indifference. [Laing, 1961:119]

That such extreme indifference is also devastating to an adult is evident in the following excerpt from a marriage counseling session (Sieburg, personal audiotape). It is perhaps significant that throughout his wife's outburst, the husband sat silent and remote:

THERAPIST: . . . and is it okay to express emotion?

WIFE: Not in my house.

THERAPIST: Has he [the husband] ever *said* it's not okay to talk about feelings?

WIFE: But he never *says* anything!

THERAPIST: But he has ways of sending you messages?

WIFE: [loudly] Yes! And the message is *shut out*—no matter what I say, no matter what I do, I get no response—zero—shut out!

THERAPIST: And does that somehow make you feel you are wrong?

WIFE: Oh, of course not wrong—just *nothing!*

THERAPIST: Then what is it that makes you feel he disapproves of you?

WIFE: Because I get nothing! [tears] If I feel discouraged—like looking for a job all day and being turned down—and I cry—zero! No touching, no patting, no "Maybe tomorrow"—just *shut out.* And if I get angry at him, instead of getting angry back, he just walks away—just nothing! All the time I'm feeling shut out and shut off!

THERAPIST: And what is it you want from him?

WIFE: [quietly] Maybe sometimes just a pat on the back would be enough. But, no!—he just shrugs me off. Where am I supposed to go to feel real? [tears]

Avoiding Involvement   Extreme instances of indifference like those above are presumed to be rare because even the slightest attention at least confirms one's presence. Lesser shows of indifference, however, still create feelings of alienation, frustration, and lowered self-worth. Although recognition is a necessary first step in confirming another, it is not in itself sufficient unless accompanied by some further indication of a willingness to be involved.

The precise ways in which one person indicates to another that he or she is interested in relating (intimacy) are not fully known, but several clear indications of *unwillingness* to relate or to become more than minimally involved have emerged from research and have been included in our systemization of disconfirming behaviors. Of particular significance are the use of:

- Impersonal language—the avoidance of first person references (I, me, my, mine) in favor of a collective "we" or "one," or the tendency to begin sentences with "there" when making what amounts to a personal statement (as, "there seems to be . . .")
- Avoidance of eye contact
- Avoidance of physical contact except in ritualized situations such as handshaking
- Other nonverbal "distancing" cues

Rejecting Communication   A third way of suggesting indifference to another is to respond in a way that is unrelated, or only minimally related, to what he or she has just said, thus creating a break or disjunction in the flow of interaction.

Totally irrelevant response is, of course, much like denial of presence in that the person whose topic is repeatedly ignored may soon come to doubt his or her very existence, and at best will feel that he or she is not heard, attended to, or regarded as significant. Perhaps for this reason Laing called relevance the "crux of confirmation," noting that only by responding relevantly can one lend significance to another's communication and accord recognition (Laing, 1961:87).

The most extreme form of communication rejection is monologue, in which one speaker continues on and on, neither hearing nor acknowledging anything the other says. It reflects unawareness and lack of concern about the other person except as a socially acceptable audience for the speaker's own self-listening. A less severe communication rejection occurs when the responder makes a connection, however slight, with what the other has said, but immediately shifts into something quite different of his or her own choosing.

Disconfirming by Imperviousness

The term "imperviousness" as used here follows Laing's usage and refers to a lack of accurate awareness of another's perceptions (Watzlawick *et al.*, 1967:91). Imperviousness is disconfirming because it denies or distorts another's self-expression and fosters dehumanized relationships in which one person perceives another as a pseudoimage rather than as what that person really is. Behaviorally, the impervious responder engages in various tactics that tend to negate or discredit the other's feeling expression. These may take the form of a flat denial that the other *has* such a feeling ("You don't really mean that"), or it may be handled more indirectly by reinterpreting the feeling in a more acceptable way, ("You're only saying that because . . ."), substituting some experience or feeling of the *listener* ("What you're trying to say is . . ."), challenging the speaker's right to have such a feeling ("How can you *possibly* feel that way after all that's been done for you?"), or some similar device intended to alter the feeling expressed. . . .

A slightly different form of imperviousness occurs when a responder creates and bestows on another an inaccurate identity, and then confirms the false identity, although it is not a part of the other's self-experience at all. Laing calls this pseudo-confirmation (1961:83). Thus a mother who insists that her daughter is always obedient and "never any trouble at all" may be able to interpret her daughter's most rebellious aggression in a way that fits the placid image she holds of her daughter, and the parents of even a murderous psychopath may be able to describe their son as a "good boy." Such a false confirmation frequently endorses the fiction of what the other is *wished* to be, without any real recognition of what the other is or how he/she feels. As noted earlier, this form of disconfirmation also appears as simply a well-meaning attempt to reassure another who is distressed, which too is usually motivated by the speaker's need to reduce his or her own discomfort.

"Don't be silly—of course you're not afraid!"

"You may think you feel that way now, but I know better."

"Stop crying—there's nothing the matter with you!"

"How can you possibly worry about a little thing like that?"

"No matter what you say, I know you still love me."

Such responses constitute a rejection of the other person's expression and often identity, raising doubts about the validity of his/her way of experiencing by suggesting, "You don't really feel as you say you do; you are only imagining that you do."

A subtle variation of the same tactic occurs when the speaker responds in a selective way, rewarding the other with attention and relevant response *only* when he or she communicates in an approved fashion, and becoming silent or indifferent if the other's speech or behavior does not meet with the responder's approval. This may mean that the speaker limits response to those topics initiated by self, ignoring any topic initiated by the other person.

Imperviousness is considered disconfirming because it contributes to a feeling of uncertainty about self or uncertainty about the validity of personal experiencing. Imperviousness occurs when a person is told how he or she feels, regardless of how he or she experiences self, when a person's talents and abilities are described without any data to support such a description, when motives are ascribed to another without any reference to the other's own experience, or when one's own efforts at self-expression are ignored or discounted unless they match the false image held by some other person. . . .

Disconfirmation by Disqualification

According to Watzlawick (1964) disqualification is a technique which enables one to say something without really saying it, to deny without really saying "no," and to disagree without really disagreeing. Certain messages, verbal and nonverbal, are included in this group because they (a) disqualify the other speaker, (b) disqualify another message, or (c) disqualify themselves.

Speaker Disqualification   This may include such direct disparagement of the other as name-calling, criticism, blame, and hostile attack, but may also take the indirect form of the sigh of martyrdom, the muttered expletive, addressing an adult in a tone of voice usually reserved for a backward child, joking "on the square," sarcasm, or any of the other numerous tactics to make the other appear and feel too incompetent or unreliable for his message to have validity. This creates a particularly unanswerable put-down by evoking strong metamessages of insignificance or worthlessness. The following examples are spouses' responses from conjoint counseling sessions:

- "Can't you ever do anything right?"
- "Here we go again!" [sigh]
- "We heard you the first time—why do you always keep repeating yourself?"
- "It's no wonder the rear axle broke, with you in the back seat!" [laughter]
- "Why do you always have to get your mouth open when you don't know what you're talking about?"

Message Disqualification   Without regard to their content, some messages tend to discredit the other person because of their irrelevance—that is, they do not "follow" the other's prior utterance in a transactional sense. (This is also a tactic of indifference and may serve a dual disconfirming purpose.) Such disjunctive responses were studied by Sluzki, Beavin, Tarnopolski, and Veron (1967) who used the term "transactional disqualification" to mean any incongruity in the response of the speaker in relation to the context of the previous message of the other. A relationship between two successive messages exists, they noted, on two possible levels: (a) continuity between the content of the two messages (are both persons talking about the same subject?), and (b) indication of reception of the prior message (what cues does the speaker give of receiving and understanding the previous message?). If a message is disjunctive at either of these levels, transactional disqualification of the prior message is said to have occurred.

A similar form of message disqualification occurs when a speaker reacts selectively to some incidental clue in another's speech, but ignores the primary theme. Thus the responder may acknowledge the other's attempt to communicate, but still appears to miss the point. This "tangential response" was identified and studied by Jurgen Ruesch (1958), who noted that a speaker often picks up on a topic presented, but then continues to spin a yarn in a different direction. The response is not totally irrelevant because it has made some connection, although perhaps slight, with the prior utterance. Because it causes the first speaker to question the value or importance of what he or she was trying to say, the tangential response is reported to affect adversely a speaker's feeling of self-significance, and is therefore included as a form of disconfirmation.

Message Disqualifying Itself

A third way in which a speaker can use disqualification to "say something without really saying it," is by sending messages that disqualify themselves. There are many ways in which this may be done, the commonest devices being lack of clarity, ambiguity, and incongruity of mode. These forms of response are grouped together here because they have all been interpreted as devices for avoiding involvement with another by generating the metamessage "I am not communicating," hence "We are not relating."

SYSTEMATIZING CONFIRMING BEHAVIORS

Responses that confirm are less clearly defined than disconfirming behaviors because there has been less motivation to study them. In fact, identification of specific acts that are generally confirming is difficult unless we simply identify confirmation as the absence of disconfirming behaviors. More research in this area is clearly needed, but, in general, confirming behaviors are those which permit people to experience their own being and significance as well as their interconnectedness with others. Following Laing (1961), these have been arranged into three clusters: recognition, acknowledgment, and endorsement.

The Recognition Cluster   Recognition is expressed by looking at the other, making frequent eye contact, touching, speaking directly to the person, and allowing the other the opportunity to respond without being interrupted or having to force his or her way into an ongoing monologue. In the case of an infant, recognition means holding and cuddling beyond basic survival functions; in the case of an adult, it may still mean physical contact (touching), but it also means psychological contact in the form of personal language, clarity, congruence of mode, and authentic self-expression. In other words, confirmation requires that a person treat the other with respect, acknowledging his or her attempt to relate, and need to have a presence in the world.

The Acknowledgment Cluster   Acknowledgment of another is demonstrated by a relevant and direct response to his or her communication. This does not require praise or even agreement, but simple conjunction. Buber (Friedman, 1960) recognized this aspect when he wrote that mutually confirming partners can still "struggle together in direct opposition," and Laing (1961) made a similar point when he said that even rejection can be confirming if it is direct, not tangential, and if it grants significance and validity to what the other says. To hear, attend, and take note of the other and to acknowledge the other by responding directly is probably the most valued form of confirmation—and possibly the most rare. It means that the other's expression is furthered, facilitated, and encouraged.

The Endorsement Cluster   This cluster includes any responses that express acceptance of the other's feelings as being true, accurate, and "okay." In general, it means simply letting the other *be*, without blame, praise, analysis, justification, modification, or denial.

Confirming response is dialogic in structure; it is a reciprocal activity involving shared talk and sometimes shared silence. It is interactional in the broadest sense of the word. It is not a one-way flow of talk; it is not a trade-off in which each speaker pauses and appears to listen only in order to get a chance to speak again. It is a complex affair in which each participates as both subject and object, cause and effect, of the other's talk. In short, confirming response, like all communication, is not something one does, it is a process in which one shares.

REVIEW QUESTIONS

1. Give one-sentence definitions of *confirmation* and *disconfirmation*.
2. Discuss the distinctions among the four elements of confirmation that Cissna and Sieburg outline—existence, relating, significance, and validity of experience.
3. According to these authors, which are more important in the confirmation/disconfirmation process, verbal cues or nonverbal cues?
4. "The most extreme form of communication rejection is _____."

5. Which kind of disconfirmation is happening in the following example:
   RAE: "Damn! I wish that test wasn't tomorrow! That really ticks me off!"
   KRIS: "You aren't mad, you're just scared because you haven't studied
   enough."
6. Give an example of a person "saying something without really saying it."
7. Explain the distinction between recognition and acknowledgment.

PROBES

1. What makes the term *disconfirmation* appropriate for what's being discussed
   here? You can confirm an airplane reservation and in some churches young
   people are confirmed. How do those meanings echo the meaning of confirmation and disconfirmation that are developed here?
2. Notice how, in the first paragraph under the heading "Dimensions of Confirmation," the authors emphasize the relational quality of the phenomenon.
   Paraphrase what you hear them saying there.
3. All of us experience disconfirmation, sometimes with destructive regularity.
   Give an example where you have given an *indifferent* response. Give an
   example where you've received one. Do the same for *imperviousness* and
   disqualification.
4. When a person is impervious, what is he or she impervious *to*? Discuss.
5. Create an example of well-meant imperviousness, that is, imperviousness
   motivated by a genuine desire to comfort or protect the other person. Do the
   same with a disqualifying response.
6. Identify five specific confirming communication events that you experienced in the last four hours.

REFERENCES

1. Buber, M. "Distance and Relation," *Psychiatry, 20* (1957): 97–104.
2. Cissna, K. N. L. "Interpersonal Confirmation: A Review of Current/Recent
   Theory and Research." Paper presented at the Central States Speech
   Association Convention, Chicago, 1976, and the International
   Communication Association Convention, Portland, Oregon, 1976.
3. Cissna, K. N. L. *Interpersonal Confirmation: A Review of Current Theory,
   Measurement, and Research.* Saint Louis: Saint Louis University, 1976.
4. Friedman, M. S. "Dialogue and the 'Essential We': The Bases of Values in
   the Philosophy of Martin Buber," *American Journal of Psychoanalysis, 20*
   (1960): 26–34.
5. Laing, R. D. *The Self and Others.* New York: Pantheon, 1961.
6. Laing, R. D. *The Politics of Experience.* New York: Ballantine, 1967.
7. Ruesch, J. "The Tangential Response," in *Psychopathology of Communication,*
   ed. P. H. Toch and J. Zuben. New York: Grune & Stratton, 1958.

8. Sieburg, E. "Dysfunctional Communication and Interpersonal Responsiveness in Small Groups." Doctoral dissertation, University of Denver, 1969.

9. Sieburg, E. "Toward a Theory of Interpersonal Confirmation," Unpublished manuscript, University of Denver, 1972.

10. Sieburg, E. *Interpersonal Confirmation: A Paradigm for Conceptualization and Measurement.* San Diego: United States International University, 1975.

11. Sieburg, E. "Confirming and Disconfirming Organizational Communication," in *Communication in Organizations,* eds. J. L. Owen, P. A. Page, and G. I. Zimmerman. St. Paul: West Publishing, 1976.

12. Sieburg, E., and C. E. Larson. "Dimensions of Interpersonal Response." Paper presented at the annual convention of the International Communication Association, Phoenix, 1971.

13. Sluzki, Carlos E., Janet Beavin, Alejandro Tarnopolsky, and Eliseo Veron. "Transactional Disqualification: Research on the Double Bind." Archives of General Psychiatry, April, 1967, *16*(4), pp. 494–504.

14. Watzlawick, P. *An Anthology of Human Communication.* Palo Alto: Science and Behavior Books, 1964.

15. Watzlawick, P., J. Beavin, and D. D. Jackson. *Pragmatics of Human Communication: A Study of Interactional Patterns, Pathologies, and Paradoxes.* New York: Norton, 1967.

Since the first edition of *Bridges Not Walls* was published in 1973, there has never been a reading that consisted of a book's table of contents. But that's what this next reading is: the table of contents of a book entitled *The 48 Laws of Power*. The reading is here because it shows how some people view power in interpersonal relationships, and how they advise people to build, hoard, manipulate, and exploit their power to gain advantage over others. This brief reading should help people avoid being naïve about how power can operate between people.

The author claims to have distilled "the laws of power in their unvarnished essence" for "those who want power, watch power, or want to arm themselves against power." The laws come from the writings of Machiavelli, a fifteenth century Italian philosopher of political expediency, Carl von Clausewitz, an eighteenth century German military strategist, and other kings, queens, dictators, and autocrats. The author reports that the book arose out of his experience with "those people in my life who have so skillfully used the game of power to manipulate, torture, and cause me pain over the years." He presents these laws in what is, for the most part, an amoral context, almost never considering the ethical or moral implications of these ideas.

As you think about how power operates in your interpersonal experience, be forewarned by these 48 "laws" distilled from various historical and contemporary writings. Some people you meet are following these laws, intentionally or unreflectively, and you could be one of their victims. Even Jesus, as he sent his disciples into the world, instructed them, ". . . be wise as serpents and innocent as doves" (Matthew 10:16).

The 48 Laws of Power

Robert Greene

LAW 1   *PAGE 1*

NEVER OUTSHINE THE MASTER

Always make those above you feel comfortably superior. In your desire to please or impress them, do not go too far in displaying your talents or you might accomplish the opposite—inspire fear and insecurity. Make your masters appear more brilliant than they are and you will attain the heights of power.

LAW 2   *PAGE 8*

NEVER PUT TOO MUCH TRUST IN FRIENDS, LEARN HOW TO USE ENEMIES

Be wary of friends—they will betray you more quickly, for they are easily aroused to envy. They also become spoiled and tyrannical. But hire a former enemy and he will be more loyal than a friend, because he has more to prove. In fact, you have more to fear from friends than from enemies. If you have no enemies, find a way to make them.

LAW 3   *PAGE 16*

CONCEAL YOUR INTENTIONS

Keep people off-balance and in the dark by never revealing the purpose behind your actions. If they have no clue what you are up to, they cannot prepare a defense. Guide them far enough down the wrong path, envelop them in enough smoke, and by the time they realize your intentions, it will be too late.

LAW 4   *PAGE 31*

ALWAYS SAY LESS THAN NECESSARY

When you are trying to impress people with words, the more you say, the more common you appear, and the less in control. Even if you are saying something banal, it will seem original if you make it vague, open-ended, and sphinxlike. Powerful people impress and intimidate by saying less. The more you say, the more likely you are to say something foolish.

LAW 5   *PAGE 37*

SO MUCH DEPENDS ON REPUTATION—GUARD IT WITH YOUR LIFE

Reputation is the cornerstone of power. Through reputation alone you can intimidate and win; once it slips, however, you are vulnerable, and will be attacked on all sides. Make your reputation unassailable. Always be alert to potential attacks and thwart them before they happen. Meanwhile, learn to destroy your enemies by opening holes in their own reputations. Then stand aside and let public opinion hang them.

LAW 6   *PAGE 44*

COURT ATTENTION AT ALL COST

Everything is judged by its appearance; what is unseen counts for nothing. Never let yourself get lost in the crowd, then, or buried in oblivion. Stand out. Be conspicuous, at all cost. Make yourself a magnet of attention by appearing larger, more colorful, more mysterious than the bland and timid masses.

LAW 7   *PAGE 56*

GET OTHERS TO DO THE WORK FOR YOU, BUT ALWAYS TAKE THE CREDIT

Use the wisdom, knowledge, and legwork of other people to further your own cause. Not only will such assistance save you valuable time and energy, it will give you a godlike aura of efficiency and speed. In the end your helpers will be forgotten and you will be remembered. Never do yourself what others can do for you.

LAW 8   *PAGE 62*

MAKE OTHER PEOPLE COME TO YOU—USE BAIT IF NECESSARY

When you force the other person to act, you are the one in control. It is always better to make your opponent come to you, abandoning his own plans in the process. Lure him with fabulous gains—then attack. You hold the cards.

LAW 9   *PAGE 69*

WIN THROUGH YOUR ACTIONS, NEVER THROUGH ARGUMENT

Any momentary triumph you think you have gained through argument is really a Pyrrhic victory: The resentment and ill will you stir up is stronger and lasts longer than any momentary change of opinion. It is much more powerful to get others to agree with you through your actions, without saying a word. Demonstrate, do not explicate.

LAW 10   PAGE 76

INFECTION: AVOID THE UNHAPPY AND UNLUCKY

You can die from someone else's misery—emotional states are as infectious as diseases. You may feel you are helping the drowning man but you are only precipitating your own disaster. The unfortunate sometimes draw misfortune on themselves; they will also draw it on you. Associate with the happy and fortunate instead.

LAW 11   PAGE 82

LEARN TO KEEP PEOPLE DEPENDENT ON YOU

To maintain your independence you must always be needed and wanted. The more you are relied on, the more freedom you have. Make people depend on you for their happiness and prosperity and you have nothing to fear. Never teach them enough so that they can do without you.

LAW 12   PAGE 89

USE SELECTIVE HONESTY AND GENEROSITY TO DISARM YOUR VICTIM

One sincere and honest move will cover over dozens of dishonest ones. Open-hearted gestures of honesty and generosity bring down the guard of even the most suspicious people. Once your selective honesty opens a hole in their armor, you can deceive and manipulate them at will. A timely gift—a Trojan horse—will serve the same purpose.

LAW 13   PAGE 95

WHEN ASKING FOR HELP, APPEAL TO PEOPLE'S SELF-INTEREST, NEVER TO THEIR MERCY OR GRATITUDE

If you need to turn to an ally for help, do not bother to remind him of your past assistance and good deeds. He will find a way to ignore you. Instead, uncover something in your request, or in your alliance with him, that will benefit him, and emphasize it out of all proportion. He will respond enthusiastically when he sees something to be gained for himself.

LAW 14   PAGE 101

POSE AS A FRIEND, WORK AS A SPY

Knowing about your rival is critical. Use spies to gather valuable information that will keep you a step ahead. Better still: Play the spy yourself. In polite social encounters, learn to probe. Ask indirect questions to get people to reveal their weaknesses and intentions. There is no occasion that is not an opportunity for artful spying.

LAW 15   *PAGE 107*

CRUSH YOUR ENEMY TOTALLY

All great leaders since Moses have known that a feared enemy must be crushed completely. (Sometimes they have learned this the hard way.) If one ember is left alight, no matter how dimly it smolders, a fire will eventually break out. More is lost through stopping halfway than through total annihilation: The enemy will recover, and will seek revenge. Crush him, not only in body but in spirit.

LAW 16   *PAGE 115*

USE ABSENCE TO INCREASE RESPECT AND HONOR

Too much circulation makes the price go down: The more you are seen and heard from, the more common you appear. If you are already established in a group, temporary withdrawal from it will make you more talked about, even more admired. You must learn when to leave. Create value through scarcity.

LAW 17   *PAGE 123*

KEEP OTHERS IN SUSPENDED TERROR: CULTIVATE AN AIR OF UNPREDICTABILITY

Humans are creatures of habit with an insatiable need to see familiarity in other people's actions. Your predictability gives them a sense of control. Turn the tables: Be deliberately unpredictable. Behavior that seems to have no consistency or purpose will keep them off-balance, and they will wear themselves out trying to explain your moves. Taken to an extreme, this strategy can intimidate and terrorize.

LAW 18   *PAGE 130*

DO NOT BUILD FORTRESSES TO PROTECT YOURSELF—ISOLATION IS DANGEROUS

The world is dangerous and enemies are everywhere—everyone has to protect themselves. A fortress seems the safest. But isolation exposes you to more dangers than it protects you from—it cuts you off from valuable information, it makes you conspicuous and an easy target. Better to circulate among people, find allies, mingle. You are shielded from your enemies by the crowd.

LAW 19   *PAGE 137*

KNOW WHO YOU'RE DEALING WITH—DO NOT OFFEND THE WRONG PERSON

There are many different kinds of people in the world, and you can never assume that everyone will react to your strategies in the same way. Deceive or outmaneuver some people and they will spend the rest of their lives seeking revenge. They are wolves in lambs' clothing. Choose your victims and opponents carefully, then—never offend or deceive the wrong person.

LAW 20   *PAGE 145*

DO NOT COMMIT TO ANYONE

It is the fool who always rushes to take sides. Do not commit to any side or cause but yourself. By maintaining your independence, you become the master of others—playing people against one another, making them pursue you.

LAW 21   *PAGE 156*

PLAY A SUCKER TO CATCH A SUCKER—SEEM DUMBER THAN YOUR MARK

No one likes feeling stupider than the next person. The trick, then, is to make your victims feel smart—and not just smart, but smarter than you are. Once convinced of this, they will never suspect that you may have ulterior motives.

LAW 22   *PAGE 163*

USE THE SURRENDER TACTIC: TRANSFORM WEAKNESS INTO POWER

When you are weaker, never fight for honor's sake; choose surrender instead. Surrender gives you time to recover, time to torment and irritate your conqueror, time to wait for his power to wane. Do not give him the satisfaction of fighting and defeating you—surrender first. By turning the other cheek you infuriate and unsettle him. Make surrender a tool of power.

LAW 23   *PAGE 171*

CONCENTRATE YOUR FORCES

Conserve your forces and energies by keeping them concentrated at their strongest point. You gain more by finding a rich mine and mining it deeper, than by flitting from one shallow mine to another—intensity defeats extensity every time. When looking for sources of power to elevate you, find the one key patron, the fat cow who will give you milk for a long time to come.

LAW 24   *PAGE 178*

PLAY THE PERFECT COURTIER

The perfect courtier thrives in a world where everything revolves around power and political dexterity. He has mastered the art of indirection; he flatters, yields to superiors, and asserts power over others in the most oblique and graceful manner. Learn and apply the laws of courtiership and there will be no limit to how far you can rise in the court.

LAW 25   *PAGE 191*

RE-CREATE YOURSELF

Do not accept the roles that society foists on you. Re-create yourself by forging a new identity, one that commands attention and never bores the audience. Be the master of your own image rather than letting others define it for you. Incorporate dramatic devices into your public gestures and actions—your power will be enhanced and your character will seem larger than life.

LAW 26   *PAGE 200*

KEEP YOUR HANDS CLEAN

You must seem a paragon of civility and efficiency: Your hands are never soiled by mistakes and nasty deeds. Maintain such a spotless appearance by using others as scapegoats and cat's-paws to disguise your involvement.

LAW 27   *PAGE 215*

PLAY ON PEOPLE'S NEED TO BELIEVE TO CREATE A CULTLIKE FOLLOWING

People have an overwhelming desire to believe in something. Become the focal point of such desire by offering them a cause, a new faith to follow. Keep your words vague but full of promise; emphasize enthusiasm over rationality and clear thinking. Give your new disciples rituals to perform, ask them to make sacrifices on your behalf. In the absence of organized religion and grand causes, your new belief system will bring you untold power.

LAW 28   *PAGE 227*

ENTER ACTION WITH BOLDNESS

If you are unsure of a course of action, do not attempt it. Your doubts and hesitations will infect your execution. Timidity is dangerous: Better to enter with boldness. Any mistakes you commit through audacity are easily corrected with more audacity. Everyone admires the bold; no one honors the timid.

LAW 29   *PAGE 236*

PLAN ALL THE WAY TO THE END

The ending is everything. Plan all the way to it, taking into account all the possible consequences, obstacles, and twists of fortune that might reverse your hard work and give the glory to others. By planning to the end you will not be overwhelmed by circumstances and you will know when to stop. Gently guide fortune and help determine the future by thinking far ahead.

LAW 30   *PAGE 245*

MAKE YOUR ACCOMPLISHMENTS SEEM EFFORTLESS

Your actions must seem natural and executed with ease. All the toil and practice that go into them, and also all the clever tricks, must be concealed. When you act, act effortlessly, as if you could do much more. Avoid the temptation of revealing how hard you work—it only raises questions. Teach no one your tricks or they will be used against you.

LAW 31   *PAGE 254*

CONTROL THE OPTIONS: GET OTHERS TO PLAY WITH THE CARDS YOU DEAL

The best deceptions are the ones that seem to give the other person a choice: Your victims feel they are in control, but are actually your puppets. Give people options that come out in your favor whichever one they choose. Force them to make choices between the lesser of two evils, both of which serve your purpose. Put them on the horns of a dilemma: They are gored wherever they turn.

LAW 32   *PAGE 263*

PLAY TO PEOPLE'S FANTASIES

The truth is often avoided because it is ugly and unpleasant. Never appeal to truth and reality unless you are prepared for the anger that comes from disenchantment. Life is so harsh and distressing that people who can manufacture romance or conjure up fantasy are like oases in the desert: Everyone flocks to them. There is great power in tapping into the fantasies of the masses.

LAW 33   *PAGE 271*

DISCOVER EACH MAN'S THUMBSCREW

Everyone has a weakness, a gap in the castle wall. That weakness is usually an insecurity, an uncontrollable emotion or need; it can also be a small secret pleasure. Either way, once found, it is a thumbscrew you can turn to your advantage.

LAW 34   *PAGE 282*

BE ROYAL IN YOUR OWN FASHION: ACT LIKE A KING TO BE TREATED LIKE ONE

The way you carry yourself will often determine how you are treated: In the long run, appearing vulgar or common will make people disrespect you. For a king respects himself and inspires the same sentiment in others. By acting regally and confident of your powers, you make yourself seem destined to wear a crown.

LAW 35   *PAGE 291*

MASTER THE ART OF TIMING

Never seem to be in a hurry—hurrying betrays a lack of control over yourself, and over time. Always seem patient, as if you know that everything will come to you eventually. Become a detective of the right moment; sniff out the spirit of the times, the trends that will carry you to power. Learn to stand back when the time is not yet ripe, and to strike fiercely when it has reached fruition.

LAW 36   *PAGE 300*

DISDAIN THINGS YOU CANNOT HAVE: IGNORING THEM IS THE BEST REVENGE

By acknowledging a petty problem you give it existence and credibility. The more attention you pay an enemy, the stronger you make him; and a small mistake is often made worse and more visible when you try to fix it. It is sometimes best to leave things alone. If there is something you want but cannot have, show contempt for it. The less interest you reveal, the more superior you seem.

LAW 37   *PAGE 309*

CREATE COMPELLING SPECTACLES

Striking imagery and grand symbolic gestures create the aura of power—everyone responds to them. Stage spectacles for those around you, then, full of arresting visuals and radiant symbols that heighten your presence. Dazzled by appearances, no one will notice what you are really doing.

LAW 38   *PAGE 317*

THINK AS YOU LIKE BUT BEHAVE LIKE OTHERS

If you make a show of going against the times, flaunting your unconventional ideas and unorthodox ways, people will think that you only want attention and that you look down upon them. They will find a way to punish you for making them feel inferior. It is far safer to blend in and nurture the common touch. Share your originality only with tolerant friends and those who are sure to appreciate your uniqueness.

LAW 39   *PAGE 325*

STIR UP WATERS TO CATCH FISH

Anger and emotion are strategically counterproductive. You must always stay calm and objective. But if you can make your enemies angry while staying calm yourself, you gain a decided advantage. Put your enemies off-balance: Find the chink in their vanity through which you can rattle them and you hold the strings.

LAW 40   *PAGE 333*

DESPISE THE FREE LUNCH

What is offered for free is dangerous—it usually involves either a trick or a hidden oblig-ation. What has worth is worth paying for. By paying your own way you stay clear of gratitude, guilt, and deceit. It is also often wise to pay the full price—there is no cutting corners with excellence. Be lavish with your money and keep it circulating, for generos-ity is a sign and a magnet for power.

LAW 41   *PAGE 347*

AVOID STEPPING INTO A GREAT MAN'S SHOES

What happens first always appears better and more original than what comes after. If you succeed a great man or have a famous parent, you will have to accomplish double their achievements to outshine them. Do not get lost in their shadow, or stuck in a past not of your own making: Establish your own name and identity by changing course. Slay the overbearing father, disparage his legacy, and gain power by shining in your own way.

LAW 42   *PAGE 358*

STRIKE THE SHEPHERD AND THE
SHEEP WILL SCATTER

Trouble can often be traced to a single strong individual—the stirrer, the arrogant un-derling, the poisoner of goodwill. If you allow such people room to operate, others will succumb to their influence. Do not wait for the troubles they cause to multiply, do not try to negotiate with them—they are irredeemable. Neutralize their influence by isolat-ing or banishing them. Strike at the source of the trouble and the sheep will scatter.

LAW 43   *PAGE 367*

WORK ON THE HEARTS AND MINDS OF OTHERS

Coercion creates a reaction that will eventually work against you. You must seduce oth-ers into wanting to move in your direction. A person you have seduced becomes your loyal pawn. And the way to seduce others is to operate on their individual psychologies and weaknesses. Soften up the resistant by working on their emotions, playing on what they hold dear and what they fear. Ignore the hearts and minds of others and they will grow to hate you.

LAW 44   *PAGE 376*

DISARM AND INFURIATE WITH THE MIRROR EFFECT

The mirror reflects reality, but it is also the perfect tool for deception: When you mirror your enemies, doing exactly as they do, they cannot figure out your strategy. The Mirror Effect mocks and humiliates them, making them overreact. By holding up a mirror to their psyches, you seduce them with the illusion that you share their values; by holding up a mirror to their actions, you teach them a lesson. Few can resist the power of the Mirror Effect.

LAW 45   *PAGE 392*

PREACH THE NEED FOR CHANGE, BUT NEVER REFORM TOO MUCH AT ONCE

Everyone understands the need for change in the abstract, but on the day-to-day level people are creatures of habit. Too much innovation is traumatic, and will lead to revolt. If you are new to a position of power, or an outsider trying to build a power base, make a show of respecting the old way of doing things. If change is necessary, make it feel like a gentle improvement on the past.

LAW 46   *PAGE 400*

NEVER APPEAR TOO PERFECT

Appearing better than others is always dangerous, but most dangerous of all is to appear to have no faults or weaknesses. Envy creates silent enemies. It is smart to occasionally display defects, and admit to harmless vices, in order to deflect envy and appear more human and approachable. Only gods and the dead can seem perfect with impunity.

LAW 47   *PAGE 410*

DO NOT GO PAST THE MARK YOU AIMED FOR; IN VICTORY, LEARN WHEN TO STOP

The moment of victory is often the moment of greatest peril. In the heat of victory, arrogance and overconfidence can push you past the goal you had aimed for, and by going too far, you make more enemies than you defeat. Do not allow success to go to your head. There is no substitute for strategy and careful planning. Set a goal, and when you reach it, stop.

LAW 48   *PAGE 419*

ASSUME FORMLESSNESS

By taking a shape, by having a visible plan, you open yourself to attack. Instead of taking a form for your enemy to grasp, keep yourself adaptable and on the move. Accept the fact that nothing is certain and no law is fixed. The best way to protect yourself is to be as fluid and formless as water; never bet on stability or lasting order. Everything changes.

REVIEW QUESTIONS

1. Why does Law 2 advise you to make enemies?
2. What does Law 4 say about self-disclosure?

3. Give an example from your own work experience of the operation of Law 7.
4. How do trial lawyers apply Law 9?
5. Give an example of how "selective honesty and generosity" might be used by a communicator to disarm a conversation partner (Law 12).
6. Who are contemporary examples of the "courtiers" discussed in Law 24?
7. How do some instances of feminism apply Law 25?
8. What are some examples of Law 38 on your college or university campus?
9. Evaluate the usefulness, in conflict situations, of law 39.
10. Give one example of a U.S. president applying law 45.

PROBES

1. Which of these laws are most obviously followed by national political figures—presidents and prime ministers?
2. In the current political environment of the United States, which national party do you observe abiding by more of these laws? Give some specific examples.
3. Give examples of the operation of these laws in the *Star Wars* or *The Lord of the Rings* trilogies.
4. "... Never appeal to truth and reality unless you are prepared for the anger that comes from disenchantment" (Law 32). Is this good advice? Explain.
5. What do these laws, taken together, suggest to you about your own interpersonal communicating?

The previous reading gives some indication of how important power can be in conflict situations, and this excerpt from a book called *Interpersonal Conflict* explains how power works in conflict situations and how you can manage it. The authors have years of practical experience helping individuals and groups deal with conflict, and *Interpersonal Conflict* has been one of the most trusted conflict texts for years.

After defining power, Wilmot and Hocker explain two different orientations toward power, one that increases difficulties and another orientation that can help resolve conflicts. The first is an "either/or" orientation to power that is common in news stories and the understandings of the person-on-the-street. From this orientation, power is force that pushes people around against their will. Almost no one thinks that he or she has enough of this kind of power, and we think that others have more than we do. In what the authors call a "distressed system," power concerns outrank concerns about rights and interests. In an effective system, by contrast, interests are primary, rights are important, and power plays a smaller role.

An effective and ethical system for exercising power is found in the second "both/and" way. This means that parties understand that everyone involved has some power and that, if the focus stays on harmony and cooperation, power relationships can be worked out. This both/and orientation is common in Japanese and Javanese cultures, and it is often the first choice of women in Western cultures. Another term for this orientation is "relational," and in the next section of the reading Wilmot and Hocker develop a relational theory of power.

The starting point of this theory is that power happens between people. One person does not "have" power on his or her own; he or she only has power *in relation to* other people, certain topics, particular times, certain contexts, and so on. As one author puts it, "power is always interpersonal"; power dynamics are fluid, changing, and dependent on the specific situation.

From this relational perspective, individuals possess various power currencies, and Wilmot and Hocker discuss four of them that spell the word RICE. R is for resource control, which is the power to control rewards or punishments. I stands for interpersonal linkages, the power to connect people to accomplish goals. A third currency is communication skills—persuasive ability, listening skills, leadership skills, and the ability to communicate caring and warmth. All these skills generate power in various contexts. The fourth power currency is *expertise*—special knowledge, skills, and talents that are useful for certain tasks. It's easy to understand how all these "RICE" elements are relational when you realize, for example, that expertise is only powerful if it's relevant. If a project or a problem involves sports, the expertise of a space scientist may be worthless. But if the project or problem has to do with physics or space travel, the scientist will have abundant power. As Wilmot and Hocker summarize, it helps to understand the power currencies available to you and other parties in a conflict because all can move from believing that they have no choice but to respond in a given way to understanding that everyone has some power.

Next, Wilmot and Hocker discuss how calm persistence can help lower-power people deal with powerful institutions or authorities. They offer four specific ways that lower-power people can cope with conflict situations.

The final section of the reading focuses on metacommunication, which basically means communication about communication. By talking explicitly about the importance and value of the relationship or by deciding in advance how the parties will handle their conflicts, power difficulties can be avoided. Metacommunication focuses the parties on the process of their communication with each other and can engage them in a joint effort to improve the situation.

Wilmot and Hocker conclude by explaining what they call the "paradox of power." To be effective, people need to take advantage of opportunities and use resources at their disposal, but within an ongoing relationship, maximizing individual power is counterproductive for everyone involved. So the paradox is that each of us needs some power, and if we have too much, communication will be difficult. Each conflict partner's goal should be to balance the power that exists between or among the parties so that power facilitates rather than prevents interpersonal communication.

Power: The Structure of Conflict

William W. Wilmot and Joyce L. Hocker

WHAT IS POWER?

In interpersonal and all other conflicts, perceptions of power are at the heart of any analysis. Hundreds of definitions of power tend to fall into three camps. Power is seen as (1) *distributive* (either/or), (2) *integrative* (both/and), or (3) *designated* (power to a certain relationship). *Distributive* definitions of power stress that "with force, control, pressure or aggression, one individual is able to carry his or her objective over the resistance of another and thus gain power" (Dahl 1957, 3). Distributive approaches focus on power over or power against the other party.

Integrative definitions of power highlight power *with* the other. Integrative views stress "joining forces with someone else to achieve mutually acceptable goals" (Lilly 1989, 281). Integrative definitions focus on "both/and"—both parties have to achieve something in the relationship. As we shall see, it is not what outsiders say about power, but the views the conflict parties have that determine the outcomes of their conflicts.

Designated power "gives" power to a certain relationship, rather than power being held by individuals or even teams. In designated power, people confer power on a marriage, a work group, a family, or a group of friends with whom one is in relationship. . . .

ORIENTATIONS TO POWER

When a dispute occurs between two people, they often talk about power, and their perspectives on how it operates will predispose them to engage in certain communicative moves. People feel passionately about power—who has it, who ought to have more or less, how people misuse power, and how justified they feel in trying to gain more power for themselves. This orientation toward power seems to be true for many reasons.

We each need enough power to live the life we want. We want to influence events that matter to us. We want to have our voices heard, and make a difference. We want to protect ourselves against perceived harm. We want to hold in high esteem ourselves and those we care about. We do not want to be victimized, misused, or demeaned. No one can escape feeling the effects of power—whether we have too much or too little, or someone else has too much or too little.

When people struggle with each other, they almost never agree on anything having to do with power. For example, if you are a student intern in a real estate firm and you feel that brokers have all the power, you are likely to keep silent even when you disagree—giving the impression that you agree when you don't. If, on the other hand, you feel that both you and the brokers have sources of power, you will be more likely to engage in discussion to work through issues. As an intern, you may have sources of power such as a different set of acquaintances, free time on weekends when the brokers are involved with their families but need to work, or a fresh outlook and a desire to learn. If you think of yourself, however, as "just a lowly intern," you may miss many opportunities to be a team member because you have assessed your power incorrectly. . . .

Either/Or Power

When you examine typical newspaper stories about power, you read about the either/or (distributive) notions of power. In fact, it is difficult to even find examples of any other orientation toward power in the popular press. Many people think that power is only "force"—pushing others around against their will. When you examine nations using military might against other nations, you see either/or power in operation.

Once a relationship begins to go downhill, concerns with power increase. As any relationship deteriorates, the parties shift to a more overt focus on power—and this shift is reflected in their discourse (Beck 1988). In fact, a characteristic of destructive power is that parties start thinking and talking about power. Almost no one thinks that he or she has more power than the other power, at least when emotions run very high. We think the other has more power, which then justifies dirty tricks and our own attempt to gain more power. We often see ourselves as blameless victims of the other's abuse of power. When partners are caught in this destructive cycle of either/or power, their communicative interactions show a lot of "one up" responses, or attempts to demonstrate conversational power over each other (Sabourin and Stamp 1995). Partners might say, "She is just trying to control me," or "I'm not going to let him push me around." People, whether married couples or work colleagues, try to "keep score"—watching the "points" they have vis-à-vis the other party (Ross and Holmberg 1992). When partners develop an overt concern with power, their struggles over power are directly related to

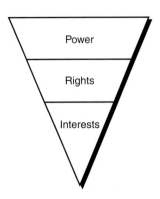

FIGURE 9–1 Power emphasized in a distressed system.
Source: From William Ury, Jeanne M. Brett, and Stephen B. Goldberg, Getting Disputes Resolved: Designing Systems to Cut the Costs of Conflict. *Copyright © 1988 Jossey-Bass Inc., Publishers, San Francisco, California. Reprinted by permission.*

relationship satisfaction (Kurdek 1994). Figure 9–1 demonstrates how concerns rank in a distressed relationship.

As Ury, Brett, and Goldberg (1988) so aptly note, the focus for a dispute becomes power—who has the right to move the other. The teenager who says, "You can't boss me around," the spouse who shouts, "Just who do you think you are?" and the co-worker who states, "Well, we'll see who the boss is around here!" are all highlighting power and giving it center stage in the dispute. These struggles often escalate. Dissatisfied couples are more than three times as likely to escalate episodes and focus on power than satisfied couples (Alberts and Driscoll 1992). . . . We are not suggesting that power shouldn't be an issue. Rather, we suggest that when power itself becomes the main focus of thinking and discussion, parties are likely to be involved in an escalating power struggle, and may well have temporarily lost sight of interests and solutions.

Notice in Figure 9–1 that disputes also involve "rights" and "interests." Rights, similar to our idea of core concerns, include not being discriminated against, being free from physical harm, and other constitutional and legal guarantees we have as citizens. Sometimes it is more appropriate that disputes get settled on the basis of rights rather than power or interests. For example, if the famous *Brown* v. *Board of Education* case in 1954 outlawing segregation in public schools had been settled on the basis of power, it would have resulted in a struggle in the streets. If, on the other hand, it had been settled on the basis of interests, Brown might have negotiated her way into school, but the country's social policy would not have changed. When we solve a dispute based on interests, the goals and desires of the parties are the key elements. For instance, if you don't want your teenage son to use the car, you can (1) tell him it is not OK as long as you pay the bills in the house (power); (2) let him know that you own the car and have all the rights to its use (rights); or (3) let him know that you are dissatisfied with how he drives, and until you are convinced he will be safe, you will not lend the car (interests). Thus, disputes can occur on any one of the three levels. When power becomes the only personal goal, the dispute is harder to resolve.

Figure 9–2 illustrates an effective system in which the emphasis is on interests with rights and power playing smaller but still important roles. As you can

FIGURE 9–2 Power de-
emphasized in an effective
system.
*Source: From William Ury,
Jeanne M. Brett, and Stephen
B. Goldberg,* Getting Disputes
Resolved: Designing
Systems to Cut the Costs of
Conflict. *Copyright © 1988
Jossey-Bass Inc., Publishers,
San Francisco, California.
Reprinted by permission.*

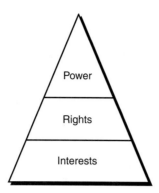

see by comparing Figure 9–1 with Figure 9–2, an overemphasis on power is
symptomatic of a distressed system.

Both/And Power

Two alternatives to viewing disputes as power struggles can help us out of the distributive power dilemma. Boulding (1989) notes that "the great fallacy, especially
of political thinking in regard to power, is to elevate threat power to the position
of dominance" (10). Interpersonal relationships reflect the same fallacy—many
people just can't envision power in terms other than "either/or," or "win/lose."
Yet a study of the dynamics of successful disputes and ongoing relationships reveals that power functions on a broader basis than either/or thinking. Disputes
become power struggles if the parties allow them to be defined as such. If we think
of power "merely in terms of threat, we will get nowhere" (250). Conceptually, the
alternative to framing disputes as power struggles is to place power in a position
subordinate to rights and needs.

    To help us understand the cultural basis of our assumptions, Augsburger
(1992) details the lack of verbal fighting in some other cultures. In these cultures,
power is activated as both/and or designated power, discussed in the next section. In Japanese and Javanese cultures, for instance, to name two obvious
examples, harmony and cooperation are basic values, and verbal contradiction
is not the automatic first choice in conflict. A more accepted process is to affirm
the strengths of each other's position, let them stand without attack, and then
join in exploring other options. Both parties search for superior options (59).

    Both/and power is often the first choice of women in our culture. Researchers
at the Stone Center at Wellesley have spent two decades explicating "relational
theory" in an attempt to balance the traditional male orientation that permeates
United States culture. In their view, relational theory is a belief system that describes how growth and effectiveness occur (Fletcher 1999). Masculine theories,
which until the last 20 years or so have been accepted as the only psychologically sound theories, often assumed that maturity and competence depend on
autonomy, or separation from constraints, other people, and group identity.

Boys, for instance, learn to relate to power through games and competition more than girls do. Boys learn to be comfortable with the hierarchy of teams, captains, coaches, and bosses. Girls learn to play with less focus on hierarchy. Many girls' games are cooperative in nature, with girls taking roles to play out, after discussing together what to do. As Heim (1993) notes, "There's no boss in dolls." For boys, conflict means competition, which often enhances relationships. For girls, competition is often painful and damages relationships. Girls often prefer to look for a win/win situation (Heim 1993, 27).

Relational theory and practice offer the idea that maturity and competence depend on growth-in-connection and mutuality. The ability to develop relationally depends on mutual empathy, mutual empowerment, responsibility to both oneself and others, and the ability to experience and express emotion, to experience and learn from vulnerability, to participate in the development of another, and to enhance each other's efforts (Fletcher 1999; Jordan et al. 1991). This approach does not need to be seen strictly as a female approach. Many effective forms of conflict resolution depend on a relational approach. Some situations in which power is heavily unbalanced also require a level of competition and assertiveness that does not come naturally for many women. If competition remains the dominant approach, however, constructive conflict resolution is unlikely to occur, except temporarily. . . .

A RELATIONAL THEORY OF POWER

A common perception is that power is an attribute of a person. If you say, "Lynn is a powerful person," you may, if she is your friend, be referring to such attributes as verbal facility, intelligence, compassion, warmth, and understanding. Or you may refer to a politician as powerful, alluding to her ability to make deals, call in favors, remember names and faces, and understand complex economic issues. In interpersonal relationships, however, excluding situations of unequal physical power and use of violence, power is a property of the social relationship rather than a quality of the individual. Lynn, for instance, has power with her friends because she has qualities they value. When she suggests something to do, like going on an annual women's backpacking trip, her friends try to clear their calendars because they like her, have fun with her, and feel understood by her. Lynn has a way of making a group feel cohesive and at ease. But if an acquaintance hated backpacking, did not like some of the other people going on the trip, and was irritated at Lynn because of a misunderstanding that had not yet been cleared up, Lynn's power with the irritated acquaintance would lessen considerably.

Similarly, if a politician did not show any interest in a bill that a human rights group was trying to get on the table in their state legislature and, furthermore, if the politician were a congresswoman representing another state, the congresswoman would have little power with the human rights group. Would she still be "a powerful person"? She would be to her constituents but not to the interest group in question.

Power is not owned by an individual but is a product of the social relationship in which certain qualities become important and valuable to others (King 1987; Rogers 1974; Harsanyi 1962a; Deutsch 1958; Dahl 1957; Soloman 1960). Deutsch (1973) states the case well: "Power is a relational concept; it does not reside in the individual but rather in the relationship of the person to his environment. Thus, the power of an agent in a given situation is determined by the characteristics of the situation" (15). Rather than residing in people, "power is always interpersonal" (May 1972, 23). In the strictest sense, except when violence and physical coercion are used, power is given from one party to another in a conflict. Power can be taken away when the situation changes. Power dynamics are fluid, changing, and dependent on the specific situation. Each person in a conflict has some degree of power, though one party may have more compared to the other, and the power can shift during a conflict. . . .

INDIVIDUAL POWER CURRENCIES

You may have had the experience of traveling in a foreign country and trying to adapt to the use of different currencies. Drachmas, used in Greece, are worthless in India, where rupees are used to buy items of value. A pocketful of rupees is worthless in France unless you exchange it for the local currency. Just as money depends on the context in which it is to be spent (the country), your power currencies depend on how much your particular resources are valued by the other persons in your relationships (Rodman 1967, 1972). You may have a vast amount of expertise in the rules of basketball, but if your fraternity needs an intramural football coach, you will not be valued as much as you would be if they needed a basketball coach. Power depends on having currencies that other people need. In the same manner, if other people possess currencies you value, such as the ability to edit a term paper or the possession of a car, they potentially maintain some degree of power over you in your relationships with them. Conflict is often confusing because people try to spend currency that is not valued in a particular relationship. . . .

R

Resource control: Often comes with one's formal position in an organization or group. An example is the controlling of rewards or punishments such as salary, number of hours worked, or firing. Parents control resources such as money, freedom, cars, and privacy for teenagers.

I

Interpersonal linkages: Your position in the larger system, such as being central to communication exchange. If you are a liaison person between two factions, serve as a bridge between two groups that would otherwise not have information about each other, or have a network of friends who like each other, you have linkage currencies.

C

Communication skills: Conversational skills, persuasive ability, listening skills, group leadership skills, the ability to communicate caring and warmth, and the ability to form close bonds with others all contribute to interpersonal power. All people need to be related to others, to matter to others, and to be understood by others. Those who communicate well gain value and thus interpersonal power.

E

Expertise: Special knowledge, skills, and talents that are useful for the task at hand. Being an expert in a content area such as budget analysis, a process area such as decision-making methods, or a relational area such as decoding nonverbal cues may give you power when others need your expertise.

Resource control often results from attaining a formal position that brings resources to you. The president of the United States, regardless of personal qualities, will always have some resources that go along with the job. Leadership and position, by their very nature, place a person in a situation in which others are dependent upon him or her, thus bringing ready-made power. Whatever your position—secretary, boss, chairperson, teacher, manager, or volunteer—you will be in a position to control resources that others desire. Many resources are economic in nature, such as money, gifts, and material possessions (Warner, Lee, and Lee 1986). Many people try to be close and supportive to those around them by buying gifts. They trade on economic currencies in order to obtain intimacy currencies from others. Their gifts are not always valued enough to bring them what they want, however. Not surprisingly, people who give gifts to each other often try to work out an agreement, probably implicitly, about the amount of money that can be spent to keep the dependence (and power) equal. If an inordinate amount of money is spent by one person, then typically the other person feels overly indebted. As Blau (1964) writes, "A person who gives others valuable gifts or renders them important services makes a claim for superior status by obligating them to himself" (108). People with little money usually have limited access to these forms of power. College graduates who cannot find jobs must remain financially dependent on parents, thus limiting independence on both sides. Elderly people whose savings shrink due to inflation lose power; mothers with children and no means of support lose most of their choices about independence, thus losing most of their potential power. Economic currencies are not the only important type of power currency, but they operate in small, personal conflicts as well as in larger social conflicts.

Another cluster of power currencies comes from one's *interpersonal linkages,* a set of currencies that depend on your interpersonal contacts and network of friends and supporters. People often obtain power based on whom they know and with whom they associate. For instance, if you have a good friend who has a mountain cabin you can share with others, then you have attained some power (if your family or friends want to go to the cabin) because of your ability to obtain things through other people. Young children try to trade on their linkage currencies when they say such things as "My Uncle Ben is a park ranger, and he will give us a tour of the park."

Interpersonal linkages help one attain power through coalition formation. Whenever you band together with another (such as a good friend) to gain some sense of strength, this coalition can be a form of power (Van de Vliert 1981). The small boy who says, "You better not hit me, because if you do, my big sister will beat you up" understands the potential value of coalitions. . . . Interpersonal linkages are a source of power when people check out their network for what classes to take, where jobs might be available, where rentals might be found, and other kinds of information. "Who you know" is often a source of power.

One's *communication skills* also serve as potential power currencies. If you can lead a group in a decision-making process, speak persuasively, write a news release for your organization, serve as an informal mediator between people who are angry with each other, or use tact in asking for what you want, you will gain power because of your communication skills. Many times, students who have developed their communication skills are employed upon graduation because of their skills. Employers are willing to teach technical and specialized skills later. Conversationally, your skills make a considerable difference, too. As Millar and Rogers (1988) demonstrated, when others allow us to dominate the conversation we have attained a source of power. Likewise, if you can facilitate the social process of a group, serve as the fun-loving joker in the family, or get conversations started at work, others typically will value you. It is not only the qualities, per se, that bring power but that these currencies are valued by others.

Communication skills also include the ability to form bonds with others through love, sex, caring, nurturing, understanding, empathic listening, warmth, attention, and other characteristics of intimate relationships. If a father provides genuine warmth and understanding to his teenage daughter who is going through a tough time at school, his support is a currency for him in their father-daughter relationship. . . .

Expertise currencies are involved when a person has some special skill or knowledge that someone else values. The worker who is the only one who can operate the boiler at a large lumber mill has power because the expertise is badly needed. The medical doctor who specializes in a particular area has expertise power because her information and skills are needed by others. Almost all professions develop specialized expertise valued by others, which serves as a basis of power for people in the profession. Family members develop expertise in certain areas that others within the family come to depend on, such as cooking, repairing the car, or babysitting.

We limit our own power by developing some currencies at the expense of others. For example, women have traditionally been most comfortable using power to bond with others (Miller 1991), providing more warmth and affection than men do (Johnson 1976). If this particular communication skill is developed at the expense of the ability to clarify a group discussion, a woman unnecessarily limits her power potential. The person who trades on currencies of interpersonal linkages, such as access to the boss, may neglect the development of expertise. The person who gains power by controlling resources, such as money or sex, may neglect the development of communication skills, resulting in a relationship based on coercive instead of shared power; withdrawing warmth in intimate relationships too often substitutes for good communication skills. A worker who focuses on the development of expertise in computer programming and systems analysis may ignore the power that can be developed through interpersonal linkages, thus furthering a tendency toward isolation in the organization. The most effective conflict participant develops several forms of power currencies and knows when to activate the different forms of power. A repertoire of currencies is a better base for sharing power than exclusive reliance on one form of power, which too often leads to misuse of that power.

Clarifying the currencies available to you and the other parties in a conflict helps in the conflict analysis. People are often unaware of their own sources of productive power, just as they do not understand their own dependence on others. Desperation and low-power tactics often arise from the feeling that one has no choice, that no power is available. Analyze your power currencies when you find yourself saying, "I have no choice." Usually, you are overlooking potential sources of power. . . .

The Power of Calm Persistence

Lower-power people in a conflict often can gain more equal power by persisting in their requests. Substantive change, when power is unequal, seldom comes about through intense, angry confrontation. Rather, change results from careful thinking and from planning for small, manageable moves based on a solid understanding of the problem (Lerner 1989, 15). When intensity is high, people react rather than observe and think. We overfocus on the other instead of an analysis of the problem, and we move toward polarization. Lower-power parties cannot afford to blow up. One source of power the lower-power person has, however, is careful, calm analysis that directs attention to the problem. If lower-power people have patience and avoid giving up out of frustration, they gain "nuisance value," and the higher-power person or group often listens and collaborates just to get them to go away. Persuasive skills become crucial. The low-power person must analyze the rhetorical situation well, taking into account what will be judged appropriate, effective, credible, and practical. . . .

Some suggestions for dealing with large, impersonal institutions are as follows:

- Identify the individuals on the phone by name and ask for them when you call back.
- Stay pleasant and calm. State clearly what you want, and ask for help in solving the problem.
- Follow the rules even if you think they are ridiculous. If they want five copies of a form, typed and folded a certain way, give it to them. Then point out that you have followed the rules and expect results.
- Write simple, clear memos summarizing what you want, what you have done, and when you expect a response.
- Tell them all the steps you took to try to get a response from them.
- Avoid taking out your frustration on low-power individuals in the organization. They may respond with "I'm just following the rules," avoiding personal responsibility—and who could blame them? Instead, be courteous and ask for help. Humor always helps if it is not at someone else's expense. . . .

Rather than remaining in self-defeating spirals, Lerner (1989, 35) suggests that people in low-power positions adopt the following moves:

- *Speak up and present a balanced picture of strengths as well as weaknesses.* One might say, "It's true that I am afraid to ask my boss for a raise, even though you want me to. But I earn a steady paycheck and budget and plan well for our family. I want some credit for what I do already contribute."
- *Make clear what one's beliefs, values, and priorities are, and then keep one's behavior congruent with these.* An entry-level accountant in a large firm was asked by the comptroller to falsify taxable deductions, hiding some of the benefits given to employees. The accountant, just out of school and a single parent, said, "When you hired me I said I was committed to doing good work and being an honest accountant. What you are asking me to do is against the code of ethics and could result in my losing my license. I can't afford to take that risk. I'm sure you'll understand my position."
- *Stay emotionally connected to significant others even when things get intense.* It takes courage for a low-power person to let another person affect him or her. One teenage son was furious and hurt when his father decided to remarry, since the son did not like the wife-to-be at all and felt disloyal to his mother. After some tough thinking, he decided to tell his father honestly how he felt, what he did not like, and what he feared about the new marriage instead of taking another way out, such as angrily leaving his father's house to live with his mother in another state. This conversation balanced the power between father and son in an entirely new way.
- *State differences, and allow others to do the same.* The easiest, but often not the best, way for a low-power person to manage conflict is to avoid engagement. Again, courage is required to bring up differences when a power imbalance is in place. Brad, a college freshman, worked at a fast-food place

during school. He was unhappy because the manager kept hiring unqualified people (without checking their references) and then expected Brad to train them and provide supervision, even though Brad was barely making more than minimum wage. Finally Brad told the manager, "I have a different way of looking at whom you should hire. I try to do a good job for you, but I have to try to work with people who have no experience and maybe don't have the personality to pitch in and work hard as part of the team. Would you consider letting me sit in on interviews and look over applications?" The manager was pleased with Brad's initiative and said yes.

Empowerment of Low-Power People by High-Power People

Sometimes it is clearly to the advantage of higher-power groups or individuals to purposely enhance the power of lower-power groups or individuals. Without this restructuring of power, working or intimate relationships may end or rigidify into bitter, silent, passive aggressive, and unsatisfactory entanglements. Currencies valued by higher-power people can be developed by lower-power people if they are allowed more training, more decision-making power, or more freedom. For instance, in one social service agency, Sharon was not doing well at directing a grant-funded program on finding housing for homeless people. Jan, the director of the agency, realized that Sharon was a good fund-raiser but not a good program director. By switching Sharon's job description, the agency gained a good employee instead of continuing a series of negative job evaluations that would have resulted in Sharon's eventual termination. . . .

Metacommunication

Another way to balance power is to transcend the win/lose structure by jointly working to preserve the relationship during conflict. By metacommunicating during or before conflicts (talking about the relationship or about how the parties will handle their conflicts), the parties can agree about behaviors that will not be allowed (such as leaving during a fight).

Metacommunication focuses the parties on the process of their communication with each other. They talk about their communication, and if that fails, they can agree to bring in outside mediators or counselors. They can agree that whenever a serious imbalance occurs, the high-power party will work actively with the low-power party to alter the balance in a meaningful way. Usually romantic partners, friends, family members, and work partners can accomplish such joint moves if they agree that the maximization of individual power, left unrestrained, will destroy the relationship. They see that individual power is based relationally, that dependence begets power, and that successful relationships necessitate a balancing of dependencies and therefore of power. The lack of a balanced arrangement is a signal to reinvest in the relationship rather than a clue that the relationship is over. The person temporarily weaker in the relationship can draw on the relationship currencies, as if the relationship were a bank and the currencies were savings. The weaker party can claim extra time, space, money, training, empathy, or other special considerations until the power is brought back into an approximation of balance. . . .

Most of us are caught in a paradox of power. To be effective people, we need to maximize our abilities, take advantage of opportunities, and use resources at our disposal so we can lead the kind of lives we desire. Yet within the confines of an ongoing relationship, *maximization of individual power is counterproductive* for both the higher-power and lower-power parties. The unrestrained maximization of individual power leads to damaged relations, destructive moves, more destructive countermoves, and the eventual ending of the relationship. Since people are going to take steps to balance power—destructively if no other means are available—we can better manage conflict by working to balance power in productive and creative ways. Equity in power reduces violence and enables all participants to continue working for the good of all parties, even in conflict.

REVIEW QUESTIONS

1. Distinguish among *distributive, integrative,* and *designated* power. Give an example of each.
2. If people are talking about how little power they have in a conflict, this can be a sign that the system they're in is what Wilmot and Hocker call "distressed." Explain.
3. What does it mean to say that both/and power is often the first choice of women in Western cultures?
4. "Power is not owned by an individual but is a product of the social relationship in which certain qualities become important and valuable to others." Explain.
5. Define resource control, interpersonal linkages, communication skills, and expertise as aspects of a person's power.
6. Paraphrase Wilmot and Hocker's advice to the low-power person in a conflict.
7. Define metacommunication.
8. Explain the "paradox of power."

PROBES

1. Wilmot and Hocker's idea of both/and power sounds good, but it may be naïve. If you are in a conflict with someone who only sees power as either/or, how can you change his or her orientation?
2. Recall a specific conflict that you have experienced in the past few weeks. Analyze your power in this conflict in R-I-C-E terms. What resource control did you have? What interpersonal linkages were important? What communication skills gave you power in this situation? What expertise did you have? How are the outcomes of that event related to the power that you had?
3. Give an example of how metacommunication can help balance power in an interpersonal conflict.

REFERENCES

1. Alberts, J., and G. Driscoll. (1992). Containment versus escalation: The trajectory of couples' conversational complaints. *Western Journal of Communication* 56: 394–412.
2. Augsburger, D. W. (1992). *Conflict mediation across cultures: Pathways and Patterns.* Louisville, Ky.: Westminster/John Knox Press.
3. Beck, A. T. (1988). *Love is never enough.* New York: Harper & Row.
4. Blau, P. M. (1964). *Exchange and power in social life.* New York: John Wiley & Sons.
5. Boulding, K. (1989). *Three faces of power.* Newbury Park, Calif.: Sage Publications.
6. Dahl, R. A. (1957). The concept of power. *Behavioral Science* 2: 201–215.
7. Deutsch, M. (1949). A theory of competition and cooperation. *Human Relations* 2: 129–151.
8. ———. (1958). Trust and suspicion. *Journal of Conflict Resolution* 2: 265–279.
9. ———. (1973). Conflicts: Productive and destructive. In *Conflict resolution through communication,* edited by F. E. Jandt. New York: Harper & Row.
10. Fletcher, J. (1999). *Disappearing acts: Gender, power, and relational practice at work.* Cambridge, Mass.: MIT Press.
11. Heim, P., and S. K. Galant. (1993). *Smashing the glass ceiling: Tactics for women who want to win in business.* New York: Simon and Schuster.
12. Johnson, P. (1976). Women and power: Toward a theory of effectiveness. *Journal of Social Issues* 32: 99–110.
13. Jordan, J., S. Kaplan, J. Miller, I. Stiver, and J. Surrey. (1991). *Women's growth in connection.* New York: Guilford Press.
14. King, A. (1987). *Power and communication.* Prospect Heights, Ill.: Waveland Press.
15. Kurdek, L. A. (1994). Areas of conflict for gay, lesbian, and heterosexual couples: What couples argue about influences relationship satisfaction. *Journal of Marriage and the Family* 56: 923–935.
16. Lerner, H. G. (1989). *The dance of intimacy.* New York: Harper & Row.
17. Lilly, E. R. (1989). The determinants of organizational power styles. *Educational Review* 41: 281–293.
18. May, R. (1972). *Power and innocence: A search for the sources of violence.* New York: Dell Publishing.
19. Millar, F. E., and L. E. Rogers. (1987). Relational dimensions of interpersonal dynamics. In *Interpersonal processes: New directions in communication research,* edited by M. E. Roloff and G. R. Miller, 117–139. Vol. 14 of *Sage Annual Reviews of Communication Research.* Newbury Park, Calif.: Sage Publications.
20. ———. (1988). Power dynamics in marital relationships. In *Perspectives on marital interaction,* edited by O. Noller and M. A. Fitzpatrick, 78–97. Clevedon, UK: Multilingual Matters.
21. Miller, J. B. (1986). What do we mean by relationships? In *Work in progress.* Stone Center Working Paper Series, no. 22. Wellesley, Mass.: Stone Center, Wellesley College.

22. ——. (1991). Women's and men's scripts for interpersonal conflict. *Psychology of Women Quarterly* 15: 15–29.

23. Rodman, H. (1967). Marital power in France, Greece, Yugoslavia, and the United States: A cross-national discussion. *Journal of Marriage and the Family* 29: 320–325.

24. ——. (1972). Marital power and the theory of resources in cultural context. *Journal of Comparative Family Studies* 3: 50–69.

25. Rogers, M. F. (1974). Instrumental and infra-resources: The bases of power. *American Journal of Sociology* 79: 1418–1433.

26. Ross, M., and D. Holmberg. (1992). Are wives' memories for events in relationships more vivid than their husbands' memories? *Journal of Social and Personal Relationships* 9: 585–604.

27. Sabourin, T. C., and G. H. Stamp. (1995). Communication and the experience of dialectical tensions in family life: An examination of abusive and nonabusive families. *Communication Monographs* 62: 213–242.

28. Soloman, L. (1960). The influence of some types of power relationships and game strategies upon the development of interpersonal trust. *Journal of Abnormal and Social Psychology* 61: 223–230.

29. Ury, W., J. Brett, and S. Goldberg. (1988). *Getting disputes resolved.* San Francisco, Calif.: Jossey-Bass.

30. Van de Vliert, E. (1981). Siding and other reactions to a conflict. *Journal of Conflict Resolution* 25, no. 3: 495–520.

31. Warner, R. L., G. R. Lee, and J. Lee. (1986). Social organization, spousal resources, and marital power: A cross-cultural study. *Journal of Marriage and the Family* 48: 121–128.

———

This final reading in the chapter about communication walls comes from a book called *The Verbally Abusive Relationship: How to Recognize it and How to Respond.* The kind of communication Patricia Evans is talking about was defined by Beverly Engel in the last reading in Chapter 6. In this reading, Evans explains how parents and others can minimize or counteract the verbal abuse that children experience.

The first section offers guidelines to parents for enhancing their children's self-esteem. The primary requirement is respect—communication that affirms the child's worth and importance, expresses admiration, and takes their concerns seriously. Four kinds of messages build esteem best: communicating confidence, appreciation, limits, and choices. Confidence is communicated when a child is allowed to meet his or her own needs as soon as the child shows an ability to do so. Appreciation is communicated when parents affirm what the child likes—music, running, bright colors, sports, and so on. When parents communicate limits, children feel safe and cared for. The challenge is to set limits while still validating the child's feelings. Esteem is also built when children understand that they have choices. The more a child learns to choose and to live with the consequences of his or her choices, the higher his or her self-esteem is likely to be.

The second section offers suggestions to parents of children who hear verbal abuse from others—relatives, coaches, teachers, or peers. It is better to say something like "I know it hurts when he talks mean" rather than "She didn't mean that." The child needs to experience an adult standing by him or her. Evans also has specific suggestions for dealing with children who indulge in verbal abuse.

The final sections of the reading discuss the kinds of verbal abuse that often accompany separation and divorce. When parents are in these painful situations, they often are unable consistently to treat their children with respect and care. Parents need to be ready to deal with their child's intense feelings without blaming. They also need to be alert for what Evans calls "stalking through the child" and, if it occurs, to respond with support and care.

You are no doubt noticing that none of the readings in this chapter provide much help for the destructive situations they discuss. But other chapters do, especially those that make up the rest of Part IV. The point of the readings in this chapter is to describe some of the more difficult "walls" or painful and hurtful communication situations that need "bridges" to be built over them.

Children and Verbal Abuse

Patricia Evans

What would it be like if all of us regarded our children as children of God—which we could do, after all?

—Alice Miller

Many questions surround the issue of children and verbal abuse. For example:

How can I encourage high self-esteem in my child?

What do I say to a child who has experienced verbal abuse from another child or from an adult?

What do I say to my child when he [she] calls me names?

How can my child best handle verbal abuse from peers?

What do I say to my child if I have left a relationship in which I experienced verbal abuse?

How can I keep myself separate when I share care of my child with my former spouse?

There are no perfect answers to these questions. The answers presented here are suggestions—models of effective ways to communicate that are meant to assist you in the process of honoring, respecting, and protecting your child from the emotional and mental harm of verbal abuse.

ENCOURAGING YOUR CHILD'S SELF-ESTEEM

When a parent faces a stressful situation and their child needs attention, the urgencies of the moment can invite a hasty response.

Even when they have time to think, a parent may overlook obvious solutions or actions because his or her mind is in turmoil.

For this reason, it is helpful for parents to remind themselves of the need to treat their child with goodwill and respect, even when they feel stressed.

When respect becomes the context for what you say, what you say is more likely to convey respect.

Courses in parenting are given in most cities, and many books on raising children are available. Sometimes it is difficult to choose between different philosophies. When you choose books on parenting and child raising, I believe the most essential criterion is that they foster respect for the child. If you give your children love and attention, are empathetic to their feelings, and are honest with them and encourage their independence, you will, in most cases, see them grow up to be loving, attentive, empathetic, honest, and independent adults.

Sometimes peer pressure or abuse from outside the home and so forth can influence the child to act out in undesirable ways. Don't be quick to blame yourself. You can only do your best. When in doubt, seek outside help through parenting classes, counselors, and/or other parents you admire.

Communicating Confidence

I believe that one of the most effective ways to impart confidence is to allow the child to meet his or her own needs as soon as the child shows an ability to do so. Parents can say:

Do you want to try using this spoon yourself?

I'll wait while you tie your shoes.

Are you ready to make your own peanut butter sandwich?

Here is the way to use the washer.

Communicating Appreciation

Children respond to appreciation. They are born good, curious, and spontaneous. Every child has unique talents and interests. As a parent, your job is to give your child the attention he or she needs. Noticing what the child likes—music, dancing, running, bright colors, quiet times, sports, and so on—and introducing and fostering the child's interests, even though they are not your own, brings forth from the child the child's own unique self. Following are ways of expressing appreciation:

What a beautiful picture.

Tell me about the book you like best.

It looks like you took extra time to make that.

Do you need some extra time to finish that?

I really appreciate your being quiet and waiting until I finished talking.

Communicating Limits

Good communication includes communicating limits to your child. Children feel safe and cared for when parents set limits for them. When they become adults, they set their own limits. They are best able to do this when they learn how during their childhood.

You can set limits for your child while still validating his or her feelings. For instance, it is natural for children to want to stay up past bedtime or to want things they can't have, but there are limits to their endurance and to the number and kinds of possessions they can have. You, as the parent, should encourage them to realize this. For example:

I hear you. You want to stay up, but now it's bedtime for five-year-olds. After you're ready, we'll read a story.

I can see that you want to watch that on TV, but that's not a kids' show. Let's pick out something else.

That's not okay.

When you're screaming I can't hear you. Let me hear your words.

Let's talk about it.

Tell me what you want.

No, I'm not buying any toys today.

I'd like you to have that, too, but I don't have the money for it.

Communicating Choices

Whenever possible, children should be given the opportunity to choose. It takes extra effort on the part of the parent—it's easier to say, "You're wearing this, like it or not." But if your child learns early on that she or he can make choices and take responsibility for them, your child will be better able to make good choices in life. Following are some examples of ways that you can present your child with the opportunity to make choices:

Do you want corn or peas?

Both your white top and your yellow top look nice with these pants—which do you want to wear?

This is the school menu. Do you want to buy lunch or take your own?

Is there anything you want to do this school year, like sports or the photography club?

Whom would you like to invite to your birthday party?

WHEN CHILDREN HEAR VERBAL ABUSE

Sometimes, even while trying to protect a child, a parent may lose sight of just how to respect the child's feelings. For example, a woman wrote, "In the past I had a grandfather who yelled at me and berated me. My own parents told me to not let Grandpa bother me—to just ignore him. I was really happy when he passed away."

In a situation like this, the child needs to hear, "What he just did [said] is not okay. Come with me while I tell him." The abuser needs to hear, "What you said to Mary [or John] is not okay. I really don't want her [him] to hear this kind of talk again."

If you are abused for speaking up, take yourself and your child out of harm's way, again acknowledging your child's feelings ("I know it hurts when he talks mean") and reiterating to your child the fact that that kind of talk is not okay.

If your child is yelled at or put down in any way, she or he needs your support. Sometimes a parent may inadvertently teach a child to put up with abuse. It is sometimes helpful to ask yourself, "Is there anything in what I've said that minimizes the abuse?"

If a child is told by a parent, "She [he] didn't mean that," the child's experience is invalidated and his or her pain discounted. The abuse is minimized and the child is taught to tolerate it.

Minimizing abuse is something most people *are* taught. To say, "Forget it. He was just having a bad day" may seem like a way to make the pain go away, but it just leaves the hurt inside. And it's crazymaking. (Does having a bad day make abuse okay?)

When you acknowledge your child's feelings and respond to verbal abuse, you validate the child's experience. And you are the all-important sympathetic witness. In this way you teach your child appropriate responses to verbal abuse and help your child to honor his or her own feelings.

On the other hand, teaching your child to pretend that words don't hurt (something males especially are taught) doesn't do anything good for the child. It even makes children doubt themselves.

Depending on your child's age and to whom she or he needs to respond, your child needs to learn appropriate responses to verbal abuse such as those covered in [Chapter 6 of] this book. Even an older child needs emotional support to respond to an adult who verbally abuses. "I'll stand by you" may be all the child needs to hear.

Children learn to abuse from adults and from each other. One of the most effective responses a child can make to a peer who puts him [her] down is to say, "That's what YOU say," with a strong emphasis on "you."

This response usually startles the other child and implies "I don't buy it. You said it. You are responsible for what you say."

Sometimes a child is verbally abused while visiting a parent after separation or divorce. I recently talked with a woman whose son would come back from visiting his father appearing very upset. When asked what was wrong, his standard reply would be, "If I tell you, even if you say you won't tell, he'll find out." Clearly, this is a serious problem. The child is suffering and feels too threatened to confide the incident.

If the parent cannot gain the child's confidence, outside intervention—a family friend, relative, or counselor who could become the child's confidant—would be of real value.

WHEN CHILDREN VERBALLY ABUSE

If you hear a child indulging in verbal abuse, you might try some of the following responses. They are appropriate to different circumstances and to different ages. See how they fit with your needs:

"That kind of talk is not okay."

"I don't want to hear that kind of talk from you."

"That kind of talk doesn't invite me to admire you."

"That's enough of that."

"There'll be no more of that kind of talk in my home."

WHEN PARENTS SEPARATE

Is there anything about your existing relationship that you know is not nurturing or healthy for you and your children and that you hope will go away if ignored?

If a child is abused or is a witness to abuse, the child suffers. A woman said to me, "Staying can hurt the child. It is totally invalid to think that staying in a marriage 'for the sake of the children' has any merit whatsoever. It is extremely detrimental. Whether the abuse shifts to the child or the child just unconsciously absorbs the mechanics of an abusive relationship, it is agonizingly painful in the long run." This woman was speaking from her own experience.

As children grow older in abusive circumstances, they may act out their frustration, pain, and confusion or try to obliterate it with drugs or other self-destructive means. They may even try suicide. Girls may be more inclined to withdraw, boys to become aggressive. If children are not raised in a peaceful and loving home, having both parents in the home does not make it healthier.

While children need both parents to treat them with respect and dignity and to attend equally to their needs, this isn't always possible. It is important to know that children can be better off in a nonabusive single-parent home than in one in which abuse takes place.

If you separate from your spouse, it is important that your child be allowed to express his or her feelings about that to you. A child may say "I hate you" meaning that he or she hates what's happened. Saying "I hate you" is not verbal abuse. It is an intense expression of feeling.

You may hear something like this when you are feeling most vulnerable. Even so, when your child is upset by changes in your relationship, it is important that you recognize his or her feelings. An appropriate response would be, "It sounds like you're angry and you feel bad. I don't blame you. I wish things were different too. I love you." Knowing what to expect can help you to respond in ways that respect your child's feelings.

Leaving an abusive situation, however, can be very difficult if the courts do not take the time to listen to children. . . .

KEEPING SEPARATE

Many women who leave abusive relationships are re-traumatized each time they see their former mate. Each time their child is picked up or left off, they may see the person who persecuted them. They may even be abused again. A woman said, "You've got a fifty/fifty shot. You don't know whether Jekyll or Hyde will be there."

One solution is to set up a neutral place—a baby-sitter's home or other safe place where your mate can leave the child ten minutes before you are to arrive, or you can leave the child minutes before your mate is to arrive.

STALKING THROUGH THE CHILD

Some partners who leave verbally and sometimes physically abusive relationships report a strange and sad phenomenon. So many women have informed me of this that it deserves to be addressed here.

When an abuser is unable to keep his agreement to put his child's needs first, even when he voices his willingness to do so, he may attempt to gain power over his partner through his child. If he is immersed in Reality I, is closed to the experience of mutuality, and has not dealt with his need for Power Over, the need will still be there. If he hasn't transferred his need to control to a new partner, his former partner may well be "it."

Stalking the mother through the child is accomplished by telling the child something like the following; "I love your mother. I want us all to be together again. If we're to get back together, I need to know what she's doing, where she goes, what she wears, who she talks to, what she says. You can't trust anyone but me."

The child wants everything to be okay. The child wants love. The child cannot know when she or he is being manipulated.

But when children grow up they sometimes know and tell. They tell of being manipulated into spying and making reports. They tell of their confusion. They tell of their mixed feelings of loyalty and guilt and sadness.

The former partners of such abusers say that such stalking of their lives is a living nightmare for themselves and for their children.

If you need to ensure your separateness from a former spouse, your child may benefit from knowing the information that follows. You may read it to your child or make a copy for your child. If you are an educator, therapist, or social worker, you may pass it out to the parents you see.

REVIEW QUESTIONS

1. Evans believes that the most important message to communicate to a child is _____.
2. How does the communication of limits build a child's self-esteem?
3. What do you remember about how your parents taught you about choices?
4. What is Evans' main message to parents about the abuse children sometimes experience when separation and divorce happens?

PROBES

1. What is the relationship between respect and agreement? Can you communicate consistent respect when you disagree with what someone is saying or doing? How?
2. Evans suggests how a parent can respond when the parent hears a child experiencing verbal abuse. What can a parent do to equip his or her child to deal with verbal abuse when the parent is not present to interpret the situation and defend the child?
3. As a child, did you experience, hear, and/or engage in verbal abuse? What do you remember about those events?

CHAPTER 10

Managing Conflict by Turning Walls into Bridges

One of the places where it is most challenging and most important to turn communication walls into bridges is in conflict. Although conflict is a natural and normal part of every work, family, roommate, and dating relationship, few people enjoy it, and even fewer believe that they manage conflict well. This chapter collects some of the best advice from nine people who can help each of us "do" conflict better.

The first reading comes from the 1996 edition of a conflict management textbook written by three speech communication teachers. It lays out some of the basic ideas that I think are important to understand if you're going to approach conflict constructively and effectively.

The authors begin with a "textbook case" that illustrates both the bad side and the potentially good side of conflict. Although they don't emphasize this point, the case shows how your view of conflict can strongly affect the ways you deal with it. For example, many people view conflict as always painful. From this point of view, unless you enjoy being blamed, put down, and shouted at, it's hard to be positive about conflicts. So if you see conflict as something entirely negative, you'll behave accordingly and will probably help create a self-fulfilling prophecy—the more you believe it's awful, the worse it will get. But as the case study shows, there are actually some benefits to conflict. Feelings get out in the open where they can be dealt with, and often people discover creative solutions to problems that had stumped them. So the first step toward handling conflict effectively is to be open to the positive values of conflict so you can, as these authors suggest, analyze "both the specific behaviors and interaction patterns involved in conflict and the forces that influence these patterns."

Folger, Poole, and Stutman define *conflict* as "the interaction of interdependent people who perceive incompatible goals and interference from each other in achieving those goals." This means that struggles inside one person's head are not "conflict" as it's defined here. Conflict always involves communication. The definition also emphasizes that conflict doesn't happen unless the people involved are interdependent. It only happens when one person's beliefs or actions have some impact on the other's. Otherwise the parties could just ignore each other.

The central section of this chapter distinguishes productive from destructive conflict interaction. One difference is that productive conflicts are *realistic,* which means that they focus on substantive problems the parties can potentially solve, while *nonrealistic* conflicts are mainly expressions of aggression designed to defeat or hurt the other. Productive conflict attitudes and behaviors are also *flexible,* while destructive ones are *inflexible.* In addition, productive conflict management is grounded in the belief that all parties can realize at least some of their goals, while destructive conflict is thoroughly win/lose. Finally, productive conflict happens when the parties are committed to working through their differences, rather than either avoiding them or simply favoring one position over the other.

In the final section the authors develop the idea that every move made in a conflict affects the other parties, and that this is why conflicts often degenerate into destructive cycles or patterns. These cycles can only be understood as unified wholes, and they can often be self-reinforcing. This means that, if you want to manage conflict effectively, you have to (a) look for the cycles, and (b) be willing and able to take unilateral action to break the destructive pattern. Subsequent readings in this chapter suggest what you can do *after* this to handle conflicts more effectively.

Conflict and Interaction

Joseph P. Folger, Marshall Scott Poole, and Randall K. Stutman

THE POTENTIAL OF CONFLICT INTERACTION

It is often said that conflict can be beneficial. Trainers, counselors, consultants, and authors of conflict textbooks point to the potential positive functions of conflict: conflicts allow important issues to be aired; they produce new and creative ideas; they release built-up tension; they can strengthen relationships; they can cause groups and organizations to reevaluate and clarify goals and missions; and they can also stimulate social change to eliminate inequities and injustice. These advantages, and others, are raised to justify conflict as a normal, healthy occurrence and to stress the importance of understanding and handling it properly.

But why must such an argument be made? Everyone has been in conflicts, and almost everyone would readily acknowledge at least some benefits. Why then do social scientists, popular authors, and consultants persist in attempting to persuade us of something we already know? Perhaps the answer can be found by studying an actual conflict. The twists and turns of a specific case often reveal why negative views of conflict persist. Consider the fairly typical case study of a conflict in a small work group in Case 1.A.

Case 1.A   The Women's Hotline Case

Imagine yourself as a staff member in this organization:
  How would you react as this conflict unfolded?
  What is it about this particular conflict that makes it seem difficult to face—let alone solve?

Women's Hotline is a rape and domestic crisis center in a medium-sized city; the center employs seven full- and part-time workers. The workers, all women, formed a cohesive unit and made all important decisions as a group; there were no formal supervisors. The hotline had started as a voluntary organization and had grown by capturing local and federal funds. The group remained proud of its roots in a democratic, feminist tradition.

The atmosphere at the hotline was rather informal. The staff saw each other as friends, but there was an implicit understanding that people should not have to take responsibility for each other's cases. Since the hotline's work was draining, having to handle each other's worries could create an unbearable strain. This norm encouraged workers to work on their own and keep problems to themselves.

The conflict arose when Diane, a new counselor who had only six months' experience, was involved in a very disturbing incident. One of her clients was killed by a man who had previously raped her. Diane had trouble dealing with this incident. She felt guilty about it; she questioned her own ability and asked herself whether she might have been able to prevent this tragedy. In the months following, Diane had increasing difficulty in coping with her feelings and began to feel that her co-workers were not giving her the support she needed. Diane had no supervisor to turn to, and, although her friends outside the hotline were helpful, she did not believe they could understand the pressure as well as her co-workers.

Since the murder, Diane had not been able to work to full capacity, and she began to notice some resentment from the other counselors. She felt the other staff were more concerned about whether she was adding to their workloads than whether she was recovering from the traumatic incident. Although Diane did not realize it at the time, most of the staff felt she had been slow to take on responsibilities even before her client was killed. They thought Diane had generally asked for more help than other staff members and that these requests were adding to their own responsibilities. No one was willing to tell Diane about these feelings after the incident, because they realized she was very disturbed. After six months, Diane believed she could no longer continue to work effectively. She felt pressure from the others at the center, and she was still shaken by the tragedy. She requested two weeks off with pay to get away from the work situation for a while, to reduce the stress she felt, and to come back with renewed energy. The staff, feeling that Diane was slacking off, denied this request. They responded by outlining, in writing, what they saw as the responsibilities of a full-time staff worker. Diane was angry when she realized her request had been denied, and she decided to file a formal work grievance.

Diane and the staff felt bad about having to resort to such a formal, adversarial procedure. No staff member had ever filed a work grievance, and the group was embarrassed by its inability to deal with the problem on a more informal basis. These feelings created additional tension between Diane and the staff.

Discussion Questions

- *Can you foresee any benefits to this conflict?*
- *Is it possible to foresee whether a conflict will move in a constructive or destructive direction?*
- *What cues would lead you to believe that conflict is going to be productive?*

The situation at the Women's Hotline has several features in common with de-structive conflicts, and might easily turn in a destructive direction. **First, the situation is tense and threatening.** The weeks during which the incident evolved were an extremely difficult time for the workers. Even for "old hands" at nego-tiation, conflicts are often unpleasant and frightening. **Second, participants are experiencing a great deal of uncertainty.** They are unable to understand many aspects of the conflict and how their behavior affects it. Conflicts are confusing; actions can have consequences quite different from those intended because the situation is more complicated than assumed. Diane did not know her co-workers thought she was slacking even before the tragedy. When she asked for time off, she was therefore surprised at their refusal, and her own angry reac-tion nearly started a major battle. **Third, the situation is extremely fragile.** The conflict may evolve in very different ways depending on the behavior of just a single worker. If, for example, the staff chooses to fire Diane, the conflict might be squelched, or it might fester and undermine relationships among the re-maining members. If, on the other hand, Diane wins allies, the staff might split over the issue and ultimately dissolve the hotline. As the case continues below, observe staff members' behavior and their method of dealing with this tense and unfamiliar situation.

Case 1.B   The Women's Hotline Case, Continued

Imagine yourself in the midst of this conflict:

What would you recommend this group do to promote a constructive outcome to this conflict?

The staff committee who received Diane's grievance suggested that they could handle the problem in a less formal way if both Diane and the staff agreed to accept a neutral third-party mediator. Everyone agreed that this suggestion had promise, and a third party was invited to a meeting where the entire staff would address the issue.

At this meeting, the group faced a difficult task. Each member offered reac-tions they had been unwilling to express previously. The staff made several pointed criticisms of Diane's overall performance. Diane expressed doubts about the staff's willingness to help new workers or to give support when it was re-quested. Although this discussion was often tense, it was well directed. At the out-set of the meeting, Diane withdrew her formal complaint. This action changed the definition of the problem from the immediate work grievance to the question of what levels of support were required for various people to work effectively in this difficult and emotionally draining setting. Staff members shared doubts and fears about their own inadequacies as counselors and agreed that something less than perfection was acceptable. The group recognized that a collective inertia had de-veloped and that they had consistently avoided giving others the support needed to deal with difficult rape cases. They acknowledged, however, the constraints on each woman's time; each worker could handle only a limited amount of stress. The group recognized that some level of mutual support was essential and felt they had fallen below that level over the past year and a half. One member suggested that any staff person should be able to ask for a "debriefing contract" whenever they felt they needed help or support. These contracts would allow someone to ask for ten minutes of another person's time to hear about a particularly disturbing issue or case. The group members adopted this suggestion because they saw it could allow members to seek help without overburdening each other. The person who was asked to listen could assist and give needed support without feeling that she had to "fix" another worker's problem. Diane continued to work at the center and found that her abilities and confidence increased as the group provided the support she needed.

Discussion Questions

- *In what ways did the parties in this conflict show "good faith"?*
- *Is "good faith" participation a necessary prerequisite to constructive conflict resolution?*

This is a "textbook" case in effective conflict management because it resulted in a solution that all parties accepted. The members of this group walked a tightrope throughout the conflict, yet they managed to avoid a fall. The tension, unpleasantness, uncertainty, and fragility of conflict situations make them hard to face. Because these problems make it difficult to deal with issues in a constructive way, conflicts are often terminated by force, by uncomfortable suppression of the issues, or by exhaustion after a prolonged fight—all outcomes that leave at least one party dissatisfied. Entering a conflict is often like making a bet against the odds: you can win big if it turns out well, but so many things can go wrong that few people are willing to chance it. It is no wonder that many writers feel a need to reassure us. They feel compelled to remind us of the positive outcomes of conflict because all too often the destructive results are all that people remember.

The key to working through conflict is not to minimize its disadvantages, or even to emphasize its positive functions, but to accept both and to try to understand how conflicts move in destructive or productive directions. Such an understanding requires a conception of conflict that calls for a careful **analysis of both the specific behaviors and interaction patterns involved in conflict and the forces that influence these patterns.** Moreover, we can only grasp the fragility of conflicts and the effects that tension and misunderstandings have in their development if we work at the level at which conflicts unfold—specific interactions among the parties.

DEFINITION OF CONFLICT

Conflict is the interaction of interdependent people who perceive incompatible goals and interference from each other in achieving those goals (Hocker and Wilmot 1985). This definition has the advantage of providing a much clearer focus than definitions that view conflict simply as disagreement, as competition, or as the presence of incompatible interests (Fink 1968). **The most important feature of conflict is that it is based in interaction.** Conflicts are constituted and sustained by the behaviors of the parties involved and their reactions to one another. Conflict interaction takes many forms, and each form presents special problems and requires special handling. The most familiar type of conflict interaction is marked by shouting matches or open competition in which each party tries to defeat the other. But conflicts can also be more subtle. Often people react to conflict by suppressing it. They interact in ways that allow them to avoid confrontation, either because they are afraid of possible changes the conflict may bring about or because the issue "isn't worth fighting over." This response is as much a part of the conflict process as the open struggles commonly associated with conflict. This book deals with the whole range of responses to conflict and how those responses affect the development of conflicts. Conflicts can best be understood and managed by concentrating on specific behavioral patterns and the forces shaping them.

People in conflict perceive that they have incompatible goals or interests and that others are a source of interference in achieving their goals. The key word here is "perceive." Regardless of whether goals are actually incompatible or if the parties believe them to be incompatible, conditions are ripe for conflict. Regardless of whether an employee really stands in the way of a co-worker or whether the co-worker interprets the employee's behavior as interference, the co-worker may move against the employee or feel compelled to skirt certain issues. Thus, the parties' interpretations and beliefs play a key role in conflicts. This does not mean that goals are always conscious as conflict develops. People can act without a clear sense of what their goals or interests are (Coser 1961). Sometimes people find themselves in strained interactions but are unsure how they got there. They realize afterward what their implicit goals were and how their goals were incompatible with those held by others (Hawes and Smith 1973). Communication looms large because of its importance in shaping and maintaining the perceptions that guide conflict behavior.

Indeed, communication problems are sometimes the cause of conflicts. Tension or irritation can result from misunderstandings that occur when people interact with very different communication styles (Tannen 1986, Grimshaw 1990). One person's inquisitive style may be perceived by someone else as intrusive and rude. One person's attempt to avoid stepping on another's toes may be perceived by someone else as distant and cold. Style differences create difficult problems that are often related to differences in cultural backgrounds (Kochman 1981, Dubinskas 1992). However, the old adage "most conflicts are actually communication problems" is not always true. The vast majority of conflicts would not exist without some real difference of interest. This difference may be hard to uncover, it may be redefined over time, and occasionally it may be trivial, but it is there nonetheless. Communication processes can cause conflicts and can easily exacerbate them, but they are rarely the sole source of the difficulty.

Conflict interaction is colored by the interdependence of the parties. For a conflict to arise, the behavior of one or both parties must have consequences for the other. Therefore, by definition, the parties involved in conflict are interdependent. The conflict at the hotline would not have occurred if Diane's behavior had not irritated the other workers and if their response had not threatened Diane's position. Furthermore, any action taken in response to the conflict affects both sides. The decision to institute a "debriefing contract" required considerable change by everyone. If Diane had been fired, that too would have affected the other workers; they would have had to "cover" Diane's cases and come to terms with themselves as co-workers who could be accused of being unresponsive or insensitive.

But interdependence implies more than this: when parties are interdependent they can potentially aid or interfere with each other. **For this reason, conflicts are always characterized by a mixture of incentives to cooperate and to compete.** Any comment during conflict interaction can be seen either as an attempt to advance the speaker's own interest or as an attempt to promote a good outcome for all involved. A party may believe that having their own point accepted is more important, at least for the moment, than proposing a mutually beneficial outcome. When Diane asked for two weeks off, she was probably thinking not of the group's best interest but of her own needs. In other cases, a participant may advance a proposal designed to benefit everyone, as when the staff member suggested the "debriefing contract." In still other instances, a participant may offer a comment with a cooperative intent, but others may interpret it as one that advances individual interests. Regardless of whether the competitive motive is intended by the speaker or assigned by other members, the interaction unfolds from that point under the assumption that the speaker may value only his or her own interests. Subsequent interaction is further likely to undermine incentives to cooperate and is also likely to weaken members' recognition of their own interdependence. The balance of incentives to compete or cooperate is important in determining the direction the conflict interaction takes.

ARENAS OF CONFLICT INTERACTION

Conflict occurs in almost all social settings. Most people learn at a very young age that conflicts arise in families, playgrounds, classrooms, Little League fields, ballet centers, scout troops, and cheerleading teams. Even as relationships become more complex and people become involved in more diverse and public settings, conflicts remain remarkably similar to those experienced in childhood. (Indeed, some argue that early experiences shape involvement in conflict throughout our lives.) Adults encounter conflict in casual work relationships and emotionally intense, intimate relationships as well as in close friendships or in political rivalries. Conflict is encountered in decision-making groups, small businesses, large corporations, church organizations, and doctors' offices. Given the diversity of conflicts typically encountered, what often is of most concern is how much is at stake in any conflict. Conflicts are assessed as pedestrian or profound, trivial or tremendous, or as major or minor maelstroms. The estimate of the significance of any conflict often influences the time and effort invested in strategizing or in developing safeguards or fallbacks.

A broad range of conflicts are examined in this book. The analysis is aimed at clarifying how conflicts emerge and unfold in three general settings. The chapters **will examine conflicts that emerge in interpersonal contexts,** that is, conflicts that occur between people who have some ongoing relationship and are interdependent in some sense (Putnam and Poole 1987, Roloff 1987a). Included in this arena are conflicts that occur between husbands and wives, or among siblings, friends, roommates, or co-workers, as well as between landlords and tenants, or supervisors and employees. These conflicts tell us a great deal about styles of conflict interaction, emotional and irrational impulses, and the diversity of resources people exchange in close or long-term relationships.

Conflicts that occur among groups of people who share long-term interdependence, such as families will also be analyzed. This arena includes work groups, small businesses, classes, clubs, juries, and even therapy or consciousness-raising groups. Since much work is done in groups, this arena has been studied extensively and offers a wide range of conflict situations for analysis. These conflicts offer insights about decision-making procedures, group cohesion, the influence of climates, coalitions, working habits, and the distribution of power.

Finally, **conflicts that occur in intergroup settings will be examined.** The focus here is on aggregates or collections of people, rather than individuals (Putnam and Poole 1987). This arena includes conflicts among different units of an organization, political action groups, or ethnic and cultural groups. In these conflicts, issues of group identity, stereotyping, and ideologies often come to the fore. . . .

Forms of interaction are patterns of actions and reactions or moves and countermoves that parties engage in during a conflict. Violent exchanges are a form of interaction that can occur in interpersonal, intragroup, or intergroup conflicts. Similarly, negotiation is a form of interaction in which parties engage in any of these settings. Negotiation, sometimes referred to as bargaining, occurs when parties agree to explicit or implicit rules for exchanging proposals or concessions to reach a mutual agreement (Pruitt 1981, Putnam and Poole 1987). People often think of negotiation as a separate arena because labor-management negotiations are the most prominent example of negotiations in most people's minds. However, negotiations can occur in any of the arenas. Husbands and wives can negotiate their divorce agreements, a professor and student can negotiate a grade, environmental groups can negotiate a land-use policy, or neighborhood groups can negotiate historical preservation standards.

There are other insights, besides those centering on forms of interaction, that apply to all the arenas of conflict covered in this book. For example, most conflicts are concerned with power because power is integral to all forms of interdependence among people. How conflict influences relationships and how climate is central to the way conflict unfolds will also be examined.

PRODUCTIVE AND DESTRUCTIVE CONFLICT INTERACTION

As previously noted, people often associate conflict with negative outcomes. However, there are times when conflicts must be addressed regardless of the apprehension they create. When differences exist and the issues are important, suppression of conflict is often more dangerous than facing it. The psychologist Irving Janis points to a number of famous political disasters, such as the Bay of Pigs invasion and the failure to anticipate the Japanese attack on Pearl Harbor, where poor decisions can be traced to the repression of conflict by key decision-making groups (Janis 1972). The critical question is: what forms of conflict interaction will yield the obvious benefits without tearing a relationship, a group, or an organization apart?

Years ago the sociologist Lewis Coser (1956) distinguished realistic from nonrealistic conflicts. **Realistic conflicts are conflicts based in disagreements over the means to an end or over the ends themselves.** In realistic conflicts, the interaction focuses on the substantive issues the participants must address to resolve their underlying incompatibilities. **Nonrealistic conflicts are expressions of aggression in which the sole end is to defeat or hurt the other.** Participants in nonrealistic conflicts serve their own interests by undercutting those of the other party. Coser argues that because nonrealistic conflicts are oriented toward the expression of aggression, force and coercion are the means for resolving these disputes. Realistic conflicts, on the other hand, foster a wide range of resolution techniques—force, negotiation, persuasion, even voting—because they are oriented toward the resolution of some substantive problem. Although Coser's analysis is somewhat of an oversimplification, it is insightful and suggests important contrasts between productive and destructive conflict interaction (Deutsch 1973). What criteria could be used to evaluate whether a conflict is productive? **In large part, productive conflict interaction depends on flexibility.** In constructive conflicts, members engage in a wide variety of behaviors ranging from coercion and threat to negotiation, joking, and relaxation to reach an acceptable solution. **In contrast, parties in destructive conflicts are likely to be much less flexible because their goal is more narrowly defined: they are trying to defeat each other.** Destructive conflict interaction is likely to have protracted, uncontrolled escalation cycles or prolonged attempts to avoid issues. In productive conflict, on the other hand, the interaction in the group will change direction often. Short cycles of escalation, de-escalation, avoidance, and constructive work on the issue are likely to occur as the participants attempt to manage the conflict.

Consider the hotline case. The group exhibited a wide range of interaction styles, from the threat of a grievance to the cooperative attempt to reach a mutually satisfactory solution. Even though Diane and the members engaged in hostile or threatening interaction, they did not persist in this mode, and when the conflict threatened to escalate, they called in a third party. The conflict showed all the hallmarks of productive interaction. In a destructive conflict the members might have responded to Diane's grievance by suspending her, and Diane might have retaliated by suing or by attempting to discredit the center in the local newspaper. Her retaliation would have hardened others' positions and they might have fired her, leading to further retaliation. Alternatively, the hot-line conflict might have ended in destructive avoidance. Diane might have hidden her problem, and the other members might have consciously or unconsciously abetted her by changing the subject when the murder came up or by avoiding talking to her at all. Diane's problem would probably have grown worse, and she might have had to quit. The center would then revert back to "normal" until the same problem surfaced again. While the damage done by destructive avoidance is much less serious in this case than that done by destructive escalation, it is still considerable: the hotline loses a good worker, and the seeds of future losses remain. In both cases, it is not the behaviors themselves that are destructive—neither avoidance nor hostile arguments are harmful in themselves—but rather the inflexibility of the parties that locks them into escalation or avoidance cycles.

   In productive conflicts, interaction is guided by the belief that all factions can attain important goals (Deutsch 1973). The interaction reflects a sustained effort to bridge the apparent incompatibility of positions. This effort is in marked contrast to destructive conflicts where the interaction is premised on participants' belief that one side must win and the other must lose. **Productive conflict interaction results in a solution satisfactory to all and produces a general feeling that the parties have gained something** (for example, a new idea, greater clarity of others' positions, or a stronger sense of solidarity). In some cases, the win-lose orientation of destructive conflict stems from fear of losing. People attempt to defeat alternative proposals because they believe that if their positions are not accepted they will lose resources, self-esteem, or the respect of others. In other cases, win-lose interaction is sparked, not by competitive motives, but by the parties' fear of working through a difficult conflict. Groups that rely on voting to reach decisions often call for a vote when discussion becomes heated and the members do not see any other immediate way out of a hostile and threatening situation. Any further attempt to discuss the alternatives or to pursue the reasons behind people's positions seems risky. A vote can put a quick end to threatening interaction, but it also induces a win-lose orientation that can easily trigger destructive cycles. Members whose proposal is rejected must resist a natural tendency to be less committed to the chosen solution and may try to "even the score" in future conflicts. **Productive conflict interaction is sometimes competitive; both parties must stand up for their own positions and strive for perceived understanding if a representative outcome is to be attained** (Cahn 1990). A great deal of tension and hostility may result as people struggle with the conflict. Although parties in productive conflicts hold strongly to their positions, they are also open to movement when convinced that such movement will result in the best decision. The need to preserve power, save face, or make the opponent look bad does not stand in the way of change. In destructive conflict, parties often become polarized, and the defense of a non-negotiable position becomes more important than working out a viable solution. This description of productive and destructive conflict interaction is obviously an idealization. It is rare that a conflict exhibits all the constructive or destructive qualities just mentioned; indeed, many conflicts exhibit both productive and destructive interaction. However, better conflict management will result if parties can sustain productive conflict interaction patterns.

CONFLICT AS INTERACTIVE BEHAVIOR

Conflict is, by nature, interactive. It is never wholly under one person's control (Kriesberg 1973). The other party's reactions and the person's anticipation of the other's response are extremely important. **Any comment made during a conflict is made with some awareness or prediction about the likely response it will elicit.** This predictive basis for any move in interaction creates a strong tendency for conflict interaction to become cyclic or repetitive. Suppose Robert criticizes Susan, an employee under his supervision, for her decreasing productivity. Susan may accept the criticism and explain why her production is down, thus reducing the conflict and moving toward a solution. Susan may also shout back and sulk, inviting escalation, or she may choose to say nothing and avoid the conflict, resulting in no improvement in the situation. Once Robert has spoken to Susan and she has responded, the situation is no longer totally under Robert's control: his next behavior will be a response to Susan's reaction. Robert's behavior, and its subsequent meaning to Susan, is dependent on the interchange between them. **A behavioral cycle of initiation-response—counterresponse results from the conflict interchange. This cycle cannot be understood by breaking it into its parts, into the individual behaviors of Robert and Susan.** It is more complex than the individual behaviors and, in a real sense, has a "life" of its own. The cycle can be self-reinforcing, if, for example, Susan shouts back at Robert, Robert tries to discipline her, Susan becomes more recalcitrant, and so on, in an escalating spiral. The cycle could also limit itself if Robert responds to Susan's shouting with an attempt to calm her and listen to her side of the story. Conflict interaction cycles acquire a momentum of their own. They tend in a definite direction—toward escalation, toward avoidance and suppression, or toward productive work on the conflict. The situation becomes even more complex when we remember that Robert formulated his criticism on the basis of his previous experience with Susan. That is, Robert's move is based on his perception of Susan's likely response. In the same way, Susan's response is based not only on Robert's criticism, but on her estimate of Robert's likely reaction to her response. Usually such estimations are "intuitive"— that is, they are not conscious—but sometimes parties do plot them out ("If I shout at Robert, he'll back down and maybe I won't have to deal with this"). They are always based on the parties' perceptions of each other, on whatever theories or beliefs each holds about the other's reactions. Because these estimates are only intuitive predictions, they may be wrong to some extent. The estimates will be revised as the conflict unfolds, and this revision will largely determine what direction the conflict takes. The most striking thing about this predictive process is the extraordinary difficulties it poses for attempts to understand the parties' thinking. When Susan responds to Robert on the basis of her prediction of Robert's answer, from the outside we see Susan making an estimate of Robert's estimate of what she means by her response. If Robert reflects on Susan's intention before answering, we observe Robert's estimate of Susan's estimate of his estimate of what Susan meant. This string of estimates can increase without bounds if one tries to pin down the originating point, and after a while the prospect is just as dizzying as a hall of mirrors.

Several studies of arms races (Richardson 1960, North, Brody, and Holsti 1963) and of marital relations (Watzlawick, Beavin, and Jackson 1967; Rubin 1983; Scarf 1987) and employee-supervisor interactions (Brown 1983) have shown how this spiral of predictions poses a critical problem in conflicts. If the parties do not take the spiral into account, they run the risk of miscalculation. However, it is impossible to calculate all the possibilities. At best, people have extremely limited knowledge of the implications their actions hold for others, and their ability to manage conflicts is therefore severely curtailed. Not only are parties' behaviors inherently interwoven in conflicts, but their thinking and anticipations are as well. The key question this chapter addresses is: **how does conflict interaction develop destructive patterns—radical escalation, prolonged or inappropriate avoidance of conflict issues, inflexibility—rather than constructive patterns leading to productive conflict management?**

REVIEW QUESTIONS

1. Describe what the authors mean when they say that the case study about Diane and her co-workers shows how conflict situations are tense and threatening, uncertain, and fragile.
2. Explain what is significant about each of the following terms in the authors' definition of conflict: *interaction, interdependent, incompatible goals, interference.*
3. Why do the authors disagree with the old adage, "most conflicts are actually communication problems"?
4. Distinguish between realistic and nonrealistic conflict.

PROBES

1. As you read the case study about Diane and her co-workers, what single feature of the situation strikes you as the most important positive move that

was made? In other words, what one thing most helped resolve this conflict productively?

2. Give an example from your own experience of the difference between a realistic and a nonrealistic conflict.

3. At one point the authors argue about the wisdom of resolving a conflict by voting. (a) What is their rationale for discouraging voting? (b) How do you respond; that is, do you agree or disagree, and why?

4. The authors end this excerpt with "the key question" of how conflicts develop destructive patterns. After you've read the other four readings in this chapter, what is your response to this key question?

REFERENCES

1. Brown, L. D. (1983). *Managing conflict at organizational interfaces.* Reading, MA: Addison-Wesley.

2. Cahn, D. 1990. *Intimates in conflict: A communication perspective.* Hillsdale, NJ: Lawrence Erlbaum.

3. Coser, L. (1956). *The functions of social conflict.* New York: Free Press.

4. Coser, L. (1961). The termination of conflict. *Journal of Conflict Resolution, 5:* 347–353.

5. Deutsch, M. (1973). *The resolution of conflict.* New Haven, CT: Yale University Press.

6. Dubinskas, F. (1992). Culture and conflict: The cultural roots of discord. In D. M. Kolb and J. M. Bartunek, Eds., *Hidden conflict in organizations:* 187–208. Newbury Park, CA: Sage.

7. Fink, C. F. (1968). Some conceptual difficulties in the theory of social conflict. *Journal of Conflict Resolution, 12:* 412–460.

8. Grimshaw, A. D., Ed. (1990). *Conflict talk: Sociolinguistic investigations of arguments in conversations.* Cambridge: Cambridge University Press.

9. Hawes, L., and Smith, D. H. (1973). A critique of assumptions underlying the study of communication in conflict. *Quarterly Journal of Speech, 59:* 423–435.

10. Hocker, J. L., and Wilmot, W. W. (1985). *Interpersonal conflict.* Dubuque, IA: Wm. C. Brown.

11. Janis, I. (1972). *Victims of groupthink.* Boston: Houghton Mifflin.

12. Kochman, T. (1981). *Black and white styles in conflict.* Chicago: The University of Chicago Press.

13. Kriesberg, L. (1973). *The sociology of social conflicts.* Englewood Cliffs, NJ: Prentice-Hall.

14. North, R. C., Brody, R. A., and Holsti, O. (1963). Some empirical data on the conflict spiral. *Peace Research Society: Papers I.* Chicago Conference: 1–14.

15. Pruitt, D. G. (1981). *Negotiating Behavior.* New York: Academic Press.

16. Putnam, L., and Poole, M. S. (1987). Conflict and negotiation. In F. Jablin, L. Putnam, K. Roberts, and L. Porter, Eds., *Handbook of organizational communication:* 549–599. Beverly Hills, CA: Sage.

17. Richardson, L. F. (1960). *Arms and insecurity.* Pittsburgh: The Boxwood Press.
18. Roloff, M. E. (1987). Communication and conflict. In C. Berger and S. H. Chaffee, Eds., *Handbook of communication science:* 484–534. Beverly Hills, CA: Sage.
19. Rubin, L. (1983). *Intimate strangers.* New York: Harper and Row.
20. Scarf, M. (1987). *Intimate partners: Patterns in love and marriage.* New York: Ballantine.
21. Tannen, D. (1986). *That's not what I meant.* New York: William Morrow.
22. Watzlawick, P., Beavin, J. H., and Jackson, D. D. (1967). *Pragmatics of Human Communication.* New York: Norton.

Bill Wilmot is an interpersonal communication and conflict management teacher and a mediator who helps people in conflict all over North America. As these excerpts from his book, *Relational Communication* illustrate, Bill has an unusually sharp sense of the complexities of interpersonal relationships. This next reading combines Bill's discussion of communication spirals and his ideas about paradoxes and conundrums (relationship puzzles). It offers some helpful advice about how to turn these particular communication walls into bridges.

The first section begins by explaining that a "communication spiral" happens when "the actions of each person in a relationship magnify those of the other." Bill gives several examples of both positive and negative spirals that can happen in family, work, and dating relationships. He emphasizes that spirals can be powerful because they pick up a momentum that feeds back on itself. This means that closeness and harmony can create more of the same, and that bitterness and hostility can operate the same way. He lists seven features of a communication spiral and then goes into some detail about generative and degenerative spirals.

An example of a generative spiral is the teacher who searches for the positive in a student and rewards it appropriately. As Bill summarizes it, "the more genuinely the teacher relates to the student, the better the student performs; the higher the quality of his or her performance, the more positive the teacher becomes."

Degenerative spirals are the mirror images of generative ones. Discord leads to more discord and the spiral intensifies. So, for example, if a person is hesitant to relate to others, he or she shuns contacts, which in turn makes it more difficult to overcome the hesitancy. Some research that Bill cites shows that one of the most common degenerative spirals in a marriage occurs when the husband withdraws emotionally, the wife expresses dissatisfaction to her husband, and the husband then withdraws even more.

Bill follows this analysis of spirals with five concrete suggestions about how to alter degenerative ones. The first is deceptively simple-sounding: "Do what comes unnaturally." Spirals are relational phenomena, which is to say that they are fed by both (or all) the parties in a relationship. Change is impossible so long as things continue as they have. At least one party has to "do what comes unnaturally."

A second suggestion is to use third parties—friends, counselors, relatives, clergy, or others whom you trust. A specific suggestion for breaking the toxic pattern can often come from an informed but not intimately involved outsider. A third suggestion is to reaffirm your relational goals. It can often help for people in a spiral to remind themselves and each other about the commitment they have to the relationship. This is a form of suggestion number four, "metacommunicating." This just means that you communicate about your communicating. You talk about the relationship and whatever has led to the degenerating series of actions.

The final two suggestions are that you try spending less time with the person and consider changing the external situation. Sometimes these moves will also break troublesome patterns.

The section of this reading on paradoxes and conundrums consists of brief discussions of twelve two-directional pulls that many people experience in their relationships. It can be reassuring to read that others feel some of the same tensions you do, and Bill also includes some suggestions about how to cope with these relational puzzles.

The first is that people want contradictory things in relationships: freedom and closeness, stability and excitement. It can be helpful to recognize that this is normal, and not necessarily problematic. A second is that both "objective" third-person observations and "subjective" insider observations about a relationship are fraught with errors. It's important to get both perspectives, and not to believe that either provides "the Truth" about the relationship.

Paradox #3 is that if you leave relationships completely alone they'll probably dissolve, and if you try to force them to happen, you can destroy them. It works best to stay in the middle of this tension. Number four is the tension between expecting a relationship to generate happiness when its purpose may be the sense of wholeness that comes from the inherently unstable dialectical encounter between two people. The fifth paradox is that we get the most pleasure *and* the most pain from our closest relationships.

Bill also discusses some paradoxes about the connection between "the self" and "the relationship" and the fact that "relationships can serve as springboards for growth or just toss you higher so you land harder." Number nine reminds us how changes in any part or level of a relationship reverberate to other levels. Number ten sketches the power inherent in and the problems created by relationship labels. And the last two emphasize the ever-changing, emergent quality of relationships.

By the time you've completed this reading you should have an appreciation for the sometimes startling complexity of the relationships you are a part of.

Communication Spirals, Paradoxes, and Conundrums

William W. Wilmot

A communication spiral occurs when the actions of each person in a relationship magnify those of the other. Communication spirals are evident almost everywhere, happening between humans, between us and other species, and among other species as well. A human–animal illustration should clarify the essential nature of spirals. My son Jason at age 3 saw a sleek, shiny cat. With the reckless abandonment of a child his age, he rushed at the cat to pet it. The wise cat, seeing potential death, moved out of Jason's reach. Not to be outdone, Jason tried harder. The cat moved farther away. Jason started running after the cat. The cat, no dummy about life, ran too. In a short 10 seconds from the initial lunge at the cat, Jason and the cat were running at full tilt. Luckily, the cat was faster and survived to run another day. Similarly, spirals occur in many contexts:

- A child disobeys the parent, the parent acts more punitively and harshly, and the child becomes even more unruly.
- A parent and 22-year-old son embark on a foreign adventure for 2 months— just the two of them. As the trip draws to a close, they both note on the plane ride home how close they feel to one another, and how easy their communication has become.
- An employee may be quiet and not forthcoming to the supervisor, the supervisor puts pressure on him to talk, and he becomes even more silent.
- Two guys are sitting in a bar; one accidentally touches the other, the first pushes him, an insult is uttered, and within a minute the two are fighting in the street.
- A supervisor is dissatisfied with an employee's performance but doesn't tell the employee. The employee is complaining to others about the supervisor. Both the employee and supervisor keep doing more of the same—the employee withdrawing and talking to others, the supervisor getting more annoyed and not telling the employee. Then 6 months later during the performance appraisal, the supervisor says, "We are reorganizing the office, and you won't be needed anymore."

- Two close friends buy a cabin midway between their two towns. Each time they go to the cabin, their relationship is reinforced, and not only do they ski better, they enjoy one another's company more.
- Two romantic partners feel that the other is pulling away. So each shares less, harbors grudges, and spends less time with the other, until there is a fight during which they end the relationship.
- Two opposite-sex friends spend a lot of time with one another. As they spend more time, they exclude others and feel closer and closer. It gets to the point that they don't want to begin other friendships because this one is so fulfilling.

All spirals, whether building in a positive or negative direction, tend to pick up a momentum that feeds back on itself—closeness and harmony builds more closeness and harmony; misunderstanding and dissatisfaction creates more misunderstanding and dissatisfaction. The responses produce a lock-step effect in relationships (Leary, 1955; Kurdek, 1991). Quality relationships, like close friendships, develop an "end in themselves"—quality—and become self-sustaining (Rose & Serafica, 1986).

Communication spirals, whether they head in positive or negative directions, are characterized by these elements:

1. The participants' meanings intertwine in such a way that each person's behavior accelerates the dynamism of the relationship. The relational synergy builds upon itself in a continuously accelerating manner.
2. *Each* person's actions contribute to the overall dynamic. Whether you talk, retreat, engage, reinvest, or disinvest in the relationship, your communication (or lack of communication) directly impacts the other person, and vice versa. Each person reacts to the other (Kurdek, 1991).
3. Bateson (1972, 1979) noted long ago that spirals manifest either (1) *symmetrical* communication moves or (2) *complementary* communication moves. In symmetrical spirals, as Person One does "more of the same" Person Two also does "more of the same"—for example, two people shouting at each other. In complementary spirals, as Person One does "more of the same" Person Two does "more of the opposite"—Person A shouts and Person B withdraws in silence (Wilden, 1980).
4. At any given period of time, a spiral is contributing to the relationship in either generative or degenerative ways. Generative spirals promote positive feelings about the relationship and more closeness; degenerative spirals induce negative feelings about the relationship and more distance.
5. Both generative and degenerative spirals tend to continue accelerating until the participants check the movement by some action.
6. Spirals can be changed, their pace quickened or slowed, or the direction reversed by the participants' actions.
7. Based on the communication spirals that unfold, relationships expand, wither, and repeat patterns of close–far.

FIGURE 10–1 A
communication spiral.

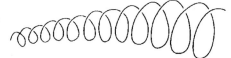

A diagram of the nature of spirals in Figure 10–1 shows how the dynamics of the communication for both persons tend to increase over time. Notice how the cycles get larger and larger across time—which is the nature of all communication spirals.

Generative Spirals

When communicative behaviors interlock to produce more positive feelings about the relationship, the participants are in a *generative spiral*. For instance, the teacher who can be open and accepting of students often experiences such spirals. Searching for the positive in a student and rewarding him or her appropriately can open a student up for teacher influence. The more genuinely the teacher relates to the student, the better the student performs; the higher the quality of his or her performance, the more positive the teacher becomes.

Generative spirals are obviously not limited to teacher–student relationships. A highly motivated worker illustrates the same ever-widening nature of spirals. As one improves working conditions, the worker's motivation increases, which cycles back and makes for an even better climate, which increases . . .

In generative spirals, the perceptions of the partners become more productive and their mutual adjustments continue to build. In romantic couples, "love generates more love, growth more growth, and knowledge more knowledge" (O'Neill & O'Neill, 1972). The favorableness builds upon itself. Trust and understanding cycle back to create more trust and understanding. The relationship is precisely like a spiral—ever-widening.

We all experience generative spirals. The student who begins doing work of a high caliber earns better grades, becomes self-motivated, and enters a generative spiral. Each piece of work brings a reward (good grades or praise) that further encourages him or her to feats of excellence. And if conditions are favorable, the spiral can continue. Teachers who retrain and become more knowledgeable discover that they have more to offer students. The excited students, in turn, reinforce the teachers' desire to work hard so they can feel even better about their profession. In generative spirals, the actions of each individual [supply] a multiplier effect in reinforcement. The better you do, the more worthwhile you feel; the more worthwhile you feel, the better you do. The effects of a simple action reverberate throughout the system. An unexpected tenderness from your loved one, for instance, will not stop there. It will recycle back to you and probably come from you again in increased dosage. A good relationship with your supervisor promotes you to want to please more, and the supervisor seeing your increased involvement, gives even more recognition to you.

Degenerative Spirals

Degenerative spirals are mirror images of generative spirals; the process is identical, but the results are opposite. In a degenerative spiral misunderstanding and discord create more and more relationship damage. As with generative spirals, degenerative spirals take many forms.

The inability to reach out and develop meaningful relationships is often compounded. The person who has reduced interest in others and does not form effective relationships suffers a lower self-esteem (because self-esteem is socially derived), which in turn cycles back and produces less interest in others. "The process is cyclical and degenerative" (Ziller, 1973). Or if one is afraid to love others, he or she shuns people, which in turn makes it more difficult to love. Also, such degenerative spirals often happen to people with regard to their sense of worth concerning work. People who have not established themselves in their profession but have been in the profession for a number of years may get caught in a spiral. They may spend time trying to appear busy, talking about others, or using various techniques to establish some sense of worth. Behavior that can change the spiral—working hard or retraining—are those least likely to occur. It is a self-fulfilling prophecy with a boost—it gets worse and worse. With each new gamut or ploy perfected (acquiring a new hobby, joining numerous social gatherings, etc.), the performance issues become further submerged.

A simple example of a degenerative spiral is the case of a lonely person. Lonely people tend to be less involved, less expressive, and less motivated in interactions. As a result, their partners in the conversation see the lonely person as uninvolved and less competent, and are less likely to initiate and maintain conversations with them. As a result, lonely people become further isolated from the social networks needed to break the cycle (Spitzberg & Canary, 1985).

Degenerative cycles are readily apparent when a relationship begins disintegrating. When distrust feeds distrust, defensiveness soars and the relationship worsens, and such "runaway relationships" become destructive for all concerned. In a "gruesome twosome," for instance, the two participants maintain a close, negative relationship. Each person receives fewer gratifications from the relationship, yet they maintain the attachment by mutual exploitation (Scheflen, 1960). When the relationship prevents one or both partners from gratifying normal needs, but the relationship is maintained, the twosome is caught in a degenerative spiral. Recent marital research demonstrates that, as love declines, negative conflict increases—a clear degenerative spiral (Lloyd & Cate, 1985).

Degenerative spirals, like generative spirals, occur in a variety of forms. A typical case involves the breakup of a significant relationship such as marriage. During a quarreling session one evening the husband says to the wife, "If you had not gone and gotten involved in an outside relationship with another man, our marriage could have made it. You just drained too much energy from us for our marriage to work." The wife responds by saying, "Yes, and had you given me the attention and care I longed for, I wouldn't have had an outside relationship." The infinite regress continues, each of them finding fault with why the other caused the termination of the marriage. The spiraling nature is clear. The more the wife retreats to an outside relationship, the less chance she has of having her needs met in the marriage. And the more the husband avoids giving her what she wants in the relationship, the more she will be influenced to seek outside relationships. One of the most common negative spirals between wives and husbands occurs when (1) the husband withdraws emotionally and (2) the wife expresses dissatisfaction to the husband (Segrin & Fitzpatrick, 1992).

Degenerative spirals are not limited to romantic relationships—they occur in all types. Parents and children often get caught up in spirals that create a dysfunctional system. The more dependent the child is on the parent, the more responsible and overburdened the parent is. And the more the parent takes responsibility for the child, the more this promotes dependence on the part of the child. It works like this: "One's actions toward other people generally effect a mirror duplication or a counter-measure from the other. This in turn tends to strengthen one's original action" (Leary, 1955). . . .

Altering Degenerative Spirals

Spirals, obviously, do change, with people going in and out of generative and degenerative spirals over the course of a relationship. And, as a relationship participant, you can have impact on the nature of the spirals—even altering degenerative spirals once they start. There are specific choices you can make that can alter the direction a relationship is flowing.

First, alter your usual response—do what comes unnaturally. For example, if you are in a relationship where you and the other tend to escalate, call each other names, you can stop the spiral by simply not allowing yourself to use negative language. Or, you can say, "This will just lead to a shouting match. I'm going to take a walk and talk with you when I come back," then exit from the normally hostile situation. Or say you have a roommate who is not very talkative and over the past 2 months you have tried to draw him out. You see that the more you talk, the more he retreats and the less he talks. Doing "more of the same" does not work, so do "less of the same." Don't act on the natural inclination to talk when he is silent; in fact, talk less and outwait him. Similarly, if you are often quiet in a group of four friends, people adapt to that by sometimes leaving you out of the decisions. Then, for the first time, begin to tell them what you would like to do. Change the patterns, and you change the spiral.

Wilmot and Stevens (1994) interviewed over 100 people who had "gone through a period of decline," and then improved their romantic, friendship, and family relationships—basically pulling out of a degenerative spiral. When asked what they did to "turn it around," it was found that a potent way of altering the patterns was to change behavior. The changes of behavior, of course, took many forms, given the particular type of relationship spiral that had occurred. Some people became more independent, some gave more "space" to the other, others changed locations or moved, and still others sacrificed for the partner or spent more time together. But the basic principle is the same—when in a degenerating or escalating set of communication patterns, change!

One last anecdote about changing patterns. I know one parent whose 11-year-old daughter was getting low grades in school. The parent had been a superb student, and the daughter, in the past, had done well. But, in the middle of the school year, the daughter started getting lower and lower grades. As the grades went down, the parent's criticism went up. Pretty soon, both the girl's grades and the mother-daughter relationship were in the cellar! After some help from an outsider, the mother took a vow to *not* talk anymore about grades, regardless of what happened. It was very difficult, for each evening the two had been arguing about grades; grades had become the focal point of the entire relationship. It only took 2 weeks, and the daughter's grades made dramatic jumps. The mother, who found "giving up" very difficult, had taken her negative part out of the communication system—and it changed.

One final note on changing your behavior. The people in the Wilmot and Stevens (1994) study noted that "persistence" was one important key to bringing about a change in the relationship. If the parent above had only stopped her criticism for one night, as soon as she resumed it, off the spiral would have gone again. The other person will be suspicious of your change at first, probably question your motives and other negative interpretations. But if you are persistent in bringing the change, it will have effects on the other person, for his or her communication patterns are interlocked with yours.

Second, you can use third parties constructively. Friends, counselors, relatives, clergy, and others can sometimes provide a different perspective for you to begin to open up a degenerative system for change. Third parties can often make specific suggestions that will break the pattern of interlocking, mutually destructive behaviors that keep adding fuel to the degenerating relationship. In one case, a husband and wife went to a marriage counselor because they had come to a standoff. He was tired of her demands to always talk to her and pay attention. She was tired of his demands for more frequent sexual activity. As a result, they became entrapped in a degenerative spiral—he talked less, and she avoided situations of physical intimacy. Upon seeing the counselor, they both realized that they were getting nowhere fast. Each was trying to get the other to change first. With the help of the counselor, they renegotiated their relationship, and each began giving a little bit. Over a period of a few days they found themselves coming out of the degenerating patterns.

Third, you can reaffirm your relational goals. Often when people get stuck in negative patterns of interaction, the other automatically assumes you want to "jump ship." If you are in a downward spiral, whether with your parents, boss, lover, child, or friend, reaffirming what you each have to gain from the relationship can promote efforts to get it back. The couple who saw the counselor found that they both had an important goal to stay together—for if either one had "won" the fight and lost the relationship, neither would have gotten what he or she wanted. Relational reaffirmation can help you focus on all the things you can do to get the relationship back to a more positive phase. Good relationships take energy to sustain; similarly, making a commitment to the relationship obvious to the other will help pull you out of the debilitating negative patterns.

Fourth, you can alter a spiral by metacommunicating. Wilmot and Stevens' (1994) respondents reported having a "Big Relationship Talk"—talking about the relationship and what had led to the degenerating series of actions. When you comment on what you see happening, it can open up the spiral itself for discussion. One can say, "Our relationship seems to be slipping—I find myself criticizing you, and you seem to be avoiding me, and it looks like it is getting worse. What can we do to turn it around?" Such metacommunication, whether pointed to the conversational episodes or the overall relationship patterns, can set the stage for productive conflict management and give participants a sense of a control over the relationship dynamics. Metacommunication, especially when coupled with a reaffirmation of your relational goals ("I don't want us to be unhappy, I want us to both like being together, but we seem to . . . "), can alter the destructive forces in a relationship. And, of course, you can use metacommunication in any type of relationship, such as on the job. J. P., for example, says, "Sally, it seems to me like our work enthusiasm is slipping away. What might we do to get that sense of fun back like we had about 6 months ago?"

Fifth, try to spend more or less time with the person. If you are on the "outs" with your co-workers, you could begin to spend more time with them—go to lunch, have coffee, take short strolls together. It is amazing what kinds of large changes can be purchased with just a small amount of time. Likewise, relationships often suffer because the people spend more time together than they can productively handle. So Tom always goes on a 3-day fishing trip with me in the summer as a way to both get more distance and independence in his marriage (and, coincidentally, to reaffirm our relationship with one another). Getting more distance and independence can bring you back refreshed and ready to relate again. Interestingly, Wilmot and Stevens (1994) found such "independence" moves as an important way to alter a degenerating spiral.

Finally, we all recognize that changing an external situation can alter a degenerating relationship. One parent has a son who got into an ongoing battle with the principal of the junior high school. The feud went on for months, with the principal (according to the mother) tormenting her boy and the boy retaliating by being mischievous. The mutually destructive actions were arrested only when the boy switched schools. He (and the principal) had a chance to start over, not contaminated by the previous interlocking patterns.

Another way to change the external situation is to stay in the presence of the other person but move to a new environment. Many married couples have gone for extended vacations in order to give themselves time to work out new solutions to relationship problems. If the relationship is important to you and you want to preserve it, effort expended to help the relationship reach productive periods is time well spent. Retreats, for business partners, romantic partners, and friends, can allow an infusion of fresh energy into a declining relationship. Because once the degenerative phases are reached, the behaviors of each person tend to be mutually reinforcing and damaging. Each person can blame the other and claim his or her own innocence, but that will not alter the degeneration. It sometimes takes long, hard work to alter a negative spiral, and it may be successful if both put in some effort. But as every counselor knows from experience, one person alone can usually not change the relationship. If that person makes changes, and the other reciprocates, you have a chance to turn the spiral around.

Woody Allen captured the essence of relational change when he said, "Relationships are like a shark. They either move forward, or they die." Our relationships are dynamic, always moving and changing either toward or away from improvement. Participants' behaviors interlock so that each one's behavior influences the others, and the mutually conjoined behaviors intensify the other's reactions.

People look at their relationships using different time frames. Some people tend to only look at the macro perspective, charting the changes in yearly units such as "do I feel as good about my job today as I did a year ago." A relationship may not look any different today than it did yesterday, but over a year's time, you can see either overall improvement or disintegration. The long-term spirals are identified by comparing the relationship to a much earlier state.

Other times one may process and categorize a relationship on an hour-by-hour basis. For example, when Jan's romantic partner announced that she wanted to "call it off," Jan spent the next 2 weeks thinking about the relationship, talking to her partner, and doing endless processing of all the changes coming her way. Rapid relational change, especially if it is unexpected, can cause intense processing of the relationship, sometimes to the point of overload. Those who suffer from an unexpected firing, termination of a romance, or disinheritance from the family find themselves processing at a depth they didn't think possible.

What is important, is to begin to sensitize yourself to the ebbs and flows inherent in all relationships, so you can make informed choices. Becoming attuned to the nature of communication spirals can increase your understanding of these processes.

TANGLES IN THE WEB: PARADOXES AND CONUNDRUMS

As you go through life, whether you are 18 or 80, the experience and understanding of your relationships is not a linear, step-by-step process. Like relationships themselves, our understanding is imperfect, and it is easy to overestimate how much we know. Relationships are elusive.

There are some relational paradoxes (statements that are both true but contradict one another) (Wilmot, 1987) and conundrums—puzzlements and elements that are inherently unsolvable. Here are a few of them.

1. We want contradictory things in relationships: freedom and closeness, openness to talk yet protection, stability and excitement. These dialectic tensions seem to be present in all relationships.

In many romantic relationships we want both freedom and connection, excitement and stability. In the family context we often want the others to accept who we are, yet we spend inordinate amounts of time centering on how we can change them. We talk openly about the importance of "communication" in relationships, but it appears to be more of a cultural belief than an actual fact (Wilmot & Stevens, 1994; Parks, 1982). Maybe we can begin to celebrate the tension inherent in all relationships rather than trying to solve the contradictory needs, flowing with the needs as they change back and forth.

2.   Both insider and outsider views of relationships are fraught with errors.

Outsiders to relationships can more accurately observe our actual communication behavior but are less accurate than we are at specifying the *meaning* of those behaviors within this particular relationship. When you, as an outsider, look at someone else's relationship, your judgments can be a good projective test for what you personally believe is the "key" to success. Think of a marriage you know that you would describe as high quality. To what would you attribute it?

- hard work
- good match on background characteristics
- being raised in non-dysfunctional families
- luck
- how well they communicate with one another
- a fine match on introversion/extroversion
- similar religious affiliations
- the support of their networks of family and friends
- both being raised in the same part of the country
- the length of time they have been together
- their ability to raise children successfully
- their mutual respect and compassion
- their intelligence
- their warmth and expressiveness
- their similar life struggles
- their commitment to one another
- their clarity about how to perform their roles
- their overriding love of one another
- their supportive friends
- similar hobbies and pastimes
- being at the same level of attractiveness

Outsiders, looking at someone else's relationship, tend to rely on external or situational factors in making their guesses (Burgoon & Newton, 1991). And we tend to evaluate others a bit more harshly than they do themselves, with us seeing the limitations of one or both of the partners: "I can't believe she stays married to him—he is so boring in public." When looking at someone's communication behavior, outsiders judge conversations less favorably than do those on the inside (Street, Mulac, & Wiemann, 1988). Outsiders generate faulty hypotheses about the intentions of the communicators—"she did that because she wants to control him" (Stafford, Waldron, & Infield, 1989). When we observe others' communication, we compensate for lack of information about their internal states by using our own personal theories—our "implicit personality theories" (Stafford, Waldron, & Infield, 1989). As an outsider, our observations are fraught with errors and overinterpretations, sort of "what we get is what we see," with most of it coming from us.

As insiders, our views aren't any less biased; we just tend to focus on different aspects (Dillard, 1987; Sillars & Scott, 1983). For example, insiders to marital relationships tend to overestimate their similarity and act with confidence on their views of the other. Yet the perceptions are not objectively accurate. Therefore, *all* views of relationships are inherently distorted—outsiders and insiders alike. Researchers and book writers (including this one) are themselves influenced by their own needs and perspectives, often looking for some order in the midst of considerable chaos.

3. Relationships are problematic—if we don't do anything about their natural dynamic, they may atrophy. If we try to force them, to "make them happen," we may destroy their essential nature.

The natural forces on relationships, marriage partners having to earn a living and nurture children, friends moving away from one another, tend to move most in the direction of decreased quality over time. In a sense, it is as if there is an energy in relationships that, if you don't continually reinvest in it, will cause the relationship to atrophy. Yet, on the other hand, we need to not try to "force" relationships. It is a rare individual in this culture who can command himself or herself to "love" someone else. The question of how to enhance a long-term relationship—whether family, romantic, or friend—looms large for all of us. . . . It is clear that, so far, there are no guarantees in relationships.

4. Committed relationships, such as marriage, may bring us much unhappiness because we think their purpose is happiness generation. Maybe their purpose is wholeness, grounded in the dialectical encounter between mates (Guggenbuhl-Craig, 1977).

In North America and most western cultures, people choose marriage partners and friends for what they do for us—make us happy, excite us sexually, provide a sense of fun and connection. Yet . . . , maybe this "what does it do for me" sets us up for disappointment and failure. From a spiritual perspective, one could say that our relationships, while started to "make us happy," have a more difficult and nobler purpose—to allow us to be challenged, to grow, and to change. Lifetime friends, for example, may serve the function of helping us correct ourselves when we get out of line in public. Romantic partners will set the stage for our unresolved issues of life and eccentricity to flourish, and see their downside. Family members will test our commitment, resilience and love, and if we move through that test we can emerge on a higher plane of relatedness.

5. The more intimacy and closeness we want, the more risk we face in the relationship. The greatest pleasure *and* pain come from those to whom we are the closest. Relationships bring both joy and suffering.

The very relationships people spend so much time processing—romantic, family, and friendships—are the ones to bring both the extremes of joy and pain. The less close relationships, while they can bring stability and meaning into life, may not address some of our deepest needs. Risk and reward seem to be opposite sides of the same coin.

6. We often see the "self" as concrete and findable. Yet relationships are no less "real" than an individual self is.

In our culture, we take, as has been noted many times, the "self" as individual, disconnected, separate, and findable. We put the locus of most things into the self—discussing "self-esteem" and "personality" as if they were real things and not abstract concepts. Relationships are neither more nor less figments of our concepts than are ourselves—but we don't tend to see it that way in this culture. It is important to note that our selves do have a conventional reality—there is a person standing there. Yet upon close examination, the "self" cannot be found. Is your brain yourself? Your torso? Your legs? Your emotions? We impose the concept of "self" onto the physical and emotional aspects and stop our analysis. Relationships, while not physically represented, are no less real than are our selves. We talk about relationships, and their "reality," upon examination, is just as findable (and no less so) than that of the self.

7. Self is produced in relationship to others; relationships are produced from two selves.

. . . It has been argued that we originate and live in-relation; we co-create our selves in relation to one another. And relationships are produced from the two persons who have a communication connection. Self and other produce, and are produced by, relationship. And self is more fruitfully viewed as "with the ecological system" rather than as the center of one's world (Broome, 1991, p. 375).

8. The greatest individual growth, and the greatest derailment of individual growth, come from the hurt and disappointment of relationships gone awry. Relationships can serve as springboards for growth or just toss you higher so you land harder.

When we face the natural traumas of life, our response determines the outcome. Trauma can bring transformation or derailment. Some people are broken when a relationship terminates, for example, or when an important person dies. Others, through grieving and slowly transforming themselves, reopen to relationships and life, reconnecting anew and building better relationships in the future.

9. We can solve problems in relationships by (1) internal, personal change; and (2) changing the external, communication connection between the two.

Change at any one level reverberates to the other level, for both us and the other person.

Like the chicken and the egg, which comes first—you or relationship? And if you have difficulties, do you "get your stuff together" and then reenter other relationships, or do you begin other relationships so you can become stronger? Both routes are used, and both can work. If you undergo change, it will reverberate in all your relationships: the boundaries are permeable. If your relationship changes, it will alter you; the influence always flows both ways.

10. We can't fully understand our relationships without concepts, and as soon as we use an abstract notion we impose its limitations on what we are seeing. Labels are essential and limiting, and cannot capture an ever-changing reality. As Wilden says, "all theories of relationship require a certain artificial closure" (Wilden, 1980, p. 114).

We can't really proceed with understanding without labels, and when you introduce your "boyfriend" to your family, it gives them a clue about the relationship. Yet when you use the label, it restricts both your and the other's views of that relationship. Each relationship contains many complex and contradictory elements, and it cannot be accurately captured by "boyfriend." Further, there is always "label lag"—the relationship changes, and the label stays the same. A "married couple" of 6 months will be very different than that very same couple at 6 years or 6 decades, yet they are still referred to as married. All concepts and labels are limiting and constricting—and essential.

11. General conclusions about gender, culture, and relationships may not apply at all to your particular relationships.

One of the problems in talking about "gender" or "cultural" effects is that we are always talking about groupings that help us "understand" on an abstract level. But your particular relationship may not reflect the general norms at all. Just like a theory of gravity cannot tell you about when a particular apple will fall from a tree, studying relational dynamics will not tell you about what will happen in your relationship. When studies on gender, for example, show that females are more expressive than males, what do you do if the woman in a cross-sex romantic relationship is the less expressive of the two? It is probably better to focus on the central issue—expressiveness, and the match or mismatch between the partners—rather than trying to reflect the general norm. Similarly, the finding that gay males have more partners than lesbians or heterosexuals does not mean that a gay man cannot live a life of commitment to another.

12. Learning about relationships occurs before, during, and after the relationship is a findable event.

Our perspectives on our relationships do not end—they only change. Just think for a moment about how you interpret events that happened to you in your childhood. As you move through time you will reinterpret them many times, focusing on different aspects, and seeing them in a different light. Likewise, the friendship that you used to see as a barometer of yourself may be later seen as not helping you at all at a stage of life. A devastating romantic termination may be seen later as the "best thing that ever happened to me." While many of us do not seek difficulties, most of us say, in retrospect, that it is what produced the learning so essential to the next stage of our life. I was once talking to a fellow on a flight from Helsinki, Finland, to Boston. He was in a long-distance relationship with a Finnish woman, and he lived in Boston, and here is what he said. "I did fatherhood and marriage, so I guess I'm doing this for awhile"—making retrospective sense of his relationship that was allowing him to collect considerable frequent flyer miles!

REVIEW QUESTIONS

1. Define *communication spiral.*
2. According to this reading, what is necessary in order to stop a spiral?
3. What's the difference between a generative and a degenerative spiral?
4. What does Wilmot and Stevens's research indicate about the role of persistence in altering a degenerative spiral?
5. What is metacommunicating?
6. What is a dialectic tension in a relationship?
7. What are the specific problems Wilmot identifies with both insider and outsider views of a relationship?

PROBES

1. Explain what Bill means when he says that, in a spiral, "each person's behavior accelerates the dynamism of the relationship." Give an example that includes a positive dynamism and one that includes a negative dynamism.
2. Could a spiral that appears to be generative to some member(s) of a relationship appear to be degenerative to others? Explain.
3. What is one generative spiral in your communication experience that you could *enhance?* What is one degenerative spiral in your communication experience that you could *break?*
4. Wilmot suggests that one of the ways you can "do what comes unnaturally" is to stop trying to make things better. Explain why this might work.
5. Wilmot suggests that you might change an external situation in order to alter a degenerating spiral. This could include changing locations—moving your home, work, or school. But some people also emphasize that, "Wherever you go, there you are," which is to say that you need to change your attitude or approach, not your location. What do you think works best?
6. Do you believe that the main purpose of a long-term relationship like a marriage is happiness generation or what Bill calls "wholeness, grounded in the dialectical encounter between mates"?

7. What is the relationship between Bill's brief discussion of the self in paradoxes 6 and 7 and Stewart, Zediker, and Witteborn's discussion of the self in Chapter 3?
8. Identify one general conclusion about gender, culture, and relationships that does *not* apply to one of your relationships.

REFERENCES

1. Bateson, G. (1972). *Steps to an Ecology of Mind.* New York: Ballantine Books.
2. Bateson, G. (1979). *Mind and Nature: A Necessary Unity.* New York: Bantam Books.
3. Broome, B. J. (1991). Building shared meaning: Implications of a relational approach to empathy for teaching intercultural communication. *Communication Education, 40,* 235–249.
4. Burgoon, J. K., & Newton, D. A. (1991). Applying a social meaning model to relational message interpretations of conversational involvement: Comparing observer and participant perspectives. *The Southern Communication Journal, 56,* 96–113.
5. Dillard, J. P. (1987). Close relationships at work: Perceptions of the motives and performance of relational participants. *Journal of Social and Personal Relationships, 4,* 179–193.
6. Guggenbuhl-Craig, A. (1977). *Marriage Dead or Alive.* Murray Stein (trans.). Dallas, TX: Spring Publication.
7. Kurdek, L. A. (1991). Marital stability and changes in marital quality in newlywed couples: A test of the contextual model. *Journal of Social and Personal Relationships, 5,* 201–221.
8. Leary, T. (1955). The theory and measurement methodology of interpersonal communication. *Psychiatry, 18,* 147–161.
9. Lloyd, S. A., & Cate, R. M. (1985). The developmental course of conflict in dissolution of premarital relationships. *Journal of Social and Personal Relationships, 2,* 179–194.
10. O'Neill, N., & O'Neill, G. (1972). *Open Marriage.* New York: M. Evans.
11. Parks, M. R. (1982). Ideology in interpersonal communication: Off the couch and into the world. In Burgoon, M. (Ed.), *Communication Yearbook 5.* New Brunswick, NJ: International Communication Association/Transaction Books, pp. 79–107.
12. Rose, S., & Serafica, F. C. (1986). Keeping and ending casual, close and best friendships. *Journal of Social and Personal Relationships, 3,* 275–288.
13. Scheflen, A. (1960). Communication and Regulation in Psychotherapy. *Psychiatry, 26,* 126–136.
14. Segrin, C., & Fitzpatrick, M. A. (1992). Depression and verbal aggressiveness in different marital types. *Communication Studies, 43,* 79–91.

15. Sillars, A. L., & Scott, M. D. (1983). Interpersonal perception between intimates: An integrative review. *Human Communication Research, 10,* 153–176.

16. Spitzberg, B. H., & Canary, D. J. (1985). Loneliness and relationally competent communication. *Journal of Social and Personal Relationships, 2,* 387–402.

17. Stafford, L., Waldron, V. R., & Infield, L. L. (1989). Actor-observer differences in conversational memory. *Human Communication Research, 15,* 590–611.

18. Street, R. L., Jr., Mulac, A., & Wiemann, J. M. (1988). Speech evaluation differences as a function of perspective (participant versus observer) and presentational medium. *Human Communication Research, 14,* 333–363.

19. Wilden, A. (1980). *System and Structure: Essays on Communication and Exchange,* 2nd ed. London: Tavistock Publication.

20. Wilmot, W. W. (1987). *Dyadic Communication.* New York: Random House.

21. Wilmot, W. W., & Stevens, D. C. (1994). Relationship rejuvenation: Arresting decline in personal relationships. In Conville, R. (Ed.), *Communication and Structure.* Philadelphia, PA: Ablex, pp. 103–124.

22. Ziller, R. C. (1973). *The Social Self.* New York: Pergamon Press.

This reading is an excerpt from a recent book that challenges one of Western culture's most basic beliefs about conflict. As you can tell by the title, the book's target is *blaming,* the widespread tendency people have to start dealing with a conflict by figuring out who or what is at fault so that they can clearly and solidly place blame. Jeffrey Kottler's attitude toward this common conviction is clear from his first sentence: "If you spent half as much time changing the ways you respond in conflict situations as you do trying to figure out who is at fault," he writes, "most of your troubles would soon vanish."

This will definitely not be easy for some people to hear. "If you don't figure out who's to blame," people often say, "how can you prevent something bad from happening again?" But as Kottler points out, this way of thinking overlooks how fault-finding and blaming actually affect communication in conflict. Most adversaries respond to blaming with more of the same, which means that the process makes the conflict worse rather than better. It is helpful to determine the causes of disastrous situations for the purposes of not repeating the same mistakes, "but only when the focus is on enlightenment rather than on assigning guilt." And there's a big difference between those two motives.

Echoing some of what I say in Chapter 2, Kottler argues that it is also often impossible to determine who is at fault, partly because "conflicted relationships tend to perpetuate themselves" until they have a life of their own. Whenever you're in this kind of relationship, the most fruitful first step is to take responsibility for your part of the whole without blaming either others or yourself.

With the help of some examples from his own life, Kottler distinguishes the "linear causality" that often operates in the natural world from the "circular causality" that governs the human world. The basic difference is that when cause-and-effect are understood to operate in a straight line (linear), cause can reliably be separated from effect and there is a predictable relationship between them. So there is linear causality between a temperature of 32°F or 0°C and water freezing. But the human world is much more complicated. One person doesn't disrespect another just "because she is insensitive." As Kottler explains, one person's perceptions and behaviors intermingle with the other person's perceptions and behaviors in a complex of expectations, attributions, and subtle nonverbal indicators that leave each person feeling that their opposite conclusions ("it's her fault"; "no, it's his fault") are entirely justified.

The best way to change this negative spiral is to take responsibility for your part of the conflict. Importantly, this does not mean blaming yourself. Taking responsibility "involves an internal process wherein you address a series of introspective inquiries," and Kottler describes how this process of internal questions and answers can work.

There are four basic questions to work through: (1) How are you disowning the problem? In what ways are you unaware of or actively denying your part in the whole? (2) In what ways are you making excuses for yourself? Just about all humans have a natural tendency to protect their own ego, and this can promote a level of defensiveness that makes problems worse. Kottler urges us to reflect on our own version of this tendency. (3) What are your favorite scapegoats for diverting blame away from yourself? This is another common defense mechanism that Kottler encourages us to work away from. (4) What might you do internally to feel more in control over what happens externally? This question can help you understand the impact of the ways you might be talking to yourself about the conflict situation.

If Kottler were a communication professional rather than a counseling psychologist, he might emphasize more strongly the interpersonal aspects of working through these four questions. It can be helpful, for example, for parties to the same conflict to help each other respond to them. But whether the questions are considered individually or in conversations, they can help conflicting parties significantly improve their communication with each other.

Taking Responsibility Without Blaming

Jeffrey Kottler

. . . If you spent half as much time changing the ways you respond in conflict situations as you do trying to figure out who is at fault, most of your troubles would soon vanish. Most people are obsessed with identifying the culprit who is responsible for a dispute. On the one hand, if you can justify that it is *they* who were negligent or irresponsible, you may rub your hands together in glee and rest easy in the knowledge that at least you are not the one who created the mess, even if you do have to live with it. If, on the other hand, you frankly admit (or you are trapped into doing so) that *you,* not they, are responsible, then you can just as easily fall into the trap of feeling guilty and remorseful.

Since most of the time adversaries are not willing to accept blame, even when all evidence points toward them, it is largely a futile exercise trying to figure out who is at fault. Of course, it is helpful to determine the causes of disastrous situations for the purposes of not repeating the same mistakes and learning from these failures, but only when the focus is on enlightenment rather than on assigning guilt.

This distinction is especially important when you consider that interpersonal conflicts are almost always the consequence of collective efforts. Even if it were possible to discern who is at fault, what difference would it make? You are still both stuck with the problem.

WHO IS TO BLAME?

. . . Determining who is at fault is an impossible task. The process described [here] requires that you identify who and what sets you off, understand the causes and origins of your entrenched patterns, and work through your discomfort until you are willing to accept greater responsibility for your troubles. You may not always be able to discover a single person or event that is causing your difficulties.

Conflicted relationships tend to perpetuate themselves, playing off interactions, carrying forward with a momentum that appears to have a life of its own. Any intention on the part of one person is predicated on the best prediction of what another person might do. If you are expecting a person to act deviously, you will prepare yourself for betrayal by cloaking your own behavior in deception. Conflicts are thus self-sustaining cycles of response and counterresponse, as illustrated in the following case of a mother- and daughter-in-law.

From the very beginning, Fran and Tina regarded one another with suspicion. Fran believed her son was making a mistake by getting married too young, and she channeled these feelings into resentment toward Tina (it is often easier to show disappointment or anger to a stranger than to a loved one). Tina, in turn, resented her mother-in-law for what she felt was excessive meddling. Each was convinced the other had ulterior motives for sabotaging her relationship with Brian, the son/husband. And, naturally, both were acting out a struggle that was a reenactment of something they had experienced before: Fran did not want her son to repeat the same mistakes she had made, and Tina had been so dominated by her own mother throughout much of her life that she was determined not to let this new mother control her life.

Tina held out an olive branch to her mother-in-law, inviting her to go to lunch one day. Fran, expecting some hidden agenda, accepted reluctantly and behaved with a certain amount of antagonism during the meal. Tina, perceiving her mother-in-law as ungrateful, launched her own defensive campaign, an attack that Fran was expecting and so interpreted as aggression on her part. When Brian heard the report that night from both combatants, each tried to convince him that the other was at fault for the conflict.

The central theme of this stage in the process, taking responsibility without blaming others or yourself, involves understanding the reciprocal nature of interpersonal difficulties. One of the most fascinating aspects of human behavior is that we do not always obey the laws of the physical world, at least with regard to what causes us to act. Whereas the laws of physics are based on a model of "linear causality," human behavior is best described as being based on "circular causality." What this means is that unlike the physical world, where it may be determined that one thing *causes* another, which in turn *causes* something else, human interactions are both causes *and* effects of what transpired previously.

This is as true for what is going on in your life now as it was for the circumstances of your past. At one time, I used to blame my mother for neglecting me, for instigating the continual arguments we had throughout my childhood and adolescence until I moved out at age seventeen. After all, she was an alcoholic. She was addicted to prescription tranquilizers, to food, to misery. When she died prematurely of cancer (and probably chronic depression), she provided me with the perfect scapegoat: it was *her* fault that I was continuously in conflict with other women in positions of authority.

Eventually, after studying the matter in depth over years of reflection, family research, journal writing, and therapy, I came to realize that my mother was only reacting to the forces of her own life—the ways she had been treated by her own parents, by my father, and even (it was difficult to admit) by my brothers and me. I realized that it was impossible to figure out who was at fault for the conflicts with my mother in the past, just as it is for those in the present.

It may appear as though a conflict results from a linear progression: I treat you disrespectfully because I am insensitive (or so you believe). Most situations are more complex: I felt slighted by you, even though you are unaware of this offense. I then approach you more tentatively in our next meeting, which you interpret as a lack of interest on my part. You begin to respond curtly, thereby reinforcing my feelings of rejection. I lash out next time, feeling totally justified but thereby appearing to be the one with the problem. You then innocently complain: "What is *his* problem?," never realizing your own role in the conflict. Most situations are even more complex than this since they involve more than two people.

You observe a family in action, for example. Thinking linearly, you see a child misbehaving, note that the parents argue between themselves before they decide what to do, and then, somewhat ineffectively, attempt to intervene to control their child. When you examine the situation in greater depth, you find that assigning blame is not as simple as you first thought. When the child misbehaves, his sister tattles to the mother, who promptly becomes angry. She then complains to the father, who punishes the child. The boy starts to pout and cry, sparking guilt in his sister, who got him in trouble. She then starts to act out herself, whining and complaining. The father and mother start arguing about whose fault this is. The boy then misbehaves again as a distraction, so his parents will stop fighting. The circular pattern continues round and round, each participant reacting to the other family members.

Who is at fault in this conflict? Is it the child who misbehaves? The sibling who manipulates the parents? The mother for being passive? The father for taking over? It is impossible to find the *single* source of this conflict, just as we cannot isolate who is causing whom to do what. All of their actions are interdependent, playing off of and reacting in response to each other's behavior. More often than not, circular causality is the most appropriate model for explaining what takes place during conflict situations.

THE INTROSPECTIVE PROCESS OF ACCEPTING RESPONSIBILITY

Tanya and Samantha, two sisters who live in the same town, continuously bicker with one another over various imagined slights. Tanya invites their parents over for dinner one night but decides not to include her sister and her family at the gathering. Samantha becomes indignant when she learns of it and vows not to include Tanya and her family the next time there is a holiday get-together.

So who is at fault in this situation: Tanya for not including her sister at the first dinner? Samantha for being so petty that she reciprocated in kind, thereby escalating the conflict? How about their parents for constantly comparing the two sisters? Each time one sister checks in with her parents, she hears an up-to-date summary of all the successes the other sister has enjoyed during the previous week.

Of course, whatever conflict exists between them has its roots in interactions that began long ago, during childhood. The sisters grew up in competition with each other—vying to be the one who could get the best grades, the most popular boyfriend, the most successful husband, the most promising career, the largest home, the fanciest car, the brightest children. Clearly, neither one of them is solely responsible for their long-standing conflicts. Nor is it relevant, at this juncture, to blame their parents for pitting them against one another, or at least failing to neutralize their mutual antagonism.

The conclusion as to who is at fault for any situation is thus predicated on answering these questions: Is anyone responsible for what happened? What is the cause of the conflict? Who is to blame? When a person is held responsible for an event, does that mean that he or she is at fault? What am I doing inside my own head to deny responsibility for what has been happening in an effort to place blame elsewhere?

These are the questions Tanya considered when she came in to see me. She was sick and tired of enduring the constant strain in her relationship with Samantha. Was there anything she could do to stop the squabbles between them?

In order to break the blaming cycle in which each sister took turns finding fault with the other, collecting evidence to prove that the other one was to blame for the situation, it was necessary for Tanya to move away from such obsessive focus on what Samantha was up to and instead concentrate on what she could do to think more constructively about what was going on. This involved figuring out what button Samantha was pushing that elicited such resentment (the implication that she wasn't good enough), discovering where the origins of their struggles lay (a reenactment of their competition for their parents' approval), and harnessing her feelings of rejection and hurt as motivators to look inward rather than outward for the source of the difficulty.

Taking responsibility for the conflict does not mean blaming yourself instead of blaming the other person. Such a strategy can be just as counterproductive, sometimes even more so since it can involve a tendency toward self-pity and helplessness. At least when you are finding fault with others you are feeling feisty in the act of fighting back instead of withdrawing into a shell surrounded by the trophies of your failures.

Taking responsibility for the relationships in your life that are not going well without accepting blame for the troubles involves an internal process wherein you address a series of introspective inquiries. This procedure proved useful for Tanya in her efforts to regain more control over her perceptions of her sister and their relationship, even if she could not change their interactive patterns.

1. How Are You Disowning the Problem?

Notice the tendency to sidestep responsibility for what has happened before and what continues to take place in the conflicted relationship. For Tanya, this task proved to be quite easy with the assistance of her husband, who had listened far too long to her list of complaints.

"My husband pointed out to me how much time I spend thinking about my sister, bitching about what she is doing. He kids me that I may forget to make the kids' lunches, or to pick him up at the car dealership, but I have never forgotten a single episode of any injustice Samantha has inflicted on me. He is right. I do spend an inordinate amount of time denying that the problem between us is in any way my fault. Yet I can provide you with the longest list of reasons as to why I am so sure she is the one who is so unreasonable. I guess that only supports the argument that I am unwilling to take some responsibility for this mess."

2. In What Ways Are You Making Excuses for Yourself?

Part of the strategy for avoiding responsibility for the conflicts in your life is to construct a list of excuses, preferably as long as possible, that get you off the hook. If you are particularly bright, then you probably have developed especially good excuses that may not easily be discounted. Even if you are an amateur at this internal activity, it is likely that you have collected a list of favorites, such as:

I didn't do it.

It was just dumb luck.

I wasn't even there.

She asked for it.

I didn't mean to do it.

It wasn't my fault.

I was just following orders.

I was just kidding.

It was just meant to be that way.

It wasn't me, it was the . . .

It wasn't me, and I don't know who did it.

It wasn't a big deal.

I had no choice.

I couldn't help it.

I didn't mean it.

Don't look at me—she did it.

Yes, but . . .

Anyone would have done the same thing.

She was asking for trouble.

I wasn't really trying.

A bad temper runs in my family.

It was just an unfortunate situation.

I didn't know the rules.

Nobody told me.

Recall a time recently when someone leveled blame at you for something that you did. What was your initial response? Before you had time to even think through your role and responsibility, to reflect on your degree of culpability, the first excuse was already out of your mouth. . . .

Such is the mechanism of excuse making as a self-protection cloak. You remain safe from criticism and keep assaults to a fragile self-image at bay, but in the process you never take the opportunity to identify the triggers that provoked your defensiveness. You are not able to understand what it is within you that feels threatened and vulnerable, nor are you able to talk things through, with yourself and others, to prevent further distortions in the future. . . .

If facing conflict without blame presents such wonderful opportunities for growth, why don't we do this more often? The answer is that it takes a tremendous amount of work. If you can get away with an excuse that deflects blame away from you, initially you keep your image clear. You stave off, at least temporarily, any of the effort associated with having to make changes. . . .

It is clearly a distortion of reality to deny your share of responsibility in *any* conflict. Even if you can convince someone you had no role in the disagreement (and that is doubtful), *you* know deep down inside that you are not totally blameless. Kidding yourself in one set of circumstances only leads to further self-deception in others. After a while, you will find it difficult to separate your fantasies about what is taking place from the actual objective events. In other words, you will believe your own lies and distortions, which further insulates you from receiving accurate information about the world and honest feedback about how you are perceived by others.

3. What Are Your Favorite Scapegoats for Diverting Blame Away from Yourself?

What are your favorite ways to divert attention and responsibility away from you and place it elsewhere? Is it poor genes? Bad luck? No support? A misunderstanding? Perhaps somebody else did it.

As with any self-respecting defense mechanism, blaming others for misdeeds allows you to maintain a positive self-image in light of attacks that are perceived as threatening. It buys you time until you can prepare a better excuse. It spreads around the focus of responsibility so that you do not bear the burden alone. Perhaps more important than rehabilitating your image in other people's eyes, blaming allows you to live with your own imperfections and still feel all right about yourself.

When a person is cornered into admitting that he or she did, in fact, do something, that it was intentional rather than accidental, and that he or she accepts responsibility for his or her actions, there is still a way to avoid blame: simply deny that there was anything wrong with what was done.

"Yes, you did tell me your concerns in confidence and ask me not to say anything to anyone else. Yes, I did promise I would honor your request. However, by keeping your feelings under wraps, by not confronting him with your concerns, by confiding in a few of us privately, you were only creating more divisiveness. I went to him and suggested that he approach you because I wanted the two of you to work things out. I felt an obligation not only to our relationship but also to the way we all get along."

Appealing to some greater good to explain one's actions is not the same as denying one's responsibility for creating a conflict. By offering a seemingly viable explanation, the individual accepts responsibility but denies any wrongdoing. The more comprehensible and rational the reasons, the more likely it is that he or she will not be held accountable.

Another means by which to disown responsibility is to *focus on the issue of intentionality:* you may have done it, but you did not mean to. This avoidance of blame goes something like this:

"There was no way I could have imagined that things would get this far out of control. I should not have been placed in this situation to begin with. I was just trying to be helpful."

A third possible response to an accusation is to imply that *you were coerced into acting this way.* You had no other choice; you were forced to do it.

"Hey, what would *you* have done? I could not risk doing anything else. I was in jeopardy, in such a vulnerable position that I was virtually forced to do it. I wish I could have acted otherwise, but there was just no other alternative."

Each of these denials of blame will only be employed when responsibility can be proven. Always the first choice is to *deny that you had anything to do with the situation in the first place.*

One of the best examples of using this type of excuse as a defense against blame comes from a favorite story of comedian Bill Cosby. It seems that one evening late at night, when Bill and his brother were supposed to be sleeping, they began wrestling around in bed. These tussles led to progressively more vigorous games, eventually culminating in "trampoline," in which they determined who could bounce the highest. When the bed came crashing down, the boys' father rushed into the room, ready to seek some revenge for his sleep being disrupted. "What is going on in here? Who broke this bed?"

Bill and his brother looked at one another. Even then showing signs that he was fast on his feet, Bill confidently proclaimed, "It was a robber! He came in through the window when we were sleeping. He woke us up jumping on the bed. Then he broke it! He escaped before we knew what happened."

"Son," his father calmly pointed out, "You don't have a window in this room. How could a robber come in through the window?"

Desperate to escape blame but never skipping a beat, Bill replied, "Well, Dad, he took it with him."

. . . It is counterproductive to blame others, but it can be just as destructive to blame yourself for unpleasant circumstances. Rather than dwelling on who is at fault, it is far better for you to accept responsibility for overcoming the problem and get on with the business of taking charge of this process and working things through. This effort is easier said than done, for the chief obstacles that get in the way of resolving conflicts are those unresolved issues that you have been ignoring.

4. What Might I Do Internally to Feel More in Control over What Happens Externally?

The consequence of accepting responsibility for a conflict is that you then have to do a tremendous amount of work on yourself in order to rectify matters. This has a lot less to do with things you do on the outside than with internal strategies you can adopt to feel more personal control and take responsibility for your internal feelings.

Attributing blame for conflict to someone or something outside of yourself represents a gross distortion of reality. Cognitive therapists (so called because they emphasize changing internal thinking patterns) have been writing for decades about the irrational beliefs people subscribe to that insist that feelings are reactions *caused* by what other people do:

"You *make* me so angry." (implying that the other person did something that created this feeling)

"You *made* me do it!" (insinuating that what the other person did necessarily caused this person's response)

"Why did you do that *to* me?" (signifying that the other person's actions were deliberately directed toward the speaker)

"If it were not for you . . . " (implying that if the other person did not exist, this person would not have any problems)

Actually, interpersonal struggles involve more than just one's chosen reaction to what has taken place. Certainly cognitive activity—that is, one's interpretation of others' actions—does influence how he or she feels about and responds to them. But in a complicated interaction between two people, individuals often trigger reactions in one another not only through their present behavior but through their unresolved issues as well.

When you attempt to assign blame for a problem, you are likely to follow one of three possible scenarios, none of which is strictly accurate.

1. *External blame:* "It is all your fault. If only you were different, then we would not have this problem between us."
2. *Scapegoat:* "We got manipulated into this conflict. If they had handled things differently, then you and I would not be having this problem."

Both of the above cognitive styles attribute blame to circumstances outside your control. You bear little responsibility for the situation, and so you have little power to change it. In the third case, you take total responsibility for the conflict.

3. *Internal blame:* "It *is* my fault. If I had reacted differently, then we would not be in this mess."

This is also a distortion of reality, since it is highly unlikely that anything is ever entirely one person's fault. Nevertheless, given a choice among the three blaming strategies, even with the remorse and guilt that accompany self-blame, this is still a more empowering way to think about your plight. At the very least, you are implying that you *choose* your reaction to what happened, meaning that you still can choose to think or act in a way that will produce a different reaction. Such personal responsibility is only possible, however, when you avoid the tendency to make excuses.

REVIEW QUESTIONS

1. What is the main practical problem with blaming that Kottler identifies?
2. Explain the difference between linear and circular causality. Give a concrete example of each.
3. What is a scapegoat, and how does scapegoating function in the process Kottler describes?

4. Blaming is important, some people say, because you have to know who was at fault to keep a bad thing from happening again. How does Kottler respond to this point?

5. "If facing conflict without blame presents such wonderful opportunities for growth," Kottler asks, "why don't we do this more often?" How does he respond to this question?

6. What is a defense mechanism?

7. What does Kottler suggest we substitute for "You make me so angry!" and "You made me do it!"?

PROBES

1. Kottler emphasizes that taking responsibility for your part in a conflict does *not* mean placing blame on yourself. What's the difference? How can you take responsibility without blaming yourself?

2. Some people make Kottler's point by encouraging conflict participants to replace the understanding of "responsibility" that leads to blaming with an understanding of responsibility as "response-ability," the ability to respond. This is one rationale for the communication skill of "nexting" that I discuss in Chapter 2. Paraphrase Kottler's advice in this chapter by using the two constructs "response-ability" and "nexting."

3. When you read about Tanya, Samantha, and their parents, who did you believe was "at fault" in this situation?

4. What relationships do you notice between what Kottler calls "the blaming cycle" and the "communication spirals" that Bill Wilmot discusses in the previous reading?

5. Which of Kottler's four questions most helps you move away from blaming?

6. Four ways to deny blame are to appeal to a greater good, claim you didn't mean to, say you were forced to, or deny any involvement. Which do you hear others using most in their conflicts with you? Which do you use most?

L ike the previous readings by Wilmot and Kottler, this one analyzes how relationships get into trouble and how they might be rescued. Steve Duck is a Brit, which is why you'll find the word "whilst" and the spelling "behaviour" here. For a number of years he's been a distinguished interpersonal communication teacher and researcher at the University of Iowa. This excerpt from the 1998 edition of his book, *Human Relationships* provides a way to understand how personal relationships come apart and how they can sometimes be put back together.

Duck explains the four typical phases that people go through when breaking up. The first is "intrapsychic" or internal, and consists of at least one member of the relationship brooding about his or her partner. The second phase is called "dyadic" because it's the time when the two partners (the dyad) talk with each other about breaking up. This leads, usually rapidly, to the third step, a "social" phase when they tell other people and seek their support. The final phase is called "grave-dressing," because it consists of communication that tries to "bury the relationship good and proper." During this phase, the people involved create an account of the relationship's history and demise. This account gives the partners and others a way to make sense out of what happened.

One benefit of this model is that it suggests what relational partners might do if they want to "put the relationship right" or rebuild it. You obviously can't just reverse the steps of the breakup, because memories of the old relationship and its demise are necessarily going to be involved in any new relationship that's developed. But the model does identify what people can do at the different stages or phases of dissolution. So, for example, Duck notes that if the relationship is at the intrapsychic phase of dissolution then "repair should aim to reestablish liking for the partner rather than to correct behavioural faults in ourselves or our nonverbal behaviour." Other strategies are appropriate at other phases of a breakup. As Duck concludes, "Different parts of the story need to be addressed at different phases of breakdown."

Handling the Break-Up of Relationships

Steve Duck

By far the most common experience of negative things in relationships is the management of minor irritations and trivial hassles that arise day to day in relationships of all kinds (Duck and Wood, 1995). The rosy picture of relational progress is thus only part of the truth (and Cupach and Spitzberg, 1994, devote a whole book to the dark side). For instance, why have researchers just focused on love and overlooked needling, bitching, boredom, complaints, harassment and enemyships (Duck, 1994b)? Why do we know more about romantic relationships than we do about troublesome relationships (Levitt et al., 1996)? Things often go wrong in relationships in all sorts of ways and cause a lot of pain when they do, some of it intentionally hurtful (Vangelisti, 1994). Sometimes it is Big Stuff and leads to break-up of the relationship, but most of the time it is relatively trivial and leads to nothing except hurt feelings and the conflicts involved in *managing* the occurrence. How does it happen?

"Handling the Break-Up of Relationships" by Steve Duck from *Human Relationships.* Reprinted by permission of Sage Publications.

When Things Go Wrong

There are several parts to acquaintance, and so we should expect there to be several parts to the undoing of acquaintance during relational dissolution. This is partly because relationships exist in time and usually take time to fall apart, so that at different times different processes are taking a role in the dissolution. It is also because, like a motor car, a relationship can have accidents for many reasons, whether the 'driver's' fault, mechanical failure or the actions of other road users. Thus, in a relationship, one or both partners might be hopeless at relating; or the structure and mechanics of the relationship may be wrong, even though both partners are socially competent in other settings; or outside influences can upset it. All of these possibilities have been explored (Baxter, 1984; Duck, 1982a; Orbuch, 1992). However, I am going to focus on my own approach to these issues and refer you elsewhere for details of the other work. . . .

The essence of my approach to relational dissolution is that there are several different phases, each with a characteristic style and concern (Duck, 1982a). Thus, as shown in Figure 10–2, the first phase is a breakdown phase where partners (or one partner only) become(s) distressed at the way the relationship is conducted. This generates an *intrapsychic phase* characterized by a brooding focus on the relationship and on the partner. Nothing is said to the partner at this point: the agony is either private or shared only with a diary or with relatively anonymous other persons (bar servers, hairdressers, passengers on the bus) who will not tell the partner about the complaint. Just before exit from this phase, people move up the scale of confidants so that they start to complain to their close friends, but do not yet present their partner with the full extent of their distress or doubts about the future of the relationship.

Once we decide to do something about a relational problem we have to deal with the difficulties of facing up to the partner. Implicit—and probably wrongly implicit—in my 1982 model was the belief that partners would tell one another about their feelings and try to do something about them. Both Lee (1984) and Baxter (1984) show that people often leave relationships without telling their partner, or else by fudging their exits. For instance, they may say: 'I'll call you' and then not do it; or 'Let's keep in touch' and never contact the partner; or 'Let's not be lovers but stay as friends' and then have hardly any contact in the future (Metts et al., 1989). Given that my assumption is partly wrong, it nevertheless assumes that partners in formal relationships like marriage will have to face up to their partner, whilst partners in other relationships may or may not do so. The *dyadic phase* is the phase when partners try to confront and talk through their feelings about the relationship and decide how to sort out the future. Assuming that they decide to break up (and even my 1982 model was quite clear that they may decide *not* to do that), they then move rapidly to a *social phase* when they have to tell other people about their decision and enlist some social support for their side of the debate. It is no good just leaving a relationship: we seek other people to agree with our decision or to prop us up and support what we have done. Other people can support us in

BREAKDOWN: Dissatisfaction with relationship

↓

| Threshold: I can't stand this any more |

↓

INTRA-PSYCHIC PHASE
Personal focus on partner's behaviour
Assess adequacy of partner's role performance
Depict and evaluate negative aspects of being in the relationship
Consider costs of withdrawal
Assess positive aspects of alternative relationships
Face 'express/repress dilemma'

↓

| Threshold: I'd be justified in withdrawing |

↓

DYADIC PHASE
Face 'confrontation/avoidance dilemma'
Confront partner
Negotiate in 'Our Relationship' Talks
Attempt repair and reconciliation?
Assess joint costs of withdrawal or reduced intimacy

↓

| Threshold: I mean it |

↓

SOCIAL PHASE
Negotiate post-dissolution state with partner
Initiate gossip/discussion in social network
Create publicly negotiable face-saving/blame-placing stories and accounts
Consider and face up to implied social network effects, if any
Call in intervention teams?

↓

| Threshold: It's now inevitable |

↓

GRAVE DRESSING PHASE
'Getting over' activity
Retrospection; reformulative post-mortem attribution
Public distribution of own version of break-up story

FIGURE 10–2 A sketch of the main phases of dissolving personal relationships.
Source: Reprinted from Duck (1982a; 16) 'A topography of relationship disengagement of dissolution', in S. W. Duck (ed.), Personal Relationships 4: Dissolving Personal Relationships. London: Academic Press. Reproduced by permission.

ways such as being sympathetic and generally understanding. More important, they can side with our version of events and our version of the partner's and the relationship's faults ('I always thought he/she was no good', 'I could never understand how you two could get along—you never seemed right for each other'). This is the *grave-dressing* phase: once the relationship is dead we have to bury it 'good and proper'—with a tombstone saying how it was born, what it was like and why it died. We have to create an account of the relationship's history and, as it were, put that somewhere so that other people can see it and, we hope, accept it. In this phase, people may strategically reinterpret their view of their partner, for example by shifting from the view of the person as 'exciting' to being 'dangerously unpredictable' or from being 'attractively reliable' to being 'boring'—exactly the same features of the person are observed, but they are given different *labels* more suited to one's present feelings about the person (Felmlee, 1995).

In breakdown of relationships as elsewhere in life, gossip plays a key role. Here it works in the social and grave-dressing phases and in a dissolving relationship we actively seek the support of members of our social networks and do so by gossiping about our partners (La Gaipa, 1982). In some instances, we look for 'arbitrators' who will help to bring us back together with our partner. In other cases, we just want someone to back up and spread around our own version of the break-up and its causes. A crucial point made by La Gaipa (1982) is that every person who leaves a relationship has to leave with 'social credit' intact for future use: that is, we cannot just get out of a relationship but we have to leave in such a way that we are not disgraced and debarred from future relationships. We must leave with a reputation for having been let down or faced with unreasonable odds or an unreasonable partner. It is socially acceptable to say 'I left because we tried hard to make it work but it wouldn't.' It is not socially acceptable to leave a relationship with the cheery but unpalatable admission: 'Well basically I'm a jilt and I got bored dangling my partner on a string so I just broke the whole thing off when it suited me.' That statement could destroy one's future credit for new relationships.

Accounts often serve the purpose of beginning the 'getting over' activity that is essential to complete the dissolution (Weber, 1983). A large part of this involves selecting an account of dissolution that refers to a fault in the partner or relationship that pre-existed the split or was even present all along (Weber, 1983). This is the 'I always thought she/he was a bit of a risk to get involved with, but I did it anyway, more fool me' story that we have all used from time to time.

However, accounts also serve another purpose: the creation of a publicly acceptable story is essential to getting over the loss of a relationship (McCall, 1982). It is insufficient having a story that we alone accept: others must also endorse it. As McCall (1982) astutely observed, part of the success of good counsellors consists in their ability to construct such stories for persons in distress about relational loss.

Putting It Right

If two people wanted to put a relationship right, then they could decide to try and make it 'redevelop'; that is, they could assume that repairing a relationship is just like acquaintance, and go through the same processes in order to regain the previous level of intimacy. This means that we have to assume that break-up of relationships is the reverse of acquaintance, and that to repair it, all we have to do is 'rewind' it. This makes some sense: developing relationships grow in intimacy whereas breaking ones decline in intimacy so perhaps we should just try to rewind the intimacy level.

However, in other ways this idea does not work. For instance, in acquaintance we get to know more about a person but in breakdown we cannot get to know less, we must just reinterpret what we already know and put it into a different framework, model, or interpretation ('Yes, he's always been kind, but then he was always after something').

I think that we need to base our ideas about repair not on our model of acquaintance but on a broader model of breakdown of relationships that takes account of principles governing formation of relationships in general. Research on relationships has begun to help us understand what precisely happens when things go wrong. By emphasizing processes of breakdown of relationships and processes of acquaintance, we have the chance now to see that there are also processes of repair. These processes do, however, address different aspects of relationships in trouble. This, I believe, also gives us the chance to be more helpful in putting things right. Bear in mind the model just covered, as you look at Figure 10–3, and you will see that it is based on proposals made earlier. There are phases to repair of relationships, and some styles work at some times and not at others (Duck, 1984a).

If the relationship is at the intrapsychic phase of dissolution, for instance, then repair should aim to reestablish liking for the partner rather than to correct behavioural faults in ourselves or our nonverbal behaviour, for instance. These latter may be more suitable if persons are in the breakdown phase instead. Liking for the partner can be reestablished or aided by means such as keeping a record, mental or physical, of the positive or pleasing behaviour of our partner rather than listing the negatives and dwelling on them in isolation (Bandura, 1977). Other methods involve redirection of attributions, that is, attempting to use more varied, and perhaps more favourable, explanations for the partner's behaviour—in brief, to make greater efforts to understand the reasons that our partner may give for what is happening in the relationship.

At other phases of dissolution, different strategies of repair are appropriate, according to this model. For instance, at the social phase, persons outside the relationship have to decide whether it is better to try to patch everything up or whether it may serve everyone's best interests to help the partners to get out of the relationship. Figure 10–2 thus indicates that the choice of strategies is between pressing the partners to stay together or helping them to save face by backing up their separate versions of the break-up. An extra possibility would

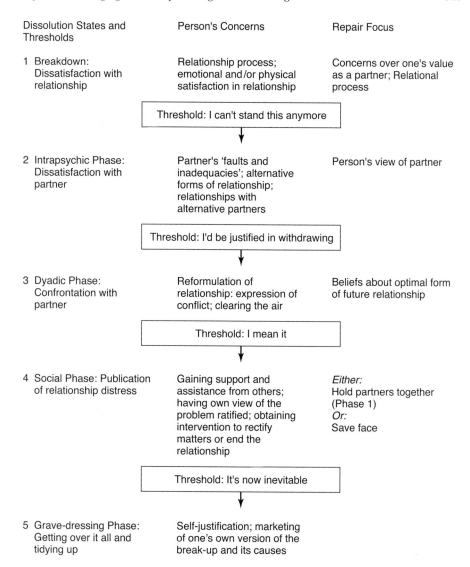

Dissolution States and Thresholds	Person's Concerns	Repair Focus
1 Breakdown: Dissatisfaction with relationship	Relationship process; emotional and/or physical satisfaction in relationship	Concerns over one's value as a partner; Relational process

Threshold: I can't stand this anymore

2 Intrapsychic Phase: Dissatisfaction with partner	Partner's 'faults and inadequacies'; alternative forms of relationship; relationships with alternative partners	Person's view of partner

Threshold: I'd be justified in withdrawing

3 Dyadic Phase: Confrontation with partner	Reformulation of relationship: expression of conflict; clearing the air	Beliefs about optimal form of future relationship

Threshold: I mean it

4 Social Phase: Publication of relationship distress	Gaining support and assistance from others; having own view of the problem ratified; obtaining intervention to rectify matters or end the relationship	*Either:* Hold partners together (Phase 1) *Or:* Save face

Threshold: It's now inevitable

5 Grave-dressing Phase: Getting over it all and tidying up	Self-justification; marketing of one's own version of the break-up and its causes	

FIGURE 10–3 A sketch of the main concerns at different phases of dissolution.
Source: Reprinted from Duck (1984: 169) 'A perspective on the repair of relationships: repair of what when?', in Duck, S. W. (ed.), Personal Relationships 5: Repairing Personal Relationships. London: Academic Press. Reproduced by permission.

be to create a story that is acceptable to both of them, such as 'It was an unworkable relationship . . . and that is nobody's fault.'

Essentially, this model proposes only three things: relationships are made up of many parts and processes, some of which 'clock in' at some points in the relationship's life and some at others; relationships can go wrong in a variety of ways; repairing of disrupted relationships will be most effective when it addresses the concerns that are most important to us at the phase of dissolution of relationships which we have reached.

The ways we change our 'stories' about a relationship provide important psychological data, and they indicate the dynamic nature of the help that outsiders have to give to relationships in trouble. Different parts of the story need to be addressed at different phases of breakdown. Is one and the same kind of intervention appropriate at all stages of a relationship's decline? Probably not. It makes more sense to look for the relative appropriateness of different intervention techniques as those dynamics unfold. There are few 'scripts' for handling break-up of relationships and many intriguing research questions surround the actual processes by which people extricate themselves (or can be helped to extricate themselves) from unwanted relationships. For example, Miller and Parks (1982) look at relationship dissolution as an influence process and show that different strategies for changing attitudes can help in dissolution. It is now a major aim in the personal relationships field to explain dissolution and repair of relationships.

REVIEW QUESTIONS

1. Define "intrapsychic," "dyadic," "social," and "grave-dressing."
2. According to Duck, what role does gossip have in the breaking-up process?
3. What are "accounts," and how do they function in the breaking-up process?
4. Why isn't the rebuilding process just the reverse of the breaking-up process?

PROBES

1. Sometimes romantic partners—especially if they're married—do try to work through their serious problems, but often the problems are so painful that they move directly from brooding to themselves to discussing with friends. How prevalent and how important do you think Duck's "dyadic" phase actually is?
2. Duck doesn't discuss the "threshold" parts of the two figures in this reading. What are they, and what is their significance?
3. Sometimes break-ups happen because of poor communication. Do you believe that a relationship ever ends because of *good* communication? Explain.

REFERENCES

1. Bandura, A. (1977). *Social Learning Theory.* Englewood Cliffs, NJ: Prentice-Hall.
2. Baxter, L. A. (1984). Trajectories of relationship disengagement, *Journal of Social and Personal Relationships*, 1: 29–48.

3. Cupach, W. R., & Spitzberg, B. Y. (1994). *The Darkside of Interpersonal Communication.* Hillsdale, NJ: Erlbaum.

4. Duck, S. (1982). A topography of relationship disengagement and dissolution, in S. W. Duck (Ed.), *Personal Relationships 4: Dissolving Personal Relationships.* London: Academic Press.

5. Duck, S. W. (1984). A perspective on the repair of personal relationships: Repair of what, when? In S. W. Duck (Ed.), *Personal Relationships 5: Repairing Personal Relationships.* London: Academic Press.

6. Duck, S. W. (1994). Stratagems, spoils, and a serpent's tooth: on the delights and dilemmas of personal relationships. In W. Cupach and B. H. Spitzberg (Eds.), *The Darkside of Interpersonal Relationships.* Hillsdale, NJ: Erlbaum.

7. Duck, S. W., & Wood, J. T. (Eds.) (1995). *Confronting Relationship Challenges, Vol. 5. Understanding Relationship Processes.* Thousand Oaks, CA: Sage.

8. Felmlee, D. H. (1995). Fatal attractions: Affection and disaffection in intimate relationships, *Journal of Social and Personal Relationships, 12,* 295–311.

9. La Gaipa, J. J. (1982). Rituals of disengagement. In S. W. Duck (Ed.), *Personal Relationships 4: Dissolving Personal Relationships.* London: Academic Press.

10. Lee, L. (1984). Sequences in separation: A framework for investigating the endings of personal (romantic) relationships, *Journal of Social and Personal Relationships, 1:* 49–74.

11. McCall, G. J. (1982). Becoming unrelated: The management of bond dissolution, in S. W. Duck (Ed.), *Personal Relationships 4: Dissolving Personal Relationships.* London: Academic Press.

12. Metts, S., Cupach, W., & Bejlovec, R. A. (1989). "I love you too much to ever start liking you": Redefining romantic relationships, *Journal of Social and Personal Relationships, 6:* 259–274.

13. Miller, G. R., & Parks, M. R., (1982). Communication in dissolving relationships. In S. W. Duck (Ed.), *Personal Relationships 4: Dissolving Personal Relationships.* London: Academic Press.

14. Orbuch, T. L. (Ed.) (1992). *Relationship Loss.* New York: Springer-Verlag.

15. Vangelisti, A. (1994). Messages that hurt. In W. R. Cupach and B. H. Spitzberg (Eds.), *The Darkside of Interpersonal Communication.* New York: Guilford, pp. 53–82.

16. Weber, A. (1983). The breakdown of relationships. Paper presented to Conference on Social Interaction and Relationships, Nags Head, North Carolina, May.

———

This reading offers a fairly complete outline of how to think about and prepare for a productive, rather than a destructive, conflict with a loved one. The authors have a long connection with *Bridges Not Walls.* When I was working on the first edition of this book in 1973, I wrote Hugh Prather asking for permission to reprint excerpts from his book *Notes to Myself.* I was struck by how his brief, journal-like notations captured several of the central points I wanted this book to make. He generously agreed to let me use some of his material, and his selections have appeared prominently in this book ever since. Now Hugh and his wife Gayle have written *A Book for Couples,* and I believe their discussion of conflict is among the best I've read.

They begin with an example of a typical everyday conflict that reveals how many issues are often buried in an argument between friends or intimates. It starts as an argument about the cat window and lasts only a couple of minutes, but the Prathers identify 17 separate issues that get raised. No wonder arguments like this create more problems than they solve!

The next important point that's made in this reading is that discussions like the one about the cat window "create the relationship's terrain." In other words, the way these discussions are carried out defines the quality of the couple's relationship. This means that *process* is vital. *How* an argument happens is more important than the outcome that emerges. Process is literally more important than product.

With their tongues firmly planted in their cheeks, the Prathers then offer seven "magic rules for ruining any discussion." You can probably recognize some of your favorite fighting moves in this list—I know I do. The point of the list is to contrast the main features of productive and destructive conflict.

Then the authors explicitly highlight the point about process that they introduced earlier. They urge you to recognize that when you are in a conflict with a person you're close to, "to agree is not the purpose." Rather, "the only allowable purpose" for this kind of discussion "is to bring you and your partner closer." This, it seems to me, is a profoundly simple but important idea. It challenges one primary assumption most of us carry into our conflicts with people we care about: that the point is to get my way, be sure the other knows how I feel, or make the other feel bad. What might happen if couples could actually internalize this idea: that the real point of our argument is to get closer?

The rest of this reading builds on this foundation. The Prathers offer five steps for preparing to argue. All of these guidelines make good sense and, taken together, as I mentioned earlier, they provide a fairly comprehensive outline of how to prepare to "do" conflict well. I won't repeat what they say here, but I do want to highlight some points.

Preparation step 2 is to "try to let go" of the issue you're thinking of raising. Although I don't think it's good to suppress genuinely felt emotions, I do believe that couples could frequently profit from applying this suggestion. I've found that it can frequently be relaxing, freeing, and empowering simply to let an irritation go.

Preparation steps 4 and 5 operationalize the Prathers' point about the only allowable purpose for a conflict. It's revealing to ask about a conflict whether "communication is your aim" rather than winning or venting. It is also helpful for me to try to be clear that "the problem is the relationship's and not your partner's."

As I read some sections of their essay I am a little frustrated by what can sound like oversimplification and naïveté. The real tough arguments are much more intense and difficult than these two authors seem to realize. But when I look again at their advice, I recognize that they understand well enough how gut-wrenching a fight with a loved one can be. They are simply convinced, as have been a great many wise people over the ages, that returning anger for anger doesn't help. Ultimately, love, which in this case means the often unromantic commitment to a relationship, is stronger than defensiveness and bitterness.

How to Resolve Issues Unmemorably

Hugh and Gayle Prather

UNFINISHED ARGUMENTS ACCUMULATE

It's not that issues don't get resolved. Indeed they are settled but settled like ketchup settles into a carpet. An uncleaned carpet can triple in weight within five years, and most relationships get so laden with undigested arguments that they collapse into a dull, angry stupor and cease to move toward their original goal.

"Albert, you've just got to install the cat window. I woke up again at 3 A.M. with Runnymede standing on my chest staring at me. I'm not getting enough alpha sleep."

"Sorry about that, Paula. I'll get to it this weekend."

"But Albert, you've been saying that for a month."

"Well, you know, honey, we could just put the cat out at night like everyone else."

"Oh, sure, and then what if he needed to get in? What if something was after him? What then?"

"What difference will the cat window make? He can still stay out all night if he wants to."

"Yes, Albert, but he can *also* get in if he *needs* to. You know, if you're not going to be a responsible pet owner, you shouldn't have a pet."

"Now there's a thought."

"I see. And I guess you don't mind breaking Gigi's heart."

"That's another thing, Paula, her name is Virginia, not Gigi. Why do we have to have a cat named Runnymede and a daughter named Gigi? Besides, I'll buy her a nice stuffed Garfield after the cat is comfortably settled in at the animal shelter."

"You know, Albert, this conversation is opening my eyes to something I've felt for a very long time."

"What's that, Paula?"

"You only care about mixed soccer. Since joining that team with the silly name you haven't been playing horsey with Gigi and you haven't been scratching Runnymede under the chin where he can't lick. You certainly pretended to like Runnymede well enough when we were dating."

"You were the one who insisted I join the team. You were the one who said it would be good for me to 'get out of the house for a change.' I like the cat. I love my daughter. But I don't want to spend my Saturdays ruining a window with a perfectly good view."

"I guess you don't really care about me either, Albert. And you can stand there calmly peeling your Snickers while wanting Runnymede to be gassed. If I didn't know how much emotion you devote to *mixed* soccer I would say you have become psychotically insensitive and unfeeling. Perhaps you should seek help."

Here Albert, proving that he is neither insensitive nor unfeeling, flings his Snickers at the window in question, grabs his soccer gear, and storms from the house, where in an afternoon match playing goalie for the Yuma Yuccas he fractures the middle three phalanges in his right hand, thus ending the question of installing anything.

EACH NEW ISSUE RESURRECTS THE OLD

We wish we could say that this dialogue was a transcript but it is a composite. If we reprinted verbatim some of the typical arguments we have heard during counseling, they would be dismissed as overwrought fiction. The large number of digressions seen here is actually commonplace and illustrates the typical residue of unsettled questions found in most long-term relationships. The difference between this and the average disagreement is that some of these words might have been thought but left unspoken. Yet the feeling of estrangement by the end of the argument would have been the same.

On this Saturday morning Paula is upset because her sleep continues to be interrupted by the cat asking to be put out. That is the sum of the issue. If the couple had sat down together instead of using the problem as a means of separating still further, they could easily have solved this one difficulty in any of a hundred different mutually acceptable ways. But a hive of older discord lies just beneath their awareness, and therefore settling just one problem in peace is harder than it would seem.

The cry of unresolved issues is strong and persistent. Any couple will feel their failure to have joined. They yearn to bridge the old gaps and fear the potential of further separation more than they welcome the opportunity to reverse the process. To bring up former differences during a discussion is not blameworthy, it is in fact a call for help, but it is mistimed.

Without realizing it—because most arguments are conducted with no deep awareness—Albert and Paula allude to seventeen other issues, none of which had to be brought up to solve *this* problem. In the order they appear, here are the questions they have left unanswered in the past, a small fraction of the total residue if you consider all the others that will be mentioned in future arguments: (1) Why has Albert's promise gone unfulfilled for a month? (2) Should the cat be left out overnight? (3) Is Albert irresponsible? (4) Should the family continue having this pet? (5) Is Albert insensitive to his daughter? (6) Should Paula continue calling Virginia "Gigi"? (7) Should the cat be renamed? (8) Would a stuffed animal sufficiently compensate? (9) Is mixed soccer affecting Albert's attitude toward his daughter and pet? (10) Does the team have a silly name? (11) Is Albert being sufficiently attentive to Paula or has he changed in some fundamental way? (12) Does Paula want Albert around the house? (13) How important is the window view to Albert's happiness? (14) Does Albert still love Paula? (15) Should Albert eat Snickers? (16) Is Albert's contact with other women on Saturdays the root cause of his, in Paula's view, wavering commitment to his family? (17) Does Albert have serious psychological problems?

As can be seen here, it is not easy for most couples to concentrate on a single issue. Nevertheless it is certainly possible and, in itself, to practice doing so will begin giving them a new kind of evidence: that within this relationship there are still grounds for unity and happiness. If one of the partners deviates from this guideline, the other should not make still another issue of this or get caught up in the irrelevant point raised, but should see instead the real desire behind the digression and treat it gently and answer it with love.

DISCUSSIONS CREATE THE RELATIONSHIP'S TERRAIN

. . . To resolve issues in the usual way is as damaging to a relationship as not resolving them at all, because the gap is not truly bridged and the unsuccessful attempt merely adds more weight to the couple's doubts about each other. In the argument over the cat window, Paula's concern about the health of her marriage surfaces, a question of far greater importance to her than how she will manage to get more sleep, and yet without fully realizing it she exacerbates this larger problem and works against her own interests. By arguing in the manner they did, this couple, as do most, merely manufactured new issues between them. Albert probably did not mean to take that hard a stand on getting rid of the cat—he may actually have wanted to keep it. And Paula did not have real doubts about Albert's mental health.

The past that drives so many relationships into the ground is built piece by piece, smallness fitted to smallness, selfishness answered with selfishness. Yet the process is largely unconscious. Each couple quickly settles into a few sad methods of conducting arguments, but seldom is the means they use thought through or the results closely examined. One person nags, the other relents. One person reasons, the other becomes silent. One person flares, the other backs down. One person cajoles, the other gives in. But where are the joy and grandeur, where is the friendship that was supposed to flourish, the companionship that through the years was to fuse an invulnerable bond, a solace and a blessing at the close of life? Instead there is a bitter and widening wedge between the two, and even the briefest of discussions contains a hundred dark echoes from the past.

No matter how entrenched are our patterns of problem solving, they can be stepped away from easily once we see that they do not serve our interests. The only interest served in most discussions is to be right. But, truly, how deep is this? Do we actually want to make our partner wrong, to defeat a friend, and slowly to defeat a friendship? It certainly may feel that way. Caught up once again in the emotions of a disagreement, we stride doggedly toward our usual means of concluding every argument: adamant silence, crushing logic, patronizing practicality, collapsed crying, quelling anger, martyred acquiescence, loveless humor, sulking retreat.

These postures and a thousand more are attempts to prove a point other than love, and as with all endeavors to show up one's partner, the friendship itself is the victim, because the friendship becomes a mere tool, a means of making the other person feel guilty. The love our partner has for us is now seen as leverage, and in our quiet or noisy way we set about making the relationship a shambles, not realizing that we ourselves are part of the wreckage.

THE MAGIC RULES FOR RUINING ANY DISCUSSION

. . . The dialogue with which we began this [reading] incorporates a few of but not all the rules for disastrous communication—yet only one or two are needed to neutralize the best of intentions. Follow these guidelines, even a little sloppily, and you are guaranteed a miserable time:

1. *Bring the matter up when at least one of you is angry.*
   Variations: Bring it up when nothing can be done about it (in the middle of the night; right before guests are due; when one of you is in the shower). Bring it up when concentration is impossible (while driving to a meeting with the IRS; while watching the one TV program you both agree on; while your spouse is balancing the checkbook).
2. *Be as personal as possible when setting forth the problem.*
   Variations: Know the answer before you ask the question. While describing the issue, use an accusatory tone. Begin by implying who, as usual, is to blame.
3. *Concentrate on getting what you want.*
   Variations: Overwhelm your partner's position before he or she can muster a defense (be very emotional; call in past favors; be impeccably reasonable). Impress on your partner what you need and what he or she must do without. If you begin losing ground, jockey for position.

4. *Instead of listening, think only of what you will say next.*
   Variations: Do other things while your partner is talking. Forget where your partner left off. In other words, listen with all the interest you would give a bathroom exhaust fan.

5. *Correct anything your partner says about you.*
   Variations: Each time your partner gives an example of your behavior, cite a worse example of his or hers. Repeat "That's not what I said" often. Do not accept anything your partner says at face value (point out exceptions; point out inaccuracies in facts and in grammar).

6. *Mention anything from the past that has a chance of making your partner defensive.*
   Variations: Make allusions to your partner's sexual performance. Remind your husband of his mother's faults. Compare what your wife does to what other women do, and after she complains, say, "I didn't mean it that way."

7. *End by saying something that will never be forgotten.*
   Variations: Do something that proves you are a madman. Let your parting display proclaim that no exposure of your partner could be amply revealing, no characterization too profane, no consequence sufficiently wretched. At least leave the impression you are a little put out.

TO AGREE IS NOT THE PURPOSE

All couples believe they know how to hold a discussion, and yet it is not an exaggeration to say that in most long-term relationships there has rarely been one wholly successful argument. Obviously they are filled with disagreements that end in agreements, but when these are examined, it can be seen that at least a small patch of reservation had to be overlooked in order for accord to be reached.

We believe this is simply how differences are settled, and so even though we sense that our partner is still in conflict, we barge ahead with our newly won concession, thinking the bad moment will pass. Later it becomes painfully clear that it has not and we judge our partner irresolute. Or if we are the one who complied, we count our little sacrifice dear and wait for reparation—which never comes or is never quite adequate, and we cannot understand why our partner feels such little gratitude.

The aim of most arguments is to reach outward agreement. Until that is replaced with a desire for friendship, varying degrees of alienation will be the only lasting outcome. Couples quickly develop a sense of helplessness over the pattern that their discussions have fallen into. They believe they are sincerely attempting to break out of it and are simply failing. They try different responses, going from shouting to silence, from interminable talking to walking out of the room, from considering each point raised to sticking tenaciously to one point, but nothing they do seems to alter the usual unhappy ending.

There is no behavioral formula to reversing the habitual course of an argument. It requires a shift in attitude, not in actions, even though actions will modify in the process. No more is needed than one partner's absolute clarity about the purpose of the argument. This is not easy but it is simple. Therefore let us look again at what the aim should be. . . .

The only allowable purpose for a discussion is to bring you and your partner closer. Minds must come together to decide instead of backing away in order to apply pressure. How is this possible, given the fact that you and your partner are deeply selfish? Fortunately, the selfishness is compartmentalized and your hearts remain unaffected. You need not eliminate it; merely bypass it because you recognize that it is not in your interests to be selfish. To the ego, this concept is insane because it sees no value in love. But love is in your interests because you *are* love, or at least part of you is, and thus each discussion is a way of moving into your real self.

A little time is obviously needed to see one's true interests. If you rush into a discussion you will operate from your insensitivity by habit and aim for a prize your heart cares nothing about. Do not kid yourself. You *do* know whether the discussion is ending with the two of you feeling closer. The selfish part of your mind will tell you that the little sadness and sense of distance you may now feel was a small price to pay for the concession you won or the point you made. Or it will argue that it was all unavoidable. This may happen many times before you begin reversing your ordinary way of participating. This transition is an important stage of growth and entails looking more and more carefully at selfish impulses and their aftermath. Is how you feel really worth it? Was the way it went truly unavoidable?

Thus you will come to see the result you want, and this deeper recognition will begin to eclipse your pettiness in the midst of an argument. Gradually you will catch the mistakes sooner, and eventually you will learn to avoid them from the start. For you *do* want these times of deciding to warm your hearts and lighten your steps. So persist in the guidelines we will give, and these little defeats to your relationship will slowly give way to friendship.

We are so used to thinking of a discussion as a symbol of separation that it can often be helpful to change its form enough that something new will appear to be happening and thus the old mind set is undercut. To take the usual process, break it into steps and put them in order is usually all that is needed to accomplish this.

An issue could be said to pass through five stages in reaching resolution. First, it must be thought of by at least one of the partners as an issue. Second, a moment is chosen to bring the matter up. Third, a decision is made as to the manner in which it will be presented. Fourth, there is an exchange of thoughts and feelings. And fifth, the discussion is concluded.

Most couples give very little thought to the first three stages. They simply find themselves in the thick of a so-called spontaneous argument and no one is certain at what point it began. Obviously you must become more conscious of the subjects you bring up so carelessly. Any sign of fear over what you are about to say is a very useful indicator. If you see you have a question about whether to say it, let this be your cue to break these preliminary choices into conscious steps. Do not begrudge the time, remember instead how strongly you want to begin building a real friendship.

FIVE STEPS IN PREPARING TO ARGUE

First, you might ask yourself if the issue you are thinking of is actually a present issue or merely one you have been reminded of. In other words, be certain this is currently a problem and not one the relationship may already be on its way to solving. Many people habitually rake over their marriage for signs of imperfection and naturally they find a great many, but it can be far more disrupting to friendship to be constantly questioning and comparing than to wait to see if the problem continues in any severe way. Meanwhile, enjoy what is already between you without telling yourself what this is. . . .

If the issue is unquestionably a present one, the second step you might try is to let go of it. Letting go is not "better," but it is an option that current values tend to underrate. However, it must be accomplished thoroughly and honestly or the issue will grow like mold in a dark unseen place. If it is done consciously dismissal is not denial. Essentially it entails examining in detail what you do not like and then making a deliberate effort to identify with another part of you that never "takes issue" with any living thing, that is still and at ease, that acts only from peace. . . .

If a couple espouses world energy consciousness or is on a tight budget, for one of the partners to habitually leave the hot water running, not turn off lights, or keep the refrigerator door open may be grating or even shocking to the other partner. Yet the spectacle of someone wasting energy and money is *not* grating or shocking. The interpretation we assign it, and not the act itself, determines the emotions we feel. Jordan, age two, is "shockingly irresponsible." He has even been known (yesterday, in fact) to flush a toilet five times in a row and then run to tell his big brother about the accomplishment. "John, I flush, I flush!" "That's nice." said John, blatantly contributing to the delinquency of a minor. The reason Jordan didn't tell his father (who is the family's conscience in these matters) was that he was the very one who kept showing him how it was done, thereby encouraging him to waste over fifteen gallons of water (plus six more his father used researching that figure). . . .

So here we have four reactions issuing from four interpretations: pride from the father, support from the seven-year-old, excitement from the two-year-old and, having no originality, curiosity from the cat. Clearly no uniform effect was produced by an external and unreachable cause. How then might you let go of your reaction to your spouse's wasteful habits in lieu of bringing it up one more time? Certainly you would not try dishonestly to convince yourself that the practice was not costing money or energy. Or that it did not really matter to you. Neither would you attempt to assign some motive to your partner's acts that you did not believe, such as not knowing any better or really trying hard but being unable to stop. Dishonesty does not end an unhappy line of thought. That is why reinterpretation is generally not effective. . . .

If in your moment of consideration you are able to see these facts deeply enough, you may open your eyes to your partner's innocence and no longer feel compelled to understand why he or she does these things. But if after making the attempt to free your mind you see that you have not let the issue go, then perhaps to bring it up would be the preferable course, for undoubtedly that is better than storing anger or fear. . . .

The third step is to consider if this is the time. If you feel an urge to bring it up quickly, be very alert to anger. Your heart is willing to wait but your ego is not, especially if it senses an opportunity to strike back. The ego is merely our love of misery, of withdrawal and loneliness, and it can feel like our own deep impulse even though it exists on the most superficial level of the mind.

For too long now our relationships have been jerked around by our own lack of awareness. There is more to your mind than selfishness. So be still a moment and let peace arise from you. Is this the time? A simple question. There need not be great soul-searching and hand-wringing over it. If your partner has just done something and this is the issue, clearly he or she is likely to be more defensive if instantly called on it. If your partner is not in a particularly happy frame of mind, is hostile, worried or depressed, a more receptive state will surely come and nothing is lost by waiting. Is this the time? Merely look and know the answer. The urge to attack when you are angry is very strong, but if you will allow yourself time to reflect on your genuine feelings, this will do more to relieve your frustration.

The fourth step is to be certain that communication is your aim. Trying to get someone to change is not communication because you have already decided what change is needed. Your partner is therefore left with nothing to say and will definitely feel your unwillingness to consider, to listen, to appreciate. So before you speak take time to hear your heart.

You are not two advocates arguing a case. You are interested in joining, not in prevailing. You are like the directors of a business you both love coming together to help it over a difficult situation. You don't care from whose lips the solution comes. You welcome the *answer.* To this end what are you willing to do if your partner becomes defensive? Are you prepared, and have you prepared, to carry through your love of the relationship? . . .

The final point to consider is whether you are clear that the problem is the relationship's and not your partner's. In our example the problem was not Paula's, because her lack of sleep was affecting Albert also. One person's jealousy, appetite, hypersensitivity, frigidity, phobia or any other characteristic that has become an issue cannot successfully be viewed as more one's responsibility than the other's because friendship is always a mutual sharing of all burdens. . . .

You must understand that unless you make a specific effort to see through the fallacy, you *will* go into a discussion thinking one of you is more to blame than the other, and this will make it very hard to listen and be open. Learn to treat every issue as an impersonal and neutral enemy and to close ranks against it. An addiction, for example, can be viewed as you would a hurricane or a deluge—you need each other's help to survive the storm. Our dog, Sunny Sunshine Pumpkin Prather (whose very name is a masterpiece of family compromise), gets sprayed by a skunk about once a month and the smell is everyone's problem. What good would it do to blame the dog? And yet we have seen other families get angry at their dog "for being so stupid." . . .

These preliminary steps, which should only take an instant or two to complete, will at least make it possible for a discussion to begin with some chance of success. Now you are ready for a *real* argument, one in which your minds can join rather than separate.

REVIEW QUESTIONS

1. What point are the Prathers making by listing 17 issues that were brought up in the argument between Albert and Paula?
2. What do the authors mean when they say that discussions "create the relationship's terrain"?
3. Paraphrase this statement: "The only allowable purpose for a discussion is to bring you and your partner closer." Do you agree or disagree with it? Explain.
4. What do the authors mean when they say that you should "learn to treat every issue as an impersonal and neutral enemy and to close ranks against it"?
5. What keeps the "protect your gains" step from being selfish?

PROBES

1. What alternative do the authors offer to "being right" in a conflict?
2. What general principle or principles are violated by the seven "magic rules for ruining any discussion"? In other words, what general attitudes make these moves destructive?
3. Which of the five steps for preparing to argue do you *least* often follow? What does that fact tell you about your way of "doing" conflict?
4. A fundamental, perhaps even a radically different, perspective or point of view is behind just about everything the Prathers say about "resolving issues unmemorably." By "different," I mean different from the attitude we normally carry into a conflict. How would you describe this alternative point of view or perspective?

This final reading in the conflict chapter adds an important idea to the others. Each of the other essays provides ways to help people cope with the disagreements that we experience every day. Lederach goes beyond all these other helpful materials to explain how people in conflict can find ways to *transform* conflict situations.

The difference between "conflict management" or "conflict resolution" and "conflict *transformation*" is that, when transformation happens, changes are made in the human system (couple, family, business organization) that enhance the future likelihood of healthy justice. In other words, when efforts are focused on "conflict resolution," they are considered successful when the specific problem is solved, even though the system that spawned it may still be unhealthy. When the goal is simply "conflict management," success means dealing with the conflict in ways that minimize friction or interpersonal difficulties without necessarily changing the conditions that led to them. Conflict transformation has some larger goals. The people who work on conflict from a transformational frame always have an eye toward larger issues of healthy relationships, productive systems, and communities marked by justice. As Lederach notes, many of these transformational efforts are grounded in faith traditions, including his own Mennonite tradition or parts of the Roman Catholic church. The main benefit of this approach is that, when it works, it can change (transform) the relationship, organization, or family into a system marked by mutual respect and creative collaboration, one that is insulated against future destructive clashes.

Lederach uses his entire book to develop his ideas, and this reading excerpts just three of his most important suggestions. He presents them as "capacities" that people can develop in order to transform conflict situations.

The first is the capacity to "pose the energies of conflict as dilemmas." Another way to put this idea is to substitute "both and" thinking for "either or" thinking. Or you can relate this idea to my discussion of "tensionality" in Chapter 2 and to Karen Zediker's and my discussion of "tensionality" in Chapter 12. The idea is to be able to think of the "sides" of a conflict as both/all-possible. Should a couple spend free weekend time on sports or shopping? Should a work group adopt the most creative solution or the least expensive one? Lederach encourages people to shift from "either/or" to "both/and" thinking.

The second is the capacity to embrace complexity. Like communication generally, which is always continuous and complex, conflict situations often get oversimplified. When people reach their tolerance for complexity, they often respond to leaving the situation, trying to find a quick fix, or ignoring some parts of the situation. Lederach urges people in conflict to make the "enemy" of complexity your "friend."

The third is the capacity to "hear and engage the voices of identity." Conflicts often appear to be about issues of content—which option is best, what "the truth" is, who actually said what. But identities, rather than content issues, are at the root of many, if not most, conflicts. The most difficult sticking points have to do with perceptions of disrespect, authority, and power. Parties don't like how they're being treated. They have different views of themselves—"I'm in charge here" "No, I am"—or conflicting definitions of each other—"You're selfish" "You're being a coward." As Karen, Saskia, and I explain in the first reading of Chapter 3, all communication involves the negotiation of identities. And when conflict occurs, it almost always centrally involves problems with this identity-negotiation process. Lederach offers some specific suggestions about how to use this insight transformationally.

His final point is that conflict management, especially if it is aimed at transformation, is not a mechanical, technique-oriented process. There are many ways to help conflict create productive changes in families, relationships, and organizations. I hope you'll use this reading to broaden your understanding of what is possible when you're dealing with conflicts. Conflict "management" is very important and helpful. And conflict "transformation" can be even better.

Conflict Transformation

John Paul Lederach

Conflict *resolution* . . . conflict *management* . . . but conflict *transformation*?

I began using the term *conflict transformation* in the 1980s, after intensive experience in Central America caused me to reexamine the language of the field. When I arrived there my vocabulary was filled with the usual terminology of conflict resolution and management. I soon found, though, that my Latin colleagues had questions, even suspicions, about what was meant by such concepts. For them, *resolution* carried with it a danger of co-optation, an attempt to get rid of conflict when people were raising important and legitimate issues. It was not clear that *resolution* left room for advocacy. In their experience, quick solutions to deep social-political problems usually meant lots of good words but no real change. "Conflicts happen for a reason," they would say. "Is this *resolution* idea just another way to cover up the changes that are really needed?"

Their concerns were consistent with my own experience and perspective. My deepest sense of vocation, and the framework that informs much of this book, arises from a faith context that is grounded in an Anabaptist/Mennonite religious-ethical framework. This perspective understands peace as embedded in justice. It emphasizes the importance of building right relationships and social structures through a radical respect for human rights and life. It advocates nonviolence as a way of life and work.

So the concerns of my Latin colleagues hit home. In my work of helping to find constructive responses to violent conflict in Central America and elsewhere, I became increasingly convinced that much of what I was doing was seeking constructive change. "Conflict transformation" seemed to convey this meaning better than conflict *resolution* or *management*.

Conflict is normal in human relationships, and conflict is a motor of change.

In the 1990s, when I helped found the Conflict Transformation Program at Eastern Mennonite University (EMU), we had extensive debates about titles and terms. *Resolution* was better known and was widely accepted in mainstream academic and political circles. *Transformation* seemed too value-laden for some, too idealistic for others, and too airy-fairy and new-age for still others. In the end, we stuck with the transformation terminology. We believed it was accurate and scientifically sound and that it provided a clear vision.

For me, *conflict transformation* is accurate because I am engaged in constructive change efforts that include, and go beyond, the resolution of specific problems. It is scientifically sound language because it is based on two verifiable realities: conflict is normal in human relationships, and conflict is a motor of change. *Transformation* provides a clear and important vision because it brings into focus the horizon toward which we journey—the building of healthy relationships and communities, locally and globally. This goal requires real change in our current ways of relating.

But the question remains, what does *transformation* really mean?

Over the past decade or so, the terminology of transformation has become increasingly common in both practitioner and academic circles. There are transformational approaches in mediation as well as in the broader discipline of peace and conflict studies. In fact, I am now part of two graduate academic programs that use this terminology, the Joan B. Kroc Institute for International Peace Studies at Notre Dame and the Conflict Transformation Program at EMU. In spite of this, conflict transformation is not as yet a school of thought. I do believe that conflict transformation is a comprehensive orientation or framework that ultimately may require a fundamental change in our way of thinking.

DEVELOPING OUR CAPACITIES

As I have moved from thinking conceptually about conflict transformation to applying it, I have found it important to cultivate [several] personal practices. Three of these practices follow.

Develop the Capacity to Pose the Energies of Conflict as Dilemmas

I tend to link two ideas with the phrases "and at the same time." This is not just a quirk in my writing; it has become part of my way of thinking and formulating perspective. It reflects my effort to shift my thinking from an either/or to a both/and frame of reference. This is what I would call the art and discipline of posing conflicts as dilemmas.

This approach initially emerged for me in settings of deeply rooted, violent conflict. Very difficult issues were demanding immediate attention and choices. The decisions we faced seemed to pose outright contradictions as framed by the people involved and even by ourselves as practitioners. For example, those of us working in relief and aid agencies in Somalia in the early 1990s struggled daily with overwhelming decisions in the middle of a disastrous war, drought, and famine. We were faced with choices about where to put our energies and responses when none of the apparent options seemed adequate. Should we send in food and relief aid even though we knew armed groups took advantage of it to continue the war, which was itself one of the key reasons why a famine existed and relief was needed? Or should we not send food, in order to avoid unintentionally contributing to the fighting, and instead work on peace initiatives, knowing that we would feel helpless about the enormous humanitarian plight? Far too often the way we posed our questions limited our strategies.

When we changed our way of framing questions to "both and," our thinking shifted. We learned to recognize the legitimacy of different, but not incompatible, goals and energies within the conflict setting. Rather than accepting a frame of reference that placed our situation as choosing between competing energies, we reframed the questions to hold both at the same time. How can we build capacities for peace in this setting *and at the same time* create responsive mechanisms for the delivery of humanitarian aid? The very formulation of the question creates a capacity to recognize the underlying energies and to develop integrative processes and responses that hold them together.

When we embrace dilemmas and paradoxes, there is the possibility that in conflict we are not dealing with outright incompatibilities. Rather, we are faced with recognizing and responding to different but interdependent aspects of a complex situation. We are not able to handle complexity well if we understand our choices in rigid either/or and contradictory terms. Complexity requires that we develop the capacity to identify the key energies in a situation and hold them up together as *interdependent goals.*

A simple formula provides us entry into the world of dilemmas and paradoxes. Its application in real time and real-life situations requires a great deal of discipline, repetition, and creativity. The formula is this: How can we address "A" and at the same time build "B"?

The ability to position situations as dilemmas, the capacity to live with apparent contradictions and paradoxes, lies at the heart of transformation. The art of dilemma-posing creates a simple way to see the bigger picture and to move us toward specific action.

Dilemmas imply complexity. This view suggests the ability to live with and to see the value of complexity. Further, it requires us to resist the push to resolve everything rationally into neat, logically consistent packages. This suggests another capacity that often needs to be cultivated.

Develop a Capacity to Make Complexity a Friend, Not a Foe

In conflicts, especially when there has been a long history of patterns and episodes that were not constructively addressed, people feel overwhelmed. You hear phrases like, "This situation is such a mess. It is just too complicated. There are too many things going on to even try to explain it." These are the signs and voices of complexity raising its head. The challenge to conflict transformation is how to make complexity a friend rather than a foe.

The capacity to live with apparent contradictions and paradoxes lies at the heart of transformation.

At times of escalated conflict, complexity describes a situation in which we feel forced to live with multiple and competing frames of reference about what things mean. We are faced with a lot happening at multiple levels between different sets of people, all at the same time. Complexity suggests multiplicity and simultaneity. By its very nature, complexity in conflict creates an atmosphere of rising ambiguity and uncertainty. Things are not clear. We feel insecure about the meaning of all that is happening, we are not sure where it is going, and we feel as if we have little or no control over what happens. No wonder we see complexity as a foe creating an interminable headache. No wonder we often believe that simplifying the issues or resolving the contradictions will bring remedy.

We all have a certain tolerance for complexity, but we all reach our point of saturation. When saturated, some of us cope by leaving, by getting out. Others of us stay but try to find a quick fix or solution that makes the complexity go away. Still others of us try to reduce the impact by ignoring the multiple meanings and faces. We settle on a single explanation about what is going on, then hold onto it doggedly and rigidly. Complexity becomes the enemy.

Paradoxically, as Abraham Lincoln observed, "The only way to truly get rid of an enemy is to make him your friend." While complexity can create a sense that there is too much to consider, it also provides untold possibilities for building desired and constructive change. One of the great advantages of complexity is that change is not tied exclusively to one thing, one action, one option. In fact, complexity can create the feeling of being a kid in a candy store: we are not limited by having too few options but by our own inability to experience the wide range of potentials afforded by all the available choices.

The key to this practice is to trust and pursue but never to be rigid. First, we must trust the capacity of systems to generate options and avenues for change and moving forward. Second, we must pursue those that appear to hold the greatest promise for constructive change. Third, we must not lock rigidly onto one idea or avenue.

Complexity often brings a multiplicity of options to the surface. If we pay careful attention to those options, we can often create new ways to look at old patterns.

Develop a Capacity to Hear and Engage the Voices of Identity

I have repeatedly suggested that we should look for and see the patterns in the context underpinning the presenting situation, in the epicenter of the conflict. But what do we look and listen for? I have consistently found that most essential is hearing and engaging the struggling, sometimes lost, voices of identity within the loud static of the conflictive environment. In my experience, issues of identity are at the root of most conflicts. Thus a capacity to understand and respect the role of identity is essential to understanding the epicenter of conflict.

Issues of identity are fundamental in protecting a sense of self and group survival, and they become particularly important during conflicts. Identity shapes and moves an expression of conflict, often in terms of deeply felt demands and preferred outcomes, to presenting issues. At the deepest level, identity is lodged in the narratives of how people see themselves, who they are, where they have come from, and what they fear they will become or lose. Thus, identity is deeply rooted in a person's or a group's sense of how that person or group is in relationship with others and what effect that relationship has on its participants' sense of self and group. Identity matters are fundamental to conflict, yet they are rarely explicitly addressed in the conflict.

Identity is not a rigid, static phenomenon. Rather, identity is dynamic and under constant definition and redefinition, especially during times of conflict. Identity is also best understood as relational. If we had no other color in the world than the color blue, then blue would be colorless. To distinguish blue we need a matrix of colors; then "blue" in relationship has identity and makes sense.

This creates a challenge for a transformational process: how do we create spaces and processes that encourage people to address and articulate a positive sense of identity in relationship to other people and groups, but not in reaction to them? In the middle of conflict, when people are often filled with great fears and unknowns, the challenge is to lower the level of reactivity and blame, while at the same time increasing a capacity to express a clear sense of self and place.

What are the disciplines that make such a practice possible?

First, we need to develop a capacity to see and hear "identity" when it appears. Be attentive to language, metaphors, and expressions that signal the distresses of identity. Sometimes these are vague: "Five years ago, not one teacher in this school would have thought of proposing such a course. What are we coming to?" Sometimes it is named by "insider" metaphor and language: "The Pioneer Street people no longer even have a voice in this church." (Pioneer Street is where the church is located, but it is also the inside label for the first-generation members of the church.) Sometimes it is explicit and mobilized: "The very survival of the Hmong community is under threat by the actions of this Police Chief." In all cases, pay attention to the concern behind the voice. It is an appeal to a sense of self, to identity, and to how a relationship is being experienced and defined. It is an appeal to take the discourse from the content to the core. You cannot touch the epicenter if you do not hear the voice. The first step: be attentive to the voice of identity.

Second, move toward, not away from, the appeals to identity. Acknowledge that the conflict requires us to address our understandings of identity and relationship. This does not take the place of a process which needs to be designed to address the specific issues and content that surfaced the conflict. Both processes are needed. Generating solutions to specific problems can alleviate anxiety temporarily, but it rarely addresses deeper identity and relational concerns directly.

Processes designed to explore these deeper issues will need to have a goal of creating spaces for exchange and dialogue, rather than the goal of creating an immediate negotiated solution. Also, in working with identity-based concerns it is important not to assume that the work is primarily that of direct inter-identity exchange. Often the most critical parts of the process are the cultivation of internal, self, or intra-group spaces, where safe and deep reflection about the nature of the situation, responsibility, hopes, and fears can be pursued.

Pushing inappropriately for inter-identity exchange without a framework of preparation and adequate support can be counterproductive and even destructive. When working with identity, I can suggest three guiding principles that should characterize the process: honesty, iterative learning, and appropriate exchange.

Honesty can never be forced. We can, however, work toward the creation of process and spaces where people feel safe enough to be deeply honest with themselves and with others about their fears and hopes, hurts and responsibilities. Cycles and episodes of escalated conflict create and reinforce an environment of insecurity that threatens identity. In turn, a threat to identity creates a tendency toward self-protection, which, while not the enemy of honesty, tends to diminish self-reflective honesty in favor of other-reflective honesty: I see clearly and honestly what is wrong with *you*. I cannot see so clearly and honestly my own responsibility. Deep honesty comes hand in hand with safety and trust. Give constant attention to how the processes are creating and assuring spaces with these characteristics.

The phrase *"iterative learning"* suggests an idea of going around. To iterate is to repeat. It requires rounds of interaction. This is especially true for issues of identity.

> Try never to ignore or talk away someone's perception. Instead, try to understand where it is rooted.

The questions "Who am I?" and "Who are we?" are foundational for understanding life and community. Yet speaking deeply about self, group, and relationship is never easy or elemental. Nor is identity rigid and fixed. Understanding and defining identity requires rounds of interaction and inner action. The development, negotiation, and definition of identity require processes of interaction with others, as well as inner reflection about self. The whole undertaking is a learning process. And the pace of learning can be very different from one person to the next. This is important because we must recognize that identity work is not a one-time decision-making process. It is an iterative process of learning, and it is done in relationship to others.

Those who support or facilitate transformational processes therefore need to think about how to create multiple forums for addressing identity. Too often we think of the transaction as a one-time event that deals with identity and then is over. Instead, it is better to see process as a platform that permits ongoing learning about self and other, while at the same time pursuing decisions about particular issues that symbolize the deeper negotiations surrounding identity. This is why, for example, conflict transformation views the dispute over a parade in

Belfast or Portadown, Northern Ireland, as simultaneously an issue requiring specific decisions related to that episode and an iterative platform to explore and shape identities of people with shared childhoods and geographic horizons. You can use the episodic issue as an opportunity to explore identity, but you cannot use the limited time and scope of the decision-making process about a specific issue as an adequate mechanism for addressing identity concerns.

As we seek appropriate forms of interaction or exchange, we can easily fall into a technique-oriented approach toward dialogue and assume that it can only happen in direct face-to-face processes. Appropriate exchange suggests there are many ways that learning and deepening understanding about identity and relationship can happen. We need not fall prey to "process" overload that suggests "dialogue-as-talk" is the only path to understanding. In deep identity work the opposite may be true. Appropriate exchange may include dialogue through music, the arts, rituals, dialogue-as-sport, fun and laughter, and dialogue-as-shared-work to preserve old city centers or parks. All of these may have greater avenues for learning and understanding than talk can possibly provide. The key to this capacity is an ability to recognize opportunity and to design response processes with innovation and creativity.

Finally, we need to be attentive to people's perceptions of how identity is linked to power and to the systems and structures which organize and govern their relationships. This is particularly important for people who feel their identity has historically been eroded, marginalized, or under deep threat. Here change processes must address the ways in which structural relationships symbolize and represent the perceptions. The key: try never to ignore or talk away someone's perception. Instead, try to understand where it is rooted. Never propose or tinker with structural arrangements as a tactic to avoid the deeper perception. When dealing with identity-based concerns encourage participants to be honest as they look at and address systemic changes, which they need in order to assure them both respect and access to the structures.

Practices such as these are not natural skills for many of us. They take commitment and discipline, but when developed they increase our capacity to think and respond transformatively to conflict.

REVIEW QUESTIONS

1. Explain the difference between conflict management or resolution and conflict transformation.
2. Explain the connection between the idea of "tensionality" in the Zediker-Stewart reading in Chapter 12 and the first "capacity" in this reading.
3. What does it mean to "make the enemy of complexity your friend"?
4. Explain the connection between the Stewart-Zediker-Witteborn reading in Chapter 3 and the third "capacity" in this reading.
5. What does it mean to "create multiple forums for addressing identity"?

PROBES

1. How do you think "the capacity to pose the energies of conflict as dilemmas" can actually help people cope with a conflict? What practical benefit can this capacity generate?
2. Recall the last conflict you experienced. Identify the identity issues that it involved. How did the parties disagree about "How I see myself, How I see you, and How I see you seeing me"?
3. In his discussion of the third capacity, Lederach writes, "I see clearly and honestly what is wrong with *you*. I cannot see so clearly and honestly my own responsibility." Explain.

CHAPTER 11

Bridging Cultural Differences

ultural differences have created human problems since recorded history began. Sometimes it seems as if the strongest tendency we humans have inherited from our non-human animal forebears is fear and hatred of anybody different from us. So it's definitely a challenge to bridge cultural differences.

The four readings in this chapter approach this problem generally and specifically. The first two readings analyze general cultural differences and show how it's possible to connect with people, even when they're not all "like us." The last two readings are specific discussions of two of the most difficult cultural differences to bridge: religion and race or ethnicity. One of these is written by an Asian woman about her white husband and the second is written by a female African-American communication teacher and scholar about contacts with white women.

For more than 25 years, educational psychologist David Johnson has been helping teachers and schools in North America, Central America, Europe, Africa, Asia, the Middle East, and the Pacific Rim take advantage of the benefits of collaborative and cooperative learning. One of the fruits of his labor is his book *Reaching Out: Interpersonal Effectiveness and Self-Actualization,* from which I've taken the next reading. This is a basic introduction to the attitudes and skills of connecting with people who are different from you.

Johnson begins with the point that although globalization is a fact that is making diversity among acquaintances, classmates, co-workers, and neighbors increasingly inevitable, it is in some ways not "natural" for humans to want to get along with diverse others. For 200,000 years, as he puts it, humans lived in small hunting and gathering groups, interacting infrequently with others. But today we are regularly thrown together with cultural strangers. Both men and women in what have traditionally been single-sex jobs (firefighter, nurse, mail carrier, parking checker) are having to team with opposite-sex colleagues. Older and younger workers are forced to collaborate, and blacks, Latinos, Asians, whites, Arabs, Pacific Islanders, and members of other ethnic groups are thrown together with those with different, and sometimes competing, identities.

The chapter this reading was taken from explains six steps for building relationships with diverse peers, and this excerpt discusses four of the six: accept yourself, lower barriers, recognize that diversity is a valuable resource, and work to clarify misunderstandings. The first step echoes some of what is in the readings about self-awareness in Chapter 3. Johnson encourages you to reflect on your own identity, which can be subdivided into your self-schema, gender identity, and ethnic identity, as a first step toward connecting effectively with people different from you.

Then he offers some suggestions about lowering three barriers: prejudice, the tendency to blame the victim, and cultural conflict. Prejudice—manifested in ethnocentrism, stereotyping, or discrimination—can be a major hurdle, and Johnson explains four specific ways to overcome it.

Blaming the victim occurs when people "attribute the cause of discrimination or misfortune to the personal characteristics and actions of the victim." In this section, Johnson reviews some of the information about external and internal attributions that is discussed by Trenholm and Jensen in Chapter 5, and shows how careful attributions can enhance your experience. Culture clash is the third barrier Johnson explains.

The next section of the reading explains some specific ways in which diversity can be openly recognized and genuinely valued. Johnson suggests four steps that can help lead toward profitable collaboration among diverse people.

The final section of this reading highlights the importance of clarifying miscommunications. Johnson could have said a great deal more here than he does, but this section does remind us how language sensitivity and a developed awareness of stylistic differences among diverse communicators can help people deal effectively with those who are different from themselves. Johnson ends this section with seven specific suggestions, and the first is, "Use all the communication skills discussed in this book." Even though "this book" he was talking about was *Reaching Out,* you can interpret it as a reference to *Bridges Not Walls.* As Johnson recognizes, the skills developed in all 16 chapters of this book can be brought to bear on the project of improving relationships among diverse people.

You may have already thought through the ideas that Johnson discusses here. But if you haven't (or if you have, and would still appreciate a reminder), this is an excellent introduction to the frame of mind and some of the specific skills that are needed in order to bridge differences between you and people you might initially think of as "strangers."

Building Relationships with Diverse Others

David W. Johnson

INTRODUCTION

We live in one world. The problems that face each person, each community, each country cannot be solved without global cooperation and joint action. Economically, for example, there has been a globalization of business reflected in the increase in multinational companies, coproduction agreements, and offshore operations. As globalization becomes the norm, more and more companies must translate their local and national perspectives into a world view. Companies that are staffed by individuals skilled in building relationships with diverse peers have an advantage in the global market.

Interacting effectively with peers from different cultures, ethnic groups, social classes, and historical backgrounds does not come naturally. For 200,000 years humans lived in small hunting and gathering groups, interacting only infrequently with other nearby small groups. Today we are required to communicate effectively with people cross-culturally, through the generations, among races, between genders, and across those subtle but pervasive barriers of class. No wonder this feels uncomfortable—we have never been required to do it before!

Diversity among your acquaintances, classmates, co-workers, neighbors, and friends is increasingly inevitable. North America, Europe, and many other parts of the world are becoming more and more diverse in terms of culture, ethnicity, religion, age, physical qualities, and gender. You will be expected to interact effectively with people with a wide variety of characteristics and from a wide variety of backgrounds. In order to build relationships with diverse peers, you must

1. Accept yourself.
2. Lower the barriers to building relationships with diverse peers.
3. Recognize that diversity exists and is a valuable resource. . . .
4. Clarify misunderstandings.

ACCEPTING YOURSELF

If I am not for myself, who will be for me? But if I am only for myself, what am I?

—The Talmud

Two basic human needs are to

1. Join with others in a cooperative effort to achieve something great.
2. Be a unique and separate individual who is valued and respected in one's own right.

In order to meet this second need, you must accept yourself as you are and build a distinct image of yourself as a certain kind of person who has an identity differentiated and discernible from others. The greater your self-acceptance, the more stable and integrated your personal identity. Building a coherent, stable, and integrated identity that summarizes who you are as a separate, autonomous, and unique individual is the first step in building constructive relationships with diverse peers.

The Person You Think You Are

What kind of person are you? How would you describe yourself to someone who does not know you? Would your description be disjointed and contradictory, or would it be organized and consistent? Would it change from day to day, or would it stay the same over a period of years? Do you like yourself, or do you feel a basic sense of shame and contempt when you think of yourself? We all need a strong and integrated sense of personal identity that serves as an anchor in life.

Early philosophers advised us to "know thyself" and poets have told us, "To thine own self be true." We have taken their advice. Hundreds of books have been written dealing with how to get to know yourself and the *Oxford English Dictionary* lists more than 100 words that focus on the self, from *self-abasement* to *self-wisdom*. When you form a conception of who you are as a person you have an identity.

Your **identity** is a consistent set of attitudes that defines who you are. It is a subjective self-image that is a type of cognitive structure called a self-schema. A **self-schema** is a generalization about the self, derived from past experience, that organizes and guides your understanding of the information you learn about yourself from interacting with others. You have multiple schemas, multiple identities, and multiple selves. They include your view of your physical characteristics (height, weight, sex, hair and eye color, general appearance), your social roles (student or teacher, child or parent, employee or employer), the activities you engage in (playing the piano, dancing, reading), your abilities (skills, achievements), your attitudes and interests (liking rock and roll, favoring equal rights for females), and your general personality traits (extrovert or introvert, impulsive or reflective, sensible or scatterbrained). Your **gender identity** is your fundamental sense of your maleness or femaleness. Your **ethnic identity** is your sense of belonging to one particular ethnic group. Your identity consists not only of various self-schemas that you currently possess but of selves that you would like to be or that you imagine you might be. These potential selves include ideals that you would like to attain and standards that you feel you should meet (the "ought" self). They can originate from your own thoughts or from the messages of others.

Each of your self-schemas is viewed as being positive or negative. You generally look at yourself in an evaluative way, approving or disapproving of your behavior and characteristics. Your self-schemas are arranged in a hierarchy. The more important an identity is, or the higher it stands in the hierarchy, the more likely it is to influence your choices and your behavior.

To cope with stress you need more than one self. The diversity and complexity of the identity reduces the stress you experience. Self-complexity provides a buffer against stressful events. If you have only one or two major self-schemas, any negative event is going to have an impact on most aspects of your identity. The woman who sees herself primarily as a wife, for example, is likely to be devastated if her husband says he wants an immediate divorce. In contrast, the individual who has a more complex representation of self may be more protected from negative events that primarily involve only one or two of several roles. The woman who sees herself not only as wife, but also as a mother, lawyer, friend, and tennis player will have other roles to fall back on when impending divorce threatens her role of spouse. People with more complex identities are less prone to depression and illness; they also experience less severe mood swings following success or failure in one particular area of performance. . . .

Some of the Benefits of Self-Acceptance

There is a common saying that goes, "I can't be right for someone else if I'm not right for me!" **Self-acceptance** is a high regard for yourself or, conversely, a lack of cynicism about yourself. There are a number of benefits to accepting yourself as you are, and a relationship exists among self-acceptance, self-disclosure, and being accepted by others. The more self-accepting you are, the greater your self-disclosure tends to be. The greater your self-disclosure, the more others accept you. And the more others accept you, the more you accept yourself. A high level of self-acceptance, furthermore, is reflected in psychological health. Psychologically healthy people see themselves as being liked, capable, worthy, and acceptable to other people. All of these perceptions are based on self-acceptance. Considerable evidence abounds that self-acceptance and acceptance of others are related. If you think well of yourself you tend to think well of others. You also tend to assume that others will like you, an expectation that often becomes a self-fulfilling prophecy.

DIFFICULTIES WITH DIVERSITY

Once you are accepting of yourself, you are in a position to be accepting of others. There are, however, a number of barriers to accepting diverse peers. They include prejudice, the tendency to blame the victim, and cultural conflict.

Prejudice

To know one's self is wisdom, but to know one's neighbor is genius.

—Minna Antrim (author)

Building relationships with diverse peers is not easy. The first barrier is prejudice. Prejudice, stereotyping, and discrimination begin with categorizing. In order to understand other people and yourself, categories must be used. **Categorizing** is a basic human cognitive process of conceptualizing objects and people as members of groups. We categorize people on the basis of *inherited traits* (culture, sex, ethnic membership, physical features) or *acquired traits* (education, occupation, lifestyle, customs). Categorizing and generalizing are often helpful in processing information and making decisions. At times, however, they malfunction and result in stereotyping and prejudice.

To be prejudiced means to prejudge. **Prejudice** can be defined as an unjustified negative attitude toward a person based solely on that individual's membership in a particular group. Prejudices are judgments made about others that establish a superiority/inferiority belief system. If one person dislikes another simply because that other person is a member of an ethnic group, sex, or religion, that is prejudice.

One common form of prejudice is ethnocentrism. **Ethnocentrism** is the tendency to regard our own ethnic group, culture, or nation as better or more correct than others. The word is derived from *ethnic,* meaning a group united by similar customs, characteristics, race, or other common factors, and *center*. When ethnocentrism is present, the standards and values of our culture are used as a yardstick to measure the worth of other ethnic groups. Ethnocentrism is often perpetuated by **cultural conditioning.** As children we are raised to fit into a particular culture. We are conditioned to respond to various situations as we see others in our culture react.

Prejudices are often associated with stereotypes. A **stereotype** is a set of beliefs about the characteristics of the people in a group that is applied to almost all members of that group. Typically, stereotypes are widely held beliefs within a group and focus on what other cultural and ethnic groups, or socioeconomic classes are "really like." Women have been stereotyped as more emotional than men. Men have been stereotyped as more competitive than women. Tall, dark, and handsome men have been stereotyped as mysterious. Stereotypes distort and exaggerate in ways that support an underlying prejudice or fundamental bias against members of other groups. Stereotypes are resistant to change because people believe information that confirms their stereotypes more readily than evidence that challenges them. Stereotypes almost always have a detrimental effect on those targeted, interfering with the victim's ability to be productive and live a high quality life.

Stereotypes reflect an **illusionary correlation** between two unrelated factors, such as being poor and lazy. Negative traits are easy to acquire and hard to lose. When you meet one poor person who is lazy you may tend to see all poor people as lazy. From then on, any poor person who is not hard at work the moment you notice him or her may be perceived to be lazy. Our prejudiced stereotype of poor people being lazy is protected in three ways. Our prejudice makes us notice the negative traits we ascribe to the groups we are prejudiced against. We tend to have a *false consensus bias* by believing that most other people share our stereotypes (i.e., see poor people as being lazy). We tend to see our own behavior and judgments as quite common and appropriate, and to view alternative responses as uncommon and often inappropriate. Finally, we often develop a rationale and explanation to justify our stereotypes and prejudices.

When prejudice is put into action, it is discrimination. **Discrimination** is an action taken to harm a group or any of its members. It is a negative, often aggressive action aimed at the target of prejudice. Discrimination is aimed at denying members of the targeted groups treatment and opportunities equal to those afforded to the dominant group. When discrimination is based on race or sex, it is referred to as racism or sexism.

Diversity among people can either be a valued resource generating energy, vitality, and creativity, or it can be a source of prejudice, stereotyping, and discrimination. To reduce your prejudices and use of stereotypes, these steps may be helpful:

1. Admit that you have prejudices (everyone does, you are no exception) and commit yourself to reducing them.
2. Identify the stereotypes that reflect your prejudices and modify them.

3. Identify the actions that reflect your prejudices and modify them.
4. Seek feedback from diverse friends and colleagues about how well you are communicating respect for and valuing of diversity.

Blaming the Victim

It is commonly believed that the world is a just place where people generally get what they deserve. If we win the lottery, it must be because we are nice people who deserve some good luck. If we are robbed, it must be because we are careless and want to be punished for past misdeeds. Any person who is mugged in a dark alley while carrying a great deal of cash may be seen as asking to be robbed. Most people tend to believe that they deserve what happens to them. Most people also believe that others also get what they deserve in the world. It is all too easy to forget that victims do not have the benefit of hindsight to guide their actions.

When someone is a victim of prejudice, stereotyping, and discrimination, all too often they are seen as doing *something* wrong. **Blaming the victim** occurs when we attribute the cause of discrimination or misfortune to the personal characteristics and actions of the victim. The situation is examined for potential causes that will enable us to maintain our belief in a just world. If the victim can be blamed for causing the discrimination, then we can believe that the future is predictable and controllable because we will get what we deserve.

Blaming the victim occurs as we try to attribute a cause to events. We constantly interpret the meaning of our behavior and events that occur in our lives. Many times we want to figure out *why* we acted in a particular way or why a certain outcome occurred. If we get angry when someone infers we are stupid, but we could care less when someone calls us clumsy, we want to know why we are so sensitive about our intelligence. When we are standing on a street corner after a rainstorm and a car splashes us with water, we want to know whether it was caused by our carelessness, the driver's meanness, or just bad luck. This process of explaining or inferring the causes of events has been termed **causal attribution.** An attribution is an inference drawn about the causes of a behavior or event. . . .

In trying to understand why a behavior or event occurred, we generally choose to attribute causes either to

1. Internal, personal factors (such as effort and ability)
2. External, situational factors (such as luck or the behavior/personality of other people)

For example, if you do well on a test, you can attribute it to your hard work and great intelligence (an internal attribution) or to the fact that the test was incredibly easy (an external attribution). When a friend drops out of school, you can attribute it to a lack of motivation (an internal attribution) or lack of money (an external attribution).

People make causal attributions to explain their successes and failures. These are *self-serving* attributions, designed to permit us to take credit for positive outcomes and to avoid blame for negative ones. We have a systematic tendency to claim our successes are due to our ability and efforts while our failures are due to bad luck, evil people, or a lack of effort. We also have a systematic tendency to claim responsibility for the success of group efforts ("It was all my idea in the first place and I did most of the work") and avoid responsibility for group failures ("If the other members had tried harder, this would not have happened."). . . .

Attributing the causes of others' failure and misfortune to their actions rather than to prejudice and discrimination can be a barrier to building constructive relationships with diverse peers. Bad things do happen to good people. Racism does exist. Innocent bystanders do get shot. It is usually a good idea to suspend any tendency to blame the victim when interacting with diverse peers.

Culture Clash

Another common barrier to building relationships with diverse peers is cultural clashes. A **culture clash** is a conflict over basic values that occurs among individuals from different cultures. The most common form is members of minority groups' questioning the values of the majority. Common reactions by majority group members when their values are being questioned are feeling:

1. *Threatened:* Their responses include avoidance, denial, and defensiveness.
2. *Confused:* Their responses include seeking more information in an attempt to redefine the problem.
3. *Enhanced:* Their responses include heightened anticipation, awareness, and positive actions that lead to solving the problem.

Many cultural clashes develop from threatening, to confusing, to enhancing. Once they are enhancing, they are no longer a barrier.

As prejudice, stereotyping, and discrimination are reduced, the tendency to blame the victim is avoided, and cultural clashes become enhancing, the stage is set for recognizing and valuing diversity.

RECOGNIZING AND VALUING DIVERSITY

In order to actualize the positive potential of diversity, you must recognize that diversity exists and then learn to value and respect fundamental differences among people. This is especially true in countries in which widely diverse groups of people live. The United States, for example, is a nation of many cultures, races, languages, and religions. In the last eight years alone, over 7.8 million people journeying from over 150 different countries and speaking dozens of different languages made the United States their new home. America's pluralism and diversity has many positive values, such as being a source of energy and creativity that increases the vitality of American society. Diversity among collaborators has been found to contribute to achievement and productivity, creative problem solving, growth in cognitive and moral reasoning, perspective-taking ability, and general sophistication in interacting and working with peers from a variety of cultural and ethnic backgrounds (Johnson & Johnson, 1989).

Within a relationship, a community, an organization, a society or a world, the goal is not to assimilate all groups so that everyone is alike. The goal is to work together to achieve mutual goals while recognizing cultural diversity and learning to value and respect fundamental differences while working together to achieve mutual goals. Creating a *unum* from *pluribus* is done in basically four steps. *First, you develop an appreciation for your own religious, ethnic, or cultural background.* Your identification with the culture and homeland of your ancestors must be recognized and valued. The assumption is that respect for your cultural heritage will translate into self-respect.

Second, you develop an appreciation and respect for the religious, ethnic, and cultural backgrounds of others. A critical aspect of developing an ethnic and cultural identity is whether ethnocentricity is inherent in your definition of yourself. An in-group identity must be developed in a way that does not lead to rejection of out-groups. There are many examples where being a member of one group requires the rejection of other groups. There are also many examples where being a member of one group requires the valuing and respect for other groups. Out-groups need to be seen as collaborators and resources rather than competitors and threats. Express respect for diverse backgrounds and value them as a resource that increases the quality of your life and adds to the viability of your society. The degree to which your in-group identity leads to respect for and valuing of out-groups depends on developing a superordinate identity that includes both your own and all other groups.

Third, you develop a strong superordinate identity that transcends the differences between your own and all other groups. Being an American, for example, is creedal rather than racial or ancestral. The United States is a nation that unites as one people the descendants of many cultures, races, religions, and ethnic groups through an identification with America and democracy. And America has grown increasingly diverse in social and cultural composition. Each cultural group is part of the whole and members of each new immigrant group, while modifying and enriching our national identity, learn they are first and foremost Americans. America is one of the few successful examples of a pluralistic society where different groups clashed but ultimately learned to live together through achieving a sense of common nationhood. In our diversity, there has always been a broad recognition that we are one people. Whatever our origins, we are all Americans.

Fourth, you adopt a pluralistic set of values concerning democracy, freedom, liberty, equality, justice, the rights of individuals, and the responsibilities of citizenship. It is these values that form the American creed. We respect basic human rights, listen to dissenters instead of jailing them, and have a multiparty political system, a free press, free speech, freedom of religion, and freedom of assembly. These values were shaped by millions of people from many different backgrounds. Americans are a multicultural people knitted together by a common set of political and moral values.

Diverse individuals from different cultural, ethnic, social class, and language backgrounds come together primarily in school, career, and community settings. Sometimes the results are positive and individuals get to know each other, appreciate and value the vitality of diversity, learn how to use diversity for creative problem solving and enhanced productivity, and internalize a common superordinate identity that binds them together. If diversity is to be a source of creativity and energy, individuals must value and seek out diversity rather than fear and reject it. Doing so will eventually result in cross-cultural friendships. . . .

CLARIFYING MISCOMMUNICATIONS

Imagine that you and several friends went to hear a speaker. Although the content was good, and the delivery entertaining, two of your friends walked out in protest. When you asked them why, they called your attention to the facts that the speaker continually said "you guys" even though half the audience was women, used only sports and military examples, only quoted males, and joked about senility and old age. Your friends were insulted.

Communication is actually one of the most complex aspects of managing relationships with diverse peers. To communicate effectively with people from a different cultural, ethnic, social class, or historical background than yours you must increase your

1. *Language sensitivity:* knowledge of words and expressions that are appropriate and inappropriate in communicating with diverse groups. The use of language can play a powerful role in reinforcing stereotypes and garbling communication. To avoid this, individuals need to heighten their sensitivity and avoid using terms and expressions that ignore or devalue others.
2. *Awareness of stylistic elements of communication:* knowledge of the key elements of communication style and how diverse cultures use these elements to communicate. Without awareness of nuances in language and differences in style, the potential for garbled communication is enormous when interacting with diverse peers.

Your ability to communicate with credibility to diverse peers is closely linked to your use of language. You must be sophisticated enough to anticipate how your messages will be interpreted by the listener. If you are unaware of nuances and innuendoes contained in your message, then you will be more likely to miscommunicate. The words you choose often tell other people more about your values, attitudes, and socialization than you intend to reveal. Receivers will react to the subtleties conveyed and interpret the implied messages behind our words. The first step in establishing relationships with diverse peers, therefore, is to understand how language reinforces stereotypes and to adjust our usage accordingly.

You can never predict with certainty how every person will react to what you say. You can, however, minimize the possibility of miscommunicating by following some basic guidelines:

1. Use all the communication skills discussed in this book.
2. Negotiate for meaning whenever you think the other persons you are talking with misinterpreted what you said.
3. Use words that are inclusive rather than exclusive such as women, men, participants.
4. Avoid adjectives that spotlight specific groups and imply the individual is an exception, such as black doctor, woman pilot, older teacher, blind lawyer.
5. Use quotes, references, metaphors, and analogies that reflect diversity and are from diverse sources, for example, from Asian and African sources as well as from European and American.
6. Avoid terms that define, demean, or devalue others, such as cripple, girl, boy, agitator.
7. Be aware of the genealogy of words viewed as inappropriate by others. It is the connotations the receiver places on the words that are important, not your connotations. These connotations change over time so continual clarification is needed. There are loaded words that seem neutral to you but highly judgmental to people of diverse backgrounds. The word lady, for example, was a complement even a few years ago, but today it fails to take into account women's independence and equal status in society and, therefore, is offensive to many women. Words such as girls or gals are just as offensive.

SUMMARY

In a global village highly diverse individuals interact daily, study and work together, and live in the same community. Diversity among your acquaintances, classmates, co-workers, neighbors, and friends is inevitable. You will be expected to interact effectively with people with a wide variety of characteristics and from a wide variety of backgrounds. In order to gain the sophistication and skills needed to do so you must accept yourself, lower the barriers to building relationships with diverse peers, recognize that diversity exists and is a valuable resource, . . . and clarify misunderstandings.

All people need to believe that they are unique and separate individuals who are valued and respected in their own right. In order to do so, you must accept yourself as you are and build a coherent, stable, and integrated identity. Your identity helps you cope with stress, it provides stability and consistency to your life, and it directs what information is attended to, how it is organized, and how it is remembered. Your identity is built through your current relationships and identifications with real, historical, and fictional people. Actually, you have many interrelated identities. You have a family identity, a gender identity, and a country identity. An important aspect of your identity is your identification with your cultural, ethnic, historical, and religious background.

The more accepting you are of yourself, the more able you are to be accepting of others. But there are barriers to building positive relationships with diverse peers. The most notable barriers are prejudice, blaming the victim, and culture clash. Minimizing these barriers makes it easier to recognize that diversity exists and fundamental differences among people are to be both respected and valued. To do so you must respect your own heritage, respect the heritages of others, develop a superordinate identity that transcends the differences, and a pluralistic set of values.

Accepting yourself, minimizing the barriers, and respecting and valuing diversity set the stage for actually gaining cross-cultural sophistication. Being able to relate effectively to people from a variety of cultures depends on seeking opportunities to interact cross-culturally, building trust, so that enough candor exists that you can learn what is and what is not disrespectful and hurtful to them. It is only through building friendships with diverse peers that the insights required to understand how to interact appropriately with people from a wide variety of backgrounds can be obtained. Two requirements for developing such friendships are highlighting cooperative efforts to achieve mutual goals and clarifying miscommunications that arise while working together.

REVIEW QUESTIONS

1. Explain what Johnson means—as specifically as you can—when he says that globalization has made diversity increasingly inevitable.
2. What is a self-schema? Give an example of one of your own self-schemas.
3. Explain the connection Johnson makes between prejudice and discrimination.
4. Explain how blaming the victim can contribute to stereotyping.
5. What does Johnson mean by "a strong superordinate identity that transcends the differences between your own and all other groups"?
6. What is a pluralistic set of values?
7. Give an example of how (a) language sensitivity and (b) awareness of stylistic elements of communication could enhance relationships with diverse others.

PROBES

1. People who belong to such organizations as a militia, skinhead, or Ku Klux Klan group often argue for the importance of ethnic purity and exclusivity. Members of men-only and women-only groups make similar arguments about gender exclusivity. Johnson's basic assumption in this reading is that these arguments for exclusivity are naïve, because diversity is a fact of the contemporary world. What specific examples can you cite to support Johnson's assumption? Where do you notice the concrete evidence of increasing diversity?

2. *Why* does Johnson say that the first step toward successfully interacting with diverse others is to learn to accept yourself?
3. Cognitive scientists pretty much agree that categorization is a basic human mental function. Our brains naturally and constantly categorize almost everything we perceive. If this is true, then we automatically categorize the people we perceive. How, then, can a person possibly avoid prejudice?
4. As Johnson defines *culture clash*, it is inevitable. Various cultures will naturally have conflicts over basic values. Tell how he suggests we respond to this inevitability.
5. Which of the previous readings in this book do you think could contribute most directly to your efforts to bridge differences with diverse others?

REFERENCE

1. Johnson, D. W. & Johnson, R. (1989). *Cooperation and competition: Theory and research.* Edina, MN: Interaction Book Company.

————————

Letty Cottin Pogrebin published an exhaustive book on friendship based on two very thorough friendship surveys, many additional published research reports, and interviews with almost 150 people ranging in age from early adolescence to 82 years and representing most of the spectrum of cultures and subcultures in the United States. The following reading consists of excerpts from Chapter 11 of her 16-chapter book. As the title indicates, the chapter deals with friendship across a variety of cultural boundaries, including color, culture, sexual preference, disability, and age. As with other readings, I chose this one because it blends sound research and straightforward writing, credible theory, and solid practice.

This rigorous but accessible flavor of Pogrebin's work emerges in the section right after the introduction. She begins with the obvious but important point that if you're going to cross a boundary, you'll find yourself doing a lot of explaining—to yourself, to each other, and to your respective communities. Then she takes a couple of pages to elaborate on what that "explaining" will probably consist of.

The next major section develops another potentially profound theme: Intercultural relationships consistently have to deal with the reality that the two persons might be "the same," but that they're also "never quite the same." She illustrates the point with examples from black/redneck white, Jewish/Irish-Catholic, Puerto Rican/white, and Spanish/Jewish relationships. Pogrebin's discussion of "moving in one another's world" extends the notion of "the same but never quite the same" to include challenges introduced by second and third languages and fundamental cultural values. She also discusses several "hazards of crossing" that emerge when fundamental differences in cultural values meet.

Under the heading "The Problem with 'Them' Is 'Us,'" Pogrebin discusses gay/straight, disabled/nondisabled, and young/aged relationships. All three topics became current only in the past decade as the minority rights movement spread to include gays and lesbians, the disabled, and "senior citizens," and government regulations made these groups increasingly visible. As the author notes, these groups warrant separate discussions, in part because "to a large degree, our society still wants to keep them out of sight—the gays and lesbians for 'flaunting their alternative lifestyles,' the disabled for not 'getting better,' and the old for reminding us of our eventual fate."

Pogrebin's outline of the kinds of explaining one has to do about his or her gay/straight relationships accurately captures the last 10 years or so of my experience communicating with some gay and lesbian people. The strong relationship Kris and I have with our friends Bill and John Paul is one example of some of the problems and much of the potential Pogrebin discusses. I also appreciate her summary of the contrasts between gay and straight views on homophobia, AIDS, lesbian politics, and acceptance.

Until recently, disabled persons in the United States made up perhaps an even more invisible subculture. Thanks in part to major changes in building codes affecting all public construction, wheelchair-bound, deaf, and blind persons are becoming increasingly visible. Pogrebin explains some of the unique problems the nondisabled can have establishing and maintaining relationships with these persons. As one quadriplegic succinctly puts it, "We need friends who won't treat us as weirdo asexual second-class children or expect us to be 'Supercrips'—miracle cripples who work like crazy to make themselves whole again. . . . We want to be accepted the way we are." Some nondisabled persons are guilty of exactly these charges and can be shocked to hear them expressed so bluntly.

In the final section of this reading, Pogrebin discusses cross-age friendships. She cites some studies that indicate that three-year-olds already have developed "ageist" perceptions of the elderly—believing that old people are sick, tired, and ugly. Other studies reveal the stereotypes older people have of children and teenagers. She discusses some of the typical reasons for cross-age miscommunication and then suggests some reasons why age can be immaterial to developing friendships. As the average age of the U.S. populace continues to increase, Pogrebin's comments will become more and more applicable and important.

I appreciate the breadth of application in this reading. I believe that Pogrebin is writing about some cutting-edge aspects of interpersonal communication and that her ideas are going to become increasingly important.

The Same and Different:

Crossing Boundaries of Color, Culture, Sexual Preference, Disability, and Age

Letty Cottin Pogrebin

On August 21, 1985, as they had done several times before, twenty-one men from a work unit at a factory in Mount Vernon, New York, each chipped in a dollar, signed a handwritten contract agreeing to "share the money equally [sic] & fairly to each other," and bought a ticket in the New York State Lottery. The next day, their ticket was picked as one of three winners of the largest jackpot in history: $41 million.

The story of the Mount Vernon 21 captivated millions not just because of the size of the pot of gold but because of the rainbow of people who won it. Black, white, yellow, and brown had scribbled their names on that contract—Mariano Martinez, Chi Wah Tse, Jaroslaw Siwy, and Peter Lee—all immigrants from countries ranging from Paraguay to Poland, from Trinidad to Thailand.

"We're like a big family here," said Peter Lee. "We thought by pooling our efforts we would increase our luck—and we were right."[1]

The men's good fortune is a metaphor for the possibility that friendships across ethnic and racial boundaries may be the winning ticket for everyone. This is not to say that crossing boundaries is a snap. It isn't. There are checkpoints along the way where psychic border guards put up a fuss and credentials must be reviewed. We look at a prospective friend and ask, "Do they want something from me?" Is this someone who sees personal advantage in having a friend of another race at his school, in her company, at this moment in history? Is it Brotherhood Week? Does this person understand that "crossing friendships" require more care and feeding than in-group friendship, that it takes extra work?

EXPLAINING

Most of the extra work can be summed up in one word: *explaining*. Whatever the boundary being crossed—race, ethnicity, or any other social category—both partners in a crossing friendship usually find they have to do a lot of explaining—to themselves, to each other, and to their respective communities.

Explaining to Yourself

One way or another, you ask yourself, "What is the meaning of my being friends with someone not like me?"

In his classic study, *The Nature of Prejudice,* Gordon Allport distinguishes between the in-group, which is the group to which you factually belong, and the reference group, which is the group to which you relate or aspire.[2] Allport gives the example of Blacks who so wish to partake of white skin privilege that they seek only white friends, disdain their own group, and become self-hating. One could as easily cite Jews who assume a WASP identity or "Anglicized Chicanos" who gain education and facility in English and then sever their ties of kinship and friendship with other Mexican-Americans.[3]

When you have a friend from another racial or ethnic group, you ask yourself whether you are sincerely fond of this person or might be using him or her as an entrée into a group that is your unconscious reference group. The explaining you do to yourself helps you understand your own motivations. It helps you ascertain whether the friend complements or denies your identity, and whether your crossing friendships are in reasonable balance with your in-group relationships.

Explaining to Each Other

Ongoing mutual clarification is one of the healthiest characteristics of crossing friendships. The Black friend explains why your saying "going ape" offends him, and the Jewish friend reminds you she can't eat your famous barbecued pork. Both of you try to be honest about your cultural sore points and to forgive the other person's initial ignorance or insensitivities. You give one another the benefit of the doubt. Step by step, you discover which aspects of the other person's "in-groupness" you can share and where you must accept exclusion with grace.

David Osborne, a white, describes his close and treasured friendship with an American Indian from Montana: "Steve was tall and athletic—the classic image of the noble full-blooded Indian chief. We were in the same dorm in my freshman year at Stanford at a time when there were only one or two other Native Americans in the whole university. He had no choice but to live in a white world. Our friendship began when our English professor gave an assignment to write about race. Steve and I got together to talk about it. We explored stuff people don't usually discuss openly. After that, we started spending a lot of time together. We played intramural sports. We were amazingly honest with each other, but we were also comfortable being silent.

"When I drove him home for spring vacation, we stopped off at a battlefield that had seen a major war between Chief Joseph's tribe and the U.S. Cavalry. Suddenly it hit me that, had we lived then, Steve and I would have been fighting on opposite sides, and we talked about the past. Another time, an owl flew onto our windowsill and Steve was very frightened. He told me the owl was a symbol of bad luck to Indians. I took it very seriously. We were so in touch, so in sync, that I felt the plausibility of his superstitions. I was open to his mysticism."

Mutual respect, acceptance, tolerance for the faux pas and the occasional closed door, open discussion and patient mutual education, all this gives crossing friendships—when they work at all—a special kind of depth.

Explaining to Your Community of Origin

Accountability to one's own group can present the most difficult challenge to the maintenance of crossing friendships. In 1950 the authors of *The Lonely Crowd* said that interracial contact runs risks not only from whites but from Blacks who may "interpret friendliness as Uncle Tomism."[4] The intervening years have not eliminated such group censure.

In her article "Friendship in Black and White," Bebe Moore Campbell wrote: "For whites, the phrase 'nigger lover' and for Blacks, the accusation of 'trying to be white' are the pressure the group applies to discourage social interaction."[5] Even without overt attacks, people's worry about group reaction inspires self-censorship. Henry, a Black man with a fair complexion, told me he dropped a white friendship that became a touchy subject during the Black Power years. "We'd just come out of a period when many light-skinned Negroes tried to pass for white and I wasn't about to be mistaken for one of them," he explains. "My racial identity mattered more to me than any white friend."

Black-white friendships are "conducted underground," says Campbell, quoting a Black social worker, who chooses to limit her intimacy with whites rather than fight the system. "I'd feel comfortable at my white friend's parties because everybody there would be a liberal, but I'd never invite her to mine because I have some friends who just don't like white people and I didn't want anybody to be embarrassed."

If a white friend of mine said she hated Blacks, I would not just keep my Black friends away from her, I would find it impossible to maintain the friendship. However, the converse is not comparable. Most Blacks have at some point been wounded by racism, while whites have not been victimized from the other direction. Understanding the experiences *behind* the reaction allows decent Black people to remain friends with anti-white Blacks. That these Blacks may have reason to hate certain whites does not excuse their hating all whites, but it does explain it. . . .

Historically, of course, the biggest enemies of boundary-crossing friendships have not been Blacks or ethnic minorities but majority whites. Because whites gain the most from social inequality, they have the most to lose from crossing friendships, which, by their existence, deny the relevance of ethnic and racial hierarchies. More important, the empowered whites can put muscle behind their disapproval by restricting access to clubs, schools, and businesses.

If you sense that your community of origin condemns one of your crossing friendships, the amount of explaining or justifying you do will depend on how conformist you are and whether you feel entitled to a happiness of your own making. . . .

THE SAME BUT NEVER QUITE THE SAME

"I go coon hunting with Tobe Spencer," said former police officer L. C. Albritton about his Black friend in Camden, Alabama. "We're good friends. We stay in town during the day for all the hullabaloo and at night we go home and load up the truck with three dogs and go way down into the swamps. We let the dogs go and sit on a log, take out our knives and a big chew of tobacco . . . and just let the rest of the world go by."

Looking at a picture of himself and Spencer taken in 1966, Albritton mused: "It's funny that a police officer like me is standing up there smiling and talking to a nigger because we were having marches and trouble at that time. . . . Old Tobe Spencer—ain't nothing wrong with that nigger. He's always neat and clean as a pin. He'll help you too. Call him at midnight and he'll come running just like that."[6]

Two friends with the same leisure-time pleasures, two men at ease together in the lonely night of the swamps. Yet race makes a difference. Not only does the white man use the derogatory "nigger," but he differentiates his friend Tobe from the rest of "them" who, presumably, are not neat and clean and helpful. The *same but never quite the same.*

Leonard Fein, the editor of *Moment,* a magazine of progressive Jewish opinion, gave me "the controlling vignette" of his cross-ethnic friendships: "An Irish-Catholic couple was among our dearest friends, but on that morning in 1967 when we first heard that Israel was being bombed, my wife said, 'Who can we huddle with tonight to get through this ordeal?' and we picked three Jewish couples. Our Irish friends were deeply offended. 'Don't you think we would have felt for you?' they asked. 'Yes,' we said, 'but it wasn't sympathy we wanted, it was people with whom, if necessary, we could have mourned the death of Israel—and that could only be other Jews.'"

"The following week, when the war was over, my wife and I went to Israel. The people who came to live in our house and take care of our children were our Irish friends. They had understood they were our closest friends yet they could never be exactly like us." . . .

For Raoul, a phenomenally successful advertising man, crossing friendships have been just about the only game in town. He reminisced with me about growing up in a Puerto Rican family in a Manhattan neighborhood populated mostly by Irish, Italians, and Jews:

"In the fifties I hung out with all kinds of guys. I sang on street corners— do-wopping in the night—played kick the can, and belonged to six different basketball clubs, from the Police Athletic League to the YMCA. My high school had 6000 kids in it—street kids who hung out in gangs like The Beacons, The Fanwoods, The Guinea Dukes, The Irish Lords, and The Diablos from Spanish Harlem and Jewish kids who never hung out because they were home studying. The gang members were bullies and punks who protected their own two-block area. They wore leather jackets and some of them carried zip guns and knives. I managed to be acceptable to all of them just because I was good at sports. I was the best athlete in the school and president of the class. So I was protected by the gangs and admired by the Jewish kids and I had a lot of friends."

Raoul's athletic prowess won him a scholarship to a large midwestern university where he was the first Puerto Rican to be encountered by some people. "They wanted me to sing the whole sound track of *West Side Story.* They asked to see my switchblade. And I was as amazed by the midwesterners as they were by me. My first hayride was a real shock. Same with hearing people saying 'Good morning' to each other. Every one of my friends—my roommate, teammates, and fraternity brothers, Blacks from Chicago and Detroit and whites from the farms—they were all gentle and nice. And gigantic and strong. Boy, if one of them had moved into my neighborhood back home, he'd have owned the block."

"After graduation, a college friend went to work in a New York City ad agency that played in a Central Park league and needed a softball pitcher. He had me brought in for an interview. Even though I knew nothing about advertising, I was a helluva pitcher, and the owner of the agency took sports seriously. So he hired me. I always say I had the only athletic scholarship in the history of advertising. I pitched for the agency, I played basketball with the owner, and I learned the business. So I found my friends and my career through sports. Even though I may have been a Spic to most everyone, sports opened all the doors."

The same but never quite the same. . . .

"At the beginning, because of difficulties of adaptation, we immigrants protect ourselves by getting together with people from the same culture who speak the same language," says Luis Marcos, a psychiatrist, who came to the United States from Seville, Spain. "Next, when we feel more comfortable, we reach out to people who do the same work we do, mostly those who help us or those we help in some way. Then we have a basis for friendship. My mentor, the director of psychiatry at Bellevue, is a native-born American and a Jew. He helped me in my area of research and now he's one of my best friends. I also began to teach and to make friends with my medical students as they grew and advanced."

That Marcos and his friends have the health profession in common has not prevented misunderstandings. "When we first went out for meals together, my impulse was to pay for both of us," he says of another doctor, a Black woman who taught him not to leave his own behavior unexamined. "It wasn't that I thought she couldn't afford to pay; we were equally able to pick up the check. It was just that the cultural habit of paying for a woman was ingrained in my personality. But she misconstrued it. She felt I was trying to take care of her and put her down as a Black, a professional, and a woman. In order for our friendship to survive, she had to explain how she experiences things that I don't even think about."

MOVING IN ONE ANOTHER'S WORLD

Ethnotherapist Judith Klein revels in her crossing friendships. "My interest in people who are different from me may be explained by the fact that I'm a twin. Many people look to be mirrored in friendship; I've had mirroring through my sister, so I can use friendship for other things. One thing I use it for is to extend my own life. People who aren't exactly like me enhance my knowledge and experience. They let me be a vicarious voyager in their world."

As much as friends try to explain one another's world, certain differences remain particular barriers to intimacy.

Luis Marcos mentions the language barrier. "No matter how well I speak, I can never overcome my accent," he says. "And some people mistake the way I talk for lack of comprehension. They are afraid I won't understand an American joke, or if I choose to use aggressive words, they don't think I mean it, they blame my 'language problem.'"

While many Americans assume people with an accent are ignorant, many ethnics assume, just as incorrectly, that someone *without* an accent is smart. Some Americans have a habit of blaming the other person for doing or saying whatever is not understandable to Americans. Ethnics also have been known to blame their own culture—to use their "foreignness" as an excuse for behavior for which an American would have to take personal responsibility. "I can't help it if we Latins are hot-tempered" is a way of generalizing one's culpability.

Of course, the strongest barrier to friendship is outright resistance. After two years of off-and-on living in Tokyo, Angie Smith came to terms with the fact that "the Japanese do not socialize the way we do." She found, as many have, that in Japan friendship is considered an obligation more than a pleasure and is almost always associated with business.[7]

"Three times I invited two couples for dinner—the men were my husband's business associates—and three times the men came and the women didn't," Smith recalls. "They sent charming little notes with flowers, but they would not have been comfortable in our house for an evening of social conversation. Yet these same Japanese women would go out to lunch with me and tell me more intimate things than they tell each other. While we were in Japan, I just had to get used to sex-divided socializing and not having any couple friendships."

When people's differences are grounded in racism rather than alien styles of socializing, it can be especially painful to move in the other person's world.

"I felt myself a slave and the idea of speaking to white people weighed me down," wrote Frederick Douglass a century ago.[8] Today, most Blacks refuse to be weighed down by whites. They do not "need" white friends. Some doubt that true friendship is possible between the races until institutional racism is destroyed. Feminists of every shade have debated the question "Is Sisterhood Possible?" Despite the issues that affect *all* women, such as sexual violence, many Black women resist working together for social change or organizing with white women because they believe most whites don't care enough about welfare reform, housing, teen pregnancies, or school dropouts—issues that are of primary concern to Blacks.

Bell Hooks, a writer and a professor of Afro-American studies, wrote: "All too frequently in the women's movement it was assumed one could be free of sexist thinking by simply adopting the appropriate feminist rhetoric; it was further assumed that identifying oneself as oppressed freed one from being an oppressor. To a very great extent, such thinking prevented white feminists from understanding and overcoming their own sexist-racist attitudes toward black women. They could pay lip service to the idea of sisterhood and solidarity be-tween women but at the same time dismiss black women."[9]

Phyllis Marynick Palmer, a historian, says white women are confounded by Black women's strong family role and work experience, which challenge the white stereotype of female incapacity. White women also criticize Black women for making solidarity with their brothers a priority rather than confronting Black men's sexism. In turn, Black women get angry at white women who ignore "their own history of racism and the benefits that white women have gained at the expense of black women."[10] With all this, how could sisterhood be possible? How can friendship be possible?

"I would argue for the abandonment of the concept of sisterhood as a global construct based on unexamined assumptions about our similarities," answers Dill, "and I would substitute a more pluralistic approach that recognizes and ac-cepts the objective differences between women."

Again the word "pluralistic" is associated with friendship. An emphasis on double consciousness, not a denial of differences. The importance of feeling both the same and different, of acknowledging "the essence of me," of understanding that friends need not *transcend* race or ethnicity but can embrace differences and be enriched by them. The people who have managed to incorporate these pre-cepts say that they are pretty reliable guidelines for good crossing friendships. But sometimes it's harder than it looks. Sometimes, the "vicarious voyage" into another world can be a bad trip.

The Hazards of Crossing

"Anglo wannabes" are a particular peeve of David Hayes Bautista. "These are Anglos who wanna be so at home with us that they try too hard to go native. For instance, Mexicans have a certain way that we yell along with the music of a mariachi band. When someone brought along an Anglo friend and yelled 'Yahoo, Yahoo' all night, every Chicano in the place squirmed."

Maxine Baca Zinn gives the reverse perspective: of a Chicano in an Anglo en-vironment. "Once, when I was to speak at the University of California, a Chicana friend who was there told me that the minute I walked into that white academic world my spine straightened up. I carried myself differently. I talked differently around them and I didn't even know it." Was Zinn just nervous about giving her speech or did she tighten up in anticipation of the tensions Chicanos feel in non-Hispanic settings? She's not certain.

When Charlie Chin, a bartender, started work in a new place, a white co-worker quipped, "One thing you have to watch out for, Charlie, are all the Chinks around here." I winced when Chin said this, but he told me, "I just smiled at the guy. I'm used to those jokes. That's the way whites break the ice with Asians. That's the American idea of being friendly.". . .

For another pair of friends, having different sensitivities did not destroy the relationship but did create a temporary misunderstanding. Yvonne, a Black woman, was offended when her white friend, Fran, came to visit, took off her shoes, and put her feet up on the couch. "I felt it showed her disregard for me and I blamed it on race," says Yvonne. "Black people believe the way you behave in someone's home indicates the respect you have for that person. Also, furniture means a lot to us because we buy it with such hard-won wages." Weeks later, Yvonne saw one of Fran's white friends do the same thing while sitting on Fran's couch. Yvonne realized that the behavior had nothing to do with lack of respect for Blacks. "For all I know millions of whites all over America put their feet up when they relax—I'd just never seen that part of their world before."

What Bill Tatum discovered about a couple of his white friends was not so easy to explain away. When the couple asked Tatum to take some food to Helen, their Black housekeeper who was sick, he asked her name and address. They knew her only as "Helen" but were able to get her address from their 6-year-old who had spent a week at her apartment when they had been on vacation.

"I arrived to find a filthy, urine-smelling building, with addicts hanging out on the front stoop. Rags were stuffed in the broken windows in Helen's apartment. She was wearing a bag of asafetida around her neck, a concoction made by southern Blacks to ward off bad luck and colds. She was old, sick, and feverish. She said she'd never been sick before and her employers—my friends—had provided her with no health insurance. Obviously, they'd never imagined where or how this poor woman might live—or else they wouldn't have left their little girl with her. They treated their Black housekeeper with none of the respect and concern they showed me, their Black *friend* and a member of their economic class."

Until that experience, if anyone had ever accused the couple of racism, Tatum says he'd have gone to the mat defending them. Now he has to square what he's seen with his old love for them and he is finding it very, very difficult.

He makes another point about moving in the world of white friends. "Some whites make me feel completely comfortable because they say exactly what they think even if it contradicts whatever I've said. But other whites never disagree with me on anything. They act as if Blacks can't defend their positions, or they're afraid it would look like a put-down to challenge what I say even though they would challenge a white person's opinion in a minute."

While Tatum resents whites' misguided protectiveness, he also finds fault with "many Blacks who are climbing socially and are too damned careful of what *they* say. They won't advance an opinion until they have a sense of what the white friend is thinking." Not only is that not good conversation, he says, "that's not good friendship."

THE PROBLEM WITH "THEM" IS "US"

If you're a young, heterosexual, nondisabled person and you do not have one friend who is either gay, old, or disabled, there might be something wrong with *you*. If you're gay, old, or disabled and all your friends are just like you, it may not be because you prefer it that way.

Gay people, the elderly, and disabled people get the same pleasure from companionship and intimacy and have the same problems with friendship as does anyone else. They merit a separate discussion in this book for the same reason that class, race, and ethnicity required special discussion: because on top of the usual friendship concerns, they experience additional barriers.

In essence, the barriers exist because we don't *know* each other. Many people—some of whom are homophobic (have a fear of homosexuality)—reach adulthood without ever to their knowledge meeting a homosexual or a lesbian. Many have neither known someone who is blind or deaf or who uses a wheelchair nor spent time with an old person other than their grandparents. That there are such things as Gay Pride marches, disability rights organizations, and the Gray Panthers does not mean that these groups have achieved equal treatment under the law or full humanity in the eyes of the world. To a large degree, our society still wants to keep them out of sight—the gays for "flaunting their alternative lifestyles," the disabled for not "getting better," and the old for reminding us of our eventual fate.

As a result of our hang-ups, these populations may be even more segregated than racial or ethnic minorities. When these groups are segregated, "we" don't have to think about "them." Out of sight, out of mind, out of friendship. People told me they had no gay, elderly, or disabled friends because "we live in two different worlds" or because "they" are so different—meaning threatening, unsettling, or strange. Closer analysis reveals, however, that we *keep* them different by making this world so hard for them to live in and by defining human norms so narrowly. It is our world—the homophobic, youth-worshipping, disability-fearing world—that is threatening, unsettling, and strange to them. In other words, their biggest problem is us.

To make friends, we have to cross our self-made boundaries and grant to other people the right to be both distinctive and equal.

Gay-Straight Friendship

Forming relationships across gay-straight boundaries can be as challenging as crossing racial and ethnic lines because it too requires the extra work of "explaining":

- Explaining to yourself why, if you're gay, you need this straight friend ("Am I unconsciously trying to keep my heterosexual credentials in order?"), or why, if you're straight, you need this gay friend ("Am I a latent homosexual?")
- Explaining to each other what your lives are like—telling the straight friend what's behind the words "heavy leather" or explaining to the gay friend just why he *cannot* bring his transvestite lover to a Bar Mitzvah
- Explaining to your respective communities why you have such a close relationship with one of "them"

Gay-straight friendship is a challenge not only because the heterosexual world stigmatizes gays but because homosexual society is a culture unto itself.

Straights who relate comfortably with their gay friends say they get along so well because they respect the distinctive qualities of gay culture—almost as if it were an ethnic group. Interestingly enough, a Toronto sociologist has determined that gay men have the same institutions, "sense of peoplehood," and friendship networks as an ethnic community; all that gays lack is the emphasis on family.[11] And in places where lesbians congregate, such as San Francisco, there are women's bars, music, bookstores, publications, folklore, and dress styles—an elaborate self-contained culture.[12]

Since gay men and lesbians have to function in a straight world during most of their lives, it's not too much to ask a straight friend to occasionally accommodate to an environment defined by homosexuals. But even when both friends accommodate, gay-straight relations can be strained by disagreements over provocative issues.

Gay-Straight Debate

The Gay's View	The Straight's View
On Homophobia	
You're not relaxed with me. You think gayness rubs off or friendship might lead to sex. You act like every gay person wants to seduce you. You fear others will think you're gay. You are repulsed by gay sex though you try to hide it. You bear some responsibility for the discrimination against gays and if you're my friend, you'll fight it with me.	I am the product of a traditional upbringing. I cannot help being afraid or ignorant of homosexuality. My religion taught me that homosexuality is a sin. I'm trying to overcome these biases and still be honest with you about my feelings. I support gay rights, but I cannot be responsible for everyone else's homophobia.
On AIDS	
Ever since the AIDS epidemic, you have not touched me or drunk from a glass in my house. I resent your paranoia. I shouldn't have to watch my gay friends die and at the same time feel that my straight friends are treating me like a leper. If I did get AIDS, I'm afraid you would blame the victim and abandon me. Can I trust a friend like that?	I *am* afraid. I don't know how contagious the AIDS virus is or how it's transmitted. From what I read, no one does. All I know is that AIDS is fatal, homosexuals are the primary victims, and you are a homosexual. I'm caught between my affection for you and my terror of the disease. I don't know what's right and you're in no position to tell me.
On Lesbian Politics	
Lesbianism is not just sexual, it's political. Every woman should call herself a lesbian, become woman-identified, and reject everything masculinist. Women who love men and live in the nuclear family contribute to the entrenchment of patriarchal power and the oppression of women. Authentic female friendship can only exist in lesbian communities. If you don't accept "lesbian" as a positive identity, it will be used to condemn all women who are not dependent on men.	I support lesbian rights and even lesbian separatism if lesbians choose it. I believe lesbian mothers must be permitted to keep their children. I oppose all discrimination and defamation of lesbians. I believe that lesbian feminists and straight women can work together and be friends, *but* I resent lesbian coercion and political strong-arming. I also resent your more-radical-than-thou attitude toward heterosexuals. Like you, what I do with my body is my business.

<table>
<tr><td colspan="2" align="center">On Acceptance</td></tr>
<tr><td>You want me to act straight whenever having a gay friend might embarrass you. I'm not going to tone down my speech or dress to please your friends or family. I do not enjoy being treated as a second-class couple when my lover and I go out with you and your spouse. If you can kiss and hold hands, we should be able to show affection in public. If straights ask each other how they met or how long they have been married, they should ask us how we met and how long we've been together.</td><td>You refuse to understand how difficult it is to explain gay lifestyles to a child or an 80-year-old. You make me feel like a square in comparison with your flashy gay friends. You treat married people like Mr. and Mrs. Tepid, as if the only true passion is gay passion. Your friends make me feel unwanted on gay turf and at political events when I'm there to support gay rights. You put down all straights before you know them. It's hard to be your friend if I can't introduce you to other people without your feeling hostile or judging their every word. . . .</td></tr>
</table>

Disabled and Nondisabled Friendship

About 36 million Americans have a disabling limitation in their hearing, seeing, speaking, walking, moving, or thinking. Few nondisabled people are as sensitive to the experiences of this population as are those with close friends who are disabled.

"Last week," recalls Barbara Spring, "I went to have a drink at a midtown hotel with a friend who uses a wheelchair. Obviously it's not important to this hotel to have disabled patrons because we had to wait for the so-called accessible elevator for thirty minutes. Anyone who waits with the disabled is amazed at how long the disabled have to wait for everything."

"In graduate school, one of my friends was a young man with cerebral palsy," says Rena Gropper. "Because he articulated slowly and with great difficulty, everyone thought he was dumb and always interrupted him, but if you let him finish, you heard how bright and original his thinking was."

Terry Keegan, an interpreter for the deaf, has become friends with many deaf people and roomed for two years with a co-worker who is deaf. "If they don't understand what we're saying it's not because they're stupid but because we aren't speaking front face or we can't sign." Keegan believes all hearing people should learn 100 basic words in Ameslan, American Sign Language. "Historically, this wonderful language has been suppressed. Deaf people were forced to use speech, lipreading, and hearing aids so they would not look handicapped and would 'fit in' with the rest of us. Their hands were slapped when they tried to sign. This deprived them of a superior communication method. Deafness is not a pathology, it's a difference. When we deny deaf people their deafness, we deny them their identity."

Many nondisabled people have become sensitized to idioms that sound like racial epithets to the disabled, such as "the blind leading the blind" or "that's a lame excuse." Some find "handicapped" demeaning because it derives from "cap in hand." A man who wears leg braces says the issue is accuracy. "*I'm* not handicapped, people's attitudes about me handicap me." Merle Froschl, a nondisabled member of the Women and Disability Awareness Project, points out that the opposite of "disabled" is "*not* disabled"; thus, "nondisabled" is the most neutral term. Disabled people are infuriated by being contrasted with "normal" people—it implies that the disabled are "abnormal" and everyone else is perfect. And the term "able-bodied" inspires the question, Able to do what: Run a marathon? See without glasses? Isn't it all relative?

"Differently abled" and "physically challenged" had a brief vogue, but, says Harilyn Rousso, those terms "made me feel I really had something to hide." Rousso, a psychotherapist who has cerebral palsy, emphasizes, "Friends who care the most sometimes think they're doing you a favor by using euphemisms or saying 'I never think of you as disabled.' The reason they don't want to acknowledge my disability is that they think it's so negative. Meanwhile, I'm trying to recognize it as a valid part of me. I'm more complex than my disability and I don't want my friends to be obsessed by it. But it's clearly there, like my eye color, and I want my friends to appreciate and accept me with it."

The point is not that there is a "right way" to talk to people who are disabled but that friendship carries with it the obligation to *know thy friends,* their sore points and their preferences. That includes knowing what words hurt their feelings as well as when and how to help them do what they cannot do for themselves.

"Each disabled person sends out messages about what they need," says Froschl. "One friend who is blind makes me feel comfortable about taking her arm crossing the street, another dislikes physical contact and wants to negotiate by cane. I've learned not to automatically do things for disabled people since they often experience help as patronizing."

"I need someone to pour cream in my coffee, but in this culture, it's not acceptable to ask for help," say Rousso, adding that women's ordinary problems with dependence are intensified by disability. "I have to feel very comfortable with my friends before I can explain my needs openly and trust that their reaction will not humiliate both of us. For some people it raises too many anxieties."

Anxieties that surround the unknown are dissipated by familiarity. Maybe that explains why so many disabled-nondisabled friendships are composed of classmates or co-workers who spend a lot of time together.

"There are those who can deal with disability and those who can't," says Phil Draper, a quadriplegic whose spinal cord was injured in a car accident. "If they can't—if they get quiet or talk nervously or avoid our eyes—the work of the relationship falls entirely on us. We need friends who won't treat us as weirdo asexual second-class children or expect us to be 'Supercrips'—miracle cripples who work like crazy to make themselves whole again. Ninety-nine percent of us aren't going to be whole no matter what we do. We want to be accepted the way we are."

To accept friends like Phil Draper, the nondisabled have to confront their unconscious fears of vulnerability and death. In one study, 80 percent of nondisabled people said they would be comfortable having someone in a wheelchair as their friend. But "being in a wheelchair" came immediately after "blind" and "deaf-mute" as the affliction they themselves would least want to have.[13] If we fear being what our friend is, that feeling is somewhere in the friendship.

Nondisabled people also have to disavow the cult of perfectability. Disabled people are not going to "get better" because they are not "sick"; they are generally healthy people who are not allowed to function fully in this society—as friends or as anything else.

"Friendship is based on people's ability to communicate," says Judy Heumann, the first postpolio person to get a teacher's license in New York City and now a leader of the disability rights movement. "But barriers such as inaccessible homes make it hard for disabled people to just drop in. Spontaneity is something disabled people enjoy infrequently and the nondisabled take for granted.

"While more public places have ramps and bathrooms that accommodate wheelchairs, many parties still occur in inaccessible spaces. If I have to be carried upstairs or if I can't have a drink because I know I won't be able to use the bathroom later, I'll probably decide not to go at all. One way I measure my friends is by whether they have put in the effort and money to make their houses wheelchair-accessible. It shows their sensitivity to me as a person.

"Good friends are conscious of the fact that a movie theater or concert hall has to be accessible before I can join them; they share my anger and frustration if it's not. They understand why I'm not crazy about big parties where all the non-disabled are standing up and I'm at ass-level. It makes me able to function more as an equal within the group if people sit down to talk to me. I can't pretend I'm part of things if I can't hear anyone. I don't want to *not* be invited to large parties—I just want people to be sensitive to my needs.

"I always need help cooking, cleaning, driving, going to the bathroom, getting dressed. I pay an attendant to do most of those things for me but sometimes I have to ask a friend for help, which presents a lot of opportunities for rejection. Often, the friends who come through best are other disabled people whose disabilities complement mine. I can help a blind woman with her reading, child care, and traveling around town; she can do the physical things I need. And we don't have to appreciate each other's help, we can just accept it.". . .

Cross-Age Friendship

I am now 46, my husband is 51. Among our good friends are two couples who are old enough to be our parents. One woman, a poet, can be counted on for the latest word on political protests and promising writers. She and I once spent a month together at a writer's colony. The other woman—as energetic and as well-read as anyone I know—is also involved in progressive causes. Although the men of both couples have each had a life-threatening illness, the one with a heart condition is a brilliant civil liberties lawyer and the one who had a stroke is a prize-winning novelist with stunning imaginative powers. The lawyer taught our son to play chess when he was 5. The novelist has encouraged our daughters to write stories ever since they could read. The men have been fine surrogate grandfathers.

When I described these couples to someone my own age, he said, "Ah, it's easy to be friends with *interesting* old people, but what about the dull ones?" The answer is, I am not friends with dull young or middle-aged people so why should I want to be friends with dull old people? And why does he immediately think in terms of old people *not* being interesting? Perhaps the crux of the problem with cross-generational friendship is this *double* double standard. First, to think we "ought" to be friends with the elderly—as a class—denies old people the dignity of individuality and devalues their friendship through condescension. But second, to assume that those who are young or in mid-life will necessarily be more interesting and attractive than those over 65 maintains a double standard of expectation that cheats younger people of friends like ours.

Ageism hurts all ages. And it begins early: Studies show that 3-year-olds already see old people as sick, tired, and ugly and don't want to associate with them.[14] Older people also have their biases about youthful behavior. Some 70-year-olds think children are undependable, unappreciative, ask too many questions, and must be told what to do. They believe teenagers are callow, impatient, and unseasoned.[15]

The authors of *Grandparents/Grandchildren* write, "We shouldn't blame adolescents for not being adults. To become adults, the young need to be around adults."[16] But age segregation keeps us apart. Without benefit of mutual acquaintance, stereotypes mount, brick by brick, until there is a wall high enough to conceal the real human beings on either side.

Another big problem is miscommunication. Conversations between young and old often founder because "sensory, physical, or cognitive differences" cause "distortion, message failure, and social discomfort."[17] That's a fancy way of saying they can't understand each other. And anyone who has ever talked with a young person whose span of concentration is the length of a TV commercial or with an old person whose mind wanders to the blizzard of '48 when asked how to dress for today's weather will understand how each generation's communication style can be a problem for the other.

But stereotypes and miscommunication do not entirely account for the gulf between young and old. Homophily—the attraction to the similar self—is the missing link. Those who are going through the same thing at the same time find it comforting to have friends who mirror their problems and meet their needs, and, usually, people of similar chronological age are going through parallel experiences with wage-earning, setting up house, child-rearing, and other life-cycle events.

Age-mates also tend to have in common the same angle of vision on history and culture. Two 65-year-olds watching a film about the Depression or World War II can exchange memories and emotional responses that are unavailable to a 30-year-old who did not live through those cataclysms. And while a person of 18 and one of 75 might both love Vivaldi, their simultaneous appreciation for Bruce Springsteen is unlikely.

Claude Fischer's studies reveal that more than half of all friend-partners are fewer than five years apart. But the span is reduced to two years if their relationship dates back to their youth when age gradations matter the most and the places where youngsters meet—school, camp, military service, and entry-level jobs—are more age-segregated. Contrary to popular wisdom, elderly people, like the rest of us, prefer friends of their own age. The more old people there are in a given community the more likely it is that each one will have a preponderance of same-age friends. And, believe it or not, a majority of old people say they think it's more important for them to have age-mates than family as their intimates.

Given this overwhelming preference for homophily at every age, why am I on the bandwagon for cross-generational friendship? Because when it's good, it's very, very good—both for friends of different ages who are undergoing similar experiences at the same time and for friends of different ages who are enjoying their differences.

- A 38-year-old woman meets 22-year-olds in her contracts class at law school.
- A couple in their early forties enrolled in a natural childbirth course make friends with parents-to-be who are twenty years younger.
- Three fathers commiserate about the high cost of college; two are in their forties, the third is a 60-year-old educating his second family.

Age-crossing friendships become less unusual as Americans follow more idiosyncratic schedules for marrying, having children, and making career decisions.

But there are other reasons for feeling that age is immaterial to friendship. Marie Wilson, a 45-year-old foundation executive who has five children of high school age or older, told me, "My friends are in their early thirties, and they have kids under 8. But these women are where I am in my head. We became close working together on organizing self-help for the poor. Most women my age are more involved in suburban life or planning their own career moves."

Sharing important interests can be as strong a basis for friendship as is experiencing the same life-cycle events. However, without either of those links, the age difference can sit between the young and the old like a stranger. I'm not asking that we deny that difference but that we free ourselves from what Victoria Secunda calls "the tyranny of age assumptions"[18] and that we entertain the possibility of enriching ourselves through our differences. . . .

As we cross all these lines and meet at many points along the life cycle, people of diverse ages, like people of every class and condition, are discovering that we who are in so many ways "the same and different" can also be friends.

REVIEW QUESTIONS

1. According to the author, when we engage in a cross-cultural relationship, what do we typically need to explain about it to ourselves? To each other? To our friends?

2. What is meant by Pogrebin's label, "the same but never quite the same"?
3. In the paragraph before the heading "The Hazards of Crossing," the author distinguishes *double consciousness* from a *denial of differences*. What do those two terms mean?
4. The essay includes a story about a white couple asking their black friend, Bill Tatum, to take some food to their black housekeeper who lived in Harlem and was sick. Tatum was shocked to discover the housekeeper living in a filthy slum. What was racist about the white couple's "generosity"?
5. How accurate is Pogrebin's summary of each side's views in the section titled "Gay-Straight Debate"?
6. What is the point of the author's discussion of the words we use to label disabled persons?
7. Paraphrase the following comment by Pogrebin: "If we fear being what our friend is, that feeling is somewhere in the friendship."

PROBES

1. Which of the three kinds of explaining that Pogrebin describes has been most difficult for you?
2. The author claims that "many Americans assume people with an accent are ignorant" and that "many ethnics assume, just as incorrectly, that someone *without* an accent is smart." How is this distorted value mirrored in the major television networks' choice of news anchors and reporters?
3. You may be surprised to read a discussion of gay/straight relationships here. What might justify putting a discussion of this topic in this book?
4. Do you commonly think about relationships with disabled persons as examples of "intercultural communication"? What happens when you do?
5. What problems have you encountered in your relationships with older persons? What is the most helpful thing Pogrebin says about these relationships?

NOTES

1. L. Rohter, "Immigrant Factory Workers Share Dream, Luck and a Lotto Jackpot," *New York Times*, August 23, 1985.
2. G. Allport, *The Nature of Prejudice*, Doubleday, Anchor Press, 1958.
3. J. Provinzano, "Settling Out and Settling In." Paper presented at annual meeting of the American Anthropological Association, November 1974.
4. D. Riesman, R. Denney, and N. Glazer, *The Lonely Crowd: A Study of the Changing American Character*, Yale University Press, 1950.
5. B. M. Campbell, "Friendship in Black and White," *Ms.*, August 1983.
6. B. Adelman, *Down Home: Camden, Alabama*, Times Books, Quadrangle, 1972.

7. R. Atsumi, "Tsukiai—Obligatory Personal Relationships of Japanese White Collar Employees," *Human Organization*, vol. 38, no. 1 (1979).
8. F. Douglass, *Narrative of the Life of Frederick Douglass, an American Slave,* New American Library, Signet, 1968.
9. B. Hooks, *Ain't I a Woman: Black Women and Feminism,* South End Press, 1981.
10. P. M. Palmer, "White Women/Black Women: The Dualism of Female Identity and Experience in the United States," *Feminist Studies,* Spring 1983.
11. S. O. Murray, "The Institutional Elaboration of a Quasi-Ethnic Community," *International Review of Modern Sociology,* vol. 9, no. 2 (1979).
12. J. C. Albro and C. Tully, "A Study of Lesbian Lifestyles in the Homosexual Micro-Culture and the Heterosexual Macro-Culture," *Journal of Homosexuality,* vol. 4, no. 4 (1979).
13. L. M. Shears and C. J. Jensema, "Social Acceptability of Anomalous Persons," *Exceptional Children,* October 1969.
14. R. K. Jantz et al., *Children's Attitudes Toward the Elderly,* University of Maryland Press, 1976.
15. A. G. Cryns and A. Monk, "Attitudes of the Aged Toward the Young," *Journal of Gerontology,* vol. 1 (1972); see also, C. Seefeld et al., "Elderly Persons' Attitude Toward Children," *Educational Gerontology,* vol. 8, no. 4 (1982).
16. K. L. Woodward and A. Kornhaber, *Grandparents, Grandchildren: The Vital Connection* (Doubleday, Anchor Press, 1981), quoted in "Youth Is Maturing Later," *New York Times,* May 10, 1985.
17. L. J. Hess and R. Hess, "Inclusion, Affection, Control: The Pragmatics of Intergenerational Communication." Paper presented at the Conference on Communication and Gerontology of the Speech Communication Association, July 1981.
18. V. Secunda, *By Youth Possessed: The Denial of Age in America,* Bobbs-Merrill, 1984.

———

Marriages between people of different races or ethnicities offer both some of the greatest potential for intercultural communication and some of its greatest challenges. In this excerpt from a book called *Talking About Identity,* an Asian-Canadian woman reflects on some of the realities of being married to a white man.

Her reflections were prompted by her experience at a fairly typical dinner party involving several professional couples. A conversation about the Canadian Ministry of Culture's policies for funding writers included some racist claims about the quality of works by Aboriginal, francophone, immigrant, and visible minority writers. As you read how Tsang recalls the conversation, it is easy to feel how close this topic is to her, even though it's about apparently anonymous others. The exchange ends when she spits, "That's like saying that because I'm yellow I should stay in Yeller-town. You're all racists. I'm leaving."

And someone followed her out the door: the white man who is now in her bed. His loving presence offers welcome security and, at the same time, makes it easy for Tsang to notice and reflect on the differences that separate them. "All through the day," she writes, "I watched him as he ate, puttered, and worked. His white skin reflected light and cast an uncomfortable feeling on me."

This is a personal reading, and it is also a reading about one of the most serious problems faced by almost every culture in the world. In every culture and each country, some people have the *unearned privileges* of majority membership, and some are "minority." This condition raises issues of identity that affect almost every communication event that minority members experience. And most of the time, in most situations, members of the majority are blissfully unaware of what's happening. As a result, feelings of discrimination, disrespect, and unfairness arise, and actions that are depersonalizing, belittling, and hostile poison relationships between groups and individuals.

There are no easy solutions offered here. There's only, "Let's take it one day at a time, alright?" But I hope Tsang's story prompts you to reflect on and talk about the racism in your community and in your life.

There's a White Man in My Bed: Scenes from an Interracial Marriage

Pui Yee Beryl Tsang

Sunday I woke to discover a white man in my bed. Once I got over the initial shock, I took a closer look and realized that the stranger sleeping in my bed really wasn't a stranger at all. He was my husband of seven years. Why had it taken me all this time to realize he was white? Was it nearsightedness, the desire not to see his colour, or just plain colour-blindness? Why did this realization hit me at this precise moment? Was it that this awareness would somehow change the nature of our relationship, hurt or even end our relationship? He—the white man in my bed—kept sleeping through my minor brainstorm. Once, I mused, I would never have paid serious attention to any of these questions; they were too deep and profound for me to ponder. On that Sunday morning, however, they seemed so pressing that I had to take the time to reflect on them.

As I threw the covers off and opened my eyes to the bright sunlight filling our bedroom, I started thinking about my realizations. In the process I couldn't help but notice the whiteness of the white man in my bed. His skin was more

"There's a White Man in My Bed" by Pui Yee Beryl Tsang from *Talking about Identity* ed. by Carl James and Adrienne Shadd, pp. 219–228. Copyright © 2001. Reprinted by permission of Between the Lines, Toronto.

than just white; it also had a translucent quality. Just beneath the surface of his skin I could see the blue traces of his veins, the purple fibres of his muscles, and the delicate red etchings of his blood vessels. Lying next to him, I could see how truly yellow my skin is, with a deep opaque richness that hides everything beneath its surface.

White skin, I thought, is different in other ways. Sunlight scorches it faster and with more vengeance than it does other skins. Illness is more easily revealed in it than with other skins. It is even injured more easily and takes longer to heal than other skins. I looked at my arm, where there were scratches from our cat; they are no longer visible. I looked at the white man's skin; the scratches from our cat were still there, even though we received them at the same time. What is it about white skin that puts me on edge? How did these feelings arise in me?

Then I remembered . . .

The night before, the white man and I had gone for drinks and dinner at the home of a distinguished Canadian poet who was also white. Most distinguished Canadian "anythings," I have come to understand, are usually white. I didn't want to go, I didn't have to go, but I went to show the white man that I supported him. After all, he had spent nearly every weekend of the last month going to rallies, marches, and conferences for yellow, red, brown, and black people.

"These people," he told me, "are very important. They can help me publish more poetry and reach wider audiences with my existing work." "I'm not sure I'm going to like them," I confessed. "It's going to be okay," he reassured me. "Just be yourself."

"That's what I'm afraid of," I commented to myself.

It began auspiciously enough. There was the mandatory ritual of "Welcome to my home. Let me take your coat." Then it moved onto the obligatory "What would you like to drink?" More people arrived and the usual "Hi, I'm so-and-so, I write such-and-such. I've recently been published in XYZ journal" took place. Things were going relatively well. They were actually not bad company. They were witty, erudite, and undeniably brilliant. Their white skin, however, reflected the light in such a way that it cast an uncomfortable feeling on me.

We were having a good time discussing our various travels around the world, the weather, and the quirks of our respective cats. (It is a stereotype to say that poets are fond of cats, but many are.) Then conversation moved on to the Ontario minister of culture's new initiative to fund artists, filmmakers, and writers who have been traditionally excluded from participating in the cultural life of the province. The new measures that he enacted were meant to benefit Aboriginals, francophones, immigrants, and visible minorities. Everyone in the room, with the exception of me, was white. Everyone in the room, with the exception of me and my husband, disagreed with the objectives of the new programs.

They didn't like them because it meant that the Ministry of Culture would stop funding existing writers, most of whom were white, and start funding other writers, most of whom were non-white. But the white men and women in the room were not willing to own up to this. Instead, they claimed that Aboriginal, francophone, immigrant, and visible minority writers did not produce quality work. The whole notion of granting people money to write about their experiences as "minorities" in this country was a bogus one. "If these people were any good they could get money and get published," the white men and women said.

I challenged these people on their notion of what was quality. "How do you define quality?" I asked. "Does it have to follow European or North American notions of what is considered good?" They looked offended and asked me what I meant by that. I could feel my yellow skin grow more yellow and bristle, but I remained unrepentant.

"What I am suggesting," I patiently explained, "is that the writers' community in Canada excludes non-white people. It was initially created for white men and changed to include white women. It judges the quality of literature in terms of white European or North American literary traditions. When it does embrace non-European or non-North American cultures, it does so by appropriation. Look at how writers like Robert Kroetsch steal Aboriginal legends to add spirituality to their books. Your organizations don't recognize the existence of racism and how it shapes the experiences of non-white writers. You invalidate non-white writing because it focuses less on the intellectual European tradition and more on personal experiences, which most non-white literary traditions—Aboriginals, African, Asian, and Caribbean writing—value. When we confront you about your exclusionary actions and your subtle but vindictive racism, you use elaborate, theoretically constructed arguments to show that racism really doesn't exist; it is merely a figment of our imagination. So what are we supposed to do if we can't convince you that racism exists? Suffer in silence? Support your appropriation of our cultures in the hopes that we will gain a foothold in the literary community through your exploitation of our traditions? Throw off our conventions and traditions and embrace yours? What the minister of culture is trying to do is make room for us in the art, filmmaking, and writing communities, and I think it's about time room was made. This country has never been entirely white but its culture always has been. It cannot remain that way. It is becoming more and more non-white by the day, and it is important that we recognize and accept this fact. If not, we will face race and ethnic war."

I took a deep breath and sat back to see their reaction. In challenging them I was only being myself, a yellow woman. My points were grudgingly acknowledged by some, but were ignored by others who went on talking about how culture in Ontario is going to the dogs. (Are the dogs us, the non-whites?)

I AM FURIOUS. This kind of reaction is typical. I have learned, as an antiracist educator, that it is meant to invalidate and segregate the non-white minority from the white majority. What they didn't know was that I wasn't going to let them get away with it. Whether they wanted to or not I was going to make them admit and confront their racism.

I spoke up and said, "This is silencing and I will not tolerate it. What I said must be addressed in your community. You must think about it."

The responses ranged from "I don't know what to say—you're right—but I don't know how to change them," to "It's certainly interesting but you really don't know anything about the writers' community," to "Look, I've had a bad day and I really don't care to get involved in your petty problems about white people." These people were in no mood to talk about racism and I knew it. It was time to stop.

The distinguished Canadian poet, though, thought that it was time to put me in my place. "I don't see," he said angrily, "what gives you the right to come here and call us all racists."

"I didn't come here to call you racists," I replied. "But when racism comes up, I call people on it. To tell the truth, though, I did expect you to be racists, given your reputations for consistently slagging non-white writers."

"Why did you bother coming, then? You had a choice not to come," was the nasty rejoinder.

"That's like saying that because I'm yellow I should stay in Yeller-town." I bit off each word. "You're all racists. I'm leaving." Tears flooded my eyes as I left. Damn it! Why did I let him get the best of me?

As I walked out the door, I realized there was a presence behind me. It was a white man. The white man I came with. Then I felt sorry. I wasn't sorry for standing up for myself, but I was sorry for him, sorry that I might have damaged his career as a writer. These people were important, influential, significant. They could have helped him with his writing career. With their sponsorship—why did I have to ruin it for him?

Something moved.

The white man woke to find me watching him and thinking. Pulling the covers closer and squinting his blue eyes against the sunlight, he grinned and said, "It's early, go back to sleep." He reached for me and pulled me close. He was no longer a white man. He had become my husband again. Being so close to him revealed the contrasts in our skin even more, and the memory of the previous evening began staining my mind with worry.

"We need to talk," I said.

"Okay," he muttered.

"It's about last night. I'm sorry I ruined your chances to get more writing published, but I was right, they were racists," I explained.

"It's okay, you were right, they were wrong. Can I go back to sleep?" he groaned. He dozed off, but his arms were still around me, trying to pacify me. I didn't feel like going back to sleep. I struggled free and heard my skin separate from his as I rolled away. I got out of bed. I glanced at him as I left the room. Even sleeping, his white body exudes a strength that is foreign to me. As I walked down the hall to the bathroom, I pondered the source of his strength.

I know where my own power came from. It developed through a combination of experience and education. New things lived and new things learned have all helped me to form my character and outlook. They made me aware of who I am, and I am a survivor. I have survived the racial inequities of this society. I have survived them with my dignity intact and I have survived them with the desire to eliminate all forms of social injustice. His strength, though, does not come from survival. It was not acquired through knowledge or reflection, but through something deeper, something that suggested a sense of self that comes from a sense of belonging.

I turned on the shower. Stepping into the steamy spray, I soaped myself. The bar of soap was blue, the lather white, but it should really be green since my skin is yellow, and blue and yellow make green. The lather, however, remained white. As I watched, the white bubbles slipped from my breast, making my body seem white. I wondered if it is the whiteness of his skin that gives him the sense of belonging he possesses. Could his white skin be a protective shield that, despite its frailties, allows him to exist safely and comfortably in the white world? Most likely. No one questions his right to be there. He can make what he wants out of his life. He can become a writer and people can admire his brilliance or condemn his impracticality. He can pursue a professional career and people can applaud his ambition or criticize his desire for respectability. He can tune out of society altogether, and people can think he's enlightened or view him as "out to lunch." No one, though, will say that all white people are like that because he's like that. He is never asked to prove his worth as a human being to anyone. The only person he has to satisfy is himself. He is secure and happy with the world.

For me the standards are different. My skin, in spite of its resiliency, is a target, drawing attention and arrows of scorn from others. People question my right to be here. I cannot do what I want. I have to agree with the existing order or else others will assume that people like me are lazy. I must become a professional or else others will conclude that people like me are stupid. I need to work hard or else others will think that people like me are useless. Everything I do has a bearing not only on me, but also on other yellow people. I am constantly asked to prove myself. I am unsure about myself and my place in the world.

Steaming water continues to spray from the silver showerhead. . . .

I pour the pink shampoo out of its equally pink bottle and lather my hair. The bubbles are also white; they should be a deep burgundy because pink and black make burgundy, but they remain white. There seems to be no way of getting around the whiteness of the world. The world is white, through and through. White men and women created the world in their image to nourish, perpetuate, and sustain themselves. The institutions they developed only made room for them, for them and no others. Those who controlled these institutions, as I witnessed the previous evening, were intensely protective of them. They had to be defended at all costs. After all, they were proof to white men and women of their power.

As I was thinking about these things, my husband came into the bathroom. He stepped into the shower as I was rinsing off, the white soap suds sliding off my body and down the drain. I made space for him, but he said there was enough. As he soaped himself, the white lather disappeared against the white of his skin.

"I'm sorry about last night," I said, "but I couldn't stand by and let them oppress me."

"It's okay," he answered, "they were wrong. Do you think that white people have a monopoly on being right?"

"But you're white," I remarked.

"Yeah, but I'm not that kind of white person."

"What kind of white person is that?" I asked.

"The kind that thinks only white people and white culture matter."

"What's it like to be white?"

He stopped washing and replied, "Embarrassing, guilty. Not very good sometimes."

"Why?" I wanted to know.

"Because you have power," he answered, "a lot of power and sometimes you don't want it. After all, you didn't ask for it. It's part of your birthright. But what the hell does that mean? Does it mean you have the right to treat 'coloured folks' like shit?" He kept on washing as I stepped out of the shower to dry off, running the yellow towel over my yellow skin, refreshing it.

All through the day I watched him as he ate, puttered, and worked. His white skin reflected light and cast an uncomfortable feeling on me. Short, fast flashes of the previous evening's events streaked through my mind all day.

When we married, I knew that racial differences would emerge some day. I just didn't expect them to erupt in such an "us-shaking" manner, forcing me to confront the difficulties of an interracial marriage.

I was worried that my belief in a racially equitable society, which was based on my experiences as a non-white minority, had cost him his dream of being a writer and would mar our relationship forever. I didn't want him resenting me for spoiling his golden opportunity. I might have swallowed the other writers' racism, if only to support him, but I could not do that and still live with myself. I know that he supported my actions and my motivations, but my uncertainty of his sincerity jabbed at me all day long. I kept asking myself what was going to happen to us.

I tried to think about times in our relationship when the question of race came up between us, but I could think of none. When we are by ourselves we think we are the only two people in the world. There is no racial dynamic, just the silly giddiness of loving each other. We can afford to be colour-blind, to ignore our differences and even make jokes about them. Once we get out into the real world, though, it is hard for us to be equal. He will always be treated one way, based on his colour, and I another, based on mine. His colour allows him to be accepted everywhere, mine only in some places. My marriage to him will grant me grudging acceptance in some places, but I will always resent the fact that this "privilege" is not accessible to everyone. Does he really understand the complexities that being married to a non-white woman can bring? Can our relationship survive the social pressures of an inherently racist society?

I'm not sure, but as I catch him looking at me, I am reminded of the things that we have been working for. He knows that the power and privilege he possesses are often unearned and must be relinquished if there is to be racial equality. This he does without hesitation. When confronted with a racist situation, he usually speaks up. (The only time he doesn't is when I am there to beat him to the proverbial punch.) Yet when he is confronted with the choices of joining the white establishment to do something he really wants to do or of denouncing it as racist, is it fair for me to insist that he take the moral high ground? Am I the one who is putting pressure on him or is he making his own decisions about what is right or wrong? Would he be anti-racist without me?

Questions flash in my mind in a brilliant kaleidoscope of colour. The pastel shades of the answers elude me. Only the colours remain.

Later that evening we watched a movie on TV, cats sleeping on our laps, a bowl of over-buttered popcorn between us. It looked like a scene from *House Beautiful*. The only difference was that such magazines show only couples who are white, not couples who are white and yellow. My husband had chosen the movie; it was about a Chinese American family trying to make it in 1949 New York. It was touching, poignant, all those words that describe good G-rated movies. This particular film made me laugh and cry at the same time. It uses every Hollywood cliché to depict people about whom Hollywood would never even think of making a film.

I looked over at my husband. He smiled. He knows me well. He understands how important it is for me to watch films like these, because they give me a sense of identity. The movie made me forget my bitter thoughts, and for the moment I felt as if we were the only two people in the world.

My doubts about our relationship returned later that evening. We were in bed. I was trying to sleep but my husband's white skin glowed dimly in the dark and made me think about our racial differences again. The white man had returned to my bed, and I didn't know what to do with him. Tired, I tried another solution to my problem.

"I love you," I said.

"I love you too," he said.

"Is my being yellow a problem for you?" I ask.

"No, not really. Is my being white?" he asks.

"Yeah, sort of," I reply.

"Oh, how?"

"I don't know," I said. (I did know.)

"So what's the problem?" he asks.

"It sometimes creates conflicts for me. Like last night. I wonder—marriage is hard enough. I don't know if the added pressure of racial difference is worth it for us," I said.

"It'll be okay. Let's take it one day at a time, alright?" he replied.

He becomes my husband again. The questions of interracial marriage still wander in my mind, but I will think of them on another day.

REVIEW QUESTIONS

1. Do you notice anything distinctly Canadian about the conversation discussed here or the points Tsang makes? Explain.
2. Who are Aboriginals?

3. In this story, what is the relationship between skin and identity?
4. Explain "unearned privilege."

PROBES

1. The topic of power discussed in Chapter 9 is a strong undercurrent in this reading. Explain how.
2. In what sense did the writers at the party "get the best of" Tsang?
3. What is communicated by the fact that Tsang does not give "the white man" a name?
4. At one point Tsang asks whether it is fair for her to insist that, when her white husband is confronted with the choice of joining the white establishment to do something he really wants to do or of denouncing it as racist, he should take the moral high ground. What do you think?

———

Marsha Houston begins this essay by illustrating how ethnicity can "trump" gender. Even though communication between women is usually more egalitarian and mutually supportive than communication between men, when one of the women is white and the other is African American, the communication often becomes, as Houston puts it, "stressful, insensitive, and in some cases even racist." She works these difficulties in this reading by identifying specific features of black women's and white women's talk that are different and by offering some concrete communication advice to white women about what to say and what not to say.

As endnote 9 explains, Houston's conclusions come from questionnaires filled out by 135 African American women and 100 white women—professionals, undergraduates, and graduate students. So what she calls "Black women's talk" and "White women's talk" may not fit every black or white woman, but it should be fairly representative of at least many women's experiences.

Black women perceive their own talk to be strong, assertive, and reflective of black experience in a white society, and they perceive white women's talk as arrogant, weak, and submissive. White women perceive their own talk as varied, appropriate, and accent-free, and they hear black women using black dialect—saying things like "young 'uns," "wif," and "wich you." This means that white women hear themselves speaking General American Speech and black women speaking dialect. Black women who speak both black dialect and General American

Speech are often perceived to speak only Black English. Black and white speakers also notice different features of each other's language.

"However," writes Houston, "there are exceptions." The bleak picture painted by her survey ignores the successful and satisfying communication that can and often does occur between black and white women. So in the last part of this reading, Houston focuses on the communication acts that bridge this particular set of cultural differences. She explains some particularly helpful communication moves by phrasing them as suggestions to white women who want to treat black women with respect and friendship. As she puts it, ". . . never utter: (1) 'I never even notice that you're black'; (2) 'You're different from most black people'; (3) 'I understand what you're going through as a black woman, because. . . .' "

If you're female and black, you can help your classmates with this material by describing the degree to which you believe Marsha Houston is right. Do your experiences resonate with hers? If you are not female and black, you can improve your ability to bridge these cultural differences not only by listening to your classmates who are, but also by bringing your own cultural experience to this reading. The most important thing, I believe, is to fully understand what is problematic about the three offending phrases. Whether or not you completely agree with Marsha Houston, try simply to understand what makes these statements offensive. Use this effort to broaden your awareness of general cultural differences and to sharpen your sense of a specific group of people who are *different* from you.

When Black Women Talk with White Women: Why Dialogues Are Difficult

Marsha Houston

My conversations with white women of equal social status involve much competition, aggression, and mutual lack of trust, intimacy, and equality. However, there are exceptions.

—A black woman graduate student

Gender and communication researchers have demonstrated that women's conversations with each other are different from their conversations with men. For example, they are more egalitarian and mutually supportive. Certainly, many conversations between African Americans[1] and white women are of this sort.

Excerpt from *Our Voices: Essays in Culture, Ethnicity, and Communication,* ed. by Conzales, Houston and Chen. © 1994 by Random House.

Yet I, and nearly every other African American woman I know, can recall many conversations with white women that were neither egalitarian nor supportive, conversations that we would describe as stressful, insensitive, and in some cases even racist. Like the graduate student quoted above, many African American women are likely to consider such "difficult dialogues"[2] with white peers to be the rule and open, satisfying conversations the exception.

The difficulties in black and white women's interracial conversations are the focus of this essay. I do not intend to give a definitive or an exhaustive analysis of women's interracial talk, but to explore two reasons why black women so often find conversations with white women unsatisfying and to suggest three statements to avoid in interracial conversation. I write from an African American woman's perspective, from within my ethnic cultural group, but I hope this essay will spark dialogue about both the differences and commonalities between black and white women speakers. . . .

MUTUAL NEGATIVE STEREOTYPES

A basic concept of contemporary communication theory is that a speaker does not merely respond to the manifest content of a message, but to his or her interpretation of the speaker's intention or meaning. In other words, I respond to what I *think* you *meant* by what you said. Such factors as the setting and occasion, the language variety or dialect, and the interpersonal relationship between speaker and listener influence message interpretation and response.

In addition, some understandings of talk are influenced by a speaker's gender or ethnicity. For example, researchers have found that when the same message is delivered in much the same manner by a woman or by a man, listeners interpret it quite differently, in part because they expect women and men to use different styles of talk and to have knowledge of different subjects.[3] Thomas Kochman has pointed out how the different nonverbal vocal cues that working-class African Americans and middle-class whites use to express the same emotion (e.g., sincerity or anger) can create diametrically opposed attributions regarding a speaker's intentions.[4] Each ethnic cultural group has come to expect the expression of various emotions or attitudes to sound a certain way. Thus, sincerity, when uttered in a high-keyed, dynamic, working-class black style, may sound like anger to middle-class whites. And when uttered in a low-keyed, non-dynamic, middle-class white style, it may sound like disinterest or deceit to working-class blacks. Because expectations for talk are culturally learned and seldom violated by speakers *within* a cultural group, they appear to be natural or normal to the members of that group. Misunderstanding and conflict can result when cultural expectations for how to express specific attitudes and emotions are violated.

By asking African American women to describe their communication style ("black women's talk" or "talking like a black woman") as well as that of white women ("white women's talk" or "talking like a white woman"), I endeavored to discover some of their expectations for talk.[5] Below are examples of these African American women's most frequent responses:

Black Women's Talk Is:

- standing behind what you say, not being afraid to speak your mind
- speaking with a strong sense of self-esteem
- speaking out; talking about what's on your mind
- getting down to the heart of the matter
- speaking with authority, intelligence, and common sense
- being very sure of oneself
- being very distinguished and educated
- reflecting black experience as seen by a black woman in a white patriarchal society

White Women's Talk Is:

- friendly (with an air of phoniness)
- arrogant
- know-it-all
- talking as if they think they're better than the average person
- mainly dealing with trivia
- talking proper about nothing
- weak, "air-headish"
- silly but educated
- illustrating fragility; seemingly dependent and helpless
- passive, submissive, delicate

I asked a comparable group of white women to describe their talk and that of black women. Here are their most frequent responses:

Black Women's Talk Is:

- using black dialect
- saying things like "young 'uns," "yous," "wif," and "wich you"
- using jive terms

White Women's Talk Is:

- all kinds of speech patterns
- distinct pronunciation
- using the appropriate words for the appropriate situations
- talking in a typical British-American language with no necessary accent and limited to "acceptable" middle-class women's topics

The above suggests that African American and white women hear very different things. Not only does each list contain positive descriptions of the group's own talk and negative descriptions of the other group's talk, but each focuses on different features. African American women concentrate on both their own and white women's interpersonal skills, strategies, and attributes. They see themselves as open, forthright, intelligent speakers and white women as duplicitous, arrogant, and frivolous. White women, on the other hand, concentrate their descriptions on language style—vocabulary, grammar, pronunciation—describing themselves as standard or correct and African American women as nonstandard, incorrect, or deviant.

Because they concentrated on language style, white women described only those African American women who use African-based black English as "talking like a black woman." Their descriptions suggest that black women who use General American Speech, the prestige variety of language in the U.S.,[6] are "talking white" (or talking "normally"). In contrast, African American women described themselves as speaking in "black women's talk" whenever they used particular interpersonal strategies (e.g., "standing behind what you say"; "getting down to the heart of the matter"), communication that is independent of language variety.

One reason why African American women perceived "black women's talk" as independent of language variety may be that many of us are bistylistic (able to speak two language varieties) while most white women are relatively monostylistic. College-educated, middle-class women who grew up and learned to speak in predominantly African American communities usually have a command of both Black English and General American Speech. Those of us who are bistylistic speakers switch language varieties to some extent[7] according to situations and conversational partners, but we do not feel that we shed our ethnic cultural identity when we use General American Speech. Barbara Smith describes black women's perspective on their two speaking styles in this way:

> Now, I don't think this is about acting white in a white context. It's about one, a lack of inspiration. Because the way you act with black people is because they inspire the behavior. And I *do* mean inspire . . . [W]hen you are in a white context, you think, 'Well, why bother? Why waste your time?' if what you're trying to do is get things across and communicate and what-have-you, *you talk in your second language.*[8]

In describing their style, African American women were able to look beneath the surface features of language choice and concentrate on underlying interpersonal skills and strategies. White women, unfamiliar with how language and interpersonal interaction work in black communities, defined only that black women's talk most different from their own in vocabulary, pronunciation, and grammar as "black."

Perhaps African American women's greater awareness of differences in language and style accounts for the final difference in the lists above. White women tended to describe their own talk as normal or universal ("all kinds of speech patterns") and African American women's talk as deviant or limited. But African American women described both their own and white women's talk as particular speaking styles.

The attention to different aspects of talk may be one reason why mutually satisfying dialogue between the two groups is often difficult. For example, researchers have noted the high value African American women place on talk that is forthright, sincere, and authentic, as did the women who responded to my questionnaire (e.g., "not being afraid to speak your mind").[9] This may sometimes conflict with the high value white women have been taught to place on politeness and propriety in speech, as several white respondents to the questionnaire indicated (e.g., "using appropriate words for the . . . situation").[10] Thus, white women may sound "phony" to black women because they have learned to be more concerned about being proper and polite than "getting down to the heart of the matter."

HOWEVER, THERE ARE EXCEPTIONS

The picture of black and white women's conversations painted here may seem particularly gloomy. The unequal power relationships that generally define the places of blacks and whites in the U.S. social order continue to intrude on our everyday interpersonal encounters. Our perceptions of one another as communicators are often riddled with stereotypes and misattributions. And yet open, satisfying conversations between African American and white women do occur; many black and white women are amicable colleagues and close friends.[11] As an African American woman who has been a student or professor at predominantly white universities for almost 30 years, I have many white women colleagues whose conversation I enjoy and a few friends whom I can count on for good talk. Even the graduate student whose stinging criticism of conversations with white women peers is quoted at the beginning of this essay admitted that "there are exceptions."

What is the nature of those exceptions? What communicative acts enable African American women to perceive white women's talk as authentic rather than "phony"? This is a complex question for which there may be as many answers as there are black women speakers (or as there are black and white women conversational partners). I would like to briefly suggest a response gleaned from my own interracial relationships and those of the members of my large network of African American women friends, relatives, students, and acquaintances.[12] I have chosen to phrase my response by offering three statements that a white woman who wants to treat black women with respect and friendship should never utter: (1) "I never even notice that you're black"; (2) "You're different from most black people"; (3) "I understand what you're going through as a black woman, because. . . ."

(1) "I Never Even Notice . . ."

The first statement sometimes comes as "We're all the same, really—just people." It expresses what I have come to call "the myth of generically packaged people." It is based on the incorrect assumption that cultural, sexual, or generational differences do not result in different social experiences and different interpretations of shared experiences.

Although intended to be nonracist, Statement 1 actually denies the uniqueness of black women's history and contemporary experiences. It suggests that the
speaker regards blackness as something negative, a problem that one "can't help"
and, therefore, as something that one's white friends should overlook. It denies
the possibility that blackness could be something to be valued, even celebrated.
Yet many black women view our blackness as a source of pride, not only because
of the many accomplished African American women and men who have overcome racism to make significant contributions, but also because of our knowledge
of how our personal histories have been influenced by our blackness.

In addition, as one white woman scholar has noted, when a white woman
says, "We're all alike. . . . ," she usually means, "I can see how *you* (a black
woman) are like *me* (a white woman)"; she does not mean, "I can see how *I* am
like *you*."[13] In other words, "just people" means "just *white* people"—that is,
people who are culturally and behaviorally similar to me, just people who share
my values and beliefs, just people who do not make me aware that they are culturally or historically different and who do not insist that I honor and respect
their way of being human. It is an ethnocentric statement.

Despite the nonracist intentions of the white women whom I have heard
utter "I never even notice. . . ," I interpret it as blatantly racist. It erases my ethnic cultural experience (a part of who I am), redefines it in white women's terms.

(2) "You're Different. . . ."

This statement is closely related to the first; I see it as an effort to subtract the
blackness from the woman. Sometimes the statement precedes other negative or
stereotypical statements about black people ("The black girls I went to high
school with in South Georgia. . . ," "Those black women on welfare . . . "). It
indicates that the speaker perceives there to be "acceptable" and "unacceptable"
black women or some groups of black women whom it is okay to hate.

Although I am anxious for white women to see that there is diversity among
African American women, and although some African American women desire
to separate themselves from elements of our community that they (and whites)
perceive as undesirable, I believe that few of us fail to see the racism lurking
behind this "divide and conquer" statement. I am different from the poor black
woman on welfare; I have a different personal history, more education, the ability to provide a better lifestyle and better life-chances for my son. But I am also
the same as her; we share an ethnic cultural history (in Africa and the U.S.), and
we share a life-long struggle with both racism and sexism. When I hear "You're
different . . .", I always wonder, "If I can respect and accept white women's differences from me, why can't they respect and accept my differences from them?"

(3) "I Understand Your Experience as a Black Woman Because. . . ."

I have heard this sentence completed in numerous, sometimes bizarre, ways, from
"because sexism is just as bad as racism" to "because I watch 'The Cosby Show,' "

to "because I'm also a member of a minority group. I'm Jewish . . . Italian . . . overweight. . . . "

The speaker here may intend to indicate her effort to gain knowledge of my cultural group or to share her own experiences with prejudice. I would never want to thwart her efforts or to trivialize such experiences. Yet I hear in such statements examples of the arrogance perceived by the black women who described "white women's talk" in the lists above. Similar experiences should not be confused with the same experience; my experience of prejudice is erased when you identify it as "the same" as yours. In addition, there are no shortcuts to interracial relationships, no vicarious ways to learn how to relate to the people of another culture (e.g., through reading or watching television). Only actual contact with individuals over an extended period of time begins to build interracial understanding.

I believe that "I understand your experience as a black woman because . . . " represents white women's attempt to express solidarity with African American women, perhaps motivated by the assumption that, before we can begin a friendship, we expect them to understand our life experiences in the way they understand their own. I make no such assumption about my white women friends, and I think they make no comparable assumption about me. There is much about white women's life experiences and perspectives that I may know about, but will never fully understand. Whether my friend is black or white, I do not presume to understand all, just to respect all.

The above three statements are words I have never heard from white women whom I count among my friends. Rather than treating our ethnic cultural differences as barriers to be feared or erased before true friendship can emerge, they embrace them as features that enrich and enliven our relationships.

REVIEW QUESTIONS

1. What does "egalitarian" mean? What are the main characteristics of egalitarian communication?
2. Give a specific example of an expression of *sincerity* in a "working-class black style" that is likely to be heard as *anger* by a white listener.
3. What is General American Speech?
4. What does Houston mean when she notes that many African American women are "bistylistic"?

PROBES

1. When describing communication differences, black women in Houston's survey focused on interpersonal skills and strategies while white women concentrated on vocabulary, grammar, and pronunciation. How do you explain this difference? What cultural barriers might this difference help intensify?

2. If General American Speech is the "second language" of many black women, how might this affect their communicating?

3. What do you believe are the differences between communicating "appropriately" and communicating in a "phony" way? How might this particular cultural difference between black and white women be bridged?

4. Explain how the statement, "We're all the same really—just people" can be interpreted to be insensitive or even racist.

5. How does the statement, "You're different from most black people" deny African American diversity?

6. "I understand your experience as a black woman because . . . ," is an attempt to establish solidarity that fails, according to Houston. Why? Explain her alternative to solidarity.

NOTES

1. Gwendolyn Etter-Lewis. (1991). Standing up and speaking out: African American women's narrative legacy, *Discourse and Society, II,* pp. 426–27.

2. Essed, pp. 144.

3. Barrie Thorne, Cheris Kramerae, & Nancy Henley. (1983). Language, gender, and society: Opening a second decade of research, in their *Language, Gender, and Society,* pp. 7–24. Rowley, Mass.

4. Thomas Kochman. (1981). Classroom Modalities in *Black and White: Styles in Conflict.* Urbana: University of Illinois Press.

5. One hundred thirty-five African American women (professionals, undergraduate, and graduate students) responded in writing to an open-ended questionnaire in which they freely described the talk of several social groups, including their own. A comparable group of 100 white women also responded to the questionnaire. Initial findings were reported in Marsha Houston (Stanback) and Carol Roach, "Sisters Under the Skin: Southern Black and White Women's Communication," and Marsha Houston, "Listening to Ourselves: African-American Women's Perspectives on Their Communication Style," both papers presented to the Southern States Communication Association, 1987 and 1992 respectively.

6. The speaking style I refer to as "General American Speech" others sometimes call "Standard English." I prefer the former term because it connotes the way of speaking (rather than writing) English that is accorded preference and prestige in the United States; thus, "General American Speech" is both a more communicatively and culturally accurate term than "Standard English."

7. Some black women change only their intonation patterns, and not their grammar or vocabulary, when they "switch" to a more black style. See discussions of the "levels" of Black English speech in Mary R. Hoover. (1978). Community attitudes toward black English. *Language in Society, 7,* pp. 65–87.

8. Barbara Smith and Beverly Smith. (1983). Across the kitchen table: A sister to sister conversation. In *This Bridge Called My Back: Writings by Radical Women of Color*, p. 119. (eds.) Cherrie Moraga and Gloria Anzaldua. New York: Kitchen Table/Women of Color Press.
9. Anita K. Foeman and Gary Pressley. (1989). Ethnic culture and corporate culture: Using black styles in organizations, *Communication Quarterly*, 33, 293–307; and Michael Hecht, Sidney Ribeau, and J. K. Alberts. (1989). An Afro-American perspective on interethnic communication, *Communication Monographs*, 56, pp. 385–410.
10. Robin Lakoff. (1975). Why women are ladies, in *Language and Woman's Place*. New York: Harper & Row.
11. Mary McCullough, Women's Friendships Across Cultures: An Ethnographic Study (Unpublished Manuscript, Temple University, 1989).
12. I admit that I chose these three statements in an "unscientific" manner, on the basis of their high experiential validity, rather than through any statistical sample. They are the statements that the women in my large network of black women friends, relatives, students, and acquaintances most often discuss as problematic in their conversations with white women; whenever I have shared my analysis of the statements with a group of black women whom I do not know (e.g., during a public speech for professional women or guest lecture at another university) they also have indicated that they hear them often and consider them insensitive.
13. Elizabeth Spelman. (1988). *Inessential Woman: Problems of Exclusion in Feminist Thought*. Boston: Beacon Press.

CHAPTER 12

Promoting Dialogue

Especially over the past ten years, many elected officials, teachers, trainers, managers, and community activists have been calling for more "dialogue." Of course, the term means different things to different people. Elected officials at national and local levels want better two-way communication with voters. Teachers on campuses across the country want less lecturing and more active involvement and open communication in their classrooms. Managers at Ford, Boeing, Motorola, Intel, and hundreds of smaller companies want to replace the command-and-control hierarchy with collaborative work teams, shared power, and "management by wandering around and talking." Community activists in Boston; Fargo; Albuquerque; Cupertino; London; Jerusalem; Aalborg, Denmark; Canberra, Australia; Cape Town, South Africa; and dozens of other cities encourage people with diverse backgrounds and radically different beliefs to talk respectfully and candidly with each other, rather than trying to shout each other down. They also try to replace distorted media campaigns, polarizing rhetoric, and violence with facilitated and mediated conversations among political enemies. But although specific definitions vary, in every case, proponents of dialogue have in mind the kind of communication that's being championed throughout this book.

For example, how might people bridge cultural differences (Chapter 11)? With dialogue. What often works in conflict (Chapter 10)? Dialogue. What's often the best communication with intimate partners (Chapter 8)? Dialogue. What's one useful and helpful way to define interpersonal communication (Chapter 2)? As dialogue. So this chapter draws from and contributes to a significant movement that's underway in many countries around the world, and it also summarizes a great deal of the rest of this book.

The first reading is from a book by best-selling author Deborah Tannen. Tannen's goal in this book is to draw attention to what she calls North America's "argument culture" and to encourage people to replace argument with dialogue. Her book shows how the argument culture is generated by media treatments of political and social issues as wars between opposing camps, and by the dominance of an "us versus them" mentality in politics. She tracks the effects of increasing litigation that extends the adversary legal system into every corner of professional, family, and private lives. She also notes how gender patterns—especially the ways boys are raised—encourage aggression and hostility. Then, in the final chapter, she suggests how the argument culture might be changed. This is the part of her book that I include here.

Tannen begins with a scene from a classroom where it looks and sounds like great learning is happening as students "engage in a heated debate." But on closer inspection it becomes apparent that only a few students are taking part, and that the process rewards the most adversarial attack-dog behaviors. She traces this educational approach to the

Greeks and early Europeans who modeled schooling after training exercises for war. She contrasts this model with Chinese and Indian educational approaches that emphasize enlightenment rather than overwhelming one's opponent.

Tannen is not against debate, but she is against the idea that adversarial communication is the *only* way to teach and learn. She uses the ancient yin-yang symbol to urge multidimensional thinking, and illustrates her point with a suggestion from anthropologist Mary Catherine Bateson that we think not in terms of "twos" but of "threes." Tannen concludes with some ideas about how this multidimensional—rather than "one side versus the other"—way of thinking can be applied in many different contexts. Fundamentally, Tannen urges her readers to remember that it is not necessary to make others wrong to prove that you are right.

This reading shows that one of this century's most respected North American writers and cultural critics believes in the powerful potential of dialogue. The other writings in this chapter spell out in much more detail how dialogue can work.

The Roots of Debate in Education and the Hope of Dialogue

Deborah Tannen

The teacher sits at the head of the classroom, feeling pleased with herself and her class. The students are engaged in a heated debate. The very noise level reassures the teacher that the students are participating, taking responsibility for their own learning. Education is going on. The class is a success.

But look again, cautions Patricia Rosof, a high school history teacher who admits to having experienced that wave of satisfaction with herself and the job she is doing. On closer inspection, you notice that only a few students are participating in the debate; the majority of the class is sitting silently, maybe attentive but perhaps either indifferent or actively turned off. And the students who are arguing are not addressing the subtleties, nuances, or complexities of the points they are making or disputing. They do not have that luxury because they want to win the argument—so they must go for the most gross and dramatic statements they can muster. They will not concede an opponent's point, even if they can see its validity, because that would weaken their position. Anyone tempted to synthesize the varying views would not dare to do so because it would look like a "cop-out," an inability to take a stand.

From *The Argument Culture* by Deborah Tannen, copyright © 1997 by Deborah Tannen. Used by permission of Random House, Inc.

One reason so many teachers use the debate format to promote student involvement is that it is relatively easy to set up and the rewards are quick and obvious: the decibel level of noise, the excitement of those who are taking part. Showing students how to integrate ideas and explore subtleties and complexities is much harder. And the rewards are quieter—but more lasting.

Our schools and universities, our ways of doing science and approaching knowledge, are deeply agonistic. We all pass through our country's educational system, and it is there that the seeds of our adversarial culture are planted. Seeing how these seeds develop, and where they came from, is a key to understanding the argument culture and a necessary foundation for determining what changes we would like to make.

ROOTS OF THE ADVERSARIAL APPROACH TO KNOWLEDGE

The argument culture, with its tendency to approach issues as a polarized debate, and the culture of critique, with its inclination to regard criticism and attack as the best if not the only type of rigorous thinking, are deeply rooted in Western tradition, going back to the ancient Greeks. This point is made by Walter Ong, a Jesuit professor at Saint Louis University, in his book *Fighting for Life*. Ong credits the ancient Greeks with a fascination with adversativeness in language and thought. He also connects the adversarial tradition of educational institutions to their all-male character. To attend the earliest universities, in the Middle Ages, young men were torn from their families and deposited in cloistered environments where corporal, even brutal, punishment was rampant. Their suffering drove them to bond with each other in opposition to their keepers—the teachers who were their symbolic enemies. Similar in many ways to puberty rites in traditional cultures, this secret society to which young men were confined also had a private language, Latin, in which students read about military exploits. Knowledge was gleaned through public oral disputation and tested by combative oral performance, which carried with it the risk of public humiliation. Students at these institutions were trained not to discover the truth but to argue either side of an argument—in other words, to debate. Ong points out that the Latin term for school, *ludus*, also referred to play or games, but it derived from the military sense of the word—training exercises for war.

If debate seems self-evidently the appropriate or even the only path to insight and knowledge, says Ong, consider the Chinese approach. Disputation was rejected in ancient China as "incompatible with the decorum and harmony cultivated by the true sage." During the Classical periods in both China and India, according to Robert T. Oliver, the preferred mode of rhetoric was exposition rather than argument. The aim was to "enlighten an inquirer," not to "overwhelm an opponent." And the preferred style reflected "the earnestness of investigation" rather than "the fervor of conviction." In contrast to Aristotle's trust of logic and mistrust of emotion, in ancient Asia intuitive insight was considered the superior means of perceiving truth. Asian rhetoric was devoted not to devising logical arguments but to explicating widely accepted propositions. Furthermore, the search for abstract truth that we assume is the goal of philosophy, while taken for granted in the West, was not found in the East, where philosophy was concerned with observation and experience.

If Aristotelian philosophy, with its emphasis on formal logic, was based on the assumption that truth is gained by opposition, Chinese philosophy offers an alternative view. With its emphasis on harmony, says anthropologist Linda Young, Chinese philosophy sees a diverse universe in precarious balance that is maintained by talk. This translates into methods of investigation that focus more on integrating ideas and exploring relations among them than on opposing ideas and fighting over them. . . .

THE SOCRATIC METHOD—OR IS IT?

Another scholar who questions the usefulness of opposition as the sole path to truth is philosopher Janice Moulton. Philosophy, she shows, equates logical reasoning with the Adversary Paradigm, a matter of making claims and then trying to find, and argue against, counterexamples to that claim. The result is a debate between adversaries trying to defend their ideas against counterexamples and to come up with counterexamples that refute the opponent's ideas. In this paradigm, the best way to evaluate someone's work is to "subject it to the strongest or most extreme opposition."

But if you parry individual points—a negative and defensive enterprise—you never step back and actively imagine a world in which a different system of ideas could be true—a positive act. And you never ask how larger systems of thought relate to each other. According to Moulton, our devotion to the Adversary Paradigm has led us to misinterpret the type of argumentation that Socrates favored: We think of the Socratic method as systematically leading an opponent into admitting error. This is primarily a way of showing up an adversary as wrong. Moulton shows that the original Socratic method—the *elenchus*—was designed to convince others, to shake them out of their habitual mode of thought and lead them to new insight. Our version of the Socratic method—an adversarial public debate—is unlikely to result in opponents changing their minds. Someone who loses a debate usually attributes that loss to poor performance or to an adversary's unfair tactics. . . .

QUESTION THE BASIC ASSUMPTION

My aim is not to put a stop to the adversarial paradigm, the doubting game, debate—but to diversify: Like a well-balanced stock portfolio, we need more than one path to the goal we seek. What makes it hard to question whether debate is truly the only or even the most fruitful approach to learning is that we're dealing with assumptions that we and everyone around us take to be self-evident.

A prominent dean at a major research university commented to me, "The Chinese cannot make great scientists because they will not debate publicly." Many people would find this remark offensive. They would object because it generalizes about all Chinese scientists, especially since it makes a negative evaluation. But I would also question the assumption that makes the generalization a criticism: the conviction that the only way to test and develop ideas is to debate them publicly. It may well be true that most Chinese scientists are reluctant to engage in public, rancorous debate. I see nothing insulting about such a claim; it derives from the Chinese cultural norms that many Chinese and Western observers have documented. But we also know that many Chinese have indeed been great scientists. The falsity of the dean's statement should lead us to question whether debate is the only path to insight. . . .

GETTING BEYOND DUALISM

At the heart of the argument culture is our habit of seeing issues and ideas as absolute and irreconcilable principles continually at war. To move beyond this static and limiting view, we can remember the Chinese approach to yin and yang. They are two principles, yes, but they are conceived not as irreconcilable polar opposites but as elements that coexist and should be brought into balance as much as possible. As sociolinguist Suzanne Wong Scollon notes, "Yin is always present in and changing into yang and vice versa." How can we translate this abstract idea into daily practice?

To overcome our bias toward dualism, we can make special efforts not to think in twos. Mary Catherine Bateson, an author and anthropologist who teaches at George Mason University, makes a point of having her class compare *three* cultures, not two. If students compare two cultures, she finds, they are inclined to polarize them, to think of the two as opposite to each other. But if they compare three cultures, they are more likely to think about each on its own terms.

As a goal, we could all try to catch ourselves when we talk about "both sides" of an issue—and talk instead about "all sides." And people in any field can try to resist the temptation to pick on details when they see a chance to score a point. If the detail really does not speak to the main issue, bite your tongue. Draw back and consider the whole picture. After asking, "Where is this wrong?" make an effort to ask "What is right about this?"—not necessarily *instead,* but *in addition.*

In the public arena, producers can try to avoid, whenever possible, structuring public discussions as debates. This means avoiding the format of having two guests discuss an issue, pro and con. In some cases three guests—or one— will be more enlightening than two.

An example of the advantage of adding a third guest was an episode of *The Diane Rehm Show* on National Public Radio following the withdrawal of Anthony Lake from nomination as director of central intelligence. White House Communications Director Ann Lewis claimed that the process of confirming presidential appointments has become more partisan and personal. Tony Blankley, former communications director for Newt Gingrich, claimed that the process has always been rancorous. Fortunately for the audience, there was a third guest: historian Michael Beschloss, who provided historical perspective. He explained that during the immediately preceding period of 1940 to 1990, confirmation hearings were indeed more benign than they have been since, but in the 1920s and the latter half of the nineteenth century, he said, they were also "pretty bloody." In this way, a third guest, especially a guest who is not committed to one side, can dispel the audience's frustration when two guests make opposite claims. . . .

MOVING FROM DEBATE TO DIALOGUE

Many of the issues I have discussed are also of concern to Amitai Etzioni and other communitarians. In *The New Golden Rule,* Etzioni proposes rules of engagement to make dialogue more constructive between people with differing views. His rules of engagement are designed to reflect—and reinforce—the tenet that people whose ideas conflict are still members of the same community. Among these rules are:

- Don't demonize those with whom you disagree.
- Don't affront their deepest moral commitments.
- Talk less of rights, which are nonnegotiable, and more of needs, wants, and interests.
- Leave some issues out.
- Engage in a dialogue of convictions: Don't be so reasonable and conciliatory that you lose touch with a core of belief you feel passionately about.

. . . producers putting together television or radio shows and journalists covering stories might consider—in at least some cases—preferring rather than rejecting potential commentators who say they cannot take one side or the other unequivocally. Information shows might do better with only one guest who is given a chance to explore an idea in depth rather than two who will prevent each other from developing either perspective. A producer who feels that two guests with radically opposed views seem truly the most appropriate might begin by asking whether the issue is being framed in the most constructive way. If it is, a third or fourth participant could be invited as well, to temper the "two sides" perspective.

Perhaps it is time to reexamine the assumption that audiences always prefer a fight. In reviewing a book about the history of *National Geographic,* Marina Warner scoffs at the magazine's policy of avoiding attack. She quotes the editor who wrote in 1915, "Only what is of a kindly nature is printed about any country or people, everything unpleasant or unduly critical being avoided." Warner describes this editorial approach condescendingly as a "happy-talk, feel-good philosophy" and concludes that "its deep wish not to offend has often made it dull." But the facts belie this judgment. *National Geographic* is one of the most successful magazines of all time—as reported in the same review, its circulation "stands at over 10 million, and the readership, according to surveys, is four times that number."

Perhaps, too, it is time to question our glorification of debate as the best, if not the only, means of inquiry. The debate format leads us to regard those doing different kinds of research as belonging to warring camps. There is something very appealing about conceptualizing differing approaches in this way, because dichotomies appeal to our sense of how knowledge should be organized.

Well, what's wrong with that?

What's wrong is that it obscures aspects of disparate work that overlap and can enlighten each other.

What's wrong is that it obscures the complexity of research. Fitting ideas into a particular camp requires you to oversimplify them. Again, disinformation and distortion can result. Less knowledge is gained, not more. And time spent attacking an opponent or defending against attacks is not spent doing something else—like original research.

What's wrong is that it implies that only one framework can apply, when in most cases many can. As a colleague put it, "Most theories are wrong not in what they assert but in what they deny." Clinging to the elephant's leg, they loudly proclaim that the person describing the elephant's tail is wrong. This is not going to help them—or their readers—understand an elephant. Again, there are parallels in personal relationships. I recall a man who had just returned from a weekend human development seminar. Full of enthusiasm, he explained the main lesson he had learned: "I don't have to make others wrong to prove that I'm right." He experienced this revelation as a liberation; it relieved him of the burden of trying to prove others wrong.

If you limit your view of a problem to choosing between two sides, you inevitably reject much that is true, and you narrow your field of vision to the limits of those two sides, making it unlikely you'll pull back, widen your field of vision, and discover the paradigm shift that will permit truly new understanding.

In moving away from a narrow view of debate, we need not give up conflict and criticism altogether. Quite the contrary, we can develop more varied—and more constructive—ways of expressing opposition and negotiating disagreement.

We need to use our imaginations and ingenuity to find different ways to seek truth and gain knowledge, and add them to our arsenal—or, should I say, to the ingredients for our stew. It will take creativity to find ways to blunt the most dangerous blades of the argument culture. It's a challenge we must undertake, because our public and private lives are at stake.

REVIEW QUESTIONS

1. According to Tannen, what are the advantages and disadvantages of using debate as a teaching tool?
2. What does "agonistic" mean?
3. Explain the difference between trusting logic (Aristotle) and treating intuition as a superior way to perceive the truth (ancient Asia).
4. True or false: Tannen wants to replace debate with dialogue. Explain.

5. Tell how the yin-yang principle works.
6. Provide a concrete example of each of the five communication rules or guidelines that Amitai Etzioni suggests.

PROBES

1. Based on your experience in schools and universities, do you agree with Tannen that "our ways of doing science and approaching knowledge, are deeply agonistic"? Explain.
2. Does it make good cultural sense to try to import Eastern ways into Western schools? Why or why not?
3. One of Tannen's concrete suggestions is this: "After asking, 'Where is this wrong?' make an effort to ask 'What is right about this?'—not necessarily *instead* but *in addition*." Give an example of making these moves in one of the subjects you are now studying.
4. How might the attitude, "I don't have to make others wrong to prove that I'm right" be evident in your communication? List half a dozen (a) verbal and (b) nonverbal ways you might live out this belief.

NOTES

1. *Going back to the ancient Greeks:* This does not mean it goes back in an unbroken chain. David Noble, in *A World Without Women,* claims that Aristotle was all but lost to the West during the early Christian era and was rediscovered in the medieval era, when universities were first established. This is significant for his observation that many early Christian monasteries welcomed both women and men who could equally aspire to an androgynous ideal, in contrast to the Middle Ages, when the female was stigmatized, unmarried women were consigned to convents, priests were required to be celibate, and women were excluded from spiritual authority.
2. *Ong credits the ancient Greeks:* There is a fascinating parallel in the evolution of the early Christian Church and the Southern Baptist Church: Noble shows that the early Christian Church regarded women as equally beloved of Jesus and equally capable of devoting their lives to religious study, so women comprised a majority of early converts to Christianity, some of them leaving their husbands—or bringing their husbands along— to join monastic communities. It was later, leading up to the medieval period, that the clerical movement gained ascendancy in part by systematically separating women, confining them in either marriage or convents, stigmatizing them, and barring them from positions of power within the church. Christine Leigh Heyrman, in *Southern Cross: The Beginnings of the Bible Belt,* shows that a similar trajectory characterized the

Southern Baptist movement. At first, young Baptist and Methodist preachers (in the 1740s to 1830s) preached that both women and blacks were equally God's children, deserving of spiritual authority—with the result that the majority of converts were women and slaves. To counteract this distressing demography, the message was changed: Antislavery rhetoric faded, and women's roles were narrowed to domesticity and subservience. With these shifts, the evangelical movement swept the South. At the same time, Heyrman shows, military imagery took over: The ideal man of God was transformed from a "willing martyr" to a "formidable fighter" led by "warrior preachers."

3. *"Incompatible with the decorum."* Ong, *Fighting for Life,* p. 122. Ong's source, on which I also rely, is Oliver, *Communication and Culture in Ancient India and China.* My own quotations from Oliver are from p. 259.

4. *"Subject it to":* Moulton, "A Paradigm of Philosophy," p. 153.

5. Suzanne Wong Scollon: Personal communication.

6. Mary Catherine Bateson: Personal communication.

7. *White House Communications Director:* At the time of this show, Ms. Lewis was deputy communications director.

8. *His rules of engagement:* Etzioni, *The New Golden Rule,* pp. 104–106. He attributes the rule "Talk less of rights . . . and more of needs, wants, and interests" to Mary Ann Glendon.

9. *In reviewing a book:* Marina Warner, "High-Minded-Pursuit of the Exotic," review of *Reading National Geographic* by Catherine A. Lutz and Jane L. Collins in *The New York Times Book Review,* Sept. 19, 1993, p. 13.

10. *"Most theories are wrong":* I got this from A. L. Becker, who got it from Kenneth Pike, who got it from . . .

These two brief excerpts are taken from a book called *Relational Responsibility: Resources for Sustainable Dialogue.* The first paragraph sketches what the authors mean by the first part of that title—"relational responsibility"—and the rest of the reading clarifies how relational responsibility is a part of dialogue.

The ideas in the first paragraph are important, because the approach to dialogue taken in this book forces a change in the meaning of the familiar term, "responsibility." Traditionally, "responsibility" means that someone is responsible, at fault, or to blame for what happens. If you "take responsibility" you admit what you did to cause something (usually) bad to happen. But if communication is truly continuous and if all humans are responding to events and actions that came before us, then this idea of "original fault" or "blame" has to be reconsidered. "Responsibility" still exists, but it means something more like "response-ability," the willingness and ability to respond.

In the second part of this reading, Eero Riikonen builds on this idea by appropriating some concepts from the Russian writer, Mikhail Bakhtin. Bakhtin is the person who reminded his readers that, since no human is Adam or Eve, who first disturbed the eternal silence of the universe, each of us is always *responding* to what's happened before us. Riikonen explains that this means speech is relational in three senses, and dialogue is speech that reflects this relational quality of speech.

Riikonen also identifies other qualities of dialogue that emerge in the writings of Australian communication researcher Robyn Penman and the British-American communication scholar John Shotter. They make one of the main points of *Bridges Not Walls*, that communication is not information transmission but the collaborative construction of worlds of meaning.

Riikonen ends by discussing what he means by "dialogical rights and responsibilities," a concept that he prefers to the notion of "relational responsibility." As a whole, this excerpt connects ideas about dialogue to efforts in many countries to promote this kind of interpersonal communicating.

Relational Responsibility and Dialogue

RELATIONAL RESPONSIBILITY

Sheila McNamee and Kenneth J. Gergen

The concept of relational responsibility derives from the . . . premise that meaningful language is generated within processes of relationship. In effect, all that we propose to be real and good . . . is born of human interchange. From this perspective, there can be no moral beliefs, no sense of right and wrong, no vision of a society worth struggling for without some basis in relational process. . . . The tradition of individual responsibility—in which single individuals are held blameworthy for untoward events—has a chilling effect on relationships. It typically isolates and alienates and ultimately invites the eradication of the other—a step toward nonmeaning. In what follows, we thus shift the focus to relational responsibility, that is, toward means of valuing, sustaining, and creating forms of relationship out of which common meanings—and thus moralities—can take wing. By using the term *responsibility*, we are not sounding the trumpet for the individual's responsibility to relationship; as we shall propose, individuals are such only by virtue of their creation in relationship. Rather, we use the term responsibility here not as a moralistic wedge but as a conversational resource; it is a term that may enter conversations in ways that might sustain and support the process

"Relational Responsibility and Dialogue" by Sheila McNamee and Kenneth J. Gergen from *Relational Responsibility*, pp. 141–149. Reprinted by permission of Sage Publications.

of constructing meaning as opposed to terminating it. The term does indeed draw moral force from our longstanding tradition of individualist morality; in the present case, we simply hope to enlist such force to render more urgent the invitation. Relational responsibility, then, lies within the shared attempt to sustain the conditions in which we can join in the construction of meaning and morality. . . .

DIALOGUE

Eero Riikonen

Dialogue, as a concept, has at least two very different senses. It can be seen cognitively, as a exchange of rational arguments among (more or less) equal persons. Or it can been seen from a perspective of connectedness and inspiration. However, it is the second view that is more interesting for me and, I think, more promising. . . . Dialogue, in this second, Bakhtinian (1981) vein, refers to joint action that ties people together and creates the temporary world they experience. Dialogue in this latter sense stands in opposition to everything that is destructive for curiosity. The main enemies seem to be objectification processes related to various forms of "knowing already." Knowing already dissolves the need to look beyond averages or categories. It is the prime source of nonparticipation.

For the dialogue to continue, it has to be appealing to all participants— genuine dialogues must be inspiring or at least interesting to continue. This is not possible if the participants are not interested in what is interesting for each other and not willing to cultivate it. This type of combination of self-interest . . . a (personal) craving for inspiring experiences and an interest in the interests of others, is essential for the birth and thriving of relationality of this central type.

There are other important things, too, such as a degree of allowed unpredictability, which is needed for freshness and interest, and a safe enough context for interaction. A prerequisite for genuine dialogue is thus allowing, to some degree or another, the expression of individual and constantly changing perspectives and individual or shared inspirations, enchantments, and desires. . . .

Bakhtin (1981) underlines consistently the essential impossibility of nonsocial or nonrelational language use. Speech is relational in (at least) a triple sense: (a) it creates, maintains, and changes relationships; (b) all utterances bear reflections of the addressees; (c) speech forms its own context and backdrop of further speech and social relations linked to it. The latter sense might be the most difficult to grasp. It refers to the fact that speech creates an environment for actual and evolving interaction, something from which and to which to respond. It is the "where we are"—the situation of the speakers. It is relatively easy to produce suffocating, sterile, oppressive, depressive, or frightening interactional environments. Correspondingly, it is possible to create enabling, empowering, and trust-enhancing conversational contexts.

What I call genuine dialogue on these pages is closely linked to the concept of relational responsibility. Dialogue, the Bakhtinian dialogue, is in fact an enactment of relational responsibility. Genuine dialogue becomes impossible when the participants cease to accept a joint responsibility for its inspiring quality. As soon as they do not see themselves anymore (at least to some extent) as a "we" having a responsibility (and good reasons) to be interested in each other's interests, the dialogue ends.

. . . The list of relevant authors who have focused on these aspects is a long one but must include people like Mikhail Bakhtin (1981), John Shotter (1993), Gaston Bachelard (1992), and Jean Baudrillard (1994). What all of these authors have in common, I think, is a belief that what makes interaction-dialogue inspiring, meaningful, or resonating, and thus capable of diminishing isolation and increasing connectedness, cannot be understood in any purely cognitive or rational way. . . .

METAPHORICAL AND DIALOGICAL
PERSPECTIVES OF CONNECTEDNESS

Communication researcher Robyn Penman (1992), who has a strong interest in how different forms of interaction allow genuine participation, has recently written about "good communication" from a postmodern perspective. She concludes that so-called goodness of communication should be defined according to moral criteria. We can say that good communication does good things to people.

Penman (1992) uses four criteria to describe this kind of communication. First, it has to start from the premise that the talk-text in which we are participating constitutes the social realities of the moment ("constitutiveness"). Second, the communication has to be open to constant revision ("contextualness"). Communication fulfilling the third criteria, "diversity," recognizes the right of the other's interpretations to exist. The fourth criteria is "incompleteness," which means that neither communication nor the meanings generated can ever be complete.

Seen from this perspective, communication is not transmitting information from one receiver or from one head to another. Rather, communication is creating common episodes, commonplaces, or common temporary worlds (see Shotter, 1993b, pp. 63–65). These often rapidly changing shared worlds have their own rules, temptations, and despairs. They always support some possibilities, some forms of meaningfulness, some types of relationships, and some moral orders— and not others.

Expert languages and scientific thinking are problematic not only because of their capability to reproduce power differences but also because they tend to obstruct the visibility of the metaphorical, inspiring, living dimension of talk. When we study any group of people in informal conversations, we see that they jump relentlessly from topic to topic and from one point of view to another; the old topics and perspectives often become stale. It is indeed typical of problematic and dehumanizing situations that some or all participants are denied the right to both thematic variation and use of metaphorical language (the use of instrumental language is preferred). Freshness and metaphoricality—which of course have many links—are in this sense basic social resources that are needed to keep interaction interesting to all participants.

Bakhtin (as cited in Morson & Emerson, 1990) says what molds and transforms dialogical interaction is its living context. It is living because it is both continuously created and changed by the talk and taken into account by it. It is, in a sense, both the background, motivator, and evaluator of dialogue. . . .

The dialogical view proposed in this article implies that we could see the processes of "solving problems," including that of isolation, in all spheres of human action. We could say that problems are areas of experience that are outside dialogue. It is evident that there are many methods by which a regeneration of genuine dialogue can happen. . . .

DIALOGICAL RIGHTS AND RESPONSIBILITIES

I prefer the concept of *dialogical rights and responsibilities* to that of *relational responsibility.* For me, it seems to tap some central issues, especially the importance of mutual rewards for connectedness. As I have claimed already, genuine dialogue does not survive without real interest and freshness.

People's moral positions and their experienced self-worth are either implicitly or explicitly involved in all dialogues and discourses, even in the most transient or technical ones. All interaction supports certain social roles and positions, not others. In interactions that arouse hopelessness or frustration, people are put into hopeless social positions; they feel that they are taken as objects in one way or another. For the same reasons, conversations (and also interaction with written texts) can in a very real sense either support or diminish experiences such as optimism, belongingness, motivation, and self-worth.

I think that the right to good interaction should really be one of the service user's basic rights. What is really at stake is everybody's right to be considered as a human being or a person. The right to be handled as a person is actualized in and by interaction.

I consider the right to participate in rewarding interaction as a very central issue indeed. From the proposed dialogical perspective, it is of course nonsensical to speak only of rights. A genuine dialogue is a form of joint action, and all participants have responsibilities for its results. The responsibility for all participants is in essence the same: be alive, be trustworthy, and be human.

I am claiming that we should be much more interested in how to develop the art of relevant, interesting, and enabling conversations . . . , even if this is a difficult task for reasons already described. Because we are dealing with a living interaction in which we are constantly immersed, these skills cannot be formulated as abstract principles. The skills should also not be seen as individual—we could also see them as parts of organization, team, and group cultures. A metaphor of a developing chamber orchestra could perhaps be a good one. To learn, develop, and practice these arts, many ways of talking and relating are needed. That is, the participants must have a multitude of ways of attempting to support beneficial and providential contexts. The knowledges needed are not exceptional. Success requires seeing, using, and developing our own existing everyday skills.

REVIEW QUESTIONS

1. Explain the difference between individual responsibility and relational responsibility.
2. Paraphrase Riikonen's definition of dialogue as "joint action that ties people together and creates the temporary world they experience."
3. Explain the three senses in which speech, according to Bakhtin, is relational.
4. Paraphrase Riikonen's point about metaphor.

PROBES

1. If responsibility is understood to be relational, as McNamee and Gergen argue it should be, what will prompt individuals to take seriously, and to be careful about their individual roles in communication events?
2. Many people say that communication is "good" if it is effective. Riikonen says that Robyn Penman defines "good communication" as morally good. Explain the difference. Which approach do you think is preferable?
3. Riikonen's notion, "dialogical rights and responsibilities" adds something important to McNamee and Gergen's "relational responsibility"; namely, the real interests of each person involved. Explain.

REFERENCES

1. Bachelard, G. (1992). *The poetics of space.* Boston: Beacon.
2. Bakhtin, M. M. (1981). *The dialogic imagination: Four essays by M. M. Bakhtin* (M. Holquist, Ed.; C. Emerson & M. Holquist, Trans.). Austin: University of Texas Press.
3. Baudrillard, J. (1994). *Pensée radicale.* Paris: Morsure.
4. Morson, G., & Emerson, C. (1990). *Mikhail Bakhtin: Creation of prosaics.* Stanford, Calif.: Stanford University Press.
5. Penman, R. (1992). Good theory and good practice: An argument in progress. *Communication Theory, 2* (3), 234–250.
6. Shotter, J. (1993a). *Conversational realities: Constructing life through language.* London: Sage.
7. Shotter, J. (1993b). *Cultural politics of everyday life: Social constructionisms, rhetoric, and knowing of the third kind.* Toronto: University of Toronto Press.

W illiam Isaacs is a teacher at the Sloan School of Management at Massachusetts Institute of Technology and president of DIA*logos,* a consulting and leadership education firm based in Cambridge, Massachusetts. Since the 1980's, he and his colleagues have been working with such major organizations as Ford, Motorola, Boeing, and Shell to enhance dialogue. This reading is taken from the first chapter of Isaacs's 1999 book, *Dialogue and the Art of Thinking Together.*

Like Deborah Tannen (the author of the first reading in this chapter), Isaacs wants to change some patterns of communication that he believes are widespread, not only in the organizations he works with but also in families, classrooms, and other settings. As he puts it, a major part of the problem is that "People do not listen, they reload." There is too much us-versus-them and not enough recognition that a conversation can be an exchange that is structured with "a center, not sides."

As Isaacs points out, the word "dialogue" comes from two Greek words. *Dia* means "through" and *logos* has a number of meanings, the most general of which is "meaning." So "dialogue" is a label for a conversation or exchange where the *meanings* that the parties held emerged *through* the exchange itself. In other words, dialogue is literally the art of *thinking together* rather than thinking separately. In a dialogue, all the parties contribute to the construction of understandings that are different from what they began with. Ideally seated in a circle facing one another, they use verbal and nonverbal communication to put their relevant beliefs, opinions, facts, information, and concerns into the center of the circle so the group can mix and "cook" them into a synthesis that's new.

This kind of dialogue is definitely not easy, especially in the corporate and organizational contexts that Isaacs works in most. Labor has a long history of being the enemy of management. Subordinates traditionally don't trust superiors, and managers are often trained to treat their workers like a drill sergeant treats privates. As Isaacs says, dialogue requires that "you relax your grip on certainty and listen to the possibilities that result simply from being in a relationship with others." Because the process is so challenging, there are endless examples in corporate, public, and political life of exactly the opposite. As Isaacs writes, "When Russians and Chechens, Northern Irish and British, management and union, husband and wife differ, they are usually defending their positions, looking for evidence that they are right and that others are wrong."

Isaacs lays out three "levels of action in dialogue," three ways people can act to help promote dialogue where it does not now occur. The first is to "produce coherent actions." The bottom line here is that you work to maintain a unity among your being, saying, and doing— among who you *are,* what you *say,* and what you *do.* The second action is to "create fluid structures of interaction." This means encouraging openness rather than closed structures, acknowledging that there are exceptions to every rule, and focusing on what happens *next* rather than on "whose fault this is." The third action is to "provide wholesome space for dialogue." The key to this action is to remember, as Isaacs puts it, that "Dividing things up is not the problem. Forgetting the connections is."

In other chapters of his book, Isaacs describes four necessary "capacities" for dialogue—listening, respecting, suspending, and voicing—and explains how to shape conversational structures to encourage it. If you're interested in these developments, I highly encourage you to get a copy of his book. But this short excerpt should illustrate pretty clearly why many very bottom-line-oriented business people are recognizing that dialogue is not some unrealistic, fuzzy-minded dream but a way of communicating that can enhance an organization's short-term and long-term success.

A Conversation with a Center, Not Sides

William Isaacs

"I never saw an instance of one or two disputants convincing the other by argument."

—*Thomas Jefferson*

When was the last time you were really listened to? If you are like most people, you will probably find it hard to recall. Think about a time when you saw others try to talk together about a tough issue. How did it go? Did they penetrate to the heart of the matter? Did they find a common understanding that they were able to sustain? Or were they wooden and mechanical, each one reacting, focusing only on their own fears and feelings, hearing only what fit their preconceptions?

Most of us, despite our best intentions, tend to spend our conversational time waiting for the first opportunity to offer our own comments or opinions. And when things heat up, the pace of our conversations resembles a gunfight on Main Street: "You're wrong!" "That's crazy!" The points go to the one who can draw the fastest or who can hold his ground the longest. As one person I know recently joked, "People do not listen, they reload." When televised sessions of the United States Congress or the British Parliament show the leaders of our society advocating, catcalling, booing, and shouting over one another in the name of reasoned discourse, we sense that something is deeply wrong. They sense the same thing, but seem powerless to do anything about it.

All too often our talk fails us. Instead of creating something new, we polarize and fight. Particularly under conditions where the stakes are high and differences abound, we tend to harden into positions that we defend by advocacy. To advocate is to speak for your point of view. Usually, people do this unilaterally, without making room for others. The Israelis and the Palestinians could not agree over settlements on the West Bank. Sales managers fight with manufacturing managers over production schedules. Executives differ over the best use of capital. Friends argue about what constitutes morality. The headlines chronicle a multitude of times when people might have come together in a new way and yet somehow failed to do so.

There are, of course, many ways in which strong advocacy like this is reasonable. We have loyalties to our tribe, to our company, to our religion, or to our country. We do not live in a neutral world at all, but, rather, one in which the landscape is thickly settled with opinions, positions, and beliefs about the right and wrong way of perceiving and interacting with the world and each other. As a result, we have interests to protect, ideas and beliefs to defend, difficult or downright crazy colleagues to avoid, and our own way in the world to make. There are certainly times when we must defend our views.

But dialogue is an altogether very different way of talking together. Generally, we think of dialogue as "better conversation." But there is much more to it. *Dialogue,* as I define it, is a *conversation with a center, not sides.* It is a way of taking the energy of our differences and channeling it toward something that has never been created before. It lifts us out of polarization and into a greater common sense, and is thereby a means for accessing the intelligence and coordinated power of groups of people.

Dialogue fulfills deeper, more widespread needs than simply "getting to yes." The aim of a negotiation is to reach agreement among parties who differ. The intention of dialogue is to reach new understanding and, in doing so, to form a totally new basis from which to think and act. In dialogue, one not only solves problems, one *dis*solves them. We do not merely try to reach agreement, we try to create a context from which many new agreements might come. And we seek to uncover a base of shared meaning that can greatly help coordinate and align our actions with our values.

The roots of the word *dialogue* come from the Greek words *dia* and *logos. Dia* means "through"; *logos* translates to "word," or "meaning." In essence, a dialogue is a *flow of meaning.* But it is more than this too. In the most ancient meaning of the word, *logos* meant "to gather together," and suggested an intimate awareness of the relationships among things in the natural world. In that sense, *logos* may be best rendered in English as "relationship." The Book of John in the New Testament begins: "In the beginning was the Word (*logos*)." We could now hear this as "In the beginning was the Relationship."

To take it one step further, dialogue is a conversation in which people think together in relationship. Thinking together implies that you no longer take your own position as final. You relax your grip on certainty and listen to the possibilities that result simply from being in a relationship with others—possibilities that might not otherwise have occurred.

Most of us believe at some level that we must fix things or change people in order to make them reachable. Dialogue does not call for such behavior. Rather, it asks us to listen for an already existing wholeness, and to create a new kind of association in which we listen deeply to all the views that people may express. It asks that we create a quality of listening and attention that can include—but is larger than—any single view.

Dialogue addresses problems farther "upstream" than conventional approaches. It attempts to bring about change at the source of our thoughts and feelings, rather than at the level of results our ways of thinking produce. . . . An analogy can be found in the environmental movement, which has moved in the past twenty years from trying to clean up waste after it spews out of the pipe to "source reduction"—eliminating toxins by redesigning core processes. Dialogue seeks to address the problem of fragmentation not by rearranging the physical components of a conversation but by uncovering and shifting the organic underlying structures that produce it. . . .

Of course thinking together is not as easy as it sounds. In my experience, most people do not even consider the possibility. Most of the time they are *thinking alone.* When Russians and Chechens, Northern Irish and British, management and union, husband and wife, differ, they are usually defending their positions, looking for evidence that they are right and that others are wrong. They assume they have to make their points without making themselves too vulnerable to the opinions of their opponent. They withhold information, feel hurt or betrayed, and lose respect for the other person or party. They want to fight or flee. In such conversations someone has to win and someone has to lose. Our meetings and our institutions can be very lonely places.

When I learned physics in high school I was taught to think of atoms as a set of microscopic billiard balls zooming past one another and sometimes colliding at high speeds. That image seems to fit the way most people interact when they're talking about difficult issues. They zoom past each other. Or they collide abruptly and then veer away. These collisions create friction—which we describe as things "heating up." We don't like the way that "heat" feels, so we respond to it by trying to cool things down, to at least get to "maybe," to compromise. We never learn to live over time in close contact with the heat, to understand why it emerges, or to explore our mutual understanding of the conditions that produced it in first place. We do not discover our resilience or our ability to completely alter the experience.

Thinking alone is so taken for granted, so deeply embedded in our modern ways of living that to suggest anything else is possible or needful often comes across as Pollyannaish. Yet it may be our headstrong belief that this is the only way to go that is getting us in trouble.

THREE LEVELS OF ACTION IN A DIALOGUE

How can we learn, as individuals, to take actions that might be conducive to evoking dialogue? How can we create dialogue in settings where people may not have initially been willing to engage in it? How can we broaden the dialogue process to include more people? How can we prevent reentrenchment? These are some of the central questions this book seeks to answer.

The key to answering them requires we address three fundamental levels of human interaction. Together these three create a foundation by which we can think together, and are the focus of the remainder of this book. We must learn to:

1. **Produce coherent actions.** One of the more puzzling things about our species is that we sometimes live in folly: We do things we do not intend. You may have noticed this about yourself. A dialogic approach requires that we learn to be aware of the contradictions between what we say and what we do. Dialogue requires that we learn four new behaviors to overcome these limits. Developing *capacity for new behavior* puts us in position to resolve incoherence and produce effects we intend.

2. **Create fluid structures of interaction.** Human beings do not always see the forces that are operating below the surface of their conversations. As individuals, this leads people to misread both what others are doing and the impact that they themselves are likely to have on others. In groups and organizations, it leads people continuously to find that efforts to make change are neutralized by other, well-intentioned individuals who have very different goals and ways of seeing the world. It is possible to develop an intuitive understanding of the nature of these forces, and to develop ways of anticipating and managing them. We can develop *"predictive intuition."* Predictive intuition is the ability to see these forces more clearly, enabling us to liberate stuck structures of interaction, free energy, and promote a more fluid means of thinking and working together.

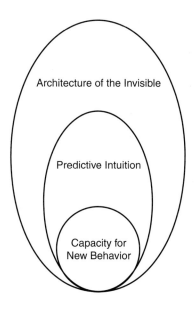

Architecture of the Invisible

Predictive Intuition

Capacity for
New Behavior

3. **Provide wholesome space for dialogue.** What is often missed when people try to create dialogue is that our conversations take place in an envelope or atmosphere that greatly influences how we think and act. The space from which people come greatly influences their quality of insight, clarity of thought, and depth of feeling. This space is composed of the habits of thought and quality of attention that people bring to any interaction. By becoming more conscious of the *architecture of the invisible* atmosphere in our conversations, we may have profound effect on our worlds.

To understand how each of these levels works, consider this example. A colleague recently told me about a major capital project in a factory of his that was supposed to cost one hundred million dollars in new investment. Very early on, the people planning the project realized that its true cost would likely be much higher than anyone had anticipated—perhaps as much as twice the initial estimates. They also quickly came to the conclusion that their senior managers and outside investors would reject any proposal that went over the number they had already publicly stated they were intending to spend. So the planners created a proposal that looked like it would work for the cost that had been stated. Do some things now and other things later, they told themselves. Within two years these same people were spending hundreds of millions of *additional* dollars to correct the problems that arose by using parts and materials that cost less but were not really designed for the purposes intended.

There is something familiar, obvious, and a little sad about a story like this.

They should have "done it right" the first time or not done it at all, right? Perhaps, except that this is far easier said than done! How often have you done something you knew was not quite right only because there did not seem to be any alternatives? Or you didn't realize until much later that the situation was awry in some crucial way?

How can we understand this situation?

First, their actions lacked coherence. These people *acted in ways that were problematic:* They judged and did not admit to it. They covered up and acted like they were not. They pushed for their point of view but resisted others who pushed for theirs. They attributed that others would not be interested or open to tackling the "real" difficulties and so did not raise them. In so acting, they remained unaware that they were doing to others what they attributed others would do to them. Despite all the questions about how to pull off a project of this size, no one really looked into how they were systematically undermining their own efforts.

Second, everyone in this story was caught in a web of traps: the senior managers who went public with their original numbers and were closed to hearing alternatives; the engineers who rearranged the project to fit the original figures out of a belief that this was what their managers wanted; the banks who were trying to get their money out of the situation; the investors who were focused only on short-range financial returns rather than on the long-range thinking and acting behind them; and the managers who felt compelled to hedge, to cover up this fact, and to jury-rig a solution for their cover-up. Clearly this problem is not unique. Everywhere we look, myopic vision, petty misunderstandings, and small deceits escalate into gross, wasteful calamities that seem like they could be avoided if people would only talk to each other with a different kind of conversational presence and "fire."

Most of the time, people do not intentionally set out to undermine their own projects. Yet this is certainly what happened in this case: Most of the managers who created the initial plan were eventually fired, costs were vastly underestimated, and a planned initial public offering (IPO) to the stock market was delayed by years. It would be easy to lay blame on a few seemingly incompetent or short-sighted managers rather than acknowledge there was a whole system of forces conspiring to limit effectiveness. What lay at the foot of this system? Blaming others for their political intrigue and failure to speak openly, while doing the same themselves.

These people were caught in certain roles and underlying *structures of interaction* that made them feel they *had* to relate together in the ways they did, but of which they were unconscious. Such structures guide people as to what counts as acceptable behavior. For instance in this case, some of the management team wanted to invite wide and open participation in the planning and decision making—including shop floor personnel who might have important roles in a new facility. But other managers and the investors wanted only the "experts" on the project to have a say, and to regulate quite carefully what got said to whom. They were concerned about the "qualifications" of the people. In the end, their approach won.

The beliefs of each of these groups are also part of the structure and led people to respond in certain ways. So, for instance, the investors believed they *had* to think first about the numbers. The engineers believed they *had* to do only what managers required of them. The managers believed they *had* to produce positive results as judged by others. These are all very real rules, ones that people feel they have to follow in this and in every situation, typically without reflection. And there can be very serious ramifications if they fail to follow them.

Third, and most important, these people had fallen into widely shared and widely taken-for-granted *habits of thinking and feeling* about their problems, what I refer to as the invisible architecture of human beings. To try to isolate one element and lay blame on it is to repeat exactly the problem that caused this disaster in the first place. It is this very *way of thinking and acting* that is at the root of the problem. It is a way of thinking that fragments, or divides, problems and fails to see the underlying interconnections and coherence of the situation. Dividing things up is not the problem. Forgetting the connections is. . . .

What is needed to bring about dialogue? Coherent new actions and behavior, fluid structures and an ability to predict problematic ones, and a wholesome atmosphere and understanding of the space out of which our conversations arise.

REVIEW QUESTIONS

1. Explain what it means to say, "People do not listen, they reload."
2. True or false: Isaacs wants to replace strong advocacy with dialogue. Explain.
3. Explain the difference Isaacs describes between negotiation ("getting to yes") and dialogue.
4. Tell what Isaacs means when he says that dialogue "addresses problems farther 'upstream' than conventional approaches."
5. Explain each of the three levels of action in a dialogue.

PROBES

1. Often "dialogue" is thought to mean a two-person conversation. Explain what's added by Isaacs's point that the Greek prefix *dia* does not mean "two" but "through."
2. How realistic is Isaacs to expect the level of trust that his notion of dialogue requires? Unions were originally created because management could not be trusted to treat workers fairly. Israelis and Palestinians have many reasons not to trust each other. How might the parties in an historically tense or even violent conflict trust enough to engage in dialogue?
3. Give two examples of what Isaacs would call "coherent" action—where the persons involved achieve a unity among their saying, being, and doing.
4. What are some specific ways a manager could help create "space for dialogue" in his or her company?

————

My colleague and friend Karen Zediker and I wrote this next selection specifically for *Bridges Not Walls*. The main ideas are taken from a journal article we published called "Dialogue as Tensional, Ethical Practice." We talk here about what we have become convinced is the main feature or characteristic of dialogue—a tension between letting another person "happen to you" while you hold your own ground in the conversation.

The first point we make is that for us, the term *dialogue* labels a particular kind or quality of communication. Dialogue is what happens between people who are connecting with each other *as persons,* as unique, reflective, choosing, valuing, thinking-and-feeling beings.

Next, the paper explains what a "tension" is. Our main point here is that there is a "both-and" quality to the experience of communicating dialogically. When you're in a tension, you feel pulled in two directions at once, *and* each pull is affected by what it's pulling against. Dialogue, we argue, is this kind of tensional event.

Then we label what we believe is dialogue's basic tension, and we describe each "moment," "pole," or "end" of this tension. "Letting the other happen to me" means being open to and actually affected by the ways that the other person is *different from* you. It doesn't take a rocket scientist to understand this idea, but it's a little strange in the Western world, because westerners are usually interested mainly in the other pole of this tension. It can take some courage and patience to let yourself be subject to someone else's influence.

"Holding your own ground" is the other pole, and it means what it sounds like. You do this when you assert your position or express your ideas. The most important point we make after we sketch these two poles is that when they are lived tensionally, *each transforms the other.* You don't just let somebody happen to you; you do that as a person who's holding your own ground. And you don't just assert your position; you do that as a person who's letting the other happen to you. In the final part of this reading, we give some concrete examples of how this tension works in order to clarify what's at stake here. One example is a story told by Martin Buber, an important writer, about dialogue. Other examples come from Karen's classes.

We hope that this brief description will clarify what you'll need to do when you want to help dialogue happen. You've undoubtedly figured out by now that there is no set recipe for dialogue. But if you can live with this tension, and if your conversation partner can, too, the chances are good that this quality of communication will happen between you.

Dialogue's Basic Tension

Karen Zediker and John Stewart

INTRODUCTION

It's exciting and confirming for us to learn about all the different people who are writing about dialogue today and trying to help dialogue happen in organizations, communities, and families. Our approach to dialogue is similar to some of theirs, and different from others'. Historically, we've been most influenced by Martin Buber's writings, so we use the term "dialogue" to refer to a particular kind or quality of communication that happens when the people involved are present to each other as persons—as unique, reflective, choosing, valuing, thinking-and-feeling beings. So when one of us can perceive and listen to you as a person while being available as a person to you, and when you can do the same thing, then the

"Dialogue's Basic Tension" excerpted from "Dialogue as Tensional, Ethical Practice" by Karen Zediker and John Stewart.

communication between us can be called "dialogic" or "dialogue." When the opposite happens—when I am only focused on getting my own ideas out and you are not listening but "reloading"—only working out your response to my ideas—then the communication between us is "monologic" or "monologue."

One significant feature of dialogue as we understand it is tensionality. This means that dialogue is not a steady state, something that is stable and predictable. When people are in dialogue, they experience a dynamic, push-pull, both-and quality in their communication. There's more to dialogue than just this tensional quality, but we believe that it's important enough that we want to take the following pages to clarify what we mean when we say that dialogue is tensional and to explain and illustrate dialogue's most basic tension.

A dictionary or thesaurus provides two different images of tension—*anxiety* (associated with stress and strain) and *tautness* (associated with force, tightness and constriction). Most of us have experienced tension in both these senses. Some characterize tension as a struggle, being pulled from a variety of directions at once, somehow knowing that if one perspective has more pull, another will lose out. Others associate tension with a headache that grips both the base of your neck and the top of your eyebrows at the same time. Or the word "tension" makes some other people think of the rod that holds curtains in place in the shower by pushing in opposite directions against two walls. None of these images is exactly what we have in mind when we say that dialogue is tensional, but they do share some common features. When something is held in tension there are at least two points of contact, and there seems to be an inherent contradiction or push-pull set of forces.

Communication teachers Barbara Montgomery and Leslie Baxter (1998) highlight one important feature of tensionality when they talk about how communicators manage "the both/andness" of privacy and disclosure across the time line of a relationship. Montgomery and Baxter explain that usually privacy isn't the most important thing at one point and then open disclosure most important at another, but that at almost every moment in a relationship the people involved are experiencing some tension between *both* privacy *and* disclosure. Montgomery and Baxter say that this primary feature of dialogue "implicate[s] a kind of in-the-moment interactive multivocality, in which multiple points of view retain their integrity as they play off each other" (p. 160). Like the tension headache that hurts both at the base of your skull and your forehead at the same time, or the tension rod that pushes out against opposite walls and is held into place by the structure of the door or window frame, dialogic tensions are characterized by both/andness.

THE PRIMARY TENSION

Our own communication experiences have taught us that moments of dialogue emerge most often when the people involved maintain one primary tension—the one between *letting the other happen to me while holding my own ground*. We are aware of other tensions as well, including one between univocality and multivocality and another tension between theory and practice. But in our opinion, other dialogic tensions are dependent on this primary tension.

In a few paragraphs, we'll highlight something misleading about this diagram. But first, let's clarify what this tension is by looking at its two ends.

Letting the other happen to me ⟵———⟶ Holding my own ground

In a few paragraphs, we'll highlight something misleading about this diagram. But first, let's clarify what this tension is by looking at its two ends.

Letting the Other Happen to Me

One moment in this dynamic—letting the other happen to me—consists of the concrete lived experience of what Buber and some other writers (e.g., Levinas, 1996) call experiencing the otherness of the Other. This means that you let someone happen to you when you allow who they are—especially their differences from you—to touch, connect with, and influence you. In his *Autobiographical Fragments,* Buber (1973)[1] reported that he recognized the basic quality of this moment when, as an 11-year-old, he cared for a "dapple-gray horse." When he was over 80 years old, he wrote,

> If I am to explain it now, beginning from the still very fresh memory of my hand, I must say that what I experienced in touch with the animal was the Other, the immense otherness of the Other, which, however, did not remain strange like the otherness of the ox and the ram, but rather let me draw near and touch it. When I stroked the mighty mane, sometimes marvelously smooth-combed, at other times just as astonishingly wild, and felt the life beneath my hand, it was as though the element of vitality itself bordered on my skin, something that was not I, was certainly not akin to me, palpably the other, not just another, really the Other itself; and yet it let me approach, confided itself to me, placed itself elementally in the relation of *Thou* and *Thou* with me. (p. 27)

In this fragment of his life, Buber provides a vivid example of letting the other happen to him. He realizes at a fundamental level that the horse is not an extension of himself, but something wholly other. Importantly, this lesson is one that Buber would have us learn about human beings as well. When we can experience other persons as unique individuals with opinions, beliefs, and values that are not simply extensions of our own, then we have the opportunity for genuine dialogue.

---

[1] We find Buber's "Autobiographical Fragments," published in 1973 as the book *Meetings,* to be a particularly fruitful source for articulating the experiential bases of his key insights and concepts. Buber collected these fragments shortly before he died, in response to the request of the editors of the *Library of Living Philosophers* to write an intellectual biography for their volume on Buber. As Buber editor and translator Maurice Friedman notes, "These 'events and meetings' are in the fullest sense of the term 'teaching' and perhaps, in the end, the most real teaching that Martin Buber has left us. . . . Not only can one discover which tales 'speak to his condition,' but also the hidden teaching contained in the restraint with which Buber retells these 'legendary anecdotes' and in the order in which he has arranged them" (1973, pp. 4–5).

Another German writer named Hans-Georg Gadamer (1989) clarifies an important aspect of this first moment of this tension when he distinguishes between two German words for "experience," *Erlebnis,* and *Erfahrung.* He explains that the first term labels experience that one "has" of something or someone. A person moves through life seeing, hearing, touching, tasting, and smelling things in order to grasp their meanings. So you might experience, in this *Erlebnis* sense, an encounter with a homeless person in which you could report where you saw her, what she said to you as you passed by, and how she smelled. *Erfahrung,* on the other hand, is the kind of experience that *happens to* one and that is the kind of experience that is consistent with Buber's notion of experiencing the otherness of the other. Gadamer describes *Erfahrung* as "experience as an event over which no one has control and which is not even determined by the particular weight of this or that observation, but in which everything is co-ordinated in a way that is ultimately incomprehensible" (p. 352). If you were to experience the homeless person in this second way, you'd experience her as a person rather than through a set of stereotypes or expectations. You might recall your eyes meeting and feeling for just that moment the sense of connection that you and she have as human beings despite the very real differences in your senses of security and community. "Experienced" people in this second sense are those who have become aware of what they have lived-through, which means in part what has *happened to* them. And Gadamer notes that one form of experience as *Erfahrung* is experience of the other, "the Thou" (1989, p. 358).

Holding My Own Ground

The other moment in the primary tension of dialogue—holding my own ground—is easier for most people raised in western traditions to understand, because of its connections with "rugged individuality." Understood as the label on one end of a continuum, holding my own ground is something that is done by an individual subject or intentional actor. You hold your own ground when you assert yourself or say exactly what's on your mind. One extreme version of this moment is present in communication teacher Barbara O'Keefe's (1997) description of the style of communication that is employed by the least developmentally sophisticated communicators she and her colleagues have studied. These people communicate in a way that O'Keefe calls "expressive." An infant communicates this way almost exclusively, but so do some adults. This way of communicating consists of

> simply thinking about the situation in relation to the self, evaluating thoughts in terms of whether they are disagreeable, repressing or misrepresenting disagreeable thoughts if uttering them might have negative consequences, but otherwise saying what comes to mind. (p. 104)

So, for example, if the baby feels bad, it cries, and if it feels good, it gurgles or smiles. What you see is what you get.

Holding my own ground presumes considerably more reflection, flexibility, and willingness to change than O'Keefe's expressive design logic, but, taken by itself, it strongly resembles of what a literature written in the 1970s and 1980s called "assertiveness." As one of the readings in Chapter 6 of *Bridges* notes, assertiveness is behavior that "promotes equality in human relationships, enabling us to act in our own best interests, to stand up for ourselves without undue anxiety, to express honest feelings comfortably, to exercise personal rights without denying the rights of others" (Alberti and Emmons, 1990, p. 7). As the definition indicates, this literature encourages the assertive person to respect the "rights of others." But it emphasizes the two-step process of mental preparation and the development of behavioral skills that results in one being able to articulate and stand up for what one wants or believes.

By itself, standing my own ground can be viewed as being assertive or expressive, and letting the other happen to me can be understood as an experience that I receive or am subject to. This oppositional way of describing the tensional poles is useful, but it can also give the impression that both ends of the continuum are all about ME: what happens to me and what I make happen. Importantly, there is more to this primary tension of dialogue than the either/or of you happening to me or me happening to you.

So here's where we need to highlight what's misleading about the diagram we've provided: It makes the tension look like a connection between simple polarities, when it's not. The most important thing about poles in dialogue is that they are *in tension,* and this means that *both ends of the continuum are transformed by their interrelation.* So the other happens to me *while* and *as* I hold my own ground, and as a result, she happens to me in relation to my own position. In addition, I hold my own ground *in her presence* as she is happening to me. As a result, my own understanding of my position is fundamentally transformed by my experience of the other person. And vise-versa; the other person's experiencing of me in relation to her is likely to transform her perception of her own identity and position. The constraints of language force us to talk about one end of this tension at a time, but our experience is that they are lived *together* or simultaneously.

This is an important point, so let us say it another way. When I live in this tension, my experience of the other person "happening to me" is strongly influenced by the position that I'm articulating (the ground that I'm holding), and the position that I'm expressing comes out as one that's strongly influenced by how the other is happening to me. In living communication, the two seemingly opposite moves (letting the other happen to me and holding my own ground) are *intimately interrelated.* And when lived in direct relation to one another, the two transform both the positions of the participants and their understanding of self and other.

Illustrations of the Tension

Here are two illustrations of how this works, one from Martin Buber's life and another from ours. Buber's autobiographical fragment called "Samuel and Agag" is a story of his lengthy conversation with "an observant Jew who followed the religious tradition in all the details of his life-pattern" (1973, p. 52). The two of them fell into a discussion of the section of the Biblical book of Samuel in which Samuel delivered to King Saul the message that his dynastic rule would be taken from him by God because he had spared the life of Agag, the conquered prince of the Amalekites. Samuel's message to Saul was that obedience to God was more important than mercy. Buber told his conversation partner how, as a boy, he had been horrified to read how the heathen king Agag went up to Samuel with the words on his lips, "Surely the bitterness of death is past," and was butchered, "hewn to pieces" by Samuel. Buber writes that his "heart compelled me to read [this passage] over again or at least to think about the fact that this stood written in the Bible." He concluded, as he put it to his conversation partner, "I have never been able to believe that this is a message of God. I do not believe it." From one thoughtful Jew to another, it was very risky to assert that one did not believe something written in the Bible. Buber described what followed:

> With wrinkled forehead and contracted brows, the man sat opposite me and his glance flamed into my eyes. He remained silent, began to speak, became silent again. "So?" he broke forth at last. "So? You do not believe it?" "No," I answered, "I do not believe it." "So? so?" he repeated almost threateningly. "You do not believe it?" And I once again: "No." "What . . . what . . . ,"—he thrust the words before him one after the other—"what do you believe then?" "I believe," I replied without reflecting, "that Samuel has misunderstood God." And he, again slowly, but more softly than before: "So? You believe that?" And I: "Yes."
>
> Then we were both silent. But now something happened the like of which I have rarely seen before or since in this my long life. The angry countenance opposite me became transformed, as if a hand had passed over it soothing it. It lightened, cleared, was now turned toward me bright and clear. "Well," said the man with a positively gentle tender clarity. "I think so too." And again we became silent, for a good while. (pp. 52–53)

Buber and the man were both believers. The fact that Buber happened to the man is most apparent in the man's final reply; "I think so, too." But the fact that the man happened to Buber is also apparent in two things. The first is Buber's choice to include this fragment among the 20 key events of his 87-year life. The second is that in this conversation, Buber tested for the first time his previously unspoken decision, as he put it, to respond to the demand to choose between the Bible and God by choosing God (p. 53). Each also held his own ground, Buber in his disbelief and the man in his challenge. In addition, the dialogue transformed both moments for each man. Buber's experience of the man (and the man's experience of Buber) was transformed from that of a conversation partner to that of a co-conspirator in a potentially damning but personally compelling heresy. Buber's experience of his own position (and the man's experience of his) was transformed from one of lonely insistence to partnered confirmation.

There are also examples of this basic tension in our classrooms. As much as is possible, we work to foster dialogue in our classes by encouraging students to simultaneously let the other happen to them and to stand their own ground, and we attempt to do the same in relation to them. Some years ago, the primary challenge seemed to be the first moment in this tension. Students often found it difficult to listen to diverse others (let the others happen to them). Today the pole of standing one's own ground seems to be more challenging. Many students come to class with the conviction that political correctness means they have to be open to all views. Rather than engaging on issues with others who express positions they find incoherent or morally lacking, they smile, nod, and offer feedback focused on something safe like vocal delivery. When asked what they find compelling in an argument or to articulate substantive points of difference, they are often unable to do so. Superficial agreement often substitutes for engaged dialogue.

As a result, at the beginning of several of our communication courses, we attempt to enhance the potential for dialogue in two ways. Although we distribute a syllabus on the first day, almost all of the class time that day is spent exploring, not the course description, but the people in the room, beginning with us. Karen starts with a round of student responses to such questions as "What do you hope to get out of this class?" or perhaps "What do you most hope we do during this course, and what do you most hope we don't do?" Then she asks groups of two to three to form questions they would like answered about her. Often for a full class period she responds to questions about her academic background, experience teaching this course, spare-time activities, approach to teaching, test design, family history, expectations, and the degree to which she is excited about or disillusioned with contemporary students. There are also opportunities these first days to talk with, whenever possible, each person taking the course. At the end of the term, students often report that this time spent exploring *all* the people in class initiates and models a dialogic quality of contact, because both Karen and her students are put in positions where they let the others happen to them and they stand their own ground.

A second move we make is to help the class identify a limited number of topics they want to focus on throughout the term. These become topics for the speeches or discussions in public dialogue or group decision-making courses, for the research projects and case studies in a course on communication ethics, or for the series of "styles" assignments in the conflict course. This move permits sustained engagement on substantive issues, slows down some elements of the idea-pace of the course, and helps create the space for student self-reflection, enabling people taking the course to identify the beliefs and especially the values that filter their research and interpretations. This pedagogical move also helps students get beyond the stage of paraphrasing someone else's approach to an issue and into the experience of taking personal responsibility for the positions they advocate. In other words, we require assignments that offer students opportunities to stand their own ground by positioning themselves *ethically* in reference to some subject matter.

Here's one example of what sometimes happens. In a recent class of Karen's a student we will call Jim took on the challenge of arguing in favor of sexual abstinence before marriage. He knew that his position was linked to his faith and his family's values, and he knew that his position was in the minority among his university peers. Others in the class were arguing against naïve "just say no" sex education programs, in favor of the morning-after pill and legalized prostitution. Jim knew that he had made an important choice for himself and that it would be an important choice for others to consider, but was unsure how to articulate his position in ways that enhanced dialogue. He knew that he did not want to portray himself as a preacher to his peers. He believed that quoting scripture would not be an effective way to engage his audience or persuade them to consider his position. Discussions with peers were part of the assigned preparation process, and in these discussions and e-mail conversations with Karen, Jim raised the concern that his position would be interpreted as a personal attack on or condemnation of his listeners. As he put it in an e-mail,

> The last thing that I want to do is make my audience feel as though I am preaching at them and telling them they are wrong and if they are having sex that they are all going to suffer huge consequences as a result of their actions. . . . All I am trying to do is make them ask questions and look inside themselves and see if what I present makes sense.

As Jim explored how to stand his ground, he realized that he did not want to give up his conviction or the opportunity to ask difficult questions simply to keep from offending anyone. One suggestion that he effectively incorporated into the first of his assigned speeches was to "steer away from being too apologetic for your position. You don't want to weaken it by worrying more about offending people than advocating for abstinence. I sense that you will get more respect than disdain."

And respect is what he gained. His listeners heard *him*—Jim—not just his position. They understood *him* and respected *him,* and this respect and understanding helped him achieve his communicative goal of getting them to ask questions and look inside themselves. Jim's ethical and moral presence helped generate the desired outcome, and the personal connection that occurred was more important than any one argument or persuasive appeal.

Importantly, Jim was also affected (transformed is only slightly too strong a word) by the communication events. As he let classmates and Karen happen to him, he was able to understand and articulate his position in ways he had not previously done. He moved from parroting the positions of his parents and the leaders of his faith community to choosing and explaining his own positions. Moments of anticipated and actual contact with others compelled Jim to reflect on his ground and to thoughtfully and assertively stand it.

The events of his preparation, presentation, and discussion of listener responses also transformed other aspects of the course. After Jim's talk, the topic of social perspectives on sex in this class was deepened beyond the superficial or selfish. Jim became a role model for standing your own ground while letting the other happen to you. Several students talked with Karen about how they too might advocate for positions they passionately and personally cared about in ways that were as direct, candid, and dialogically engaging as Jim had. They were particularly interested in prompting discussion that engaged not only arguments but also the value systems of the arguers themselves—as choice-making, ethically present persons.

CONCLUSION

In our experience, dialogue involves the negotiation of a variety of tensions, the most fundamental of which is holding my own ground and being open to the otherness of the other. To say that dialogue is tensional reminds us that (a) it is a dynamic, emergent process rather than any kind of steady state, and (b) it can be understood as happening *between* distinguishable moments or poles, each of which transforms the other. We understand that not all communication is dialogic—in fact, much of it is a series of monologues in which one end of the continuum we identify is emphasized over the other. Either the persons involved are only standing their own ground—asserting or expressing to their heart's content, almost regardless of who is present—or they are going along with what's said, regardless of their true beliefs. Dialogue, however, is made manifest when the fundamental tension between letting the other happen to me and holding my own ground is in play for all the parties involved. This tension characterizes dialogue in every context where we have experienced it—intimate contact, student advising, psychotherapy, mentoring, group decision making, public deliberation, patient–provider contact, conflict management, mediation, and superior–subordinate negotiation.

REVIEW QUESTIONS

1. How do we define "dialogue"?
2. Explain what "letting the other happen to me" means. Give an example.
3. Explain what "holding my own ground" means. Give an example.
4. Give an example from your own communication experience of holding your own ground *while* you were letting the other happen to you, and of letting the other happen to you *as* you were holding your own ground.
5. Explain how having the class identify a limited set of topics for the term can help them experience dialogue's central tension.

PROBES

1. Before you work on the tension we discuss here, think about how you negotiate both "privacy" and "disclosure" in your dating relationship(s). Notice how you work both sides of this tension at the same time. Notice how your privacy moves are affected by your disclosures and vice-versa. All this is also true about the basic tension of dialogue.

2. Identify and briefly discuss two different kinds of *experience* you've had, one that is obviously what German speakers would call *Erlebnis* and one that is obviously *Erfahrung*.
3. Some time in the next 48 hours, make a real effort to live this tension in one of your communication encounters. Immediately afterwards, write down what you experience. Bring your reflections to class and discuss them with one to two classmates who have tried the same thing. What do you notice?

REFERENCES

1. Alberti, R. E., & Emmons, M. L. (1990). *Your perfect right: A guide to assertive living.* San Luis Obispo, CA: Impact Publishers.
2. Baxter, L. A., & Montgomery, B. W. (1996). *Relating: Dialogue and dialectics.* Mahwah, NJ: Lawrence Erlbaum.
3. Buber, M. (1970). *I and thou* (W. Kaufmann, Trans). New York: Scribners.
4. Buber, M. (1973). *Meetings* (M. Friedman, Ed.). LaSalle, IL: Open Court Press.
5. Cissna, K. N., & Anderson, R. (1998). Theorizing about dialogic moments: The Buber-Rogers position and postmodern themes. *Communication Theory, 9,* 63–104.
6. Gadamer, H-G. (1989). *Truth and method* (2nd rev. ed.) (J. Weinsheimer & D. G. Marshall, Trans.) New York: Crossroad.
7. Levinas, E. (1996). *Emmanuel Levinas: Basic writings* (R. Bernasconi, S. Critchley, & A. Peperzak, Eds.). Bloomington, IN: Indiana University Press.
8. Montgomery, B. W., & Baxter, L. A. (Eds.). (1998). *Dialectical approaches to studying personal relationships.* Mahwah, NJ: Lawrence Erlbaum.
9. O'Keefe, B. (1997). Variation, adaptation, and functional explanation in the study of message design. In G. Philipsen & T. L. Albrecht (Eds.), *Developing communication theories* (pp. 85–118). Albany: State University of New York Press.

This final reading in the Dialogue chapter explains a kind of communication that work groups or teams can practice when the demands of pure dialogue can't be met. It's called "skillful discussion." The word "discussion" comes from a Latin term that means "to smash to pieces,"[1] and often discussions get bogged down in talk about the things that *separate* the people involved. But "skillful discussion" differs from unproductive discussion because the participants work collaboratively.

In this reading, Rick Ross emphasizes the practical value of skillful discussion to help a team come to a pressing conclusion, decision, or plan. He notes that a skillful discussion can usually progress without a facilitator, so long as the team members agree to follow five basic guidelines or "protocols."

The first is to "pay attention to your intentions," and here the key is to be willing to be influenced by others. The second is to "balance advocacy with inquiry," and Ross offers some very specific advice about what to say and what to do in order to achieve this balance. The third protocol or guideline is to "build shared meaning," which requires using language carefully, in ways to minimize misunderstanding. The fourth is to "use self-awareness as a resource." This protocol takes discipline, because it requires each person in the discussion to keep tabs on what he or she specifically is thinking, feeling, and what he or she wants, moment by moment. The fifth protocol is to "explore impasses," to pay attention in nondefensive ways to areas of disagreement and, as Ross puts it, to "Ask yourself (and everyone else): What do we need to do to move forward?"

The reading ends with some additional specific suggestions for preparing the ground for skillful discussion and for listening effectively. Notice that the first and the last "rule" for effective listening is "Stop talking."

Skillful Discussion

Protocols for Reaching a Decision—Mindfully

Rick Ross

From the standpoint of building shared meaning within teams or between groups, traditional discussion is dangerously oriented toward advocacy. People "discuss" to win; they heave ideas against each other, as Bill Isaacs puts it, to see whose ideas will be the strongest. It is a dismal way to conduct teamwork, not just because it undermines learning, but because ideas and "solutions" rarely get the consideration they deserve. They are judged according to who said them, and whether or not they match conventional wisdom. Most teams need new tools and skills to both broaden and focus the scale and scope of their conversations—to make them both more divergent and more convergent—when appropriate.

The most effective vehicle I know is the form of conversation which I call "skillful discussion." You can think of it as a midpoint on the continuum between dialogue and "raw," advocacy-filled discussion:

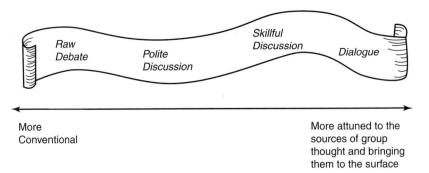

More
Conventional

More attuned to the
sources of group
thought and bringing
them to the surface

The primary difference between dialogue and skillful discussion involves intention. In skillful discussion, the team intends to come to some sort of closure—either to make a decision, reach agreement, or identify priorities. Along the way, the team may explore new issues and build some deeper meaning among the members. But their intent involves convergent thinking.

In dialogue the intention is exploration, discovery, and insight. Along that path, the group may in fact sometimes come to a meeting of the minds and reach some agreement—but that isn't their primary purpose in coming together.

Teams unquestionably benefit from dialogue—from exploring shared meaning—but they also have the everyday need to come to a pressing conclusion, decision, or plan. To accomplish this work productively, skillful discussion incorporates some of the techniques and devices of dialogue and action learning, but always focused on tasks. Meetings have agendas; people leave with priorities and work assignments in hand. Nonetheless, the team also learns to make their thought processes visible, to surface and challenge assumptions, and to look more closely at sources of disagreement. Gradually, within their team setting, they improve the quality of their collective thinking and interacting.

For the past two years, I've been training teams to conduct their business this way, and most of them have found it a far more effective means of getting to the results they want. Practicing the tools and techniques encourages openness and teamwork, builds trust within the group, and makes visible unseen assumptions which typically block progress toward the results the team members want.

Personally, I believe that everyone should conduct *all* their meetings using these tools and techniques. And I would also encourage them to engage in dialogue on a regular basis, because the two types of conversation enrich each other. But far too few teams in organizations, particularly in business, are willing to experiment with either form. Many teams will spend hours improving their billing or materials-handling processes, but will not construct the practice fields they need to improve the quality of their thinking processes, which might then leverage the quality of everything else they produce.

A facilitator is not as essential to skillful discussion as for dialogue. . . . The most essential ingredient is an agreement which team members make: to follow five basic protocols. The protocols are clear, and not difficult to grasp; but they require practice. Any team using the protocols will observe its own behavior and effectiveness improve dramatically.

1. PAY ATTENTION TO YOUR INTENTIONS

As an individual, make sure you understand what you hope to accomplish in this discussion. Ask yourself: "What is my intention?" and "Am I willing to be influenced?" If you are not, what is the purpose of the conversation? Be clear on what *you* want, and do not mislead others as to your intentions.

2. BALANCE ADVOCACY WITH INQUIRY

In most management teams, the pendulum between advocacy and inquiry has swung far over on the advocacy side. Some teams take great pride in "challenging each other," but they don't actually challenge each other in any meaningful way. They're merely "in your face" with each other, one-upping each other with trivialities. Other teams pride themselves on how constructively they deal with confrontation. My experience, however, is that they just sit there and listen, in turn, to each other's position statements. Assumptions are not even surfaced, much less challenged. What they are really thinking will be heard only after the meeting—in the hallways or in the bathrooms. While there is essentially nothing wrong with this sort of advocacy, it is the lack of balance that causes misunderstanding, miscommunication, and poor decisions.

1. PROTOCOLS FOR IMPROVED ADVOCACY:

Make your thinking process visible (walk up the ladder of inference slowly).

What to do	What to say
State your assumptions, and describe the data that led to them.	*"Here's what I think, and here's how I got there."*
Explain your assumptions.	*"I assumed that . . ."*
Make your reasoning explicit.	*"I came to this conclusion because . . ."*
Explain the context of your point of view: who will be affected by what you propose, how they will be affected, and why.	
Give examples of what you propose, even if they're hypothetical or metaphorical.	*"To get a clear picture of what I'm talking about, imagine that you're the customer who will be affected . . ."*
As you speak, try to picture the other people's perspectives on what you are saying.	

Publicly test your conclusions and assumptions.

What to do	**What to say**
Encourage others to explore your model, your assumptions, and your data.	*"What do you think about what I just said?" or "Do you see any flaws in my reasoning?" or "What can you add?"*
Refrain from defensiveness when your ideas are questioned. If you're advocating something worthwhile, then it will only get stronger by being tested.	
Reveal where you are least clear in your thinking. Rather than making you vulnerable, it defuses the force of advocates who are opposed to you, and invites improvement.	*"Here's one aspect which you might help me think through . . ."*
Even when advocating: listen, stay open, and encourage others to provide different views.	*"Do you see it differently?"*

2. PROTOCOLS FOR IMPROVED INQUIRY:

Ask others to make their thinking process visible.

What to do	**What to say**
Gently walk others down the ladder of inference and find out what data they are operating from.	*"What leads you to conclude that?" "What data do you have for that?" "What causes you to say that?"*
Use unaggressive language, particularly with people who are not familiar with these skills. Ask in a way which does not provoke defensiveness or "lead the witness."	Instead of *"What do you mean?"* or *"What's your proof?"* say, *"Can you help me understand your thinking here?"*
Draw out their reasoning. Find out as much as you can about why they are saying what they're saying.	*"What is the significance of that?" "How does this relate to your other concerns?" "Where does your reasoning go next?"*
Explain your reasons for inquiring, and how your inquiry relates to your own concerns, hopes, and needs.	*"I'm asking you about your assumptions here because . . ."*

Compare your assumptions to theirs.

What to do	What to say
Test what they say by asking for broader contexts, or for examples.	*"How would your proposal affect . . . ?" "Is this similar to . . . ?" "Can you describe a typical example . . . ?"*
Check your understanding of what they have said.	*"Am I correct that you're saying . . . ?"*
Listen for the new understanding that may emerge. Don't concentrate on preparing to destroy the other person's argument or promote your own agenda.	

3. PROTOCOLS FOR FACING A POINT OF VIEW WITH WHICH YOU DISAGREE:

What to do	What to say
Again, inquire about what has led the person to that view.	*"How did you arrive at this view?" "Are you taking into account data that I have not considered?"*
Make sure you truly understand the view.	*"If I understand you correctly, you're saying that . . ."*
Explore, listen, and offer your own views in an open way.	*"Have you considered . . ."*
Listen for the larger meaning that may come out of honest, open sharing of alternative mental models.	
Raise your concerns and state what is leading you to have them.	*"I have a hard time seeing that, because of this reasoning . . ."*

3. BUILD SHARED MEANING

All words are symbols, and as such are abstractions. They often have different meanings to different people. If most people understood this—if they assumed that they did not understand what an individual meant by a particular word unless they inquired about it—then everyone would routinely check the meanings behind the words being spoken more often and there would be far less miscommunication. In most teams, the discussion moves at such a fast clip, and people use words so loosely, that it becomes very hard to build shared meaning. People walk away with vague ambiguous understandings, or even gross misunderstandings, of who meant what and who will do what. Decisions made in such an environment won't stick.

Thus it is important to use language with great precision, taking care to make evident the meaning—or lack of meaning—in a word. Avoid having phrases in your team lexicon where you assume everyone agrees on the definition, but nobody actually has any idea what it is. This practice is most important with the simplest phrases:

"You said 'Get it done.' But what's 'done'?"

"Well, finish the marketing plan."

"Oh. So you're not including shipping."

"I hadn't intended to. But what leads you to suggest that our definition of 'done' should include shipping?"

When talking about definitions, particularly for abstract concepts like 'inferences' and 'mental models,' it helps to start out with some sloppiness—so that everyone gets a chance to "feel around" for the right meaning of the word you are using together. "I just want to exaggerate for a minute," you might say, "so take this with a grain of salt, but I think when we say 'empowerment,' we're actually talking about . . ." As you talk around the issue, you may get closer to a precise definition which you can all agree on. If the word is important to you, then converge on the meaning with as much precision as possible.

4. USE SELF-AWARENESS AS A RESOURCE

Ask yourself, at moments when you are confused, angry, frustrated, concerned, or troubled:

1. What am I thinking? (pause)
2. What am I feeling? (pause)
3. What do I want at this moment?

You will often end up with insights about the team's assumptions or your own concerns, which you can then raise before the group, without casting blame: *"You know, this action implies an assumption about our customers . . ."* or *"When you say such-and-such, I find myself disagreeing because . . ."* or simply, *"I notice that I'm feeling uncomfortable, and I'm not sure why."*

5. EXPLORE IMPASSES

Ask yourself: What do we agree on, and what do we disagree on? Can we pinpoint the source of the disagreement or impasse? Often the sources of disagreement fall into four categories:

1. Facts—What exactly has happened? What is the "data"?
2. Methods—How should we do what we need to do?

3. Goals—What is our objective? (A "vision" exercise may help bring the disagreement over this into clarity.)
4. Values—Why do we think it must be done in a particular way? What do we believe in?

Simply agreeing on the source of disagreement often allows people to learn more about the situation, clarify assumptions that previously were below awareness, and move forward.

Three moves in particular will help:

Listen to ideas as if for the first time. Work at being open to new ideas.

Consider each person's mental model as a piece of a larger puzzle. Look at the issue from the other person's perspective.

Ask yourself (and everyone else): What do we need to do to move forward?

THE SKILLFUL DISCUSSION TENT CARD TEMPLATE

I have found it helpful to print the protocols on the back of name (tent) cards, so that team members have them handy throughout meetings. It's hokey, but it works!

A sample card might read:

1. Pay attention to my intentions
   What do I want from this conversation? Am I willing to be influenced?

2. Balance advocacy with inquiry
   "What led you to that view?" "What do you mean by that view?"

3. Build shared meaning
   "When we use the term———, what are we really saying?"

4. Use self-awareness as a resource
   What am I thinking? What am I feeling? What do I want at this moment?

5. Explore impasses
   What do we agree on, and what do we disagree on?

PREPARING THE GROUND FOR SKILLFUL DISCUSSION

1. Create a safe haven for participants. Because people from different parts of the organization may join this team, the "turf" of the meeting must belong to no one. The symbols and trappings of power, prestige, and status should be minimized. As another power equalizer, all participants in a skillful discussion should expressly agree to "treat each other as colleagues." Curiosity, respect of, and support for each other's opinions and feelings are essential.
2. Make openness and trust the rule rather than the exception. People must feel secure that they can speak freely, without fear of being the target of criticism,

ridicule, or retribution. Thus, there must be a ground rule that people will not have their remarks attributed to them outside the room, unless they agree. Everyone who attends must be given complete immunity for what they say during these discussions.

Agreeing on a set of ground rules is only the beginning. Trust develops only if every participant continues to act in a trustworthy manner.

3. Encourage and reward the injection of new perspectives. For groups which meet often, it is useful to find external sources of new perspectives—such as outsiders invited to join in for one or several sessions. Regardless of who is present, the discussion will broach issues, ideas, and approaches typically given short shrift in day-to-day work. Right and wrong are not of concern. The exchange of perspectives and points of view, not the selling of them, is the issue.

4. Plan the agenda, time, and context to allow for concentrated deliberation. The best way to assure a single focus is to make sure that every partici-pant expects to talk about the same subject. Agendas should be devel-oped and agreed upon in advance. Also, creative discussions take time. Less than two hours is unacceptable, even for the most experienced groups. Keep distractions—especially phone calls, other appointments, and interruptions—to a minimum.

HOW TO LISTEN IN SKILLFUL DISCUSSION
(OR ANY TIME)

1. Stop talking: To others and to yourself. Learn to still the voice within. You can't listen if you are talking.
2. Imagine the other person's viewpoint. Picture yourself in her position, doing her work, facing her problems, using her language, and having her values. If the other person is younger or more junior, remember your early days in the company.
3. Look, act, and be interested. Don't read your mail, doodle, shuffle, or tap papers while others are talking.
4. Observe nonverbal behavior, like body language, to glean meanings beyond what is said to you.
5. Don't interrupt. Sit still past your tolerance level.
6. Listen between the lines, for implicit meanings as well as explicit ones. Consider connotations as well as denotations. Note figures of speech. Instead of accepting a person's remarks as the whole story, look for omissions—things left unsaid or unexplained, which should logically be present. Ask about these.
7. Speak only affirmatively while listening. Resist the temptation to jump in with an evaluative, critical, or disparaging comment at the moment a re-mark is uttered. Confine yourself to constructive replies until the context has shifted, and criticism can be offered without blame.

8. To ensure understanding, rephrase what the other person has just told you at key points in the conversation. Yes, I know this is the old "active listening" technique, but it works—and how often do you do it?
9. Stop talking. This is first and last, because all other techniques of listening depend on it. Take a vow of silence once in a while.

SUMMARY

Ross recognizes, as do the authors of the other readings in this chapter, that dialogue is the best kind of communication to strive for. But he also understands that it isn't always possible, and he offers skillful discussion as a helpful way for a team or work group to work together.

REVIEW QUESTIONS

1. Explain the basic difference between "discussion" and "skillful discussion."
2. Explain the basic difference between "skillful discussion" and "dialogue."
3. What does it mean to "balance advocacy with inquiry"?
4. What's an "impasse," and what does it mean to "explore" an impasse?
5. How do agendas function in skillful discussion?

PROBES

1. Why do people in skillful discussions need to pay attention to their intentions? What does this accomplish?
2. Which of the "what to say" suggestions sound most genuine to you? Which ones can you actually imagine yourself saying during a discussion? Which sound most awkward or phony?
3. How can a discussant "use language with great precision" and still be spontaneous and responsive?
4. Ross emphasizes that trust is important for skillful discussion. What are some ways that organizations build trust and what are some ways organizations tear it down?

Approaches to Interpersonal Communication

CHAPTER 13

A Teacher's Approach

C. Roland Christensen was a teacher at the Harvard Business School and senior editor of a book called *Education for Judgment: The Artistry of Discussion Leadership.* The book is a collection of essays by teachers who have given up lecturing in favor of collaborative learning through focused discussion. I like his book and use it as a text partly because its title acknowledges that facilitating a good classroom discussion is an *art*, not a *science*, which is to say that it includes some *unmeasurable* aspects and some *mystery.* Christensen is a teacher who clearly recognizes this, and who applies to his teaching large chunks of the approach to interpersonal communication that's been laid out in the earlier chapters of *Bridges Not Walls.*

One of these chunks is the commitment to the idea that communication is a relational thing, something that happens mutually, *between people.* Christensen expresses his version of this idea as the "fundamental insight" that "teaching and learning are inseparable, [a] reciprocal giving and receiving." As he discovered firsthand, when you apply this insight to an 80-student classroom, the results can create cognitive overload. But they can also be gratifying as you find that students are deeply involved "both intellectually and with their guts." As a result of his first experiences, Christensen reports, he wanted to find out how this electrifying, yet overwhelming, process works.

When other teachers could only tell him, "Play it by ear," he went to those responsible for his survival, his students. He discovered that, directly or indirectly, they would let him know what worked and what didn't. He also figured out that the complex process could be understood in terms of three basic activities: questioning, listening, and responding to student responses. He explains some of the insights students taught him about these activities under six headings. First, students can play a significant role in constructing the day's agenda. Second, student logic can be different from—but nonetheless as useful as—the teacher's logic. Third, timing is crucial, and fourth, the types of questions affect how the discussion goes. Fifth, students can often communicate more effectively than the instructor because of their "rough and ready emotional profiles of one another," and finally, students build a class *culture* that affects all the class activities. These are all specific ways students contribute materially to the "teaching" process, and, Christensen believes, successful teaching begins when you recognize them.

In the major section of this essay, Christensen discusses five main "lessons" that he has learned about this approach to teaching. I could spend pages on each, but since he discusses them well, I'll just summarize here. (1) *A teacher's openness and caring increase the students' learning opportunities.* Caring teachers don't just "coddle" students; they actually help them learn. (2) *Effective discussions require the classroom to become a learning space.* Intellectual hospitality and the safety that encourages risk-taking are two of the main features. (3) *Modest expectations are the most powerful of all.* Rather than trying to cover every possible topic or every possible reading, it works best to just help everybody learn a few ideas well. What a revolutionary idea! (4) *Instructors' patience promotes students' learning.* Inquiry and growth flourish under low pressure. The story in this section about the butterfly is super. (5) *Faith is the most essential ingredient in good teaching practice.* And to flesh out this idea, Christensen concludes with 10 items of "faith" that guide his teaching. I'll just mention a couple: "Involvement is critical to enduring learning." "Teaching is a moral act." "What my students become is as important as what they learn." "Fun has a critical place in teaching."

It's hard to read this essay without wishing that all your classes could be taught by Christensen, or somebody who approaches teaching and learning as he does. But I hope you can also see how this approach to classroom discussion is one exciting way to synthesize this book's approach to interpersonal communication.

Every Student Teaches and Every Teacher Learns:

The Reciprocal Gift of Discussion Teaching

C. Roland Christensen

It has been said that we live life forward but understand it backward. Looking back over years of discussion teaching, I see how intensely its process has intrigued, baffled, and intellectually nourished this practitioner—and the fascination shows no signs of abating. At its core lies a fundamental insight: teaching and learning are inseparable, parts of a single continuum—more Möbius strip than circle—of reciprocal giving and receiving. In discussion pedagogy students share the teaching task with the instructor and one another. All teach, and all learn. This view of the dynamic has implications for every aspect of discussion teaching, from fundamental assumptions to the finest points of classroom behavior. I make no claim to understand them all. But looking at teaching through the prism of reciprocity has allowed me to discern certain components of the process than can be named, described, studied, and communicated.

The reader should not be surprised to find "what I know," and, in particular, my descriptions of how I think while teaching, in the form of questions rather than statements. Four decades of discussion teaching leave their mark—in my case, an aversion to divorcing knowledge from challenge, dialogue, emotional engagement, and personal development. The quest for wisdom, as distinct from knowledge, will always remain open-ended.

This essay will present insights I have collected about the discussion teaching process with some details about the context that allowed me to see them. It will begin in the past, with my very first discussion class and fledgling efforts to learn how to learn about its mysteries. It will then continue with hypotheses about the nature of the process and the very powerful role students play in sharing its leadership with their instructors. And it will conclude in the present, with overarching "lessons learned" about values and the essential ingredient in all good teaching: faith.

EARLY YEARS: HOW I LEARNED TO LEARN ABOUT DISCUSSION TEACHING

Exploring the discussion process has been a wondrous adventure, a long journey within the confines of classroom walls. Like any productive educational enterprise, mine was aided by a fortunate synergy between instructor and institution. My colleagues on the faculty of the Harvard Business School honored teaching as a legitimate subject to be studied, as well as an action to be performed—an attitude that affected my perspective on everything that I saw, heard, and sensed as I taught, and my decisions on the best investment of my own intellectual resources.

My personal chain of discovery began with the first discussion class I ever taught: Tuesday, February 14, 1947. Yesterday. Remembered painfully, it was a bit like a session with a dental surgeon, sans novocaine. I was to teach an eighty-student section of the required second-year Business Policy course. The course mission was complex: to help students learn the functions, roles, and knowledge requirements of a general manager, with emphasis on the qualitative intricacies of strategic decision making. Underlying all this was the more basic goal of promoting the development of essential personal qualities: judgment, wisdom, and ethics.

Promptly at 8:30 A.M., having sweated through the weekend and Monday, I opened the door to Baker Library 101. It was a thin, cold room, with windows that rattled in the northeast wind and metal blinds stuck in various positions of closure. A slightly curved amphitheater format barely allowed space at the front for a platform, replete with brass rail and curtain that but partially hid the instructor's chair and desk. My suit coat over one arm—army exercise had changed my body frame and Harvard's salary did not allow for wardrobe refurbishment—and a folder of class notes in the other, I walked to the small platform, started up the three steps, tripped, and fell.

I blushed a bright red and knelt to gather my scattered papers. The room was quiet, except for an embarrassed half-laugh from the right, so brief it must have been squelched. I took a deep breath and, finally, stood up to look around at "them": scores of almost indistinguishable faces. A few smiled at me, thank heavens. My opening question—"Mr. Adams [you can imagine my reason for selecting him to start off], what is your diagnosis of the Consolidated Vultee situation?"—went well. But the remainder of the eighty minutes was a blur. My carefully prepared teaching plan, crafted to direct the group through an efficient analysis of the case that would reveal both the principles of Business Policy and my own indispensability to the discussion process, had minimal impact.

We were discussing a case about a company organizing for rapidly expanded military production during wartime, a topic still of high interest in 1947. The students wanted to pursue their own concerns and questions in ways that were meaningful to them. They agreed, disagreed, expressed confidence in (or incredulity at the naiveté of) their associates' suggestions. Infrequently, someone would admit confusion—a predicament appreciated and shared by the instructor. A few seemed bored, but most were deeply involved in the case, both intellectually and with their guts. There was no antagonism—all were polite—but the group permitted neither plan nor professor to get in its way.

When the class was over, I had heard hundreds and hundreds of words—verbal exchanges between and among the students, a multiplicity of conclusions, and an explosion of suggestions as to what the president of Consolidated Vultee should do. For me, it had been an academic Tower of Babel, a throw of conversational confetti. Most puzzling, however, was the reaction of the students. Seemingly, the class had made sense to them. Small groups stayed in the classroom after the discussion. Others left still carrying on their dialogue with an intensity that would have been difficult to contrive. Several commented, "Good class, professor." I thought, "Good class? Come on!"

The few steps back to my office felt like a stroll through a sandstorm. All I could remember of what had happened but minutes before were a few major themes and some dramatic statements. Students' comments fused; I couldn't recall who had said what or the responses those comments had triggered. A psychologist might have diagnosed my condition as cognitive overload: too much information to process too fast. How could I lead such a confusing process as this discussion had been? "It can't be done," I thought. "It simply can't be done!"

The only sensible course of action was to get help. Our faculty was the best, artists of the classroom, the teaching equivalents of Monet, Miró, and Jasper Johns. I asked senior colleagues to explain the discussion teaching process to me. Unfortunately, mastery of a creative activity does not guarantee the ability to explain it or help another master it. "Play it by ear, just play it by ear," was a typical response. For all their classroom genius, my colleagues treated teaching like the proverbial "black box": a container full of powerful mechanisms, but sealed.

During that first year of teaching, succeeding classes continued to listen much like the first one. The weeks marched by: dozens of class meetings, three times a week, with two eighty-person class groups. The discussions were spirited—decibels galore, dialogue, orations, even disquisitions. Crisp comments and pauses, murmurs, and mumbles. Themes did emerge in class, and the group often obtained reasonable consensus by the end of the session. Assumptions were tested and points proved. I had a good notion that cooperation powered the process, but even so, its dynamic eluded me. It was still a noisy mystery "out there." I felt like a stranger in the midst of the familiar. Nietzsche somewhere notes that all that is profound wears a mask. I wanted to look behind the mask that the learning process wore every day in the classroom.

Getting help became a puzzle, a pedagogical Rubik's cube. By now I had guessed that the students were responsible for my survival, thus far, in the classroom. Slowly this realization became a clue to learning about the mysterious process of discussion teaching. If colleagues couldn't "give" me the answer, perhaps I might find it with the students. After all, they were the reason it was working. I wondered if, somehow, those whom I supposedly led could help me learn how to lead. Perhaps I could work out a way to study what we all did in discussions and discover order in the apparent chaos. This would mean observing other teachers' classes and, as far as possible, my own.

I soon learned that mastery of course content wasn't the key. At the very beginning, I had, like most instructors, assumed that my job was to devise the clearest, most insightful analysis of the material possible, compose a list of questions to elicit that analysis in class, and then lead the students through my list in a courteous but authoritative manner. How starkly that assumption clashed with what I observed in class! When I tried to figure out what distinguished higher-from lower-quality discussion classes, I noticed that the better discussions were those in which the students asked particularly good questions—questions that often eclipsed those I had prepared. And the best discussions often modified or completely abandoned my neatly sequenced teaching plans. I was intrigued to realize that this aspect of good classes lay largely beyond my control, as did another common feature of productive discussions: students' listening to one another with attention and care. Good discussions frequently took paths that the group found reasonable but I had not foreseen. It seemed increasingly obvious that I neither could nor should try to control the discussion process. The students were my co-teachers.

Over time, such glimmers of insight brightened to beams of light that illuminated at least a portion of the contents of the black box of the discussion process. My early, overwhelmed conclusion, "It can't be done," evolved to, "It *can* be done, but not alone." But if the students were teaching, what was my job? To help them teach better. This meant that I needed not only to master the skills of leading the discussion process but also to devise ways to describe and explain the process to others.

Self-knowledge is the beginning of all knowledge. I had to find the teacher in myself before I could find the teacher in my students and gain understanding of how we all taught one another. Slowly, I learned to make my classroom observations more productive by focusing them. I started to try out tiny experiments. Instead of waiting for the class to assemble before making my appearance, for example, I tried arriving early to see what that might teach me about my students. The exercise proved valuable. Talking with students and watching them enter the room revealed much about their lives and interests—who played sports before class, who was under the weather or visibly fatigued that day, who had special interest in the day's topic (or, conversely, an apparent desire to hide). Coming to class early also allowed me to prepare a genial, cooperative atmosphere by welcoming students by name, and it gave me an opportunity to note students' subgroups.

Some other early experiments: I dropped my initial practice of calling opening speakers in alphabetical order and made choices based on some knowledge of students' backgrounds and interests. And I took a tip from a student who noted a preponderance of "whats" among my questions and tried more "whys." Simple, simple steps, rooted in practicality. But these were my first glimpses of the workings of the black box.

Finding time to reflect on the discussion as it unfolded in class was still like trying to meditate on a speeding fire engine. The after-class reprise was equally difficult. But I now had some ideas about why certain classes seemed more productive than others. Much of what we teachers do in the classroom seems intuitive. My task was to examine this apparently automatic behavior, show its workings, and identify areas in which judgment might play a part. "Process," whatever it might be, was clearly going to be the major focus of my attention.

Like most academics, I assumed that abstract principles of some sort would be my best guides. But my initial attempts, directed at understanding "process" in its purest sense, brought little practical reward. It seemed that the farther down the "abstraction ladder" I climbed, the closer I came to my real goal, an ever-deeper understanding of process. Near the bottom of the ladder, on the operational (how to) level, I began to make observations that truly dispelled confusion. When I came to class with a simple, practical teaching experiment in mind—something like evaluating the effect of calling on students seated in different parts of the room—I got results. Sometimes I focused on the art of questioning. What happens when I ask the same question of two students in succession? What is the effect of asking a delayed question—one to be answered after a moment of reflection—compared with asking the same question "cold"? Sometimes I concentrated on phrasing. What is the difference between using a student's name and simply gesturing? Or I concentrated on timing: How long can a silence last before restlessness sets in? I repeated these experiments from class to class, year to year, trying, like any researcher, to hold as many things constant as possible each time in order to evaluate the variable element.

Once I learned to focus on what a teacher says and does in the classroom, possibilities for experimentation and learning began to proliferate. The classroom proved to be a perfect laboratory for my nuts-and-bolts experiments with the discussion process. As an observer, of myself and other instructors in action, I truly began to learn. My experimental approach to the discussion process revealed that all participants, instructor included, spent most of their time either asking questions, listening to people's answers, or making some sort of response to those answers. I began to appreciate that these activities—questioning, listening, and response—were the most basic "stuff" of process. I also realized that every discussion produced rehearsals of data, analysis, questions, challenges, and syntheses, but not necessarily in a predictable sequence. This insight suggested that one of the instructor's most crucial tasks is linking—explicitly relating, and helping the students to relate, current points of argument to others that may have appeared earlier that day or in a previous discussion. This point, I realized, had important implications for teaching preparation as well as discussion management.

What I found inside the black box of the discussion process was an ever-changing flow of activities that resisted abstract analysis but yielded to disciplined observation and the application of very specific skills. To some extent, all of the essays in [*Education for Judgment*] examine aspects of these skills from the points of view of experienced practitioners, teachers at work. And what is our work? To create a favorable learning climate, to set a teaching/learning contract, to ask and respond to questions, listen to contributions, and promote the formation of groups in which students can teach themselves and one another. All these are practical approaches to a process that cannot be abstracted without substantial loss of identity, for the discussion process is a true slice of life. Guiding it takes skill, patience, and a basic faith that one may learn, with time and effort, to preside over disorder without disorientation.

SOME INSIGHTS ABOUT PROCESS AND STUDENTS' ROLE IN ITS LEADERSHIP

Seen in retrospect, my attempts to understand the workings of the discussion teaching process have much in common with the process itself. Both exhibit the disorderliness of discovery: even the most steadfast explorer cannot march straight through a jungle. Most attempts to capture the essence of the discussion process produce frustrations as well as insights. The very meaning of the phrase, for example, still teases our profession. The totality of a discussion includes the intellectual and emotional experiences of a whole roomful of people: material to occupy psychologists, neurologists, sociologists, anthropologists, and philosophers for years to come. My own quest for an enlightening definition produced little to help me choose which of ten vigorously waving hands to recognize. All processes are flows, either of activities or thoughts, but this basic definition gives one no handle on why some opening questions inspire lively debate while others trigger alienation or apathy, or why the comments of "student experts" sometimes help and sometimes hinder a discussion. Nor does it distinguish what happens in a discussion classroom from what happens on an assembly line.

I found the exercise of drawing distinctions more fruitful. Contrasting process with content provided practical help. Confusing mastery of material with mastery of the discussion process produces a common error: a controlling teaching style that creates bilateral frustration when students inevitably try to go their own ways. This lesson became clear to me as my students continued to offer polite, but stubborn resistance to my attempts to shepherd them through the meticulous analyses that had cost me so many hours of preparation. And when I examined my own initial inclination to choose opening speakers alphabetically from my class list, I found that it showed another typical novice's confusion: the failure to distinguish process from procedure. Procedures are logical and rigid sequences of actions, indispensable in making an arrest, performing an appendectomy, or accessing a computer file—but fatal to leading a meaningful group discussion. Discussions are liquid. They do not move in straight lines; they undulate.

Over the years, I have found the use of metaphor enriching to my understanding of the discussion process. What is a discussion, if not a voyage of exploration, with the leader as both captain and crew member? To appreciate the frequent reversals and indirections of the process, one may imagine a discussion class as a mountain climb, where even apparent reversals produce ascent. In the discussion process, "wrong" can be more helpful than "right"; an obtuse statement can spark a charged, enlightening debate that straightforward analysis could never provoke.

Discussion teaching is noisy. Messy, too. It greets an observer with a verbal cacophony—an unnerving scene for teachers unprepared for its energy. Good discussions unfold in unexpected ways that modify the programmed logic of a teaching plan. They pose new questions, uncover and gnaw away at sanctified assumptions, rejuvenate old topics with fresh insights, broaden perspectives, and create new paths of inquiry. But focused observation and systematic analysis can reveal meaning in the noise and logic in the disorder. The rough-and-tumble of classroom interchange contains opportunities that enhance the learning of both students and instructors. What unsettles a teacher may energize the students: less disorder, than new order. Discussion teaching demands a milieu of freedom, an openness that encourages students to share power over, and responsibility for, the leadership and conduct of a class.

In discussion teaching, tidiness can tyrannize. Messiness can work miracles. To succeed, the enterprise requires the active contribution, not merely cooperation, of the discussion group. Mutual collaboration—reciprocity of effort—is not only engaging and exciting for students, it is also imperative for the discussion leader. However impressive your experience or skills, you will have difficulty in questioning, listening, and responding while simultaneously observing, synthesizing, reflecting, and evaluating the discussion dialogue, and planning for the rest of the class. A teacher would need more than one pair of eyes and ears to carry out such a task—it really *can't* be done alone!

This realization suggests a further point: a great deal of essential information—factors that condition the instructional choices of the moment—emerges only in action as the process unfolds. Should an idea be explored in greater depth or overviewed in a hurry? Should the class move on to another topic? Would it be helpful to raise or lower the abstraction level of the argument? What does the group understand? What is missing? What topics need to be covered again? What questions are bothering or intriguing the group? What new avenues of exploration should we investigate now? It helps to remember that the teacher does not bear the sole responsibility for answering these questions. Students control a surprisingly large part of the turf of discussion leadership. They participate in critical "framework" decisions by influencing the agenda, sequence of topics, and allocation of time to various topics. They help determine the minute-by-minute direction of the discussion process and the quality of the dialogue. They contribute to the creation of a class culture, accept responsibility for their own involvement, and teach their peers. They develop and practice the skills of leading and following. Without their co-leadership, there is no true discussion.

I have found it helpful to consider students' contribution to the leadership of the discussion process under six broad categories. First, when responsibility is collective, the students play a significant role in constructing the agenda of the day. The instructor may find his or her preclass teaching plan influenced by the addition of new topics of interest to students, suggestions for restating issues in ways that provoke different questions, or requests that materials from previous discussions be combined with the dialogue of the day. Sometimes the class will simply reject the instructor's program. In these cases capitulation is advisable, if not inevitable. Teaching is difficult enough when students want to learn, virtually impossible if they are uninterested. Given these circumstances, discussion teachers do not, like lecturers, set the agenda; they manage its emergence, direction, and evolution.

Second, the students affect the sequence in which topics of the day are discussed. Teachers and students prepare differently. Instructors' plans exploit a flow of inquiry that seems logical to them, consistent with course objectives, and built on past experience with the material and students. But the instructor's teaching logic may not match the students' learning logic. In discussion leadership, efficiency does not always equal effectiveness. Last year's—or last hour's—discussion of a particular topic will never exactly predict the one that's about to begin. Even very experienced instructors, who have been teaching longer than their students have been studying (sometimes longer than their students have been alive), have an inferior command of one essential topic: their students' agendas and learning styles. As a result, questions that an instructor may wish to consider early may well be out of sync with the students' wishes and needs.

Accordingly, a wise instructor prepares twice: both from his or her point of view and, more important, from the students' point of view. How will participants be likely to approach the material? What paths of inquiry might they follow? When the instructor's approach differs from that of the students, the discussion may well tilt in the students' direction. The professor proposes, but the class disposes.

The third aspect of the discussion that students influence is timing. When their involvement in a question or topic is intense, it will be difficult for an instructor to redirect their energy. One can force a shift in topic, but students' interests, though denied, do not disappear. They reemerge, deftly inserted into their responses to the instructor's new questions. The sensitive instructor will "hear" the discontinuity and act accordingly.

Fourth, the types of questions students ask of one another and of the instructor play a critical role in directing the minute-by-minute flow of dialogue. Their questions may be directionally neutral—"Where do we go next?"—or may shift the discussion to another topic. The phrasing, tone, and delivery of their questions and comments influence the mood and tempo of the class, encourage conflict, excitement, resolution, or reflection. The astute instructor will listen carefully, and on several levels, to students' questions and also respectfully note the directive power in the students' choice of which individual or subgroup to address. This choice is another, crucial contribution students make to determining both the style and content of discussion.

Working and playing together over a period of time, students get to know their associates better than the instructor can—their itches and ouches, blind spots, areas of experience and wisdom, cares and concerns. And students possess current information about their peers to augment this background information. They are familiar with Rosa's or Juan's circumstances today, this minute. They know Herman's special interest in the topic and his mood. Was he worked over in an earlier class today? Is there a family crisis going on? This sort of student intelligence (in the military sense) lies mainly beyond an instructor's reach. But its power to maintain continuity or produce radical change in the direction of dialogue will show up in the classroom.

Such information can improve the quality of the group's communication. Effective communication—in which words encourage and advance understanding for others as well as the speaker—is difficult to achieve under the best of circumstances. Indeed, as the late Fritz Roethlisberger observed, the first law of communication is to expect miscommunication. Communication is even more complex in crowded classrooms, where dialogue is rapid-fire, personal commitment—even passion—accompanies many comments, and reflection time is limited. In such situations, students' intelligence does more to influence the flow of dialogue than the instructor's directions can.

Fifth, because students relate to one another as peers, they can often communicate more effectively than the instructor in class. Why? Not because they are more rigorous in thought, skilled in semantics and phonetics, or expert in their artistry of explanation. Rather, because they possess rough and ready emotional profiles of one another. In what fields does Ms. Peterson feel confident, have the knack of explaining, and the interest, patience, and ingenuity to state her message in a variety of ways? What are the barriers, the ignorance, bias, lack of interest, that limit Mr. Ripley's understanding and ability to listen?

Students also tend to share the language system of their generation, a common idiom of "go" and "no go" words and relevant metaphors ("needle in a haystack" might resonate less well than "contact lens in a swimming pool," for example). This, plus their knowledge of fellow students, brings them swiftly to the core of effective communication, speaking *to*, not *at*, one another.

Equally important, it is simpler and less threatening for participants to check and recheck each other's meaning than for the instructor to do so. They can accept "I don't understand what you said" more easily from a friend than a potential judge. Correction of the inevitable miscommunication is less complicated when it comes from a classmate than a teacher. When a fellow student says, "You didn't read me right. I meant this," or "Give me that again, Bill. Your assumptions are off base," the remark is less likely to be perceived as an accusation of ignorance or error, and more likely to be seen as a low-key request for help.

Finally, the sixth aspect of the discussion process that students influence heavily is class culture. Discussion groups derive tone and character from the way students work together in the daily routines of class. What is to be the balance between cooperation and competition? Where are the boundaries? What is acceptable and nonacceptable behavior? What are the responsibilities of a class member to himself or herself and the group? Obviously, all students should prepare, attend, and participate. It is difficult to experience a discussion in absentia. But what more? How will these particular participants work out the fundamental challenges of a member of a discussion group—when to stand out, when to blend in, when to lead, when to follow? How members of the group help one another through these complexities affects the context in which the discussions take place. The resolution of these problems contributes to the quality of the learning milieu.

The apparent disorder of a discussion class is, then, but a mask for a complicated teaching and learning process in which students play a vital, but far from obvious role in leadership. Only appreciation of, and attention to, process can help us teachers understand students' essential teaching contribution—a key understanding for effective educational discussions. Most important, the mask blinds us, as teachers, to a fundamental fact: we not only teach a course, but also simultaneously help the students learn how to teach one another. It is not enough to ask "good questions"; we must understand the art of questioning, listening, and responding constructively; model those skills in class for our students and, by so doing, demonstrate our respect for their importance.

LESSONS LEARNED

Years after that first disorienting class, I still regard the mysterious power of discussion teaching with awe. I have shed the youthful naiveté that led me to search for "the answer," but I still work away at pedagogical questions. Accommodation is the order of the years, but the decades have brought a measure of understanding. My belief in the essential magnificence of teaching grows ever stronger. What I have learned about the abiding conundrums of discussion pedagogy makes me even more certain that teaching is a great learning experience. And for the study of teaching, what better research laboratory than the classroom, where the teacher can experiment with the real "stuff" and test, modify, and retest all hypotheses? I have stressed the rewards of this pursuit, but I am also aware of its price. The gains in depth and specificity that come from "knowing more" increase the pressure for yet higher standards. As hands-on classroom knowledge builds, one can no longer turn to easy excuses—the students just didn't like the material; another course had a long report due this week; or (most common of all) I just had a bad day. None of these explanations works when one grasps the dynamics of classroom process. Higher standards are a constant reminder to do better.

In working up a "wish I had learned this earlier" list, I asked myself: Does my experience suggest one quintessential lesson? Perhaps the answer is yes. Teaching is a human activity. Intellect does not teach intellect; people teach people.

No matter how factually accurate and time-tested our data, how clear cut and disciplined our analytical methods, or how practiced and skillful our pedagogical techniques, true learning emerges only when we honor the human factor. One measure of pedagogical maturity is the ability to augment technical expertise with attention to people.

Given this overarching proposition, I would like to offer some lessons learned from students, colleagues, and day-to-day classroom practice. Some of these lessons have been purchased at substantial personal cost. Many lessons had to be both learned and relearned. On reflection, I find none of them surprising. Why didn't I think of them earlier? No one reason. But is a lifetime in the classroom really long enough to figure out what effective teaching is all about?

1. A teacher's openness and caring increase the students' learning opportunities.   When students perceive the instructor at the front of the room as distant and impersonal—a figurehead, not a friend—their learning opportunities suffer. "He lives in another world, guys; I don't know what turns his flame up. . . . I'm just line twelve on the class list." Enduring learning needs a human context, an emotional matrix, in which to grow. The teacher who provides that context and encourages it in the learning group must let students know him or her as more than an intellectual resource or mobile data base.

Our educational conventions put distance between teachers and students. Without sacrificing propriety or relinquishing our role as guides, we teachers need to open our worlds to students. Far too many people in public view become, as Dr. Grete Bibring put it, "individuals with faces that have never been lived in." Our students want and need to know what we stand for. The opposite side of this coin is our need to understand students as people. What are their ambitions, uncertainties, blind spots, and areas of excellence? When we open our wider worlds and appear "in the round," we also maximize our possibilities for learning about them. Openness brings mutual advantage because it permits mutual learning.

But openness is not enough. We must combine it with caring. Teachers must do more than feel concerned; we must actively look after and provide for the welfare of students. We must not only appreciate, but also become personally involved in, their progress. By so doing, we measurably enhance the potential for learning on both sides. One experienced associate noted that most students want to know how much you care before they care how much you know. His judgment, though paradoxical, makes sense to me. Caring converts impersonal offers of academic assistance into gifts, and every gift of learning enriches the giver as much as the recipient. Students sense the difference between perfunctory offers of help and true personal willingness to teach and learn with them. Openness increases a discussion leader's opportunities to help students. Caring makes the process work.

2. Effective discussions require the classroom to become a learning space. As a novice instructor I would have defined "learning space" physically, as the classroom. Baker 101 was an adequate room—satisfactory acoustics, lights in working order, enough chairs. I looked for nothing more. Over the years, however, my view of the classroom has grown metaphorical and far more demanding. A true learning space is psychological, not physical, and the teacher bears the primary responsibility for creating it.

I now view the discussion classroom as a joining ground where students, instructor, and ideas meet and commingle; a space where, as Henri Nouwen suggests, "students and teachers can enter into a fearless communication with each other and allow their respective life experiences to be their primary and most valuable source of growth and maturation."[1] The creation of such space requires a mutual trust in which teachers and learners (those shifting roles) can present themselves as colleagues in a common quest for truth. A genuine learning space is more than a container for this quest; it is a place where all feel free to question one another constructively and where an aggregation of competitive individuals, dedicated to personal goals, can become a learning group.

When we teachers create and support an atmosphere of intellectual hospitality, we help students believe that they have something of value to contribute. This belief, in turn, encourages them to risk trying out ideas—the risk that makes learning possible. Perhaps most important, it is only within a welcoming classroom space that we can obtain students' active involvement in discussions. Discussions that take place in true learning spaces engage students verbally and reflectively, intellectually and emotionally.

Above all, such spaces make risk-taking safe—as safe as it can be, that is. And safety—students' anticipation of aid and comfort in tough situations—is the greatest antidote to the discussion leader's ever-present, always unsettling challenge: silence. Joe isn't contributing very much anymore. What's going on? Is he reflecting on points made earlier, contemplating new questions to ask, wrestling with uncertainty, just feeling turned off—or is he scared? We teachers sometimes forget how difficult it is for students to develop the capacity for what Donald Schön calls cognitive risk-taking. A glance backward at our own student days may help us remember. Didn't we use silence to protect ourselves from questions—by peers, instructors, or ourselves (these last often the most painful)? In a safe space, members of a group with especially complex needs and concerns (that includes most of us, doesn't it?) can reveal their sensitivities and needs. When this happens, community is strengthened, and all benefit.

The creation and maintenance of a safe space is not very arduous, and its rewards are bountiful. David Riesman's metaphor of the teacher as host, or welcomer of guests, may serve as a useful guide. There is little cost but great value in learning something about students' backgrounds and current circumstances in time to welcome them personally to the upcoming dialogue. Similarly, the few moments we instructors devote to weaving "safety nets"—techniques for supporting students who run into trouble by taking on complex or unpopular points of argument—are well spent. Safety nets enable participants to walk the high wire of adventuresome thought and argument with daring bolstered by a sense of security.

When the instructor fosters the creation of a learning space in the classroom, everyone gains. The class becomes a community. A working partnership emerges between teacher and students, and risk-taking increases on both sides. We sometimes forget that instructors are as risk-averse as students. We hesitate to reveal our own uncertainties and areas of ignorance. We hold back from presenting positions in their early stages of development. We resist challenging popular points of view. But in a safe learning space, we can reveal what we know and need to know, and also what we are and would like to be.

3. Modest expectations are the most powerful of all.   Teachers select their life's work for complex reasons, unique in every case. But one basic circumstance of our vocation unites us all: our work simultaneously allows us to serve the wider community and make significant contributions to the lives of the individual students entrusted to our care. Stories about master teachers give us pictures of what the great can do. Each of us has had some personal experience of the impact a teacher can make on a life by stimulating interest in a topic or field of study, providing a role model, or molding our basic values and beliefs. Teachers can accomplish so much of importance. But the contemplation of that accomplishment can overwhelm as well as inspire.

As my years in the classroom have multiplied, I have made the paradoxical discovery that modest expectations, particularly in the realm of content, trigger more effective learning than ambitious ones. Material learned in depth—with heart as well as head—stays with students, but broad-based lists of facts, techniques, and theories tend to fade. J. D. Salinger noted that the mark of immaturity is a desire to die nobly for a cause, but maturity brings the willingness to live humbly for one. Our colleague Abby Hansen suggests that discussion leaders' best songs are anthems of modest expectations. I have found that teaching practice improves when I fit my expectations about how much the group should cover in a given period to a quite modest standard. Thoroughness and depth compensate abundantly for the sacrifice of breadth. Retention of a few crucial things over time brings far more benefit than superficial mastery.

There are few tasks more difficult than evaluating the effect of our teaching. Trying to gauge success is like tossing coins into the Grand Canyon and waiting to hear the clink. How can we ever know just what we have contributed to a student's education? Teachers have much in common with performing artists, but our applause (or boos and hisses) may not come for years, if ever. Who knows what students retain a day, week, year, or decade after a seminar? It is chastening to be thanked by an alumnus for all you taught him only to realize, as the conversation continues, that he is praising a colleague, not you.

Gradually I have abandoned my interest in final outcomes—whatever they may be—and begun to derive satisfaction from the act of teaching itself. When I consider the innumerable gradations that intervene between success and failure, the complex natures of the parties involved, and the magnitude of the daily efforts that go unevaluated, I marvel at the imponderability of long-term effects. I have learned that wisdom and effectiveness lie in a constant struggle for improvement, rather than a quest for final results. Like virtue, teaching is its own reward. For me this means that if I practice and hone my skills, welcome observation and constructive criticism, and experiment and grow, my efforts may very well have an impact. Minor miracles do happen—often enough, in fact, to justify this hope.

4. Instructors' patience promotes students' learning.   Patience, though a virtue of restraint, has the effect of energizing students. Inquiry, growth, and learning flourish under low pressure. Concepts and ideas are difficult to plant in our intellectual garden. They have erratic, individualized growing circles, and harvesting is always under the student's control—exam schedules to the contrary notwithstanding. Yet I found this simple lesson difficult to learn. Patience is not readily acquired.

Impatience comes more easily. Having worked through the process of understanding the applicability and limits of the ideas under study, we feel we know our subjects. The material is ours, and we forget the missteps we took on the way to this possession. But discussion teaching is not a straightforward dispensing of knowledge. Students have their own missteps to make; their journeys will not necessarily parallel ours. Discussion leaders who fail to appreciate the constructiveness of inefficiency make a serious error. Efficient teaching does not always equate with effective learning. On the contrary, students often discover valuable lessons at the ends of blind alleys—lessons that we teachers cannot anticipate before they unfold in the discussion. What seems like a digression may link the challenge of the moment to prior explorations. Apparent tangents examine questions of the students' creation, not because of any obvious link to the assignment of the day, but because they hold high, continuing intellectual interest for the students.

The syllabi we develop contribute to our impatience. There is always more to be taught than time to teach. A rigid, daily roster of material to cover pressures us to ignore crucial elements of context—school events, local and national circumstances, and personal matters. A colleague tells of a friend, a Civil War historian, who puts the point well: "In my class Grant has to arrive at Richmond before Thanksgiving, no matter what!"

The costs of such rigidity can be high, even cruel. As an unknown poet once said, "All the flowers of all the tomorrows are planted in the seeds of today." We need to nurture, tend, and let them mature at their own pace. Forcing can kill. Nikos Kazantzakis makes the point tellingly in *Zorba the Greek:*

> I remembered one morning when I discovered a cocoon in the bark of a tree, just as a butterfly was making a hole in its case and preparing to come out. I waited awhile, but it was too long appearing and I was impatient. I bent over it and breathed on it to warm it. I warmed it as quickly as I could and the miracle began to happen before my eyes, faster than life. The case opened, the butterfly started slowly crawling out and I shall never forget my horror when I saw how its wings were folded back and crumpled; the wretched butterfly tried with its whole trembling body to unfold them. Bending over it, I tried to help it breathe. In vain.
>
> It needed to be hatched out patiently and the unfolding of the wings should be a gradual process in the sun. Now it was too late. My breath had forced the butterfly to appear, all crumpled before its time. It struggled desperately and a few seconds later, died in the palm of my hand.

> That little body is, I do believe, the greatest weight I have on my conscience. For I realize today that it is a mortal sin to violate the great laws of nature. We should not hurry, we should not be impatient, but we should confidently obey the eternal rhythm.[2]

This lesson has special meaning for teachers. We must bring to each class infinite patience, and moderate our critical judgments about students' progress. Walter Jackson Bate reminds us, in his biography of Samuel Johnson, how difficult it is to appreciate "the actual process and daily crawl of other people's experience."[3] But it is precisely this "daily crawl" that we must respect, protect, and honor. And we must, I submit, do it in a context of positive belief in students.

5. Faith is the most essential ingredient in good teaching practice.   Thus far I have discussed in depth two essentials of discussion teaching: knowledge of pedagogical concepts and mastery of process skills. It is now time to consider the third essential: faith. Faith in the fundamental worth of our vocation, in the values that govern our relations with individual students and classes, and in the likelihood that at least some of the results we desire will be achieved. To me, faith is the indispensable dimension of teaching life. Why, then, is it so rarely mentioned? Perhaps because academicians may feel more comfortable with hard facts, logical analysis, and readily observable skills than with intangibles like belief. But without these intangibles—the "soul," if you will, that animates that mechanism inside the black box of discussion teaching—technique becomes mechanical, skills manipulative, and attitudes suspect.

Can faith be codified? I have found that certain insights have not only endured but assumed increasing significance for my teaching practice while other observations and theoretical constructs have faded or been replaced. I offer these articles of faith—so meaningful to me—not as prescriptions or dogma, but as a purely personal testament: *credo*, after all, means "I believe."

- I believe that the profession of teaching is crucial to the maintenance and advancement of civilization. Only our most talented—master crafts-people who perform to the highest possible standards—should undertake it. As Theodore Roethke put it in "Words for Young Writers," we need "more people that specialize in the impossible,"[4] and that is what teachers do. To me, teaching carries an awesome responsibility to encourage students to want to know, to show them how to know, and to insist that they ask and answer the question "For what purpose do *I* need to know?"
- I believe in the teachability of teaching. For the past two decades my pedagogical research, statements, and teaching objectives have centered on this fundamental conviction: good teachers are made, not born. We can observe, analyze, and communicate the artistry of discussion leadership to other practitioners. Effective teachers both practice and constantly search and research their own activities; their classrooms are both instructional arenas and laboratories.
- I believe that active involvement is critical to enduring learning. In discussion classes, students and teachers alike must give of themselves.

Without involvement, the discussion of the day is but noise and its leadership a charade. There's a world of difference between a lackadaisical game of "Simon Says" and the muscle-building that takes place when a committed coach leads an eager team through a workout. Involvement transforms passive, received knowledge into the active ability to apply that knowledge effectively.

- I believe that discussion leaders need to master both process skills as well as the substantive knowledge of their course. Without knowledge of process, instructors are limited in their effort to help students discover, assimilate, and retain course content. It is through command of process that the primacy of content is realized.

- I believe that teaching is a moral act. Ethical commitment must temper the balance we strike in selecting materials and working with them in class. Morality must shape our treatment of students—David Riesman calls teaching "power, with sympathy"—and the values we develop for the classroom community. As the late Professor Lon Fuller suggested, we must distinguish between a morality of duty—that which is formally and/or legally appropriate—and a morality of aspiration—a striving for excellence and idealism. The latter must govern.

- I believe that what my students become is as important as what they learn. The endpoint of teaching is as much human as intellectual growth. Where qualities of person are as central as qualities of mind—as is true in all professional education—we must engage the whole being of students so that they become open and receptive to multiple levels of understanding. And we must engage our whole selves as well. I teach not only what I know, but what I am.

- I believe that, in the words of Professor Charles Gragg, "teachers must also learn!"[5] We cannot truly teach unless we let ourselves experience the vicissitudes and exhilaration of exploration—the mastery and communication of ideas, coupled with the reception of new insights, and the never-ending desire to know more. Teaching and learning are inseparable; the process of education is a reciprocal gift.

- I believe that fun has a critical place in teaching. Great classes include multiple moods—verbal pyrotechnics, moments of stillness, measured, cadenced analyses, and flights of fancy—but always in a context of celebration. Fun permits breakouts from routine. It enlivens the humdrum and sustains generosity as all participants give and receive enjoyment along with wisdom. And fun can heal: it is difficult to dislike someone with whom you share a laugh. Humor can broaden the scope of the possible, but, as Samuel Johnson noted, "Nothing is more hopeless than a scheme of merriment."[6] In a context of good nature, fun will emerge unplanned from the inevitable incongruities of all extended conversations: the extrapolations that take comments to maximum exaggeration and the implosions that carry words and images to absurdity.

- I believe that the teacher's challenge in evaluating students is less to separate the gifted from the ordinary than to find the gifts of the ordinary. And I believe that we must communicate our evaluations in a manner that helps students understand their competence, or lack thereof, without destroying their confidence. Robert Frost said it well: "No figure [or letter] has ever caught the whole of it." At best, grades are imprecise measures even of academic achievement. They do not weigh the worth of a student as a person, now or in the future.
- I believe in the unlimited potential of every student. At first glance they range, like instructors, from mediocre to magnificent. But potential is invisible to the superficial gaze. It takes faith to discern it, but I have witnessed too many academic miracles to doubt its existence. I now view each student as "material for a work of art."

If I have faith, deep faith, in students' capacities for creativity and growth, how very much we can accomplish together. If, on the other hand, I fail to believe in that potential, my failure sows seeds of doubt. Students read our negative signals, however carefully cloaked, and retreat from creative risk to the "just possible." When this happens, everyone loses.

One student—call him Andy—was tottering between Low Pass and Unsatisfactory in my Business Policy course. Together we devised a remedial program. He would write five "dry run" exams before a "make-or-break" final that could determine whether he would graduate with his class. After each remedial exam, we would meet to discuss what he had written. Andy worked hard, but progress came slowly. At our last meeting, somewhat discouraged, I asked, "Andy, do you think you can handle the exam tomorrow?" He looked at me and said, oh so softly, "Professor Christensen, Professor Christensen, that's not it. The question is, do *you* think I can handle the exam? Do *you believe in me?*" His comment hit home—helped me. It reminded me of his strengths and the gains he had made. "Andy," I said, "would I spend this much time on a hopeless cause? Yes, I think you can pass this exam and take your degree. What's more, I know you will have a wonderful career. *I believe in you.*"

My words affected him visibly. He smiled, and I thought I could see his back straighten a bit as he left my office. He passed the final exam, graduated with his class, and went on to great success, in both business and civic affairs. Many people have benefited from Andy's capability and generosity—his family, our school, his community, and society in general.

We learn so much from our students. Andy and others like him taught me that if I round out my knowledge of Business Policy and skill at discussion management with faith in them, they can accomplish the improbable and enable me to do the same. For the reciprocity of teaching and learning—their inseparability—makes us share in our students' successes, just as we share in their failures. To give up on students is to give up on ourselves, and that I have never done.

REVIEW QUESTIONS

1. What is a Möbius strip? How does it help make Christensen's point in the first paragraph?
2. Christensen says he "soon learned that mastery of course content wasn't the key" to effective teaching. What was?
3. Describe the distinction Christensen makes between content and process and between process and procedures.
4. Paraphrase: "In discussion teaching, tidiness can tyrannize. Messiness can work miracles." "In discussion leadership, efficiency does not always equal effectiveness."
5. Explain the connection Christensen makes between a teacher's openness and his or her caring.
6. Give two clear examples of what Christensen means by "patience."
7. What does it mean to say that "teaching is a moral act?"

PROBES

1. It was relatively easy for Christensen to build this approach in a business-school class based on the case-study method. But other chapters of the book this essay appears in discuss applications of discussion teaching in political science, literature, and medical school (microscopic anatomy class). How might this approach be applied to each of the courses you are registered for this term?
2. On the one hand, Christensen emphasizes the application of specific, even mechanical skills—like asking questions of students in various parts of the room or using the student's name in the question versus not using his or her name. On the other hand, he clearly believes that excellent teaching involves more than just mechanics. How would you describe his view of this tension between mechanics, or rules, and intuition, or art?
3. What do you believe makes up the "class culture" Christensen talks about near the end of the essay? How does this culture affect what goes on in the classroom?
4. I think one of Christensen's most important insights is this: "Teaching is a human activity. Intellect does not teach intellect; people teach people." Paraphrase what you think this means and then respond. What would you expect the teacher who believes this to do, for example, with a syllabus, required readings, tests, office hours, and grading?
5. Give an example from your own experience of the importance of the classroom being a space where it is safe to take a cognitive risk.
6. Christensen says that he has gradually given up any interest in final outcomes—the degree to which his students achieve some particular goal in their education or in the "real world." What is his rationale for giving this up, and what has he substituted for it? How do you respond to this part of his essay?

7. How do you respond to all Christensen's talk about faith? Isn't this a pretty imprecise, abstract, and maybe even dangerous topic for something as concrete and practical as teaching? What justifies his discussion of it?

NOTES

1. Henri J. M. Nouwen, *Reaching Out* (Garden City, NY: Image Books, 1986), p. 85.
2. Nikos Kazantzakis, *Zorba the Greek,* tr. Carl Wildman (New York: Simon & Schuster, 1952), p. 120.
3. Walter Jackson Bate, *Samuel Johnson* (New York: Harcourt Brace Jovanovich, 1977), p. 233.
4. Theodore Roethke, *Straw for the Fire: From the Notebooks of Theodore Roethke, 1943–63,* selected and arranged by David Wagoner (Garden City, NY: Doubleday, 1972), p. 185.
5. Charles I. Gragg, "Teachers Also Must Learn," *Harvard Educational Review,* vol. 10 (1940), pp. 30–47.
6. Samuel Johnson, "The Idler," in vol. 2, no. 58, *The Works of Samuel Johnson,* ed. Robert Lynam (London: George Cowre, 1825).

CHAPTER 14

A Counselor's Approach

C arl Rogers was a psychotherapist and communication theorist who influenced many of the authors represented in this book. I highly recommend that you read at least one of his books—for example, *On Becoming a Person, Person to Person: The Process of Becoming Human,* or his most recent book, *A Way of Being.* In the 1950s, Rogers was one of the half-dozen persons responsible for moving psychology away from an exclusive focus on Freudian psychodynamics and quantifiable variables to a concern with the whole person and communication relationships. By the time of his death in the late 1980s, he was known all over the world as a psychotherapist, group facilitator, and teacher.

This reading is made up of excerpts from a chapter in *A Way of Being.* Like many of his writings, this one was originally a talk he gave, in this case an invited speech at the California Institute of Technology. Rogers reports that as he prepared for the occasion, he became frustrated at his own efforts to describe what he believed about communication. So he decided to demonstrate rather than simply discuss, to endeavor, as he put it, "to *communicate,* rather than just to speak about the subject of communication."

In another place, Rogers wrote that over his lifetime he had discovered that "what is most personal is most general." This talk is evidence of this same insight. Rogers tries to stick close to his personal experiences with communication, and as he describes them, he finds himself talking about my experience—and probably yours, too. So this essay demonstrates how "what is most personal is most general."

One of the reasons I like much of what Rogers says is that he begins discussing communication by focusing not on talk but on listening. He describes what it means really to hear someone and to be heard, to be listened to by another. Over his 40 years as a psychotherapist, Rogers learned that complete hearing—listening, clarifying, and responding to all the levels at which the other is communicating—is one key to a therapeutic, growth-promoting relationship. The therapist, he argues, doesn't primarily need to be able to administer psychometric tests or interpret dreams. The most important thing is that he or she needs to make contact, to communicate interpersonally. As Rogers summarizes, "a creative, active, sensitive, accurate, emphatic, nonjudgmental listening is for me terribly important in a relationship."

The second of Rogers's three main points involves what he calls "congruence." This is his label for the state where "my experiencing of this moment is present in my awareness and when what is present in my awareness is present in my communication." As he explains in other writings, this does not mean that you impulsively blurt out every thought that enters your mind. Especially when you're experiencing mixed feelings, it's important to reflect on the dimensions of experience that deserve communicating. Rogers also believes that incongruence is often an outgrowth of fear.

The flip side of congruence, of course, is allowing and encouraging the other to be congruent too. As Rogers says, this is often the ultimate test for the leader, teacher, and parent. But when at least some measure of congruence characterizes both sides of a relationship, the communication is enriched by it.

Rogers's third learning is that what he's called "unconditional positive regard" or "nonpossessive warmth" is also vital to effective communication. People typically experience so much evaluation and criticism that when they feel accepted for who they are, they often blossom. As he notes, people can be appreciated just as we appreciate a sunset.

In other writings, Rogers has also clarified that he doesn't mean we should go around in a naïve fog, loving every terrorist, rapist, and sociopath who makes the front page. He worked extensively with "sick" persons, and he knew what it was like to apply the principle of unconditional positive regard to his communication with them. Often the key is to separate the person and the behavior so that you can accept the former while rejecting the latter. It is also important to remember that persons act in ways that make the most sense to them at the time they act. Observers may not be able to fathom the sense that some actions make, but if we want to communicate with these persons—without necessarily condoning what they do—positive regard helps.

When Rogers gave this talk, it was remarkable to hear a person being so open and straightforward in such a relatively "formal" situation. Rogers was often disarmingly direct in just that way. I hope his directness enables you to hear what he has to say. Carl Rogers had an approach to interpersonal communication that is very much worth getting to know.

Rogers is another "classic" writer who used "he" to mean "everyone." As with the essays by Gibb and Buber, I hope you can read beyond this language for the good ideas that are here.

Experiences in Communication

Carl R. Rogers

. . . What I would like to do is very simple indeed. I would like to share with you some of the things I have learned for myself in regard to communication. They are personal learnings growing out of my own experience. I am not attempting at all to say that you should learn or do these same things but I feel that if I can report my own experience honestly enough, perhaps you can check what I say against your own experience and decide as to its truth or falsity for you. . . . Another way of putting this is that some of my experiences in communicating with others have made me feel expanded, larger, enriched, and have accelerated my own growth. Very often in these experiences I feel that the other person has had similar reactions and that he too has been enriched, that his development and his functioning have moved forward. Then there have been other occasions in which the growth or development of each of us has been diminished or stopped or even reversed. . . .

The first simple feeling I want to share with you is my enjoyment when I can really *hear* someone. I think perhaps this has been a long-standing characteristic of mine. I can remember this in my early grammar school days. A child would ask the teacher a question and the teacher would give a perfectly good answer to a completely different question. A feeling of pain and distress would always strike me. My reaction was, "But you didn't hear him!" I felt a sort of childish despair at the lack of communication which was (and is) so common.

I believe I know why it is satisfying to me to hear someone. When I can really hear someone, it puts me in touch with him; it enriches my life. It is through hearing people that I have learned all that I know about individuals, about personality, about interpersonal relationships. . . .

When I say that I enjoy hearing someone, I mean, of course, hearing deeply. I mean that I hear the words, the thoughts, the feeling tones, the personal meaning, even the meaning that is below the conscious intent of the speaker. Sometimes too, in a message which superficially is not very important, I hear a deep human cry that lies buried and unknown far below the surface of the person.

So I have learned to ask myself, can I hear the sounds and sense the shape of this other person's inner world? Can I resonate to what he is saying so deeply that I sense the meanings he is afraid of yet would like to communicate, as well as those he knows?

I think, for example, of an interview I had with an adolescent boy. Like many an adolescent today he was saying at the outset of the interview that he had no goals. When I questioned him on this, he insisted even more strongly that he had no goals whatsoever, not even one. I said, "There isn't anything you want to do?" *"Nothing.* . . . Well, yeah, I want to keep on living." I remember distinctly my feeling at that moment. I resonated very deeply to this phrase. He might simply be telling me that, like everyone else, he wanted to live. On the other hand, he might be telling me—and this seemed to be a definite possibility—that at some point the question of whether or not to live had been a real issue with him. So I tried to resonate to him at all levels. I didn't know for certain what the message was. I simply wanted to be open to any of the meanings that this statement might have, including the possibility that he might at one time have considered suicide. My being willing and able to listen to him at all levels is perhaps one of the things that made it possible for him to tell me, before the end of the interview, that not long before he had been on the point of blowing his brains out. This little episode is an example of what I mean by wanting to really hear someone at all the levels at which he is endeavoring to communicate. . . .

I find, both in therapeutic interviews and in the intensive group experiences which have meant a great deal to me, that hearing has consequences. When I truly hear a person and the meanings that are important to him at that moment, hearing not simply his words, but him, and when I let him know that I have heard his own private personal meanings, many things happen. There is first of all a grateful look. He feels released. He wants to tell me more about his world. He surges forth in a new sense of freedom. He becomes more open to the process of change. . . .

Let me move on to a second learning that I would like to share with you. I like to *be heard.* A number of times in my life I have felt myself bursting with insoluble problems, or going round and round in tormented circles or, during one period, overcome by feelings of worthlessness and despair. I think I have been more fortunate than most in finding at these times individuals who have been able to hear me and thus to rescue me from the chaos of my feelings, individuals who have been able to hear my meanings a little more deeply than I have known them. These persons have heard me without judging me, diagnosing me, appraising me, evaluating me. They have just listened and clarified and responded to me at all the levels at which I was communicating. I can testify that when you are in psychological distress and someone really hears you without passing judgment on you, without trying to take responsibility for you, without trying to mold you, it feels damn good! At these times it has relaxed the tension in me. It has permitted me to bring out the frightening feelings, the guilts, the despair, the confusions that have been a part of my experience. When I have been listened to and when I have been heard, I am able to reperceive my world in a new way and to go on. It is astonishing how elements that seem insoluble become soluble when someone listens, how confusions that seem irremediable turn into relatively clear flowing streams when one is heard. I have deeply appreciated the times that I have experienced this sensitive, empathic, concentrated listening.

I dislike it myself when I can't hear another, when I do not understand him. If it is only a simple failure of comprehension or a failure to focus my attention on what he is saying or a difficulty in understanding his words, then I feel only a very mild dissatisfaction with myself. But what I really dislike in myself is not being able to hear the other person because I am so sure in advance of what he is about to say that I don't listen. It is only afterward that I realize that I have heard what I have already decided he is saying; I have failed really to listen. Or even worse are those times when I catch myself trying to twist his message to make it say what I want him to say, and then only hearing that. This can be a very subtle thing, and it is surprising how skillful I can be in doing it. Just by twisting his words a small amount, by distorting his meaning just a little, I can make it appear that he is not only saying the thing I want to hear, but that he is the person I want him to be. Only when I realize through his protest or through my own gradual recognition that I am subtly manipulating him, do I become disgusted with myself. I know too, from being on the receiving end of this, how frustrating it is to be received for what you are not, to be heard as saying something which you have not said. This creates anger and bafflement and disillusion.

This last statement indeed leads into the next learning that I want to share with you: I am terribly frustrated and shut into myself when I try to express something which is deeply me, which is a part of my own private, inner world, and the other person does not understand. When I take the gamble, the risk, of trying to share something that is very personal with another individual and it is not received and not understood, this is a very deflating and a very lonely experience. I have come to believe that such an experience makes some individuals psychotic. It causes them to give up hoping that anyone can understand them. Once they have lost that hope, then their own inner world, which becomes more and more bizarre, is the only place where they can live. They can no longer live in any shared human experience. I can sympathize with them because I know that when I try to share some feeling aspect of myself which is private, precious, and tentative, and when this communication is met by evaluation, by reassurance, by distortion of my meaning, my very strong reaction is, "Oh, what's the use!" At such a time, one knows what it is to be alone.

So, as you can readily see from what I have said thus far, a creative, active, sensitive, accurate, empathic, nonjudgmental listening is for me terribly important in a relationship. It is important for me to provide it; it has been extremely important, especially at certain times in my life, to receive it. I feel that I have grown within myself when I have provided it; I am very sure that I have grown and been released and enhanced when I have received this kind of listening.

Let me move on to another area of my learnings.

I find it very satisfying when I can be real, when I can be close to whatever it is that is going on within me. I like it when I can listen to myself. To really know what I am experiencing in the moment is by no means an easy thing, but I feel somewhat encouraged because I think that over the years I have been improving at it. I am convinced, however, that it is a lifelong task and that none of us ever is totally able to be comfortably close to all that is going on within our own experience.

In place of the term "realness" I have sometimes used the word "congruence." By this I mean when my experiencing of this moment is present in my awareness and when what is present in my awareness is present in my communication, then each of these three levels matches or is congruent. At such moments I am integrated or whole, I am completely in one piece. Most of the time, of course, I, like everyone else, exhibit some degree of incongruence. I have learned, however, that realness, or genuineness, or congruence—whatever term you wish to give it—is a fundamental basis for the best of communication.

What do I mean by being close to what is going on in me? Let me try to explain what I mean by describing what sometimes occurs in my work as a therapist. Sometimes a feeling "rises up in me" which seems to have no particular relationship to what is going on. Yet I have learned to accept and trust this feeling in my awareness and to try to communicate it to my client. For example, a client is talking to me and I suddenly feel an image of him as a pleading little boy, folding his hands in supplication, saying, "Please let me have this, please let me have this." I have learned that if I can be real in the relationship with him and express this feeling that has occurred in me, it is very likely to strike some deep note in him and to advance our relationship. . . .

I feel a sense of satisfaction when I can dare to communicate the realness in me to another. This is far from easy, partly because what I am experiencing keeps changing every moment. Usually there is a lag, sometimes of moments, sometimes of days, weeks or months, between the experiencing and the communication: I experience something; I feel something, but only later do I dare to communicate it, when it has become cool enough to risk sharing it with another. But when I can communicate what is real in me at the moment that it occurs, I feel genuine, spontaneous, and alive.

I am disappointed when I realize—and of course this realization always comes afterward, after a lag of time—that I have been too frightened or too threatened to let myself get close to what I am experiencing, and that consequently I have not been genuine or congruent. There immediately comes to mind an instance that is somewhat painful to reveal. Some years ago I was invited to be a Fellow at the Center for Advanced Study in the Behavioral Sciences at Stanford. The Fellows are a group of brilliant and well-informed scholars. I suppose it is inevitable that there is a considerable amount of one-upmanship, of showing off one's knowledge and achievements. It seems important for each Fellow to impress the others, to be a little more assured, to be a little more knowledgeable than he really is. I found myself doing this same thing—playing a role of having greater certainty and greater competence than I really possess. I can't tell you how disgusted with myself I felt as I realized what I was doing: I was not being me, I was playing a part.

I regret it when I suppress my feelings too long and they burst forth in ways that are distorted or attacking or hurtful. I have a friend whom I like very much but who has one particular pattern of behavior that thoroughly annoys me. Because of the usual tendency to be nice, polite, and pleasant I kept this annoyance to myself for too long and, when it finally burst its bounds, it came out not only as annoyance but as an attack on him. This was hurtful, and it took us some time to repair the relationship.

I am inwardly pleased when I have the strength to permit another person to be his own realness and to be separate from me. I think that is often a very threatening possibility. In some ways I have found it an ultimate test of staff leadership and of parenthood. Can I freely permit this staff member or my son or my daughter to become a separate person with ideas, purpose, and values which may not be identical with my own? I think of one staff member this past year who showed many flashes of brilliance but who clearly held values different from mine and behaved in ways very different from the ways in which I would behave. It was a real struggle, in which I feel I was only partially successful, to let him be himself, to let him develop as a person entirely separate from me and my ideas and my values. Yet to the extent that I was successful, I was pleased with myself, because I think this permission to be a separate person is what makes for the autonomous development of another individual.

I am angry with myself when I discover that I have been subtly controlling and molding another person in my own image. This has been a very painful part of my professional experience. I hate to have "disciples," students who have molded themselves meticulously into the pattern that they feel I wish. Some of the responsibility I place with them, but I cannot avoid the uncomfortable probability that in unknown ways I have subtly controlled such individuals and made them into carbon copies of myself, instead of the separate professional persons they have every right to become.

From what I have been saying, I trust it is clear that when I can permit realness in myself or sense it or permit it in another, I am very satisfied. When I cannot permit it in myself or fail to permit it in another, I am very distressed. When I am able to let myself be congruent and genuine, I often help the other person. When the other person is transparently real and congruent, he often helps me. In those rare moments when a deep realness in one meets a realness in the other, a memorable "I-thou relationship," as Martin Buber would call it, occurs. Such a deep and mutual personal encounter does not happen often, but I am convinced that unless it happens occasionally, we are not living as human beings.

I want to move on to another area of my learning in interpersonal relationships—one that has been slow and painful for me.

I feel warmed and fulfilled when I can let in the fact, or permit myself to feel, that someone cares for, accepts, admires, or prizes me. Because of elements in my past history, I suppose, it has been very difficult for me to do this. For a long time I tended almost automatically to brush aside any positive feelings aimed in my direction. My reaction was, "Who, me? You couldn't possibly care for me. You might like what I have done, or my achievements, but not me." This is one respect in which my own therapy helped me very much. I am not always able even now to let in such warm and loving feelings from others, but I find it very releasing when I can do so. I know that some people flatter me in order to gain something for themselves; some people praise me because they are afraid to be hostile. But I have come to recognize the fact that some people genuinely appreciate me, like me, love me, and I want to sense that fact and let it in. I think I have become less aloof as I have been able to take in and soak up those loving feelings.

I feel enriched when I can truly prize or care for or love another person and when I can let that feeling flow out to that person. Like many others, I used to fear being trapped by letting my feelings show. "If I care for him, he can control me." "If I love her, I am trying to control her." I think that I have moved a long way toward being less fearful in this respect. Like my clients, I too have slowly learned that tender, positive feelings are not dangerous either to give or to receive. . . .

I think of one governmental executive in a group in which I participated, a man with high responsibility and excellent technical training as an engineer. At the first meeting of the group he impressed me, and I think others, as being cold, aloof, somewhat bitter, resentful, and cynical. When he spoke of how he ran his office, it appeared that he administered it "by the book," without any warmth or human feeling. In one of the early sessions he was speaking of his wife, and a group member asked him, "Do you love your wife?" He paused for a long time and the questioner said, "O.K. That's answer enough." The executive said, "No. Wait a minute. The reason I didn't respond was that I was wondering, 'Have I ever loved anyone?' I don't really think I have ever *loved* anyone."

A few days later, he listened with great intensity as one member of the group revealed many personal feelings of isolation and loneliness and spoke of the extent to which he had been living behind a facade. The next morning the engineer said, "Last night I thought and thought about what he told us. I even wept quite a bit myself. I can't remember how long it has been since I have cried, and I really felt something. I think perhaps what I felt was love."

It is not surprising that before the week was over, he had thought through different ways of handling his growing son, on whom he had been placing very rigorous demands. He had also begun to really appreciate the love his wife had extended to him—love that he now felt he could in some measure reciprocate.

Because of having less fear of giving or receiving positive feelings, I have become more able to appreciate individuals. I have come to believe that this ability is rather rare; so often, even with our children, we love them to control them rather than loving them because we appreciate them. One of the most satisfying feelings I know—and also one of the most growth-promoting experiences for the other person—comes from my appreciating this individual in the same way that I appreciate a sunset. People are just as wonderful as sunsets if I can let them *be*. In fact, perhaps the reason we can truly appreciate a sunset is that we cannot control it. When I look at a sunset as I did the other evening, I don't find myself saying, "Soften the orange a little on the right hand corner, and put a bit more purple along the base, and use a little more pink in the cloud color." I don't do that. I don't *try* to control a sunset. I watch it with awe as it unfolds. I like myself best when I can appreciate my staff member, my son, my daughter, my grandchildren, in this same way. I believe this is a somewhat Oriental attitude; for me it is a most satisfying one.

Another learning I would like to mention briefly is one of which I am not proud but which seems to be a fact. When I am not prized and appreciated, I not only *feel* very much diminished, but my behavior is actually affected by my feelings. When I am prized, I blossom and expand, I am an interesting individual. In a hostile or unappreciative group, I am just not much of anything. People wonder, with very good reason, how did he ever get a reputation? I wish I had the strength to be more similar in both kinds of groups, but actually the person I am in a warm and interested group is different from the person I am in a hostile or cold group.

Thus, prizing or loving and being prized or loved is experienced as very growth enhancing. A person who is loved appreciatively, not possessively, blooms and develops his own unique self. The person who loves nonpossessively is himself enriched. This, at least, has been my experience.

I could give you some of the research evidence which shows that these qualities I have mentioned—an ability to listen emphatically, a congruence or genuineness, an acceptance or prizing of the other—when they are present in a relationship make for good communication and for constructive change in personality. But I feel that, somehow, research evidence is out of place in a talk such as I have been giving.

REVIEW QUESTIONS

1. What does Rogers mean by "hearing deeply"?
2. According to Rogers, what is the primary outcome of someone's being fully or deeply heard?
3. What does congruence mean? What does it *not* mean?
4. How does the fact that I am changing from moment to moment affect my being congruent?
5. At what points in his talk does Rogers suggest that the communication he is discussing is appropriate in nonintimate—that is, business or professional— settings?

PROBES

1. Which discussion of listening in Chapter 5 is closest to Rogers's description of hearing another and being heard?
2. How is Rogers's concept of congruence related to what McKay, Davis, and Fanning say about expressing in Chapter 6?
3. Do you think congruence helps create a defensive or a supportive communication climate (see Chapter 9)?
4. Did you ever feel uncomfortable as you read Rogers's words? What do those feelings tell you about one of the topics of Chapter 6, self-disclosure?
5. How do you think Anita Vangelisti, the author of "Messages That Hurt," in Chapter 9, would respond to what Rogers says here?

CHAPTER 15

A Spiritual Approach

I t may surprise you to learn that this approach I've called "Spiritual" could also have been labeled "A Business or Management Approach," but it could. This reading comes from a book called *Spirit at Work: Discovering the Spirituality in Leadership,* which is edited by one of the world's most sought-after management school professors for corporate education programs, Jay Conger. Conger put the book together because of his conviction developed through years of experience with many different businesses that spirituality offers concrete solutions to some of the increasing demands being made on today's business organizations.

Parker J. Palmer, the author of this reading, is a writer, teacher, and activist who agrees with Conger and who works on issues in education, community, leadership, spirituality, and social change. He is a senior associate of the American Association of Higher Education, so he's especially interested in spirituality in educational organizations. Palmer has published 6 widely-used books, over 100 essays, and 10 poems. When I've heard him speak I've been impressed with his down-to-earth, common sense approach to spirituality.

Palmer begins this selection with a quotation from Vaclav Havel, the playwright who, after several years as a political prisoner, became the president of Czechoslovakia. Havel emphasizes that he has learned a key lesson from his experiences as a writer and political activist: "the salvation of the world lies in the human heart." In other words, material conditions do not determine human realities at all as much as conceptual and spiritual conditions do. Thought and spirit are "the deep sources of freedom and power with which oppressed peoples historically have been able to move immense boulders and create remarkable change." So if you want to be a leader—of your living group, at work, in an organization, as a professional, in politics, or even in your family—you'll want to pay attention to your spiritual understanding and your spiritual health.

Palmer has his own spiritual tradition—Christianity—and he offers some examples of how it plays an important role in his life. But his central point is about how *any* historically developed spiritual tradition can anchor effective human action. Fundamentally, Palmer argues, we "share responsibility for creating the external world by projecting either a spirit of light or a spirit of shadow on that which is other than us." Consciousness, our thinking and spiritual lives, can help "deform, or reform, our world."

Leaders—in classrooms, families, and businesses—fail when they work only from extroversion and ignore what's going on inside themselves. One of the most important ways to develop your spirituality is to plumb some of your own depths. This means that you develop the courage to think and feel deeply about your own core strengths and your own core fears or "monsters." Palmer gives an example of what this means from his own experience in an Outward Bound program. He found himself dangling from a thin, frayed rope 110 feet above ground and having to lean out, into space, rather than hugging the rock wall, which felt much more natural. The only way to get out of his predicament was to "get into it."

Leaders need to be willing to undertake such a spiritual journey—*into* rather than away from their inner lives. When they do, they can often discover a common "shadow," an insecurity about their identity. Especially male leaders often have their identities hooked up with external, institutional markers like the difference between "Dr. Jones" and "Nancy," the secretary. Spiritual maturity clarifies, though, that who I am is not a function of what I do. A second insight it clarifies is that life is not a battleground. "Our commitment to competition," Palmer writes, "is a self-fulfilling prophecy." But if we move spiritually we can discover that "the structure of reality is not the structure of a battle. A third learning from spiritual reflection is that the ultimate responsibility for everything does not rest "with me." As Palmer puts it, "the great gift we receive on the inner journey is the certain knowledge that ours is not the only act in town." Leaders can also learn from the spiritual journey that they do not have to live in fear, of either chaos—total disorganization—or death—public failure. "The best organizations and leaders are asking people to take risks that may sometimes lead to failure, because they understand that from failure we can learn."

Palmer encourages us to help each other with our spiritual journeys, because even though the work is deeply personal, "it is not necessarily a *private* matter." As those in the Quaker tradition know, human support is a vital part of spiritual reflection.

You might wonder what a chapter on spiritual reflection is doing in a book about interpersonal communication. Spirituality is "inside" one person, and communication is "between" two or more, right? Well, yes and no. Spiritual reflection, regardless of whether it is Jewish, Christian, Sufi, Buddhist, Hindu, or New Age, is not simply an inner, private journey, because it connects you with insights and truths that are confirmed in *many people's* lives. Not only can your inner journey be supported and assisted by others, but as you take it you will discover important *connections* with the people around you. In addition, most people can tell when they are communicating with a spiritually aware, spiritually active, or spiritually mature person. Those qualities can't help but leak out in many different parts of your communicating.

Leading from Within

Out of the Shadow, into the Light[1]

Parker J. Palmer

In the last decade or two, we have done a lot of moaning about the lack of moral, humane, and visionary leadership in the public arena. But today, if we have eyes to see, we can look around the world and find those moral, visionary, humane

Excerpted from, *Spirit at Work: Discovering the Spirituality in Leadership*, by Parker J. Palmer. Reprinted by permission of Jossey-Bass, Inc.; a subsidiary of John Wiley & Sons, Inc.

leaders. We can find them in South Africa, we can find them in Latin America, and we can find them in eastern Europe.

I want to begin these reflections with the words of one of those people, someone whose credentials for leadership are far more authentic than mine. Vaclav Havel (playwright, dissident, prisoner, and then president of Czechoslovakia) addressed the U.S. Congress in early 1990. It was surely one of the most remarkable speeches ever delivered on the floor of our national legislative body.

> *As long as people are people, democracy, in the full sense of the word, will always be no more than an ideal. In this sense, you too are merely approaching democracy uninterruptedly for more than 200 years, and your journey toward the horizon has never been disrupted by a totalitarian system.*
>
> *The communist type of totalitarian system has left both our nations, Czechs and Slovaks, as it has all the nations of the Soviet Union and the other countries the Soviet Union subjugated in its time, a legacy of countless dead, an infinite spectrum of human suffering, profound economic decline, and, above all, enormous human humiliation. It has brought us horrors that fortunately you have not known. [I think we Americans should confess that some in our country have known such horrors.—P.J.P.]*
>
> *It has given us something positive, a special capacity to look from time to time somewhat further than someone who has not undergone this bitter experience. A person who cannot move and lead a somewhat normal life because he is pinned under a boulder has more time to think about his hopes than someone who is not trapped that way.*
>
> *What I'm trying to say is this: We must all learn many things from you, from how to educate our offspring, how to elect our representatives, all the way to how to organize our economic life so that it will lead to prosperity and not to poverty. But it doesn't have to be merely assistance from the well-educated, powerful and wealthy to someone who has nothing and therefore has nothing to offer in return.*
>
> *We too can offer something to you: Our experience and the knowledge that has come from it. The specific experience I'm talking about has given me one certainty: Consciousness precedes being, and not the other way around, as the Marxists claim. For this reason, the salvation of this human world lies nowhere else than in the human heart, in the human power to reflect, in human meekness and in human responsibility. Without a global revolution in the sphere of human consciousness, nothing will change for the better in the sphere of our beings as humans, and the catastrophe toward which this world is headed—be it ecological, social, demographic or a general breakdown of civilization—will be unavoidable.*[2]

I doubt there has ever been, from a more remarkable source, a stronger affirmation of the link between spirituality and leadership than Havel's words, "consciousness precedes being" and "the salvation of the world lies in the human heart." He points us toward the heart of the matter—the formation of the human heart, the reformation of the human heart, and the rescuing of the human heart from all its deformations.

Material realities, he tells us, are not the fundamental factor in the movement of history. Consciousness is. Human awareness is. Thought is. Spirit is. Those are the deep sources of freedom and power with which oppressed people historically have been able to move immense boulders and create remarkable change. . . .

The great insight of our spiritual traditions is that external reality does not impinge upon us as a prison or as an ultimate constraint. Instead we *co-create* that reality. We live in and through a complex interaction of spirit and matter, a complex interaction of what is inside of us and what is "out there." The wisdom of our spiritual traditions is not to deny the reality of the outer world, but to help us understand that we create the world, in part, by projecting our spirit on it—for better or worse.

Vaclav Havel has said some hard things to his own people about how they conspired in the domination of a tyrannical communist system through their own passivity. We too are responsible for the existence of tyrannical conditions, of external constraints that crush our spirits, because we too co-create reality through the projection of our internal limitations. Our complicity in world-making is a source of awesome and sometimes painful responsibility and at the same time a source of profound hope for change.

The great spiritual traditions are not primarily about values and ethics, not primarily about doing right or living well. The spiritual traditions are primarily about *reality.* The spiritual traditions all strive to penetrate the illusions of the external world and to name its underlying truth—what it is, how it emerges, and how we relate to it.

In my own tradition, I have been rereading some of Jesus's sayings that I was taught as ethical exhortations, as guides to what we *ought* to do: "The person who seeks life will lose it; but the person who is willing to lose life will find it." But that is not an ethical exhortation. It is not an "ought" statement. It is simply a description of what *is!* Time and again, things Jesus said that we take as ethical pronouncements are simply his statements of what is real. That is the nature of great spiritual teaching.

The insight that I want to draw from the spiritual traditions, and from Havel, may be best summarized in a word from depth psychology: *projection.* We share responsibility for creating the external world by projecting either a spirit of light or a spirit of shadow on that which is other than us. We project either a spirit of hope or a spirit of despair, either an inner confidence in wholeness and integration or an inner terror about life being diseased and ultimately terminal. We have a choice about what we are going to project, and in that choice we help create the world that is. Consciousness precedes being, and consciousness can help deform, or reform, our world.

LEADERS HAVE A SHADOW SIDE

What does all of this have to do with leadership and with the relation of leadership to spirituality? Here is a quick definition of a leader: A leader is a person who has an unusual degree of power to project on other people his or her shadow, or his or her light. A leader is a person who has an unusual degree of power to create the conditions under which other people must live and move and have their being, conditions that can either be as illuminating as heaven or as shadowy as hell. A leader must take special responsibility for what's going on inside his or her own self, inside his or her consciousness, lest the act of leadership create more harm than good.

I want to look here at the shadow side of leadership. Many books on leadership seem to be about the power of positive thinking. I fear they feed a common delusion among leaders that their efforts are always well intended, their power always benign. I suggest that the challenge is to examine our consciousness for those ways in which we leaders may project more shadow than light.

By *leaders,* I do not mean simply the heads of nation-states. I am talking, for example, about a classroom teacher who has the power to create the conditions under which young people must spend half of their waking hours, five days a week, week in and week out. We know that there are classrooms where the leader projects a welcoming light under which new growth flourishes. But we also know of classrooms where the leader casts an ominous shadow under which nothing can grow. I am talking also about a parent who can generate the same effects in a family, about a clergyperson who can create a congregation that lurks in the leader's shadow or thrives in his or her light. I am talking about the CEO of a corporation who faces the same choice every day but who often does not even know that a choice is being made, let alone know how to reflect upon the process.

The problem is that people rise to leadership in our society by a tendency toward extroversion, which too often means ignoring what is going on inside themselves. Leaders rise to power by operating very competently and effectively in the external world, sometimes at the cost of internal awareness. Leaders, in the very way they become leaders, tend to screen out the inner consciousness that Vaclav Havel is calling us to attend to. I have met too many leaders whose confidence in the external world is so high that they regard the inner life as illusory, a waste of time, a magical fantasy trip into a region that does not even exist. But the link Havel makes between consciousness and reality, between leadership and spirituality, calls us to reexamine that common denial of the inner life.

I think leaders often feed themselves on the power of positive thinking because their jobs are hard. They face many external discouragements and they get little affirmation. Thus they feel a need to psych themselves up even if it means ignoring the inner shadow. Of course, leaders are supported in this by an American culture that wants to externalize everything, that wants (just as much as Marx ever did) to see the good life more as a matter of outer arrangements than of inner well-being.

I have looked at some training programs for leaders, and I am discouraged by how often they focus on the development of skills to manipulate the external world rather than the skills necessary to go within and make the spiritual journey. I find that discouraging because it feeds a dangerous syndrome among leaders who already tend to deny their inner world.

THE NATURE OF SPIRITUALITY

Spirituality, like leadership, is a very hard concept to pin down. These are probably two of the vaguest words you can find in our language, and when you put them together you get something even more vague.

So let me share a remarkably concrete quote from Annie Dillard's wonderfully titled book, *Teaching a Stone to Talk.* Never have I read a more evocative description of the inner journey:

> In the deeps are the violence and terror of which psychology has warned us. But if you ride these monsters down, if you drop with them farther over the world's rim, you find what our sciences cannot locate or name, the substrate, the ocean or matrix or ether which buoys the rest, which gives goodness its power for good, and evil its power for evil, the unified field: our complex and inexplicable caring for each other, and for our life together here. This is given. It is not learned.[3]

Annie Dillard is saying several things that are very important for a spirituality of leadership. She is saying, first of all, that the spiritual journey moves inward and downward, not outward and upward toward abstraction. It moves downward toward the hardest concrete realities of our lives—a reversal of what we traditionally have understood spirituality to be.

Why must we go in and down? Because as we do so, we will meet the violence and terror that we carry within ourselves. If we do not confront these things inwardly, we will project them outward onto other people. When we have not understood that the enemy is within ourselves, we will find a thousand ways of making someone "out there" into the enemy—people of a different race, a different gender, a different sexual orientation. We will deal with our fears by killing the enemy, when what we really fear is the shadow within ourselves.

Annie Dillard is saying we have to go down and in, and on the way we will meet our own monsters. But if we ride those monsters all the way down, we find the most precious thing of all: "the unified field, our complex and inexplicable caring for each other," the community we have underneath our brokenness—which, Dillard says, is given, not learned. Great leadership comes from people who have made that downward journey through violence and terror, who have touched the deep place where we are in community with each other, and who can help take the rest of us to that place. *That* is what great leadership is all about.

That is also what Vaclav Havel is talking about, because the downward journey is what you take when you are under a stone for forty years. That is what you have a chance to do when you are a victim of oppression. Is it not remarkable that Nelson Mandela used decades in prison to prepare himself for leadership rather than for despair? Under the most destructive circumstances, he went down, he went in, he dealt with the violence and terror, and he emerged as a leader able to take people toward "our complex and inexplicable caring for each other." It seems to me that this is a powerful image for the spiritual journey, the journey that leaders must take if Havel and Dillard are right.

Now the question is, why would anybody want to take such a difficult and dangerous journey? Everything in us cries out against it. That is why we externalize everything—it is far easier to deal with the external world. It is easier to spend your life manipulating an institution than dealing with your own soul. We make institutions sound complicated and hard and rigorous, but they are simplicity itself compared with our inner labyrinths!

Let me tell you a little parable about why one might want to take the inner journey, a parable from my own life. About ten years ago, when I was in my early forties, I decided to go on that amazing program called Outward Bound. I was in the midst of a midlife crisis, and I thought Outward Bound might be a useful challenge.

I elected to spend ten days at a place called Hurricane Island. I should have known from the name what was in store for me. Next time I will choose the program at Pleasant Valley or Happy Gardens! It was a week of sheer terror. It was also a week of amazing growth and great teaching and a deep sense of community, the likes of which I have seldom experienced.

In the middle of that Outward Bound course I faced the challenge that I had most feared. The leaders backed me up to the edge of a cliff 110 feet above solid ground. They tied a frayed and very thin rope to my waist, and told me to back down that cliff.

So I said, "Well, what do I do?"

The instructor, in typical Outward Bound fashion, said, "Just *go!*"

So I went, and slammed down onto a small ledge, with considerable force. The instructor looked down at me. "I don't think you quite have it yet."

"Right. *Now* what do I do?"

"The only way to do this is to lean back as far as you can. You have to get your feet at right angles to the rock face so you'll have your full weight on them."

Of course I *knew* that he was wrong. I knew that the trick was to hug the mountain, to stay as close to the rock face as I could. So I tried it again, and *BOOM!* I hit the next ledge, hard.

"You still don't have it," the instructor said.

And I said, "Well, what do I do?"

And he said, "Lean way back and take the next step."

The next step was a very big one, but I took it. Wonder of wonders, I began to get the knack. I leaned back, and sure enough, I was moving down the rock face, eyes on the heavens, making tiny, tiny, tiny movements with my feet but gaining confidence with every step.

When I got about halfway down, a second instructor called up from below. "Parker," she said, "I think you better stop and look at what's happening beneath your feet."

Very slowly I lowered my eyes, and there beneath my feet a large hole was opening up in the rock.

To get around the hole, I was going to have to change directions. I froze, completely paralyzed in sheer terror.

The second instructor let me hang there for what seemed like a very long time, and finally she shouted up, "Parker, is anything wrong?"

To this day, I do not know where these words came from, though I have twelve witnesses that I spoke them. But in a high, squeaky voice I said, "I don't want to talk about it."

"Then I think it's time you learned the motto of the Outward Bound School."

"Oh, great," I thought. "I'm about to die, and she's giving me a motto!"

But then she yelled up to me words that I will never forget, words that have been genuinely empowering for me ever since. "The motto of the Outward Bound Hurricane Island School is, 'If you can't get out of it, get into it!'"

I have believed in the idea of "the word became flesh" for a long time, but I had never had a real experience of it. But those words seemed so profoundly true to me at that existential moment that they entered my body, bypassed my mind, and animated my legs and feet. It was just so clear that there was no way out of that situation except to get into it. No helicopter was going to come; they were not going to haul me up on the rope; I was not going to float down. I had to get into it, and my feet started to move.

Why would anyone ever want to take the inner journey about which Annie Dillard and Vaclav Havel write? The answer is: There is no way out of my inner life so I'd better get into it. On the inward and downward spiritual journey, the only way out is in and through.

OUT OF THE SHADOW, INTO THE LIGHT

The shadow lives of leaders are inevitably projected onto institutions and society. If they are to create less shadow and more light, leaders need to ride certain monsters all the way down. I have five of them as a sampler, and a few thoughts on how the inner journey might transform our leadership at these five points.

One of the biggest shadows inside a lot of leaders is deep insecurity about their own identity, their own worth. That insecurity is hard to see in extroverted people. But the extroversion is often there precisely because they are insecure about who they are and are trying to prove themselves in the external world rather than wrestling with their inner identity.

This insecurity takes a specific form that I have seen many times, especially in men, and I see it in myself: We have an identity that is so hooked up with external, institutional functions that we may literally die when those functions are taken away from us. We live in terror of what will happen to us if our institutional identity were ever to disappear.

When leaders operate with a deep, unexamined insecurity about their own identity, they create institutional settings that deprive *other* people of *their* identity as a way of dealing with the unexamined fears in the leaders themselves.

Here is a simple example. I am astonished at the number of times I call an office and hear "Dr. Jones's office; this is Nancy speaking." The boss has decreed it be done that way. The leader has a title and a last name; the person who answers the phone has neither. This is a small but powerful example of depriving someone else of an identity in order to enhance your own.

Everywhere I look I see institutions depriving large numbers of people of their identity so that a few people can enhance theirs. I look at schools and I see hundreds of thousands of students passively memorizing information delivered by experts. These students have been deprived of an identity by the educational system so that teachers can have more identity for themselves, as if this were a zero-sum game, a win-lose situation. As I go around the country talking to people in higher education, I always ask students, "When was the last time that you were asked to relate your life story to the things you are studying?" They say, "What? Our life story doesn't count here." The whole idea in higher education is to replace their "little" life stories with the "big" story of the disciplines. The whole idea in an expert-dominated, technocratic form of education is to devalue those little parochial stories on behalf of the "true" one. And think of what we do to patients in a hospital. Talk about depriving people of identity so that leaders can have more for themselves!

It is not always this way. There are organizations led by people who know who they are "all the way down," whose identity does not depend on a specific role that might be taken away at any moment. If you are in that kind of organization, you are with people and in settings that *give* you identity, that empower you to be someone. I think that is a core issue in the spirituality of leadership. The great spiritual gift that comes as one takes the inward journey is to know for certain that who I am does not depend on what I do. Identity does not depend on titles, or degrees, or function. It depends only on the simple fact that I am a child of God, valued and treasured for what I am. When a leader knows that, then the classroom is different, the hospital is different, and the office is different.

The second shadow of leadership that is inside a lot of us (and please understand that I am talking about myself and my struggles here as much as anybody else's) is the perception that the universe is essentially hostile to human interests and that life is fundamentally a battleground.

Have you ever noticed how often people use "battle" images as they go about the work of leadership? We talk about "do or die" tactics and strategy, about using our big guns, about allies and enemies, about wins and losses. The imagery suggests that if we fail to be fiercely competitive, we will lose, because the basic structure of the universe is a vast combat. The tragedy of that inner shadow, that unexamined inner fear of failing, is that it helps create situations where people actually have to live that way.

Our commitment to competition is a self-fulfilling prophecy. Yes, the world is competitive, but only because we make it that way. Some of the best operations in our world, some of our best corporations, some of our best schools, are learning that there is another way of going about things, a way that is consensual, cooperative, communal. They are fulfilling a different prophecy and creating a different reality.

The spiritual gift we receive as we take the inward journey is the knowledge that the universe is working together for good. The universe is not out to get anybody; the structure of reality is not the structure of a battle. Yes, there is death, but it is part of the cycle of life, and when people learn to move with that cycle there is coherence and great harmony in our lives. That is the spiritual insight that can transform this particular dimension of leadership and thus transform our institutions.

The third shadow in leaders I call "functional atheism"—the belief that ultimate responsibility for everything rests with *me*. It is the unconscious, unexamined conviction within us that if anything decent is going to happen here, I am the one who needs to make it happen.

Functional atheism leads to dysfunctional behavior on every level of our lives: workaholism, burnout, stressed and strained and broken relationships, unhealthy priorities. It is the reason the average group can tolerate only fifteen seconds of silence; people believe that if they are not making noise, nothing is happening!

The great gift we receive on the inner journey is the certain knowledge that ours is not the only act in town. Not only are there other acts in town, but some of them, from time to time, are even better than ours. On this inner journey we learn that we do not have to carry the whole load, that we can be empowered by sharing the load with others, and that sometimes we are even free to lay our part of the load down. We learn that co-creation leaves us free to do only what we are called and able to do, and to trust the rest to other hands.

The fourth shadow among leaders is fear. There are many kinds of fear, but I am thinking especially of our fear of the natural chaos of life. Many leaders have a deep devotion to eliminating all remnants of chaos from the world. They want to order and organize things so thoroughly that the nasty stuff will never bubble up around us—such nasty stuff as dissent, innovation, challenge, change. In an organization, this particular shadow gets projected outward as rigidity of rules and procedures. It creates corporate cultures that are imprisoning rather than empowering.

What we forget from our spiritual traditions is that chaos is the precondition to creativity. Any organization (or any individual) that does not have a safe arena for creative chaos is already half dead. When a leader is so fearful of chaos as not to be able to protect and nurture that arena for other people, there is deep trouble. The spiritual gift of the inner journey is to know that creation comes out of chaos, and that even what has been created needs to be turned to chaos every now and then so that it can be recreated in a more vital form. The spiritual gift on this inner journey is the knowledge that people and organizations not only survive but thrive in chaos, that there is vitality in the play of chaotic energy.

The final example of the shadows that leaders can project on others involves the denial of death. We live in a culture that simply does not want to talk about things dying. Leaders everywhere demand that they themselves, and the people who work for them, artificially maintain things that are no longer alive, maybe never have been. Projects and programs that should have been laid down ten years ago are still on the life-support system.

There is fear in this denial of death—the fear of negative evaluation, the fear of public failure. Surprisingly, the people in our culture who are least afraid of death, in this sense, are the scientists. The scientific community really honors the failure of a hypothesis because the death of an idea produces new learning. But in many organizations, if you fail at what you are doing, you will find a pink slip in your box. Again, the best organizations and leaders are asking people to take risks that may sometimes lead to failure, because they understand that from failure we can learn.

The spiritual gift on the inner journey is the knowledge that death is natural and that death is not the final word. The spiritual gift is to know that allowing something to die is also allowing new life to emerge.

Can we, should we, help each other deal with the spiritual issues inherent in leadership? We *must* help each other because these are critical issues. The failure of leaders to deal with their own inner lives is creating conditions of real misery for lots and lots of folks and unfulfilled missions for lots and lots of institutions. Too many organizations in our society are in deep trouble around the leadership shadows I have tried to name. One way out of trouble is for us to start helping each other recover the power of the inner journey. How might that happen?

To begin, we could strive to elevate the value of "inner work." It would be wonderful if the phrase "inner work" could become a central term in our schools, in our businesses, and in our churches—if we could help people understand that the phrase really means something. The activities that constitute "inner work" are as real and as important as any outer project or task—activities like journaling, reflective reading, spiritual friendship, and meditation. We must come to understand that if we skimp on our inner work, our outer work will be diminished as well.

A second thing we can do is to remind each other that while inner work is a deeply personal matter, it is not necessarily a *private* matter. There are ways to come together in community to help each other with that inner work. I have been very touched by the Quaker tradition, where they know how to come together in support of people engaged in deep inner work. They come together in a way that is supportive but not invasive, that asks a lot of probing questions but never renders judgment or gives advice. They come together in a way that respects the mystery of the human heart but still allows people to challenge and stretch one another in that mystery. . . .

Finally, we need to remember that all of the great spiritual traditions at their core say one simple thing: Be not afraid. They do not say you cannot *have* fears; we all have fears, and leaders have fears aplenty. But they say you do not have to *be* your fears; you do not have to lead from fear and thus create a world in which fear dominates the lives of far too many people. We can lead, instead, from an inner place of trust and hope, thus creating a world that is more hopeful and more trustworthy.

REVIEW QUESTIONS

1. Explain what Vaclav Havel means when he says that "Consciousness precedes being, and not the other way around, as the Marxists claim."
2. Palmer argues that the great spiritual traditions are not primarily about values or ethics, but about *"reality."* That sounds odd; we often think of spiritual traditions about something beyond "reality." Explain what Palmer means here.
3. Palmer makes it clear that he is not just writing about leaders of businesses and organizations. What are two positions of leadership in your own life that are included in Palmer's discussion?
4. A first problem with leaders, Palmer writes, is that they give themselves power by taking it away from others. What are two more of these "shadow sides of leadership"?
5. What does it mean to say that "chaos is the precondition to creativity"? What are some implications for communication of this statement?

PROBES

1. What kinds of experiences taught Havel and other Czechs that "Consciousness precedes being, and not the other way around"? What do you suppose is the relationship between their often-painful experiences and this conclusion about spirituality?
2. Palmer says that people have a choice about what they project, and that "in that choice we help create the world that is." Explain how a choice about projecting either a spirit of hope or a spirit of despair can help create "the world that is."
3. The quotation by Annie Dillard indicates that spirituality is about "our complex and inexplicable caring for each other, and for our life together here." Explain what this means.
4. Palmer's Outward Bound experience helped him "go down and in." What experience has functioned for you in a similar way? What experiences might help you do this in the future?
5. Explain how your effectiveness as a leader could be enhanced if you were able to reject the necessity of competition.
6. Palmer's essay is clearly about a spiritual approach to leadership. How is it also about a spiritual approach to interpersonal communication?

NOTES

1. An earlier version of this chapter appeared as a pamphlet entitled *Leading from Within: Reflections on Spirituality and Leadership,* published by the Indiana Office for Campus Minorities in Indianapolis with support from the Lilly Endowment, 1990.
2. V. Havel, "The Revolution Has Just Begun," *Time* (Mar. 5, 1990): 14–15.
3. A. Dillard, *Teaching a Stone to Talk* (New York: Harper & Row, 1982), 94–95.

CHAPTER 16

A Philosopher's Approach

Martin Buber, a Jewish philosopher and teacher, was born and raised in Austria and Germany and died in 1965 in Israel. Throughout his life, Buber was both a "scholar," or "intellectual," and an intensely practical person interested in everyday life experiences. As an intellectual, he was hungry to learn and to write all he could about how humans relate with one another. As a practical person, he was determined to keep all his theorizing and scholarship firmly based on the concrete events he experienced every day. Because he was raised by his grandparents in Europe during the late-nineteenth and early-twentieth centuries (Buber's parents were divorced), lived through both world wars, was active in several political movements, and was a well-known, even famous, citizen of Israel, his life experiences are different in many ways from yours and mine. But for me, Buber's peculiar genius is that he can sense the part of his experience that is universal and can project that universal knowledge about human meetings through his European heritage and his "foreign" native language in such a way that he talks to me directly. In other words, even though he is in many ways very different from me, he says, "this is my experience; reflect on it a little and you might find that it's your experience too." Sometimes I stumble over Buber's language, the way he puts things. For example, like some other older authors in this book, Buber uses "man" when he means "human." But when I listen to him and do what he asks, I discover that he's right. It *is* my experience, only now I understand it better than I did before.

I don't know whether this one excerpt from Buber's writing will work this way for you. But the possibility is there if you will open yourself to hear him.[1] That's one thing about Buber's writings. Although he's a philosopher, some scholars criticize him because he doesn't state philosophical propositions and then try to verify and validate them with "proof." Instead, Buber insists that his reader try to meet him in a *conversation,* a dialogue. The main thing is for the reader to see whether his or her life experiences resonate with Buber's. This resonance is the only "proof" of the validity of Buber's ideas that the reader will receive. So far, millions of people have experienced this resonance. Books by and about Buber, especially his *I and Thou,* have been translated into over 20 languages and are read around the world.

In almost all his writing, Buber begins by observing that each of us lives a twofold reality. One "fold" is made up of our interaction with objects—human and otherwise—in the world. In this model of living, we merely need to develop and maintain our ability to be "objective," to explain ourselves and the world with accurate theories and valid cause-and-effect formulations. But the other "fold" occurs when we become fully human *persons* in genuine relationships with others, when we meet another and "make the other present as a whole and as a unique being, as the person that he is."

The genuine relationship Buber talks about is the "highest form" of what I've been calling interpersonal communication. You've probably heard of Buber's term for it—an "*I-Thou* relationship."[2] According to Buber, the individual lives always in the world of *I-It;* the person can enter the world of *I-Thou.* Both worlds are necessary. You can't expect to communicate interpersonally with everyone in every situation. But you can only become a fully human person by sharing genuine interpersonal relationships with others. As Buber puts it, without *It* the person cannot live. But he who lives with *It* alone is not a person.

This article is taken from a talk Buber gave when he visited the United States in 1957. It's especially useful because it is a kind of summary of much of what he had written in the first 79 years of his life (he died when he was 87).

I've outlined the article to simplify it some and to show how clearly organized it actually is. As you can see from the outline, Buber's subject is interpersonal relationships, which he calls "man's personal dealings with one another," or "the interhuman." Like the rest of this book, Buber's article doesn't deal with some mystical spirit world in which we all become one. Rather, he's writing about communication between today's teachers and students, politicians and voters, dating partners, and between you and me. First, he explains some attitudes and actions that keep people from achieving "genuine dialogue." Then he describes the characteristics of this dialogue, or *I-Thou* relationship. In the outline I've paraphrased each point that he makes.

When you read the essay, you'll probably be able to see where several of the other writers in this book got some of their ideas. For example, compare Carl Rogers's explanation of "congruence" in chapter 14 with what Buber says about "being and seeming."

Whether or not you note that kind of thing, however, read this article as thoughtfully as you can. It sums up everything in this book. And I know from the experience I have lived that it's worth understanding.

A reminder about his language: I pointed out in the Introduction that a few of the readings in *Bridges Not Walls* were written before we had learned about the destructive potential of the male bias in the English language. This is one of these readings. When I paraphrase Buber I remove this bias, and I have tried to soft-pedal it when I quote him. But it's still part of his writing, at least as it is now translated. Given what he believed about human beings—and given the strong intellectual influence his wife, Paula, had on him—I am sure that Buber would have been quick to correct the gender bias in his language if he had lived long enough to have the opportunity. I hope you can overlook this part of his writing and can hear his insights about *persons.*

OUTLINE OF MARTIN BUBER'S
"ELEMENTS OF THE INTERHUMAN"

I.   Interhuman relationships are not the same as "social relationships."
  A. Social relationships can be very close, but no *existential* or person-to-person relation is necessarily involved.
  B. This is because the collective or social suppresses individual persons.
  C. But in the interhuman, person meets person. In other words, "the only thing that matters is that for each of the two [persons] the other happens as the particular other, that each becomes aware of the other and is thus related to him in such a way that he does not regard and use him as his object, but as his partner in a living event, even if it is no more than a boxing match."
  D. In short, "the sphere of the interhuman is one in which a person is confronted by the other. We [i.e., Buber] call its unfolding the dialogical."

II.   There are three problems that get in the way of dialogue.
  A. The first problem is the duality of *being* and *seeming*. Dialogue won't happen if the people involved are only "seeming." They need to try to practice "being."
    1. "Seeming" in a relationship involves being concerned with your image, or front—with how you wish to appear.
    2. "Being" involves the spontaneous and unreserved presentation of what you really are in your personal dealings with the other.
    3. These two are generally found mixed together. The most we can do is to distinguish between persons in whose essential attitude one or the other (being or seeming) predominates.
    4. When seeming reigns, real interpersonal communication is impossible: "Whatever the meaning of the word 'truth' may be in other realms, in the interhuman realm it means that [people] communicate themselves to one another as what they are."
    5. The tendency toward seeming, however, is understandable.
      a. We *essentially* need personal confirmation, that is, we can't live without being confirmed by other people.
      b. Seeming often appears to help us get the confirmation we need.
      c. Consequently, "to yield to seeming is [the human's] essential cowardice, to resist it is his [or her] essential courage."
    6. This view indicates that there is no such thing as "bad being," but rather people who are habitually content to "seem" and afraid to "be." "I have never known a young person who seemed to me irretrievably bad."
  B. The second problem involves the way we perceive others.
    1. Many fatalists thinkers, such as Jean-Paul Sartre, believe that we can ultimately know *only* ourselves, that "man has directly to do only with himself and his own affairs."

2. But the main prerequisite for dialogue is that you get in direct touch with the other, "that each person should regard his partner as the very one he is."
   a. This means becoming aware of the other person as an essentially unique being. "To be aware of a [person] . . . means in particular to perceive his wholeness as a person determined by the spirit: it means to perceive the dynamic centre which stamps his every utterance, action, and attitude with the recognizable sign of uniqueness."
   b. But this kind of awareness is impossible so long as I objectify the other.
3. Perceiving the other in this way is contrary to everything in our world that is scientifically analytic or reductive.
   a. This is not to say that the sciences are wrong, only that they are severely limited.
   b. What's dangerous is the extension of the scientific, analytic method to all of life, because it is very difficult for science to remain aware of the essential uniqueness of persons.
4. This kind of perception is called "personal making present." What enables us to do it is our capacity for "imagining the real" of the other.
   a. Imagining the real "is not a looking at the other but a bold swinging— demanding the most intensive stirring of one's being—into the life of the other."
   b. When I *imagine* what the other person is *really* thinking and feeling, I can make direct contact with him or her.

C. The third problem which impedes the growth of dialogue is the tendency toward imposition instead of unfolding.
   1. One way to affect a person is to impose yourself on him or her.
   2. Another way is to "find and further in the soul of the other the disposition toward" that which you have recognized in yourself as right.
      a. Unfolding is not simply "teaching," but rather *meeting*.
      b. It requires believing in the other person.
      c. It means working as a helper of the growth processes already going on in the other.
   3. The propagandist is the typical "imposer"; the teacher *can* be the correspondingly typical "unfolder."
   4. The ethic implied here is similar to Immanuel Kant's, that is, persons should never be treated as means to an end, but only as ends in themselves.
      a. The only difference is that Buber stresses that persons exist not in isolation but in the interhuman, and
      b. for the interhuman to occur, there must be:
         (1) as little seeming as possible.
         (2) genuine perceiving ("personal making present") of the other, and
         (3) as little imposing as possible.

III. Summary of the characteristics of genuine dialogue:
  A. Each person must turn toward and be open to the other, a "turning of the being."
  B. Each must make present the other by imagining the real.
  C. Each confirms the other's being; however, confirmation does not necessarily mean approval.
  D. Each must be authentically himself or herself.
      1. Each must say whatever she or he "has to say."
      2. Each cannot be ruled by thoughts of his or her own effect or effectiveness as a speaker.
  E. Where dialogue becomes genuine, "there is brought into being a memorable common fruitlessness which is to be found nowhere else."
  F. Speaking is not always essential; silence can be very important.
  G. Finally, all participants must be committed to dialogue; otherwise, it will fail.

Again, Buber's language sometimes can get in the way of understanding him. But if you listen carefully, I think you will be able to resonate with at least some of what he says.

Elements of the Interhuman

Martin Buber

THE SOCIAL AND THE INTERHUMAN

It is usual to ascribe what takes place between men to the social realm, thereby blurring a basically important line of division between two essentially different areas of human life. I myself, when I began nearly fifty years ago to find my own bearings in the knowledge of society, making use of the then unknown concept of the interhuman, made the same error. From that time it became increasingly clear to me that we have to do here with a separate category of our existence, even a separate dimension, to use a mathematical term, and one with which we are so familiar that its peculiarity has hitherto almost escaped us. Yet insight into its peculiarity is extremely important not only for our thinking but also for our living.

We may speak of social phenomena wherever the life of a number of men, lived with one another, bound up together, brings in its train shared experiences and reactions. But to be thus bound up together means only that each individual existence is enclosed and contained in a group existence. It does not mean that between one member and another of the group there exists any kind of personal relation. They do feel that they belong together in a way that is, so to speak,

"Elements of the Interhuman," by Martin Buber from *The Knowledge of Man*. Edited by Maruice Friedman and translated by Maurice Friedman and Ronald Gregor Smith. © 1965 by Martin Buber. Reprinted by permission of the Balkin Agency.

fundamentally different from every possible belonging together with someone outside the group. And there do arise, especially in the life of smaller groups, contacts which frequently favour the birth of individual relations, but, on the other hand, frequently make it more difficult. In no case, however, does membership in a group necessarily involve an existential relation between one member and another. It is true that there have been groups in history which included highly sensitive and intimate relations between two of their members—as, for instance, in the homosexual relations among the Japanese samurai or among Doric warriors—and these were countenanced for the sake of the stricter cohesion of the group. But in general it must be said that the leading elements in groups, especially in the later course of human history, have rather been inclined to suppress the personal relation in favour of the purely collective element. Where this latter element reigns alone or is predominant, men feel themselves to be carried by the collectivity, which lifts them out of loneliness and fear of the world and lostness. When this happens—and for modern man it is an essential happening—the life between person and person seems to retreat more and more before the advance of the collective. The collective aims at holding in check the inclination to personal life. It is as though those who are bound together in groups should in the main be concerned only with the work of the group and should turn to the personal partners, who are tolerated by the group, only in secondary meetings.

The difference between the two realms became very palpable to me on one occasion when I had joined the procession through a large town of a movement to which I did not belong. I did it out of sympathy for the tragic development which I sensed was at hand in the destiny of a friend who was one of the leaders of the movement. While the procession was forming, I conversed with him and with another, a good-hearted "wild man," who also had the mark of death upon him. At that moment I still felt that the two men really were there, over against me, each of them a man near to me, near even in what was most remote from me; so different from me that my soul continually suffered from this difference, yet by virtue of this very difference confronting me with authentic being. Then the formations started off, and after a short time I was lifted out of all confrontation, drawn into the procession, falling in with its aimless step; and it was obviously the very same for the two with whom I had just exchanged human words. After a while we passed a café where I had been sitting the previous day with a musician whom I knew only slightly. The very moment we passed it the door opened, the musician stood on the threshold, saw me, apparently saw me alone, and waved to me. Straightway it seemed to me as though I were taken out of the procession and of the presence of my marching friends, and set there, confronting the musician. I forgot that I was walking along with the same step; I felt that I was standing over there by the man who had called out to me, and without a word, with a smile of understanding, was answering him. When consciousness of the facts returned to me, the procession, with my companions and myself at its head, had left the café behind.

The realm of the interhuman goes far beyond that of sympathy. Such simple happenings can be part of it as, for instance, when two strangers exchange glances in a crowded streetcar, at once to sink back again into the convenient state of wishing to know nothing about each other. But also every casual encounter between opponents belong to this realm, when it affects the opponent's attitude—that is, when something, however imperceptible, happens between the two, no matter whether it is marked at the time by any feeling or not. The only thing that matters is that for each of the two men the other happens as the particular other, that each becomes aware of the other and is thus related to him in such a way that he does not regard and use him as his object, but as his partner in a living event, even if it is no more than a boxing match. It is well known that some existentialists assert that the basic factor between men is that one is an object for the other. But so far as this is actually the case, the special reality of the interhuman, the fact of the contact, has been largely eliminated. It cannot indeed be entirely eliminated. As a crude example, take two men who are observing one another. The essential thing is not that the one makes the other his object, but the fact that he is not fully able to do so and the reason for his failure. We have in common with all existing things that we can be made objects of observation. But it is my privilege as man that by the hidden activity of my being I can establish an impassable barrier to objectification. Only in partnership can my being be perceived as an existing whole.

The sociologist may object to any separation of the social and the interhuman on the ground that society is actually built upon human relations, and the theory of these relations is therefore to be regarded as the very foundation of sociology. But here an ambiguity in the concept "relation" becomes evident. We speak, for instance, of a comradely relation between two men in their work, and do not merely mean what happens between them as comrades, but also a lasting disposition which is actualized in those happenings and which even includes purely psychological events such as the recollection of the absent comrade. But by the sphere of the interhuman I mean solely actual happenings between men, whether wholly mutual or tending to grow into mutual relations. For the participation of both partners is in principle indispensable. The sphere of the interhuman is one in which a person is confronted by the other. We call its unfolding the dialogical.

In accordance with this, it is basically erroneous to try to understand the interhuman phenomena as psychological. When two men converse together, the psychological is certainly an important part of the situation, as each listens and each prepares to speak. Yet this is only the hidden accompaniment to the conversation itself, the phonetic event fraught with meaning, whose meaning is to be found neither in one of the two partners nor in both together, but only in their dialogue itself, in this "between" which they live together.

BEING AND SEEMING

The essential problem of the sphere of the interhuman is the duality of being and seeming. Although it is a familiar fact that men are often troubled about the impression they make on others, this has been much more discussed in moral philosophy than in anthropology. Yet this is one of the most important subjects for anthropological study.

We may distinguish between two different types of human existence. The one proceeds from what one really is, the other from what one wishes to seem. In general, the two are found mixed together. There have probably been few men who were entirely independent of the impression they made on others, while there has scarcely existed one who was exclusively determined by the impression made by him. We must be content to distinguish between men in whose essential attitude the one or the other predominates.

This distinction is most powerfully at work, as its nature indicates, in the interhuman realm—that is, in men's personal dealings with one another.

Take as the simplest and yet quite clear example the situation in which two persons look at one another—the first belonging to the first type, the second to the second. The one who lives from his being looks at the other just as one looks at someone with whom he has personal dealings. His look is "spontaneous," "without reserve"; of course, he is not uninfluenced by the desire to make himself understood by the other, but he is uninfluenced by any thought of the idea of himself which he can or should awaken in the person whom he is looking at. His opposite is different. Since he is concerned with the image which his appearance, and especially his look or glance, produces in the other, he "makes" this look. With the help of the capacity, in greater or lesser degree peculiar to man, to make a definite element of his being appear in his look, he produces a look which is meant to have, and often enough does have, the effect of a spontaneous utterance—not only the utterance of a physical event supposed to be taking place at that very moment, but also, as it were, the reflection of a personal life of such-and-such a kind.

This must, however, be carefully distinguished from another area of seeming whose ontological legitimacy cannot be doubted. I mean the realm of "genuine seeming," where a lad, for instance, imitates his heroic model and while he is doing so is seized by the actuality of heroism, or a man plays the part of a destiny and conjures up authentic destiny. In this situation there is nothing false; the imitation is genuine imitation and the part played is genuine; the mask, too, is a mask and no deceit. But where the semblance originates from the lie and is permeated by it, the interhuman is threatened in its very existence. It is not that someone utters a lie, falsifies some account. The lie I mean does not take place in relation to particular facts, but in relation to existence itself, and it attacks interhuman existence as such. There are times when a man, to satisfy some stale conceit, forfeits the great chance of a true happening between I and Thou.

Let us now imagine two men, whose life is dominated by appearance, sitting and talking together. Call them Peter and Paul. Let us list the different configurations which are involved. First, there is Peter as he wishes to appear to Paul, and Paul as he wishes to appear to Peter. Then there is Peter as he really appears to Paul, that is, Paul's image of Peter, which in general does not in the least coincide with what Peter wishes Paul to see; and similarly there is the reverse situation. Further, there is Peter as he appears to himself, and Paul as he appears to himself. Lastly, there are the bodily Peter and the bodily Paul. Two living beings and six ghostly appearances, which mingle in many ways in the conversation between the two. Where is there room for any genuine interhuman life?

Whatever the meaning of the word "truth" may be in other realms, in the interhuman realm it means that men communicate themselves to one another as what they are. It does not depend on one saying to the other everything that occurs to him, but only on his letting no seeming creep in between himself and the other. It does not depend on one letting himself go before another, but on his granting to the man to whom he communicates himself a share in his being. This is a question of the authenticity of the interhuman, and where this is not to be found, neither is the human element itself authentic.

Therefore, as we begin to recognize the crisis of man as the crisis of what is between man and man, we must free the concept of uprightness from the thin moralistic tones which cling to it, and let it take its tone from the concept of bodily uprightness. If a presupposition of human life in primeval times is given in man's walking upright, the fulfillment of human life can only come through the soul's walking upright, through the great uprightness which is not tempted by any seeming because it has conquered all semblance.

But, one may ask, what if a man by his nature makes his life subservient to the images which he produces in others? Can he, in such a case, still become a man living from his being, can he escape from his nature?

The widespread tendency to live from the recurrent impression one makes instead of from the steadiness of one's being is not a "nature." It originates, in fact, on the other side of interhuman life itself, in men's dependence upon one another. It is no light thing to be confirmed in one's being by others, and seeming deceptively offers itself as a help in this. To yield to seeming is man's essential cowardice, to resist it is his essential courage. But this is not an inexorable state of affairs which is as it is and must so remain. One can struggle to come to oneself—that is, to come to confidence in being. One struggles, now more successfully, now less, but never in vain, even when one thinks he is defeated. One must at times pay dearly for life lived from the being; but it is never too dear. Yet is there not bad being, do weeds not grow everywhere? I have never known a young person who seemed to me irretrievably bad. Later indeed it becomes more and more difficult to penetrate the increasingly tough layer which has settled down on a man's being. Thus there arises the false perspective of the seemingly fixed "nature" which cannot be overcome. It is false; the foreground is deceitful; man as man can be redeemed.

Again we see Peter and Paul before us surrounded by the ghosts of the semblances. A ghost can be exorcized. Let us imagine that these two find it more and more repellent to be represented by ghosts. In each of them the will is stirred and strengthened to be confirmed in their being as what they really are and nothing else. We see the forces of real life at work as they drive out the ghosts, till the semblance vanishes and the depths of personal life call to one another.

PERSONAL MAKING PRESENT

By far the greater part of what is today called conversation among men would be more properly and precisely described as speechifying. In general, people do not really speak to one another, but each, although turned to the other, really speaks to a fictitious court of appeal whose life consists of nothing but listening to him. Chekhov has given poetic expression to this state of affairs in *The Cherry Orchard,* where the only use the members of a family make of their being together is to talk past one another. But it is Sartre who has raised to a principle of existence what in Chekhov still appears as the deficiency of a person who is shut up in himself. Sartre regards the walls between the partners in a conversation as simply impassable. For him it is inevitable human destiny that a man has directly to do only with himself and his own affairs. The inner existence of the other is his own concern, not mine; there is no direct relation with the other, nor can there be. This is perhaps the clearest expression of the wretched fatalism of modern man, which regards degeneration as the unchangeable nature of *Homo sapiens* and the misfortune of having run into a blind alley as his primal fate, and which brands every thought of a breakthrough as reactionary romanticism. He who really knows how far our generation has lost the way of true freedom, of free giving between I and Thou, must himself, by virtue of the demand implicit in every great knowledge of this kind, practice directness—even if he were the only man on earth who did it—and not depart from it until scoffers are struck with fear and hear in his voice the voice of their own suppressed longing.

The chief presupposition for the rise of genuine dialogue is that each should regard his partner as the very one he is. I become aware of him, aware that he is different, essentially different from myself, in the definite, unique way which is peculiar to him, and I accept whom I thus see, so that in full earnestness I can direct what I say to him as the person he is. Perhaps from time to time I must offer strict opposition to his view about the subject of our conversation. But I accept this person, the personal bearer of a conviction, in his definite being out of which his conviction has grown—even though I must try to show, bit by bit, the wrongness of this very conviction. I affirm the person I struggle with: I struggle with him as his partner, I confirm him as creature and as creation, I confirm him who is opposed to me as him who is over against me. It is true that it now depends on the other whether genuine dialogue, mutuality in speech arises between us. But if I thus give to the other who confronts me his legitimate standing as a man with whom I am ready to enter into dialogue, then I may trust him and suppose him to be also ready to deal with me as his partner.

But what does it mean to be "aware" of a man in the exact sense in which I use the word? To be aware of a thing or a being means, in quite general terms, to experience it as a whole and yet at the same time without reduction or abstraction, in all its concreteness. But a man, although he exists as a living being among living beings and even as a thing among things, is nevertheless something categorically different from all things and all beings. A man cannot really be grasped except on the basis of the gift of the spirit which belongs to man alone among all things, the spirit as sharing decisively in the personal life of the living man, that is, the spirit which determines the person. To be aware of a man, therefore, means in particular to perceive his wholeness as a person determined by the spirit; it means to perceive the dynamic centre which stamps his every utterance, action, and attitude with the recognizable sign of uniqueness. Such an awareness is impossible, however, if and so long as the other is the separated object of my contemplation or even observation, for this wholeness and its centre do not let themselves be known to contemplation or observation. It is only possible when I step into an elemental relation with the other, that is, when he becomes present to me. Hence I designate awareness in this special sense as "personal making present."

The perception of one's fellow man as a whole, as a unity, and as unique—even if his wholeness, unity, and uniqueness are only partly developed, as is usually the case—is opposed in our time by almost everything that is commonly understood as specifically modern. In our time there predominates an analytical, reductive, and deriving look between man and man. This look is analytical, or rather pseudo analytical, since it treats the whole being as put together and therefore able to be taken apart—not only the so-called unconscious which is accessible to relative objectification, but also the psychic stream itself, which can never, in fact, be grasped as an object. This look is a reductive one because it tries to contract the manifold person, who is nourished by the microcosmic richness of the possible, to some schematically surveyable and recurrent structures. And this look is a deriving one because it supposes it can grasp what a man has become, or even is becoming, in genetic formulae, and it thinks that even the dynamic central principle of the individual in this becoming can be represented by a general concept. An effort is being made today radically to destroy the mystery between man and man. The personal life, the ever-near mystery, once the source of the stillest enthusiasms, is levelled down.

What I have just said is not an attack on the analytical method of the human sciences, a method which is indispensable wherever it furthers knowledge of a phenomenon without impairing the essentially different knowledge of its uniqueness that transcends the valid circle of the method. The science of man that makes use of the analytical method must accordingly always keep in view the boundary of such a contemplation, which stretches like a horizon around it. This duty makes the transportation of the method into life dubious; for it is excessively difficult to see where the boundary is in life.

If we want to do today's work and prepare tomorrow's with clear sight, then we must develop in ourselves and in the next generation a gift which lives in man's inwardness as a Cinderella, one day to be a princess. Some call it intuition, but that is not a wholly unambiguous concept. I prefer the name "imagining the real," for in its essential being this gift is not a looking at the other, but a bold swinging—demanding the most intensive stirring of one's being—into the life of the other. This is the nature of all genuine imagining, only that here the realm of my action is not the all-possible, but the particular real person who confronts me, whom I can attempt to make present to myself just in this way, and not otherwise, in his wholeness, unity, and uniqueness, and with his dynamic centre which realizes all these things ever anew.

Let it be said again that all this can only take place in a living partnership, that is, when I stand in a common situation with the other and expose myself vitally to his share in the situation as really his share. It is true that my basic attitude can remain unanswered, and the dialogue can die in seed. But if mutuality stirs, then the interhuman blossoms into genuine dialogue.

IMPOSITION AND UNFOLDING

I have referred to two things which impede the growth of life between men: the invasion of seeming, and the inadequacy of perception. We are now faced with a third, plainer than the others, and in this critical hour more powerful and more dangerous than ever.

There are two basic ways of affecting men in their views and their attitude to life. In the first a man tries to impose himself, his opinion and his attitude, on the other in such a way that the latter feels the psychical result of the action to be his own insight, which has only been freed by the influence. In the second basic way of affecting others, as man wishes to find and to further in the soul of the other the disposition toward what he has recognized in himself as the right. Because it is the right, it must also be alive in the microcosm of the other, as one possibility. The other need only be opened out in this potentiality of his; moreover, this opening out takes place not essentially by teaching, but by meeting, by existential communication between someone that is in actual being and someone that is in a process of becoming. The first way has been most powerfully developed in the realm of propaganda, the second in that of education.

The propagandist I have in mind, who imposes himself, is not in the least concerned with the person whom he desires to influence, as a person; various individual qualities are of importance only in so far as he can exploit them to win the other and must get to know them for this purpose. In his indifference to everything personal the propagandist goes a substantial distance beyond the party for which he works. For the party, persons in their difference are of significance because each can be used according to his special qualities in a particular function. It is true that the personal is considered only in respect of the specific use to which it can be put, but within these limits it is recognized in practice. To propaganda as such, on the other hand, individual qualities are rather looked on as a burden, for propaganda is concerned simply with *more*— more members, more adherents, an increasing extent of support. Political methods, where they rule in an extreme form, as here, simply mean winning power over the other by depersonalizing him. This kind of propaganda enters upon different relations with force; it supplements it or replaces it, according to the need or the prospects, but it is in the last analysis nothing but sublimated violence, which has become imperceptible as such. It places men's souls under a pressure which allows the illusion of autonomy. Political methods at their height mean the effective abolition of the human factor.

The educator whom I have in mind lives in a world of individuals, a certain number of whom are always at any one time committed to his care. He sees each of these individuals as in a position to become a unique, single person, and thus the bearer of a special task of existence which can be fulfilled through him and through him alone. He sees every personal life as engaged in such a process of actualization, and he knows from his own experience that the forces making for actualization are all the time involved in a microcosmic struggle with counter-forces. He has come to see himself as a helper of the actualizing forces. He knows these forces; they have shaped and they still shape him. Now he puts this person shaped by them at their disposal for a new struggle and a new work. He cannot wish to impose himself, for he believes in the effect of the actualizing forces, that is, he believes that in every man what is right is established in a single and uniquely personal way. No other way may be imposed on a man, but another way, that of the educator, may and must unfold what is right, as in this case it struggles for achievement, and help it to develop.

The propagandist, who imposes himself, does not really believe in his own cause, for he does not trust it to attain its effect of its own power without his special methods, whose symbols are the loudspeaker and the television advertisement. The educator who unfolds what is there believes in the primal power which has scattered itself, and still scatters itself, in all human beings in order that it may grow up in each man in the special form of that man. He is confident that this growth needs at each moment only that help which is given in meeting and that he is called to supply that help.

I have illustrated the character of the two basic attitudes and their relation to one another by means of two extremely antithetical examples. But wherever men have dealings with one another, one or the other attitude is to be found to be in more or less degree.

These two principles of imposing oneself on someone and helping someone to unfold should not be confused with concepts such as arrogance and humility. A man can be arrogant without wishing to impose himself on others, and it is not enough to be humble in order to help another unfold. Arrogance and humility are dispositions of the soul, psychological fact with a moral accent, while imposition and helping to unfold are events between men, anthropological facts which point to an ontology, the ontology of the interhuman.

In the moral realm Kant expressed the essential principle that one's fellow man must never be thought of and treated merely as a means, but always at the same time as an independent end. The principle is expressed as an "ought" which is sustained by the idea of human dignity. My point of view, which is near to Kant's in its essential features, has another source and goal. It is concerned with the presuppositions of the interhuman. Man exists anthropologically not in his isolation, but in the completeness of the relation between man and man; what humanity is can be properly grasped only in vital reciprocity. For the proper existence of the interhuman it is necessary, as I have shown, that the semblance does not intervene to spoil the relation of personal being to personal being. It is further necessary, as I have also shown, that each one means and makes present the other in his personal being. That neither should wish to impose himself on the other is the third basic presupposition of the interhuman. These presuppositions do not include the demand that one should influence the other in his unfolding; that is, however, an element that is suited to lead to a higher stage of the interhuman.

That there resides in every man the possibility of attaining authentic human existence in the special way peculiar to him can be grasped in the Aristotelian image of entelechy, innate self-realization; but one must note that it is an entelechy of the work of creation. It would be mistaken to speak here of individuation alone. Individuation is only the indispensable personal stamp of all realization of human existence. The self as such is not ultimately the essential, but the meaning of human existence given in creation again and again fulfills itself as self. The help that men give each other in becoming a self leads the life between men to its height. The dynamic glory of the being of man is first bodily present in the relation between two men each of whom in meaning the other also means the highest to which this person is called, and serves the self-realization of this human life as one true to creation without wishing to impose on the other anything of his own realization.

GENUINE DIALOGUE

We must now summarize and clarify the marks of genuine dialogue.

In genuine dialogue the turning to the partner takes place in all truth, that is, it is a turning of the being. Every speaker "means" the partner of partners to whom he turns as this personal existence. To "mean" someone in this connection is at the same time to exercise that degree of making present which is possible to the speaker at that moment. The experiencing senses and the imagining of the real which completes the findings of the senses work together to make the other present as a whole and as a unique being, as the person that he is. But the speaker does not merely perceive the one who is present to him in this way; he receives him as his partner, and that means that he confirms this other being, so far as it is for him to confirm. The true turning of his person to the other includes this confirmation, this acceptance. Of course, such a confirmation does not mean approval; but no matter in what I am against the other, by accepting him as my partner in genuine dialogue I have affirmed him as a person.

Further, if genuine dialogue is to arise, everyone who takes part in it must bring himself into it. And that also means that he must be willing on each occasion to say what is really in his mind about the subject of the conversation. And that means further that on each occasion he makes the contribution of his spirit without reduction and without shifting his ground. Even men of great integrity are under the illusion that they are not bound to say everything "they have to say." But in the great faithfulness which is the climate of genuine dialogue, what

I have to say at any one time already has in me the character of something that wishes to be uttered, and I must not keep it back, keep it in myself. It bears for me the unmistakable sign which indicates that it belongs to the common life of the word. Where the dialogical word genuinely exists, it must be given its right by keeping nothing back. To keep nothing back is the exact opposite of unreserved speech. Everything depends on the legitimacy of "what I have to say." And of course I must also be intent to raise into an inner word and then into a spoken word what I have to say at this moment but do not yet possess as speech. To speak is both nature and work, something that grows and something that is made, and where it appears dialogically, in the climate of great faithfulness, it has to fulfill ever anew the unity of the two.

Associated with this is that overcoming of semblance to which I have referred. In the atmosphere of genuine dialogue, he who is ruled by the thought of his own effect as the speaker of what he has to speak has a destructive effect. If, instead of what has to be said, I try to bring attention to my I, I have irrevocably miscarried what I had to say; it enters the dialogue as a failure and the dialogue is a failure. Because genuine dialogue is an ontological sphere which is constituted by the authenticity of being, every invasion of semblance must damage it.

But where the dialogue is fulfilled in its being, between partners who have turned to one another in truth, who express themselves without reserve and are free of the desire for semblance, there is brought into being a memorable common fruitfulness which is to be found nowhere else. At such times, at each such time, the word arises in a substantial way between men who have been seized in their depths and opened out by the dynamic of an elemental togetherness. The interhuman opens out what otherwise remains unopened.

This phenomenon is indeed well known in dialogue between two persons; but I have also sometimes experienced it in a dialogue in which several have taken part.

About Easter of 1914 there met a group consisting of representatives of several European nations for a three-day discussion that was intended to be preliminary to further talks. We wanted to discuss together how the catastrophe, which we all believed was imminent, could be avoided. Without our having agreed beforehand on any sort of modalities for our talk, all the presuppositions of genuine dialogue were fulfilled. From the first hour immediacy reigned between all of us, some of whom had just got to know one another; everyone spoke with an unheard-of unreserve, and clearly not a single one of the participants was in bondage to semblance. In respect of its purpose the meeting must be described as a failure (though even now in my heart it is still not a certainty that it had to be a failure); the irony of the situation was that we arranged the final discussion for the middle of August, and in the course of events the group was soon broken up. Nevertheless, in the time that followed, not one of the participants doubted that he shared in a triumph of the interhuman.

One more point must be noted. Of course it is not necessary for all who are joined in a genuine dialogue actually to speak; those who keep silent can on occasion be especially important. But each must be determined not to withdraw when the course of the conversation makes it proper for him to say what he has to say. No one, of course, can know in advance what it is that he has to say; genuine dialogue cannot be arranged beforehand. It has indeed its basic order in itself from the beginning, but nothing can be determined, the course is of the spirit, and some discover what they have to say only when they catch the call of the spirit.

But it is also a matter of course that all the participants, without exception, must be of such nature that they are capable of satisfying the presuppositions of genuine dialogue and are ready to do so. The genuineness of the dialogue is called in question as soon as even a small number of those present are felt by themselves and by the others as not being expected to take any active part. Such a state of affairs can lead to very serious problems.

I had a friend whom I account one of the most considerable men of our age. He was a master of conversation, and he loved it: his genuineness as a speaker was evident. But once it happened that he was sitting with two friends and with the three wives, and a conversation arose in which by its nature the women were clearly not joining, although their presence in fact had a great influence. The conversation among the men soon developed into a duel between two of them (I was the third). The other "duelist," also a friend of mine, was of a noble nature; he too was a man of true conversation, but given more to objective fairness than to the play of the intellect, and a stranger to any controversy. The friend whom I have called a master of conversation did not speak with his usual composure and strength, but he scintillated, he fought, he triumphed. The dialogue was destroyed.

REVIEW QUESTIONS

1. What distinction does Buber make between the social and the interhuman?
2. What feature of interpersonal contact does Buber say can characterize even "a boxing match"?
3. What does Buber mean when he says that "it is basically erroneous to try to understand the interhuman phenomena as psychological"?
4. Does Buber say that a person can practice "being" consistently, all the time? Explain.
5. Paraphrase the last sentence in the first paragraph under the heading, "Personal Making Present." What is Buber challenging his reader to do here?
6. Identify three possible things that a person who is imposing could impose on his or her conversational partner. In other words, what is (are) imposed when a person is imposing? What is unfolded when a person is unfolding?
7. What does Buber mean when he says that "to keep nothing back is the exact opposite of unreserved speech"?

PROBES

1. What does it mean to you when Buber says that social contacts don't involve an existential relation, but that interhuman contacts do?

2. How is Buber's discussion of "being" and "seeming" similar to and differ-ent from Rogers's discussion of "congruence" (Chapter 14)?
3. For Buber, does "being" mean total honesty? Is "seeming" lying?
4. What circumstances make it difficult for you to "be"? How can you best help others to "be" instead of "seem"?
5. How do Buber's comments about the way we perceive others relate to the discussion of person perception in Chapter 5?
6. It sounds as if Buber is saying that science *cannot* be used to study human life. Is he saying that? Do you agree with him? Why or why not?
7. How is Buber's discussion of "imagining the real" related to what Stewart and Logan (Chapter 5) and Rogers (Chapter 14) say about empathy?
8. Which teacher that you've had has functioned most as an "imposer?" Which teacher has been most consistently an "unfolder?"
9. What does "personal making present" mean to you? What do you need to do in order to perceive someone that way?
10. Have you ever experienced a silent "dialogue" of the kind Buber mentions here? What happened?

NOTES

1. You might also be interested in other things written by or about Buber. For starters I recommend Aubrey Hodes, *Martin Buber: An Intimate Portrait* (New York: Viking, 1971); or Hilary Evans Bender, *Monarch Notes: The Philosophy of Martin Buber* (New York: Monarch, 1974). Maurice Friedman has written the definitive Buber biography, and I'd especially recommend the third volume, *Martin Buber's Life and Work: The Later Years, 1945–1965* (New York: Dutton, 1983). Buber's most important and influential book is *I and Thou,* trans. Walter Kaufmann (New York: Scribner, 1970).
2. Buber's translators always point out that this "thou" is not the religious term of formal address. It is a translation of the German *Du*, the familiar form of the pronoun "you." As Walter Kaufmann, one of Buber's translators, explains, "German lovers say *Du* to one another and so do friends. Du is spontaneous and unpretentious, remote from formality, pomp, and dignity."

> *Ideas are clean. They soar in the serene supernal. I can take*
> *them out and look at them, they fit in books, they lead me*
> *down that narrow way. And in the morning they are there.*
> *Ideas are straight—*
> *But the world is round, and a*
> *messy mortal is my friend.*
> *Come walk with me in the mud. . . .*

> —*Hugh Prather*

Photo Credits

Index